AMC

White Mountain Guide

26th Edition

Hiking trails in the White Mountain National Forest

Compiled and edited by
Gene Daniell and Jon Burroughs

APPALACHIAN MOUNTAIN CLUB BOOKS
BOSTON, MASSACHUSETTS

Cover Photograph: Robert Kozlow
Cover Design: Alicia Ozyjowski

EDITIONS
First edition, 1907, Second Edition 1916, Third Edition 1917, Fourth Edition 1920,
Fifth Edition 1922, Sixth Edition 1925, Seventh Edition 1928, Eighth Edition 1931,
Ninth Edition 1934, Tenth Edition 1936, Eleventh Edition 1940, Twelfth Edition 1946,
Thirteenth Edition 1948, Fourteenth Edition 1952, Fifteenth Edition 1955, Sixteenth
Edition 1960, Seventeenth Edition 1963, Eighteenth Edition 1966, Nineteenth Edition
1969, Twentieth Edition 1972, Twenty-First Edition 1976, Twenty-Second Edition 1979,
Twenty-Third Edition 1983, Twenty-Fourth Edition 1987, Twenty-Fifth Edition 1992,
Twenty-Sixth Edition 1998.

Library of Congress Cataloging-in-Publication Data
White mountain guide: hiking trails in the White Mountain National Forest / compiled
and edited by Gene Daniell and Jon Burroughs. — 26th ed.
p. cm.
Rev. ed. of: AMC White Mountain guide / Appalachian Mountain Club. 25th ed. 1992.
Includes index.
ISBN 1-878239-65-1 (alk. paper)
1. Hiking—White Mountains (N.H. and Me.)—Guidebooks. 2. Trails—White Mountains
(N.H. and Me.)—Guidebooks. 3. White Mountains (N.H. and Me.)—Guidebooks.
I. Daniell, Gene. II. Burroughs, Jon. III. Appalachian Mountain Club.
AMC White Mountain guide.
GV199.42.W47A67   1998
796.51'09742'2—dc21   98-27283
                                                       CIP

The paper used in this publication meets the minimum requirements of the American
National Standard for Information Sciences—Permanence of Paper for Printed Library
Materials, ANSI Z39.48-1984. ∞

**Due to changes in conditions, use of the information
in this book is at the sole risk of the user.**

Printed in the United States of America. Printed on recycled paper using soy-based inks.

10 9 8 7 6 5 4 3 2 1   98 99 00 01 02 03 04

Contents

Key to Maps

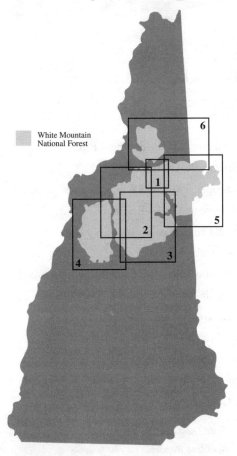

White Mountain
National Forest

Map 1: Presidential Range
Map 2: Franconia–Pemigewasset
Map 3: Crawford Notch–Sandwich
    Range
Map 4: Moosilauke–Kinsman
Map 5: Carter Range–Evans Notch
Map 6: North Country–Mahoosuc
    Range

To the Owner of this Book

This book aims for complete coverage of hiking trails located in the White Mountain National Forest in New Hampshire and Maine, and also includes descriptions of the more important trails outside the national forest in the northern part of New Hampshire, with a small amount of coverage of immediately adjacent parts of Maine. For other regions in Maine, consult the *AMC Maine Mountain Guide*. The *White Mountain Guide* also covers the entire Appalachian Trail and its side trails from the New Hampshire–Vermont boundary at the Connecticut River to Grafton Notch in Maine, just east of the Maine–New Hampshire boundary. The new *AMC Guide to Southern and Central New Hampshire* includes a number of mountains and areas (such as Mt. Cardigan, Monadnock, and the Belknaps) that were previously covered by the *White Mountain Guide*. NH 25, the highway that runs west to east across the state of New Hampshire and roughly separates the White Mountain Region from the Lakes Region and the Dartmouth-Sunapee Region, has been chosen as the southern boundary of the areas covered in the *White Mountain Guide*; however, the Middle Connecticut River region, which is crossed by the Appalachian Trail between Hanover and Glencliff, is included—although it lies south of NH 25—in order to provide complete coverage of the Appalachian Trail in New Hampshire in this book.

No attempt is made to cover any kind of skiing (alpine, downhill, or cross-country), although several cross-country (ski-touring) trails are mentioned where they happen to intersect hiking trails. Rock climbs are not described in this book, since they require special techniques and equipment and should be undertaken only by roped parties under qualified leaders, due to the high degree of danger to inexperienced or insufficiently equipped climbers or groups.

The mountains themselves may seem virtually changeless, but the lands of the White Mountains are constantly subjected to the powerful forces of nature and the pervasive effects of contacts with human visitors and their management policies. Since change is therefore the rule, no source of information can be perfectly trustworthy, and a guidebook to this region can never be more than a record of the way things were at a given moment in time. Though great care has been taken to make this book as accurate as possible, it will be a useful tool only if its owner employs constant good judgment and vigilance. In the woods, we are visitors who must accept that this environment can only be partly adapted to our convenience—and in fact most of us prefer to visit a backcountry relatively undisturbed by human interference—so we must make up the difference by adapting our behavior as circumstances demand.

While trails vary greatly in the amount of use they receive and the ease with which they can usually be followed, it cannot be emphasized too strongly that there is almost no trail that might not be closed unexpectedly or suddenly become obscure or hazardous under certain conditions. Trails can be rerouted or abandoned or closed by landowners. Signs are stolen or fall from their posts. Storms may cause blowdowns or landslides, which can obliterate a trail for an entire climbing season or longer. Trails may not be cleared of fallen trees and brush until late summer, and not all trails are cleared every year. Logging operations can cover trails with slash and add a bewildering network of new roads. In addition, even momentary inattention to trail markers, particularly arrows at sharp turns or signs at junctions, or misinterpretation of signs or guidebook descriptions, can cause hikers to become separated from all but the most heavily traveled paths—or at least lead them into what may be a much longer or more difficult route. So please remember that this book is an aid to planning, not a substitute for observation and judgment.

As a consequence, all the trail-maintaining organizations, including the AMC, reserve the right to discontinue any trail without notice and expressly disclaim any legal responsibility for the condition of any trail. Most organizations give priority to heavily used trails, so lightly used trails quite often do not receive their share of attention and following them may require great care.

Note: **A major ice storm in January of 1998 caused great damage in many parts of New Hampshire and Maine.** Some areas and trails were practically untouched by this storm, but many others were severely damaged. While trail-maintaining organizations plan to have most of the important trails open at some point during the summer of 1998, some trails that normally receive only infrequent use may not be cleared for two to three years. Hikers should consult the AMC or WMNF offices for the latest information on trail clearing and closures.

By a program initiated in 1997, the WMNF requires the purchase of a recreational permit for visitors who wish to park vehicles anywhere on WMNF land (including roadsides and other areas in addition to official trailheads). These permits are available for a week or for an entire season. Since this is an experimental program, many of the details may change from year to year. Many important trailheads are located just outside the WMNF and are thus not subject to the fee, and there is some doubt about other trailheads, but signs notifying visitors about the permit program are posted at most of the trailheads and at the beginning of the roadside areas where the permits are required. Because of uncertainty as to the status of some trailheads, and because the AMC does not wish to encourage overuse of free parking areas by those wishing to avoid the permit fee (which may cause serious parking problems in some places), no attempt has been made in this book to indicate which trailheads or other areas are subject to the permit requirement.

We request your help in keeping the *White Mountain Guide* accurate. New editions are published at intervals of about four or five years. This book belongs to the entire hiking community, not just to the AMC and the people who produce it. If you encounter a problem with a trail, or with a map or description in this book, please let us know. The comments of a person who is inexperienced or unfamiliar with a trail are often particularly useful. Any comments or corrections can be sent to the *White Mountain Guide,* AMC, 5 Joy St., Boston, MA 02108.

TRIP PLANNING

The descriptions in this book are intended to apply in the conditions that are usually encountered during the normal hiking season, which runs approximately from Memorial Day to Columbus Day. In some years ice or snowdrifts may remain at higher elevations until the early part of June—or even longer—and possibly much later than that in some of the major ravines, on north-facing slopes, and in other sheltered places such as Mahoosuc Notch. Such conditions vary greatly from year to year and place to place; one year most trails may be fairly clear by mid-May, but the next year hikers may find icy patches and even significant drifts well into June. When snow or ice are present, trails are often far more difficult to follow, and usually far more arduous, or even dangerous, to hike on.

Winter-like conditions can occur above treeline in any month of the year. Even in midsummer, hikers above treeline should be prepared for cold weather with a wool sweater, hat, mittens, and a wind parka, which will give comfort on sunny but cool days and protection against sudden storms. Spring and fall are particularly difficult seasons in the mountains, since the weather may be pleasant in the valleys and brutal on the summits and ridges. A great number of the serious incidents in the mountains occur in the spring and fall, when hikers deceived by mild conditions at home or even at trailheads may find themselves facing unanticipated severe, perhaps life-threatening, hazards.

Plan your trip schedule with safety in mind. Consider the strength of your party and the general strenuousness of the trip: the overall distance, the amount of climbing, and the roughness of the terrain. Get a weather report, but be aware of the fact that most forecasts are not intended to apply to the mountain region; a day that is sunny and pleasant in the lowlands may well be inclement in the mountains. The National Weather Service in Gray ME issues a recreational forecast for the White Mountain region and broadcasts it on its short-wave radio station each morning approximately from 5 A.M. to 10 A.M.; this forecast is posted at Pinkham Notch Camp at about 8 A.M., and is also carried on the National Weather Service telephone line (603-225-5191). Mountain weather information is also available on the AMC Web site (www.outdoors.org).

Plan to finish your hike with daylight to spare (remember that days grow shorter rapidly in late summer and fall). Hiking after dark, even with flashlights (which frequently fail), makes finding trails more difficult and crossing streams hazardous. Let someone else know where you will be hiking, and do not let inexperienced people get separated from the group. Many unpaved roads are not passable until about Memorial Day, and from November to May the WMNF closes with locked gates many of its roads that are normally open during the summer season; many trips are much longer when the roads are not open.

FOLLOWING TRAILS

Hikers should always carry a map and compass and carefully keep track of their approximate location on the map. The maps included with this guide are topographic maps (maps with the shape of the terrain represented by contour lines). They are designed as an aid to planning trips and following well-established trails, and for determining a reasonable course of action in an emergency. They therefore cover fairly large areas, which necessarily limits the amount of detail that can be shown on them. In particular, on trails that closely follow streams, it is often difficult to show accurately the number and location of crossings; the text of the trail's description should also be consulted for this information. Due to this limited detail, these maps are not generally suitable for following obscure trails or for bushwhacks (planned trips away from trails). Maps with more detail (which necessarily cover much smaller areas) are published by the US Geological Survey (see Introduction).

The best compass for hiking is the protractor type: a circular, liquid-filled compass that turns on a rectangular base made of clear plastic. Excellent compasses of this type, with leaflets that give ample instructions for their use, are available for less than $10. Such a compass is easily set to the bearing you wish to follow, and then it is a simple matter of keeping the compass needle aligned to north and following the arrow on the base. More sophisticated and expensive compasses have features designed for special applications that are often not useful in the woods; they are normally harder to use and apt to cause confusion in an emergency situation. Directions of the compass given in the text are based on true north instead of magnetic north, unless otherwise specified. There is a deviation of 16° to 17° between true north and magnetic north in the White Mountains. This means that true north will be about 17° to the right of (clockwise from) the compass's north needle. If you take a bearing from a map, you should add 17° to the bearing when you set your compass. On the maps included with this guide, the black lines that run from bottom to top are aligned with true north and south.

In general, trails are maintained to provide a clear pathway while protecting the environment by minimizing erosion and other damage. Some may offer rough and difficult passage. Most hiking trails are marked with paint on trees or rocks, though a few still only have axe blazes cut into trees. The trails that compose the Appalachian Trail through the White Mountains are marked with vertical rectangular white paint blazes throughout. Side trails off the Appalachian Trail are usually marked with blue paint. Other trails are marked in other colors, the most popular being yellow. Except for the Appalachian Trail and its side trails, and trails maintained by certain clubs such as the Chocorua Mountain Club and the Wonalancet Outdoor Club, the color of blazing has no significance and may change without notice; therefore blazing color is not a reliable means of distinguishing particular trails from intersecting ones. Above timberline, cairns (piles of rocks) mark the trails. Where hikers have trodden out the vegetation, the footway is usually visible except when it is covered by snow or fallen leaves. In winter, signs at trailheads and intersections and blazes also are often covered by snow. Trails following or crossing logging roads require special care at intersections in order to distinguish the trail from diverging roads, particularly since blazing is usually very sparse while the trail follows the road. Around shelters or campsites, beaten paths may lead in all directions, so look for signs and paint blazes.

If you lose a trail and it is not visible to either side, it is usually best to backtrack right away to the last mark seen and look again from there; this will be made much easier if you carefully note each trail marking and keep track of where and how long ago you saw the most recent one. Even when the trail cannot be immediately found, it is a serious but not desperate situation. Few people become truly lost in the White Mountains; a moment's reflection and five minutes with the map will show that you probably know at least your approximate location and the direction to the nearest road, if nothing else. Most cases in which a person has become lost for any length of time involve panic and aimless wandering, so the most important first step is to stop and take a break, make an inventory of useful information, decide on a course of action and stick to it. (The caution against allowing inexperienced persons to become separated from a group should be emphasized here, since they are most likely to panic and wander aimlessly. Make sure also that all party members are familiar with the route of the trip and the names of the trails to be used, so that if they do become separated they will have some prospect of rejoining the group.) If you have carefully kept track of your location on the map, it will usually be possible to find a nearby stream, trail, or road to which a compass course may be followed. Most distances are short enough (except in the North Country north of NH 110) that it is possible, in the absence of alternatives, to reach a highway in half a day, or at most in a whole day, simply by going downhill, carefully avoiding any dangerous cliffs (which will normally be found in areas where the map's contour lines are unusually close together), until you come upon a river or brook. The stream should then be followed downward.

WHAT TO CARRY

Adequate equipment for a hike in the White Mountains varies greatly according to the length of the trip and the difficulty of getting to the nearest trailhead if trouble arises. If you are only strolling in to a pond or waterfall a mile or so from the road in good weather, then perhaps a light jacket, a candy bar, and a bottle of water will suffice. If, however, you are going above treeline and are not inclined to turn back at the first sign of questionable weather, you will need a good pack filled with plenty of warm clothing and food for emergency use, and other equipment. No determination of what one needs to take along can be made without considering the length of a trip and the hazards of the terrain it will cross.

Good things to have in your pack for an ordinary summer day hike in the White Mountains include guidebook, maps, water bottle (ordinary plastic soft-drink bottles, with or without original contents, work well), compass, knife (good-quality stainless steel, since ordinary steel rusts very quickly), rain gear, windbreaker, wool sweater(s), wool hat and mittens, waterproof matches, enough food for your usual needs plus extra high-energy foods in reserve (such as dried fruit or candy), first-aid supplies (including personal medicines, a non-prescription painkiller [such as aspirin, acetaminophen, or ibuprofen], adhesive bandages, gauze, and antiseptic), needle and thread, safety pins, nylon cord, trash bag, toilet paper, and a (small) flashlight with extra batteries and a spare bulb.

Wear comfortable hiking boots. Lightweight boots, somewhat more sturdy than sneakers, are popular these days. Experienced hikers can often wear sneakers quite safely and comfortably on easy to moderate hikes. Unfortunately, most of the people who actually do wear sneakers on the trails are inexperienced and not accustomed to walking on rough trails, and have legs and ankles that are not trail-toughened. As a result, many leg injuries occur on short, relatively easy trails because of the large numbers of inexperienced hikers who wear sneakers when they need the support of boots.

Blue jeans, sweatshirts, and other cotton clothes are popular but, once wet, dry very slowly and may be uncomfortable; in adverse weather conditions they often seriously drain a cold and tired hiker's heat reserves. While such clothes are worn by most hikers on most summer trips, people who are planning to travel to remote places or above treeline should seriously consider wearing (or at least carrying) wool or synthetics instead. Wool keeps much of its insulation value even when wet, and it (or one of several modern synthetic materials) is indispensable for hikers who want to visit places from which return to civilization might require substantial time and effort if conditions turn bad. Not only do hats, mittens, and other such gear provide safety in adverse conditions, but they also allow one to enjoy the summits in comfort on those occasional crisp, clear days when the views are particularly fine, when the other hikers who snickered at one's bulging pack are driven from the magnificent vistas with terse greetings forced through chattering teeth.

BACKCOUNTRY HAZARDS

In emergencies call the toll-free New Hampshire State Police number (800-852-3411) or Pinkham Notch Camp (603-466-2727).

Hypothermia, the most serious danger to hikers in the White Mountains, is the loss of ability to preserve body heat because of injury, exhaustion, lack of sufficient food, and inadequate or wet clothing. Most of the dozens of deaths on Mt. Washington have resulted from hypothermia. It is important to understand that the victim does not "freeze to death," since death occurs at a body temperature of about 80° F. Many cases occur in temperatures above freezing; the most dangerous weather conditions involve rain, with wind, with temperatures below 50° F. The symptoms include uncontrolled shivering, impaired speech and movement, lowered body temperature, and drowsiness. The result is death, unless the victim (who will not understand the situation, due to impaired mental function) is rewarmed. In mild cases the victim should be given dry clothing and placed in a sleeping bag (perhaps with someone else in it to provide body heat), then quick-energy food and something warm (not hot) to drink. In severe cases only prompt hospitalization offers reasonable hope for recovery. It is not unusual for a victim to resist treatment and even combat rescuers. It should therefore be obvious that prevention of hypothermia is the only truly practical course. Uncontrollable shivering should be regarded as a sure sign of hypothermia; this shivering will eventually cease on its own, but that is merely the sign that the body has given up the struggle and is sinking toward death.

Much has been written about hypothermia, and some of the advice has been confusing, largely because a victim in an advanced state of hypothermia requires radically different treatment from one in the early stages of the illness. Basically, chronic hypothermia—the form usually encountered in hiking situations—develops over the course of several hours when a person loses body heat faster than it can be generated. The body uses a number of means to prevent the temperature of vital organs from dropping to a level where proper functioning will be impaired; most important of these is the withdrawal of blood supply from the extremities of the body into the core. This is the reason that poor coordination of hands and legs is an important sign of a developing problem. As the situation becomes more serious, the body goes into violent shivering, which produces a substantial amount of heat but consumes the body's last remaining energy reserves very rapidly. At this point rapid and decisive application of the treatments mentioned above may still save the victim's life. (Unfortunately, an exhausted hiker, or one who has not been eating or drinking properly, may not possess the energy reserves for violent shivering.) Violent shivering is the body's last response; once the shivering ceases the body has no more weapons to use and the descent toward death is quite rapid. This is profound hypothermia; and profound hypothermia cannot be treated in the field, since it requires advanced techniques such as circulating warm water through the abdominal cavity to rewarm the victim from the body core outward. Any attempt to rewarm such a person in the field will cause cold blood from the extremities to return to the heart, almost certainly causing death from heart failure. Extreme care must also be used in attempting to transport such a person to a trailhead, since even a slight jar can bring on heart failure. Since successful rescue of a profoundly hypothermic person from the backcountry is so difficult, the need for prevention or early detection must be obvious. In almost all cases, the advent of hypothermia is fairly slow, and in cold weather all members of a hiking group must be aware of the signs of developing hypothermia and pay constant attention to the first appearance of such signs—which may be fairly subtle—in all fellow party members, so as to detect the condition in one of their companions well before it becomes a serious matter. Those who do not pay attention to the well-being of their companions may well have the experience of standing by helplessly while a friend dies.

In sum, a person who is shivering violently must be treated for hypothermia immediately and aggressively. Since victims do not always exhibit violent shivering, as a general rule it is safe to render this sort of treatment to anyone who is able to eat or drink voluntarily, perhaps with minor assistance. Once violent shivering has ceased, or when a victim is unable to eat or drink without exceptional assistance, the existence of a state of profound hypothermia must be assumed. The victim should be protected from further heat loss as much as possible and handled with extreme gentleness, and trained rescue personnel should be called for assistance unless the party is capable of providing an advanced litter evacuation themselves.

For those interested in more information, a thorough treatment of the subject is contained in *The Basic Essentials of Hypothermia* by William W. Forgey, M.D., published by The Basic Essentials Series, ICS Books, One Tower Plaza, Merrillville, IN 46410 (1991).

Lightning is another serious hazard, particularly on the Presidential and Franconia ranges and on any bare ridge or summit. In other mountain ranges throughout the world, where thunderstorms are more common and shelter often much farther away, fairly elaborate advice is often provided for finding the least unsafe place to sit out a storm. In the White Mountains the best course of action is to avoid the dangerous places when thunderstorms are likely, and to go down the mountain to shelter in thick woods as quickly as possible if an unexpected "thumper" is detected. Most thunderstorms occur when a cold front passes, or on very warm days; those produced by cold fronts are typically more sudden and violent. Weather forecasts that mention cold fronts or predict temperatures much above 80° in the lowlands and valleys should arouse concern.

The most risky part of hiking in the White Mountains, in the opinion of many people, has always been the drive to the trailhead, and the recent rapid increase in New Hampshire's moose population has added a significant new hazard. During the first nine months of one recent year, for example, collisions between moose and automobiles caused the deaths of four people and more than 160 moose. The great majority of these collisions occurs in the period from early May to the middle of July, when the moose leave the woods to avoid the black flies and seek out the road salt that has accumulated in ditches near highways. Motorists need to be aware of the seriousness of the problem, particularly at night when these huge, dark-colored animals are both active and very difficult to see. Instinct often causes them to face an auto rather than run from it, and they are also apt to cross the road unpredictably as a car approaches. It is thus safest to assume that moose will behave in the most inconvenient manner possible. Otherwise they probably constitute little threat to hikers on foot, though it would be wise to give bulls a wide berth during the fall mating season.

Bears are common but tend to keep well out of sight. The last known case of a human killed by a bear in New Hampshire was in 1784—a 10-year-old boy in the town of Londonderry—and since that time many thousands of bears have perished from attacks by humans or their automobiles. Nevertheless, the bear is a large and unpredictable animal that must be treated with respect, though not fear. Several recent serious incidents have been unnecessarily provoked by deliberate feeding of bears, or by harassment by a dog leading to an attack on people nearby. Bears live mostly on nuts, berries, and other plants, and dead animals, and rarely kill anything larger than a mouse. Since the closing of many of the town dumps in the White Mountain region, where some bears routinely foraged for food, bears have become a nuisance and even a hazard at some popular campsites; any bear that has lost its natural fear of humans and gotten used to living off us is extremely dangerous.

The philosophy of dealing with bears has undergone some modification in recent years. Formerly the usual advice was that, if approached by a bear, one should throw down one's pack and back away slowly. This advice works, but unfortunately it teaches the bear that people have food and that very little effort and risk is required to make them part with it. The result is a bear that is likely to be more aggressive toward the next visitor, which may result in injury to the human (who may be you) and frequently results in a death sentence for the bear. Most hikers regard bears as an indispensable feature of wild country in New England, and preservation of the bears requires us to make sure that they remain wild, so feeding them either deliberately or through carelessness should be regarded as tantamount to bringing about their execution. Thus the current advice is that a hiker confronted by a bear should attempt to appear neither threatening nor frightened, and should back off slowly but not abandon food unless the bear appears irresistibly aggressive. A loud noise, such as one made by a whistle or by banging metal pots, is often useful. Careful protection of food at campsites is mandatory; it must never be kept overnight in a tent, but should be hung between trees well off the ground.

Deer-hunting season (with rifles) is in November, when you'll probably see many more hunters than deer. Seasons involving muzzle-loader and bow-and-arrow hunters extend from mid-October through mid-December. Most hunters usually stay fairly close to roads, and, in general, the harder it would be to haul a deer out of a given area, the lower the probability that a hiker will encounter hunters there. In any case, avoid wearing brown or anything that might give a hunter the impression of the white flash of a white-tailed deer running away. Wearing hunter's-orange clothing is strongly recommended.

There are no poisonous snakes in the White Mountains. Mosquitoes and black flies are the woodland residents most frequently encountered by hikers. Mosquitoes are worst throughout the summer in low, wet areas, and black flies are most bloodthirsty in June and early July; at times these winged pests can make life in the woods virtually unbearable. Fishermen's head-nets can be useful. The most effective repellents are based on the active ingredient diethyl-meta-toluamide, generally known as "DEET," but there are growing doubts about its safety. Hikers should probably apply repellents with DEET to clothing rather than skin where possible, and avoid using them on small children. There are other effective repellents available. There is also a good deal of folklore and tradition on the subject: people who seek true solitude in the woods often employ the traditional creosote-scented recipes, reasoning that anything that repels fellow humans might have the same effect on insects.

Cars parked at White Mountain trailheads are frequently targets of break-ins, so valuables or expensive equipment should never be left in cars while you are off hiking, particularly overnight.

BROOK CROSSINGS

Rivers and brooks are often crossed without bridges, and it is usually possible to jump from rock to rock; a hiking staff or stick is a great aid to balance. Use caution; several fatalities have resulted from hikers (particularly solo hikers) falling on slippery rocks and suffering an injury that rendered them unconscious, causing them to drown in relatively shallow streams. If you need to wade across (often the safer course), wearing boots, but not necessarily socks, is recommended. Note that many crossings that may only be a nuisance in summer may be a serious obstacle in cold weather when one's feet and boots must be kept dry. Higher waters, which can turn innocuous brooks into virtually uncrossable torrents, come in the spring as snow melts, or after heavy rainstorms, particularly in the fall when trees drop their leaves and take up less water. Avoid trails with potentially dangerous stream crossings during these high-water periods. If you are cut off from roads by swollen streams, it is better to make a long detour, even if you need to wait and spend a night in the woods. Rushing current can make wading extremely hazardous, and several deaths have resulted. Flood waters may subside within a few hours, especially in small brooks. It is particularly important not to camp on the far side of a brook from your exit point if the crossing is difficult and heavy rain is predicted.

DRINKING WATER

The pleasure of quaffing a cup of water fresh from a pure mountain spring is one of the traditional attractions of the mountains. Unfortunately, in many mountain regions, including the White Mountains, the presence of cysts of the intestinal parasite *Giardia lamblia* in water sources is thought to be common, though difficult to prove. It is impossible to be completely sure whether a given source is safe, no matter how clear the water or remote the location. The safest course is for day hikers to carry their own water, and for those who use sources in the woods to treat the water before drinking it. There are also various kinds of filters available, which are constantly becoming less bulky and expensive and more effective; they also remove impurities from water, often making it look and taste better, so that sources that are unappealing in the untreated state can be made to produce drinkable water. Water may also be boiled for five minutes or disinfected with an iodine-based disinfectant. Chlorine-based products, such as Halazone, are ineffective in water that contains organic impurities, and all water-purification chemicals tend to deteriorate quickly in the pack. Remember to allow extra contact time (and use twice as many tablets) if the water is very cold. The symptoms of giardiasis are severe intestinal distress and diarrhea, but such discomforts can have many other causes, making the disease difficult to diagnose accurately. The principal cause of the spread of this noxious ailment in the woods is probably careless disposal of human waste. Keep it at least 200 ft. away from water sources. If there are no toilets nearby, dig a hole 6 to 8 in. deep (but not below the organic layer of the soil) for a latrine and cover it completely after use. The bacteria in the organic layer of the soil will then decompose the waste naturally. Many people unknowingly carry the *Giardia* parasites, which have sometimes been present in municipal water supplies and frequently do not produce symptoms. Some authorities feel that the disease is more likely to be spread by party members to each other than by contaminated water. For this reason it would be advisable to be scrupulous about washing hands after answering calls of nature.

DISTANCES, TIMES, AND ELEVATION GAINS

The distances, times, and elevation gains that appear in the tables at the end of trail descriptions are cumulative from the starting point at the head of each table. Elevation gains are given for the reverse direction only when they are significant, *and are not cumulative*—they apply only to the interval between the current entry and the next one (which will be the entry *before* the current one in the list). Reverse elevation gains are not given for trails which have summaries in both directions. All trails in this book have been measured with a surveyor's wheel within the past few years. Minor inconsistencies sometimes occur when measured distances are rounded, and the distances given often differ from those on trail signs. Elevation gains are estimated and rounded to the nearest 50 ft.; some elevation gains can be determined almost to the foot, while others (such as where several minor ups and downs are traversed) are only roughly accurate. Elevations of places are estimated as closely as possible when not given precisely by our source maps. The USGS maps are used as the basis for all such information except for the area covered by Bradford Washburn's map of the Presidential Range, where that map supersedes the USGS maps.

There is no reliable method for predicting how much time a particular hiker or group of hikers will actually take to complete a particular hike on a particular day. The factors that influence the speed of an individual hiker or hiking group are simply too numerous and too complex. Most hikers will observe that their own individual speed varies from day to day, often by a significant amount, depending on a number of factors, many of which—such as fatigue, weight of pack, or weather conditions—are fairly easy to identify. (Hikers often forget to consider that a given segment of trail will usually require more time—perhaps much more—when encountered at the end of a strenuous day compared to what it might have required if encountered at the start of the day.)

However, in order to give inexperienced hikers a rough basis for planning, estimated times have been calculated for this book by allowing a half-hour for each mile of distance or 1000 ft. of climbing. No attempt has been made to adjust these times for the difficulties of specific trails, since fine-tuning an inherently limited method would probably only lead to greater unjustified reliance on it. In many cases, as hikers gain experience, they find that they usually require a fairly predictable percentage of book time to hike most trails, but eventually they are almost certain to encounter a significant exception. Therefore, all hikers using this book should be well aware of the limitations of the time-estimating formula, and should always regard book times with a critical eye and check each trail description thoroughly for trail conditions that might render the given times misleading; these times may be very inadequate for steep or rough trails, for hikers with heavy packs, or for large groups, particularly with inexperienced hikers. Average descent times vary even more greatly, with agility and the condition of the hiker's knees being the principal factors; times for descending are given in this book only for segments of ridgecrest trails that have substantial descents in both directions. In winter, times are even less predictable: on a packed trail, travel may be faster than in summer, but with heavy packs or in deep snow it may take two or three times the summer estimate.

FIRE REGULATIONS

Campfire permits are no longer required in the WMNF, but hikers who build fires are still legally responsible for any damage they may cause. Fires are not permitted on state lands except at explicitly designated sites, and on private land the owner's permission is required. During periods when there is a high risk of forest fires, the Forest Supervisor may temporarily close the entire WMNF against public entry. Such general closures apply only as long as the dangerous conditions prevail. Other forest lands throughout New Hampshire or Maine may be closed during similar periods through proclamation by the governors. These special closures are given wide publicity so that local residents and visitors alike may realize the danger of fires in the woods.

PROTECTING THE BEAUTY OF THE MOUNTAINS

Please use special care above timberline. Extreme weather and a short growing season make the vegetation in these areas especially fragile. Mere footsteps can destroy the toughest natural cover, so please try to stay on the trail or walk on rocks. And, of course, don't camp above timberline—it is illegal and very damaging to alpine vegetation.

Once every campsite had a dump, and many trails became unsightly with litter. Now visitors are asked to bring trash bags and carry out everything—food, paper, glass, cans—they carry in. Cooperation with the "carry in/carry out" program has been outstanding, resulting in a great decrease in trailside litter over the past few years, and the concept has grown to "carry out more than you carried in." We hope you will join in the effort. Your fellow backcountry users will appreciate it.

A FINAL NOTE

Hiking is a sport of self-reliance. Its high potential for adventure and relatively low level of regulation have been made possible by the dedication of most hikers to the values of prudence and independence. This tradition of self-reliance imposes an obligation on each of us: at any time we may have to rely on our own ingenuity and judgment, aided by map and compass, to reach our goals or even make a timely exit from the woods. While the penalty for error rarely exceeds an unplanned and uncomfortable night in the woods, more serious consequences are possible. Most hikers find a high degree of satisfaction in obtaining the knowledge and skills that free them from blind dependence on the next blaze or trail sign and enable them to walk in the woods with confidence and assurance. Those who learn the skills of getting about in the woods, the habits of studious acquisition of information before the trip and careful observation while in the woods, soon find that they have earned "the Freedom of the Hills."

The AMC earnestly requests that those who use the trails, shelters, and campsites heed the rules (especially those having to do with camping) of the WMNF, NHDP, and SPNHF. The same consideration should be shown to private landowners. In many cases the privileges enjoyed by hikers today could be withdrawn if rules and conditions are not observed. Trails must not be cut in the WMNF without the approval of the Forest Supervisor, nor elsewhere without consent of the owners and definite provision for maintenance.

The trails that we use and enjoy are only in part the product of government agencies and public nonprofit organizations; there is ultimately no "they" responsible for providing the hiking public with a full variety of interesting, convenient, well-maintained trails. Many trails are cared for by one dedicated person, or a small group. Funds for trail work are scarce, and unless hikers contribute both time and money to the maintenance of trails, the diversity of trails available to the public is almost certain to experience a sad decline. Every hiker can make some contribution to the improvement of the trails, if nothing more than pushing a blowdown off the trail rather than walking around it. They are our trails, and without our participation in their care they will languish. (Write to AMC Trails, Pinkham Notch Camp, Box 298, Gorham, NH 03581, for more information regarding volunteer trail-maintenance activities, or see the AMC Web site, www.outdoors.org.)

Introduction

According to Ticknor's *White Mountains,* published in 1887, the higher peaks "seem to have received the name of White Mountains from the sailors off the coast, to whom they were a landmark and a mystery lifting their crowns of brilliant snow against the blue sky from October until June."

CLIMATE AND VEGETATION

The climate gets much cooler, windier, and wetter at higher elevations. The summit of Mt. Washington is under cloud cover about 55 percent of the time. On an average summer afternoon, the high temperature on the summit is only about 52° F (11° C); in the winter, about 15° F (-9° C). The record low temperature is -46° F. Average winds throughout the day and night are 26 mph in summer and 44 mph in winter. Winds have gusted over 100 mph in every month of the year, and set the world record of 231 mph on April 12, 1934. During the storm of February 24–26, 1969, the observatory recorded a snowfall of 97.8 in. Within a 24-hour period during that storm, a total of 49.3 in. was recorded, at that time a record for the mountain and for all weather observation stations in the United States. Other mountains also experience severe conditions in proportion to their height and exposure.

The forest on the White Mountains is of two major types: the northern hardwood forest (birch, beech, and maple), found at elevations of less than about 3000 ft., and the boreal forest (spruce, fir, and birch), found from about 3000 ft. to the timberline. At low elevations oaks and white pines may be seen, and hemlocks are found in some deep valleys; red pines may grow up to elevations of about 2000 ft. in ledgy areas. Above the timberline is the "krummholz," the gnarled and stunted trees that manage to survive wherever there is a bit of shelter from the violent winds, and the tiny wildflowers, some of which are extremely rare. Hikers are encouraged to be particularly careful in their activities above treeline, as the plants that grow there already have to cope with the severity of the environment. For information about these trees and plants, consult *Trees and Shrubs of Northern New England,* published by the SPNHF, and *At Timberline* and the *AMC Guide to the New England Alpine Summits,* both published by AMC Books.

MAPS

Detailed maps are available from the United States Geological Survey for most of the United States, including all of New Hampshire and Maine. They are published in rectangles of several standard sizes called quadrangles ("quads"). Most areas in the regions covered in this guide are now covered by the recent, more detailed 7.5-minute quads—some in metric format—which have largely replaced the old 15-minute quads. Although topography on the newer maps is excellent, some recent maps are very inaccurate in showing the location of some trails. These maps can be obtained at a number of local outlets and from USGS Map Sales, Federal Center, Box 25286, Denver, CO 80225 (800-USA-MAPS). Index maps showing the available USGS quads in any state (specify states) and an informative pamphlet entitled "Topographic Maps" are available free on request from the USGS. USGS maps are now also available on compact disk from a number of sources.

This 26th edition of the *AMC White Mountain Guide* features 6 new maps that were designed on a computer, using a variety of digital data. The most valuable source of data comes from global position system (GPS) technology. Every mile of trail in the White Mountain National Forest and surrounding areas (except the trails surveyed by Brad Washburn in the 1980's) was hiked and electronically recorded with GPS technology. The resulting maps accurately depict trail locations. All previous maps, including USGS quadrangle maps, relied on less precise techniques to determine a trail's location.

The six maps featured in the guidebook now provide complete coverage of the White Mountain National Forest for the first time. These new maps (except the #1 Presidential Range) are designed at the same size and scale, allowing the user to easily read from one map to the next. Universal Transverse Mercator (UTM) grid coordinates are included on the map sheets to facilitate the use of GPS receivers in the field. Additionally, a mileage scale runs around the outer frame of each map to help users estimate distance.

Digital technology also allows the maps to be printed with five colors, making them easier to read. All National Forest lands are shown in green, with designated Scenic and Wilderness Areas highlighted in darker shades. The hiker and backcountry user should be aware that certain regulations may apply to any lands within the WMNF. It is the responsibility of the individual to be aware of land use restrictions for both public and private land.

Although the original GPS data is very exact, certain features (including roads, streams, and trails) may have been approximated and/or exaggerated in order to show their proper relationships at map scale. We would appreciate your assistance by reporting corrections to: AMC White Mountain Guidebook Committee, Appalachian Mountain Club, 5 Joy Street, Boston, MA 02108.

Extra copies of AMC maps may be purchased at the AMC's Boston and Pinkham Notch offices and at some book and outdoor equipment stores.

Other maps of specific areas of the White Mountains are mentioned in the relevant individual sections of this guide.

CAMPING

Those who camp overnight in the backcountry tend to have more of an impact on the land than day hikers. In the past some popular sites suffered misuse and began to resemble disaster areas as campers left piles of trash and devastated the surrounding trees by stripping them for firewood. For this reason backpacking hikers should take great care to minimize their effect on the mountains by practicing low-impact camping and making conscious efforts to preserve the natural forest. One alternative is to camp in well-prepared, designated sites; the popular ones are supervised by caretakers. The other alternative has come to be called "clean camping": to disperse camping over a wide area, out of sight of trails and roads, and to camp with full respect for wilderness values. Repeated camping on one site compacts the soil and makes it difficult for vegetation to survive. The objective of clean camping is to leave no trace of one's presence, so that the site will not be reused before it has a chance to recover.

There are more than fifty backcountry shelters and tentsites in the White Mountain area, open on a first-come, first-served basis. Some sites have summer caretakers who collect an overnight fee to help defray expenses. Most sites have shelters, a few have only tent platforms, and some have both. Shelters are intended as overnight accommodations for persons carrying their own bedding and cooking supplies. The more popular shelters are often full, so be prepared to camp at a legal site off-trail with tents or tarps. Make yourself aware of regulations and restrictions prior to your trip. Unless one plans carefully, it is quite possible to find oneself far from any legal, practical campsite with night swiftly approaching.

If you camp away from established sites, look for a spot more than 200 ft. from the trail and from any surface water, and observe Forest Service camping regulations for the area. Bring all needed shelter, including whatever poles, stakes, ground insulation, and cord are required. Try to choose a clear, level site for pitching your tent. Use a compass, and check landmarks carefully to find your way to and from your campsite. Do not cut boughs or branches for bedding.

Avoid clearing vegetation and never make a ditch around the tent. Wash your dishes and yourself well away from streams, ponds and springs. Heed the rules of neatness, sanitation, and fire prevention, and carry out everything—food, paper, glass, cans, etc.—that you carry in (and whatever trash less thoughtful campers may have left). Food should not be kept in your tent; if possible, hang it from a tree—well down from a high, sturdy branch and well away from the tree trunk—to protect it from raccoons and bears.

In some camping areas, a "human browse line" where people have gathered firewood over the years is quite evident: limbs are gone from trees, the ground is devoid of dead wood, and vegetation has been trampled as people scoured the area for the smallest burnable twig. The use of portable stoves is practically mandatory in popular areas, and is encouraged elsewhere to prevent damage to vegetation. Operate stoves with great caution—fuels can be explosive. Wood campfires should not be made unless there is ample dead and down wood available near your site; never cut green trees. Such fires must be made in safe, sheltered places and not in leaves or rotten wood or against logs, trees, or stumps. Before you build a fire, clear a space at least 5 ft. in radius of all flammable material down to the mineral soil. Under no circumstances should a fire be left unattended. All fires must be completely extinguished with earth or water before you leave a campsite, even temporarily. Campers should restore the campfire site to as natural an appearance as possible before leaving the campsite.

Roadside Campgrounds

The WMNF operates a number of roadside campgrounds with limited facilities; fees are charged, and several of these campgrounds are now managed by private concessionaires. Consult the WMNF offices for details. Many of these campgrounds are full on summer weekends. Reservations for sites at some WMNF campgrounds can be made through MISTIX (800-283-CAMP). Several New Hampshire state parks also have campgrounds located conveniently for hikers in the White Mountains and other parts of the state. No reservations can be made at state campgrounds. For details on state parks and campgrounds, contact the Office of Vacation Travel, Box 856, Concord, NH 03301 (603-271-2665). Brochures on state parks and state and private campgrounds are usually available at New Hampshire highway rest areas throughout the normal camping season.

Camping Regulations

Trailside camping is really practical only within the WMNF, with a few limited exceptions, such as the established campsites on the Appalachian Trail. The laws of the states of Maine and New Hampshire require that permission be obtained from the owner to camp on private land, and that permits be obtained to build campfires anywhere outside the WMNF, except at officially designated campsites. Camping and campfires are not permitted in New Hampshire state parks except in campgrounds.

Overnight camping is permitted in almost all of the WMNF. To limit or prevent some of the adverse impacts of concentrated, uncontrolled camping, the USFS has adopted regulations for a number of areas in the WMNF that are threatened by overuse and misuse. The objective of the Forest Protection Area (FPA) program (formerly called the Restricted Use Area program) is not to hinder backpackers and campers, but to disperse their use of the land so that people can enjoy themselves in a clean and attractive environment without causing deterioration of natural resources. By protecting the plants, water, soil, and wildlife of the White Mountains, these restrictions should help to provide a higher quality experience for all visitors. Because hikers and backpackers have cooperated with FPA rules, many areas once designated as FPAs have recovered and are no longer under formal restrictions. However, common sense and self-imposed restrictions are still necessary to prevent damage.

Stated briefly, the 1997 FPA rules prohibit camping and wood or charcoal fires above timberline (where trees are less than 8 ft. in height), or within a specified distance of certain roads, trails, streams, and other locations, except at designated sites. Some of these restrictions are in force throughout the year and others only from May 1 to November 1. This guide provides information on FPAs as of 1997 in each relevant section, but since the list of restricted areas changes from year to year, hikers should contact the USFS in Laconia NH (603-524-6450) or any Ranger District office for up-to-date information.

WINTER CLIMBING

Snowshoeing and cross-country skiing on White Mountain trails and peaks have steadily become more popular in the last decade. Increasing numbers of hikers have discovered the beauty of the woods in winter, and advances in clothing and equipment have made it possible for experienced winter travelers to enjoy great comfort and safety. The greatest danger is that it begins to look too easy and too safe, while snow, ice, and weather conditions are constantly changing, and a relatively trivial error of judgment may have grave, even fatal, consequences. Conditions can vary greatly from day to day, and from trail to trail; therefore, much more experience is required to foresee and avoid dangerous situations in winter than in summer. Trails are frequently difficult or impossible to follow, and navigation skills are hard to learn in adverse weather conditions (as anyone who has tried to read a map in a blizzard can attest). "Breaking trail" on snowshoes through new snow can be strenuous and exhausting work. Some trails go through areas that may pose a severe avalanche hazard. In a "white-out" above treeline, it may be almost impossible to tell the ground from the sky, and hikers frequently become disoriented.

Winter on the lower trails in the White Mountains may require only snowshoes or skis and some warm clothing. Even so, summer hiking boots are usually inadequate, flashlight batteries fail quickly (a headlamp with battery pack works better), and water in canteens freezes unless carried in an insulated container or wrapped in a sock or sweater. The winter hiker needs good physical conditioning from regular exercise, and must dress carefully in order to avoid overheating and excessive perspiration, which soaks clothing and soon leads to chilling. Cotton clothes are useful only as long as they can be kept perfectly dry (an impossible task, thus the winter climbers' maxim "cotton kills"); only wool and some of the newer synthetics retain their insulating values when wet. Fluid intake must increase, as dehydration can be a serious problem in the dry winter air.

Above timberline, conditions often require specialized equipment, and also skills and experience of a different magnitude. The conditions on the Presidential Range in winter are as severe as any in North America south of the great mountains of Alaska and the Yukon Territory. On the summit of Mt. Washington in winter, winds average 44 mph and daily high temperatures average 15° F. There are few calm days, and even on an average day conditions will probably be too severe for any but the most experienced and well-equipped climbers. The Mt. Washington Observatory routinely records wind velocities in excess of 100 mph, and temperatures are often far below zero. The combination of high wind and low temperature has such a cooling effect that the worst conditions on Mt. Washington are approximately equal to the worst reported from Antarctica, despite the much greater cold in the latter region. Extremely severe storms can develop suddenly and unexpectedly. But the most dangerous aspect of winter in the White Mountains is the extreme variability of the weather: it is not unusual for a cold, penetrating, wind-driven rain to be followed within a few hours by a cold front that brings below-zero temperatures and high winds.

No book can begin to impart all the knowledge necessary to cope safely with the potential for such brutal conditions, but helpful information can be found in *Winterwise: A Backpacker's Guide* by John M. Dunn (1988, Adirondack Mountain Club) and the *AMC Guide to Winter Camping* by Stephen Gorman (1991, AMC Books), which despite their titles are also quite useful for those primarily interested in day-hiking. Hikers who are interested in extending their activities into the winter season are strongly advised to seek out organized parties with leaders who have extensive winter experience. Each year the AMC and Adirondack Mountain Club operate a week-long winter school that exposes participants to techniques and equipment for safe winter travel. The AMC and several of its chapters also sponsor numerous workshops on evenings and weekends, in addition to introductory winter hikes and regular winter schedules through which participants can gain experience. Information on such activities can be obtained from the AMC information center at 5 Joy St., Boston, MA 02108 (617-523-0636; www.outdoors.org).

WHITE MOUNTAIN NATIONAL FOREST

Most of the higher White Mountains are within the White Mountain National Forest (WMNF), which was established under the Weeks Act and now comprises about 770,000 acres, of which about 47,000 acres are in Maine and the rest in New Hampshire. It is important to understand that this is not a national *park,* but a national *forest*; parks are established primarily for preservation and recreation, while national forests are managed for multiple use. In the administration of national forests, the following objectives are considered: recreation development, timber production, watershed protection, and wildlife propagation. It is the policy of the USFS to manage logging operations so that trails, streams, camping places, and other spots of public interest are protected. Mountain recreation has been identified as the most important resource in the WMNF. The boundaries of the WMNF are usually marked wherever they cross roads or trails, usually by red-painted corner posts and blazes. Hunting and fishing are permitted in the WMNF under the state laws; state licenses are required. Organized groups, including those sponsored by nonprofit organizations, must apply for an Outfitter-Guide Permit if they conduct trips on WMNF land for which they charge any kind of fee; contact any WMNF office for details. Much informational literature has been published by the WMNF and is available free of charge at the Forest Supervisor's office in Laconia, the Ranger District offices (list below), and other information centers.

The national Wilderness Preservation System, which included the Great Gulf, was established in 1964 with passage of the Wilderness Act. The Presidential Range–Dry River Wilderness, the Pemigewasset Wilderness, the Sandwich Range Wilderness, and the Caribou–Speckled Mountain Wilderness have since been added to the system, making a total of about 115,000 acres of designated Wilderness in the WMNF—about 15 percent of its area. Regulations for these areas prohibit logging and road building, as well as any use of mechanized equipment or vehicles, including bicycles. It should be noted that Wilderness areas are established by an act of Congress, not simply by USFS administrative action, though the recommendations of the USFS are a critical part of the process of selecting areas for congressional designation. Management of these areas in accordance with guidelines contained in the Wilderness Act is entrusted to the USFS. Most important is the protection of the natural environment, and among other qualities that the USFS is charged with preserving is the opportunity for visitors to enjoy solitude and challenge within this natural environment. As a consequence, for example, "structures for user convenience" such as shelters are not permitted in Wilderness. In general, Wilderness visitors should look forward to a rougher, wilder, more primitive experience than in other parts of the WMNF, and should expect USFS regulations to emphasize the preservation of Wilderness qualities even when substantial inconvenience to hikers results. Those who are mainly looking for a pleasant hiking experience in scenic surroundings, perhaps with a group of cherished friends, would do well to look elsewhere—there are many wild, beautiful places outside of designated Wilderness. It is one of the ironies of Wilderness protection that such designation often draws crowds of people who imagine they can enjoy a true wilderness experience simply by visiting a piece of land with this official certification, and as a result the wildness that caused the area to be designated as Wilderness is severely compromised.

The USFS has also established nine Scenic Areas in the WMNF to preserve lands of outstanding or unique natural beauty: Gibbs Brook, Nancy Brook, Greeley Ponds, Pinkham Notch, Lafayette Brook, Rocky Gorge, Lincoln Woods, Sawyer Pond, and Snyder Brook. Furthermore, camping is restricted in many areas under the Forest Protection Area (FPA) program to protect vulnerable areas from damage. To preserve the rare alpine plants of the Mt. Washington Range and other significant and uncommon ecosystems within the entire WMNF, rules prohibit removal of any tree, shrub, or plant without written permission. Cultural sites and artifacts on public lands are also protected by federal law. If you discover such remains, please leave them undisturbed.

WMNF Offices and Ranger Districts (R.D.s)

Note: The WMNF plans, at some time in the near future, to construct a new central office in the Lincoln area and then move all operations now conducted at Laconia to the Lincoln site. The Pemigewasset and Ammonoosuc Ranger Districts would then be combined and located at the Lincoln facility. (Also, the Evans Notch Ranger District has been absorbed by the Androscoggin Ranger District.) Until these plans are carried out, the information listed below will be valid.

The Androscoggin and Saco Ranger District offices have sometimes been open seven days a week in the summer, occasionally with evening hours. Otherwise, the offices are open during normal business hours.

Forest Supervisor, PO Box 638, Laconia, NH 03247 (on North Main St., across railroad tracks from downtown section). Tel. 603-528-8721; TDD (for hearing impaired) 603-528-8722.

Ammonoosuc R.D., Trudeau Rd., Bethlehem, NH 03574 (just north of US 3 opposite Gale River Rd.). Tel. 603-869-2626; TDD 603-869-3104.

Androscoggin R.D., 300 Glen Rd., Gorham, NH 03581 (at south end of town along NH 16). Tel. 603-466-2713; TDD 603-466-2856.

Pemigewasset R.D., RFD 3, Box 15, Rte. 175, Plymouth, NH 03264 (from I-93 Exit 25, turn left uphill, bear left at fork at top of hill onto NH 175 (north), then on left in 1 mi.). Tel. 603-536-1310.

Saco R. D., RFD 1, Box 94, Conway, NH 03818 (on Kancamagus Highway just west of NH 16). Tel. 603-447-5448; TDD 603-447-1989.

As noted, the Evans Notch R.D. has been absorbed by the Androscoggin R.D., but the former office on US 2 east of the village of Bethel ME is still open as a visitor center and is the appropriate source for information on trails and areas in the Evans Notch–Speckled Mtn. region: RFD #2, Box 2270, Bethel, ME 04217 (207-824-2134).

APPALACHIAN TRAIL (AT)

This footpath runs more than 2000 mi. from Springer Mtn. in Georgia to Katahdin in Maine, and traverses the White Mountains for about 170 mi. in a southwest to northeast direction, from the New Hampshire–Vermont boundary in the Connecticut River Valley at Hanover to Grafton Notch, a short distance past the Maine–New Hampshire boundary. Its route traverses many of the major peaks and ranges of the White Mountains, following many historic and scenic trails. Except for a few short segments between Hanover and Glencliff, the trails that make up the AT in the White Mountains are all described in this book. In each section of this guide through which the AT passes, its route through the section is described in a separate paragraph near the beginning. (South to north, the trail passes consecutively through Sections 13, 6, 5, 3, 1, 2, 1 again, 9, and 11.) Those interested in following the AT as a continuous path should also consult the Appalachian Trail Conference's *Guide to the Appalachian Trail in New Hampshire and Vermont*. Information on the Appalachian Trail and the several guidebooks that cover its entire length can be obtained from the Appalachian Trail Conference, PO Box 236, Harpers Ferry, WV 25425.

With the passage of the National Trails System Act by Congress on October 2, 1968, the Appalachian Trail became the first federally protected footpath in this country and was officially designated the Appalachian National Scenic Trail. Under this act the Appalachian Trail is administered primarily as a footpath by the secretary of the interior in consultation with the secretary of agriculture and representatives of the several states through which it passes. In addition, an Advisory Council for the Appalachian National Scenic Trail was appointed by the secretary of the interior. It includes representatives of each of the states and the several hiking clubs recommended by the Appalachian Trail Conference.

SOCIETY FOR THE PROTECTION OF NEW HAMPSHIRE FORESTS (SPNHF)

This organization has worked since 1901 to protect the mountains, forests, wetlands, and farm lands of New Hampshire, and to encourage wise forestry and land-use practices. It owns Lost River in Kinsman Notch, a substantial reservation on Monadnock, and a number of other lands. In cooperation with the AMC, it protects and maintains the Monadnock–Sunapee Greenway. Its headquarters building in Concord NH was designed as a showcase of the latest techniques of energy conservation. For membership information, contact the SPNHF, 54 Portsmouth St., Concord, NH 03301 (603-224-9945).

ABBREVIATIONS

The following abbreviations are used in trail descriptions.

hr.	hour(s)
min.	minutes(s)
mph	miles per hour
in.	inch(es)
ft.	foot, feet
km.	kilometer(s)
yd.	yard(s)
est.	estimated
AMC	Appalachian Mountain Club
AT	Appalachian Trail
CMC	Chocorua Mountain Club
CTA	Chatham Trails Association
CU	Camp Union
DOC	Dartmouth Outing Club
FR	Forest Road (WMNF)
HA	Hutmen's Association
JCC	Jackson Conservation Commission
MBPL	Maine Bureau of Public Lands
NC	Nature Conservancy
NHDP	New Hampshire Division of Parks
PEAOC	Phillips Exeter Academy Outing Club
RMC	Randolph Mountain Club
SLA	Squam Lakes Association
SPNHF	Society for the Protection of New Hampshire Forests
SSOC	Sub Sig Outing Club
USFS	United States Forest Service
USGS	United States Geological Survey
WMNF	White Mountain National Forest
WODC	Wonalancet Outdoor Club
WVAIA	Waterville Valley Athletic and Improvement Association

ACKNOWLEDGMENTS

A book like the *White Mountain Guide* is the product of the efforts of many people, including those who contributed to the previous 25 editions over the period of 90 years since it was first brought into being. The editors constantly have in mind the enthusiastic mountain-walkers who trod the trails before us and created and preserved this magnificent tradition that is now our cherished responsibility. Properly recognizing everyone, past and present, who made some contribution to this book would require a small book of its own, but the editors would like to recognize a few people whose contributions were especially indispensible.

First, we would like to thank our families, and particularly our wives, Anita Burroughs and Debi Clark. Their contributions to this book, though not outwardly visible, were immense. Without their constant assistance, encouragement, and support, as well as companionship on many hikes—and tolerance for two husbands who are obsessed by the project of maintaining this book and could argue for half an hour the question of whether a particular trail segment is steep or merely rather steep—we would never have been able to give this book the time and energy we feel it deserves. Therefore we dedicate our part of the life of this venerable book to them, with love and gratitude.

Among the others who made unusually important contributions to this book, we wish to recognize the following:

First, we want to thank the publications staff of the AMC, including Gordon Hardy, Mark Russell, Elisabeth Brady, and Ola Frank. Not only did they assume all the myriad (and frequently tedious) professional responsibilities of publishing this book so that we could concentrate on preparing the text, they managed to cope with the eccentricities and frailties of the editors without complaint, giving generous support and assistance even when we made their jobs harder.

Also, we want to thank Larry Garland, who turned our fantasy of bright, beautiful new computer-generated maps into a reality. His obsession with making things right is at least equal to our own, and as a result he has managed to digest a staggering amount of detail and overcome many difficulties inherent to such a pioneering effort in order to produce maps that will actually help hikers plan their trips and complete them successfully. Larry deserves more appreciation than we will ever be able to give him.

Larry, in turn, would like to thank the following individuals and concerns that contributed to this immense effort. Producing the new digital maps would not have been possible without the committment and support of the AMC Leadership Team, and especially Ken Kimball and Gordon Hardy who mentored the project from its inception in 1994.

Many people assisted with the mapping project, and the cartographer would like to thank his trail mappers/GPS assistants: Matt Bowman; Craig Collins; Linda Comeau; John DeLeo and students at Lyndon State College, VT; Brian Gehan; Sarah Giffen; Kenneth Hockert; Eric, Ken and Sarah Kimball; Bo Miller; Brendan O'Reilly; Steve Piotrow; Nicole Robillard; and Mike Stevens.

Thanks are also due to Sharon O'Neill and Susan Peterson, who helped with issues of digitizing. Steve Engle, Brendan O'Reilly, Mark Russell, and Dave Salisbury generously provided their time and expertise as map reviewers. Technical assistance was offered by Brad Beeler, Maine Technical Source; Steve Burgess, HEB Engineers; Patrick Dunlavey; Ken Rancourt and the Mount Washington Observatory; and Fay Rubin, Complex Systems Research Center.

Products and services were provided by Mike Margolis, Trimble Navigation; Kathy Rogers, Hewlett-Packard Co.; and Robert White, Whitestar Corp.

Finally, Larry would like to thank the members of the US Forest Service, White Mountain National Forest, most notably Rebecca Oreskes and Norma Sorgman.

Then, we want to thank those who made other contributions to this book. For helping review sections of the manuscript and making numerous suggestions for improvements in details of both fact and style, we want to thank John Egsgard, Roioli Schweiker, Roy Schweiker, and Steve Smith. For providing numerous corrections and suggestions of the same sort, we want to thank Mike Bromberg and Nicole Cormen, as well as the others, too numerous to mention, who helped in some way to make this a better, more accurate book. We also want to thank those individuals from the trail-maintaining organizations who provided information and advice: Rebecca Oreskes, Dave Pratt, Brad Ray, and Eric Swett of the USFS; George Zink and Peter Smart of the WODC; Ruth Antonides of the WVAIA; and Martha Carlson of the Sandwich Land Trust Committee.

Section 1

Mount Washington and the Southern Ridges

This section includes the summit of Mt. Washington and the major ridges that run south from it, which constitute the southern portion of the Presidential Range. It is bounded on the north approximately by the line formed by the Mt. Washington Cog Railway and the Mt. Washington Auto Rd., on the east by NH 16, on the south by US 302, and on the west by US 302 and the Base Rd. The northern portion of the Presidential Range, including Mts. Clay, Jefferson, Adams, and Madison, and the Great Gulf, is covered in Section 2 of this book. Many of the trails described in Section 2 also provide routes to Mt. Washington.

The AMC Presidential Range map (map #1) covers this entire section except for the Iron Mountain Trail and several trails in the Southern Montalban region in the south part of the section. All these trails (and much of the rest of this section as well) are covered by the AMC Crawford Notch–Sandwich Range map (map #3). The Davis Path is the only trail not completely covered by one map or the other; however, all but the southern end is on map #1 and all but the northern end on map #3.

Note: No hotel or overnight lodging for the public is available on the summit of Mt. Washington. No camping is permitted above treeline in summer. In winter, above-treeline camping is permitted in places where there is at least two feet of snow cover on the ground, but not on frozen bodies of water nor on the east face of Mt. Washington's summit cone (the area above Tuckerman and Huntington ravines and the Alpine Garden, running up to the summit).

In this section the Appalachian Trail follows the entire Webster Cliff Trail from Crawford Notch to its intersection with the Crawford Path near the summit of Mt. Pierce, then follows the Crawford Path to the summit of Mt. Washington. On the way it also crosses the summits of Mts. Webster, Jackson, and Pierce, and passes near Mts. Eisenhower, Franklin, and Monroe. From Mt. Washington, it descends to the Gulfside Trail (see Section 2) via the Trinity Heights Connector. Then, after passing over the ridge of the Northern Peaks (although missing most of the summits) and through the Great Gulf—areas also covered in Section 2—it returns to Section 1 at the Mt. Washington Auto Rd. and follows the Old Jackson Road to Pinkham Notch Visitor Center and NH 16.

MOUNTAIN SAFETY

Caution: Mt. Washington has a well-earned reputation as the most dangerous small mountain in the world. Storms increase in violence with great rapidity toward the summit. The highest wind velocity ever recorded at any surface weather station (231 mph on April 12, 1934) was attained on Mt. Washington. Judged by the wind-chill temperatures, the worst conditions on Mt. Washington are approximately equal to the worst reported from Antarctica, although actual temperatures on Mt. Washington are not as low. If you begin to experience difficulty from weather conditions, remember that the worst is yet to come, and turn back, without shame, before it is too late. (This warning applies as well to all peaks above timberline, particularly the Northern Peaks.) Each hiker should carry, as a bare minimum, a good rain suit with a hood (or equivalent outfit) that will also protect from wind, an extra sweater, a wool hat, and mittens. Cotton clothes, and blue jeans in particular, while popular and generally suitable for summer ascents of lower mountains, become a threat to survival in bad conditions above treeline due to cotton's propensity for promoting rapid heat loss when wet, which therefore contributes greatly to the development of hypothermia.

Ascents of the mountain in winter are sometimes easy enough to deceive inexperienced hikers into false confidence, but the worst conditions are inconceivably brutal and can materialize with little warning. Safe ascent of the mountain in winter requires much warm clothing, some special equipment such as crampons and an ice ax, and experienced leadership. From Columbus Day to Memorial Day, no building is open to provide shelter or refuge to hikers.

Inexperienced hikers sometimes misjudge the difficulty of climbing Mt. Washington by placing too much emphasis on the relatively short distance from the trailheads to the summit. To a person used to walking around the neighborhood, the trail distance of 4 mi. or so sounds rather tame. But the most important factor in the difficulty of the trip is the altitude gain of around 4000 ft. from base to summit, give or take a few hundred feet depending on the route chosen. To a person unused to mountain trails or in less than excellent physical condition, this unrelenting uphill grind can be grueling and intensely discouraging. If you are not an experienced hiker or a trained athlete, you will almost certainly enjoy the ascent of Mt. Washington a great deal more if you build up to it with easier climbs in areas with less exposure to potentially severe weather.

Visitors ascending the mountain on foot should carry a compass and should take care to stay on the trails. If you are forced to travel in conditions of reduced visibility, favor the main trails with their large yellow-topped cairns over the less-used connecting trails that are often far less clearly marked. The hiker who becomes lost from the trails above treeline in dense fog or a white-out, particularly if the weather is rapidly deteriorating, is in a grave predicament. There is no completely satisfactory course of action in this situation, since the objective is to get below treeline as quickly as possible—with or without a trail—but the weather exposure is generally worse to the west while cliffs are more prevalent in the ravines to the east. If you know where the nearest major trail should be, then it is probably best to try to find it. If you have adequate clothing, it may be best to find a scrub patch and shelter yourself in it. In the absence of alternatives, take note that the cog railway on the western slope and the Mt. Washington Auto Rd. on the eastern slope make a line, although a rather crooked one, from west to east. These landmarks are difficult to miss in even the darkest night or the thickest fog, except in winter conditions when they may be concealed by snowdrifts. Remember which side of the mountain you are on, and travel clockwise or counter-clockwise to the closer of the two, skirting the tops of the ravines; sooner or later you will reach one or the other. Given a choice, aim for the auto road, as the railroad is on the side of the mountain that faces the prevailing winds.

Whether, as is often stated, Mt. Washington has the worst weather in the world, or at least in North America, is subject to debate. But the dozens of people who have died on its slopes in the last century furnish adequate proof that the weather is vicious enough to kill those who are foolish enough to challenge the mountain at its worst. This appalling and needless loss of life has been due, almost without exception, to the failure of robust but incautious hikers to realize that winter-like storms of incredible violence occur frequently, even during the summer months. Winds of hurricane force exhaust even the strongest hiker, and cold rain driven horizontally by the wind penetrates clothing and drains heat from the body. Temperatures in the 30s and low 40s can be even more dangerous than those below freezing, since rain penetrates and soaks clothing much more rapidly than snow, although at colder temperatures sleet and freezing rain on rocks can further obstruct a belated attempt to return to safety.

As the victim's body temperature falls, brain function quickly deteriorates; this is one of the first, and most insidious, effects of excessive heat loss (hypothermia). Eventually the victim loses coordination, staggers, and then falls, numb and dazed, never to rise again. At this point, any form of first aid in the field is likely to do more harm than good, and even immediate access to the best medical treatment obtainable will not assure the victim's survival. Prevention is the only sure cure. It is true that those who misjudge conditions and their own endurance almost always get away with their mistakes, and thus many hikers are lulled into overconfidence. The mountain spares most of those who underestimate it, including many who are guilty of the most grievous foolishness, but now and then it suddenly claims one or two (who may have been guilty of only minor errors of judgment, or even just of inexperience) without warning, or mercy.

All water sources in this heavily used area should be suspected of being unfit to drink; the safest course is to avoid drinking from trailside sources. Water is available at the Sherman Adams summit building during the months in which it is open, roughly from Memorial Day to Columbus Day.

SUMMIT BUILDINGS

No hotel or overnight lodging for the public is available on the summit of Mt. Washington. From Columbus Day to Memorial Day no buildings are open to hikers for shelter or refuge. The principal summit building serving tourists and hikers was named to honor Sherman Adams, a former New Hampshire governor and special assistant to President Eisenhower who was also a legendary White Mountain woodsman and, in his youth, trailmaster of the AMC Trail Crew. Operated by the NH Division of Parks and Recreation during the summer season (mid-May to mid-October), it has food service, a pack room, a souvenir shop, public restrooms, telephones, and a post office. It houses the Mt. Washington Observatory, the Mt. Washington Museum, and facilities for park personnel.

The first Summit House on Mt. Washington was built in 1852. The oldest building still standing on the summit is the Tip Top House, a hotel first built in 1853 and rebuilt after it suffered a fire in 1915. This stone building, now owned by the state of New Hampshire and part of Mt. Washington State Park, has been restored and is open to the public as a historical site when the public summit facilities are in operation, but is not available for lodging or emergency shelter. The second Summit House, 1873–1908, was destroyed by fire.

There are several other buildings on the summit of Mt. Washington, none of them open to the general public. The Yankee Building, built in 1941 to house transmitter facilities for the first FM station in northern New England, is now leased by WMTW-TV and houses two-way radio equipment for various state, federal, and local organizations. The transmitter building and powerhouse for WMTW-TV and WHOM-FM, built in 1954 and designed to withstand winds of 300 mph, provides living quarters for station personnel and houses television and microwave equipment. The Stage Office, built in 1975 to replace a similar building constructed in 1908, is owned by the Mt. Washington Auto Road Company.

MT. WASHINGTON OBSERVATORY

There has been a year-round weather observatory on Mt. Washington from 1870 to 1886, and from 1932 onward. The observatory maintains museum exhibits in the Sherman Adams summit building on Mt. Washington and in a new location on NH 16 just south of North Conway village. The Mt. Washington Observatory is operated by a nonprofit corporation, and individuals from the general public are invited to become members and contribute to the support of its important work. For details contact the Mt. Washington Observatory, Development Dept., PO Box 2448, North Conway, NH 03581 (800-706-0432).

MT. WASHINGTON AUTO ROAD

This road from the Glen House site on NH 16 to the summit, often called the Carriage Road, was constructed in 1855–61. Vehicles are charged a toll at the foot of the mountain. With long zigzags and an easy grade, the road climbs the prominent northeast ridge named for Benjamin Chandler, who died of exposure (as hypothermia was then called) on the upper part in 1856. Hiking on the road is not forbidden, but despite easier grades and smoother footing than hiking trails, the distance is long and the competition with automobile traffic is annoying and potentially dangerous. After dark, however, its advantages increase markedly while its disadvantages decrease greatly, so this road may well be the best escape route for hikers faced with the likelihood of becoming benighted on the trails of Mt. Washington. In winter, severe icing and drifting, along with ruts from official snow-vehicle traffic, make the section above treeline a less pleasant and more difficult route than might be anticipated, particularly for skiers. The emergency shelters that were formerly located along the upper part of the road have been removed. The first four miles of the road (below treeline), although still used by snow vehicles, is now officially maintained as a part of the Great Glen cross-country ski trail network and receives considerable use by skiers.

Because of the continual theft and destruction of trail signs, they are often placed on the trails at some distance from the Auto Rd. The names of some trails are painted on rocks at the point where they leave the road.

The Auto Rd. leaves NH 16 opposite the Glen House site (elevation about 1600 ft.), crosses the Peabody River, and starts the long climb. Just above the 2-

mi. mark, after sharp curves right and then left, the Appalachian Trail (AT) crosses. To the south, the AT follows the Old Jackson Road (now a foot trail) past junctions with the Nelson Crag Trail and the Raymond Path to Pinkham Notch Visitor Center. To the north the AT follows the Madison Gulf Trail toward the Great Gulf and the Northern Peaks. Lowe's Bald Spot, a fine viewpoint, can be reached by an easy walk of about 0.3 mi. from the road via the Madison Gulf Trail and a short side path.

The Auto Rd. continues to treeline, passing to the left of the site of the Halfway House (3840 ft.), and soon swings around the Horn, skirting a prominent shoulder known as the Ledge, where there is a fine view to the north. A short distance above the Ledge, the Chandler Brook Trail descends into the Great Gulf on the right, and soon the route used by snow vehicles in winter diverges right.

Just above the 5-mi. mark, on the right exactly at the sharp turn, there are some remarkable folded strata in the rocks beside the road. Here, near Cragway Spring, the Nelson Crag Trail comes close to the left side of the road. At about 5.5 mi. the road passes through the patch of high scrub in which Dr. B. L. Ball survived two nights in a winter storm in October 1855. A short distance above the 6-mi. mark, where the winter route rejoins, the Wamsutta Trail descends on the right to the Great Gulf, and the Alpine Garden Trail diverges left. The trench-like structures near the road are the remains of the old Glen House Bridle Path, built in 1853. The road soon makes a hairpin turn and circles the left edge of a lawn sometimes called the Cow Pasture, where the Huntington Ravine Trail enters on the left and the remains of an old corral are visible on the right a little farther along. Beyond the 7-mi. post, the Cog Railway approaches and runs above the road on the right; near the tracks, just below the summit, the Bourne monument stands at the spot where Lizzie Bourne perished in September 1855 at the age of 23, the second recorded death on the mountain. Soon the road crosses the Nelson Crag Trail, which enters on the left and climbs to the summit from the right side. The Tuckerman Ravine Trail enters on the left just below the parking-lot complex at about 8 mi. (13 km.), from which the summit buildings are reached by a wooden stairway.

MT. WASHINGTON COG RAILWAY

The Mt. Washington Cog Railway, an unusual artifact of 19th-century engineering with a fascinating history, was completed in 1869. It roughly follows the route of Abel Crawford's second trail up the mountain, which he cut to provide a shorter and more direct route to Mt. Washington than the Crawford Path over the Southern Peaks. Its maximum grade, 13.5 inches to the yard, is equaled by only one other railroad in the world (excluding funicular roads), the railroad on Pilatus in the Alps. The location of the Base Station is called Marshfield, in honor of Sylvester Marsh, an inventor of meat-packing machinery who was the chief promoter and builder of the railway, and Darby Field, leader of the first recorded ascent of Mt. Washington. When the cog railway is in operation, walking on the track is not permitted; at other times it is a poor pedestrian route at best. A new public parking area is located on the Base Rd. about 0.5 mi. west of Marshfield. Hikers who wish to visit or park at the Base Station itself should expect to pay an admission fee.

The cog railway ascends a minor westerly ridge in a nearly straight line to the treeline, which is reached near the trestle called Jacob's Ladder (4800 ft.). This trestle, standing as much as 30 ft. above the mountainside, is the steepest part of the railroad. After crossing the shoulder that extends toward Mt. Clay, the line curves to the right and runs close to the edge of the Great Gulf; there is a fine view across the gulf toward the Northern Peaks from the vicinity of the Gulf Tank (5600 ft.). It is 3 mi. from Marshfield to the summit, and trains ascend in about 1 hr. 10 min.

SKIING IN THE MT. WASHINGTON AREA

A number of cross-country ski trails have been constructed in the vicinity of Pinkham Notch Visitor Center, making it a fine destination for those who wish to enjoy this sport. In addition, several of the hiking trails in the area are also suitable for ski touring. Information on these trails can be obtained at the Center's Trading Post.

The slopes of Tuckerman Ravine and the snowfields on and near the summit cone are justly famous for the opportunities they offer for alpine skiing. The skiing season on the Tuckerman headwall starts about the middle of March and may last into June in some years. The ravine area and the John Sherburne Ski Trail (see below) are patrolled by Forest Service rangers and the Mt. Washington Volunteer Ski Patrol. Warning notices about sections that are unsafe because of ice or possible avalanche danger are posted at Pinkham Notch Visitor Center and in the Tuckerman shelter area. Several lives have been lost in recent years from failure to read and heed these warnings. Skiing areas in the ravine, and also those in the Gulf of Slides or on any part of the mountain above timberline, are subject to wide temperature variations within short periods of time. The difference between corn snow and ice, or between bathing suits and parkas, may be an hour—or even less—when clouds roll in or the afternoon sun drops behind a shoulder of the mountain, so skiers should prepare accordingly. There is a sun deck at Hermit Lake but no longer a warming room open to the public.

The Tuckerman Ravine Trail affords an easy ascent route on foot since it is normally well packed, but skiing downhill on it is prohibited because people walking on the trail would be put in jeopardy. Skiers should descend from Tuckerman Ravine on the John Sherburne Ski Trail (WMNF). This trail—named for John H. Sherburne Jr., whose efforts contributed greatly to its establishment— leaves the south end of the parking lot at Pinkham Notch Visitor Center at the same point as the Gulf of Slides Ski Trail. It ascends by a zigzag course, always to the left (south) of the Tuckerman Ravine Trail and the Cutler River, to the foot of the Little Headwall of the ravine, above the shelter area, where it ends. It is 10 to 50 ft. wide, and although the slope is suitable for expert and intermediate skiers at some points, many less expert skiers can also negotiate this trail because of its width.

The Gulf of Slides, which is situated somewhat similarly to Tuckerman Ravine, receives a large volume of snow that remains in the ravine, so open-slope skiing is possible well into the spring (April and May). Its slopes, though less severe than those in Tuckerman Ravine, are more uniform and avalanche frequently. The Gulf of Slides Ski Trail leaves the south end of the parking lot at Pinkham Notch Visitor Center at the same point as the John Sherburne Ski Trail, and ascends west about 2200 ft. in 2.5 mi. to the bowl of the Gulf of Slides.

The Old Jackson Road is a good run for intermediate skiers. It drops 650 ft. and can be run in 30 min. The ascent takes 1 hr. Skiers should use the old trail route instead of the relocation; enter the old route below the 2-mi. mark, about 0.2 mi. below where the relocated section and the Madison Gulf Trail meet at the Auto Rd.

The upper half of the Mt. Washington Auto Rd. is not usually suitable for skiing due to windblown bare and icy spots and ruts from snow-vehicle traffic. The snowfields between the top of the Tuckerman headwall and the summit cone, and also those on Chandler Ridge near the 6-mi. mark on the Auto Rd., afford good spring skiing at all levels of skill, but are far more exposed to bad weather and require much more effort to reach because of their elevation. The lower half of the Auto Rd. is maintained as a cross-country ski trail by the Great Glen Ski Area. In particular, it affords a link between the Old Jackson Road at the 2-mi. mark and Connie's Way, a ski trail that runs from Pinkham Notch Visitor Center to the 1-mi. mark on the road.

GEOGRAPHY

Mt. Washington (6288 ft.), the highest peak east of the Mississippi River and north of the Carolinas, was seen from the ocean as early as 1605. Its first recorded ascent was in June 1642 by Darby Field of Exeter NH and one or two Algonkian natives, who may have reached the summit by way of the Southern Peaks—though no conclusive case can be made for any of the several reasonably practical routes, since only two rather meager second-hand accounts of this expedition have survived. Field made a second ascent a month later, and several other ascents were made that year, including one by Thomas Georges and Richard Vines of Maine. However, the discovery that the mountain's slopes were not strewn with precious stones led to a sharp decline in interest after this flurry of visits, and it was almost two centuries before visits to Mt. Washington returned to this level. The mountain has a long and varied history of human activity, having been the site of several hotels, a road and a railway, a weather observatory, a daily newspaper, a radio station and a television station, and an assortment of auto, foot, and ski races. *The Story of Mt. Washington* by F. Allen Burt treats the entertaining (and frequently unusual) human history of the mountain in great detail, while Peter Randall's *Mount Washington* is a much shorter and less detailed handbook of human and natural history.

Mt. Washington is a broad, massive mountain with great ravines cut deeply into its steep sides, leaving buttress ridges that reach up through the timberline and support the great upper plateau. The timberline occurs at an elevation of 4500 to 5000 ft., depending on the degree of exposure to the mountain's fierce weather. The upper plateau, varying in elevation from 5000 to 5500 ft., bears comparatively gentle slopes interspersed with wide grassy areas strewn with rocks, which are called lawns. The summit cone, covered with fragments of rock and almost devoid of vegetation, rises steeply above this plateau. The upper part of the mountain has a climate similar to that of northern Labrador, and its areas of alpine tundra support a fascinating variety of plant and animal life adapted to the extreme conditions of the alpine environment. Many of these species are found only on other high mountaintops or in the tundra many hundreds of miles farther north, and a few plants are found only or primarily on the Presidential Range. The alpine plants in particular have attracted many professional and amateur scientists (including, among the well-known amateurs, Henry David Thoreau), and many of the features of the mountain are named for early botanists such as Manasseh Cutler, Jacob Bigelow, Francis Boott, William Oakes, and Edward Tuckerman. Great care should be exercised not to damage the plant life in these areas, as their struggle for survival is already sufficiently severe. Hikers should avoid unnecessary excursions away from the trails, and should step on rocks rather than vegetation wherever possible. The AMC publishes the *AMC Field Guide to the New England Alpine Summits,* a handbook covering the ecological relations of the plants and animals found above treeline, and *At Timberline,* which includes mountain geology and animal life as well as plants. The New Hampshire Department of Resources and Economic Development (PO Box 856, Concord, NH 03301) publishes booklets on geology intended for the general public. The Presidential Range area is covered by *The Geology of the Mt. Washington Quadrangle* and *The Geology of the Crawford Notch Quadrangle.*

The slopes of Mt. Washington are drained by tributaries of three major rivers: the Androscoggin, the Connecticut, and the Saco. The high, massive **Northern Presidentials** or **Northern Peaks** (see Section 2) continue the rocky alpine terrain of Mt. Washington to the north and northeast in an arc that encloses the **Great Gulf,** the largest glacial cirque in the White Mtns. (A glacial cirque is a landform that results when a glacier excavates a typical V-shaped brook valley with a narrow floor and fairly uniform slopes, turning it into the classic U-shaped cirque with a broad, fairly flat floor and almost vertical walls.)

Moving clockwise from the Great Gulf around the east side of the mountain, **Chandler Ridge** (by which the Mt. Washington Auto Rd. ascends the upper part of the mountain) passes over the small peak of **Nelson Crag** before merging into the summit cone; this ridge divides the Great Gulf from the great ravines of the east face: **Huntington Ravine,** the **Ravine of Raymond Cataract, Tuckerman Ravine** (which is one of the finest examples of the glacial cirque), and the **Gulf of Slides.** Chandler Ridge also forms the north boundary of the lawn that is called the **Alpine Garden** for its colorful displays of alpine flowers in late June, which lies at the foot of the summit cone just above the three eastern ravines. **Lion Head,** a pinnacled buttress named for its appearance when seen from points on NH 16 just north of Pinkham Notch Visitor Center, caps the north wall of Tuckerman Ravine.

The steep eastern slopes of the mountain bear several notable waterfalls. **Raymond Cataract** falls through a series of wild and beautiful cascades in the Ravine of Raymond Cataract, but brush has covered a former footway, so this series of falls can be reached only by those intrepid explorers who are skilled in off-trail travel. **Crystal Cascade** is easily reached from Pinkham Notch Visitor Center by a walk of about 0.4 mi. on the Tuckerman Ravine Trail. **Glen Ellis Falls,** located deep in the Ellis River valley, can be easily reached from the parking area located on NH 16, 0.8 mi. south of Pinkham Notch Visitor Center, by a gravel path 0.3 mi. long, with rock steps and handrails, that passes under the highway through a tunnel. The main fall is 70 ft. high, and below it are several pools and smaller falls.

Boott Spur (5500 ft.), the great southeast shoulder of Mt. Washington, forms the south wall of Tuckerman Ravine and the north wall of the Gulf of Slides. The flat ridge connecting Boott Spur with the cone of Mt. Washington bears **Bigelow Lawn,** the largest of the Presidential Range lawns. Both the **Montalban Ridge** anΔd the **Rocky Branch Ridge** descend from Boott Spur and quickly drop below treeline, continuing south in thick woods with occasional open summits. **Oakes Gulf,** at the headwaters of the Dry River, lies west of Boott Spur and east of Mt. Monroe. The **Southern Presidentials** or **Southern Peaks,** running southwest from Mt. Washington, form the second most prominent ridge in the range (after the Northern Peaks), dropping to the treeline slowly and rising above it again several times before the final descent into the woods below Mt. Pierce. The Mt. Washington Cog Railway ascends the minor unnamed ridge that separates the much less spectacular (but still quite impressive) principal ravines of Mt. Washington's western face, **Ammonoosuc Ravine** and **Burt Ravine,** which lie between the Southern Peaks and the Northern Peaks.

Day trips to the summit of Mt. Washington can be made by a great variety of routes, but the vast majority of climbers use only a very few trails. From the west, the mountain is most frequently ascended from the parking area (about 2500 ft.) on the Base Rd. near the Cog Railway base station by the Ammonoosuc Ravine Trail and the Crawford Path, or by the Jewell and Gulfside trails (see Section 2), or by a loop using both routes. The Ammonoosuc Ravine Trail has a long very steep section but offers the shelter of Lakes of the Clouds Hut, just above treeline, if a storm arises. The Jewell Trail provides an easier ascent or descent, but reaches the Gulfside Trail high on the slope of Mt. Clay, a more dangerous place in bad weather—particularly when afternoon thunderstorms threaten. Both of these routes are used heavily, with the Jewell Trail providing what is probably the least strenuous and challenging of any of the routes to the summit. Because of the very high elevation (3000 ft.) of its trailhead on the Jefferson Notch Rd., the Caps Ridge Trail is frequently used for a one-day hike to Mt. Washington, in combination with the Gulfside Trail and the Cornice (see Section 2). It offers fine scenery and the opportunity to climb Mt. Jefferson as well with little extra effort, but as a route to Mt. Washington it is longer, rougher, and more exposed to bad weather than the Jewell Trail, and thus saves no effort despite its higher start. The Boundary Line Trail (see Section 2) connects the Base Rd. parking area with the Jefferson Notch Rd., and thus makes possible loop trips involving the Caps Ridge Trail and either the Ammonoosuc Ravine Trail or the Jewell Trail.

Most hikers ascend Mt. Washington from the east. The Tuckerman Ravine Trail from Pinkham Notch Visitor Center (2032 ft.) is by far the most popular route, affording the least arduous ascent of the east side of Mt. Washington, with moderate grades for most of its length and spectacular views of the ravine. Other routes from Pinkham Notch are all either longer or steeper, but have good views and are often less crowded. In the spring and early summer the section of the Tuckerman Ravine Trail that ascends the ravine headwall is often closed by the WMNF on account of dangerous snow or ice conditions; notice of its closure is posted at Pinkham Notch Visitor Center. In this case the Lion Head Trail, which runs along the prominent Lion Head buttress north of Tuckerman Ravine, is usually the best alternative route. This trail (using a newly constructed bypass of the lower section that is open only when winter conditions prevail) is also the most popular and least dangerous route of ascent in winter conditions.

Three major ridges run southwest or south from Mt. Washington, separated by deep river valleys from each other and from the ranges to the west and east. The most impressive of these ridges, formed by the **Southern Peaks,** runs southwest from Mt. Washington and ends abruptly at the cliffs of Mt. Webster, which make up the most impressive section of the eastern wall of Crawford Notch. The peaks that rise along this ridge are (from northeast to southwest) Mts. Monroe, Franklin, Eisenhower (formerly called Pleasant), Pierce (also commonly known as Clinton), Jackson, and Webster. To the northwest, the headwaters of the Ammonoosuc River (a Connecticut River tributary) flow across the Fabyan Plain—a broad, relatively flat expanse that separates the Southern Peaks from the much lower Cherry-Dartmouth Range; on the other side of the Southern Peaks ridge, the Dry River begins high on Mt. Washington in Oakes Gulf and runs to the Saco River below Crawford Notch through a deep, steep-sided valley between the Southern Peaks and the Montalban Ridge. Beyond the Dry River valley rises the Montalban Ridge, the longest of all Mt. Washington's subsidiary ridges, extending about 20 mi. from the summit. This ridge first runs generally south over Boott Spur, Mt. Isolation, Mt. Davis, Stairs Mtn., Mt. Resolution, and Mt. Parker, then swings east to Mts. Langdon, Pickering, and Stanton, the low peaks above the intervales of Bartlett and Glen near the confluence of the Rocky Branch and Saco River. The Bemis Ridge is a significant spur running from Mt. Resolution southwest over Mt. Crawford, then south to Hart Ledge, which overlooks the great bend in the Saco. East of the Montalbans lies the Rocky Branch of the Saco River, and to the east of that stream rises the Rocky Branch Ridge, a long, wide-spreading assortment of humps and flat ridges running south from Boott Spur via Slide Peak, with no noteworthy summit except Iron Mtn. at the far south end. Still farther east the Ellis River flows down from Pinkham Notch, with NH 16 running through the valley and the ridges of Wildcat Mtn. rising on the opposite side.

The **Southern Presidentials** or **Southern Peaks**—the names are used interchangeably—form a great ridge that extends about 8 mi. southwest from the summit of Mt. Washington to the Webster Cliffs above Crawford Notch. The Ammonoosuc River lies to the northwest and the Dry River to the southeast. The summits on this ridge decrease steadily in elevation from northeast to southwest.

Mt. Monroe (5372 ft.), the highest of the Southern Peaks, is a sharply pointed pyramid that rises abruptly from the flat area around the Lakes of the Clouds, with a secondary summit, a small crag sometimes called **Little Monroe** (5225 ft.), on its west ridge. The summit, crossed by the Mount Monroe Loop, is completely above treeline and affords fine views of the deep chasm of Oakes Gulf on the east, the **Lakes of the Clouds,** and the nearby summit of Mt. Washington. The Lakes of the Clouds are two small alpine tarns that lie in a small bowl on the northwest side of the ridge near the low point between Mt. Washington and Mt. Monroe. The larger lake, often called the Lower Lake, is at an elevation of 5025 ft., while the much smaller Upper Lake lies to the north of the Lower Lake at an elevation of 5050 ft. The flat region between Mt. Monroe and the Lakes of the Clouds supports a bountiful number of alpine plants, making it the most significant and thus the most vulnerable habitat in the White Mtns. Part of this area is closed to all public entry due to damage caused in the past by hikers coming to admire these plants, which can withstand the full violence of above-treeline weather but not the tread of hikers' boots. Sadly, we can now pay homage to some of these rare survivors only from a distance.

Mt. Franklin (5001 ft.) is a flat shoulder of Monroe that appears impressive only when seen from below, in the Franklin-Eisenhower col. The summit's exact location (and even existence) among a group of low, rolling ridges is not entirely obvious; it lies a short distance to the east of the Crawford Path and commands an excellent view straight down into Oakes Gulf.

Mt. Eisenhower (4760 ft.), previously called Mt. Pleasant, was renamed after the former president's death. While there is a good deal of scrub on the lower slopes of this dome-shaped mountain, the top is completely bald. Its summit is crossed by the Mount Eisenhower Loop.

Mt. Pierce (4310 ft.) was named for Franklin Pierce, the only United States president born in New Hampshire, by act of the New Hampshire legislature in 1913. Although this name is officially recognized by the Board of Geographic Names and appears on all USGS maps, it was not universally accepted, and the mountain's former name, Mt. Clinton, persists in the Mt. Clinton Rd. and the Mount Clinton Trail, which ascends the southeast slope of the mountain. Mt. Pierce is wooded almost to the top of its flat summit on the west, but a broad open area on the east side affords fine views. Its summit lies on the Webster Cliff Trail just above its junction with the Crawford Path.

Mt. Jackson (4052 ft.)—named for Charles Jackson, a 19th-century New Hampshire state geologist, and not (as many would suppose) for President Andrew Jackson—has a square, ledgy summit with steep sides and a flat top, affording possibly the finest views overall among the Southern Peaks. Its summit is crossed by the Webster Cliff Trail and is also reached by the Jackson branch of the Webster-Jackson Trail.

Mt. Webster (3910 ft.), once called Notch Mtn., was renamed for Daniel Webster, the great 19th-century orator, United States senator, secretary of state, and unsuccessful aspirant to the presidency, probably the best-known and most eminent native the state of New Hampshire can claim. Webster visited the summit of Mt. Washington once with Ethan Allen Crawford as his guide, but unfortunately found the summit swathed in its customary blanket of clouds. Undaunted, the great orator delivered a short address to his large audience, the mountain itself: "Mount Washington, I have come a long distance, have toiled hard to arrive at your summit, and now you seem to give me a cold reception, for which I am extremely sorry, as I shall not have time enough to view this grand prospect which now lies before me, and nothing prevents but the uncomfortable atmosphere in which you reside!" Thousands of visitors have shared his experience of Mt. Washington and his regrets for the lack of a view, though few presumably have remonstrated so directly and eloquently with the mountain itself. The summit of Mt. Webster is crossed by the Webster Cliff Trail, which is intersected by the Webster branch of the Webster-Jackson Trail not far from the top.

To the southeast of the Southern Peaks lies the **Dry River,** running down the central valley of the Presidential–Dry River Wilderness. This river has also been called the Mt. Washington River, but Dry River has won the battle, possibly because of the ironic quality of the name. The Dry River runs from Oakes Gulf to the Saco through a deep, narrow, steep-walled ravine. Though in a dry season the flow is a bit meager, with lots of rocks lying uncovered in the stream bed, its watershed has extremely rapid runoff and its sudden floods are legendary—it has drowned unwary hikers. No other logging railroad ever constructed in the White Mtns. had as many river crossings in so short a distance as the railroad that was built up this valley, and no other logging railroad ever had all its trestles swept away by floods so quickly after ceasing operations.

Access to the Dry River area has always been somewhat difficult, and ascents of the Southern Peaks from this side have always been relatively arduous. But since the Presidential Range–Dry River Wilderness was established and the number of wilderness-seeking visitors increased sharply, the WMNF has made access somewhat easier by eliminating many river crossings through trail relocations and the construction of a major suspension bridge at the first (and usually most difficult) remaining crossing. However, it is still an area where visitors need to keep a careful watch on the weather and take account of any substantial rainfall in the previous few days.

The **Montalban Ridge** extends southward from Boott Spur, forming the longest subsidiary ridge in the Presidential Range, running for about 20 mi. between the Rocky Branch on the east and the Dry River and Saco River on the west. At Mt. Resolution the main ridge curves to the east along the Saco valley, while the short **Bemis Ridge** carries the line of the upper ridge south to the great bend in the Saco. The peaks of the Montalban Ridge, in order from the north, include **Mt. Isolation** (4003 ft.), **Mt. Davis** (3819 ft.), **Stairs Mtn.** (3463 ft.), **Mt. Resolution** (3415 ft.), **Mt. Parker** (3004 ft.), **Mt. Langdon** (2390 ft.), **Mt. Pickering** (1930 ft.), and **Mt. Stanton** (1716 ft.). The peaks of the Bemis Ridge include **Mt. Crawford** (3119 ft.), **Mt. Hope** (2505 ft.), and **Hart Ledge** (2020 ft.). **Cave Mtn.** (1439 ft.), a low spur of the range near Bartlett village, is much better known for the cave on its south face than for its summit.

The views from the summits of Mts. Isolation, Davis, and Crawford are among the finest in the White Mtns., and Mts. Resolution and Parker also offer excellent outlooks. The **Giant Stairs** are a wild and picturesque feature of the region, offering a spectacular view from the top of the cliff that forms the upper stair. These two great step-like ledges at the south end of the ridge of Stairs Mtn. are quite regular in form, and are visible from many points. A third and somewhat similar cliff, sometimes called the Back Stair, lies east of the main summit but has no trail. Mt. Stanton and Mt. Pickering are wooded, but several open ledges near their summits afford interesting views in various directions.

All of the peaks named above are reached by well-maintained trails, except Mt. Hope and Hart Ledge. Mt. Hope is heavily wooded and very seldom climbed. The fine cliff of Hart Ledge rises more than 1000 ft. above the meadows at the great bend in the Saco River just above Bartlett and affords commanding views to the east, west, and south. There is no regular trail, but intrepid bushwhackers may follow the roads that run west along the north side of the river, passing under the cliffs, then climb up the slope well to the west of the cliffs.

East of the Montalban Ridge, beyond the Rocky Branch but west of the Ellis River valley, lies the **Rocky Branch Ridge.** This heavily wooded ridge runs south from Slide Peak, and is sharply defined for only about 3 mi., then spreads out and flattens. It has no important peaks. **Iron Mtn.** (2726 ft.), a small mountain near Jackson with a fine north outlook and a magnificent bare ledge at the top of its south cliff, is the most significant summit on this long stretch of uplands between the Rocky Branch and the Ellis River—though the Rocky Branch Ridge ceases to be an outstanding ridge long before it reaches Iron Mtn. **Green Hill** (2181 ft.) is a shoulder of Iron Mtn. with an interesting view reached by an unofficial path.

HUTS

For current information on AMC huts, Pinkham Notch Visitor Center, or Crawford Notch Hostel, contact the Reservation Office, Pinkham Notch Visitor Center, PO Box 298, Gorham, NH 03581 (603-466-2727) or www.outdoors.org.

Pinkham Notch Visitor Center (AMC)

Pinkham Notch Visitor Center is a unique mountain sports facility in the heart of the WMNF. This facility, originally built in 1920 and greatly enlarged since then, is located on NH 16 practically at the height-of-land in Pinkham Notch, about 20 mi. north of Conway and 11 mi. south of Gorham. It is also 0.8 mi. north of Glen Ellis Falls and 0.5 mi. south of the base of the Wildcat Mtn. Ski Area. Pinkham Notch Visitor Center offers food and lodging to the public throughout the year and is managed similarly to the AMC huts. Pets are not allowed inside any building of the Visitor Center. The telephone number for the Reservation Office is 603-466-2727; the number for general information is 603-466-2721. Concord Trailways offers daily bus service to and from Logan Airport and South Station in Boston, and the AMC operates a hiker shuttle bus from the Visitor Center to most of the principal trailheads in the White Mtns. during the summer.

The Joe Dodge Lodge accommodates more than one hundred guests in rooms with double beds or two, three, or four bunks. It also offers overnight guests a library that commands a spectacular view of the nearby Wildcat Ridge, and a living room where accounts of the day's activities can be shared around an open fireplace. The Center features a 65-seat conference room equipped with audiovisual facilities.

The Trading Post, a popular meeting place for hikers, has been a center of AMC educational and recreational activities since 1920. Weekend workshops, seminars, and lectures are conducted throughout the year. The building houses a dining room, and an information desk where basic equipment, guidebooks, and AMC publications are available. The pack room downstairs is open 24 hours a day for hikers to stop in, relax, use the coin-operated showers, and repack their gear.

Pinkham Notch Visitor Center is the most important trailhead on the east side of Mt. Washington. Free public parking is available, although sleeping in cars is not permitted. Additional parking is available in designated areas along NH 16 in both directions, but a USFS recreational permit is required since these areas are on WMNF land. The Tuckerman Ravine Trail, the Lost Pond Trail, and the Old Jackson Road all start at the camp, giving access to many more trails, and a number of walking trails have been constructed for shorter, easier trips in the Pinkham vicinity. Among these are the Crew-Cut Trail, George's Gorge Trail, Liebeskind's Loop, and the Square Ledge Trail. There are also several ski-touring trails; for information consult personnel at the Trading Post main desk.

Crawford Notch Hostel (AMC)

Located at the head of historic Crawford Notch in the heart of the White Mountain National Forest, the Crawford Notch Hostel provides low-cost overnight accommodations for hikers and other visitors. The hostel, consisting of buildings that were once part of the Crawford House grand hotel complex, is located on NH 302 about 20 mi. west of North Conway and 10 mi. east of Twin Mountain village. The nearby Crawford Notch Depot Visitor Center is also operated by the AMC during the summer hiking season.

The main hostel building, known as the Shapleigh studio (since it was once the studio of a well-known White Mountain artist named Shapleigh), includes a natural history library; a meeting room for small groups; a small store that stocks last-minute hiker supplies and souvenir items; toilet facilities and showers; and a complete kitchen with stove, refrigerator, and sinks. It is heated in fall, winter, and spring. These amenities make it an excellent choice for families and small groups, and a convenient base to begin or end any hut experience. There is a caretaker in residence. Two adjacent cabins, heated by propane, each accommodate 12 persons. Winter workshops in snowshoeing, backcountry skiing, and ice climbing are regularly conducted with the hostel as a base. Operating as a traditional hostel, the Shapleigh building is open to the public from 6:00–10:00 A.M. and from 4:00–9:30 P.M. Overnight lodging is available year-round, and AMC members receive a discount. Reservations are encouraged, and may be made through the Pinkham Notch Visitor Center Reservation Office (603-466-2727).

The Depot Visitor Center, the former train station renovated by the AMC in 1984, houses educational displays, an information desk, and a small store that stocks last-minute hiker supplies and souvenir items. It is also a major stop and transfer point for the AMC hiker shuttle bus, which operates during the summer and early fall, and serves as a depot for the excursion trains that run on the Crawford Notch line during the tourist season.

The AMC's Crawford Notch property includes a major parking area for trailheads on the west side of the highway, including the Mount Willard Trail and the A–Z Trail. Parking next to the Depot Visitor Center is limited to 30 minutes. Parking for hostel overnight guests is located between the main building and the cabins. Parking for the Crawford Path is available in the USFS lot (recreational permit required) located just off Mt. Clinton Rd. near its junction with US 302.

Lakes of the Clouds Hut (AMC)

The original stone hut was built in 1915 and has been greatly enlarged since then. It is located on a shelf near the foot of Mt. Monroe about 50 yd. west of the larger lake at an elevation of 5012 ft. It is reached by the Crawford Path or the Ammonoosuc Ravine Trail, and has accommodations for 90 guests. Pets are not permitted in the hut. The hut is open to the public from June to mid-September, and closed at all other times. Space for backpackers is available at a lesser cost. A refuge room in the cellar is left open in the winter *for emergency use only.*

Mizpah Spring Hut (AMC)

The newest of the AMC huts was completed in 1965 and is located at about 3800 ft. elevation on the site formerly occupied by the Mizpah Spring Shelter, at the junction of the Webster Cliff Trail and the Mount Clinton Trail, near the Mizpah Cutoff. The hut accommodates 60 guests, with sleeping quarters in eight rooms containing from four to ten bunks. This hut is open to the public from mid-May to mid-October (caretaker basis in May). Pets are not permitted in the hut. There are tentsites nearby (caretaker, fee charged).

CAMPING

Presidential Range–Dry River Wilderness

Wilderness regulations, intended to protect Wilderness resources and promote opportunities for challenge and solitude, prohibit use of motorized equipment or mechanical means of transportation of any sort. Camping and wood or charcoal fires are not allowed within 200 ft. of any trail except at designated campsites. Hiking and camping group size must be no larger than 10 people. Camping and fires are also prohibited above treeline (where trees are less than 8 ft. tall) except in winter, when camping is permitted above treeline in places where snow cover is at least two feet deep, but not on any frozen body of water. Many shelters have been removed, and the remaining ones will be dismantled when major mainte-nance is required; one should not count on using any of these shelters.

Forest Protection Areas

The WMNF has established a number of Forest Protection Areas (FPAs)—for-merly known as Restricted Use Areas—where camping and wood or charcoal fires are prohibited throughout the year. The specific areas are under continual review, and areas are added to or subtracted from the list in order to provide the greatest amount of protection to areas subject to damage by excessive camping, while imposing the lowest level of restrictions possible. A general list of FPAs in this section follows, but since there are often major changes from year to year, one should obtain current information on FPAs from the WMNF.

(1) No camping is permitted above treeline (where trees are less than 8 ft. tall), except in winter, and then only in places where there is at least two feet of snow cover on the ground—but not on any frozen body of water, and not on the east face of Mt. Washington's summit cone from Boott Spur to Nelson Crag (the area above Tuckerman and Huntington ravines, including the Alpine Garden area). The point where the above-treeline restricted area begins is marked on most trails with small signs, but the absence of such signs should not be construed as proof of the legality of a site.

(2) No camping is permitted within a quarter-mile of any trailhead, picnic area, or any facility for overnight accommodation such as a hut, cabin, shelter, tentsite, or campground, except as designated at the facility itself. In the area covered by Section 1, camping is also forbidden within a quarter-mile of Glen Ellis Falls.

(3) No camping is permitted within 200 ft. of certain trails. In 1997, designated trails included the Ammonoosuc Ravine Trail.

(4) No camping is permitted on WMNF land within a quarter-mile of certain roads (camping on private roadside land is illegal except by per-mission of the landowner). In 1997, these roads included US 302 west of

Bartlett NH, NH 16 north of Glen Ellis Falls, Jefferson Notch Rd. from the Base Rd. to the Caps Ridge Trail trailhead, and the Rocky Branch Rd. (also known as Jericho Rd.).

(5) In Tuckerman and Huntington ravines (Cutler River drainage, including the Alpine Garden and the east face of the Mt. Washington summit cone), camping is prohibited throughout the year; the only year-round exception is the Hermit Lake Shelters and adjoining tent platforms (management policies described below under campsites). Visitors in the ravine areas may not kindle charcoal or wood fires; people intending to cook must bring their own small stoves. Day visitors and shelter users alike are required to carry out all their own trash and garbage—no receptacles are provided. This operating policy is under continual review, so it can change from time to time; current information is available at Pinkham Notch Visitor Center or the Tuckerman Ravine caretaker's residence, or from WMNF offices. There is no warming room open to the public, and refreshments are not available.

Crawford Notch State Park

No camping is permitted in Crawford Notch State Park, except at the public Dry River Campground (fee charged).

Established Trailside Campsites

Hermit Lake Campsite (AMC/WMNF), located in Tuckerman Ravine, consists of ten open-front shelters with a capacity of 86 and three tent platforms open to the public. Tickets for shelter and tentsite space (non-transferable and non-refundable) must be purchased for a nominal fee at Pinkham Notch Visitor Center in person (first come, first served). Campers are limited to a maximum of seven consecutive nights, and pets are not allowed to stay overnight.

Nauman Tentsite (AMC) consists of seven tent platforms near Mizpah Spring Hut. In summer there is a caretaker and a fee is charged.

Lakes of the Clouds Hut (AMC) has limited space available for backpackers at a substantially lower cost than the normal hut services.

Rocky Branch Shelter #1 and Tentsite (WMNF) is located near the junction of the Rocky Branch and Stairs Col trails, just outside the Presidential Range–Dry River Wilderness.

Rocky Branch Shelter #2 (WMNF) is located at the junction of the Rocky Branch and Isolation trails, within the Presidential Range–Dry River Wilderness.

Following the established policy for management of Wilderness, this shelter will be removed when major maintenance is required.

Dry River Shelter #3 (WMNF) is located on the Dry River Trail, 6.3 mi. from US 302, within the Presidential Range–Dry River Wilderness. This shelter will be removed when major maintenance is required.

Resolution Shelter (AMC) is located on a spur path that leaves the Davis Path at its junction with the Mount Parker Trail, within the Presidential Range–Dry River Wilderness. The water source is scanty in dry seasons. This shelter will be removed when major maintenance is required.

Mt. Langdon Shelter (WMNF) is located at the junction of the Mount Langdon and Mount Stanton trails, at the edge of the Presidential Range–Dry River Wilderness.

Trails to Mt. Washington from Pinkham Notch

List of Trails	Map	Page
Tuckerman Ravine Trail	1:F9	23
Lion Head Trail	1:F9	25
Huntington Ravine Trail	1:F9	27
Nelson Crag Trail	1:F9	28
Boott Spur Trail	1:F9	29
Boott Spur Link	1:F9	30
Gulf of Slides Ski Trail	1:F9–G9	31
Glen Boulder Trail	1:G9	31
The Direttissima	1:F9–G9	32

Trails on the Upper Cone of Mt. Washington

List of Trails	Map	Page
Alpine Garden Trail	1:F9	33
Southside Trail	1:F9	34
Tuckerman Crossover	1:F9	34
Lawn Cutoff	1:F9	35
Camel Trail	1:F9	35
Westside Trail	1:F9	36
Trinity Heights Connector	1:F9	36

Trails North of Pinkham Notch Visitor Center

Trails on the Main Ridge of the Southern Peaks

Trails to the Southern Peaks from the West and South

Trails of the Dry River Valley

Trails of the Montalban Ridge

Trails of the Jackson Area

THE TRAILS

Tuckerman Ravine Trail (WMNF)

This trail to the summit of Mt. Washington from NH 16 at Pinkham Notch Visitor Center is probably the most popular route of ascent on the mountain. From Pinkham Notch Visitor Center, it uses a rocky tractor road to the floor of Tuckerman Ravine. From there to the top of the headwall it is a well-graded path, steady but not excessively steep. Its final section ascends the cone of Mt. Washington steeply over fragments of rock. In the spring and early summer the WMNF often closes the section of trail on the ravine headwall because of snow and ice hazards, and notice is posted at Pinkham Notch Visitor Center. In these circumstances, the Lion Head Trail is usually the most convenient alternative route. In winter conditions the headwall is often impassable except by experienced and well-equipped technical snow and ice climbers, and it is frequently closed by the WMNF even to such climbers due to avalanche and icefall hazards. The winter route of the Lion Head Trail, which now begins on the Huntington Ravine Fire Road 0.1 mi. from the Tuckerman Ravine Trail, bypasses the headwall and usually provides the easiest and safest route for ascending Mt. Washington from the east in winter.

The Tuckerman Ravine Trail starts behind the Trading Post at Pinkham Notch Visitor Center; the Old Jackson Road diverges right 50 yd. from here. Be careful to avoid numerous side paths, including the Blanchard Ski Trail, in this area. In 0.3 mi. it crosses a bridge to the south bank of Cutler River, begins its moderate but relentless climb, and soon passes a side path leading 20 yd. right to the best viewpoint for Crystal Cascade. The Boott Spur Trail diverges on the left at a sharp curve to the right, 0.4 mi. from Pinkham Notch Visitor Center, and at 1.3 mi. the Huntington Ravine Trail diverges on the right. At 1.5 mi. the Tuckerman Ravine Trail crosses a tributary, then at 1.6 mi. the main branch of the Cutler River. At 1.7 mi. the Huntington Ravine Fire Road, which is the easiest route to Huntington Ravine in winter but offers very rough footing on some parts in summer, leaves on the right. The Lion Head winter route now begins about 0.1 mi. up this road. At 2.1 mi. the Raymond Path enters on the right at a point where the Tuckerman trail turns sharp left, and at 2.3 mi. the Lion Head Trail leaves on the right. In another 0.1 mi. the Boott Spur Link leaves on the left, opposite the buildings located at the floor of Tuckerman Ravine near Hermit Lake. Views from the floor of the ravine are impressive: the cliff on the right is Lion Head, while the more distant crags on the left are the Hanging Cliffs of Boott Spur.

The main trail keeps to the right (north) of the main stream and ascends a well-constructed footway into the upper floor of the ravine. At the foot of the headwall it bears right and ascends a steep slope, where the Snow Arch can be seen on the left in the spring and early summer of most years. In the early part of the hiking season, the snowfield above the Snow Arch usually extends across the trail, and the trail is often closed to hiking until this potentially hazardous snow-slope has melted away. Some snow may persist in the ravine until late summer. The arch (which does not always form) is carved by a stream of snow-melt water that flows under the snowfield. *Caution:* Do not approach too near the arch and under no circumstances cross over it or venture beneath it, since sections weighing many tons may break off at any moment. One death and several narrow escapes have occurred. When ascending the headwall, be careful not to dislodge rocks and start them rolling—this may put hikers below you in serious danger. There have been several serious accidents in recent years involving hikers who slipped off the side of the trail on the upper part of the headwall, often in adverse weather conditions, especially when the trail was slippery. Though the trail itself is relatively easy and quite safe, it passes within a very short distance of some extremely dangerous terrain, so a minor misstep off the side of the trail can have grave consequences.

Turning sharp left at the top of the debris slope and traversing under a cliff, the trail emerges from the ravine and climbs almost straight west up a grassy, ledgy slope. At 3.4 mi., a short distance above the top of the headwall, the Alpine Garden Trail diverges right. At Tuckerman Junction, located on the lower edge of Bigelow Lawn at 3.6 mi., the Tuckerman Crossover leads almost straight ahead (southwest) to the Crawford Path near the Lakes of the Clouds Hut; the Southside Trail diverges from the Tuckerman Crossover in 30 yd. and leads west, skirting the cone to the Davis Path; and the Lawn Cutoff leads left (south) toward Boott Spur. The Tuckerman Ravine Trail turns sharp right at this junction and ascends the steep rocks, marked by cairns and paint on ledges. At 3.8 mi., at Cloudwater Spring about a third of the way up the cone, the Lion Head Trail re-enters on the right. The Tuckerman trail continues to ascend to the Auto Rd. a few yards below the lower parking area, from which wooden stairways lead to the summit area.

Tuckerman Ravine Trail (map 1:F9)

Distances from Pinkham Notch Visitor Center (2032')

> *to* Boott Spur Trail (2275'): 0.4 mi., 250 ft., 20 min.

> *to* Huntington Ravine Trail (3031'): 1.3 mi., 1000 ft., 1 hr. 10 min.

> *to* Huntington Ravine Fire Road (3425'): 1.7 mi., 1400 ft., 1 hr. 35 min.

> *to* Raymond Path (3675'): 2.1 mi., 1650 ft., 1 hr. 55 min.

> *to* Lion Head Trail (3825'): 2.3 mi., 1800 ft., 2 hr. 5 min.

> *to* Boott Spur Link and Hermit Lake shelters (3875'): 2.4 mi., 1850 ft., 2 hr. 10 min.

> *to* Snow Arch (4525'): 3.1 mi., 2500 ft., 2 hr. 50 min.

> *to* Alpine Garden Trail (5125'): 3.4 mi., 3100 ft., 3 hr. 15 min.

> *to* Tuckerman Junction (5383'): 3.6 mi., 3350 ft., 3 hr. 30 min.

> *to* Lion Head Trail, upper junction (5675'): 3.8 mi., 3650 ft., 3 hr. 45 min.

> *to* Mt. Washington summit (6288'): 4.2 mi. (6.8 km.), 4250 ft., 4 hr. 15 min.

Lion Head Trail (AMC)

The Lion Head Trail follows the steep-ended ridge—aptly named for the appearance of its upper portion when viewed from points on NH 16 north of Pinkham Notch Visitor Center—that forms the north wall of Tuckerman Ravine. The trail begins and ends on the Tuckerman Ravine Trail and thus provides an alternative route to that heavily used trail, although it is much steeper in parts. It is especially important as an alternative when the Tuckerman Ravine Trail over the headwall is closed on account of snow or ice hazard. The winter route of the Lion Head Trail is considered the least dangerous route for ascending Mt. Washington in winter conditions, and is the most frequently used winter ascent route. An avalanche late in 1995 destroyed the former winter route, and a new winter route has been constructed; this route leaves the Huntington Ravine Fire Road just past the crossing of the Raymond Path, about 0.1 mi. from the Tuckerman Ravine Trail, and rejoins the summer Lion Head Trail at treeline. The signs and markings are changed at the beginning and end of the winter season to ensure that climbers take the proper route for prevailing conditions; the winter route is not open for summer use.

The Lion Head Trail diverges right from the Tuckerman Ravine Trail 2.3 mi. from Pinkham Notch Visitor Center and 0.1 mi. below Hermit Lake. Running north, it passes a side path on the left to one of the Hermit Lake shelters and crosses the outlet of Hermit Lake. It soon begins to climb the steep slope by switchbacks, scrambling up several small ledges with very rough footing. It reaches treeline at 0.4 mi., where the winter route enters on the right as the main trail bears left. (Descending, the summer trail turns right and the winter route descends almost straight ahead.) The trail then ascends an open slope to the lower Lion Head and continues to the upper Lion Head at 0.9 mi., where it runs mostly level, with impressive views from the open spur, until it crosses the Alpine Garden Trail at 1.1 mi. After passing through a belt of scrub, it ascends to the Tuckerman Ravine Trail, which it enters at Cloudwater Spring about a third of the way up the cone of Mt. Washington, about 0.4 mi. and 600 ft. below the summit.

Lion Head Trail (map 1:F9)

Distances from lower junction with Tuckerman Ravine Trail (3825')

> *to* Alpine Garden Trail (5175'): 1.1 mi., 1350 ft., 1 hr. 15 min.

> *to* upper junction with Tuckerman Ravine Trail (5675 ft.): 1.6 mi. (2.5 km.), 1850 ft., 1 hr. 45 min.

Distance from Pinkham Notch Visitor Center (2032')

> *to* Mt. Washington summit (6288') via Lion Head Trail and Tuckerman Ravine Trail: 4.1 mi. (7.0 km.), 4250 ft., 4 hr. 10 min.

Huntington Ravine Trail (AMC)

Caution: This is the most difficult regular hiking trail in the White Mtns. Many of the ledges demand proper use of handholds for safe passage, and extreme caution must be exercised at all times. Although experienced hikers who are reasonably comfortable on steep rock will probably encounter little difficulty when conditions are good, the exposure on several of the steepest ledges is likely to prove extremely unnerving to novices and to those who are uncomfortable in steep places. Do not attempt this trail if you tend to feel queasy or have difficulty on ledges on ordinary trails. Hikers encumbered with large or heavy packs may experience great difficulty in some places. This trail is very dangerous when wet or icy, and its use for descent at any time is strongly discouraged. Since retreat under unfavorable conditions can be extremely difficult and hazardous, one should never venture beyond the Fan in deteriorating conditions or when weather on the Alpine Garden is likely to be severe. During late fall, winter, and early spring, this trail (and any part of the ravine headwall) should be attempted only by those with full technical ice-climbing training and equipment. In particular, the ravine must not be regarded as a feasible escape route from the Alpine Garden in severe winter conditions.

This trail diverges right from the Tuckerman Ravine Trail 1.3 mi. from Pinkham Notch Visitor Center. In 0.2 mi. it crosses the Cutler River and, at 0.3 mi., the brook that drains Huntington Ravine. At 0.5 mi. it goes straight across the Raymond Path. It crosses the Huntington Ravine Fire Road and then climbs to meet it again, turning left on the road; at this junction a fine view of the ravine can be obtained by following the road to a small rise about 100 yd. in the opposite direction. Above this point the trail and road separate, rejoin, or cross several times; the junctions are not always well marked, but both routes lead to the same objective and the major advantage of the trail is somewhat better footing. At 1.3 mi. the first-aid cache in the floor of the ravine is reached. Just beyond here there are some interesting boulders near the path whose tops afford good views of the ravine. Beyond the scrubby trees is a steep slope covered with broken rock, known as the Fan, whose tip lies at the foot of the deepest gully. To the left of this gully are precipices; the lower one is called the Pinnacle.

After passing through the boulders, the path ascends to the left side of the Fan and, marked by yellow blazes on the rocks, crosses the talus diagonally. It then turns left and ascends in scrub along the north (right) side of the Fan to its tip at 1.8 mi., crossing a small brook about two-thirds of the way up. The trail then recrosses the brooklet and immediately attacks the rocks to the right of the main gully, climbing about 650 ft. in 0.3 mi. The route up the headwall follows the line of least difficulty and should be followed carefully over the ledges, which are dangerous, especially when wet. The first pitch above the Fan—a large, fairly smooth, steeply sloping ledge—is probably the most difficult scramble on the trail. Above the first ledges the trail climbs steeply through scrub and over short sections of rock, including some fairly difficult scrambles. About two-thirds of the way up it turns sharp left at a promontory with a good view, then continues to the top of the headwall, where it crosses the Alpine Garden Trail at 2.1 mi. From this point it ascends moderately, and at 2.3 mi. it crosses the Nelson Crag Trail, by which the summit can be reached in 0.8 mi. by turning left at this junction. Soon the Huntington Ravine Trail reaches the Mt. Washington Auto Rd. just below the 7-mi. mark, 1.1 mi. below the summit.

Huntington Ravine Trail (map 1:F9)

Distances from Tuckerman Ravine Trail (3031')

   to Raymond Path (3425'): 0.5 mi., 400 ft., 25 min.

   to first-aid cache in ravine floor (4075'): 1.3 mi., 1050 ft., 1 hr. 10 min.

   to Alpine Garden Trail crossing (5475'): 2.1 mi., 2450 ft., 2 hr. 15 min.

   to Auto Rd. (5725'): 2.4 mi. (3.8 km.), 2700 ft., 2 hr. 35 min.

Distance from Pinkham Notch Visitor Center (2032')

   to Mt. Washington summit (6288') via Tuckerman Ravine, Huntington
      Ravine, and Nelson Crag trails: 4.3 mi. (6.9 km.), 4250 ft., 4 hr. 15 min.

Nelson Crag Trail (AMC)

This trail, which now runs to the summit of Mt. Washington, begins on the Old Jackson Road at a point 1.7 mi. from Pinkham Notch Visitor Center and 0.2 mi. from the Auto Rd. It is an attractive trail, relatively lightly used, fairly steep in the lower part and greatly exposed to weather in the upper part.

   Leaving the Old Jackson Road, this trail follows and soon crosses a small brook, then climbs steadily, soon becoming quite steep. At about 1.1 mi. it rises out of the scrub, emerging on the crest of Chandler Ridge, from which there is an unusual view of Pinkham Notch in both directions. From this point the trail is above treeline and very exposed to the northwest winds. It then bears northwest, climbs moderately over open ledges, and passes close by the Auto Rd. near Cragway Spring (unreliable), at the sharp turn about 0.3 mi. above the 5-mi. mark. The trail then climbs steeply to the crest of the ridge. It passes over Nelson Crag and crosses the Alpine Garden Trail, swings left and travels across the Huntington Ravine Trail and up the rocks to Ball Crag (6112 ft.), then finally runs across the Auto Rd. and the Cog Railway to the summit. To descend on this trail, follow the walkway down along the lower side of the Sherman Adams summit building.

Nelson Crag Trail (map 1:F9)

Distances from Old Jackson Road (2625')

> *to* closest approach to the Auto Rd. near Cragway Spring (4825'): 1.7 mi., 2200 ft., 1 hr. 55 min.

> *to* Huntington Ravine Trail (5725'): 2.8 mi., 3100 ft., 2 hr. 55 min.

> *to* Mt. Washington summit (6288'): 3.6 mi. (5.8 km.), 2700 ft., 3 hr. 30 min.

Boott Spur Trail (AMC)

This trail runs from the Tuckerman Ravine Trail near Pinkham Notch Visitor Center to the Davis Path near the summit of Boott Spur. It follows the long ridge that forms the south wall of Tuckerman Ravine and affords fine views. Grades are mostly moderate, but the trail is above treeline and thus greatly exposed to any bad weather for a considerable distance.

This trail diverges left from the Tuckerman Ravine Trail at a sharp right turn 0.4 mi. from Pinkham Notch Visitor Center, about 150 yd. above the side path to Crystal Cascade. It immediately crosses the John Sherburne Ski Trail, then climbs through a ledgy area, crosses a tiny brook, and climbs steeply up a crevice in a ledge to the ridgecrest. At 0.5 mi., after a slight descent, there is a sharp right turn where a side trail (left) leads in 50 yd. down to a restricted view east. The trail next passes through some interesting woods, crosses a moist region, and then ascends northwest up a steeper slope toward a craggy shoulder. Halfway up this section, a side trail leads left 100 yd. to a small brook (last water). At the ridgecrest, 1.0 mi. from the Tuckerman Ravine Trail, the main trail turns left and a side trail leads right (east) 25 yd. to an interesting though restricted outlook to Huntington Ravine. The main trail continues upward at moderate grades, reaching a ledgy ridgecrest that affords some views, and at 1.7 mi. a side trail on the right leads in 30 yd. to Harvard Rock, which provides an excellent view of Tuckerman Ravine and of Lion Head directly in front of the summit of Mt. Washington.

The trail emerges from the scrub at 1.9 mi., then soon bears left and angles up the slope to Split Rock, which one can pass through or go around, at 2.0 mi.

The trail then turns right, passes through a final patch of fairly high scrub, and rises steeply over two minor humps to a broad, flat ridge, where, at 2.2 mi., the Boott Spur Link descends on the right to the Tuckerman Ravine Trail near Hermit Lake. Above this point the trail follows the ridge, which consists of a series of alternating step-like levels and steep slopes. The views of the ravine are excellent, particularly where the path skirts around the potentially dangerous Hanging Cliff, 1500 ft. above Hermit Lake. After passing just to the right (north) of the summit of Boott Spur, the trail ends at the Davis Path.

Boott Spur Trail (map 1:F9)

Distances from Tuckerman Ravine Trail (2275')

> *to* Harvard Rock (4046'): 1.7 mi., 1750 ft., 1 hr. 45 min.

> *to* Split Rock (4337'): 2.0 mi., 2050 ft., 2 hr.

> *to* Boott Spur Link (4650'): 2.2 mi., 2400 ft., 2 hr. 20 min.

> *to* Davis Path junction (5450'): 2.9 mi. (4.7 km.), 3200 ft., 3 hr. 5 min.

Distances from Pinkham Notch Visitor Center (2032')

> *to* Davis Path junction (5450'): 3.4 mi., 3400 ft., 3 hr. 25 min.

> *to* Mt. Washington summit (6288') via Davis and Crawford paths: 5.4 mi. (8.7 km.), 4300 ft., 4 hr. 50 min.

Boott Spur Link (AMC)

This steep but interesting trail climbs the south wall of Tuckerman Ravine, connecting the main floor of the ravine with the upper part of Boott Spur. The lower trailhead has been recently relocated to a point about 0.1 mi. farther up the Tuckerman Ravine Trail, so the Boott Spur Link now leaves the south side of the Tuckerman trail at the southeast corner of the clearing opposite the buildings at Hermit Lake, 2.4 mi. from Pinkham Notch Visitor Center. From this clearing it descends south-southeast and soon crosses the Cutler River on a bridge, then crosses the John Sherburne Ski Trail and swings to the left, reaching a junction with the old route of the trail at 0.2 mi. Here it turns right and climbs straight up the slope very steeply through woods and scrub, with rapidly improving views back into the ravine. It then continues to climb steeply over open rocks to the crest of Boott Spur, where it meets the Boott Spur Trail.

Boott Spur Link (map 1:F9)

Distance from Tuckerman Ravine Trail (3875')

> *to* Boott Spur Trail (4650'): 0.6 mi. (1.0 km.), 850 ft., 45 min.

Gulf of Slides Ski Trail (WMNF)

This trail leads from Pinkham Notch Visitor Center on NH 16 into the Gulf of Slides, a ravine somewhat similar to Tuckerman Ravine but far less well known and crowded than its illustrious neighbor on the other side of Boott Spur. While this trail is not specifically maintained as a summer hiking trail and may be wet in spots, it still provides an interesting route to a relatively secluded valley. This is a dead-end trail, so hikers must return by the same route unless they choose to make the challenging trailless ascent of the ravine headwall.

The trail leaves the south end of the parking lot at Pinkham Notch Visitor Center in common with the John Sherburne Ski Trail. In a short distance it turns left where the Blanchard Ski Trail continues straight, crosses Cutler River and a smaller side channel on bridges, and immediately turns left where the Sherburne Trail turns right. After crossing a branch of New River on a bridge, it bears right along this stream, passes a junction where the Avalanche Brook Ski Trail diverges left, recrosses the stream, and climbs moderately up into the Gulf of Slides, staying mostly well to the north of New River. At 1.9 mi. it swings left where the Graham Ski Trail (marked by can tops) goes right toward Tuckerman Ravine. At 2.2 mi. it passes a first-aid cache, ascends roughly for a short distance, then descends for a short distance to the headwaters of New River near the base of the steep slopes of the ravine's headwall. Soon the trail reaches the base of ski trails leading into the major gullies and ends.

Gulf of Slides Ski Trail (map 1:F9–G9)

Distance from Pinkham Notch Visitor Center (2032')

   to Gulf of Slides (3900'): 2.6 mi. (4.2 km.), 1900 ft., 2 hr. 15 min.

Glen Boulder Trail (AMC)

This trail ascends past the famous Glen Boulder to the Davis Path 0.4 mi. below Boott Spur. It begins on the west side of NH 16 at the Glen Ellis Falls parking area south of Pinkham Notch Visitor Center. Parts of it are rather rough, but it reaches treeline and views relatively quickly.

The trail leaves the parking area and ascends gradually for about 0.4 mi. to the base of a small cliff, then climbs around to the right of the cliff and meets the Direttissima, which enters from the right (north) coming from Pinkham Notch Visitor Center. At this junction the trail turns sharp left (south) and soon passes a short branch trail that leads left to an outlook on the brink of a cliff, which commands a fine view of Wildcat Mtn. and Pinkham Notch. The main trail turns west, rises gradually, then steepens. At 0.8 mi. it crosses the Avalanche Brook Ski Trail, which is marked with blue plastic markers (but not maintained for hiking). The Glen Boulder Trail soon reaches the north bank of a brook draining the minor ravine south of the Gulf of Slides. After following the brook, which soon divides, the trail then turns southwest and crosses both branches. It is level for 200 yd., then rapidly climbs the northeast side of the spur through conifers, giving views of the minor ravine and spur south of the Gulf of Slides. Leaving the trees, it climbs over open rocks and at 1.6 mi. reaches the Glen Boulder, an immense rock perched on the end of the spur that is a familiar landmark for travelers through Pinkham Notch. The view is wide, from Chocorua around to Mt. Washington, and is particularly fine of Wildcat Mtn.

From the boulder the trail climbs steeply up the open ridgecrest to its top at 2.0 mi., then re-enters high scrub and ascends moderately. At 2.3 mi. a side trail descends right about 60 yd. to a fine spring. The main trail continues to Slide Peak (also called Gulf Peak), the rather insignificant peak heading the Gulf of Slides, at 2.6 mi. It then turns north and descends slightly, leaving the scrub, and runs entirely above treeline—greatly exposed to the weather—to the Davis Path just below a minor crag.

Glen Boulder Trail (map 1:G9)

Distances from Glen Ellis Falls parking area on NH 16 (1975')

   to The Direttissima (2300'): 0.4 mi., 350 ft., 25 min.

   to Avalanche Brook Ski Trail (2600'): 0.8 mi., 650 ft., 45 min.

   to Glen Boulder (3729'): 1.6 mi., 1750 ft., 1 hr. 40 min.

   to Slide Peak (4806'): 2.6 mi., 2850 ft., 2 hr. 45 min.

   to Davis Path junction (5175'): 3.2 mi. (5.2 km.), 3200 ft., 3 hr. 10 min.

   to Boott Spur Trail (5450') via Davis Path: 3.7 mi., 3500 ft., 3 hr. 35 min.

   to Mt. Washington summit (6288') via Davis and Crawford paths: 5.7 mi. (9.2 km.), 4400 ft., 5 hr. 5 min.

The Direttissima (AMC)

For hikers desiring access to the Glen Boulder Trail from Pinkham Notch Visitor Center, this trail eliminates a road walk on NH 16. Although in general it is almost level, there are several significant ups and downs. The trail begins about 0.2 mi. south of Pinkham Notch Visitor Center, just south of the highway bridge over the Cutler River, indicated by a sign at the edge of the woods. Marked by paint blazes, the trail turns sharp left about 30 yd. into the woods and follows a cleared area south. It turns slightly west at the end of this clearing and winds generally south, crossing a small brook. It skirts through the upper (west) end of a gorge and then crosses the gorge on a bridge at 0.5 mi. The trail continues past an excellent viewpoint looking down Pinkham Notch, passes along the top of a cliff and then the bottom of another cliff, and ends at the Glen Boulder Trail.

The Direttissima (map 1:F9–G9)

Distance from NH 16 near Cutler River bridge (2025')

   to Glen Boulder Trail (2300'): 1.0 mi. (1.6 km.), 400 ft., 40 min.

Alpine Garden Trail (AMC)

This trail leads from the Tuckerman Ravine Trail to the Mt. Washington Auto Rd. through the grassy lawn called the Alpine Garden. Although its chief value is the beauty of the flowers (in season) and the views, it is also a convenient connecting link between the trails on the east side of the mountain, making up a part of various routes for those who do not wish to visit the summit. It is completely above treeline and exposed to bad weather, although it is on the mountain's east side, which usually bears somewhat less of the brunt of the mountain's worst weather.

   The tiny alpine flowers that grow here are best seen in the middle to late part of June. Especially prominent in this area are the five-petaled white diapensia, the bell-shaped pink-magenta Lapland rosebay, and the very small pink flowers of the alpine azalea. (See the AMC's *Field Guide to the New England Alpine Summits* and *At Timberline: A Nature Guide to the Mountains of the Northeast.*) No plants should ever be picked or otherwise damaged. Hikers are urged to stay on trails or walk very carefully on rocks so as not to kill the fragile alpine vegetation.

   The trail diverges right from the Tuckerman Ravine Trail a short distance above the ravine headwall, about 0.2 mi. below Tuckerman Junction. It leads northeast, bearing toward Lion Head, and crosses the Lion Head Trail at 0.3 mi. Beyond this junction the trail ascends gradually northward, its general direction from here to the Auto Rd. It traverses the Alpine Garden and crosses a tiny stream that is the headwater of Raymond Cataract. (This water may be contaminated by drainage from the summit buildings.) The trail soon approaches the top of Huntington Ravine and crosses the Huntington Ravine Trail at 1.2 mi. Here, a little off the trail, there is a fine view down into this impressive ravine. In winter and spring, take care not to approach too close to the icy gullies that drop precipitously from the edge of the Alpine Garden. Rising to the top of the ridge leading from Nelson Crag, the trail crosses the Nelson Crag Trail at 1.4 mi., then descends and soon enters the old Glen House Bridle Path, constructed in 1853, whose course is still plain although it was abandoned more than a century ago. In a short distance the Alpine Garden Trail turns left and in a few yards enters the Auto Rd. a short distance above the 6-mi. mark, opposite the upper terminus of the Wamsutta Trail.

Alpine Garden Trail (map 1:F9)
Distances from Tuckerman Ravine Trail (5125')

  to Lion Head Trail (5175'): 0.3 mi., 50 ft., 10 min.

  to Huntington Ravine Trail (5475'): 1.2 mi., 350 ft., 45 min.

  to Nelson Crag Trail (5575'): 1.4 mi., 450 ft., 55 min.

  to Auto Rd. junction (5305'): 1.8 mi. (2.9 km.), 450 ft. (rev. 250 ft.), 1 hr. 10 min.

Southside Trail (AMC)

This trail forms a direct link between Tuckerman Ravine and the Crawford Path and Westside Trail. It diverges right (west) from the Tuckerman Crossover about 30 yd. southwest of the Tuckerman Ravine Trail at Tuckerman Junction and, skirting the southwest side of Mt. Washington's summit cone, enters the Davis Path near its junction with the Crawford Path.

Southside Trail (map 1:F9)
Distance from Tuckerman Junction (5383')

  to Davis Path (5575'): 0.3 mi. (0.5 km.), 200 ft., 15 min.

Tuckerman Crossover (AMC)

This trail connects Tuckerman Ravine with Lakes of the Clouds Hut. It is totally above treeline and crosses a high ridge where there is much exposure to westerly winds. It leaves the Tuckerman Ravine Trail left (southwest) at Tuckerman Junction, where the latter trail turns sharp right to ascend the cone. In 30 yd. the Southside Trail diverges to the right. The Tuckerman Crossover then rises gradually across Bigelow Lawn, crosses the Davis Path, and descends moderately to the Crawford Path, which it meets along with the Camel Trail a short distance above the upper Lake of the Clouds. Turning left on the Crawford Path, the Lakes of the Clouds Hut is reached in 0.2 mi.

Tuckerman Crossover (map 1:F9)

Distances from Tuckerman Junction (5383')

   to Davis Path (5475'): 0.5 mi., 100 ft., 20 min.

   to Crawford Path (5125'): 0.8 mi. (1.3 km.), 100 ft. (rev. 350 ft.), 25 min.

   to Lakes of the Clouds Hut (5012') via Crawford Path: 1.0 mi. (1.6 km.),
     100 ft. (rev. 100 ft.), 30 min.

Lawn Cutoff (AMC)

This trail provides a direct route between Tuckerman Junction and Boott Spur, entirely above treeline. It leaves the Tuckerman Ravine Trail at Tuckerman Junction and ascends gradually southward across Bigelow Lawn to the Davis Path about 0.5 mi. north of Boott Spur.

Lawn Cutoff (map 1:F9)

Distance from Tuckerman Junction (5383')

   to Davis Path (5475'): 0.4 mi. (0.6 km.), 100 ft., 15 min.

Camel Trail (AMC)

This trail, connecting Boott Spur with the Lakes of the Clouds Hut, is named for ledges on Boott Spur that resemble a kneeling camel when seen against the skyline.

   This is the right-hand trail of the two that diverge right (east) from the Crawford Path 0.2 mi. northeast of Lakes of the Clouds Hut (the Tuckerman Crossover, the other trail that also diverges here, is the left-hand trail of the two). The Camel Trail ascends easy grassy slopes, crosses the old location of the Crawford Path, and continues in a practically straight line across the level stretch of Bigelow Lawn. It aims directly toward the ledges that form the camel, passes under the camel's nose, and joins the Davis Path about 200 yd. northwest of the Lawn Cutoff.

Camel Trail (map 1:F9)

Distance from Crawford Path (5125')

   to Davis Path (5475'): 0.7 mi. (1.1 km.), 350 ft., 30 min.

Westside Trail (WMNF)

This trail was partly constructed by pioneer trail-maker J. Rayner Edmands; as was Edmands's practice, many segments are paved with carefully placed stones. It is wholly above timberline, very much exposed to the prevailing west and northwest winds. However, as a shortcut between the Gulfside Trail and Crawford Path that avoids the summit of Mt. Washington, it saves about 0.7 mi. in distance and 600 ft. in elevation between objectives in the Northern Peaks and Southern Peaks regions.

The trail diverges left from the Crawford Path at the point where the latter path begins to climb the steep part of the cone of Mt. Washington. It skirts the cone, climbing for 0.6 mi. at an easy grade, then descends moderately, passes under the tracks of the Mt. Washington Cog Railway, and soon ends at the Gulfside Trail.

Westside Trail (map 1:F9)
Distance from Crawford Path (5625')

    to Gulfside Trail (5500'): 0.9 mi. (1.4 km.), 50 ft. (rev. 150 ft.), 30 min.

Trinity Heights Connector (NHDP)

This trail was created to allow the Appalachian Trail to make a loop over the summit of Mt. Washington; formerly the true summit was a side trip, albeit a very short one, from the AT, so technically the AT did not pass over it. Trinity Heights is a name formerly used for the summit region of Mt. Washington. From the true summit (marked by a large sign), the path runs approximately northwest over the rocks to the Gulfside Trail less than 0.1 mi. to the north of its junction with the Crawford Path.

Trinity Heights Connector (map 1:F9)
Distance from true summit of Mt. Washington (6288')

    to Gulfside Trail (6100'): 0.2 mi. (0.3 km.), 0 ft. (rev. 200 ft.), 5 min.

Raymond Path (AMC)

This trail, one of the older paths in the region, begins on the Old Jackson Road 1.7 mi. from Pinkham Notch Visitor Center and 0.3 mi. from the Auto Rd., at a point about 100 yd. south of the beginning of the Nelson Crag Trail. It ends at the Tuckerman Ravine Trail about 0.3 mi. below Hermit Lake. Its grades are mostly easy to moderate.

After diverging from the Old Jackson Road the trail crosses several small branches of the Peabody River, climbing moderately to the crest of a small ridge at 0.8 mi. where there is an excellent view to Lion Head and Boott Spur. It then descends moderately for a short distance to a small mossy brook, then begins to ascend easily, crossing Nelson Brook at 1.2 mi. and the Huntington Ravine Trail at 1.8 mi. From here it drops down a steep bank to cross the brook that drains Huntington Ravine on a ledge at the brink of Vesper Falls—one should use great care here in high water or icy conditions, and perhaps consider a detour upstream. (This crossing can be avoided entirely by following the Huntington Ravine Trail north 0.1 mi. to the Huntington Ravine Fire Road, then following the Fire Road south until it crosses the Raymond Path.) Soon the path crosses the brook coming from the Ravine of Raymond Cataract (sign) and then the Huntington Ravine Fire Road, then climbs 0.3 mi. at a moderate grade to the Tuckerman Ravine Trail.

Raymond Path (map 1:F9)

Distances from Old Jackson Road (2625')

    to Huntington Ravine Trail (3425'): 1.8 mi., 800 ft., 1 hr. 20 min.

    to Tuckerman Ravine Trail (3675'): 2.4 mi. (3.9 km.), 1050 ft., 1 hr. 45 min.

    to Hermit Lake (3850') via Tuckerman Ravine Trail: 2.7 mi., 1250 ft., 2 hr.

Old Jackson Road (AMC)

This trail runs north from Pinkham Notch Visitor Center to the Mt. Washington Auto Rd., providing access to a number of other trails along with the most direct route from the Visitor Center to the Great Gulf. It is part of the Appalachian Trail and is blazed in white. Since it is used as a cross-country ski trail in winter, it is usually also marked with blue diamonds year-round.

It diverges right from the Tuckerman Ravine Trail about 50 yd. from the trailhead at the rear of the Trading Post. After about 0.3 mi. the Blanchard and Connie's Way ski trails cross, and at 0.4 mi. the Link Ski Trail enters right just before a bridge and the Crew-Cut Trail leaves right (east) just after the bridge. Soon the Old Jackson Road begins to ascend moderately—more steeply in fact than one would expect of an old road—and crosses a small brook that runs in an interesting gorge with a small waterfall just above the trail. At 0.9 mi., George's Gorge Trail enters on the right (east), and the Old Jackson Road rises easily across the flat divide between the Saco and Androscoggin drainages and then descends slightly, crossing several small brooks. Just before reaching a larger brook it makes a sharp left turn uphill, then after a short, steep climb it turns right and runs nearly level. At 1.7 mi. the Raymond Path leaves on the left, and in another 100 yd., just after a small brook is crossed, the Nelson Crag Trail leaves on the left. Continuing north, the trail climbs slightly up an interesting little rocky hogback, passes through an old gravel pit, and meets the Auto Rd. just above the 2-mi. mark, at a small parking area opposite the Madison Gulf Trail trailhead.

Old Jackson Road (map 1:F9)

Distance from Pinkham Notch Visitor Center (2032')

    to Mt. Washington Auto Rd. (2675'): 1.9 mi. (3.1 km.), 700 ft., 1 hr. 20 min.

Crew-Cut Trail (AMC)

The Crew-Cut Trail, George's Gorge Trail, and Liebeskind's Loop, a small network of paths in the region north of Pinkham Notch Visitor Center, were originally located and cut by Bradford Swan. These trails provide pleasant walking at a modest expenditure of effort, passing through fine woods with small ravines and ledges.

    The Crew-Cut Trail leaves the Old Jackson Road on the right about 0.4 mi. from the Visitor Center, just after a stream crossing and just before the point where the Old Jackson Road starts to climb more steeply. After crossing a stony, dry brook bed it runs generally east-northeast, crossing two small brooks. On the east bank of the second brook, at 0.2 mi., the George's Gorge Trail leaves left. The Crew-Cut Trail continues generally northeast, rising gradually up the slope through open woods and crossing several gullies. It skirts southeast of the steeper rocky outcroppings until, at 0.5 mi. from the Old Jackson Road, Liebeskind's Loop enters left, coming down from George's Gorge Trail. The spur path to Lila's Ledge, which affords fine views, leaves Liebeskind's Loop less than 0.1 mi. from this junction. The Crew-Cut Trail passes under the base of a cliff and turns right, then descends steeply over a few small ledges and through open woods until it passes east of a small high-level bog formed by an old beaver dam. Shortly thereafter, it crosses a small stream and Connie's Way Ski Trail, and goes through open woods again, emerging at the top of the grassy embankment on NH 16 almost exactly opposite the south end of the Wildcat Ski Area parking lot.

Crew-Cut Trail (map 1:F9–F10)

Distances from Old Jackson Road (2075')

    to Liebeskind's Loop (2350'): 0.5 mi., 300 ft., 25 min.

    to NH 16 (1950'): 1.0 mi. (1.6 km.), 300 ft. (rev. 400 ft.), 35 min.

George's Gorge Trail (AMC)

This trail leaves the Crew-Cut Trail on the left 0.2 mi. from the Old Jackson Road, on the east bank of a small brook (the infant Peabody River). It leads up the brook, steeply in places, passing Chudacoff Falls and crossing the brook twice, then swings rather sharply away from the brook. Liebeskind's Loop leaves on the right at 0.5 mi., and George's Gorge Trail then climbs nearly to the top of a knob and descends west to the Old Jackson Road in the flat section near its halfway point, 0.9 mi. from Pinkham Notch Visitor Center.

George's Gorge Trail (map 1:F9)
Distance from Crew-Cut Trail (2100')

   to Old Jackson Road (2525'): 0.8 mi. (1.3 km.), 600 ft. (rev. 150 ft.), 40 min.

Liebeskind's Loop (AMC)

Liebeskind's Loop makes possible a loop hike (using the Crew-Cut, George's Gorge, Loop, and Crew-Cut trails) without resorting to returning either by NH 16 or by the section of the Old Jackson Road that is markedly steeper than the rest of the trail. This loop hike is best made in the sequence referred to above, since George's Gorge is more interesting on the ascent and Liebeskind's Loop is more interesting on the descent.

   Liebeskind's Loop leaves right (east) near the high point of the George's Gorge Trail, 0.3 mi. from Old Jackson Road, and descends to a swampy flat, then rises through a spruce thicket to the top of a cliff, where there is a fine lookout called Brad's Bluff with a good view to the south down Pinkham Notch. Here the trail turns left and runs along the edge of the cliff, finally descending by an easy zigzag in a gully to a beautiful open grove of birches. The trail continues east, descending through two gorges and skirting the east end of several small swells until it finally climbs a ridge to its crest. Here a spur trail leads left 0.1 mi. to Lila's Ledge (named by Brad Swan in memory of his wife), which affords excellent views of Pinkham Notch and the eastern slope of Mt. Washington. Liebeskind's Loop then descends on the other side of the ridge to join the Crew-Cut Trail, which can then be followed back to the starting point.

Liebeskind's Loop (map 1:F9–F10)
Distances from George's Gorge Trail (2575')

   to Crew-Cut Trail (2350'): 0.6 mi. (1.0 km.), 0 ft. (rev. 250 ft.), 20 min.

for complete loop from Pinkham Notch Visitor Center (2032') via Old Jackson Road, Crew-Cut Trail, George's Gorge Trail, Liebeskind's Loop, Crew-Cut Trail, and Old Jackson Road: 1.8 mi. (2.9 km.), 550 ft., 1 hr. 10 min.

Crawford Path (WMNF)

This trail is considered to be the oldest continuously maintained footpath in America. The first section, leading up Mt. Pierce (Mt. Clinton), was cut in 1819 by Abel Crawford and his son Ethan Allen Crawford. In 1840 Thomas J. Crawford, a younger son of Abel, converted the footpath into a bridle path, but more than a century has passed since its regular use for ascents on horseback ended. The trail still follows the original path, except for the section between Mt. Monroe and the Westside Trail, which was relocated to take it off the windswept ridge and down past the shelter at Lakes of the Clouds. From the junction just north of Mt. Pierce to the summit of Mt. Washington, the Crawford Path is part of the Appalachian Trail and is blazed in white.

Caution: Parts of this trail are dangerous in bad weather. Several lives have been lost on the Crawford Path due to failure to observe proper precautions. Below Mt. Eisenhower there are a number of ledges exposed to the weather, but they are scattered and shelter is usually available in nearby scrub. From the Eisenhower-Franklin col the trail runs completely above treeline, exposed to the full force of all storms. The most dangerous part of the path is the section on the cone of Mt. Washington, beyond Lakes of the Clouds Hut. Always carry a compass and study the map before starting. If trouble arises on or above Mt. Monroe, take refuge at Lakes of the Clouds Hut or go down the Ammonoosuc Ravine Trail. The Crawford Path is well marked above treeline with large cairns topped by yellow-painted rocks, and in poor visibility great care should be exercised to stay on it, since many of the other paths in the vicinity are much less clearly marked. If the path is lost in bad weather and cannot be found again after diligent effort, one should travel west, descending into the woods and following streams downhill to the roads. On the southeast, toward the Dry River valley, nearly all the slopes are more precipitous, the river crossings are potentially dangerous, and the distance to a highway is much greater.

The main parking area at the south end of this trail is now located on the Mt. Clinton Rd. a short distance from its junction with US 302. The former parking lot on US 302 has been closed, and Crawford Path hikers are requested to use the Mt. Clinton Rd. lot, since the parking spaces at other lots in the area are needed for the trails that originate from them. For historical reasons the name Crawford Path continues to be attached to the old route of the trail that leads directly from US 302, and the short path that connects the Crawford Path to the Mt. Clinton Rd. parking lot is called the Crawford Connector. However, in the descriptions that follow, the main route will be described and distances given starting from Mt. Clinton Rd. via the Crawford Connector, which will now be the usual route for most hikers using this trail.

The following description of the path is in the northbound direction (toward Mt. Washington). See below for a description of the path in the reverse direction.

Leaving the parking lot and soon crossing Mt. Clinton Rd., the Crawford Connector climbs gradually for 0.4 mi. until it reaches the bridge over Gibbs Brook. Here the Crawford Cliff Spur diverges left.

Crawford Cliff Spur. This short side path leaves the Crawford Connector at the west end of the bridge over Gibbs Brook and follows the brook to a small flume and pool. It then climbs steeply above the brook, turns left at an old illegible sign, becomes very rough, and reaches a ledge with an outlook over Crawford Notch and the Willey Range, 0.4 mi. (20 min.) from the Crawford Path.

The Crawford Connector continues across the bridge and ends at the Crawford Path 0.2 mi. from its trailhead on US 302 opposite the AMC Crawford Notch Hostel. To continue ascending on the Crawford Path, turn left here. The Crawford Path follows the south bank of Gibbs Brook, and at 0.6 mi. a side path leads 40 yd. left to Gibbs Falls. Soon the trail passes an information sign for the Gibbs Brook Scenic Area, then climbs moderately but steadily. At about 1.2 mi. from Mt. Clinton Rd. the trail begins to climb away from the brook, angling up the side of the valley. At 1.9 mi. the Mizpah Cutoff diverges east for Mizpah Spring Hut. The Crawford Path continues to ascend at easy to moderate grades, crossing several small brooks, then reaches its high point on the shoulder of Mt. Pierce and runs almost level, breaking into the open with fine views. At 3.1 mi. it reaches the junction with the Webster Cliff Trail, which leads right (south) to the summit of Mt. Pierce in about 0.1 mi.

From Mt. Pierce to Mt. Eisenhower the path runs through patches of scrub and woods with many open ledges that give magnificent views in all directions. Cairns and the marks left by many feet on the rocks indicate the way. The path winds about heading generally in a northeasterly direction, staying fairly near the poorly defined crest of the broad ridge, which is composed of several rounded humps. At 3.8 mi. the trail crosses a small stream in the col, then ascends mostly on ledges to the junction with the Mount Eisenhower Loop, which diverges left at 4.3 mi. The trip over this summit adds only 0.2 mi. and 300 ft. of climbing and provides excellent views in good weather. The Crawford Path bears somewhat to the right at this junction and runs nearly level—though with somewhat rough footing—through scrub on the southeast side of the mountain; this is the better route in bad weather. The Mount Eisenhower Loop rejoins the Crawford Path on the left at 4.8 mi., just above the sag between Mt. Eisenhower and Mt. Franklin, on a ledge that overlooks Red Pond, a small alpine tarn of stagnant water. The Edmands Path can be reached from this junction by following the Mount Eisenhower Loop for a short distance.

At 5.0 mi. the Mount Eisenhower Trail from the Dry River valley enters right. The Crawford Path then begins the ascent of the shoulder called Mt. Franklin, first moderately, then steeply for a short distance near the top. At 5.5 mi. the trail reaches the relatively level shoulder and continues past an unmarked path on the right at 6.0 mi. that leads in 130 yd. to the barely noticeable summit of Mt. Franklin, from which there are excellent views, particularly into Oakes Gulf. At 6.2 mi. the Mount Monroe Loop diverges left to cross both summits of Monroe, affording excellent views. It is about the same length as the parallel section of the Crawford Path but requires about 350 ft. more climbing. The Crawford Path is safer in inclement conditions, since it is much less exposed to the weather. The Crawford Path continues along the edge of the precipice that forms the northwest wall of Oakes Gulf, then follows a relocated section, passing an area that has been closed to public entry to preserve the habitat of the dwarf cinquefoil, an endangered species of plant. The area between the two ends of the Mount Monroe Loop is one of great fragility and botanical importance. To protect this area—probably the most significant tract of rare vegetation in the entire White Mtn. region—the most scrupulous care is required on the part of visitors. At 6.9 mi. the Mount Monroe Loop rejoins on the left, and the Crawford Path descends easily to Lakes of the Clouds Hut at 7.0 mi.

The Ammonoosuc Ravine Trail enters on the left at the corner of the hut, and in another 30 yd. the Dry River Trail enters on the right. The Crawford Path crosses the outlet of the larger lake and passes between it and the second lake, and in a short distance the Camel Trail to Boott Spur and the Tuckerman Crossover to Tuckerman Ravine diverge right at the same point. The Crawford Path then ascends moderately on the northwest side of the ridge, always some distance below the crest. The Davis Path, which has been following the original, less-sheltered location of the Crawford Path, enters on the right at 7.9 mi., at the foot of the cone of Mt. Washington. In another 50 yd. the Westside Trail, a shortcut to the Northern Peaks, diverges left. The Crawford Path runs generally north, switching back and forth as it climbs the steep cone through a trench in the rocks. At the plateau west of the summit, it meets the Gulfside Trail at 8.3 mi., then turns right, passes through the old corral in which saddle horses from the Glen House used to be kept, and from there ascends past buildings to the summit.

Crawford Path (map 1:G8–F9)

Distances from Mt. Clinton Rd. parking area (1920') via Crawford Connector

to Mizpah Cutoff (3380'): 1.9 mi., 1450 ft., 1 hr. 40 min.

to Webster Cliff Trail (4250'): 3.1 mi., 2350 ft., 2 hr. 45 min.

to south end of Mount Eisenhower Loop (4425'): 4.3 mi., 2650 ft., 3 hr. 30 min.

to Mount Eisenhower Trail (4475'): 5.0 mi., 2750 ft., 3 hr. 55 min.

to Lakes of the Clouds Hut (5012'): 7.0 mi., 3450 ft., 5 hr. 15 min.

to Westside Trail (5625'): 7.9 mi., 4050 ft., 6 hr.

to Gulfside Trail (6150'): 8.3 mi., 4600 ft., 6 hr. 30 min.

to Mt. Washington summit (6288'): 8.5 mi. (13.7 km.), 4750 ft., 6 hr. 40 min.

Crawford Path (WMNF) [in reverse]

Descending from the summit of Mt. Washington, the path is on the right (west) side of the railroad track. After passing between the buildings it leads generally south, then west. After passing the old corral it reaches a junction where the Gulfside Trail turns sharp right. Here the Crawford Path turns sharp left and zigzags downward through a trench in the rocks. At 0.6 mi. the Westside Trail enters on the right and in another 50 yd. the Davis Path diverges left, following the original, less-sheltered route of the Crawford Path. The Crawford Path now descends moderately on the northwest side of the ridge well below the crest, and the Tuckerman Crossover and the Camel Trail enter on the left at the same point just before the trail reaches the Lakes of the Clouds. It then passes between the lakes and reaches Lakes of the Clouds Hut at 1.5 mi., where the Dry River Trail enters on the left and the Ammonoosuc Ravine Trail enters on the right.

The Crawford Path now climbs up to the base of Mt. Monroe, where the north end of the Mount Monroe Loop diverges right to cross both summits of Monroe, affording excellent views. The loop over the summits is about the same length as the parallel section of the Crawford Path but requires about 350 ft. more climbing. The Crawford Path is safer in inclement conditions, as it is much less exposed to the weather. It circles around the foot of this sharp peak, following a relocated section past an area that has been closed to public entry to preserve the habitat of the dwarf cinquefoil, an endangered species of plant. The area between the two ends of the Mount Monroe Loop is one of great fragility and botanical importance. To protect this area—probably the most significant tract of rare vegetation in the entire White Mtn. region—the most scrupulous care is required on the part of visitors. The Crawford Path continues along the edge of the precipice that forms the northwest wall of Oakes Gulf, the Mount Monroe Loop rejoins on the right, and the main path continues along the flat ridge, passing an unmarked path on the left at 2.6 mi. that leads in 130 yd. to the barely noticeable summit of Mt. Franklin, from which there are excellent views, particularly into Oakes Gulf. At 3.0 mi. the trail drops rather steeply off the end of the shoulder, then descends moderately to the sag, passing the Mount Eisenhower Trail on the left at 3.5 mi. The Mount Eisenhower Loop leaves on the right at 3.7 mi. on a small ledge overlooking Red Pond, a small alpine tarn of stagnant water. The Edmands Path can be reached from this junction by following the Mount Eisenhower Loop for a short distance. The trip over Mt. Eisenhower adds only 0.2 mi. and 300 ft. of climbing and provides excellent views in good weather. The Crawford Path bears left and runs nearly level—though with somewhat rough footing—through scrub on the southeast side of the mountain; this is the better route in bad weather.

The Mount Eisenhower Loop rejoins on the right at 4.2 mi., and the Crawford Path descends on ledges to cross a small stream in the col, then climbs moderately to the junction with the Webster Cliff Trail at 5.4 mi., on an open ledge just below the summit of Mt. Pierce. From here the trail soon enters the scrub and then full woods, descends moderately past the Mizpah Cutoff at 6.6 mi., and continues through the Gibbs Brook Scenic Area. At 8.1 mi., where the Crawford Path continues straight another 0.2 mi. to US 302 opposite the AMC Crawford Notch Hostel, the main route turns right on the Crawford Connector, immediately crosses a bridge over Gibbs Brook and passes the side path on the right to Crawford Cliff (see above), and continues 0.4 mi. to the Mt. Clinton Rd. parking area.

Crawford Path (map 1:G8–F9)

Distances from the summit of Mt. Washington (6288')

to Gulfside Trail (6150'): 0.2 mi., 0 ft., 5 min.

to Westside Trail (5625'): 0.6 mi., 0 ft., 20 min.

to Lakes of the Clouds Hut (5012'): 1.5 mi., 0 ft., 45 min.

to Mount Eisenhower Trail (4475'): 3.5 mi., 150 ft., 1 hr. 50 min.

to south end of Mount Eisenhower Loop (4425'): 4.2 mi., 200 ft., 2 hr. 10 min.

to Webster Cliff Trail (4250'): 5.4 mi., 350 ft., 2 hr. 55 min.

to Mizpah Cutoff (3380'): 6.6 mi., 350 ft., 3 hr. 30 min.

to Mt. Clinton Rd. parking area (1920') via Crawford Connector: 8.5 mi. (13.7 km.), 350 ft., 4 hr. 25 min.

Mount Eisenhower Loop (AMC)

This short trail parallels the Crawford Path, climbing over the bare, flat summit of Mt. Eisenhower, which provides magnificent views. It diverges from the Crawford Path 4.3 mi. from Mt. Clinton Rd. at the south edge of the summit dome, climbs easily for 0.1 mi., then turns sharp left in a flat area and ascends steadily to the summit at 0.4 mi. From there it descends moderately to a ledge overlooking Red Pond, then drops steeply over ledges, passes through a grassy sag just to the left of Red Pond, and finally climbs briefly past a junction on the left with the Edmands Path to rejoin the Crawford Path on a small, rocky knob.

Mount Eisenhower Loop (map 1:G8)

Distances from south junction with Crawford Path (4425')

to Mt. Eisenhower summit (4760'): 0.4 mi., 350 ft., 25 min.

to north junction with Crawford Path (4475'): 0.8 mi. (1.2 km.), 350 ft. (rev. 300 ft.), 35 min.

Mount Monroe Loop (AMC)

This short trail runs parallel to the Crawford Path and passes over the summits of Mt. Monroe and Little Monroe. The views are fine but the summits are very exposed to the weather. The trail diverges from the Crawford Path 6.3 mi. from Mt. Clinton Rd. and quickly ascends the minor crag called Little Monroe, then descends into the shallow, grassy sag beyond. It then climbs steeply to the summit of Mt. Monroe at 0.4 mi., follows the northeast ridge to the end of the shoulder, and drops sharply to the Crawford Path 0.1 mi. south of Lakes of the Clouds Hut.

Mount Monroe Loop (map 1:F9)

Distances from south junction with Crawford Path (5075')

to summit of Mt. Monroe (5372'): 0.4 mi., 350 ft., 20 min.

to north junction with Crawford Path (5075'): 0.7 mi. (1.1 km.), 350 ft. (rev. 350 ft.), 30 min.

Ammonoosuc Ravine Trail (WMNF)

The Ammonoosuc Ravine Trail ascends to Lakes of the Clouds Hut from a parking lot on the Base Rd., about 1 mi. east of its junction with the Mt. Clinton Rd. and the Jefferson Notch Rd. It can also be reached on foot from the Jefferson Notch Rd. via the Boundary Line Trail (see Section 2). Together with the upper section of the Crawford Path, this trail provides the shortest route to Mt. Washington from the west. The trail follows the headwaters of the Ammonoosuc River with many fine falls, cascades, and pools, and affords excellent views from its upper section. It is the most direct route to Lakes of the Clouds Hut, and the best route to or from the hut in bad weather, since it lies in woods or scrub except for the last 200 yd. to the hut. The section above Gem Pool is extremely steep and rough, and is likely to prove quite arduous to many hikers, particularly those with limited trail-walking experience. Many hikers also find it somewhat unpleasant to descend this section because of the steep, often slippery rocks and ledges.

Leaving the parking lot, this trail follows a path through the woods, crossing Franklin Brook at 0.3 mi. then passing over a double pipeline as it skirts around the Base Station area. It joins the old route of the trail at the edge of the Ammonoosuc River at 1.0 mi., after a slight descent. (The lower section of the old route, marked by a sign, leads left from here 0.3 mi. to the Base Station.) The main trail bears right along the river, following the old route for the rest of the way. It ascends mostly by easy grades, though with some rough footing, crossing Monroe Brook at 1.7 mi. At 2.1 mi. it crosses the outlet of Gem Pool, a beautiful emerald pool at the foot of a cascade.

Now the very steep, rough ascent begins. At 2.3 mi. a side path (sign) leads right about 80 yd. to a spectacular viewpoint at the foot of the gorge. Above this point the main brook falls about 600 ft. down a steep trough in the mountainside at an average angle of 45 degrees, while another brook a short distance to the north does the same, and these two spectacular water slides meet in a pool at the foot of the gorge. The main trail continues its steep ascent, passes an outlook over the cascades to the right of the trail, and at 2.5 mi. crosses the main brook on flat ledges at the head of the highest fall, a striking viewpoint. The grade now begins to ease, and the trail crosses several more brooks. Ledges become more frequent and the scrub becomes smaller and more sparse. At 3.0 mi. the trail emerges from the scrub and follows a line of cairns directly up some rock slabs (which are slippery when wet), passes through one last patch of scrub, and reaches the Crawford Path at the south side of Lakes of the Clouds Hut.

Ammonoosuc Ravine Trail (map 1:F8–F9)

Distances from the Base Rd. parking lot (2500')

> *to* Gem Pool (3450'): 2.1 mi., 950 ft., 1 hr. 30 min.

> *to* brook crossing on flat ledges (4175'): 2.5 mi., 1700 ft., 2 hr. 5 min.

> *to* Lakes of the Clouds Hut (5012'): 3.1 mi. (5.0 km.), 2500 ft., 2 hr. 50 min.

> *to* Mt. Washington summit (6288') via Crawford Path: 4.5 mi. (7.2 km.), 3800 ft., 4 hr. 10 min.

Edmands Path (WMNF)

The Edmands Path climbs to the Mount Eisenhower Loop near its junction with the Crawford Path in the Eisenhower-Franklin col, starting from a parking lot on the east side of the Mt. Clinton Rd. 2.3 mi. north of its junction with US 302. This trail provides the shortest route to the summit of Mt. Eisenhower, and a relatively easy access to the middle portion of the Crawford Path and the Southern Presidentials. The last 0.2-mi. segment before it joins the Mount Eisenhower Loop and Crawford Path is very exposed to northwest winds and, although short, can create a serious problem in bad weather. The ledgy brook crossings in the upper part of the trail can be treacherous in icy conditions.

J. Rayner Edmands, the pioneer trail-maker, relocated and reconstructed this trail in 1909. The rock cribbing and paving in the middle and upper sections of the trail testify to the diligent labor that Edmands devoted to constructing a trail with constant comfortable grades in rather difficult terrain. Most of his work has survived the weather and foot traffic of many decades well, and though erosion has made the footing noticeably rougher in recent years, the trail retains what is probably the easiest grade and footing of any comparable trail in the White Mtns. It is nearly always comfortable, and almost never challenging.

From its trailhead the path runs nearly level across two small brooks, then at 0.4 mi. it crosses Abenaki Brook and turns sharp right onto an old logging road on the far bank. At 0.7 mi. the trail diverges left off the old road and crosses a wet area. Soon it begins to climb steadily, undulating up the west ridge of Mt. Eisenhower, carefully searching out the most comfortable grades. At 2.2 mi. the trail swings left and angles up the mountainside on a footway supported by extensive rock cribbing, then passes through a tiny stone gateway. At 2.5 mi. it crosses a small brook running over a ledge, and soon the grade becomes almost level as the trail contours around the north slope of Mt. Eisenhower, affording excellent views out through a fringe of trees. At 2.8 mi. it breaks into the open, crosses the nose of a ridge on a footway paved with carefully placed stones, and reaches the Mount Eisenhower Loop a few yards from the Crawford Path.

Edmands Path (map 1:G8)

Distances from Mt. Clinton Rd. (2000')

> *to* stone gateway (4000'): 2.2 mi., 2000 ft., 2 hr. 5 min.

> *to* Mount Eisenhower Loop junction (4450'): 2.9 mi. (4.7 km.), 2450 ft., 2 hr. 40 min.

> *to* Mt. Eisenhower summit (4760') via Mount Eisenhower Loop: 3.3 mi. (5.3 km.), 2750 ft., 3 hr.

Webster-Jackson Trail (AMC)

This trail connects US 302 at a small parking area just south of the Crawford Depot information center with the summits of both Mt. Webster and Mt. Jackson, and provides the opportunity for an interesting loop trip, since the two summits are linked by the Webster Cliff Trail.

The trail, blazed in blue, leaves the east side of US 302 0.1 mi. south of the Crawford Depot and 0.1 mi. north of the Gate of the Notch. It runs through a clearing, enters the woods, and at 0.1 mi. from US 302 passes the side path leading right to Elephant Head.

Elephant Head Spur. Elephant Head is an interesting ledge that forms the east side of the Gate of the Notch, a mass of gray rock striped with veins of white quartz providing a remarkable likeness to an elephant's head and trunk. The path runs through the woods parallel to the highway at an easy grade, then ascends across the summit of the knob and descends 40 yd. to the top of the ledge, which overlooks Crawford Notch and affords fine views; it is 0.2 mi. (10 min.) from the Webster-Jackson Trail.

The main trail climbs along the south bank of Elephant Head Brook, well above the stream, then turns right, away from the brook, at 0.2 mi. Angling up the mountainside roughly parallel to the highway, nearly level stretches alternating with sharp uphill pitches, it crosses Little Mossy Brook at 0.3 mi., and at 0.6 mi. from US 302 a side path leads right 60 yd. to Bugle Cliff. This is a massive ledge overlooking Crawford Notch, where the view is well worth the slight extra effort required; if ice is present, exercise extreme caution. The main trail rises fairly steeply and crosses Flume Cascade Brook at 0.9 mi. At 1.4 mi., within sound of Silver Cascade Brook, the trail divides, the left branch for Mt. Jackson and the right for Mt. Webster.

Mount Webster Branch

The Webster (right) branch immediately descends steeply to Silver Cascade Brook, crosses it just below a beautiful cascade and pool, then bears left and climbs steeply up the bank. The trail then climbs steadily south 1.0 mi., meeting the Webster Cliff Trail on the high plateau northwest of the summit of Mt. Webster, 2.4 mi. from US 302. The ledgy summit of Mt. Webster, with an excellent view of Crawford Notch and the mountains to the west and south, is 0.1 mi. right (south) via the Webster Cliff Trail. For Mt. Jackson and Mizpah Spring Hut, turn left.

Mount Jackson Branch

The Jackson (left) branch ascends gradually until it comes within sight of Silver Cascade Brook, then begins to climb moderately. About 0.5 mi. above the junction, it crosses three branches of the brook in quick succession. At 1.0 mi. from the junction, a short distance below the base of the rocky summit cone, it passes Tisdale Spring (unreliable, often scanty and muddy). The trail soon swings right and ascends steep ledges to the open summit, 2.6 mi. from US 302.

Webster-Jackson Trail (map 1:G8)

Distances from US 302 (1900')

   to Bugle Cliff (2450'): 0.6 mi., 550 ft., 35 min.

   to Flume Cascade Brook (2500'): 0.9 mi., 600 ft., 45 min.

   to Mt. Webster–Mt. Jackson fork (2800'): 1.4 mi., 900 ft., 1 hr. 10 min.

   to Webster Cliff Trail (3840') via Webster branch: 2.4 mi., 2050 ft., 2 hr. 15 min.

   to summit of Mt. Webster (3910') via Webster Cliff Trail: 2.5 mi. (4.1 km.), 2100 ft., 2 hr. 20 min.

   to summit of Mt. Jackson (4052') via Jackson branch: 2.6 mi. (4.2 km.), 2150 ft., 2 hr. 25 min.

   for loop trip over summits of Webster and Jackson (via Webster Cliff Trail): 6.5 mi. (10.5 km.), 2500 ft., 4 hr. 30 min.

Webster Cliff Trail (AMC)

This trail, a part of the Appalachian Trail, leaves the east side of US 302 opposite the road to Willey House Station, about 1 mi. south of the Willey House Recreation Area at the Willey House site. It ascends along the edge of the spectacular cliffs that form the east wall of Crawford Notch, then leads over Mts. Webster, Jackson, and Pierce to the Crawford Path 0.1 mi. north of Mt. Pierce.

From US 302, it runs nearly east 0.1 mi. to a bridge across the Saco River. Then the trail climbs steadily up the south end of the ridge, winding up the steep slope, swinging more to the north and growing steeper as it approaches the cliffs. At 1.8 mi. from US 302 it reaches the first open ledge, and from here on, as the trail ascends the ridge with easier grades, there are frequent outlook ledges giving ever-changing perspectives of the notch and the mountains to the south and west. At 2.4 mi. a ledge affords a view straight down to the state park buildings, and at 3.3 mi. the jumbled, ledgy summit is reached.

The trail then descends north, and in 0.1 mi. the Webster branch of the Webster-Jackson Trail from Crawford Depot on US 302 enters left. The Webster Cliff Trail swings east and crosses numerous wet gullies, finally ascending the steep, ledgy cone of Mt. Jackson to reach the summit at 4.7 mi., where the Jackson branch of the Webster-Jackson Trail enters left.

The trail leaves the summit of Mt. Jackson toward Mt. Pierce, following a line of cairns running north, and descends the ledges at the north end of the cone quite rapidly into the scrub, then enters and winds through open alpine meadows. At 5.2 mi., where a side path leads right 40 yd. to an outlook, the trail turns sharp left and drops into the woods. It continues up and down along the ridge toward Mt. Pierce, then descends gradually to the junction at 6.3 mi. with the Mizpah Cutoff, which leads left (west) to the Crawford Path. At 6.4 mi. Mizpah Spring Hut (where there are also tentsites for backpackers) is reached, and the Mount Clinton Trail to the Dry River valley diverges right (southeast), starting off diagonally down the hut clearing. Continuing past the hut, the trail soon ascends very rapidly, passes an outlook toward Mt. Jackson, and reaches an open ledge with good views at 6.6 mi. The grade lessens, and after a sharp right turn in a ledgy area the trail reaches the summit of the southwest knob of Mt. Pierce, which affords a view of the summit of Mt. Washington rising over Mt. Pierce. The trail descends into a sag and ascends easily through scrub to the summit of Mt. Pierce at 7.2 mi., where it comes into the open. It then descends moderately in the open in the same direction (northeast) about 150 yd. to its junction with the Crawford Path.

Webster Cliff Trail (map 1:G8)
Distances from US 302 (1275')

to first open ledge (3100'): 1.8 mi., 1850 ft., 1 hr. 50 min.

to summit of Mt. Webster (3910'): 3.3 mi., 2700 ft., 3 hr.

to summit of Mt. Jackson (4052'): 4.7 mi., 3050 ft. (rev. 250 ft.), 3 hr. 50 min.

to Mizpah Spring Hut (3800'): 6.4 mi., 3000 ft. (rev. 250 ft.), 4 hr. 40 min.

to Crawford Path (4250'): 7.3 mi. (11.7 km.), 3550 ft. (rev. 100 ft.), 5 hr. 25 min.

Mizpah Cutoff (AMC)

This short trail provides a direct route from the Crawford Depot area to Mizpah Spring Hut. It diverges right (east) from the Crawford Path 1.9 mi. from the Mt. Clinton Rd. parking area, climbs the ridge at a moderate grade, passes through a fairly level area, and descends slightly to join the Webster Cliff Trail 0.1 mi. south of Mizpah Spring Hut.

Mizpah Cutoff (map 1:G8)
Distance from Crawford Path (3380')

to Mizpah Spring Hut (3800'): 0.7 mi. (1.1 km.), 400 ft., 35 min.

Distance from Mt. Clinton Rd. parking area (1920')

to Mizpah Spring Hut (3800') via Crawford Connector, Crawford Path and Mizpah Cutoff: 2.6 mi. (4.2 km.), 1900 ft., 2 hr. 15 min.

Saco Lake Trail (AMC)

This very short trail makes a loop around the east shore of Saco Lake, beginning and ending on US 302. It starts opposite the AMC Crawford Notch Hostel and ends after crossing the dam at the south end of Saco Lake. In addition to being an attractive short walk, it provides an alternative to part of the road walk between the beginning points of the Crawford Path and Webster-Jackson Trail.

Saco Lake Trail (map 1:G8)
Distance from north junction with US 302 (1890')

to south junction with US 302 (1890'): 0.3 mi. (0.5 km.), 0 ft., 10 min.

Dry River Trail (WMNF)

The Dry River Trail is the main trail from US 302 up the valley of Dry River and through Oakes Gulf to Lakes of the Clouds Hut, giving access to Mt. Washington, the Southern Peaks, and the upper portion of the Montalban Ridge. It leaves the east side of US 302, 0.3 mi. north of the entrance to Dry River Campground and 2.6 mi. south of the Willey House site. This trail in general is somewhat rougher than most similar valley trails elsewhere in the White Mtns. The first 5 mi. follows fairly close to the route of an old logging railroad, although the river and its tributaries have eradicated much of the old roadbed, and the relocations cut to eliminate the numerous potentially hazardous river crossings have bypassed much of the remaining grade. When water levels are high, the few Dry River crossings that remain on this trail—and on the trails that diverge from it— are at best difficult and can be very dangerous. At such times it is prudent not to descend into this valley if major stream crossings lie between you and your destination. This trail is almost entirely within the Presidential Range–Dry River Wilderness. Dry River Shelters #1 and #2 have been removed; Dry River Shelter #3 will be removed whenever major maintenance is required (contact Saco Ranger District office for information).

From the highway the trail follows a wide woods road generally northeast for 0.5 mi. to its junction with the bed of the old logging railroad, which reaches this point from Dry River Campground in 0.3 mi. From here the trail follows the railroad bed, enters the Presidential Range–Dry River Wilderness at 0.7 mi., and leaves the railroad grade sharp left at 0.9 mi., staying on the west side of the river where the railroad formerly crossed it. Just downstream from this point there is a pleasant pool. The trail climbs over a low bluff, rejoins the roadbed, then leaves it again and climbs over a higher bluff, where there is a restricted but beautiful outlook up the Dry River to Mt. Washington, Mt. Monroe, and the headwall of Oakes Gulf. At 1.7 mi. the trail crosses the Dry River on a suspension bridge and continues up the east bank, occasionally using portions of the old railroad grade. At 2.9 mi. it turns sharp right off the railroad grade where the Mount Clinton Trail diverges left to cross the river and ascend to Mizpah Spring Hut. At 4.2 mi. the Dry River Trail makes a sharp turn away from the river, then turns left and continues along the bank at a higher level. At 4.9 mi. it crosses Isolation Brook, turns right along the brook bank, and in 60 yd. the Isolation Trail diverges right, heading up along the brook.

The Dry River Trail continues straight along the high east bank of the Dry River and passes a cleared outlook over the river; at 5.2 mi. the Mount Eisenhower Trail diverges sharp left and descends the steep bank to cross the river and climb to the Crawford Path. The Dry River Trail continues along the east bank, passing at 5.4 mi. a side path (sign) on the left that leads down 40 yd. to the pool at the foot of Dry River Falls, a very attractive spot. The top of the falls, with an interesting pothole, can also be reached from here. At 5.6 mi. the trail crosses the river to the west side; the crossing is normally fairly easy but could be a serious problem at high water. At 6.3 mi. Dry River Shelter #3 is passed; it will be removed when major maintenance is required. In another 60 yd. the trail crosses a major tributary of Dry River at the confluence and continues along the bank of the main stream, gradually rising higher above the river.

At 7.4 mi. the trail begins to swing away from the river, which has been at least audible to this point, and gradually climbs into Oakes Gulf. After it crosses a small ridge and descends sharply on the other side, views begin to appear, although the trail remains well sheltered in the scrub. At 8.7 mi. there is a good outlook perch just to the right of the trail. The trail soon climbs out of the scrub, turns left, and crosses a small brook at a right angle. At 9.1 mi. the trail turns sharp right from the gully it once ascended, where signs forbid public entry into the area formerly crossed by the trail. (The closed area is the habitat of the dwarf cinquefoil, an endangered plant species.) The trail continues to climb, passing the Presidential Range–Dry River Wilderness boundary sign in a patch of scrub, and reaches the height-of-land on the southwest ridge of Mt. Washington at 9.4 mi. It then descends to the larger of the two Lakes of the Clouds, follows its south edge, and ends at Lakes of the Clouds Hut.

Dry River Trail (map 1:H8–F9)

Distances from US 302 (1205')

   to suspension bridge (1600'): 1.7 mi., 500 ft., 1 hr. 5 min.

   to Mount Clinton Trail (1900'): 2.9 mi., 800 ft., 1 hr. 50 min.

   to Isolation Trail (2600'): 4.9 mi., 1500 ft., 3 hr. 10 min.

   to Mount Eisenhower Trail (2650'): 5.2 mi., 1550 ft., 3 hr. 25 min.

   to Dry River Shelter #3 (3125'): 6.3 mi., 2000 ft., 4 hr. 10 min.

   to Lakes of the Clouds Hut (5012'): 9.6 mi. (15.5 km.), 4000 ft., 6 hr. 50 min.

Mount Clinton Trail (WMNF)

This trail connects the lower part of the Dry River to Mizpah Spring Hut and the southern part of the Southern Peaks, and lies almost entirely within the Presidential Range–Dry River Wilderness. *Caution:* The crossing of Dry River on this trail near its junction with the Dry River Trail can vary from an easy skip over the stones to a waist-high ford in a torrent, and there may be no safe way across. In high water conditions, it would be prudent not to descend from Mizpah Spring Hut by this trail, since the only safe course on reaching Dry River (other than returning to the hut) might be a rough bushwhack south along the river bank for about 1.2 mi.

The trail diverges left from the Dry River Trail 2.9 mi. from US 302, and immediately makes the potentially hazardous crossing of the Dry River. On the west side of the river it follows a short stretch of old railroad grade, then swings left up the bank of a major tributary, following an old logging road at a moderate grade much of the way. At 0.5 mi. the trail crosses this brook for the first of seven times, then scrambles up a washed-out area on the other bank. At 1.2 mi. the trail turns sharp left off the road and descends to the brook, crosses at a ledgy spot, and soon regains the road on the other side. It follows close to the brook, crossing many tributaries as well as the main brook, to the seventh crossing of the main brook at 1.8 mi. Above an eroded section where a small brook has taken over the road, the walking on the old road becomes very pleasant, and the Dry River Cutoff enters on the right at 2.5 mi. From here the trail ascends past a large boulder to the Presidential Range–Dry River Wilderness boundary at 2.9 mi., and soon enters the clearing of Mizpah Spring Hut, where it joins the Webster Cliff Trail.

Mount Clinton Trail (map 1:G8)

Distances from Dry River Trail (1900')

to Dry River Cutoff (3425'): 2.5 mi., 1550 ft., 2 hr.

to Mizpah Spring Hut (3800'): 3.0 mi. (4.8 km.), 1900 ft., 2 hr. 25 min.

Mount Eisenhower Trail (WMNF)

This trail connects the middle part of the Dry River valley to the Crawford Path at the Eisenhower-Franklin col and lies almost entirely within the Presidential Range–Dry River Wilderness. Its grades are mostly easy to moderate and it runs above treeline for only a short distance at the ridgecrest.

The trail diverges left from the Dry River Trail about 5.2 mi. from US 302, and descends rather steeply on a former route of the Dry River Trail through an area with many side paths; care must be taken to stay on the proper trail. The trail crosses Dry River (may be difficult or impassable at high water), and follows the bank downstream. At 0.2 mi. it joins its former route and bears right up a rather steep logging road, and the Dry River Cutoff diverges left at 0.3 mi. Soon the grade on the Mount Eisenhower Trail eases as it leads generally north, keeping a bit to the west of the crest of the long ridge that runs south from a point midway between Mts. Franklin and Eisenhower. At 1.3 mi. it passes through a blowdown patch with views of Mt. Pierce, and from here on there are occasional views to the west from the edge of the ravine. At 1.8 mi. it turns sharp right, then left, and soon ascends more steeply for a while. At 2.4 mi. the trail finally gains the crest of the ridge, and winds among rocks and scrub, passing the Presidential Range–Dry River Wilderness boundary 50 yd. before reaching the Crawford Path in the Eisenhower-Franklin col, at a point 0.2 mi. north of the Crawford Path's northern junction with the Mount Eisenhower Loop.

Mount Eisenhower Trail (map 1:G8)

Distances from Dry River Trail (2650')

> *to* Dry River Cutoff (2650'): 0.3 mi., 100 ft. (rev. 100 ft.), 10 min.

> *to* Crawford Path (4475'): 2.7 mi. (4.3 km.), 1950 ft., 2 hr. 20 min.

Dry River Cutoff (AMC)

This trail connects the middle part of the Dry River valley to Mizpah Spring Hut and the southern section of the Southern Peaks. Grades are mostly easy with some moderate sections. This trail is entirely within the Presidential Range–Dry River Wilderness.

The trail diverges left from the Mount Eisenhower Trail 0.3 mi. from the latter trail's junction with the Dry River Trail. In 0.1 mi. it crosses a substantial brook after a slight descent, then turns sharp left and climbs the bank, crosses a tributary, then swings back and climbs above the bank of the tributary. It crosses several branches of the tributary and gains the height-of-land on the southeast ridge of Mt. Pierce at 1.3 mi., then runs almost on the level to its junction with the Mount Clinton Trail at 1.7 mi. Mizpah Spring Hut is 0.5 mi. to the right from this junction via the Mount Clinton Trail.

Dry River Cutoff (map 1:G8)

Distance from Mount Eisenhower Trail (2650')

> *to* Mount Clinton Trail (3425'): 1.7 mi. (2.8 km.), 800 ft., 1 hr. 15 min.

Davis Path (AMC)

The Davis Path, completed by Nathaniel P. T. Davis in 1845, was the third (and longest) bridle path constructed to the summit of Mt. Washington. It was in use until 1853 or 1854, but became impassable soon afterward, and eventually went out of existence entirely until it was reopened as a foot trail by the AMC in 1910. At that time it was so overgrown that some sections could be located only by one of the original laborers, then a very old man, who relied on his memory of where the path had been built. The sections leading up the dauntingly steep southern slopes of Mt. Crawford and Stairs Mtn. give some idea of the magnitude of the task Davis performed in building a trail passable to horses along this ridge. The resolution that enabled Davis to push forward with this apparently hopeless task was the inspiration for the naming of Mt. Resolution. This trail is almost entirely within the Presidential Range–Dry River Wilderness.

The path leaves US 302 on the west side of the Saco River at a paved parking lot near the Notchland Inn, 5.6 mi. south of the Willey House site in Crawford Notch State Park. It follows the bank of the river about 200 yd. upstream to the suspension footbridge (Bemis Bridge). Beyond the east end of the bridge, the trail passes through private land, continuing straight east across an overgrown field near a camp, then turns left into a path along a power line and crosses a small brook. It then enters the woods and the WMNF, and soon joins and follows a logging road along the bed of a small brook (normally dry in summer). It crosses the brook bed at a point where there may be running water upstream, soon recrosses it, and begins to climb away from it, shortly passing into the Presidential Range–Dry River Wilderness. At 0.9 mi. it turns sharp right and soon enters the old, carefully graded bridle path and begins to ascend the steep ridge between Mt. Crawford and Mt. Hope by zigzags. Attaining the crest at 1.9 mi., the Davis Path follows this ridge north, rising over bare ledges with good outlooks, particularly to Carrigain and Tripyramid.

At 2.2 mi. from US 302, at the foot of a large, sloping ledge, a side trail diverges left and climbs 0.3 mi. (15 min.) to the bare, peaked summit of Mt. Crawford, from which there is a magnificent view of Crawford Notch, the Dry River valley, and the surrounding ridges and peaks.

From this junction the Davis Path turns northeast, descends slightly to the col between the peak of Mt. Crawford and its ledgy, domelike east knob (sometimes called Crawford Dome), and resumes the ascent. It soon passes over a ledgy shoulder of Crawford Dome, with good views back to the impressively precipitous face of the small peak of Mt. Crawford, and dips to the Crawford-

Resolution col. Leaving this col, the path runs north, rises slightly, and keeps close to the same level along the steep west side of Mt. Resolution.

At 3.7 mi., the Mount Parker Trail diverges right (east) and leads in about 0.6 mi. to open ledges near the summit of Mt. Resolution, then continues to the Mount Langdon Trail and Bartlett village. Fine views can be obtained from open ledges by ascending this trail for only a little more than 0.1 mi. from the Davis Path junction.

At this junction also, a spur trail leaves opposite the Mount Parker Trail and descends steeply for about 120 yd. to the AMC Resolution Shelter, an open camp with room for eight, situated on a small branch of Sleeper Brook. (WMNF Wilderness policies call for removal of this shelter when major maintenance is required.) Ordinarily there is water just behind the shelter, but in dry seasons it may be necessary to go down the brook a short distance. In most seasons, this is the first water after the brook at the base of the climb up from the Saco valley; in dry seasons it may be the last water available on the entire remainder of the trail unless one descends well down one of the branches of the Isolation Trail, since all of the water sources near this ridgecrest trail are unreliable.

At 4.0 mi. the path passes just west of Stairs Col, the small, wild pass between Mt. Resolution and Stairs Mtn. Here the Stairs Col Trail to the Rocky Branch diverges right. The Davis Path now veers northwest, passing west of the precipitous Giant Stairs, ascending gradually along a steep mountainside, then zigzagging boldly northeast toward the flat top of Stairs Mtn. As the path turns sharp left shortly before reaching the top of the slope, a branch trail leads right a few steps to the Down-look, a good viewpoint at the brink of a cliff. (On the descent, where the main trail turns sharp right, take care not to follow this side path inadvertently since it ends at the drop-off very abruptly.) At the top of the climb, 4.4 mi. from US 302, a branch trail leads right (southeast) 0.2 mi., passing just south of the summit of Stairs Mtn., to the top of the Giant Stairs, where there is an inspiring view.

The Davis Path continues down the north ridge of Stairs Mtn. for 1.0 mi., then runs east in a sag for about 0.1 mi. Turning north again and crossing a small brook (watch for this turn), it passes over a small rise and descends into another sag. The path next begins to ascend the long north and south ridge of Mt. Davis, keeping mostly to the west slopes. At 6.1 mi. there is a small spring on the right, and at 6.5 mi. a small brook is crossed. At 8.5 mi. a branch trail diverges right (east) 0.2 mi. to the summit of Mt. Davis, which commands perhaps the finest view on the Montalban Ridge and one of the best in the mountains. The main path now descends to the col between Mt. Davis and Mt. Isolation, where it crosses a small brook and then ascends Mt. Isolation. At 9.7 mi. a spur path (which is signed, but easily missed) diverges left at a ledgy spot, leading in 125 yd. to the open summit of Mt. Isolation, which provides magnificent views in all directions.

At 10.5 mi. the path leads past the site of the former Isolation Shelter, and at 10.6 mi. the east branch of the Isolation Trail enters on the right from the Rocky Branch valley. Water can be obtained by going down the Isolation Trail to the right (east); decent-appearing water (which is nevertheless unsafe to drink without treatment) may be a considerable distance down. The Davis Path continues to climb steadily, and at 10.9 mi., as it reaches the top of the ridge and the grade decreases, the west branch of the Isolation Trail diverges and descends to the left into the Dry River valley. The Davis Path passes over a hump and runs through a sag at 11.5 mi., then ascends steadily to treeline at 12.1 mi. From here the trail is above treeline and completely exposed to the weather. At 12.5 mi. the Glen Boulder Trail joins on the right just below a small crag, and at 13.0 mi. the path passes just west of the summit of Boott Spur, and the Boott Spur Trail from AMC Pinkham Notch Visitor Center enters on the right (east).

Turning northwest, the path leads along the almost level ridges of Boott Spur and crosses Bigelow Lawn. At 13.6 mi. the Lawn Cutoff diverges right to Tuckerman Junction, and, 200 yd. farther on, the Camel Trail diverges left (west) to the Lakes of the Clouds Hut. At 14.0 mi. the Davis Path begins to follow the original location of the Crawford Path and crosses the Tuckerman Crossover, and in another 0.3 mi. the Davis Path is joined on the right by the Southside Trail. At 14.4 mi. the Davis Path ends at the present Crawford Path, which climbs to the summit of Mt. Washington in another 0.6 mi.

Davis Path (maps 1/3:H8–F9)

Distances from parking area near US 302 (1000')

    to Mt. Crawford spur path (2960'): 2.2 mi., 1950 ft., 2 hr. 5 min.

    to Mount Parker Trail (3100'): 3.7 mi., 2500 ft. (rev. 400 ft.), 3 hr.

    to Stairs Col Trail (3040'): 4.0 mi., 2500 ft. (rev. 50 ft.), 3 hr. 15 min.

    to Giant Stairs spur path (3450'): 4.4 mi., 2900 ft., 3 hr. 40 min.

    to Mt. Davis spur path (3720'): 8.5 mi., 4000 ft. (rev. 800 ft.), 6 hr. 15 min.

    to Mt. Isolation spur path (3950'): 9.7 mi., 4400 ft. (rev. 150 ft.), 7 hr. 5 min.

    to Isolation Trail, east branch (3850'): 10.6 mi., 4550 ft. (rev. 250 ft.), 7 hr. 35 min.

    to Isolation Trail, west branch (4150'): 10.9 mi., 4850 ft., 7 hr. 55 min.

to Glen Boulder Trail (5175'): 12.5 mi., 5900 ft. (rev. 100 ft.), 9 hr. 10 min.

to Boott Spur Trail (5425'): 13.0 mi., 6150 ft., 9 hr. 35 min.

to Lawn Cutoff (5475'): 13.6 mi., 6200 ft. (rev. 100 ft.), 9 hr. 55 min.

to Crawford Path (5625'): 14.4 mi. (23.2 km.), 6400 ft. (rev. 50 ft.), 10 hr. 10 min.

to Lakes of the Clouds Hut (5012') via Camel Trail: 14.4 mi., 6200 ft. (rev. 450 ft.), 10 hr. 20 min.

to Mt. Washington summit (6288') via Crawford Path: 15.0 mi. (24.1 km.), 7000 ft., 11 hr.

Stairs Col Trail (AMC)

This trail connects the Rocky Branch valley with Stairs Col on the Davis Path, providing, in particular, the easiest route to the Giant Stairs. Note that there is usually water in small streams in the upper part of this trail, but very little on the Davis Path. This trail is almost entirely within the Presidential Range–Dry River Wilderness.

It leaves the Rocky Branch Trail opposite the side path to the Rocky Branch Shelter #1 area and follows an old railroad siding for 50 yd. It then turns sharp left, crosses a swampy area, and climbs briefly to a logging road, where it enters the Presidential Range–Dry River Wilderness. From here nearly to Stairs Col, the trail follows logging roads along the ravine of Lower Stairs Brook, becoming quite steep at 1.3 mi. and crossing the headwaters of the brook at about 1.5 mi., where it enters a birch glade. The trail becomes gradual as it approaches Stairs Col, then it crosses this small, ferny pass below the cliffs of Stairs Mtn. and continues down the west slope a short distance to meet the Davis Path. For the Giant Stairs, turn right.

Stairs Col Trail (map 1:H9)

Distance from Rocky Branch Trail (1420')

to Davis Path junction (3040'): 1.8 mi. (2.9 km.), 1600 ft., 1 hr. 40 min.

Rocky Branch Trail (WMNF)

This trail provides access to the valley of the Rocky Branch of the Saco River, which lies between the two longest subsidiary ridges of Mt. Washington: the Montalban Ridge to the west and the Rocky Branch Ridge to the east. In the upper part of the valley, the forest is still recovering from fires that swept the slopes in 1914 to 1916. The lack of mature trees, particularly conifers, is evident in many areas. *Caution:* There are four river crossings between the junctions with the Stairs Col Trail and the Isolation Trail, and one just beyond the Isolation Trail junction; these crossings are wide, difficult, and possibly dangerous at high water. The northeast terminus of this trail is located at a paved parking lot on NH 16 about 5 mi. north of Jackson, just north of the highway bridge over the Ellis River. The Jericho (south) trailhead is reached by following Jericho Rd.—called Rocky Branch Rd. (FR 27) by the USFS—which leaves US 302 just east of the bridge over the Rocky Branch, 1 mi. west of the junction of US 302 and NH 16 in Glen; it is paved for about 1 mi., then a good gravel road up to the beginning of the trail about 4.4 mi. from US 302.

At the northeast terminus, on NH 16 below Pinkham Notch, the trail leaves the north end of the parking lot (avoid a gravel road that branches left just below the parking lot) and climbs moderately on an old logging road. At about 0.5 mi. the Avalanche Brook Ski Trail enters from the left and leaves on the right at 0.7 mi. At 1.3 mi. the trail swings left, away from the bank of a small brook, and continues to ascend, then turns sharp left at 1.8 mi. and follows an old, very straight road on a slight downhill grade. After about 0.5 mi. on this road, it swings gradually right and climbs moderately, following a brook part of the way, and reaches the Presidential Range–Dry River Wilderness boundary just east of the ridge top. Passing the almost imperceptible height-of-land at 2.8 mi., the trail follows a short bypass to the left of a very wet area and runs almost level, then descends easily, with small brooks running in and out of the trail.

At 3.5 mi. the trail begins to swing left, descends gradually to the Rocky Branch and follows it downstream for a short distance, then crosses it at 3.7 mi. This crossing may be very difficult, and the trail can be difficult to follow from this crossing for travelers going toward NH 16, since it is poorly marked and there are well-beaten side paths to campsites—heading for NH 16, the main trail first parallels the river going upstream and then swings gradually away from the river on a well-defined old road. (*Note:* If you are climbing to Mt. Isolation from NH 16, and the river is high, you can avoid two possibly difficult crossings by bushwhacking upstream along the east side of the river for 0.4 mi., since the Isolation Trail, which begins on the opposite bank, soon crosses back to the east bank.)

On the west bank of the river at this crossing is the junction with the Isolation Trail, which turns right (north), following the river bank upstream on the old railroad grade. The Rocky Branch Trail turns left downstream, also following the old railroad grade from this junction, and passes Rocky Branch Shelter #2 in 60 yd. (USFS Wilderness policies call for removal of this shelter when major maintenance is required.) The trail then runs generally south along the west bank for about 2.4 mi., at times on the old railroad grade, then follows the grade more closely, crossing the river four times. These crossings are difficult at high water, but it may be practical to avoid some or all—particularly the upstream pair, which are a bit more than 0.1 mi. apart, while the downstream pair are 0.4 mi. apart—by bushwhacking along the west bank. Passing out of the Presidential Range–Dry River Wilderness, the trail reaches a junction at 7.8 mi. with the Stairs Col Trail on the right, and, 20 yd. farther along the trail, a spur path on the left leads 60 yd. to WMNF Rocky Branch Shelter #1 and tentsite. Continuing south along the river on the railroad grade, the trail eventually enters a new gravel logging road and follows it for another 0.4 mi. to Jericho Rd., crossing the river and Otis Brook on logging-road bridges just before reaching its south terminus. In the reverse direction, where the new road swings to the left about 0.4 mi. from Jericho Rd., the trail continues straight ahead on the old railroad grade, which looks like an old grassy road.

Rocky Branch Trail (map 3:G10–H9)

Distances from parking lot off NH 16 (1200')

   to height-of-land (3100'): 2.8 mi., 1900 ft., 2 hr. 20 min.

   to Isolation Trail (2800'): 3.7 mi., 1900 ft. (rev. 300 ft.), 2 hr. 50 min.

   to Stairs Col Trail (1420'): 7.8 mi., 1900 ft. (rev. 1400 ft.), 4 hr. 50 min.

   to Jericho Rd. (1100'): 9.8 mi. (15.8 km.), 1900 ft. (rev. 300 ft.), 5 hr. 50 min.

Isolation Trail (WMNF)

This trail links the Dry River valley (Dry River Trail), the Montalban Ridge (Davis Path), and the Rocky Branch valley (Rocky Branch Trail), crossing the ridgecrest north of Mt. Isolation. It is entirely within the Presidential Range–Dry River Wilderness.

   This trail diverges from the Rocky Branch Trail just north of Rocky Branch Shelter #2 (which will be removed when major maintenance is required), on the west bank of the river at the point where the Rocky Branch Trail crosses it. The Isolation Trail follows the river north along the west bank on what is left of the old railroad grade, crossing the river at 0.4 mi. At 0.7 mi. the trail turns sharp right off the railroad grade, climbs briefly, then follows a logging road that at first runs high above the river. The trail crosses the river three more times; the next two crossings are only 70 yd. apart and so can be fairly easily avoided by a short bushwhack along the river bank. The last crossing comes at 1.7 mi., after which the trail swings away from the main stream and climbs easily along a tributary, reaching the Davis Path at 2.6 mi. after passing through an area of confusing side paths among bootleg campsites where the main trail must be followed with care.

Now coinciding with the Davis Path, the Isolation Trail climbs steadily north for about 0.3 mi. until it approaches the ridgecrest and the grade decreases, where it turns left off the Davis Path. It runs level for 0.2 mi., then descends moderately southwest into the Dry River valley. At 4.3 mi. the trail reaches Isolation Brook, a branch of the Dry River, and follows its northwest bank on an old logging road disrupted by numerous small slides until it ends at the Dry River Trail, 4.9 mi. from US 302.

Isolation Trail (map 1:G9–G8)

Distances from Rocky Branch Trail (2800')

>   *to* fourth crossing of the Rocky Branch (3423'): 1.7 mi., 600 ft., 1 hr. 10 min.

>   *to* Davis Path, south junction (3850'): 2.6 mi., 1050 ft., 1 hr. 50 min.

>   *to* Davis Path, north junction (4150'): 2.9 mi., 1350 ft., 2 hr. 10 min.

>   *to* Isolation Brook (3300'): 4.3 mi., 1400 ft. (rev. 900 ft.), 2 hr. 50 min.

>   *to* Dry River Trail (2600'): 5.3 mi. (8.6 km.), 1400 ft. (rev. 700 ft.), 3 hr. 20 min.

Distances from Rocky Branch Trail at parking area on NH 16 (1200')

>   *to* Isolation Trail (2800') via Rocky Branch Trail: 3.8 mi., 1900 ft. (rev. 300 ft.), 2 hr. 50 min.

>   *to* Davis Path, south junction (3850'): 6.4 mi., 2950 ft., 4 hr. 40 min.

>   *to* Mt. Isolation summit (4004') via Davis Path: 7.3 mi. (11.8 km.), 3250 ft. (rev. 150 ft.), 5 hr. 15 min.

Mount Langdon Trail (WMNF)

This trail runs to the Mt. Langdon Shelter from the road on the north side of the Saco near Bartlett village, meeting both the Mount Parker Trail and the Mount Stanton Trail, and thus gives access to both the higher and lower sections of the Montalban Ridge. It should be noted that despite its name this trail does not get particularly close to the summit of Mt. Langdon, which is crossed by the Mount Stanton Trail. Most of this trail is either within or close to the boundary of the Presidential Range–Dry River Wilderness; Mt. Langdon Shelter is just outside the Wilderness.

From the four corners at the junction of US 302 and the Bear Notch Rd. in Bartlett village, follow the road that leads north across a bridge over the Saco to an intersection at 0.4 mi. The trail begins almost straight ahead; there are two entrances that very soon converge (no sign). The trail follows a fairly recent gravel logging road, and at 0.3 mi. the path to Cave Mtn. (unsigned and easily missed) diverges left. The road gradually becomes older and less evident. The trail enters the Presidential Range–Dry River Wilderness and passes a trail register just before it crosses a good-sized brook at 1.0 mi., after which it climbs more steadily, bearing sharp right twice as the road fades away.

The Mount Langdon Trail crosses Oak Ridge at 2.2 mi. and descends, sharply at times, to the Oak Ridge–Mt. Parker col, where it bears right at 2.5 mi. at the junction with the Mount Parker Trail. The Mount Langdon Trail then descends gradually to the WMNF Mt. Langdon Shelter, capacity eight, where this trail and the Mount Stanton Trail both end. Some care is required to follow the trail near the shelter. Water may be found in a brook 60 yd. from the shelter on the Mount Stanton Trail, although in dry weather the brook bed may have to be followed downhill for a distance.

Mount Langdon Trail (map 3:I9–H9)

Distances from the road on the north bank of the Saco River (700')

   to Mount Parker Trail (1894'): 2.5 mi., 1450 ft. (rev. 250 ft.), 2 hr.

   to Mt. Langdon Shelter (1760'): 2.9 mi. (4.7 km.), 1450 ft. (rev. 100 ft.), 2 hr. 10 min.

   to high point on Mt. Langdon (2380') via Mount Stanton Trail: 3.7 mi., 2050 ft., 2 hr. 55 min.

Mount Parker Trail (SSOC)

This pleasant, rugged, lightly used trail passes several excellent viewpoints, and provides access from Bartlett to Mt. Parker, Mt. Resolution, the Stairs Col area, and the upper Montalban Ridge. It runs almost entirely within or close to the boundary of the Presidential Range–Dry River Wilderness. There is no reliable water on this trail.

This trail begins in the Oak Ridge–Mt. Parker col 2.5 mi. from Bartlett, continuing straight ahead to the north where the Mount Langdon Trail turns right (east). It climbs moderately with many switchbacks through beech and oak woods, descends briefly, and then continues its winding ascent to the open summit of Mt. Parker at 1.4 mi., where there are excellent views.

Continuing north, the trail follows the long ridge between Mt. Parker and Mt. Resolution and passes over three bumps, alternating between spruce woods and semi-open ledges with restricted views. It then runs along the west and south slopes of the remainder of the ridge (swinging inside the Presidential Range–Dry River Wilderness for the rest of its length) until it reaches the southeast corner of Mt. Resolution. Here it turns sharp right and zigzags up to the col between the main summit ridge and a southerly knob at 3.2 mi., where a branch trail leads left 0.1 mi. to the top of this knob, which is an open ledge with excellent views. Beyond this junction the trail winds along the flat top of Mt. Resolution until it reaches a large cairn on an open ledge with excellent views at 3.8 mi. The true summit is probably just above this cairn; there is another knob of almost equal elevation about 0.1 mi. east-northeast that affords excellent views north, but there is no path to it. From the cairn the trail descends into a gully where it crosses a small, sluggish brook (unreliable water), then heads down northwest over fine open ledges and finally drops steeply to the Davis Path, opposite the branch trail to Resolution Shelter.

Mount Parker Trail (map 3:H9)

Distances from Mount Langdon Trail (1894')

> *to* summit of Mt. Parker (3004'): 1.4 mi., 1100 ft., 1 hr. 15 min.
>
> *to* branch trail to open southerly knob (3200'): 3.2 mi., 1500 ft. (rev. 300 ft.), 2 hr. 20 min.
>
> *to* high point on Mt. Resolution (3400'): 3.8 mi., 1700 ft., 2 hr. 45 min.
>
> *to* Davis Path junction (3100'): 4.3 mi. (6.8 km.), 1700 ft. (rev. 300 ft.), 3 hr.

Mount Stanton Trail (SSOC)

This trail passes over the low eastern summits of the Montalban Ridge and affords many views from scattered ledges. To reach the east trailhead (the west trailhead is at Mt. Langdon Shelter), leave the north side of US 302 1.8 mi. west of its junction with NH 16 in Glen and a short distance east of the bridge over the Saco River. Follow a paved road west about 0.2 mi., then bear right on Oak Ridge Drive, and almost immediately turn sharp right onto Hemlock Drive. (In winter, continue on Oak Ridge Drive and take the next right after Hemlock Drive.) Park at the trail sign near a crossroads 0.6 mi. from US 302; the trail begins just uphill on the left side of the driveway that leads to the right from the crossroads. This is an area of new home construction, so the sequence of roads may change. As of 1997, the turns at road junctions on the summer access route were well marked with unobtrusive signs.

In 100 yd. the trail passes to the right of a red-blazed WMNF boundary corner, and at 0.3 mi. it turns sharp left with yellow blazes where the red-blazed WMNF boundary continues straight ahead. The trail climbs steeply at times, but there are gentler sections, and the outlooks from White's Ledge begin at about 0.8 mi. The trail climbs steeply again after passing a large boulder on the right of the trail, and at 1.2 mi. it turns sharp right on a ledge as climbing becomes easier. At 1.4 mi. it passes about 15 yd. to the right of the true summit of Mt. Stanton. The summit area is covered with a fine stand of red (Norway) pines, and there are good views from nearby scattered ledges.

The trail descends to the Stanton-Pickering col, then ascends steadily, crosses a ledgy ridge and descends slightly, then climbs again and at 2.1 mi. passes 30 yd. to the right of the true summit of Mt. Pickering. It then leads to ledges on a slightly lower knob, where there are excellent views. The trail descends to a minor col, then crosses over several interesting small humps sometimes called the Crippies (the origin of this peculiar name is one of the mysteries of White Mtn. nomenclature). These humps have scattered outlook ledges, and the best view is from the fourth and last Crippie, which is crossed at 3.3 mi.

After the last Crippie the trail may be less well cleared and harder to follow. It descends somewhat along the north side of the ridge toward Mt. Langdon, then climbs north moderately with a few steep pitches, passing an outlook to Carter Dome, Carter Notch, and Wildcat Mtn. At 4.5 mi. the trail passes about 35 yd. to the right of the summit of Mt. Langdon, which is wooded and viewless, then descends easily to a gravel slope, turns right, and continues downward to a brook that is crossed 60 yd. east of Mt. Langdon Shelter, where the Mount Stanton Trail ends.

Mount Stanton Trail (map 3:H10–H9)

Distances from the trailhead off Hemlock Drive (1700')

> *to* high point on Mt. Stanton (1700'): 1.4 mi., 1000 ft., 1 hr. 10 min.
>
> *to* high point on Mt. Pickering (1900'): 2.1 mi., 1400 ft. (rev. 200 ft.), 1 hr. 45 min.
>
> *to* fourth Crippie (1888'): 3.3 mi., 1750 ft. (rev. 300 ft.), 2 hr. 30 min.

   to high point on Mt. Langdon (2380'): 4.5 mi., 2450 ft. (rev. 200 ft.), 3 hr. 30 min.

   to Mount Langdon Trail at Mt. Langdon Shelter (1760'): 5.3 mi. (8.5 km.), 2450 ft. (rev. 600 ft.), 3 hr. 55 min.

Cave Mountain Path

Cave Mtn. (located on private property) is remarkable for the shallow cave near its wooded summit. It is reached from Bartlett by following the Mount Langdon Trail for 0.3 mi. to an unsigned branch path that forks left (watch for it carefully) and skirts the east side of Cave Mtn. After 0.3 mi. this path swings right and leads up a steep gravel slope to the cave. A rough, poorly marked trail to the right of the cave leads, after a short scramble, to the top of the cliff in which the cave is located, where there is a good view of Bartlett and the Saco River.

Cave Mountain Path (map 3:H9)

Distances from Mount Langdon Trail (800')

   to cave (1200'): 0.3 mi., 400 ft., 20 min.

   to outlook (1350'): 0.4 mi. (0.6 km.), 550 ft., 30 min.

Winniweta Falls Trail (WMNF)

This trail provides easy access to an interesting waterfall. Its trailhead (limited parking) is located on the west side of NH 16, 3 mi. north of the bridge over the Ellis River in Jackson. Hikers using this trail must ford the wide bed of the Ellis River, which is often a rather shallow stream, but the crossing can require wading in even moderate flow and may be dangerous or impassable at high water. During the winter months, the crossing is even more treacherous, since there is often considerable running water under a seemingly stable snow and ice pack. This trail makes use of several cross-country ski trails maintained by the Jackson Ski Touring Foundation. During the winter months hikers should avoid walking on ski tracks and should yield to skiers, who have the right of way.

   After reaching the far bank of the Ellis River, this trail bears right and skirts the north side of an open field, crossing the Ellis River Ski Trail at 0.2 mi. It then follows the Winniweta Falls Ski Trail upstream along the north bank of Miles Brook on an old logging road. At an arrow, the path turns left from the road and soon reaches the falls. The ski trail continues uphill along the logging road for over a mile and ends at the Hall Ski Trail, which connects Dana Place with Green Hill Rd.

Winniweta Falls Trail (map 1:G10)
Distance from NH 16 (950')

　to Winniweta Falls (1350'): 0.9 mi. (1.4 km.), 400 ft., 40 min.

Iron Mountain Trail (JCC)

The summit of this mountain is wooded with somewhat restricted views, but an outlook on the north side and the fine south cliffs provide very attractive views for relatively little effort. Somewhat down the slope to the east of the cliffs are abandoned iron mines. A prominent easterly ridge, on which there was once a trail, descends over the open summit of Green Hill to the cliff called Duck's Head, named for its shape when seen from the vicinity of the Iron Mtn. House, which lies at its foot on NH 16. The trail is reached by leaving NH 16 in Jackson, next to the golf links and nearly opposite the red covered bridge, and following a road prominently signed Green Hill Rd. At 1.2 mi. the pavement ends, and at 1.4 mi. the road (FR 119) bears left at a fork where FR 325 bears right. The road now becomes fairly steep, a bit rough, and very narrow (be prepared to back up if required for other cars to pass); above the fork the road is not passable in mud season and winter. At 2.7 mi. from NH 16, swing left at a sign as the road ahead becomes very poor, and park in a small designated field behind the house of the former Hayes Farm (now a summer residence).

　The trail crosses the field, passes through a narrow band of trees, and crosses a second field, entering the woods at the top edge. The path climbs steadily and the footing is good. At 0.6 mi. there is a side path right 20 yd. to a fine outlook up the Rocky Branch valley to Mt. Washington, with the Southern Presidentials visible over the Montalban Ridge. The main trail continues to the summit at 0.8 mi., where there are remains of the former fire tower and a rickety wooden tower. The trail descends steadily along a rocky ridge, dropping about 300 ft., then crosses several small humps in thick woods. At 1.5 mi. a faintly marked side path descends left 0.2 mi. and 250 ft. to the old mines (tailings, water-filled shaft, tunnel), while the main trail ascends in a short distance to ledges and the edge of the cliffs, where wide views to the south and west can be enjoyed.

Iron Mountain Trail (map 3:H10)
Distances from Hayes Farm (1920')

　to summit of Iron Mtn. (2726'): 0.8 mi., 800 ft., 50 min.

　to south cliffs (2430'): 1.6 mi. (2.6 km.), 850 ft. (rev. 250 ft.), 1 hr. 15 min.

Section 2

The Northern Peaks
and the Great Gulf

This section covers the high peaks of Mt. Washington's massive northern ridge, which curves north and then northeast as a great arm embracing the magnificent glacial cirque called the Great Gulf. This ridge runs for 5 mi. with only slight dips below the 5000 ft. level, and each of the three main peaks rises at least 500 ft. above the cols. The AMC Presidential Range map (map #1) covers the entire area, except for the Pine Mountain Trail which is covered by the AMC Carter Range–Evans Notch map (map #5). The Randolph Mountain Club (RMC) publishes a map of the Randolph Valley and Northern Peaks, printed on plastic-coated paper, and a guidebook, *Randolph Paths,* which can be obtained from the RMC, Randolph, NH 03570. The map covers the dense trail network on the northern slope of this region at a larger scale than map #1, and it is useful for people who want to explore some of the attractive, less crowded paths in this section. The RMC maintains a considerable number of paths on the Northern Peaks; many of these paths are very lightly used and are wilder and rougher than most trails in the WMNF. They are also less plainly marked, cleared, and trampled out, so they may not be suitable for the inexperienced, but adventurous hikers with good trail-following skills will find them a delightful alternative to the heavily used principal throughways on the range. This network of paths also provides opportunities for less strenuous, varied walks to the many waterfalls and other interesting places on the lower slopes of the range.

Caution: The peaks and higher ridges of this range are nearly as exposed to the elements as Mt. Washington, and should be treated with the same degree of respect and caution. Severe winter-like storms can occur at any time of the year, and many lives have been lost in this area from failure to observe the basic principles of safety. In addition, all of the major peaks are strenuous climbs by even the easiest routes. The distances quoted may not seem long to a novice, but there is only one route to a major peak, the Caps Ridge Trail to Mt. Jefferson, that involves less than 3000 ft. of climbing, and that trail is not an easy one. Although the Caps Ridge Trail is relatively short, it is also quite steep with numerous scrambles on ledges that a person unfamiliar with mountain trails might find daunting. Most other routes to the summits involve 4000 to 4500 ft. of climbing, due to the lower elevations of the major trailheads, thus making these ascents roughly equivalent in strenuousness to the ascent of Mt. Washington. The substantial amount of effort required to climb these peaks, together with the threat of sudden and violent storms, should make the need to avoid overextending oneself quite apparent.

The highest points from which to climb the Northern Peaks, not including the summit of Mt. Washington, are Jefferson Notch Rd. at the Caps Ridge Trail (3008 ft.); the parking lot on the Cog Railway Base Rd., 1.1 mi. east of the Jefferson Notch Rd., for the Jewell Trail (2500 ft.); at Pinkham Notch Visitor Center (2030 ft.); and the Pinkham B Rd. (Dolly Copp Rd.) at the Pine Link (1650 ft.). Other important parking areas are at a newly constructed area serving the Great Gulf trails located 1.5 mi. south of Dolly Copp Campground on NH 16; at Randolph East, on Pinkham B (Dolly Copp) Rd. near its junction with US 2; at Appalachia, on US 2 about 1 mi. west of Pinkham B Rd.; at Lowe's Store on US 2 (nominal fee charged by owner); and at Bowman, on US 2 about 1 mi. west of Lowe's Store. Several of the trailheads in the region, such as Randolph East, Appalachia, and Bowman, owe their names and locations to their former status as stations on the railroad line, whose tracks were removed in the summer of 1997. The USFS requires a parking permit (fee) for areas located on WMNF land.

The Northern Peaks were observed by Thomas Gorges and Richard Vines from the summit of Mt. Washington in 1642, but they evidently considered these peaks to be merely a part of Mt. Washington, for on their return the explorers wrote, with considerable geographical confusion, "The mountain runs E. and W. 30 miles, but the peak is above all the rest." In the early summer of 1820, a party consisting of Adino N. Brackett, John W. Weeks, Gen. John Wilson, Charles J. Stuart, Noyes S. Dennison, Samuel A. Pearson, Philip Carrigain, and Ethan Allen Crawford visited Mt. Washington, and from that summit named Mts. Jefferson, Adams, and Madison, but did not explore them. On August 31st, 1820, Brackett, Weeks, and Stuart made a second visit to the summit of Mt. Washington in company with Richard Eastman, Amos Legro, Joseph W. Brackett, and Edward B. Moore. Two members of this party spent a part of the day on the Northern Peaks and were probably the first persons of European extraction to visit these summits. In 1828 a more thorough exploration was made by Dr. J. W. Robbins who spent considerable time there, collecting botanical and other specimens.

The first trail on the Northern Peaks was probably the Stillings Path, which was cut about 1852 primarily for transporting building materials from Randolph to the summit of Mt. Washington and did not cross any of the summits. In 1860 or 1861 a partial trail was made over the peaks to Mt. Washington, of which some sections still exist as parts of current trails. Lowe's Path was cut in 1875–76, the branch path through King Ravine was made in 1876, and the Osgood Path was opened in 1878. Many trails were constructed between 1878 and the beginning of lumbering in about 1902, but this network was greatly damaged by the timber cutting, and many trails were obliterated, at least temporarily. The more important ones were restored after the most intensive period of lumbering ceased.

In the Randolph Valley, where the Amphibrach and the Link cross Cold Brook just below scenic Cold Brook Falls, Memorial Bridge stands as a memorial to J. Rayner Edmands, Eugene B. Cook, and other pioneer pathmakers who helped construct the superb trail network in the Presidential Range, including Thomas Starr King, James Gordon, Charles E. Lowe, Laban M. Watson, William H. Peek, Hubbard Hunt, William G. Nowell, and William Sargent.

In this section, the Appalachian Trail follows the Gulfside Trail to Madison Hut from its junction with the Trinity Heights Connector near the summit of Mt. Washington. It then follows the Osgood Trail over Mt. Madison and down into the Great Gulf, proceeding to the Auto Rd. via the Osgood Cutoff, Great Gulf Trail (for a very short distance), and Madison Gulf Trail.

GEOGRAPHY

The upper part of the mass of the **Northern Peaks** is covered with rock fragments; above 5000 ft. there are no trees and little scrub. The southeast side of the range is dominated by the **Great Gulf** and the two smaller cirques that branch off from it, **Jefferson Ravine** and **Madison Gulf.** The two Jefferson "knees," fairly prominent buttresses truncated by the Great Gulf, are the only significant ridges on this side of the range that survived the massive excavations by the glaciers which hollowed out the gulf. Many ridges and valleys radiate from this range on the north and west sides, the most important being, from north to south: on **Mt. Madison,** the **Osgood Ridge, Howker Ridge, Bumpus Basin, Gordon Ridge,** and the **ravine of Snyder Brook,** which is shared with Mt. Adams; on **Mt. Adams, Durand Ridge, King Ravine, Nowell Ridge, Cascade Ravine,** the **Israel Ridge,** and **Castle Ravine,** which is shared with Mt. Jefferson; on **Mt. Jefferson,** the **Castellated Ridge** and the **Ridge of the Caps;** and on **Mt. Clay,** an **unnamed but conspicuous ridge extending westerly.** The Great Gulf, Bumpus Basin, King Ravine, and Castle Ravine are glacial cirques, a landform that results when a glacier excavates a typical V-shaped brook valley with a narrow floor and fairly uniform slopes, turning it into the classic U-shaped cirque with a broad, fairly flat floor and almost vertical walls.

The **Great Gulf** is the largest cirque in the White Mtns., lying between Mt. Washington and the Northern Peaks and drained by the **West Branch of the Peabody River.** The headwall, bounded on the south by the slopes of Mt. Washington and on the west by the summit ridge of Mt. Clay, rises about 1100 to 1600 ft. above a bowl-shaped valley enclosed by steep walls that extend east for about 3.5 mi. The gulf then continues as a more open valley about 1.5 mi. farther east. The glacial action that formed the Great Gulf and its tributary gulfs is believed to have occurred mainly prior to the most recent ice age. The views from its walls and from points on its floor are among the best in New England, and steep slopes and abundant water result in a great number of cascades. The first recorded observation of the Great Gulf was by Darby Field in 1642, and the name probably had its origin in 1823 from a casual statement made by Ethan Allen Crawford, who, having lost his way in cloudy weather, came to "the edge of a great gulf." For a time it was sometimes called the "Gulf of Mexico," but this name is no longer used. The region was visited in 1829 by J. W. Robbins, a botanist, but was little known until Benjamin F. Osgood blazed the first trail, from the Osgood Trail to the headwall, in 1881.

Mt. Clay (5533 ft.) is the first peak on the ridge north of Mt. Washington. Strictly speaking it is only a shoulder, comparable to Boott Spur on the southeast ridge of its great neighbor, since it rises barely 150 ft. above the connecting ridge. But it offers superb views from the cliffs that drop away practically at the summit to form the west side of the Great Gulf headwall.

Mt. Jefferson (5716 ft.) has three summits a short distance apart, in line northwest and southeast, with the highest in the middle. Perhaps the most striking view is down the Great Gulf with the Carter Range beyond (better views of the gulf itself are obtained from points on the Gulfside Trail to the north of the summit). There are other fine views from the peak, most notably those to Mt. Washington and the other Northern Peaks, to the Fabyan Plain on the southwest, and down the broad valley of the Israel River on the northwest. The **Castellated Ridge,** sharpest and most salient of the White Mtn. ridges, extends northwest, forming the southwest wall of Castle Ravine; the view of the Castles from US 2 near the hamlet of Bowman is unforgettable. The **Ridge of the Caps,** similar in formation but less striking, extends to the west from the base of the summit cone.

Jefferson's Knees, the two eastern ridges that are cut off abruptly by the Great Gulf, have precipitous wooded slopes and gently sloping tops. South of the peak of Mt. Jefferson is a smooth, grassy plateau called **Monticello Lawn** (about 5400 ft.). In addition to its share of the Great Gulf proper, Jefferson's slopes are cut by two other prominent glacial cirques: **Jefferson Ravine,** a branch of the Great Gulf northeast of the mountain, and **Castle Ravine,** drained by a branch of **Israel River,** on the north. The boundary between these two cirques is the narrow section of the main Northern Presidential ridge that runs from Mt. Jefferson through **Edmands Col** to Mt. Adams.

Mt. Adams (5799 ft.), second highest of the New England summits, has a greater variety of interesting features than any other New England mountain except Katahdin: its sharp, clean-cut profile; its large area above treeline; its inspiring views, the finest being across the Great Gulf to Mts. Washington, Jefferson, and Clay; its great northern ridges, sharp, narrow **Durand Ridge** and massive, broad-spreading **Nowell Ridge;** and its four glacial cirques, **King Ravine** and the three that it shares with its neighbors, which are the **Great Gulf, Madison Gulf,** and **Castle Ravine.** Mt. Adams also has several lesser summits and crags, of which the two most prominent are **Mt. Sam Adams** (5585 ft.), a rather flat mass to the west, and **Mt. Quincy Adams** or **J. Q. Adams** (5410 ft.), a sharp, narrow shark-fin ridge to the north.

Mt. Madison (5366 ft.) is the farthest northeast of the high peaks of the Presidential Range, remarkable for the great drop of more than 4000 ft. to the river valleys east and northeast from its summit. The drop to the Androscoggin River at Gorham (4580 ft. in about 6.5 mi.) is probably the closest approach in New England, except at Katahdin, of a major river to a high mountain. The views south and southwest to the neighboring Presidential peaks and into the Great Gulf are very fine; the distant view is excellent in all other directions, and it includes Chocorua, which is visible just to the left of Mt. Washington.

Edmands Col (4938 ft.), named for pioneer trail-maker J. Rayner Edmands, lies between Mt. Adams and Mt. Jefferson, and **Sphinx Col** (4959 ft.) lies between Mt. Jefferson and Mt. Clay. The col between Mt. Adams and Mt. Madison has an elevation of about 4890 ft., so there is a range of only about 70 ft. between the lowest and highest of the three major cols on this ridge. In the **unnamed Adams-Madison col** lies **Star Lake,** a small, shallow body of water among jagged rocks, with impressive views, particularly up to Mt. Madison and Mt. Quincy Adams. Nearby is the **Parapet,** a small crag that offers magnificent views into the Great Gulf.

Pine Mtn. (2405 ft.) is a small peak lying to the northeast, between Mt. Madison and the great bend of the Androscoggin River at Gorham. Though low compared to its lofty neighbors, it is a rugged mountain with a fine cliff on the southeast side, and it offers magnificent, easily attained views of its Northern Presidential neighbors and of the mountains and river valleys to the north and east.

HUTS
Madison Hut (AMC)

In 1888 at Madison Spring (4800 ft.), a little north of the Adams-Madison col, the AMC built a stone hut that was later demolished. The present hut, rebuilt and improved after a fire in 1940, accommodates 50 guests in two bunkrooms operated on a coed basis. It is open to the public from early June to mid-September and is closed at all other times. Pets are not permitted in the hut. It is located 6.0 mi. from the summit of Mt. Washington via the Gulfside Trail, and 6.8 mi. from Lakes of the Clouds Hut via the Gulfside Trail, Westside Trail, and Crawford Path. In bad weather the best approach (or exit) is via the Valley Way, which is sheltered to within a short distance of the hut. Nearby points of interest include Star Lake and the Parapet, a crag overlooking Madison Gulf. For current information contact the Reservation Office, Pinkham Notch Visitor Center, PO Box 298, Gorham, NH 03581 (603-466-2727) or www.outdoors.org.

CAMPING
Great Gulf Wilderness

Wilderness regulations, intended to protect Wilderness resources and promote opportunities for challenge and solitude, prohibit use of motorized equipment or mechanical means of transportation of any sort. No camping is allowed within 200 ft. of any trail except at designated campsites (of which there are several between the Bluff and the Sphinx Trail), and wood or charcoal fires are not permitted at any place in the Great Gulf Wilderness. Camping is prohibited on the Great Gulf Trail south of its junction with the Sphinx Trail, including Spaulding Lake and its vicinity. Hiking and camping group size must be no larger than 10 people. Camping and fires are also prohibited above treeline (where trees are less than 8 ft. tall), except in winter, when camping is permitted above treeline in places where snow cover is at least two feet deep, but not on any frozen body of water. All former shelters have been removed.

Forest Protection Areas

The WMNF has established a number of Forest Protection Areas (FPAs)—formerly known as Restricted Use Areas—where camping and wood or charcoal fires are prohibited throughout the year. The specific areas are under continual review, and areas are added to or subtracted from the list in order to provide the greatest amount of protection to areas subject to damage by excessive camping, while imposing the lowest level of restrictions possible. A general list of FPAs in this section follows, but since there are often major changes from year to year, one should obtain current information on FPAs from the WMNF.

(1) No camping is permitted above treeline (where trees are less than 8 ft. tall) except in winter, and then only where there is at least two feet of snow cover on the ground—but not on any frozen body of water. The point where the above-treeline restricted area begins is marked on most trails with small signs, but the absence of such signs should not be construed as proof of the legality of a site.

(2) No camping is permitted within a quarter-mile of any trailhead, picnic area, or any facility for overnight accommodation such as a hut, cabin, shelter, tentsite, or campground, except as designated at the facility itself.

(3) No camping is permitted within 200 ft. of certain trails. In 1991, designated trails included the Valley Way south of its junction with the Scar Trail, from that junction up to Madison Hut.

(4) No camping is permitted on WMNF land within a quarter-mile of certain roads (camping on private roadside land is illegal except by permission of the landowner). In 1997, these roads included NH 16 north of Glen Ellis Falls, Jefferson Notch Rd. from the Cog Railway Base Rd. to the Caps Ridge Trail trailhead, and the Pinkham B Rd. (also known as Dolly Copp Rd.).

Established Trailside Campsites

The Log Cabin (RMC), first built about 1890 and totally rebuilt in 1985, is located at a spring at 3300 ft. elevation, beside Lowe's Path at the junction with the Cabin-Cascades Trail. The cabin is partly enclosed, has room for about ten guests, and is open to the public. A fee is charged. There is no stove, and no wood fires are permitted in the area. Guests are requested to leave the cabin clean and are required to carry out all trash.

The Perch (RMC) is an open log shelter located at about 4300 ft. on the Perch Path between the Randolph Path and Israel Ridge Path, but much closer to the former. It is open to the public and accommodates eight, and there are also four tent platforms at the site. The caretaker at Gray Knob often visits to collect the overnight fee. Wood fires are not allowed in the area, and all trash must be carried out.

Crag Camp (RMC) is situated at the edge of King Ravine near the Spur Trail at about 4200 ft. It is open to the public, and a fee is charged. It is an enclosed cabin, newly rebuilt, supplied with cooking utensils and a gas stove in the summer, with room for about fourteen guests. During July and August it is maintained by a caretaker. Hikers are required to limit groups to ten and stays to two nights. Wood fires are not allowed in the area, and all trash must be carried out.

Gray Knob (Town of Randolph and RMC) is an enclosed, winterized cabin on Gray Knob Trail at its junction with Hincks Trail, near Lowe's Path, at about 4400 ft. It has been renovated recently and is open to the public. It is staffed by a caretaker year-round, and a fee is charged at all times. Gray Knob has room for about twelve guests and is supplied with a gas stove and cooking utensils in the summer. Rules are the same as for Crag Camp.

These RMC shelters are all in Forest Protection Areas, and no camping is allowed within a quarter-mile except in the shelters and on the tent platforms themselves. Fees should be mailed to the Randolph Mountain Club, Randolph, NH 03570, if not collected by the caretakers. Any infraction of rules or acts of vandalism should be reported to the above address.

Osgood Campsite (WMNF), consisting of tent platforms, is located near the junction of the Osgood Trail and Osgood Cutoff (which is on the Appalachian Trail).

Trails on the Main Ridge

List of Trails	Map	Page
Gulfside Trail	1:F9	78
Mount Jefferson Loop	1:F9	87
Mount Clay Loop	1:F9	87
Edmands Col Cutoff	1:F9	88
The Cornice	1:F9	88

Linking Trails on the North and West Slopes of the Range

Trails in the Great Gulf Wilderness

Trails on Mount Madison

Trails on Mount Adams

List of Trails	Map	Page
Air Line	1:E9–F9	112
Scar Trail	1:E9	114
Star Lake Trail	1:F9	115
Short Line	1:E9	115
King Ravine Trail	1:E9–F9	116
Chemin des Dames	1:F9	117
Great Gully Trail	1:F9	118
The Amphibrach	1:E9	119
Cliffway	1:E9	120
Monaway	1:E9	121
Spur Trail	1:E9–F9	121
Hincks Trail	1:E9–F9	122
Gray Knob Trail	1:F9	122
Perch Path	1:F9	123
Lowe's Path	1:E9–F9	123
Cabin-Cascades Trail	1:E9–F9	125
Israel Ridge Path	1:E8–F9	125
Emerald Trail	1:F9	126

Trails on Mount Jefferson

List of Trails	Map	Page
Castle Ravine Trail	1:E8–F9	127
Castle Trail	1:E8–F9	128
Caps Ridge Trail	1:F8–F9	130
Boundary Line Trail	1:F8	131

Trail on Mount Clay

Trail	Map	Page
Jewell Trail	1:F8–F9	132

Trails on Pine Mountain

Pleasure Paths on the Lower North Slopes of the Range

THE TRAILS

Gulfside Trail (WMNF)

This trail, the main route along the Northern Presidential ridgecrest, leads from Madison Hut to the summit of Mt. Washington. It threads its way through the principal cols, avoiding the summits of the Northern Peaks, and offers extensive, ever-changing views. Its elevations range from about 4800 ft. close to the hut to 6288 ft. on the summit of Mt. Washington. The name Gulfside was given by J. Rayner Edmands who, starting in 1892, located and constructed the greater part of the trail, sometimes following trails that had existed before. All but about 0.8 mi. of the trail was once a graded path, and parts were paved with carefully placed stones—a work cut short by Edmands's death in 1910. The whole trail is part of the Appalachian Trail, except for a very short segment at the south end. For its entire distance it forms the northwestern boundary of the Great Gulf Wilderness, though the path itself is not within the Wilderness.

The trail is well marked with large cairns, each topped with a yellow-painted stone, and, though care must be used, it can often be followed even in dense fog. Always carry a compass and study the map before starting, so you will be aware of your alternatives if a storm strikes suddenly. The trail is continuously exposed to the weather; dangerously high winds and low temperatures may occur with little warning at any season of the year. If such storms threaten serious trouble on the Gulfside Trail, do not attempt to ascend the summit cone of Mt. Washington, where conditions are usually far worse. If you are not close to either of the huts (at Madison Spring or Lakes of the Clouds), descend into one of the ravines on a trail if possible, or without trail if necessary. A night of discomfort in the woods is better than exposure on the heights, which may prove fatal. Slopes on the Great Gulf (southeast) side are more sheltered but generally steeper and farther from highways. It is particularly important not to head toward Edmands Col in deteriorating conditions; there is no easy trail out of this isolated mountain pass (which often acts like a natural wind tunnel) in bad weather, and hikers have sometimes been trapped in this desolate and isolated place by a storm. The emergency refuge shelter that was once located here was removed in 1982 after years of misuse and abuse (including illegal camping) by thoughtless visitors. In order to enjoy a safe trip through this spectacular but often dangerous area, there is no substitute for studying the map carefully and understanding the hazards and options before setting out on the ridge.

The following description of the path is in the southbound direction (toward Mt. Washington). See below for a description of the path in the reverse direction.

Part I. Madison Hut–Edmands Col

The trail begins about 30 yd. from Madison Hut at a junction with the Valley Way and Star Lake Trail and leads southwest through a patch of scrub. It then aims to the right (north) of Mt. Quincy Adams and ascends its steep, open north slope. At the top of this slope, on the high plateau between King Ravine and Mt. Quincy Adams, it is joined from the right by the Air Line, which has just been joined by the King Ravine Trail. Here there are striking views back to Mt. Madison, and into King Ravine at the Gateway a short distance down on the right. The Gulfside and Air Line coincide for less than 100 yd., then the Air Line branches left toward the summit of Mt. Adams. Much of the Gulfside Trail for about the next 0.5 mi. is paved with carefully placed stones. It rises moderately southwest, then steepens, and at 0.9 mi. from the hut reaches a grassy lawn in the saddle (5490 ft.) between Mt. Adams and Mt. Sam Adams. Here several trails intersect at a spot called Thunderstorm Junction, where there is a massive cairn that once stood about 10 ft. high. Entering the junction on the right is the Great Gully Trail, coming up across the slope from the southwest corner of King Ravine. Here, also, the Gulfside is crossed by Lowe's Path, ascending from Lowe's Store on US 2 to the summit of Mt. Adams. About 100 yd. down Lowe's Path, the Spur Trail branches right for Crag Camp. The summit of Mt. Adams is about 0.3 mi.

from the junction (left) via Lowe's Path; a round trip to the summit requires about 25 min.

An unofficial trail, known as the White Trail because its cairns are topped with white rocks, will be seen running from Thunderstorm Junction to the summit of Mt. Sam Adams, and then following its south ridge to the Gulfside at the point where the Israel Ridge Path enters from US 2. Sam Adams is an interesting viewpoint, well worth a visit, but in good weather the cairned path is not necessary, since the route over the rocks between Sam Adams and either starting point is quite plain. However, the cairns are neither prominent enough nor close enough together to be followed reliably when visibility is poor, and the Sam Adams ridge is much more exposed to the wind and weather than the Gulfside.

Continuing southwest from Thunderstorm Junction and beginning to descend, the Gulfside Trail passes a junction on the left with the Israel Ridge Path, which ascends a short distance to Lowe's Path and thence to the summit of Mt. Adams. For about 0.5 mi. the Gulfside Trail and Israel Ridge Path coincide, passing Peabody Spring (unreliable) just to the right in a small, grassy flat; more-reliable water is located a short distance beyond at the base of a conspicuous boulder just to the left of the path. Soon the trail climbs easily across a small ridge, where the Israel Ridge Path diverges right at a point 1.5 mi. from Madison Hut. Near this junction in wet weather there is a small pool called Storm Lake. The Gulfside bears a bit left toward the edge of Jefferson Ravine, and, always leading toward Mt. Jefferson, descends southwest along the narrow ridge that divides Jefferson Ravine from Castle Ravine, near the edge of the southeast cliffs, from which there are fine views into the Great Gulf. This part of the Gulfside was never graded. At the end of this descent the trail reaches Edmands Col at 2.2 mi. from the hut, with 3.8 mi. to go to Mt. Washington.

At Edmands Col (4938 ft.) there is a bronze tablet in memory of J. Rayner Edmands, who made most of the graded paths on the Northern Peaks. Gulfside Spring is 50 yd. south of the col on the Edmands Col Cutoff, and Spaulding Spring (reliable) is about 0.2 mi. north near the Castle Ravine Trail. The emergency shelter once located at this col has been dismantled, and none of the trails leaving this area is an entirely satisfactory escape route in bad weather. From the col, the Edmands Col Cutoff leads south, entering scrub almost immediately, affording the quickest route to this rough form of shelter in dangerous weather; it then continues about 0.5 mi. to the Six Husbands Trail leading down into the Great Gulf, but it is very rough and the Six Husbands Trail is fairly difficult to descend, making it a far less than ideal escape route unless the severity of the weather leaves no choice. The Randolph Path leads north into the Randolph valley, running above treeline with great exposure to northwest winds for more than 0.5 mi. It is nevertheless probably the fastest, safest route to civilization unless high winds make it too dangerous to cross through Edmands Col. Branching from this path about 0.1 mi. north of the col are the Cornice, a very rough trail leading west entirely above treeline to the Castle Trail, and the Castle Ravine Trail, which descends steeply over very loose talus and may be hard to follow.

•

Part II. Edmands Col–Sphinx Col

South of Edmands Col the Gulfside Trail ascends steeply over rough rocks, with Jefferson Ravine on the left. It passes flat-topped Dingmaul Rock, from which there is a good view down the ravine, with Mt. Adams on the left. This rock is named for a legendary alpine beast to which it is reputed to bear a remarkable resemblance—the more remarkable since there has never been a verified sighting of the beast. About 100 yd. beyond, the Mount Jefferson Loop branches right and leads 0.4 mi. to the summit of Mt. Jefferson (5716 ft.). The views from the summit are excellent, and the Mount Jefferson Loop is only slightly longer than the parallel section of the Gulfside, though it requires about 300 ft. of extra climbing and about 10 min. more hiking time.

The path now rises less steeply. It crosses the Six Husbands Trail and soon reaches its greatest height on Mt. Jefferson, about 5400 ft. Curving southwest and descending a little, it crosses Monticello Lawn, a comparatively smooth, grassy plateau. Here the Mount Jefferson Loop rejoins the Gulfside about 0.3 mi. from the summit. A short distance beyond the edge of the lawn, the Cornice enters right from the Caps Ridge Trail. The Gulfside descends to the south, and from one point there is a view of the Sphinx down the slope to the left. A few yards north of the low point in Sphinx Col, the Sphinx Trail branches left (east) into the Great Gulf through a grassy passage between ledges. Sphinx Col is 3.7 mi. from Madison Hut, with 2.3 mi. left to the summit of Mt. Washington. In bad weather, a fairly quick descent to sheltering scrub can be made via the Sphinx Trail, though once treeline is reached this trail becomes rather steep and difficult.

Part III. Sphinx Col–Mount Washington

From Sphinx Col the path leads toward Mt. Washington, and soon the Mount Clay Loop diverges left to climb over the summits of Mt. Clay, with impressive views into the Great Gulf. The Mount Clay Loop adds about 300 ft. of climbing and 10 min.; the distance is about the same. The Gulfside Trail is slightly easier and passes close to a spring, but misses the best views. It bears right from the junction with the Mount Clay Loop, runs south, and climbs moderately, angling up the west side of Mt. Clay. About 0.3 mi. above Sphinx Col, a loop leads to water a few steps down to the right. The side path continues about 30 yd. farther to Greenough Spring (more reliable), then rejoins the Gulfside about 100 yd. above its exit point. The Gulfside continues its moderate ascent, and the Jewell Trail from the Cog Railway Base Rd. enters from the right at 4.6 mi. From this junction the ridgecrest of Mt. Clay can be reached in good weather by a short scramble up the rocks without trail. The Gulfside swings southeast and soon descends slightly to a point near the Clay-Washington col (5391 ft.), where the Mount Clay Loop rejoins it from the left. A little to the east is the edge of the Great Gulf, with fine views, especially of the east cliffs of Mt. Clay.

The path continues southeast, rising gradually on Mt. Washington. About 0.1 mi. above the col, the Westside Trail branches right, crosses the Cog Railway, and leads to the Crawford Path and Lakes of the Clouds Hut. The Gulfside continues southeast between the Cog Railway on the right and the edge of the gulf on the left. If the path is lost, the railway can be followed to the summit. At the extreme south corner of the gulf, the Great Gulf Trail joins the Gulfside from the left, 5.5 mi. from Madison Hut. Here the Gulfside turns sharp right, crosses under the railway, and continues west to the plateau just west of the summit. Here it passes a junction with the Trinity Heights Connector, a link in the Appalachian Trail, which branches left and climbs for 0.2 mi. to the true summit of Mt. Washington. In another 0.1 mi. the Gulfside joins the Crawford Path just below (north of) the old corral, and the two trails turn left and coincide to the summit.

Gulfside Trail (map 1:F9)

Distances from Madison Hut (4825')

> *to* Air Line (5125'): 0.3 mi., 300 ft., 20 min.
>
> *to* Thunderstorm Junction (5490'): 0.9 mi., 650 ft., 45 min.
>
> *to* Israel Ridge Path, north junction (5475'): 1.0 mi., 650 ft., 50 min.
>
> *to* Israel Ridge Path, south junction (5225'): 1.5 mi., 650 ft., 1 hr. 5 min.
>
> *to* Edmands Col (4938'): 2.2 mi., 650 ft., 1 hr. 25 min.
>
> *to* Mount Jefferson Loop, north end (5125'): 2.4 mi., 850 ft., 1 hr. 40 min.
>
> *to* Six Husbands Trail (5325'): 2.7 mi., 1050 ft., 1 hr. 55 min.
>
> *to* Mount Jefferson Loop, south end (5375'): 3.1 mi., 1100 ft., 2 hr. 5 min.
>
> *to* the Cornice (5325'): 3.2 mi., 1100 ft., 2 hr. 10 min.
>
> *to* Sphinx Trail (4975'): 3.7 mi., 1100 ft., 2 hr. 25 min.

to Mount Clay Loop, north end (5025'): 3.8 mi., 1150 ft., 2 hr. 30 min.

to Jewell Trail (5400'): 4.6 mi., 1550 ft., 3 hr. 5 min.

to Mount Clay Loop, south end (5400'): 4.9 mi., 1600 ft., 3 hr. 15 min.

to Westside Trail (5500'): 5.0 mi., 1700 ft., 3 hr. 20 min.

to Great Gulf Trail (5925'): 5.5 mi., 2150 ft., 3 hr. 50 min.

to Trinity Heights Connector (6100'): 5.7 mi., 2300 ft., 4 hr.

to Crawford Path (6150'): 5.8 mi. (9.3 km.), 2350 ft., 4 hr. 5 min.

to Mt. Washington summit (6288') via Crawford Path: 6.0 mi. (9.7 km.), 2500 ft., 4 hr. 15 min.

to Lakes of the Clouds Hut (5012') via Westside Trail and Crawford Path: 6.8 mi. (10.9 km.), 1850 ft., 4 hr. 20 min.

Gulfside Trail (WMNF) [in reverse]

Part I. Mount Washington–Sphinx Col

Descending from the summit of Mt. Washington, coinciding with the Crawford Path, the trail is on the right (west) side of the railroad track. After passing between the buildings it leads generally northwest; avoid random side paths toward the south. Shortly it reaches its point of departure from the Crawford Path, just below the remains of an old corral, and turns sharp right. In 0.1 mi. it passes a junction with the Trinity Heights Connector, a link in the Appalachian Trail, which branches right and climbs for 0.2 mi. to the true summit of Mt. Washington. The Gulfside Trail then descends steadily, crossing under the railroad, and at 0.4 mi., as the Gulfside turns sharp left at the extreme south corner of the Great Gulf, the Great Gulf Trail joins on the right. The Gulfside continues northwest between the Cog Railway on the left and the edge of the gulf on the right. At 1.0 mi. the Westside Trail branches left, crosses under the Cog Railway, and leads to the Crawford Path and Lakes of the Clouds Hut. The Gulfside descends gradually to a point near the Clay-Washington col (5391 ft.), where the Mount Clay Loop diverges right to traverse the summits of Mt. Clay, with impressive views into the Great Gulf. The Mount Clay Loop adds about 300 ft. of climbing and 10 min.; the distance is about the same. The Gulfside Trail is slightly easier and passes close to a spring, but misses the best views. A little to the east at this col is the edge of the Great Gulf, with fine views, especially of the east cliffs of Mt. Clay.

After a slight ascent, the Gulfside begins to angle down the west side of Mt. Clay, and the Jewell Trail from the Cog Railway Base Rd. enters from the left at 1.4 mi. From this junction the ridgecrest of Mt. Clay can be reached by a short scramble up the rocks without trail. At about 0.5 mi. beyond this junction, a loop leads left to Greenough Spring (reliable), then rejoins the Gulfside about 100 yd. below its exit point. As the grade levels approaching Sphinx Col, the Mount Clay Loop rejoins on the right. At Sphinx Col, it is 2.3 mi. from Mt. Washington and 3.7 mi. to Madison Hut. In bad weather, a fairly quick descent to sheltering scrub can be made via the Sphinx Trail, though once treeline is reached this trail becomes rather steep and difficult.

Part II. Sphinx Col–Edmands Col

A few yards north of the low point in Sphinx Col, the Sphinx Trail branches right (east) into the Great Gulf through a grassy passage between ledges. The Gulfside ascends to the north, and from one point there is a view of the Sphinx down the slope to the right. The Cornice enters left from the Caps Ridge Trail a short distance before the Gulfside begins to cross Monticello Lawn, a comparatively smooth, grassy plateau. Here the Mount Jefferson Loop branches left and leads 0.3 mi. to the summit of Mt. Jefferson (5716 ft.). The views from the summit are excellent, and the Mount Jefferson Loop is only slightly longer than the parallel section of the Gulfside, though it requires about 300 ft. of extra climbing and about 10 min. more hiking time.

The path now turns northeast and rises less steeply. It crosses the Six Husbands Trail soon after reaching its greatest height on Mt. Jefferson, about 5400 ft., then descends moderately to the point where the Mount Jefferson Loop rejoins on the left about 0.3 mi. from the summit. The trail now descends steeply north over rough rocks, with Jefferson Ravine on the right, and about 100 yd. beyond the junction, it passes flat-topped Dingmaul Rock, from which there is a good view down the ravine, with Mt. Adams on the left. The trail reaches Edmands Col at 3.8 mi. from Mt. Washington, with 2.2 mi. to go to Madison Hut.

At Edmands Col (4938 ft.) there is a bronze tablet in memory of J. Rayner Edmands, who made most of the graded paths on the Northern Peaks. Gulfside Spring (unreliable in dry seasons) is 50 yd. south of the col, and Spaulding Spring (reliable) is about 0.2 mi. north near the Castle Ravine Trail. The emergency shelter once located at this col has been dismantled, and none of the trails leaving this area is a particularly satisfactory escape route in bad weather. From the col, the Edmands Col Cutoff leads south, entering scrub almost immediately, affording the quickest route to this rough form of shelter in dangerous weather; it then continues about 0.5 mi. to the Six Husbands Trail leading down to the Great Gulf, but it is very rough and the Six Husbands Trail is fairly difficult to descend, making it a far less than ideal escape route unless the severity of the weather leaves no choice. The Randolph Path leads north into the Randolph valley, running above treeline with great exposure to northwest winds for more than 0.5 mi. It is nevertheless probably the fastest, safest route to civilization unless high winds make it too dangerous to cross through Edmands Col. Branching from this path about 0.1 mi. north of the col are the Cornice, a very rough trail leading west entirely above treeline to the Castle Trail, and the Castle Ravine Trail, which descends steeply over very loose talus and may be hard to follow.

Part III. Edmands Col–Madison Hut

Leaving Edmands Col, the Gulfside climbs moderately along the edge of Jefferson Ravine, ascending northeast along the narrow ridge that divides Jefferson Ravine from Castle Ravine near the edge of the southeast cliffs, from which there are fine views into the Great Gulf. This part of the Gulfside was never graded. About 0.7 mi. above Edmands Col, the trail reaches the crest of a small ridge, where the Israel Ridge Path enters left. Near this junction in wet weather there is a small pool called Storm Lake. For about 0.5 mi. the Gulfside Trail and Israel Ridge Path coincide, passing reliable water at the base of a conspicuous boulder just to the right of the path; Peabody Spring (unreliable) is just beyond on the left in a small, grassy flat. The Gulfside Trail continues to ascend and, as it levels out on a grassy lawn in the saddle (5490 ft.) between Mt. Adams and Mt. Sam Adams, the Israel Ridge Path diverges right and ascends a short distance to Lowe's Path and thence to the summit of Mt. Adams.

In another 0.1 mi. several trails intersect at a spot called Thunderstorm Junction, where there is a massive cairn that once stood about 10 ft. high. Entering the junction on the left is the Great Gully Trail, coming up across the slope from the southwest corner of King Ravine. Here, also, the Gulfside is crossed by Lowe's Path, ascending from Lowe's Store on US 2 to the summit of Mt. Adams. About 100 yd. down Lowe's Path, the Spur Trail branches right for Crag Camp. The summit of Mt. Adams is about 0.3 mi. from the junction (right) via Lowe's Path; a round trip to the summit requires about 25 min.

An unofficial trail, known as the White Trail because its cairns are topped with white rocks, runs from Thunderstorm Junction to the summit of Mt. Sam Adams, and then follows its south ridge to the Gulfside at the point where the Israel Ridge Path enters from US 2. Sam Adams is an interesting viewpoint, well worth a visit, but in good weather the cairned path is not necessary, since the route over the rocks between Sam Adams and either starting point is quite plain. However, the cairns are neither prominent enough nor close enough together to be followed reliably when visibility is poor, and the Sam Adams ridge is much more exposed to the wind and weather than the Gulfside.

From Thunderstorm Junction the Gulfside descends northeast, gradually at first, and enters a section about 0.5 mi. long that is paved with carefully placed stones. At the end of this section, on the high plateau between King Ravine and Mt. Quincy Adams, the Air Line enters on the right, descending from Mt. Adams, and the trails coincide for less than 100 yd. Then the Air Line branches left at the top of the steep, open north slope of Mt. Quincy Adams, and just below this junction the King Ravine Trail branches left from the Air Line. Here there are striking views ahead to Mt. Madison, and into King Ravine at the Gateway a short distance down on the left. The Gulfside then descends the slope and passes through a patch of scrub to a junction with the Valley Way and Star Lake Trail about 30 yd. from Madison Hut.

Gulfside Trail (map 1:F9)

Distances from the summit of Mt. Washington (6288')

to Crawford Path junction (6150'): 0.2 mi., 0 ft., 5 min.

to Trinity Heights Connector (6100'): 0.3 mi., 0 ft., 10 min.

to Great Gulf Trail (5925'): 0.5 mi., 0 ft., 15 min.

to Westside Trail (5500'): 1.0 mi., 0 ft., 30 min.

to Mount Clay Loop, south end (5400'): 1.1 mi., 0 ft., 35 min.

to Jewell Trail (5400'): 1.4 mi., 50 ft., 45 min.

to Mount Clay Loop, north end (5025'): 2.2 mi., 50 ft., 1 hr. 5 min.

to Sphinx Trail (4975'): 2.3 mi., 50 ft., 2 hr. 10 min.

to the Cornice (5325'): 2.8 mi., 400 ft., 1 hr. 35 min.

to Mount Jefferson Loop, south end (5375'): 2.9 mi., 450 ft., 1 hr. 40 min.

to Six Husbands Trail (5325'): 3.3 mi., 450 ft., 1 hr. 55 min.

to Mount Jefferson Loop, north end (5125'): 3.6 mi., 450 ft., 2 hr.

to Edmands Col (4938'): 3.8 mi., 450 ft., 2 hr. 10 min.

to Israel Ridge Path, south junction (5225'): 4.5 mi., 750 ft., 2 hr. 40 min.

to Israel Ridge Path, north junction (5475'): 5.0 mi., 1000 ft., 3 hr.

to Thunderstorm Junction (5490'): 5.1 mi., 1000 ft., 3 hr. 5 min.

to Air Line (5125'): 5.6 mi., 1000 ft., 3 hr. 20 min.

to Madison Hut (4825'): 6.0 mi. (9.7 km.), 1000 ft., 3 hr. 30 min.

Distance from Lakes of the Clouds Hut (5012')

    to Madison Hut (4825') via Westside Trail, Crawford Path, and Gulfside
       Trail: 6.8 mi. (10.9 km.), 1650 ft., 4 hr. 15 min.

Mount Jefferson Loop (AMC)

This trail provides access to the summit of Mt. Jefferson from the Gulfside Trail.
It diverges right (west) from the Gulfside, 0.2 mi. south of Edmands Col, and
climbs steeply almost straight up the slope. Just below the summit, the Six Husbands Trail enters on the left, then the Castle Trail enters on the right, and soon
the junction with Caps Ridge Trail is reached at the base of the summit crag. The
true summit is 40 yd. right (west) on the Caps Ridge Trail. The Mount Jefferson
Loop then descends to rejoin the Gulfside Trail on Monticello Lawn.

Mount Jefferson Loop (map 1:F9)
Distances from north junction with Gulfside Trail (5125')

    to Mt. Jefferson summit (5716'): 0.4 mi., 600 ft., 30 min.

    to south junction with Gulfside Trail (5375'): 0.7 mi. (1.1 km.), 600 ft. (rev.
       350 ft.), 40 min.

Mount Clay Loop (AMC)

This trail traverses the summit ridge of Mt. Clay roughly parallel to the Gulfside
Trail, providing access to the superb views into the Great Gulf from Clay's east
cliffs. The entire trail (except for its end points) is within the Great Gulf Wilderness.

    The trail diverges left (east) from the Gulfside Trail about 0.1 mi. south of
Sphinx Col, and ascends a somewhat steep, rough slope to the ragged ridgecrest.
After crossing the summit and passing over several slightly lower knobs, the trail
descends easily to the flat col between Mt. Clay and Mt. Washington, where it
rejoins the Gulfside Trail.

Mount Clay Loop (map 1:F9)
Distances from north junction with Gulfside Trail (5025')

    to summit of Mt. Clay (5533'): 0.5 mi., 500 ft., 30 min.

    to north junction with Gulfside Trail (5400'): 1.2 mi. (1.9 km.), 650 ft. (rev.
       300 ft.), 55 min.

Edmands Col Cutoff (RMC)

This important link, connecting the Gulfside Trail and Randolph Path at Edmands Col with the Six Husbands Trail, makes possible a quick escape from Edmands Col into plentiful sheltering scrub on the lee side of Mt. Jefferson; it also provides a route to civilization through the Great Gulf via Six Husbands Trail, and although this route is long, with a steep, rough, and rather difficult descent, it may be the safest escape route from the vicinity of Edmands Col in severe weather. Footing on this trail is very rough and rocky. It is almost entirely within the Great Gulf Wilderness.

Leaving Edmands Col, the trail passes Gulfside Spring in 50 yd., then begins a rough scramble over rockslides and through scrub, marked by cairns. The trail is generally almost level but has many small rises and falls over minor ridges and gullies, with good views to the Great Gulf and out to the east. It ends at the Six Husbands Trail 0.3 mi. below that trail's junction with the Gulfside Trail.

Edmands Col Cutoff (map 1:F9)

Distance from Edmands Col (4938')

> *to* Six Husbands Trail (4925'): 0.5 mi. (0.8 km.), 100 ft., 20 min.

The Cornice (RMC)

This trail circles the west slope of Mt. Jefferson, running completely above treeline, with many interesting views. It starts near Edmands Col, crosses the Castle Trail and the Caps Ridge Trail, and returns to the Gulfside at Monticello Lawn, linking the trails on the west and northwest slopes of Jefferson. Its southern segment, which has good footing, provides an excellent shortcut from the Caps Ridge Trail to the Gulfside on Monticello Lawn south of Mt. Jefferson. However, the section leading from Edmands Col to the Caps Ridge Trail is extremely rough, with a large amount of tedious and strenuous rock-hopping, which is very hard on knees and ankles. This section of the trail, therefore, may take considerably more time than the estimates below. As a route between Edmands Col and the Caps Ridge Trail, the Cornice saves a little climbing compared to the route over the summit of Jefferson, but it is much longer, requires more exertion, and is just as exposed to the weather. This makes its value as a route to avoid Jefferson's summit in bad weather very questionable.

The Cornice diverges west from the Randolph Path near Spaulding Spring, 0.1 north of the Gulfside Trail in Edmands Col, where the Castle Ravine Trail also diverges from the Randolph Path. It crosses a small grassy depression where there may be no perceptible footway until it climbs the rocky bank on the other side. It then ascends moderately over large rocks, passing above a rock formation that resembles a petrified cousin of the Loch Ness monster, and circles around the north and west sides of Mt. Jefferson, crossing the Castle Trail above the Upper Castle. It continues across the rocky slope, intersects the Caps Ridge Trail above the Upper Cap, and turns left (east) up the Caps Ridge Trail for about 20 yd., then diverges right (south) and climbs gradually with improved footing to the Gulfside Trail just below Monticello Lawn.

The Cornice (map 1:F9)

Distances from Randolph Path (4900')

to Castle Trail (5100'): 0.6 mi., 200 ft., 25 min.

to Caps Ridge Trail (5025'): 1.3 mi., 200 ft. (rev. 100 ft.), 45 min.

to Gulfside Trail junction (5325'): 1.8 mi. (2.9 km.), 500 ft., 1 hr. 10 min.

Randolph Path (RMC)

This graded path extends southwest from the Pinkham B (Dolly Copp) Rd. near Randolph village, ascending diagonally up the slopes of Mt. Madison and Mt. Adams to the Gulfside Trail in Edmands Col between Mt. Adams and Mt. Jefferson. In addition to providing a route from Randolph to Edmands Col it crosses numerous other trails along the way and thus constitutes an important linking trail between them. Some sections are heavily used and well beaten, while others bear very little traffic and must be followed with care. It was made by J. Rayner Edmands from 1893 to 1899. Parts of it were reconstructed in 1978 as a memorial to Christopher Goetze, an active RMC member and former editor of *Appalachia,* the AMC's journal.

    The path begins at the parking space known as Randolph East, located on the Pinkham B Rd. 0.2 mi. south of US 2 and 0.3 mi. west of the crossing of the former Boston and Maine Railroad grade (tracks removed in the summer of 1997). Coinciding with the Howker Ridge Trail, it bears sharp left and quickly crosses the former railroad grade, and 30 yd. beyond turns right (west) where the Howker Ridge Trail diverges left (southeast). The Randolph Path runs along the south edge of the power line clearing for about 0.3 mi., then swings southwest. (Logging activity in this area has disrupted this trail somewhat in recent years, and trail markings must be observed and followed with great care.) Soon the trail enters a logging road, turns right and follows it for about 150 yd., then leaves it on the right, though continuing to parallel it for a while longer. It crosses the Sylvan Way at 0.7 mi., and at 1.4 mi. it reaches Snyder Brook, where the Inlook Trail and Brookside join on the left. The Brookside and the Randolph Path cross the brook together on a bridge, then the Brookside diverges right and leads down to the Valley Way. After a short climb the Randolph Path crosses the Valley Way, and soon after that joins the Air Line, coincides with it for 20 yd., then leaves it on the right.

At 1.9 mi. the Short Line enters right; by this shortcut route it is 1.3 mi. to US 2 at Appalachia. The Short Line coincides with the Randolph Path for 0.4 mi., then branches left for King Ravine. The Randolph Path descends slightly and crosses Cold Brook on Sanders Bridge, and the Cliffway diverges right just beyond. At 3.1 mi. the King Ravine Trail is crossed at its junction with the Amphibrach, an intersection called the Pentadoi. The Randolph Path continues across Spur Brook on ledges just below some interesting pools and cascades, and just beyond the brook the Spur Trail diverges left. The Randolph Path climbs around the nose of a minor ridge and becomes steeper. Soon the Log Cabin Cutoff diverges right and runs 0.2 mi. to the Log Cabin, and in another 0.2 mi. an unmaintained branch of the Log Cabin Cutoff diverges to the right from the Randolph Path and descends steeply and directly to the Log Cabin.

At 3.9 mi. from Randolph East, Lowe's Path is crossed and the grade moderates as the trail angles up the steep west side of Nowell Ridge. At 4.7 mi. good outlooks begin to appear, providing particularly notable views of the Castles nearby and Mt. Lafayette in the distance to the southwest. At 4.9 mi. the Perch Path crosses, leading left (north) to the Gray Knob Trail and right (south) to the Perch and Israel Ridge Path; a small brook runs across the Perch Path about 60 yd. south of the Randolph Path. Above this junction the Randolph Path rises due south through high scrub. At 5.4 mi. the Gray Knob Trail from Crag Camp and Gray Knob enters left at about the point where the Randolph Path rises out of the high scrub. In another 70 yd. the Israel Ridge Path enters right (west), ascending from US 2, and the trails coincide for about 150 yd.; then the Israel Ridge Path branches left for Mt. Adams in an area where views to Jefferson and the Castles are particularly fine. From this point the Randolph Path is nearly level to its end at Edmands Col, curving around the head of Castle Ravine, offering continuous excellent views. It is above treeline, much exposed to the weather, and its footway is visible for a long distance ahead. Near Edmands Col is Spaulding Spring (reliable water), in a small grassy depression on the right, which the Castle Ravine Trail from US 2 comes up through and the Cornice to the Caps and Castles crosses. In 0.1 mi. more the Randolph Path joins the Gulfside Trail in Edmands Col.

Randolph Path (map 1:E9–F9)

Distances from Randolph East parking area (1225')

   to Valley Way (1953'): 1.5 mi., 750 ft., 1 hr. 5 min.

   to Air Line (2000'): 1.6 mi., 800 ft., 1 hr. 10 min.

   to Short Line, north junction (2275'): 1.9 mi., 1050 ft., 1 hr. 30 min.

   to King Ravine Trail and Amphibrach (2925'): 3.1 mi., 1700 ft., 2 hr. 25
      min.

   to Lowe's Path (3600'): 3.9 mi., 2400 ft., 3 hr. 10 min.

   to Perch Path (4325'): 4.9 mi., 3100 ft., 4 hr.

   to Israel Ridge Path, north junction (4825'): 5.4 mi., 3600 ft., 4 hr. 30 min.

   to Edmands Col and Gulfside Trail (4938'): 6.1 mi. (9.8 km.), 3700 ft., 4 hr.
      55 min.

   to Mt. Washington summit (6288') via Gulfside Trail and Crawford Path:
      9.9 mi. (15.9 km.), 5550 ft. (rev. 450 ft.), 7 hr. 45 min.

The Link (RMC)

This path links the Appalachia parking area and the trails to Mt. Madison with
the trails ascending Mt. Adams and Mt. Jefferson, connecting with the Amphibrach, Cliffway, Lowe's Path, and Israel Ridge Path, and the Castle Ravine,
Emerald, Castle, and Caps Ridge trails. It is graded as far as Cascade Brook. The
section between the Caps Ridge and Castle trails, although very rough, makes
possible a circuit of the Caps and the Castles from Jefferson Notch Rd. Though
some sections are heavily used, much of the trail is very lightly used with little
evident footway, and such segments must be followed with care.

   The Link, coinciding with the Amphibrach, diverges right from the Air Line
100 yd. south of Appalachia, just after entering the woods beyond the power line
clearing, and runs west, fairly close to the edge of this clearing. At 0.6 mi. it
enters a logging road and bears left, then Beechwood Way diverges left, and, just
east of Cold Brook, Sylvan Way enters left. Cold Brook is crossed at 0.7 mi. on
the Memorial Bridge, where there is a fine view upstream to Cold Brook Fall,
which can be reached in less than 100 yd. by Sylvan Way or by a spur from the
Amphibrach. Memorial Bridge is a memorial to J. Rayner Edmands, Eugene B.
Cook, and other pioneer pathmakers: Thomas Starr King, James Gordon,
Charles E. Lowe, Laban M. Watson, William H. Peek, Hubbard Hunt, William
G. Nowell, and William Sargent.

Just west of the brook the Amphibrach diverges left and the Link continues straight ahead. The Link then follows old logging roads southwest with gradually increasing grades and occasional wet footing. At 2.0 mi. the Cliffway leads left (east) to White Cliff, a fine viewpoint on Nowell Ridge, and the Link swings to the south and climbs at easy grades, crossing Lowe's Path at 2.7 mi. It crosses the north branch of the Mystic Stream at 3.1 mi. and the main Mystic Stream, in a region of small cascades, at 3.3 mi. It soon curves left, rounds the western buttress of Nowell Ridge, and, running southeast nearly level, enters Cascade Ravine on the mountainside high above the stream. At 4.0 mi. it joins the Israel Ridge Path coming up on the right from US 2; the two trails coincide for 50 yd., then the Israel Ridge Path diverges sharp left for Mt. Adams, passing the Cabin-Cascades Trail in about 60 yd. The Link continues straight from this junction, descending sharply to Cascade Brook, which it crosses on a large flat ledge at the top of the largest cascade, where there are fine views down the valley. This crossing may be difficult at high water. The trail makes a steep and very rough climb up the bank of the brook, then swings right, and the grade eases and the footing gradually improves as it rounds the tip of Israel Ridge and runs generally south into Castle Ravine.

At 5.1 mi. the Link joins the Castle Ravine Trail, with which it coincides while the two trails pass the Emerald Trail and cross Castle Brook, then at 5.4 mi. the Link diverges sharp right and ascends steeply west, angling up the southwest wall of Castle Ravine. At 6.0 mi. it crosses the Castle Trail below the first Castle at about 4050 ft., then runs south, generally descending gradually, over a very rough pathway with countless treacherous roots, rocks, and hollows that are very tricky and tedious to negotiate. At 6.5 mi. the trail crosses a gravelly slide with good views, and at 7.0 mi. it crosses a fair-sized brook flowing over mossy ledges. At 7.6 mi. it turns sharp left uphill and in 50 yd. reaches the Caps Ridge Trail 1.1 mi. above the Jefferson Notch Rd., about 100 yd. above the famous ledge with the potholes and the fine view up to Jefferson.

The Link (map 1:E9–F8)

Distances from Appalachia parking area (1306')

    to Memorial Bridge (1425'): 0.7 mi., 100 ft., 25 min.

    to Cliffway (2170'): 2.0 mi., 850 ft., 1 hr. 25 min.

    to Lowe's Path (2475'): 2.7 mi., 1150 ft., 1 hr. 55 min.

    to Israel Ridge Path (2800'): 4.0 mi., 1500 ft., 2 hr. 45 min.

    to Castle Ravine Trail, lower junction (3125'): 5.1 mi., 1800 ft., 3 hr. 25 min.

to Castle Trail (4025'): 6.0 mi., 2700 ft., 4 hr. 20 min.

to Caps Ridge Trail (3800'): 7.6 mi. (12.2 km.), 2850 ft. (rev. 400 ft.), 5 hr. 15 min.

Great Gulf Trail (WMNF)

This trail begins at the new parking area on NH 16, about 1.5 mi. south of its junction with Pinkham B (Dolly Copp) Rd. near Dolly Copp Campground. It follows the West Branch of the Peabody River through the Great Gulf, climbs up the headwall, and ends at a junction with the Gulfside Trail 0.5 mi. below the summit of Mt. Washington. Ascent on the headwall is steep and rough. Except for first 1.6 mi. this trail is in the Great Gulf Wilderness; camping is prohibited above the junction with the Sphinx Trail, and below that point it is limited to designated trailside sites or sites at least 200 ft. away from the trail.

Leaving the new parking lot, the trail descends slightly to cross the Peabody River on a suspension bridge, then ascends to a junction at 0.3 mi. with the former route from Dolly Copp Campground, now called the Great Gulf Link Trail. The Great Gulf Trail turns sharp left here and follows a logging road along the northwest bank of the West Branch of the Peabody River, at first close to the stream and later some distance away from it. An alternate route of the trail for skiing diverges right at 0.6 mi. and rejoins at 1.0 mi., where the main trail turns sharp left. At 1.6 mi. the Hayes Copp Ski Trail diverges right, the Great Gulf Trail soon crosses into the Great Gulf Wilderness, and the Osgood Trail diverges right at 1.8 mi.; Osgood Campsite is 0.9 mi. from here via the Osgood Trail. The Great Gulf Trail returns to the West Branch and follows it fairly closely for 0.7 mi., then climbs to the high gravelly bank called the Bluff, where there is a good view of the gulf and the mountains around it. The trail follows the edge of the Bluff, then at 2.7 mi. the Osgood Cutoff (which is part of the Appalachian Trail) continues straight ahead while the Great Gulf Trail descends sharp left; for a short distance this trail is also part of the Appalachian Trail. In 50 yd. it crosses Parapet Brook on a bridge, then climbs to the crest of the little ridge that separates Parapet Brook from the West Branch, where the Madison Gulf Trail (as recently relocated) enters right, coming down from the vicinity of Madison Hut through Madison Gulf. The two trails coincide for a short distance, descending to cross the West Branch on a suspension bridge and ascending the steep bank on the south side. Here, the Madison Gulf Trail branches left, taking the Appalachian Trail designation with it, while the Great Gulf Trail turns right, leading up the south bank of the river past Clam Rock, a huge boulder on the left, at 3.1 mi.

At 3.9 mi. the Great Gulf Trail crosses Chandler Brook, and on the far bank the Chandler Brook Trail diverges left and ascends to the Mt. Washington Auto Rd. The Great Gulf Trail continues close to the river, passing in sight of the mouth of the stream that issues from Jefferson Ravine on the north, to join the Six Husbands Trail (right) and Wamsutta Trail (left) at 4.5 mi. At 5.2 mi. the trail climbs up ledges beside a cascade and continues past numerous other attractive cascades in the next 0.2 mi. After crossing over to the northwest bank of the West Branch (may be difficult), it soon crosses the brook that descends from Sphinx Col and at 5.6 mi. reaches the junction where the Sphinx Trail, leading to the Gulfside Trail, diverges right. Camping is prohibited above this junction. The Great Gulf Trail soon crosses again to the southeast bank of the West Branch, passing waterfalls, including Weetamoo Falls, the finest in the gulf. There are remarkable views up the gulf to Mt. Adams and Mt. Madison. The trail crosses an eastern tributary and, after a slight ascent, reaches Spaulding Lake (4228 ft.) at 6.5 mi. from NH 16 and about 1.4 mi. by trail from the summit of Mt. Washington.

The Great Gulf Trail continues on the east side of the lake, and a little beyond begins to ascend the steep headwall. The trail runs south and then southeast, rising 1600 ft. in about 0.8 mi. over fragments of stone, many of which are loose. The way may be poorly marked, because snow slides may sweep away cairns, but paint blazes are usually visible on the rocks. The trail generally curves a little to the left until within a few yards of the top of the headwall; then, bearing slightly right, it emerges from the gulf and ends at the Gulfside Trail near the Cog Railway. It is 0.4 mi. from here to the summit of Mt. Washington by the Gulfside Trail.

Great Gulf Trail (map 1:F10–F9)

Distances from new parking area on NH 16 (1350')

  to Osgood Trail (1850'): 1.8 mi., 500 ft., 1 hr. 10 min.

  to Osgood Cutoff (2300'): 2.7 mi., 950 ft., 1 hr. 50 min.

  to Madison Gulf Trail, south junction (2300'): 2.8 mi., 1000 ft., 1 hr. 55 min.

  to Six Husbands and Wamsutta trails (3100'): 4.5 mi., 1800 ft., 3 hr. 10 min.

  to Sphinx Trail (3625'): 5.6 mi., 2350 ft., 4 hr.

  to Spaulding Lake (4228'): 6.5 mi., 2950 ft., 4 hr. 45 min.

  to Gulfside Trail junction (5925'): 7.5 mi. (12.1 km.), 4650 ft., 6 hr. 5 min.

  to Mt. Washington summit (6288') via Gulfside Trail and Crawford Path: 7.9 mi. (12.7 km.), 5000 ft., 6 hr. 25 min.

Great Gulf Link Trail (WMNF)

This trail was formerly a segment of the Great Gulf Trail. It leaves Dolly Copp Campground at the south end of the main camp road, which is a dead end. The trail enters the woods, and in 0.1 mi. turns sharp left onto an old logging road that has cross-country ski markers in both directions. It follows the logging road south along the west bank of the Peabody River, passing some interesting pools, and at 0.7 mi. it passes a junction with a branch of the Hayes Copp Ski Trail on the right. It ends at a junction with the Great Gulf Trail, which comes in on the left from the parking lot on NH 16 and continues straight ahead into the gulf.

Great Gulf Link Trail (map 1:F10)

Distance from Dolly Copp Campground (1250')

   to Great Gulf Trail (1375'): 1.0 mi. (1.6 km.),150 ft., 35 min.

Madison Gulf Trail (AMC)

This trail begins on the Mt. Washington Auto Rd. a little more than 2 mi. from the Glen House site, opposite the Old Jackson Road. It first crosses a low ridge then descends gently to the West Branch, where it meets the Great Gulf Trail, then ascends along Parapet Brook to the Parapet, where it ends at a point 0.3 mi. from Madison Hut. From the Auto Rd. to its departure from the Great Gulf Trail, the Madison Gulf Trail is part of the Appalachian Trail and therefore blazed in white; the rest is blazed in blue. It is almost entirely within the Great Gulf Wilderness.

   Caution: The section of this trail on the headwall of Madison Gulf is one of the most difficult in the White Mtns., going over several ledge outcrops, bouldery areas, and a chimney with loose rock. The steep slabs may be slippery when wet, and several ledges require scrambling and the use of handholds—hikers with short arms may have a particular problem reaching the handholds. Stream crossings may be very difficult in wet weather. The trail is not recommended for the descent, for hikers with heavy packs, or in wet weather. Allow extra time, and do not start up the headwall late in the day. The ascent of the headwall may require several hours more than the estimated time; parties frequently fail to reach the hut before dark on account of slowness on the headwall.

   This trail is well marked, well protected from storms, and has plenty of water. Combined with the Old Jackson Road, it is the shortest route (7.1 mi.) from Pinkham Notch Visitor Center to Madison Hut via the Great Gulf, but not usually the easiest; there are several reasonable alternative routes, though none of them is without drawbacks. The route via the Osgood Cutoff and Osgood Trail, 7.5 mi. long, is steep in parts but has no hard brook crossings or difficult scrambles; however, it is very exposed to weather in the upper part, even if the rough but more sheltered Parapet Trail is used to bypass Mt. Madison's summit. The route via the Buttress Trail is 8.4 mi. long, and has two significant brook crossings and somewhat more weather exposure than the Madison Gulf Trail, though substantially less than the Osgood-Parapet route. In any event, for parties traveling to the hut from the Great Gulf side, there is no way to avoid the 0.3-mi. walk to Madison Hut across the windswept col between Madison and Adams, except by going over the summit of Madison where conditions may well be much worse. Therefore choice of route comes down to a trade-off among the factors of distance, weather exposure, brook crossings, and rock scrambles; hikers must consider which factors they feel better prepared to deal with, taking current and expected conditions into account. The main advantage that the Madison Gulf Trail has in bad weather, compared to the Buttress Trail, is that the brook crossings on the Madison Gulf Trail, while they may be difficult, are unlikely to be impassable, whereas those on the Buttress Trail may be impossible to cross without an unacceptable risk of drowning. However, in rainy conditions the deep streams and steep slippery ledges on the Madison Gulf Trail would pose great difficulty. In sum, hikers who are not prepared for this level of challenge would be well advised to change their plans rather than attempt any of the direct routes between Pinkham Notch Visitor Center and Madison Hut in adverse conditions, and even in favorable conditions the Madison Gulf Trail must be treated with serious caution and vigilance.

The Madison Gulf Trail leaves the Auto Rd. above the 2-mi. mark, opposite the Old Jackson Road junction, and enters the Great Gulf Wilderness. In 0.2 mi. a side path branches right in a little pass west of Lowe's Bald Spot and climbs 0.1 mi. to this little ledgy knob, an excellent viewpoint. The Madison Gulf Trail bears left and ascends over a ledge with a limited view, then descends, first rapidly for a short distance, then easily, crossing many small brooks. The trail curves into the valley of the West Branch of the Peabody River and continues descending gently until it meets the Great Gulf Trail on the south bank at 2.1 mi. The two trails now run together, descending the steep bank to the West Branch, crossing a suspension bridge to the north bank, and climbing to the crest of the little ridge that divides Parapet Brook from the West Branch. Here the Great Gulf Trail continues straight ahead, leading to NH 16 or (via the Osgood Cutoff) to the Osgood Trail for Mt. Madison and Madison Hut. The Madison Gulf Trail turns left up the narrow ridge and continues between the two streams until it enters its former route near the bank of Parapet Brook at 2.5 mi. At 2.8 mi. it crosses one channel of the divided brook, runs between the two for 0.1 mi., then crosses the other to the northeast bank. It follows the brook bank for a little way; then it turns right, away from the brook, then turns left and ascends along the valley wall at a moderate grade, coming back to the brook at the mouth of the branch stream from Osgood Ridge. From here it follows Parapet Brook rather closely, and at 3.5 mi. crosses the brook for the first of three times in less than 0.5 mi., ascending to the lower floor of the gulf where it reaches Sylvan Cascade, a fine waterfall, at 4.1 mi.

The Madison Gulf Trail then ascends to the upper floor of the gulf, where it crosses numerous small brooks. From the floor it rises gradually to Mossy Slide at the foot of the headwall, then ascends very rapidly alongside a stream, which becomes partly hidden among the rocks as the trail rises. The trail then reaches the headwall of the gulf and climbs very steeply, with some difficult scrambles on the ledges. As it emerges on the rocks at treeline, it bears right and the grade moderates, and soon it ends at the Parapet Trail. For the Parapet (0.1 mi.) and Madison Hut (0.3 mi.), turn left; for the Osgood Trail via the Parapet Trail, turn right.

Madison Gulf Trail (map 1:F9)

Distances from Mt. Washington Auto Rd. (2625')

> *to* Great Gulf Trail (2300'): 2.1 mi., 200 ft. (rev. 500 ft.), 1 hr. 10 min.

> *to* foot of Madison Gulf headwall at Sylvan Cascade (3900'): 4.1 mi., 1800 ft., 2 hr. 55 min.

> *to* Parapet Trail (4850'): 4.8 mi. (7.7 km.), 2750 ft., 3 hr. 45 min.

> *to* Madison Hut (4825') via Parapet and Star Lake trails: 5.2 mi., 2800 ft., 4 hr.

Distance from Pinkham Notch Visitor Center (2032')

> *to* Madison Hut (via Old Jackson Road and Madison Gulf, Parapet, and Star Lake trails): 7.1 mi. (11.4 km.), 3500 ft., 5 hr. 20 min.

Chandler Brook Trail (AMC)

This wild, rough, and beautiful trail passes many cascades as it climbs from the Great Gulf Trail to the Auto Rd. just above the 4-mi. post. It is almost entirely within the Great Gulf Wilderness. It diverges south from the Great Gulf Trail 3.9 mi. from NH 16, just above its crossing of Chandler Brook, and follows the brook rather closely, crossing three times, passing fine waterfalls that can be seen from the trail. From the last crossing it runs southeast, rising over a jumbled mass of stones and keeping west of interesting rock formations. The trail enters the Auto Rd. near a ledge of white quartz at the Horn, 0.3 mi. above the 4-mi. post. (Descending, look for this white ledge, which is close to the Auto Rd. The trail is marked by cairns here and is visible from the road.)

Chandler Brook Trail (map 1:F9)
Distance from Great Gulf Trail (2800')

   to Mt. Washington Auto Rd. (4125'): 0.9 mi. (1.4 km.), 1300 ft., 1 hr. 5 min.

Wamsutta Trail (AMC)

This wild, rough, and beautiful trail begins on the Great Gulf Trail and ascends to the Auto Rd. just above the 6-mi. marker and opposite the Alpine Garden Trail, with which it provides routes to Tuckerman Junction, Lakes of the Clouds Hut, and other points to the south. It is almost entirely within the Great Gulf Wilderness. The trail was named for Wamsutta, the first of six successive husbands of Weetamoo, a queen of the Pocasset tribe, for whom a beautiful waterfall in the Great Gulf is named.

   Leaving the Great Gulf Trail opposite the Six Husbands Trail, 4.5 mi. from NH 16, the trail crosses a small stream, then ascends gradually. Soon it climbs the very steep and rough northerly spur of Chandler Ridge. Passing a quartz ledge on the right, the trail continues steeply to a small, open promontory on the crest of the spur, which offers a good view, at 0.9 mi. It then ascends gradually through woods, passing a spring on the right. Continuing along the ridgecrest at a moderate grade, the trail emerges at treeline and climbs to a point near the top end of the winter shortcut of the Auto Rd. After turning right along this road, it ends in another 100 yd. at the Auto Rd. just above the 6-mi. post.

Wamsutta Trail (map 1:F9)
Distances from Great Gulf Trail (3100')

   to outlook on promontory (4350'): 0.9 mi., 1250 ft., 1 hr. 5 min.

   to Mt. Washington Auto Rd. (5305'): 1.7 mi. (2.7 km.), 2200 ft., 1 hr. 55 min.

Sphinx Trail (AMC)

This wild, beautiful, and very rough trail runs from the Great Gulf Trail below Spaulding Lake to the Gulfside Trail in Sphinx Col, between Mt. Jefferson and Mt. Clay. This trail is particularly important because it affords the quickest escape route for anyone overtaken by storm in the vicinity of Sphinx Col. It diverges east from the Gulfside Trail 40 yd. north of the lowest point in the col, running through a grassy, rock-walled corridor, and descends to the Great Gulf Trail. Once below the col, the hiker is quickly protected from the rigor of west and northwest winds. For a considerable part of its length this trail climbs very steeply; there is a long section of very slippery rocks in a brook bed, very tedious particularly on the descent, and some of the scrambles on the ledges in the upper part are challenging. The trail's name is derived from the profile of a rock formation seen from just below the meadow where water is found. This trail is almost entirely within the Great Gulf Wilderness.

The trail branches northwest from the Great Gulf Trail 5.6 mi. from NH 16, near the crossing of the brook that flows down from Sphinx Col through the minor ravine between Mt. Clay and Mt. Jefferson. It soon turns due west and ascends close to the brook, first gradually, then very steeply, passing several attractive cascades and pools. For about 100 yd. it runs directly in the brook bed, where the rocks are extremely slippery. At 0.6 mi., at the foot of a broken ledge with several small streams cascading over it, the trail turns left away from the brook and angles up across two more small brooks. It climbs a small chimney where views out from the scrubby slope start to appear, then scrambles up ledges with several rock pitches of some difficulty. About 100 yd. above the chimney, after a slight descent, the trail crosses a small meadow where there is usually water under a rock just downhill to the north of the trail. The trail then climbs steeply up a rocky cleft, ascends easily over the crest of a small rocky ridge and descends into a slight sag. It finally climbs to the ridgecrest and traverses a grassy passage at the base of a rock wall to the Gulfside just north of Sphinx Col.

Sphinx Trail (map 1:F9)
Distance from Great Gulf Trail (3625')

    to Gulfside Trail (4975'): 1.1 mi. (1.7 km.), 1350 ft., 1 hr. 15 min.

Six Husbands Trail (AMC)

This wild, rough, beautiful trail provides magnificent views of the inner part of the Great Gulf. It diverges from the Great Gulf Trail 4.5 mi. from NH 16, opposite the Wamsutta Trail, and climbs up the north knee of Jefferson, crosses the Gulfside Trail, and ends at the Mount Jefferson Loop a short distance northeast of the summit. It is very steep and is not recommended for descent except to escape bad conditions above treeline. Up to the Gulfside Trail junction, it is entirely within the Great Gulf Wilderness. The name honors the six successive husbands of Weetamoo, queen of the Pocasset tribe.

Leaving the Great Gulf Trail, it descends directly across the West Branch, avoiding side paths along the stream. In times of high water this crossing may be very difficult, but there may be a better crossing upstream. The trail climbs easily northward across a low ridge to join Jefferson Brook, the stream that flows from Jefferson Ravine, and ascends along its southwest bank. At 0.5 mi. the Buttress Trail branches right and crosses the stream. The Six Husbands Trail swings away from the brook (last sure water) and runs through an area containing many large boulders. Soon it begins to attack the very steep main buttress, the north knee of Jefferson, passing by one boulder cave and through another. At 1.0 mi. it ascends a steep ledge on a pair of ladders, then climbs under an overhanging ledge on a second pair, with a tricky spot at the top that might be dangerous if wet or icy. In another 100 yd. it reaches a promontory with a fine view, and begins a moderately difficult scramble up the crest of a rocky ridge.

At 1.3 mi. the trail reaches the top of the knee approximately at treeline, and the grade moderates. Across the bare stretches the trail is marked by cairns. At 1.7 mi. the Edmands Col Cutoff branches right, leading in 0.5 mi. to Edmands Col, and the trail becomes steeper as it begins to climb the cone of Mt. Jefferson. Soon it passes over a talus slope that is usually covered well into July by a great drift of snow, conspicuous for a considerable distance from viewpoints to the east. Marked by cairns, the trail crosses the Gulfside Trail and continues west toward the summit of Mt. Jefferson, joining the Mount Jefferson Loop 0.1 mi. below the summit.

Six Husbands Trail (map 1:F9)

Distances from Great Gulf Trail junction (3100')

> *to* Buttress Trail (3350'): 0.5 mi., 250 ft., 25 min.

> *to* Edmands Col Cutoff (4925'): 1.7 mi., 1850 ft., 1 hr. 45 min.

> *to* Gulfside Trail (5325'): 2.0 mi., 2150 ft., 2 hr. 5 min.

> *to* Mount Jefferson Loop (5625'): 2.3 mi. (3.6 km.), 2450 ft., 2 hr. 25 min.

Buttress Trail (AMC)

This trail leads from the Six Husbands Trail to the Star Lake Trail near Madison Hut, and is the most direct route from the upper part of the Great Gulf to Madison Hut. It is mostly well sheltered until it nears the hut, and grades are moderate; in bad weather, or for hikers with heavy packs, or for descending, it is probably the best route from the lower part of the gulf to the hut, in spite of the somewhat greater distance. (See Madison Gulf Trail, the principal alternative, for a discussion of the options.) It is almost entirely within the Great Gulf Wilderness.

The trail diverges north from the Six Husbands Trail 0.5 mi. from the Great Gulf Trail, and immediately crosses Jefferson Brook (last sure water), the brook that flows out of Jefferson Ravine. It bears right (east) in 0.1 mi., and climbs diagonally across a steep slope of large, loose, angular fragments of rock (care must be taken not to dislodge the loose rocks). At the top of this talus slope there is a spectacular view up the Great Gulf, and to the steep buttress of Jefferson's north knee rising nearby across a small valley. The trail continues east, rising gradually along a steep, wooded slope, then at 0.5 mi. it reaches a ridge corner and swings left (north) and runs across a gently sloping upland covered with trees, passing a spring (reliable water) on the left at 1.0 mi. At 1.2 mi. the trail passes through a boulder cave formed by a large boulder across the path, then reaches the foot of a steep ledge, swings left, and climbs it. At 1.4 mi. the trail swings right after passing between two ledges; the ledge on the right provides a fine view. The trail now ascends less steeply on open rocks above the scrub line, crosses a minor ridge, and descends moderately. After passing under an overhanging rock, it re-enters high scrub that provides shelter almost all the way to the junction with the Star Lake Trail, which is reached in the gap between the Parapet and Mt. Quincy Adams, just southwest of Star Lake and 0.3 mi. from Madison Hut.

Buttress Trail (map 1:F9)

Distances from Six Husbands Trail junction (3350')

   to Star Lake Trail (4900'): 1.9 mi. (3.1 km.), 1600 ft., 1 hr. 45 min.

   to Madison Hut (4825') via Star Lake Trail: 2.2 mi. (3.6 km.), 1600 ft., 1 hr. 55 min.

Osgood Trail (AMC)

This trail runs from the Great Gulf Trail, 1.8 mi. from the new Great Gulf Wilderness parking area on NH 16, up the southeast ridge of Mt. Madison to the summit, then down to Madison Hut. Made by Benjamin F. Osgood in 1878, this is the oldest trail now in use to the summit of Mt. Madison. Above the Osgood Cutoff it is part of the Appalachian Trail. The section of the trail that formerly ran from the Great Gulf Trail to the Mt. Washington Auto Rd. has been abandoned. The Osgood Trail begins in the Great Gulf Wilderness, but for most of its length it is just outside the boundary (in fact, it constitutes the northern section of the eastern boundary of the Great Gulf Wilderness).

This trail leaves the Great Gulf Trail and ascends at an easy to moderate grade. At 0.3 mi. it crosses a small brook, follows it, recrosses, and bears away from it to the left. At 0.8 mi. the Osgood Cutoff comes in from the left, and a spur path leads right over a small brook (last sure water) and continues about 100 yd. to Osgood Campsite. From this junction to Madison Hut, the Osgood Trail is part of the Appalachian Trail.

At 1.4 mi. the trail begins to climb a very steep section, then at about 1.6 mi. it gradually but steadily becomes less steep, and the grade is easy by the time the trail emerges on the crest of Osgood Ridge at treeline at 2.1 mi. Ahead, on the crest of the ridge, ten or twelve small, rocky peaks curve to the left in a crescent toward the summit of Mt. Madison; the trail, marked by cairns, follows this ridgecrest. At 2.8 mi. from the Great Gulf Trail, the Osgood Trail reaches Osgood Junction in a small hollow. Here, the Daniel Webster–Scout Trail enters on the right, ascending from Dolly Copp Campground, and the Parapet Trail diverges left on a level path marked by cairns and passes around the south side of the cone of Madison with little change of elevation, making a very rough but comparatively sheltered route to Madison Hut.

From Osgood Junction the Osgood Trail climbs over a prominent crag, crosses a shallow sag, and starts up the east ridge of Madison's summit cone, where it is soon joined on the right by the Howker Ridge Trail. Hikers planning to descend on the Howker Ridge Trail must take care to distinguish that trail from beaten side paths that lead back to the Osgood Trail. The Osgood Trail ascends to the summit of Mt. Madison at 3.3 mi., where the Watson Path enters on the right, then follows the crest of the ridge past several large cairns, drops off to the left (south), and continues to descend westward just below the ridge crest and above the steep slopes falling off into Madison Gulf on the left. Soon it crosses to the north side of the ridge and descends steeply, and, 30 yd. before it reaches Madison Hut, the Pine Link joins on the right.

Osgood Trail (map 1:F10–F9)

Distances from Great Gulf Trail (1850')

to Osgood Cutoff (2486'): 0.8 mi., 650 ft., 45 min.

to Osgood Junction (4822'): 2.8 mi., 3000 ft., 2 hr. 55 min.

to Mt. Madison summit (5366'): 3.3 mi., 3550 ft., 3 hr. 25 min.

to Madison Hut (4825'): 3.8 mi. (6.1 km.), 3550 ft. (rev. 550 ft.), 3 hr. 40 min.

Osgood Cutoff (AMC)

This link trail, a part of the Appalachian Trail, provides a convenient shortcut from the Great Gulf and Madison Gulf trails to the Osgood Trail. It is entirely within the Great Gulf Wilderness. This trail leaves the Great Gulf Trail on the Bluff, continuing straight ahead where the Great Gulf Trail turns sharp left to descend to Parapet Brook. The Osgood Cutoff climbs moderately for 0.2 mi. to its former junction with the Madison Gulf Trail, then turns sharp right and runs nearly on contour east across several small brooks to the Osgood Trail at its junction with the spur path to Osgood Campsite, where there is reliable water.

Osgood Cutoff (map 1:F9)

Distance from Madison Gulf Trail (2300')

to Osgood Trail (2486'): 0.6 mi. (1.0 km.), 200 ft., 25 min.

Daniel Webster–Scout Trail (WMNF)

This trail, cut in 1933 by Boy Scouts from the Daniel Webster Council, leads from Dolly Copp Campground to the Osgood Trail at Osgood Junction, 0.5 mi. below the summit of Mt. Madison. It begins on the main campground road 0.9 mi. south of the campground entrance on the Pinkham B (Dolly Copp) Rd., with adequate parking available on the left in another 0.1 mi. For most of its length its grades are moderate and its footing is somewhat rocky but not unusually rough; however, the upper part of this trail is very steep and very exposed to the weather.

The trail starts out through a section of open woods with some very large trees, soon crosses the Hayes Copp Ski Trail (here a grassy logging road), and swings northwest almost to the bank of Culhane Brook. Veering away from the brook just before reaching it, the trail climbs moderately up the east slope of Madison, mostly angling upward and carefully avoiding a more direct assault on the steeper parts of the mountainside. At 2.0 mi. it reaches the base of a little buttress, where the forest changes rather abruptly from hardwoods to evergreens. It winds steeply up this buttress to its top, switchbacks upward a bit farther, then resumes its moderate ascent, angling northwest across the steep slope, becoming steeper and rockier. At 2.9 mi. it begins a very steep and rough climb nearly straight up the slope with ever-increasing amounts of talus and decreasing amounts of scrub, where views begin to appear and improve. At 3.2 mi. the trail reaches treeline and moderates somewhat, though it is still steep. As it approaches the ridgecrest, it turns left and ascends directly up the slope for the last 100 yd. to Osgood Junction and the Osgood Trail.

Daniel Webster–Scout Trail (map 1:F10–F9)

Distances from Dolly Copp Campground (1250')

> *to* foot of little buttress (2800'): 2.0 mi., 1550 ft., 1 hr. 45 min.
>
> *to* Osgood Junction (4822'): 3.5 mi., 3600 ft., 3 hr. 35 min.
>
> *to* Mt. Madison summit (5366') via Osgood Trail: 4.1 mi. (6.6 km.), 4100 ft., 4 hr. 5 min.

Parapet Trail (AMC)

This trail, marked with cairns and blue paint, runs at a roughly constant elevation around the south side of the cone of Mt. Madison, from the Osgood and Daniel Webster–Scout trails at Osgood Junction to the Star Lake Trail between the Parapet and Madison Hut. Although above timberline and extremely rough, particularly in its eastern half, in bad weather the Parapet Trail is mostly sheltered from the northwest winds. The rocks can be very slippery, the trail may be hard to follow if visibility is poor, and the extra effort of rock-hopping more than expends the energy saved by avoiding the climb of about 500 ft. over the summit of Mt. Madison. Therefore it is probably a useful bad-weather route only if strong northwest or west winds are a major part of the problem.

From Osgood Junction the trail rises very slightly, marked by cairns across the open rocks; at the start care must be taken to distinguish its cairns from those ascending the ridgecrest on the right, which belong to the Osgood Trail. At 0.8 mi. the Madison Gulf Trail enters left at the bottom of a little gully, and the Parapet Trail ascends a ledge and then makes a sharp right turn at 0.9 mi., where a spur path leads left 30 yd. onto the Parapet, a ledge that commands excellent views over the Great Gulf and Madison Gulf to the mountains beyond. The Parapet Trail then runs north, passing above Star Lake, and joins the Star Lake Trail 0.1 mi. south of Madison Hut.

Parapet Trail (map 1:F9)

Distances from Osgood Junction (4822')

> *to* Madison Gulf Trail (4850'): 0.8 mi., 150 ft. (rev. 100 ft.), 30 min.
>
> *to* Star Lake Trail (4900'): 1.0 mi. (1.5 km.), 200 ft., 35 min.
>
> *to* Madison Hut (4825') via Star Lake Trail: 1.1 mi. (1.8 km.), 200 ft., 40 min.

Pine Link (AMC)

The Pine Link ascends Mt. Madison from the highest point of the Pinkham B (Dolly Copp) Rd., almost directly opposite the private road to the Horton Center on Pine Mtn., 2.4 mi. from US 2 at the foot of the big hill west of Gorham and 1.9 mi. from NH 16 near Dolly Copp Campground. It is an interesting trail that provides an unusual variety of views from its outlook ledges and from the section above treeline on Madison's northwest slope. Combined with the upper part of the Howker Ridge Trail, it provides a very scenic loop. In general it is not unusually steep, but the footing is often rough and consumes an unusual amount of attention and energy in comparison to most trails of similar steepness. The part above the treeline is continuously exposed to the full force of northwest winds for about 0.7 mi. and might be difficult to follow if visibility is poor, and also requires a considerable amount of fairly strenuous rock-hopping. The result is that the trail generally proves more challenging than its statistical details might indicate.

The trail first ascends the northwest slope of a spur of Howker Ridge, climbing by a series of short steep pitches interspersed with level sections. At 1.0 mi. it crosses a flat, swampy area and ascends another steep pitch, then climbs to the ridgecrest of the spur and follows it. At 1.7 mi. it passes an outlook with good views from the south side of the trail, the result of a 1968 fire. At 1.9 mi., just before the trail descends into a sag, a spur path leads left 20 yd. to a bare crag with fine views up to Madison and out to the Carters. At 2.4 mi., after a fairly long section of trail that has a brook running in and out of it, the Pine Link turns right and joins the Howker Ridge Trail in a shady little glen. Turning left at this junction, the Pine Link coincides with the Howker Ridge Trail. The two trails pass over a ledgy minor knob (a "Howk") that offers a good view and then descend from the ledge down a steep cleft to a wet sag. After passing a small cave on the right of the trail, the Pine Link branches right at 2.8 mi. at the foot of the most prominent Howk. The fine viewpoint at the top of this crag is only about 0.1 mi. above the junction and is well worth a visit. From the junction the

Pink Link runs nearly level across a wet area, then rises moderately on the slope above Bumpus Basin, crossing several small brooks. Climbing out of the scrub at 3.3 mi., it runs above treeline with fine views and great exposure. After crossing the Watson Path at 3.5 mi. (0.3 mi. below the summit of Mt. Madison), the Pine Link descends gradually, frequently crossing jumbles of large rocks that require strenuous rock-hopping, to the Osgood Trail 30 yd. from Madison Hut.

Pine Link (map 1:E10–F9)

Distances from Pinkham B (Dolly Copp) Rd. (1650')

> *to* Howker Ridge Trail, lower junction (3850'): 2.4 mi., 2300 ft., 2 hr. 20 min.
>
> *to* Watson Path (4950'): 3.5 mi., 3500 ft., 3 hr. 30 min.
>
> *to* Madison Hut (4825'): 4.0 mi. (6.5 km.), 3600 ft. (rev. 200 ft.), 3 hr. 50 min.

Howker Ridge Trail (RMC)

This wild, rough, very scenic trail was built by Eugene B. Cook and William H. Peek, although the lower part no longer follow the original route. It leads from the Pinkham B (Dolly Copp) Rd. at the Randolph East parking area, 0.2 mi. south of US 2, to the Osgood Trail near the summit of Mt. Madison. It is an interesting trail with a great variety of attractive scenery and woods, passing three fine cascades in the lower part of the trail and offering excellent outlooks at different altitudes higher up. Howker Ridge is the long, curving northeast ridge of Mt. Madison that partly encloses the deep, bowl-shaped valley called Bumpus Basin. The trail follows the crest of the ridge, on which there are four little peaks called the Howks. The ridge gets its name from a Howker family that once had a farm at its base.

Coinciding with the Randolph Path, the trail bears sharp left and quickly crosses the railroad grade, and 30 yd. beyond diverges left (southeast) where the Randolph Path turns right (west). (Logging activity has disrupted this part of the trail somewhat in recent years, and trail markings must be observed and followed with great care.) It crosses a recent logging road near a yarding area, then enters a shallow gully and turns right, going up through it. At 0.4 mi. it reaches the bank of Bumpus Brook and follows it, passing Stairs Fall, a cascade on a tributary that enters Bumpus Brook directly across from the viewpoint. The trail continues along the brook, passing a small rocky gorge called the Devil's Kitchen and other interesting pools and cascades. At Coosauk Fall the Sylvan Way enters on the right, and in less than 0.1 mi. the Kelton Trail diverges on the right. At 1.0 mi. the Howker Ridge Trail crosses Bumpus Brook at the foot of Hitchcock Fall, then climbs steeply up the bank on the other side, levels off, descends slightly, and reaches a junction with a spur trail that leads right 40 yd. to the Bear Pit, a natural cleft in the ledge that forms a trap-like box. The main trail climbs steeply through conifer woods, then moderates, reaching a rocky shoulder and descending into a slight sag. It resumes climbing and passes over a ledgy ridgecrest called Blueberry Ledge—now far too overgrown to produce many blueberries— then continues up the ridge. It continues to climb, steeply at first and then moderately as it approaches the crest of the first Howk, a long, narrow, densely wooded ridge capped by a number of small peaks. Following the ridge at easy grades, it passes a good though limited outlook ahead to Mt. Madison and crosses the ledgy but viewless summit of the first Howk at 2.3 mi., then descends steeply for a short distance. After crossing through a long, fairly level sag, the trail climbs seriously again, and at 3.0 mi. it passes over the ledgy summit of the second Howk, where there are fine views, especially into Bumpus Basin. Descending into the woods again, it passes through the shady glen where the Pink Link enters on the left; there is water down this trail in less than 100 yd.

From this junction the two trails coincide for 0.3 mi., ascending over one of a group of several small, ledgy knobs that constitute the third Howk, affording another good view. Descending a steep cleft to a wet sag, the trail passes a small cave to the right of the path and then ascends to a junction where the Pine Link branches right. Bearing slightly left, the Howker Ridge Trail climbs rather steeply up ledges to the open summit of the highest, most prominent Howk (4315 ft.) at 3.6 mi., where there are fine views in all directions. The trail descends back into the scrub, climbs over another minor crag, and passes through one last patch of high scrub before breaking out above treeline for good. The ensuing section of trail is very exposed to northwest winds and may be difficult to follow in poor visibility; however, if the trail is lost in conditions that do not dictate a retreat below treeline, it is easy enough to reach the Osgood Trail simply by climbing up to the ridgecrest, as the Osgood Trail follows that crest closely. From treeline the trail climbs steeply up the rocks, generally angling a bit to the left and aiming for the notch between the most prominent visible crag and the lower crag to its left. As it approaches the ridgecrest it turns more to the right, heading for the most prominent visible crag, and enters the Osgood Trail about 100 yd. above a small sag and 0.2 mi. below the summit of Mt. Madison.

On the descent, at the junction of the Howker Ridge and Osgood trails, care must be taken to avoid beaten paths that lead back into the Osgood Trail. On leaving the junction one should keep well to the left, descending only slightly, until the RMC sign a short distance down the path has been sighted.

Howker Ridge Trail (map 1:E9–F9)
Distances from Pinkham B (Dolly Copp) Rd. (1225')

to Hitchcock Fall (1875'): 1.0 mi., 650 ft., 50 min.

to first Howk (3425'): 2.3 mi., 2200 ft., 2 hr. 15 min.

to Pine Link, lower junction (3850'): 3.1 mi., 2750 ft., 2 hr. 55 min.

to Osgood Trail (5100'): 4.2 mi. (6.8 km.), 4100 ft., 4 hr. 10 min.

to Mt. Madison summit (5366') via Osgood Trail: 4.5 mi., 4350 ft., 4 hr. 25 min.

Kelton Trail (RMC)

This path runs from the Howker Ridge Trail just above Coosauk Fall to the Brookside just below Salmacis Fall, from which the Watson Path and Valley Way can be quickly reached. It passes several fine viewpoints, notably the Upper Inlook.

The trail branches right from the Howker Ridge Trail 0.8 mi. from the Pinkham B (Dolly Copp) Rd. It climbs steeply with some slippery sections to Kelton Crag, then ascends toward the finger-like north spur of Gordon Ridge, reaching an upper crag at the edge of a very old burn. From both crags there are restricted views; there is usually water between them on the right. Ascending, with good views east, the trail reaches the Overlook at the edge of the old burn, then runs west to the Upper Inlook at 0.9 mi., where the Inlook Trail enters right from Dome Rock. The Kelton Trail then runs south, nearly level but rough in places, through dense woods. It crosses Gordon Rill (reliable water) and Snyder Brook, and enters the Brookside 0.1 mi. below the foot of Salmacis Fall.

Kelton Trail (map 1:E9)
Distances from Howker Ridge Trail (1700')

to Kelton Crag (2075'): 0.3 mi., 400 ft., 25 min.

to Inlook Trail (2732'): 0.9 mi., 1050 ft., 1 hr.

to the Brookside (2750'): 1.7 mi. (2.7 km.), 1100 ft., 1 hr. 25 min.

Inlook Trail (RMC)

This path ascends the ridge that leads northwest from the end of the finger-like north spur of Gordon Ridge, offering excellent views from the brink of the line of cliffs that overlook Snyder Brook and culminate in Dome Rock. It begins at the junction of the Randolph Path and the Brookside on the east bank of Snyder Brook. It ascends, steeply at the start, soon reaching the first of several "inlooks" up the valley of Snyder Brook to Mt. John Quincy Adams and Mt. Adams. After passing Dome Rock, which offers an excellent view north from the tip of the finger, the trail continues up to the Upper Inlook near the crest of the finger, where it ends at its junction with the Kelton Trail.

Inlook Trail (map 1:E9)

Distances from Randolph Path (1900')

   to Dome Rock (2662'): 0.6 mi., 750 ft., 40 min.

   to Kelton Trail (2732'): 0.7 mi. (1.1 km.), 850 ft., 45 min.

The Brookside (RMC)

This trail follows Snyder Brook, offering views of many cascades and pools. It begins at the junction with the Inlook Trail and the Valley Way, at the point where the Valley Way leaves the edge of the brook 0.9 mi. from the Appalachia parking area, and climbs along the brook to the Watson Path 100 yd. south of Bruin Rock.

The Brookside begins by continuing straight about 30 yd. above its junction with the Beechwood Way, where the Valley Way turns uphill to the right. After a short washed-out section the Randolph Path joins on the right, and the two trails cross Snyder Brook together on a bridge. Here the Randolph Path turns left, the Inlook Trail leaves straight ahead, and the Brookside turns right, continuing up the bank of the brook. At 0.3 mi. the Brookside recrosses the brook and climbs along the west bank at a moderate grade, rising well above the brook, with occasional views through the trees to cliffs on the valley wall on the other side of the brook. Returning gradually to brook level, it comes to the junction with the Kelton Trail, which enters from the left at 1.2 mi. Above this point the Brookside becomes steeper and rougher, and again runs close to the brook, passing Salmacis Fall and continuing along a wild and beautiful part of the brook, with cascades and mossy rocks in a fine forest. It then climbs away from the brook and finally ascends sharply to the Watson Path 100 yd. south of Bruin Rock.

The Brookside (map 1:E9)

Distance from the Valley Way and Inlook Trail (1900')

  to Watson Path (3250'): 1.7 mi. (2.7 km.), 1350 ft., 1 hr. 30 min.

Watson Path (RMC)

The original Watson Path, completed by Laban M. Watson in 1882, led from the Ravine House to the summit of Mt. Madison. The present path begins at the Scar Trail, leads across the Valley Way to Bruin Rock, and then follows the original route to the summit. It is an interesting route to Mt. Madison, but it is steep and rough, and, on the slopes above treeline, exposed to the full fury of northwest winds in a storm. The cairns above treeline are not very prominent, and the trail may be hard to follow when visibility is poor. Therefore, in bad weather it is potentially one of the most dangerous routes on the Northern Peaks.

  Branching from the Scar Trail 0.3 mi. from the Valley Way, it runs level, turning sharp left at 0.1 mi. and crossing the Valley Way at 0.2 mi., at a point 2.4 mi. from the Appalachia parking area via the Valley Way. This first section is seldom used and is rather difficult to follow. After crossing the Valley Way, the trail continues at an easy grade to Bruin Rock—a large, flat-topped boulder on the west bank of Snyder Brook—and in another 100 yd. the Brookside enters on the left. In another 80 yd. the Lower Bruin branches to the right toward the Valley Way, and the Watson Path crosses the brook at the foot of Duck Fall. The trail soon attacks the steep flank of Gordon Ridge on a very steep and rough footway. At 1.0 mi. it emerges from the scrub onto the grassy, stony back of the ridge, crosses the Pine Link at 1.4 mi., and ascends to the summit of Mt. Madison over rough and shelving stones.

Watson Path (map 1:E9–F9)

Distances from Scar Trail (3200')

  to Valley Way (3175'): 0.2 mi., 0 ft., 5 min.

  to Pine Link (4950'): 1.4 mi., 1750 ft., 1 hr. 35 min.

  to Mt. Madison summit (5366'): 1.7 mi. (2.7 km.), 2200 ft., 1 hr. 55 min

Distance from Appalachia parking area (1306')

  to Mt. Madison summit (5366') via Valley Way and Watson Path: 4.1 mi. (6.6 km.), 4050 ft., 4 hr. 5 min.

Valley Way (WMNF)

This is the most direct and easiest route from the Appalachia parking area to Madison Hut, well sheltered almost to the door of the hut. In bad weather it is the safest route to or from the hut. It was constructed by J. R. Edmands in his unmistakable style in 1895–97, using parts of earlier trails constructed by Laban Watson and Eugene Cook.

The trail, in common with the Air Line, begins at Appalachia and crosses the former railroad grade to a fork, where the Valley Way leads to the left and the Air Line to the right across the power line clearing into the woods. Just into the woods, the Maple Walk diverges left, and at 0.2 mi. Sylvan Way crosses. The trail enters the WMNF at 0.3 mi., and at 0.5 mi. the Fallsway comes in on the left, soon departs on the left for Tama Fall and the Brookbank, then re-enters the Valley Way in a few yards—a short but worthwhile loop.

The Valley Way leads nearer Snyder Brook and is soon joined from the right by the Beechwood Way. About 30 yd. above this junction the Brookside continues straight, while the Valley Way turns right and climbs 100 yd. to the crossing of the Randolph Path at 0.9 mi., then climbs at a comfortable grade high above Snyder Brook. At 2.1 mi. the Scar Trail branches right, leading to the Air Line via Durand Scar, an excellent outlook on the Scar Loop only about 0.2 mi. above the Valley Way, well worth the small effort required to visit it. At 2.4 mi. the Watson Path crosses, leading left to the summit of Mt. Madison. The Valley Way angles up the rather steep slopes of Durand Ridge at a moderate grade considerably above the stream. At 2.8 mi. the Lower Bruin enters left, coming up from Bruin Rock and Duck Fall. At 3.1 mi. a path formerly led to Valley Way Campsite, which may be reopened if sanitation problems can be solved; at present camping on the site is prohibited. Soon the trail passes a spring to the right of the trail. At 3.3 mi. the Upper Bruin branches steeply right, leading in 0.2 mi. to the Air Line at the lower end of the Knife-edge.

Now the Valley Way steepens and approaches nearer to Snyder Brook. High up in the scrub, the path swings to the right, away from the brook, then swings back toward the stream and emerges from the scrub close to the stream, reaching a junction with the Air Line Cutoff 50 yd. below the hut. It ends in another 10 yd. at a junction with the Gulfside and Star Lake trails.

Valley Way (map 1:E9–F9)

Distances from Appalachia parking area (1306')

to Randolph Path crossing (1953'): 0.9 mi., 650 ft., 45 min.

to Watson Path crossing (3175'): 2.4 mi., 1900 ft., 2 hr. 10 min.

to Upper Bruin junction (4150'): 3.3 mi., 2900 ft., 3 hr. 5 min.

to Madison Hut (4825'): 3.8 mi. (6.1 km.), 3550 ft., 3 hr. 40 min.

to Mt. Madison summit (5366') via Osgood Trail: 4.2 mi. (6.8 km.), 4100 ft., 4 hr. 10 min.

Lower Bruin (RMC)

This short trail branches right from the Watson Path on the west bank of Snyder Brook, where the Watson Path crosses the brook at Duck Fall. It ascends rapidly, passes through a campsite area, and turns right uphill away from the brook. It soon turns left and continues to climb rather steeply, then becomes gradual and ends at the Valley Way. In the reverse direction, care should be taken to turn left into the campsite area rather than following a beaten path down to the brook.

Lower Bruin (map 1:E9)
Distance from Watson Path (3325')

to Valley Way (3584'): 0.2 mi. (0.3 km.), 250 ft., 15 min.

Upper Bruin (RMC)

This short but steep trail and its companion, the Lower Bruin, are the remnants of the original trail to Mt. Adams from Randolph. It branches to the right from the Valley Way 3.3 mi. from Appalachia and climbs to the Air Line near treeline, 3.1 mi. from Appalachia.

Upper Bruin (map 1:F9)
Distance from Valley Way (4150')

to Air Line (4400'): 0.2 mi. (0.3 km.), 250 ft., 15 min.

Air Line (AMC /WMNF)

This trail, completed in 1885, is the shortest route to Mt. Adams from a highway. It runs from the Appalachia parking area up Durand Ridge to the summit. The middle section is rather steep, and the sections on the knife-edged crest of Durand Ridge and above treeline are very exposed to weather but afford magnificent views.

The trail, in common with the Valley Way, begins at Appalachia and crosses the former railroad grade to a fork near the edge of the power line clearing, where the Air Line leads right and Valley Way left. In 40 yd., just after the Air Line enters the woods, the Link and the Amphibrach diverge right. The Air Line crosses the Sylvan Way at 0.2 mi. and the Beechwood Way and Beechwood Brook at 0.6 mi. At 0.8 mi. from Appalachia the Short Line diverges right, and at 0.9 mi. the Air Line enters the Randolph Path, coincides with it for 15 yd., then diverges left uphill. At 1.6 mi. there may be water in a spring 30 yd. left (east) of the path (sign). From here the path becomes steeper for 0.5 mi., then eases up and reaches an old and now completely overgrown clearing known as Camp Placid Stream (water unreliable) at 2.4 mi., where the Scar Trail enters on the left, coming up from the Valley Way.

At 3.0 mi. the Air Line emerges from the scrub, and at 3.1 mi. the Upper Bruin comes up left from the Valley Way. The Air Line now ascends over the bare, ledgy crest of Durand Ridge known as the Knife-edge, passing over crags that drop off sharply into King Ravine on the right and descend steeply but not precipitously into Snyder Glen on the left. At 3.2 mi., just south of the little peak called Needle Rock, the Chemin des Dames comes up from King Ravine. The Air Line now climbs steadily up the ridge toward Mt. Adams. From several outlooks along the upper part of this ridge, one can look back down the ridge for a fine demonstration of the difference between the U-shaped glacial cirque of King Ravine on the left (west), and the ordinary V-shaped brook valley of Snyder Glen on the right (east). At 3.5 mi. the Air Line Cutoff diverges left (southeast) to Madison Hut, which is visible from this junction in clear weather.

Air Line Cutoff (AMC). This short branch path provides a direct route 0.2 mi. (10 min.) long, fully sheltered by scrub, from the Air Line high on Durand Ridge to the Valley Way just below Madison Hut. Water can be obtained on this trail not far from the Air Line.

The Air Line now departs a little from the edge of the ravine, going left of the jutting crags at the ravine's southeast corner, and rises steeply. Since there is no single well-beaten footway in this section, following the trail in poor visibility requires great care. At 3.7 mi. it passes the Gateway of King Ravine, where the King Ravine Trail diverges right and plunges between two crags into that gulf. Here there is a striking view of Mt. Madison. In 60 yd. the path enters the Gulfside Trail, turns right, and coincides with it for 70 yd. on the high plateau at the head of the ravine. Then the Air Line diverges to the left (southwest), passing northwest of Mt. Quincy Adams, up a rough way over large, angular stones to the summit of Mt. Adams, where it meets Lowe's Path and the Star Lake Trail.

Air Line (map 1:E9–F9)

Distances from Appalachia parking area (1306')

  to Randolph Path (2000'): 0.9 mi., 700 ft., 50 min.

  to Scar Trail (3700'): 2.4 mi., 2400 ft., 2 hr. 25 min.

  to Chemin des Dames (4475'): 3.2 mi., 3150 ft., 3 hr. 10 min.

  to Air Line Cutoff (4800'): 3.5 mi., 3500 ft., 3 hr. 30 min.

  to Gulfside Trail (5125'): 3.7 mi., 3850 ft., 3 hr. 45 min.

  to Mt. Adams summit (5799'): 4.3 mi. (6.9 km.), 4500 ft., 4 hr. 25 min.

  to Madison Hut (4825') via Air Line Cutoff: 3.7 mi. (6.0 km.), 3550 ft., 3 hr. 40 min.

Scar Trail (RMC)

This trail runs from the Valley Way 2.1 mi. from Appalachia to the Air Line at Camp Placid Stream, an old overgrown clearing 2.4 mi. from Appalachia. It provides a route to Mt. Adams that includes the spectacular views from Durand Ridge while avoiding the steepest section of the Air Line, and it also has excellent outlooks of its own from Durand Scar, reached by the Scar Loop.

The trail ascends moderately and divides 0.2 mi. above the Valley Way. The Scar Loop, an alternative route to the right, climbs up a natural ramp between two sections of rock face, turns sharp left, and 40 yd. above the loop junction reaches Durand Scar, which commands excellent views both up and down the valley of Snyder Brook; those up to Adams and Madison are especially fine. The Scar Loop then scrambles up the ledge, passes another fine outlook up the Snyder Brook valley toward Mt. Madison, and descends slightly to rejoin the main path 0.4 mi. above the Valley Way.

The main Scar Trail, which is easier but misses the best views, bears left at the loop junction. In 0.1 mi. it turns sharp right as the Watson Path diverges left, then climbs across a small brook to the upper loop junction where the Scar Loop re-enters. From here the trail winds its way up the mountainside to the Air Line with mostly moderate grades and good footing.

Scar Trail (map 1:E9)

Distances from Valley Way (2811')

  to Durand Scar (3200') via Scar Loop: 0.2 mi., 400 ft., 20 min.

  to Watson Path (3200') via main trail: 0.3 mi., 400 ft., 20 min.

to Air Line (3700') via either main trail or loop: 1.0 mi. (1.6 km.), 900 ft., 55 min.

Distance from Appalachia parking area (1306')

to Mt. Adams summit (5799') via Valley Way, Scar Trail or Scar Loop, and Air Line: 5.1 mi. (8.2 km.), 4550 ft., 4 hr. 50 min.

Star Lake Trail (AMC)

This trail leads from Madison Hut to the summit of Mt. Adams, much of the way angling up the steep southeast side of Mt. John Quincy Adams. It is often more sheltered from the wind than the Air Line, but it is steep and rough, especially in the upper part where it rock-hops a great deal of large talus and then tackles some fairly challenging rock scrambles on the steep section just below the summit ridge. It may also be difficult to follow when descending.

The trail runs south from the hut, rising gently, and at 0.2 mi. the Parapet Trail branches to the left, passing east of Star Lake and leading to the Parapet and to the Madison Gulf and Osgood trails. The Star Lake Trail passes along the west shore of the lake, and beyond it at 0.3 mi. the Buttress Trail diverges left and descends into the Great Gulf. The Star Lake Trail ascends southwest on the steep southeast slope of Mt. Quincy Adams, leaving the scrub and passing a good spring below the trail. It becomes progressively steeper and rougher as it angles up the steep, rocky slope, and the rocks become larger and require more strenuous hopping. Approaching the crest of a minor easterly ridge, it turns right and climbs very steeply with some fairly difficult scrambles to the top of the shoulder, then ascends moderately along the ridgecrest to the summit of Adams, where it meets Lowe's Path and the Air Line.

Star Lake Trail (map 1:F9)

Distances from Madison Hut (4825')

to Buttress Trail (4900'): 0.3 mi., 100 ft., 10 min.

to Mt. Adams summit (5799'): 1.0 mi. (1.6 km.), 1000 ft., 1 hr.

Short Line (RMC)

This graded path, leading from the Air Line to the King Ravine Trail below Mossy Fall, was made in 1899–1901 by J. Rayner Edmands. It offers direct access to the Randolph Path and to King Ravine from the Appalachia parking area.

The Short Line branches right from the Air Line 0.8 mi. from Appalachia. At 0.5 mi. it unites with the Randolph Path, coincides with it for 0.4 mi., then branches left and leads south up the valley of Cold Brook toward King Ravine, keeping a short distance east of the stream. At 2.7 mi. from Appalachia, the path joins the King Ravine Trail just below Mossy Fall.

Short Line (map 1:E9)

Distances from Air Line junction (1825')

> *to* Randolph Path, lower junction (2275'): 0.5 mi., 450 ft., 30 min.
>
> *to* Randolph Path, upper junction (2500'): 0.9 mi., 700 ft., 50 min.
>
> *to* King Ravine Trail (3150'): 1.9 mi. (3.1 km.), 1350 ft., 1 hr. 40 min.

King Ravine Trail (RMC)

This trail through King Ravine was constructed as a branch of Lowe's Path by Charles E. Lowe in 1876. It is very steep and rough on the headwall of the ravine, but it is one of the most spectacular trails in the White Mtns., offering an overwhelming variety of wild and magnificent scenery. It is not a good trail to descend on account of steep, rough, slippery footing, and extra time should be allowed in either direction due to the roughness—and the views. The trip to the floor of the ravine is well worth the effort even if you do not choose to ascend the headwall. Though the King Ravine Trail begins on Lowe's Path, a more direct route to the most scenic part of the trail leads from Appalachia via the Air Line and Short Line.

The King Ravine Trail diverges left from Lowe's Path 1.8 mi. from US 2 and rises over a low swell of Nowell Ridge. At 0.8 mi. it crosses Spur Brook below some cascades, and in another 0.2 mi. it crosses the Randolph Path at its junction with the Amphibrach, a spot called the Pentadoi. Skirting the east spur of Nowell Ridge, it enters King Ravine and descends slightly, crosses a western branch of Cold Brook, goes across the lower floor of the ravine, and crosses the main stream. At 1.8 mi., near the foot of Mossy Fall (last sure water), it is joined by the Short Line, the usual route of access from the Appalachia parking area. Just above this fall, Cold Brook, already a good-sized stream, gushes from beneath the boulders that have fallen into the ravine.

So far the path has been fairly gradual, but in the next 0.3 mi. it rises about 500 ft. and gains the upper floor of the ravine (about 3700 ft.). The grandeur of the views of the ravine from the jumbled rocks that the trail passes around amply rewards the trip to this area, even if one does not continue up the headwall. The

Chemin des Dames, leading very steeply up to the Air Line, branches sharp left at 2.2 mi. The King Ravine Trail turns sharp right here and then divides in another 10 yd. The main trail, called the Subway, leads to the right from this junction; it is one of the celebrated features of White Mtn. trails, very strenuous, winding through boulder caves over and under boulders ranging up to the size of a small house. The path to the left, called the Elevated, avoids some of the main boulder caves and is thus much easier; it also offers some good views of the ravine. The paths rejoin after 220 yd. on the Subway or 140 yd. on the Elevated, and soon the Great Gully Trail diverges right, then the King Ravine Trail divides again. The left fork is the main trail and the right is a loop path, about 30 yd. shorter than the main trail, that leads to boulder caves near the foot of the headwall which have ice that remains throughout the year. After the paths rejoin at about 0.7 mi. from the Short Line junction, the ascent of the headwall begins. It is very steep and rough, rising about 1100 ft. in 0.5 mi. over large blocks of rock marked with paint. It climbs to the Gateway, where the trail emerges from the ravine between two crags and immediately joins the Air Line just below its junction with the Gulfside Trail. From the Gateway there is a striking view of Mt. Madison. Madison Hut is in sight and can be reached by taking the Gulfside Trail left. The summit of Mt. Adams is 0.6 mi. away via the Air Line.

King Ravine Trail (map 1:E9–F9)

Distances from Lowe's Path (2575')

  to Randolph Path and the Amphibrach (2925'): 1.0 mi., 350 ft., 40 min.

  to Short Line (3150'): 1.8 mi., 700 ft. (rev. 100 ft.), 1 hr. 15 min.

  to foot of King Ravine headwall (3825'): 2.5 mi., 1400 ft., 1 hr. 55 min.

  to Air Line (5100'): 3.1 mi. (5.0 km.), 3700 ft., 2 hr. 45 min.

Distance from Appalachia parking area (1306')

  to summit of Mt. Adams (5799') via Air Line, Short Line, King Ravine Trail, and Air Line: 4.6 mi. (7.4 km.), 4600 ft., 4 hr. 35 min.

Chemin des Dames (RMC)

This trail leads from the floor of King Ravine up its east wall and joins the Air Line just above treeline. It is the shortest route out of the ravine, but is nevertheless very steep and rough, climbing about 750 ft. in 0.4 mi. over gravel and talus, some of which is loose; it is also a difficult trail to descend.

Leaving the King Ravine Trail just before the point where the Subway and Elevated divide, it winds through scrub and boulders to the east side of the ravine, where it climbs steeply over talus through varying amounts of scrub, permitting plentiful though not constant views. About halfway up the steep slope it passes through a boulder cave called Tunnel Rock. Above this there are many fine views out across King Ravine and up to the towering crags of Durand Ridge. High up, the trail angles to the right across the top of a small slide and along the base of a rock face, reaching the Air Line in a little col.

Chemin des Dames (map 1:F9)

Distance from King Ravine Trail (3700')

to Air Line junction (4450'): 0.4 mi. (0.6 km.), 750 ft., 35 min.

Great Gully Trail (RMC)

This remarkably wild and beautiful trail provides an alternative route between the floor of King Ravine and the Gulfside Trail, reaching the latter at Thunderstorm Junction. It is extremely steep and rough, and, like the other trails in the ravine, especially difficult to descend. It is lightly used and sparsely marked, and must be followed with great care. It has one particularly difficult scramble, and should not be attempted in wet or icy conditions.

Leaving the King Ravine Trail just past the point where the Subway and Elevated rejoin, the Great Gully Trail leads across a region damaged by an avalanche, and at 0.3 mi. it reaches the brook that flows down the gully but does not cross it. At the base of an attractive high cascade the trail turns right, away from the brook, and climbs up rocks to the spine of a narrow ridge and to a promontory with a spectacular view. The trail then passes under an overhanging rock on a ledge with a high sheer drop close by on the left, forcing the faint of heart to crawl on their bellies, possibly dragging their packs behind them. After negotiating this pitch the climber is rewarded with a fine view of the cascade. Here the trail turns sharp right and climbs to another viewpoint, then crosses the brook above the cascade at a spot where *Arnica mollis*, an herb of the aster family sought by Thoreau on his trips to the mountains, grows in profusion. The trail continues to climb steeply to treeline, then begins to moderate as it runs almost due south across a grassy area marked by cairns that might be hard to follow in poor visibility, and finally meets the Gulfside and Lowe's Path at Thunderstorm Junction.

Great Gully Trail (map 1:F9)

Distance from King Ravine Trail (3775')

to Gulfside Trail (5490'): 1.0 mi. (1.6 km.), 1700 ft., 1 hr. 20 min.

The Amphibrach (RMC)

This trail runs from the Appalachia parking area to Memorial Bridge, then swings south and parallels Cold Brook to the five-way junction with the Randolph Path and King Ravine Trail known as the Pentadoi. The trail takes its unusual name from the marking that was used when it was first made, about 1883: three blazes—short, long, and short—arranged vertically. It is a good alternative approach to King Ravine or to any point reached via the Randolph Path or the Link—and also, via the Beechwood Way, to points reached by the Short Line, the Air Line, or the Valley Way. Its moderate grade and relative smoothness make it comparatively less difficult when descent after dark is necessary. It is, in fact, one of the kindest trails to the feet in this region.

The Amphibrach, coinciding with the Link, diverges right from the Air Line 100 yd. south of Appalachia, just after entering the woods beyond the power line clearing, and runs west, fairly close to the edge of this clearing. At 0.6 mi. it enters a logging road and bears left, then the Beechwood Way diverges left and, just east of Cold Brook, the Sylvan Way enters left. Cold Brook is crossed at 0.7 mi. on the Memorial Bridge, dedicated to the pioneer pathmakers of the Randolph Valley. Here there is a fine view upstream to Cold Brook Fall, which can be reached in less than 100 yd. by the Sylvan Way or by a spur from the Amphibrach. Just west of the brook the Amphibrach diverges left and the Link continues straight ahead.

The Amphibrach now follows the course of Cold Brook, ascending west of the stream but generally not in sight of the water. In 20 yd. from the junction a side trail branches left 50 yd. to the foot of Cold Brook Fall. Soon the Amphibrach enters the WMNF. At 1.8 mi. the Monaway crosses, leading right to the Cliffway and left to Coldspur Ledges, pleasant flat ledges at the confluence of Cold and Spur brooks reached about 80 yd. from this junction. The Amphibrach soon crosses Spur Brook on the rocks and then bears away to the left (east), ascending the tongue of land between the two brooks, climbing moderately. At 2.2 mi. it crosses the Cliffway, which leads right (west) less than 0.2 mi. to picturesque Spur Brook Fall. Becoming a bit rougher, the Amphibrach continues upward to join the King Ravine Trail a few steps below the Pentadoi.

The Amphibrach (map 1:E9)

Distances from Appalachia parking area (1306')

to Memorial Bridge (1425'): 0.7 mi., 100 ft., 25 min.

to Monaway (2200'): 1.8 mi., 900 ft., 1 hr. 20 min.

to Randolph Path and King Ravine Trail (2925'): 2.6 mi. (4.2 km.), 1600 ft., 2 hr. 5 min.

Cliffway (RMC)

This path begins on the Link, 2.0 mi. from the Appalachia parking area, and runs across the Amphibrach to the Randolph Path, 2.1 mi. from Appalachia. Many of its former viewpoints from the cliffs and ledges of the low swell of Nowell Ridge are now overgrown, but White Cliff still offers an excellent view of the Randolph valley and the Pliny and Crescent ranges to the north. The trail has generally easy grades, but it is very lightly used and poorly marked, and great care is required to follow it.

Leaving the Link, the Cliffway climbs gradually to the fine viewpoint at White Cliff, where it turns sharp right. Here the Ladderback Trail diverges left along the cliff top.

Ladderback Trail (RMC). This short link trail—named for Ladderback Rock, a large boulder in the woods—connects the Monaway to the Cliffway at White Cliff, permitting a short loop hike including White Cliff and the overgrown Bog Ledge and King Cliff. It is rough and must be followed with great care. It leaves White Cliff and in a short distance, as it turns sharp right, it is joined from the left by Along the Brink, a path only 20 yd. long that parallels the Ladderback Trail a few steps closer to the brink of White Cliff. The Ladderback Trail then descends past Ladderback Rock to the Monaway 0.2 mi. (5 min.) from White Cliff.

At 1.0 mi. the Cliffway crosses overgrown Bog Ledge, where a tantalizing glimpse of King Ravine barely filters through the trees, then descends sharply for a short distance and turns left through a boggy area where the path is rather obscure. It then turns sharp left again and soon meets the Monaway at the edge of overgrown King Cliff. The Monaway continues straight, while the Cliffway turns sharp right and drops down a small broken ledge that resembles a ruined stairway, then runs nearly level across a moist area to Spur Brook at the base of picturesque Spur Brook Fall. It then climbs beside the fall, crosses Spur Brook above the fall, and runs across the Amphibrach to the Randolph Path at the west end of Sanders Bridge over Cold Brook.

Cliffway (map 1:E9)

Distances from the Link (2170')

> *to* White Cliff (2484'): 0.7 mi., 300 ft., 30 min.

> *to* Spur Brook Fall (2550'): 1.7 mi., 450 ft., 1 hr. 5 min.

> *to* Randolph Path (2575'): 2.1 mi. (3.4 km.), 450 ft., 1 hr. 15 min.

Monaway (RMC)

This short link trail affords the shortest route from the Randolph area to the Cliffway at White Cliff or King Cliff. It begins on the Amphibrach just below that trail's crossing of Spur Brook. At this junction, a short segment of the Monaway leads downhill (east) about 80 yd. to pleasant Coldspur Ledges at the confluence of Cold and Spur brooks. The main part of the Monaway runs uphill (west) from the Amphibrach at a moderate grade, passes a junction on the right at 0.3 mi. with the Ladderback Trail to White Cliff, then swings south along the brink of overgrown King Cliff and meets the Cliffway. Turn left here for Spur Brook Fall or continue straight to Bog Ledge and White Cliff.

Monaway (map 1:E9)

Distance from the Amphibrach (2200')

   to Cliffway (2550'): 0.4 mi. (0.6 km.), 350 ft., 25 min.

Spur Trail (RMC)

This trail leads from the Randolph Path, just above its junction with the King Ravine Trail, to Lowe's Path just below Thunderstorm Junction. It ascends the east spur of Nowell Ridge near the west edge of King Ravine, passing Crag Camp (cabin). At several points below treeline there are fine outlooks into King Ravine, and above treeline views into King Ravine and up to Madison and Adams are continuous and excellent. The lower part is steep and rough, while the upper part runs completely in the open, very exposed to weather.

The Spur Trail diverges south from the Randolph Path about 100 yd. west of its junction with the King Ravine Trail, on the west bank of Spur Brook, and climbs rather steeply along Spur Brook past attractive cascades and pools. At 0.2 mi. a short branch path leads left 90 yd. to Chandler Fall, where the brook runs down a steep, smooth slab of rock. At 0.3 mi. the Hincks Trail to Gray Knob (cabin) diverges right, and the Spur Trail crosses to the east side of the brook, the last water until Crag Camp. It ascends the spur that forms the west wall of King Ravine, passing a side path that leads left 10 yd. to the Lower Crag, a good outlook to the ravine and Mts. Madison and Adams. At 0.9 mi. it reaches the Upper Crag, where it passes Crag Camp and soon reaches the junction on the right with the Gray Knob Trail, which leads west 0.4 mi. to Gray Knob.

The trail continues to climb quite steeply up the ridge, but not so near the edge of the ravine. At 1.1 mi. a side path (sign, hard to see on the descent) leads left 100 yd. to Knight's Castle, a spectacular perch high up on the ravine wall.

Here the Spur Trail passes into high scrub, and in another 0.2 mi. it breaks out above treeline, commanding excellent views; those to King Ravine are better in the lower portion, while those to Madison and Adams are better higher up. The grade moderates as it joins Nowell Ridge, ascending well to the east of the crest. It finally merges with Lowe's Path 100 yd. below the Gulfside Trail at Thunderstorm Junction.

Spur Trail (map 1:E9–F9)
Distances from Randolph Path (2950')

> *to* Crag Camp (4247'): 0.9 mi., 1300 ft., 1 hr. 5 min.

> *to* Lowe's Path (5425'): 2.0 mi. (3.2 km.), 2500 ft., 2 hr. 15 min.

> *to* Mt. Adams summit (5799') via Lowe's Path: 2.4 mi., 2850 ft., 2 hr. 40 min.

Hincks Trail (RMC)

This short link trail connects the Spur Trail and Randolph Path to Gray Knob cabin. It is fairly steep and rough. It diverges right from the Spur Trail immediately before the crossing of Spur Brook, about 0.3 mi. above the Randolph Path. Soon it comes to the edge of Spur Brook near a pleasant little cascade over mossy rocks, then winds rather steeply up the valley, passing through several patches of woods damaged by wind, to Gray Knob.

Hincks Trail (map 1:E9–F9)
Distance from Spur Trail (3450')

> *to* Gray Knob (4375'): 0.7 mi. (1.1 km.), 950 ft., 50 min.

Gray Knob Trail (RMC)

This trail connects three of the four RMC camps (Crag Camp, Gray Knob, and the Perch) with each other. It also links the upper parts of the Spur Trail and Lowe's, Randolph, and Israel Ridge paths, affording in particular a route from Crag Camp and Gray Knob to Edmands Col without loss of elevation. Grades are mostly easy but the footing is frequently rough, and south of Lowe's Path it has substantial weather exposure, although some sheltering scrub is usually close by.

Leaving the Spur Trail 50 yd. above Crag Camp, it soon works around a jutting ledge at a ridge corner on log bridges, then passes a side path on the right leading down 25 yd. to a good piped spring. It traverses a rough slope nearly on the level; then, soon after passing a spring (left), it ascends a short pitch to Gray Knob cabin (left) at 0.4 mi., where the Hincks Trail enters on the right. The Gray Knob Trail then runs almost level, passing a short spur right to an outlook up to the crag for which the cabin is named. It continues past the Quay, a shortcut path on the right that runs 50 yd. to Lowe's Path at a fine outlook ledge. The Gray Knob Trail crosses Lowe's Path at 0.5 mi. and almost immediately enters scrub of variable height, offering a mixture of shelter and weather exposure with nearly constant views, and begins to climb moderately. At 0.8 mi. the Perch Path diverges right. The Gray Knob Trail continues to climb moderately up the slope, then levels off and runs nearly on contour to the Randolph Path just before its junction with the Israel Ridge Path.

Gray Knob Trail (map 1:F9)

Distances from Spur Trail (4250')

> *to* Lowe's Path (4400'): 0.5 mi., 150 ft., 20 min.
>
> *to* Randolph Path (4825'): 1.7 mi. (2.7 km.), 600 ft., 1 hr. 10 min.

Perch Path (RMC)

This path runs from the Gray Knob Trail across the Randolph Path and past the Perch (lean-to) to the Israel Ridge Path. It diverges right from the Gray Knob Trail 0.3 mi. south of Lowe's Path, then descends moderately and crosses the Randolph Path at 0.3 mi. It soon passes a small brook, then the Perch and its tent platforms, and runs nearly level to the Israel Ridge Path at a sharp curve.

Perch Path (map 1:F9)

Distances from Gray Knob Trail (4550')

> *to* the Perch (4313'): 0.4 mi., 0 ft. (rev. 200 ft.), 10 min.
>
> *to* Israel Ridge Path junction (4300'): 0.5 mi. (0.8 km.), 0 ft., 15 min.

Lowe's Path (RMC)

This trail, cut in 1875–76 by Charles E. Lowe and Dr. William G. Nowell from Lowe's house in Randolph to the summit of Mt. Adams, is the oldest of the mountain trails that ascend the peaks from the Randolph valley. It begins on the south side of US 2, 100 yd. west of Lowe's Store, at which cars may be parked (small fee). It is perhaps the easiest way to climb Mt. Adams, with mostly moderate grades, good footing, and excellent views, but it still has considerable exposure to weather in the part above treeline.

Leaving US 2, Lowe's Path follows a broad woods road for 100 yd., then diverges right at a sign giving the history of the trail. It passes through a logged area, crosses the former railroad grade and then the power lines, and ascends through woods at a moderate grade, heading at first southwest and then southeast, and crossing several small brooks. At 1.7 mi. the Link crosses, and at 1.8 mi. the King Ravine Trail branches left. Lowe's Path continues to ascend, and at 2.4 mi. it passes just to the right of the Log Cabin. Here the Log Cabin Cutoff runs left 0.2 mi. to the Randolph Path, and the Cabin-Cascades Trail to the Israel Ridge Path in Cascade Ravine leaves on the right. Water is always found at the Log Cabin and midway between the cabin and treeline. The path now begins to ascend more seriously, and after crossing the Randolph Path at 2.7 mi. it climbs steeply up to the crest of Nowell Ridge, then moderates. At a fine outlook ledge at 3.2 mi., the short path called the Quay diverges left to Gray Knob Trail, and 30 yd. farther the Gray Knob Trail crosses. The cabin at Gray Knob is 0.1 mi. left (east) by either route.

Soon the trail breaks out of the scrub, and from here onward it is above treeline and completely exposed to wind. Views are very fine. At 4.1 mi., after the steady ascent up Nowell Ridge, the trail reaches the crag known as Adams 4 (5355 ft.), descends into a little sag, then rises moderately again, keeping to the left (east) of Mt. Sam Adams. The Spur Trail joins on the left 100 yd. below Thunderstorm Junction, the major intersection with the Gulfside at 4.4 mi., where the Great Gully Trail also enters on the left. Lowe's Path climbs moderately up the jumbled rocks of the cone of Mt. Adams, passing the junction where the Israel Ridge Path enters right at 4.5 mi. Climbing almost due east, it reaches the summit of Mt. Adams at 4.7 mi., where it meets the Air Line and Star Lake Trail.

Lowe's Path (map 1:E9–F9)

Distances from US 2 near Lowe's Store (1375')

to the Link (2475'): 1.7 mi., 1100 ft., 1 hr. 25 min.

to King Ravine Trail (2575'): 1.8 mi., 1200 ft., 1 hr. 30 min.

to Log Cabin (3263'): 2.4 mi., 1900 ft., 2 hr. 10 min.

to Randolph Path (3600'): 2.7 mi., 2250 ft., 2 hr. 20 min.

to Gray Knob Trail (4400'): 3.2 mi., 3050 ft., 3 hr. 10 min.

to Adams 4 summit (5355'): 4.1 mi., 4000 ft., 4 hr. 5 min.

to Gulfside Trail (5490'): 4.4 mi., 4150 ft., 4 hr. 15 min.

to Mt. Adams summit (5799'): 4.7 mi. (7.6 km.), 4450 ft., 4 hr. 35 min.

Cabin-Cascades Trail (RMC)

One of the earliest trails constructed by the AMC (1881), the Cabin-Cascades Trail leads from the Log Cabin on Lowe's Path to the Israel Ridge Path near the cascades on Cascade Brook, descending almost all the way. It is generally rough with one rather steep, very rough section.

The trail begins at Lowe's Path 2.4 mi. from US 2, opposite the Log Cabin. It runs gradually downhill, with minor ups and downs, crossing the Mystic Stream at 0.3 mi. At 0.7 mi. it enters Cascade Ravine and descends a steep pitch, passing a rocky outlook with a good view to the Castles and Mt. Bowman rising over Israel Ridge. It then begins the final steep, rough descent to Cascade Brook, ending at the Israel Ridge Path just above its upper junction with the Link. The first and highest cascade can be reached by descending on the Israel Ridge Path 60 yd. to the Link, then following it downward to the left another 60 yd. to the ledges at the top of the cascade. The second cascade can be seen by following the Israel Ridge Path about 150 yd. upward.

Cabin-Cascades Trail (map 1:E9–F9)

Distance from Lowe's Path (3263')

   to Israel Ridge Path (2825'): 1.0 mi. (1.6 km.), 0 ft. (rev. 450 ft.), 30 min.

Israel Ridge Path (RMC)

This trail runs to the summit of Mt. Adams from the Castle Trail, 1.3 mi. from US 2 at Bowman (which is 1.0 mi. west of Lowe's Store). It was constructed as a graded path by J. Rayner Edmands beginning in 1892. Although hurricanes and slides have severely damaged the original trail, and there have been many relocations, the upper part is still one of the finest and most beautiful of the Randolph trails. Some brook crossings may be difficult in high water.

From Bowman follow the Castle Trail for 1.3 mi. Here, the Israel Ridge Path branches left and at 0.1 mi. crosses to the east bank of the Israel River. It follows the river, then turns left up the bank at 0.4 mi., where the Castle Ravine Trail diverges right and continues along the river. The Israel Ridge Path bears southeast up the slope of Nowell Ridge into Cascade Ravine, and at 1.2 mi. the Link enters left. The trails coincide for 50 yd., and then the Link diverges right to cross Cascade Brook. The highest of the cascades can be reached by following the Link 60 yd. downhill to the right. In another 60 yd. the Cabin-Cascades Trail enters left from the Log Cabin. The Israel Ridge Path now enters virgin growth. From this point to treeline, the forest has never been disturbed by lumbering, though slides and windstorms have done much damage.

The path continues to ascend on the north side of Cascade Brook to the head of the second cascade at 1.4 mi., where it crosses the brook, turns right downstream for a short distance, then turns left and climbs. It ascends steeply up Israel Ridge, sometimes also called the Emerald Tongue, which rises between Cascade and Castle ravines. At 2.2 mi. the path turns sharp left (east) where the Emerald Trail diverges right to descend steeply into Castle Ravine. Emerald Bluff, a remarkable outlook to the Castles and Castle Ravine that is well worth a visit, can be reached from this junction in less than 0.2 mi. by following the Emerald Trail and a spur path that turns right before the main trail begins its steep descent. The Israel Ridge Path angles up a rather steep slope, then turns right at 2.4 mi. where the Perch Path enters left (east), 0.1 mi. from the Perch. The main path ascends south to treeline, where it joins the Randolph Path at 2.8 mi. The junction of the Gray Knob Trail with the Randolph Path is 80 yd. to the left (north) at this point. For 0.1 mi. the Israel Ridge and Randolph paths coincide, then the Israel Ridge Path branches to the left and, curving east, ascends the southwest ridge of Mt. Adams and joins the Gulfside Trail at 3.3 mi., near Storm Lake. It coincides with the Gulfside for 0.5 mi., running northeast past Peabody Spring to the Adams–Sam Adams col. At 3.8 mi., with the cairn at Thunderstorm Junction in sight ahead, the Israel Ridge Path branches right from the Gulfside Trail, and at 3.9 mi. enters Lowe's Path, which leads to the summit of Mt. Adams at 4.1 mi. The cairns between the Gulfside Trail and Lowe's Path are rather sketchy, so in poor visibility it might be better to follow Lowe's Path from Thunderstorm Junction to the summit.

Israel Ridge Path (map 1:E8–F9)

Distances from Castle Trail (1900')

   to Castle Ravine Trail (2100'): 0.4 mi., 200 ft., 20 min.

   to the Link (2800'): 1.2 mi., 900 ft., 1 hr. 5 min.

   to Perch Path (4300'): 2.4 mi., 2400 ft., 2 hr. 25 min.

   to Randolph Path, lower junction (4825'): 2.8 mi., 2950 ft., 2 hr. 55 min.

   to Gulfside Trail (5225'): 3.3 mi., 3350 ft., 3 hr. 20 min.

   to Mt. Adams summit (5799'): 4.1 mi. (6.7 km.), 3800 ft., 3 hr. 55 min.

   to Edmands Col (via Randolph Path): 3.5 mi., 3050 ft., 3 hr. 15 min.

Emerald Trail (RMC)

This steep, rough, wild trail connects Israel Ridge Path with the Castle Ravine Trail, passing Emerald Bluff, a fine viewpoint to the Castles and Castle Ravine.

The short section between Israel Ridge Path and Emerald Bluff is uncharacteristically gradual and easy. The path is lightly used and blazed, and must be followed with care. Emerald Bluff can be visited from US 2 by a wild, scenic loop hike using the Castle Ravine Trail, Emerald Trail, and Israel Ridge Path.

This trail leaves the combined Castle Ravine Trail and Link 0.2 mi. from their lower junction and descends slightly across a channel of Castle Brook, then climbs a very steep and rough slope. As the trail levels off on the crest of Israel Ridge just south of Emerald Bluff, it turns sharp right. Here a side path turns left and leads 50 yd. to the viewpoint on Emerald Bluff. The main trail runs at easy grades to the Israel Ridge Path 0.2 mi. below its junction with the Perch Path.

Emerald Trail (map 1:F9)

Distances from Castle Ravine Trail and the Link (3225')

   to Emerald Bluff (4025'): 0.5 mi., 800 ft., 40 min.

   to Israel Ridge Path (4050'): 0.6 mi. (1.0 km.), 850 ft., 45 min.

Castle Ravine Trail (RMC)

This scenic, challenging trail diverges from the Israel Ridge Path 1.7 mi. from US 2 at Bowman and leads through wild and beautiful Castle Ravine to the Randolph Path near Edmands Col. While it is reasonably well sheltered except for the highest section, parts of the trail are very rough, especially where it crosses a great deal of unstable talus on the headwall, which makes footing extremely poor for descending or when the rocks are wet. It is lightly used and sparsely marked, and must be followed with great care. Some of the brook crossings may be very difficult at moderate to high water, and the ravine walls are very steep, making rapid flooding likely during heavy rain. Except for very experienced hikers, it would almost certainly prove to be a very difficult escape route from Edmands Col in bad weather conditions.

From Bowman follow the Castle Trail and then the Israel Ridge Path to a point 1.7 mi. from Bowman. Here the Israel Ridge Path turns left up a slope, while the Castle Ravine Trail leads straight ahead near the river. It crosses to the west bank (difficult at high water and not easy at other times) and soon reaches a point abreast of the Forks of Israel, where Cascade and Castle brooks unite to form Israel River. The trail crosses to the east bank of Castle Brook, passes a fine cascade, and recrosses to the west bank. In general, it follows the route of an old logging road, now almost imperceptible. After entering Castle Ravine, the trail crosses to the east bank and climbs at a moderate grade well above the brook. At 1.5 mi. the Link enters from the left, and the two trails coincide, passing at 1.7

mi. the junction with the Emerald Trail left (north) from Israel Ridge. After crossing to the southwest side of the brook in a tract of enchanted cool virgin forest beloved of *musca nigra,* the Link diverges right for the Castle Trail at 1.8 mi., while the Castle Ravine Trail continues up the ravine close to the brook, crossing it several times and once using its bed for a short distance. It recrosses Castle Brook near the foot of the headwall, close to where the stream emerges from under the mossy boulders that have fallen into the ravine, then winds through a rocky area where water can often be heard running underground. The trail then turns left and mounts the steep slope, and at 2.1 mi. it passes under Roof Rock, a large flat-bottomed boulder that would provide some shelter in a rainstorm.

Rising very steeply southeast with very rough footing, the trail soon winds up a patch of bare rocks marked by small cairns and dashes of paint, where there are good views up to the Castles and down the valley northward to the Pliny Range. It re-enters the scrub at a large cairn, and in 100 yd. it re-emerges from the scrub at the foot of a steep slope of very loose rock (use extreme care, particularly when descending). It climbs very steeply to the top of the headwall, marked by cairns and paint on rocks, then ascends gradually in a grassy little valley with little evident footway and sparsely placed cairns, passing Spaulding Spring and joining the Randolph Path (sign) on the rocks to the left of the grassy valley, 0.1 mi. north of Edmands Col.

Descending, follow the Randolph Path north from Edmands Col to the small grassy valley, then descend along it until the line of cairns is found leading down the headwall.

Castle Ravine Trail (map 1:E8–F9)
Distances from Israel Ridge Path (2100')

> *to* the Link, lower junction (3125'): 1.5 mi., 1050 ft., 1 hr. 15 min.
>
> *to* Roof Rock (3600'): 2.1 mi., 1500 ft., 1 hr. 50 min.
>
> *to* Randolph Path (4900'): 2.8 mi. (4.5 km.), 2800 ft., 2 hr. 50 min.

Castle Trail (AMC)

This trail follows the narrow, serrated ridge that runs northwest from Mt. Jefferson, providing magnificent views in a spectacular setting. The part that traverses the Castles is rough with some difficult rock scrambles. In bad weather it can be a dangerous trail due to long and continuous exposure to the northwest winds at and above the Castles. The path was first cut in 1883–84 but most of it has since been relocated.

The Castle Trail begins at Bowman on US 2, 3 mi. west of the Appalachia parking area and 4.2 mi. east of the junction of US 2 and NH 115. Park on the north side of the former railroad grade, cross the track, and follow the right-hand driveway for 150 yd. to where the trail enters woods on the right (signs). The trail circles left, crosses a power line, and at 0.4 mi. crosses the Israel River (may be difficult at high water) at the site of an old bridge.

At 1.3 mi. the Israel Ridge Path branches left (east) toward the brook. The last sure water is a short distance along this trail. The Castle Trail continues to rise above the brook on the northeast flank of Mt. Bowman, and at 1.5 mi. it turns sharp right away from the brook. Now climbing up the slope at a steeper angle, it ascends a long series of rock steps, passes a very large boulder on the left at 2.2 mi., and becomes much steeper for the next 0.3 mi. At 2.5 mi. it enters a blowdown area near the crest of the ridge connecting Mt. Bowman and the Castellated Ridge and becomes almost level. Soon it ascends easily with excellent footing through open woods with abundant ferns, and gradually becomes steeper again as it climbs the main ridge below the Castles to a densely wooded shoulder with a sharp, ragged crest. Here it winds along the steep slopes near the ridgecrest to a little gap at 3.5 mi., where the Link crosses, coming up from Castle Ravine on the left and leading off to the Caps Ridge Trail on the right.

The ridge becomes very narrow and the trail becomes steep and rough with some fairly difficult scrambles. After passing over two ledges with a good outlook from each, it reaches treeline and climbs to the foot of the first and most impressive Castle, a pair of 20-ft. pillars, at 3.8 mi. The view is very fine. The trail leads on past a slightly higher but less impressive Castle, runs through a small col filled with scrub that would provide reasonable shelter in a storm, and continues to ascend over several higher but lesser crags as the Castellated Ridge blends into the main mass of Mt. Jefferson. At 4.5 mi. the Cornice crosses, leading northeast to the Randolph Path near Edmands Col and south to the Caps Ridge and Gulfside trails. The Castle Trail ascends moderately over the rocks and joins the Mount Jefferson Loop in a small flat area just north of the summit crag.

Castle Trail (map 1:E8–F9)

Distances from Bowman (1500')

to Israel Ridge Path (1900'): 1.3 mi., 400 ft., 50 min.

to the Link junction (4025'): 3.5 mi., 2550 ft., 3 hr.

to first Castle (4450'): 3.8 mi., 2950 ft., 3 hr. 20 min.

to Mt. Jefferson summit (5716'): 5.0 mi. (8.1 km.), 4200 ft., 4 hr. 35 min.

Caps Ridge Trail (AMC)

The Caps Ridge Trail makes a direct ascent of Mt. Jefferson from the height-of-land (3008 ft.) on the road through Jefferson Notch, the pass between Mt. Jefferson and the Dartmouth Range. This is the highest trailhead on a public through road in the White Mtns., making it possible to ascend Mt. Jefferson with much less elevation gain than on any other trail to a Presidential peak over 5000 ft., except for a few trails that begin high on the Mt. Washington Auto Rd. However, the Caps Ridge Trail is steep and rough with numerous ledges that require rock scrambling and are slippery when wet, and the upper part is very exposed to weather. Therefore the route is more strenuous than might be anticipated from the relatively small distance and elevation gain. (One should take note that it is not easier to ascend Mt. Washington via the Caps Ridge Trail than via the Jewell Trail, because the descent from Monticello Lawn to Sphinx Col mostly cancels out the advantage of the higher start.)

The south end of Jefferson Notch Rd. is located directly opposite Mt. Clinton Rd. at a crossroads on Base Rd. (the road that runs from US 302 to the Cog Railway). The north end is on Valley Rd. in Jefferson (which runs between US 2 and NH 115). The high point in the notch is about 5.5 mi. from Valley Rd. on the north and 3.4 mi. from Base Rd. on the south. Jefferson Notch Rd. is a good gravel road, open in summer and early fall, but due to the high elevation it reaches, snow and mud disappear late in the spring and ice returns early. Drive with care, since it is winding and narrow in places, and watch out for logging trucks. The southern half is usually in better condition than the northern half, which is often very rough (but still sound).

The trail leaves the parking area and crosses a wet section on log bridges, then ascends steadily up the lower part of the ridge. At 1.0 mi. there is an outcrop of granite on the right that provides a fine view, particularly of the summit of Jefferson and the Caps Ridge ahead. There are several potholes in this outcrop; such potholes are normally formed only by torrential streams, and such streams occur on high ridges like the Ridge of the Caps only during the melting of a glacier, so these potholes indicate to geologists that the continental ice sheet once covered this area.

About 100 yd. beyond this outcrop, the Link enters from the left, providing a nearly level but rough path that runs 1.6 mi. to the Castle Trail just below the Castles, making possible a very scenic though strenuous loop over the Caps and Castles. The Caps Ridge Trail follows the narrow crest of the ridge, becoming steeper and rougher as it climbs up into scrub, and views become more and more frequent. At 1.5 mi. the trail reaches the lowest Cap after a steep scramble up ledges, and it runs entirely in the open from here on. The trail ascends very steeply up the ridge to the highest Cap at 1.9 mi., then continues to climb steeply as the ridge blends into the summit mass. At 2.1 mi. the Cornice enters left, providing a very rough route to the Castle Trail and Edmands Col, and then diverges right in 20 yd., providing an easy shortcut to Monticello Lawn and points to the south. The Caps Ridge Trail continues east, keeping a little south of the crest of the ridge, to the summit of Mt. Jefferson, then descends east 40 yd. to the base of the little conical summit crag, where it meets the Mount Jefferson Loop just above its junctions with the Castle and Six Husbands trails.

Caps Ridge Trail (map 1:F8–F9)

Distances from Jefferson Notch Rd. (3008')

> *to* the Link (3800'): 1.1 mi., 800 ft., 55 min.

> *to* lower Cap (4422'): 1.5 mi., 1400 ft., 1 hr. 25 min.

> *to* upper Cap (4830'): 1.9 mi., 1800 ft., 1 hr. 50 min.

> *to* Cornice (5025'): 2.1 mi., 2000 ft., 2 hr. 5 min.

> *to* Mt. Jefferson summit (5716'): 2.5 mi., 2700 ft., 2 hr. 35 min.

> *to* junction with Mount Jefferson Loop (5700'): 2.6 mi. (4.1 km.), 2700 ft., 2 hr. 40 min.

> *to* Gulfside Trail (5325') via Cornice: 2.5 mi., 2300 ft., 2 hr. 25 min.

> *to* Mt. Washington summit (6288') via Cornice, Gulfside Trail, and Crawford Path: 5.2 mi. (8.4 km.), 3700 ft. (rev. 400 ft.), 4 hr. 25 min.

> *for* loop over Caps and Castles (via Caps Ridge Trail, Castle Trail, Link, and Caps Ridge Trail): 6.7 mi. (10.8 km.), 2850 ft., 4 hr. 25 min.

Boundary Line Trail (WMNF)

This trail connects the Jefferson Notch Rd., 1.4 mi. south of the Caps Ridge Trail, to the new parking area on the Cog Railway Base Rd., 1.1 mi. from its junction with the Jefferson Notch Rd. It thus provides a shortcut between the trailheads of the Caps Ridge Trail and the Jewell Trail or the Ammonoosuc Ravine Trail (Section 1), though it is lightly used and often poorly marked, and must be followed with care. It diverges left (north) from the Jewell Trail 0.4 mi. from the Base Rd. parking lot and runs north, nearly level, closely following the straight boundary line between two unincorporated townships. At 0.5 mi. it crosses Clay Brook, then continues to its end at the Jefferson Notch Rd.

Boundary Line Trail (map 1:F8)

Distance from Jewell Trail (2525')

 to Jefferson Notch Rd. (2525'): 0.9 mi. (1.4 km.), 50 ft. (rev. 50 ft.), 30 min.

Distance from Cog Railway Base Rd. parking area (2500')

 to Caps Ridge Trail (3008') via Jewell Trail, Boundary Line Trail, and Jefferson Notch Rd.: 2.7 mi. (4.3 km.), 550 ft., 1 hr. 40 min.

Jewell Trail (WMNF)

This trail begins at the new parking area on the Cog Railway Base Rd., 1.1 mi. from its junction with Jefferson Notch Rd. Base Rd. is the road that leads from US 302 to the Cog Railway Base Station at Marshfield. The trail ascends the unnamed ridge that leads west from Mt. Clay and ends at the Gulfside Trail high on the west slope of Mt. Clay, 0.3 mi. north of the Clay-Washington col and 1.4 mi. north of the summit of Mt. Washington. The grade is constant but seldom steep, there are no rock scrambles, and the footing is generally very good below treeline and only moderately rough and rocky in the last section below the Gulfside. It provides the easiest route to Mt. Washington from the west, featuring a great length of ridge walking above treeline with fine views, but this part is also greatly exposed to the weather and offers no shelter between the summit and treeline. In bad weather, or if afternoon thunderstorms threaten, it is safer to descend from Mt. Washington via Lakes of the Clouds Hut and the Ammonoosuc Ravine Trail, despite the steep and slippery footing on the latter trail; descent by the Jewell Trail offers much easier footing and thus may be preferred when the weather cooperates. The trail is named for Sergeant Winfield S. Jewell, once an observer for the Army Signal Corps on Mt. Washington, who perished on the Greeley expedition to the Arctic in 1884.

 The Jewell Trail enters the woods directly across the road from the parking area, crosses the Ammonoosuc River at 0.1 mi., then swings northeast and ascends at an easy grade. At 0.4 mi. the Boundary Line Trail diverges left, while the Jewell Trail ascends the crest of the low ridge between the Ammonoosuc River and Clay Brook, joining the old route of the trail at 1.0 mi. The old path (sign) can be followed right 0.4 mi. to the Base Station. From the junction the main trail descends slightly to Clay Brook, crosses on a footbridge, then climbs northeast by long switchbacks. At 2.0 mi. it passes through a blowdown patch at the edge of the steep wall of Burt Ravine, where there are interesting though limited views. It then swings somewhat to the north side of the ridge and climbs east, staying well below the ridgecrest until near the treeline. Reaching treeline at about 3.0 mi., it zigzags at a moderate grade with rough, rocky footing up the ridgecrest, which quickly becomes less prominent and blends into the slope of Mt. Clay. At 3.5 mi. the trail swings to the right away from what remains of the ridge and angles up the slope at an easy grade to the Gulfside Trail. For Mt. Washington, follow the Gulfside right. In good weather, the fine views from the cliffs of Mt. Clay can be reached fairly easily by a scramble directly up the rocks above the junction.

Jewell Trail (map 1:F8–F9)

Distances from Cog Railway Base Rd. parking area (2500')

   to Clay Brook crossing (2850'): 1.1 mi., 400 ft., 45 min.

   to Gulfside Trail (5400'): 3.7 mi. (5.9 km.), 2950 ft., 3 hr. 20 min.

   to Mt. Washington summit (6288') via Gulfside Trail: 5.1 mi. (8.2 km.), 3900 ft., 4 hr. 30 min.

Pine Mountain Trail (WMNF)

This new trail is a restoration of an abandoned section of the Pine Link that once linked an old route of the Appalachian Trail in Gorham with the Northern Presidentials via Pine Mtn. The trailhead can be reached by turning west onto Promenade St. from NH 16 at a point 0.1 mi. south of its junction with US 2 at the eastern edge of the Gorham business district. Follow this road past a small cemetery on the right and an equipment shed on the left at 0.5 mi., then a larger cemetery on the right. The road becomes gravel at 0.6 mi. and continues to a gravel pit at 0.7 mi. from NH 16, where cars may be parked (no sign).

The trail first follows an old gravel road that starts on the left side of the pit, then swings right and then left uphill above and behind the open pit, passing through an overgrown section of the pit until it intersects a snowmobile trail along the natural gas pipeline clearing at 0.2 mi. Here trail signs will be found. The trail follows an old road (also a snowmobile trail) for 0.3 mi., bearing left twice. The trail then leaves this road on the right (sign) and passes through a recently logged area, then swings left onto a small ridge (arrow) and ascends. At 1.3 mi. the trail descends briefly, enters the WMNF, and angles up the northwest slope of Pine Mtn., crossing several old logging roads. At 2.1 mi. there is a spur path leading left to a limited view to the north. At 2.3 mi. the grade eases and the trail swings left under utility lines; here an unmarked path ascends to the left along the power line clearing and in 0.1 mi. reaches the north summit and the Horton Center worship area, where there is an excellent view from a rocky pinnacle called Chapel Rock. Hikers are welcome to enjoy the views and meditate, but are requested to avoid disturbing religious activities that may be in progress there. After crossing the power lines, the main trail bears right and ascends to the old Pine Mountain Trail at 2.4 mi. A right turn here leads to the Pine Mountain Road in 0.1 mi. Turning left, the main trail leads to the summit of Pine Mtn. and the junction with the Ledge Trail.

Pine Mountain Trail (map 5:E10)
Distance from gravel pit on Promenade Rd. (825')

   to Pine Mtn. summit (2405'): 2.7 mi. (4.3 km.), 1600 ft., 2 hr. 10 min.

Pine Mountain Road

This trail uses the private automobile road to the Horton Center on Pine Mtn. most of the way to the summit of Pine Mtn. (The WMNF has plans to extend the Ledge Trail so that, at some point in the future, hikers will no longer need to use this road.) The road begins a little northwest of the highest point of the Pinkham B (Dolly Copp) Rd., opposite the Pine Link trailhead (where parking is available), 2.4 mi. from US 2 at the foot of the big hill west of Gorham and 1.9 mi. from NH 16 near Dolly Copp Campground. It is closed to public vehicular use and has a locked gate, but is open to the public as a foot trail to the summit; hikers should watch out for automobiles. The Ledge Trail, a foot trail over the top of the south cliff, diverges from the road and runs to the summit; it is frequently used to make a loop over the summit. The views from the summit are fine, both to the much higher surrounding peaks and to the valleys of the Androscoggin, Moose, and Peabody rivers. The Douglas Horton Center, a center for renewal and education operated by the New Hampshire Conference of the United Church of Christ (Congregational), occupies a tract of 100 acres on the summit. The center consists of six buildings and an outdoor chapel on the more precipitous northeast peak (which has excellent views and can be reached by a spur path from the new Pine Mountain Trail). Although camping is not permitted on this mountain, day hikers are welcome to use the trails and appreciate the views but should be careful to avoid disturbing religious activities that may be in progress there.

   The road runs northeast from Pinkham B Rd. across the col and winds its way up the south and west flanks of the mountain. At 0.9 mi. the Ledge Trail branches right to climb to the summit by way of the south cliff. About 1.6 mi. from Pinkham B Rd., the trail turns to the right off the gravel road and follows the old tractor road, which swings south past a spur on the left to a northeast outlook and ascends easily to the summit, where it meets the Ledge Trail.

Pine Mountain Road (map 1:E10)
Distances from Pinkham B (Dolly Copp) Rd. (1650')

> *to* Ledge Trail (1800'): 0.9 mi., 200 ft., 35 min.

> *to* Pine Mtn. summit (2405'): 2.0 mi. (3.2 km.), 800 ft., 1 hr. 25 min.

> *for* loop to Pine Mtn. via Ledge Trail with return via Pine Mountain Road: 3.5 mi., 800 ft., 2 hr. 10 min.

Ledge Trail (WMNF)

This trail runs to the summit of Pine Mtn. from the Pine Mountain Road (a private road, closed to public vehicles), making possible an attractive loop with a sporty ascent past excellent views and an easy return. It diverges from the Pine Mountain Rd. 0.9 mi. from the Pinkham B (Dolly Copp) Rd., runs under the south cliff, and then climbs up to the east of the cliff to its top, with beautiful views to the south and west. It then continues to meet the Pine Mountain Road at the summit.

Ledge Trail (map 1:E10)
Distance from Pine Mountain Road (1800')

> *to* summit (2405'): 0.6 mi. (1.0 km.), 600 ft., 35 min.

Town Line Brook Trail (RMC)

This good but steep path gives access to Triple Falls from Pinkham B (Dolly Copp) Rd., 1.4 mi. southeast of the former railroad grade crossing. Triple Falls are beautiful cascades on Town Line Brook named Proteus, Erebus, and Evans. The watershed is steep and the rainwater runs off very rapidly, so the falls should be visited during or immediately after a rainfall.

Town Line Brook Trail (map 1:E10)
Distance from Pinkham B (Dolly Copp) Rd. (1475')

> *to* the end of the path above Triple Falls (1725'): 0.2 mi. (0.3 km.), 250 ft., 15 min.

Sylvan Way (RMC)

The Sylvan Way departs from the Link and Amphibrach at Memorial Bridge, 0.7 mi. from the Appalachia parking area, and leads over Snyder Brook to the Howker Ridge Trail just above Coosauk Fall. Leaving Memorial Bridge, after 80 yd. it turns left away from Cold Brook at the base of Cold Brook Fall, where a beaten path continues ahead up the brook. The Sylvan Way crosses the Beechwood Way at 0.1 mi., the Air Line at 0.6 mi., and the Valley Way 100 yd. farther. At 0.7 mi., within a space of 30 yd., the Maple Walk enters left, the Fallsway crosses, the Sylvan Way crosses Snyder Brook on ledges 60 yd. above Gordon Fall, and the Brookbank crosses. From here the Sylvan Way ascends gradually, crossing the Randolph Path at 1.1 mi. It then passes through a recently logged area, where it must be followed with care, then enters the WMNF and continues to the Howker Ridge Trail.

Sylvan Way (map 1:E9)
Distance from Memorial Bridge (1425')

  to Howker Ridge Trail (1625'): 1.7 mi. (2.7 km.), 250 ft., 1 hr.

Fallsway (RMC)

The Fallsway is an alternative route to the first 0.6 mi. of the Valley Way, following close to Snyder Brook and passing several falls. From the east end of the Appalachia parking area it goes east for 60 yd., then turns right on a gravel road and crosses the former railroad grade and the power lines. Here the Brookbank diverges left as the Fallsway enters the woods and continues straight ahead. At 0.2 mi. from Appalachia, the path reaches Snyder Brook and soon passes Gordon Fall, where the Gordon Fall Loop diverges right. In 60 yd. the Sylvan Way crosses and the Maple Walk enters right as the trail continues up the brook in hemlock woods. Lower and Upper Salroc Falls are passed, and soon the Fallsway enters the Valley Way at 0.6 mi., below Tama Fall. In 30 yd. the Fallsway leaves the Valley Way and passes Tama Fall, where the Brookbank enters, and in another 60 yd. the Fallsway ends at the Valley Way.

Fallsway (map 1:E9)
Distance from Appalachia parking area (1306')

  to Valley Way junction above Tama Fall (1700'): 0.7 mi. (1.2 km.), 400 ft., 35 min.

Brookbank (RMC)

The Brookbank diverges from the Fallsway near the former railroad grade and rejoins the Fallsway above Tama Fall. It leaves the Fallsway at the edge of the woods just beyond the power lines, 0.1 mi. from the Appalachia parking lot. It runs parallel to the railroad grade for about 0.1 mi., then crosses Snyder Brook, turns sharp right (south), and enters the woods. It runs up the east side of the brook, passing Gordon Fall, Sylvan Way, Lower and Upper Salroc Falls, and Tama Fall. Above Tama Fall it recrosses the brook and re-enters the Fallsway.

Brookbank (map 1:E9)

Distance from lower junction with Fallsway (1310')

  to upper junction with Fallsway (1675'): 0.7 mi. (1.2 km.), 350 ft., 30 min.

Maple Walk (RMC)

The Maple Walk diverges left from the Valley Way a few yards from the Appalachia parking area and soon passes a junction, where the Gordon Fall Loop diverges left and runs 70 yd. to the Fallsway at Gordon Fall. The Maple Walk continues to the junction of the Fallsway and the Sylvan Way just above Gordon Fall.

Maple Walk (map 1:E9)

Distance from Valley Way (1310')

  to Sylvan Way and Fallsway (1400'): 0.2 mi. (0.3 km.), 100 ft., 5 min.

Beechwood Way (RMC)

This path runs from the Link and Amphibrach 0.6 mi. from Appalachia to the Valley Way 0.9 mi. from Appalachia, just below its junctions with the Brookside and the Randolph Path. It follows a good logging road with moderate grades. It leaves the Amphibrach, crosses the Sylvan Way in 100 yd. and then the Air Line at 0.6 mi., and ends at the Valley Way.

Beechwood Way (map 1:E9)

Distance from Link and Amphibrach (1400')

  to Valley Way (1850'): 0.8 mi. (1.3 km.), 450 ft., 40 min.

Section 3

The Franconia, Twin, and Willey Ranges

The central region of the White Mtns. is a great wooded area studded with fine peaks, with no through highways and only a few gravel roads near the edges. The vast expanses of unbroken forest compensate for mountains that are, except for the Franconia Range and the cliffs of Mt. Bond, generally less rugged than the Presidentials. The region is bordered on the west and northwest by US 3 (and I-93), on the north by US 302, on the east by NH 16, and on the south by the Kancamagus Highway (NH 112). Section 3 includes the west and northwest portion of this central region, including the Franconia Range, Twin Range, and Willey Range. Most of the Pemigewasset Wilderness is also covered here. Please note that in this book the term Pemigewasset Wilderness is used strictly to refer to the officially designated Wilderness area, not to the somewhat broader but less clearly defined area that has traditionally borne this name. Section 3 is divided from Section 4, which covers the eastern portion of the central region, by the Wilderness Trail (described in Section 3), and by a continuation of the line of the Wilderness Trail east from its terminus at Stillwater Junction, over the plateau between Mt. Bemis and Mt. Willey, to US 302 in Crawford Notch. There are only two points of contact between trails described in Section 3 and those described in Section 4: first, where the Cedar Brook Trail (Section 4) meets the Wilderness Trail, just east of the latter's crossing of the East Branch of the Pemigewasset River on a suspension bridge; and second, where the Carrigain Notch Trail (Section 4) meets the Wilderness Trail and Shoal Pond Trail at Stillwater Junction. All of Section 3 is covered by the AMC Franconia–Pemigewasset map (map #2).

In this section the Appalachian Trail follows the Liberty Spring Trail and the Franconia Ridge Trail over Little Haystack Mtn. and Mt. Lincoln to Mt. Lafayette. It then runs along the Garfield Ridge Trail to Galehead Hut, passing close to the summit of Mt. Garfield along the way. After following the Twinway over South Twin Mtn. and Mt. Guyot and passing near the summit of Zealand

Mtn., it reaches Zealand Falls Hut, then takes the Ethan Pond Trail to US 302 in Crawford Notch.

FRANCONIA NOTCH AND THE FLUME

Franconia Notch lies between the Franconia Range on the east and the Kinsman Range and Cannon Mtn. on the west. The region includes many interesting and accessible natural features such as the Profile (Old Man of the Mountain); Indian Head; Profile, Echo, and Lonesome lakes; and the Flume, the Pool, and the Basin. The Flume and the Pool are described below; the others, which are west of US 3, are discussed in Section 5. From the Flume area north to Echo Lake, the valley bottom and lower slopes on both sides lie within Franconia Notch State Park. Information regarding trails and other facilities is available during the summer and fall tourist season at the Flume Visitor Center at the south end of the park, and throughout the year (except for the late fall and early spring "off-seasons") at the Cannon Mtn. Tramway. The New Hampshire Department of Parks (NHDP) maintains an information booth during the summer and on fall weekends at the Lafayette Place trailhead parking area to provide information about weather, trail conditions, facilities, and regulations. Hiker parking is available at the Flume Visitor Center, Basin, Lafayette Place, Old Man, Cannon Mtn. Tramway, and Echo Lake parking lots. There is no parking at the Appalachian Trail crossing near the former Whitehouse Bridge site, which is now reached by the Whitehouse Trail from the hikers' parking lot on US 3 just north of the Flume Visitor Center. A paved bike path runs the entire length of the notch from the parking area at the Flume to the Skookumchuck Trail and is available for pedestrian use, though those on foot should be careful not to unnecessarily impede bicycle traffic. Concord Trailways has bus service from Boston at Logan Airport and South Station to Lincoln and Franconia, which may operate only on weekends. In the summer, connections to trailheads may be made by using the AMC hiker shuttle bus.

The Flume, one of the best-known features in the Franconia region, is a narrow gorge that can be reached from the Flume Visitor Center by graded trails or by an NHDP bus. A network of graded trails connects points of interest, and a boardwalk runs up through the Flume itself. It is open to visitors from about May 15 to October 15; there is an admission fee for the Flume and the Pool during this time. In the Flume, one can see broad ledges worn smooth by the action of the water and scoured by an avalanche in June 1883 that swept away the once-famous suspended boulder. Avalanche Falls at the upper end is also worth visiting. The Pool is an interesting pothole formation in the Pemigewasset River, more than 100 ft. in diameter and 40 ft. deep; it can be reached by a path of about 0.5 mi. from the visitor center. In the winter this is an easy, popular, and beautiful area to walk in, and there is no admission fee; however, several of the boardwalks are removed for the season, restricting access to some parts of the Flume.

GEOGRAPHY

The **Pemigewasset Wilderness** is a vast forested area surrounded by high mountains and drained by the **East Branch of the Pemigewasset River.** A bit more than a century ago it was an untracked wilderness, but lumber operations in the period from about 1890 to 1940 left it a virtual wasteland, logged and burned almost to total destruction, often referred to as the "so-called Pemigewasset Wilderness." Though the birch forests that clothe its slopes in many areas still testify subtly to the devastation of the not-so-distant past, the beauty of the area is almost completely restored, and the act of Congress establishing the Pemigewasset Wilderness has once again officially entitled it to the name of Wilderness. The history of the logging, and of the railroads that made it possible, is recounted in C. Francis Belcher's *Logging Railroads of the White Mountains,* published by AMC Books but now out of print.

The main part of the Pemigewasset Wilderness, north of the East Branch, is divided into two lobes by the long ridge of Mt. Bond.

The **Franconia Range** and the **Twin Range** are the two high ridges that form a great horseshoe enclosing the western lobe of the Pemigewasset Wilderness. This lobe is drained by Franconia and Lincoln brooks, which almost encircle the long wooded ridge called Owl's Head Mtn. Starting at the southwest end of the horseshoe and running almost due north, the main ridge rises over several lower mountains to the high peaks of the Franconia Range: Mts. Flume, Liberty, Little Haystack, Lincoln, and Lafayette, the high point on the ridge. Swinging around to the east, the ridge crosses Mt. Garfield, Galehead Mtn., and South Twin Mtn., passing its lowest point (other than the ends), about 3400 ft., between Garfield and Galehead. Rising again to South Twin Mtn., where a major spur ridge leads north to North Twin Mtn., the main ridge runs southeast to Mt. Guyot. Here another major spur, Zealand Ridge, runs east. Before Zealand Ridge comes to an abrupt end at Zealand Notch, another ridge runs north from it over the **Little River Mtns.,** which consist of Mt. Hale and the Sugarloaves. From Mt. Guyot the main ridge runs south over Mt. Bond and Bondcliff before dropping to the East Branch. To the east of the great horseshoe lies the **Willey**

Range, forming the west wall of Crawford Notch and the east wall of the broad, flat eastern lobe of the Pemigewasset Wilderness. The **Rosebrook Range** is a lower northwest spur of the Willey Range. Running south from the Willey Range is the broad plateau that connects the Willey Range to the Nancy Range and Mt. Carrigain. Slopes rise steeply to this plateau from Crawford Notch, bearing the highest waterfalls in the White Mtns., then incline gradually westward into the Pemigewasset Wilderness.

The **Franconia Range** ranks second among the ranges of the White Mtns. only in elevation. Its sharp, narrow ridge contrasts strikingly with the broad, massive Presidential Range. **Mt. Lafayette** (5260 ft.) was called "Great Haystack" on Carrigain's map of 1816 but was renamed in honor of the Marquis de Lafayette in gratitude for his assistance in the War of Independence. The highest part of the ridge, from Mt. Lafayette over **Mt. Lincoln** (5089 ft.) to **Little Haystack Mtn.** (4780 ft.), rises well above treeline. This part of the ridge is a Gothic masterpiece. Especially when seen from the west (particularly from North Kinsman), it suggests the ruins of a gigantic medieval cathedral. The peaks along the high, serrated ridge are like towers supported by soaring buttresses that rise from the floor of the notch. Part of the ridge between Lincoln and Little Haystack is a knife-edge with interesting rock formations. To the south rise the sharp, ledgy peaks of **Mt. Liberty** (4459 ft.) and **Mt. Flume** (4328 ft.), which are connected to each other and to Little Haystack Mtn. by long, graceful parabolic ridges. Both these peaks have very fine views in all directions, particularly to the east to rugged Mt. Bond and over the vast expanse of the Pemigewasset Wilderness. **Eagle Cliff** (3420 ft.), a northwesterly spur of Mt. Lafayette, is remarkable for its sheer cliffs and for the "Eaglet," a detached finger of rock that can be seen best from the vicinity of the Cannon Mtn. Tramway parking area. At the south end of the range, the ledges of **Little Coolidge Mtn.** (2421 ft.) overlook the town of Lincoln. There is no maintained trail to these ledges, but they can be reached by bushwhacking from Lincoln village.

The **Twin Range** is connected to the Franconia Range by the **Garfield Ridge.** This jumbled, mostly densely wooded ridge runs north from Lafayette, then swings to the east and culminates in the fine rocky peak of **Mt. Garfield** (4500 ft.), which rises like a sphinx watching over the valleys of Franconia and Lincoln brooks to the south and provides one of the finest views in the White Mtns., including a spectacular panorama of the higher Franconias to the south. After passing **Galehead Mtn.** (4024 ft.), a wooded hump with a restricted but excellent view of the Franconias, the ridge reaches **South Twin Mtn.** (4902 ft.), where the views from the open summit are similar to Garfield's and equally fine, but from a different perspective. The summit of **North Twin Mtn**. (4761 ft.) is densely wooded, but a ledge almost at the summit on the west and another a short distance northeast provide magnificent views. **Haystack Mtn.** (2713 ft.), also sometimes called the **Nubble,** is a small but very prominent rocky peak that rises sharply from the lower end of North Twin's north ridge; it has no maintained trail.

The main ridge now swings southeast, then south, crossing the bare summits of **Mt. Guyot** (4580 ft.) and **Mt. Bond** (4698 ft.), and then **Bondcliff** (4265 ft.), the fine series of crags and ledges southwest of Mt. Bond. These three peaks, in addition to the spur of Bond called **West Bond** (4540 ft.), command views unequaled in the White Mtns. for their expansive vistas of forests and mountains with virtually no sign of roads or buildings. For example, from the summit of Mt. Bond only the summit buildings on Mt. Washington and the Loon Mtn. ski slopes give visible evidence of human intrusion. Arnold Guyot was the geographer who made the first accurate map of the White Mtns., supplanting the previous best map, the work of Prof. G. P. Bond of Harvard; thus the most remote set of peaks in the White Mtns. bear the names of these two pioneer mapmakers. Guyot himself named several important White Mtn. peaks, including Mt. Tripyramid. Wherever there were mountains to be explored, Guyot could be found—there are also mountains named for him in several other ranges, including the Great Smoky Mtns., the Colorado Rockies, and the Sierra Nevada of California, and even a crater on the moon bears his name.

The interior of the western lobe is a relatively narrow valley surrounded by steep slopes and occupied mainly by the long wooded ridge of **Owl's Head Mtn.** (4025 ft.), one of the more remote major peaks in the White Mtns., named for the shape of its south end. The summit is wooded, but the great western slide provides some very fine views up to the Franconia Ridge and the isolated valley of Lincoln Brook.

The high point of the **Zealand Ridge, Zealand Mtn.** (4260 ft.), is wooded and viewless, but there is a magnificent outlook from **Zeacliff**, which overlooks Zealand Notch and the eastern part of the Pemigewasset Wilderness from the east end of the ridge. Originally called the New Zealand Valley, presumably owing to its remoteness, the name was shortened to Zealand for the convenience of the railroad and post office. Much of **Zealand Notch** and the area to the north was reduced to a jumble of seared rock and sterile soil by a series of intensely hot fires around 1900. It has now made a reasonably complete recovery, a remarkable and outstanding testimony to the infinite healing powers of nature. Nowhere else in New England is there a better example of regeneration after disaster. At the height-of-land in Zealand Notch is **Zealand Pond,** which has beaver dams as well as outlets at both ends; its waters eventually flow to the sea in both the Merrimack and the Connecticut rivers.

The **Little River Mtns.,** lying between the **Zealand River** and **Little River,** offer excellent and easily attained panoramas of the surrounding summits from **Mt. Hale** (4054 ft.), **Middle Sugarloaf** (2539 ft.), and **North Sugarloaf** (2310 ft.). Mt. Hale was named for the Rev. Edward Everett Hale, author of the well-known patriotic tale "The Man without a Country."

The **Willey Range** is a high ridge that rises sharply out of Crawford Notch. The ridge is rather narrow with steep sides, giving it a rugged appearance from many viewpoints, but its crest undulates gently for about 2.5 mi. with relatively broad summits and shallow cols. The main peaks (from south to north) are **Mt. Willey** (4285 ft.), named for the family whose members were all killed by a landslide that swept down its east face in 1826; **Mt. Field** (4340 ft.), named for Darby Field, leader of the first recorded ascent of Mt. Washington; and **Mt. Tom** (4051 ft.), named for Thomas Crawford, younger brother of Ethan Allen Crawford and fellow White Mtn. innkeeper. All these peaks are wooded to the top, but Willey has fine outlooks to the east over Crawford Notch and to the south into the eastern lobe of the Pemigewasset Wilderness. Tom temporarily offers good views from a blowdown patch at the summit; a similar blowdown patch on Field is now almost completely grown up. A westerly spur of the Willey Range ends abruptly at Zealand Notch with the cliffs of **Whitewall Mtn.** (3405 ft.). **Mt. Avalon** (3442 ft.) and **Mt. Willard** (2850 ft.) are easterly spurs offering fine views for relatively little exertion; in fact probably no other spot in the White Mtns. affords so grand a view as Mt. Willard for so little effort. The **Rosebrook Range** continues northwest from Mt. Tom over **Mt. Echo** (3084 ft.), **Mt. Stickney** (3070 ft.), **Mt. Rosebrook** (3004 ft.), and **Mt. Oscar** (2746 ft.). There are no hiking trails on these peaks, but the summit ledges of Mt. Oscar, with magnificent views over the Zealand Valley, can be reached by following ski slopes of the Bretton Woods Ski Area to a point close to the col between Mt. Oscar and Mt. Rosebrook. The ridge can then be followed northwest (no maintained trail) about 0.3 mi. to the ledges.

Arethusa Falls and **Ripley Falls** are situated on brooks that flow down the steep west side of Crawford Notch; in times of high water, these waterfalls can be quite spectacular. Between them stands **Frankenstein Cliff,** named for George L. Frankenstein, an artist whose work in the White Mtns. was once well known. A network of trails connects these features and affords the opportunity for a variety of shorter day hikes.

The interior of the eastern lobe is broad and relatively flat, with no important mountains, but **Thoreau Falls, Ethan Pond,** and **Shoal Pond** are interesting features. This region was the site of the most extensive logging in the White Mtns.; in the wake of the devastation that resulted, part of the eastern lobe was commonly referred to as the Desolation region.

HUTS

For information concerning AMC huts or Crawford Notch Hostel, including opening and closing schedules, contact the Reservation Office, Pinkham Notch Visitor Center, PO Box 298, Gorham, NH 03581 (603-466-2727) or www.outdoors.org.

Greenleaf Hut (AMC)

Greenleaf Hut was built in 1929 and is located at about 4200 ft. at the junction of the Old Bridle Path and Greenleaf Trail on Mt. Lafayette, overlooking Eagle Lake. It is reached from US 3 via the Greenleaf Trail (2.5 mi.) or Old Bridle Path (2.9 mi.), and is 1.1 mi. from the summit of Mt. Lafayette and 7.7 mi. from Galehead Hut. The hut accommodates 48 guests and is open to the public from mid-May to mid-October (caretaker basis in May). Pets are not permitted in the hut.

Galehead Hut (AMC)

Galehead Hut, built in 1932, is located at about 3800 ft. on a little hump on the Garfield Ridge, near the Twinway and the Garfield Ridge, Frost, and Twin Brook trails. It is reached in 4.6 mi. from the Gale River Loop Rd. (FR 25 and FR 92) via the Gale River and Garfield Ridge trails. It accommodates 38 guests and is open to the public from mid-May to mid-October (caretaker basis in May). Pets are not permitted in the hut.

Zealand Falls Hut (AMC)

This hut, built in 1932, is located at about 2700 ft. beside Zealand Falls on Whitewall Brook, at the north end of Zealand Notch, near the Twinway and the Zealand and Ethan Pond trails. It is reached from the Zealand Rd. via the Zealand Trail in 2.8 mi.; in winter Zealand Rd. is closed, which increases the approach walk to 6.3 mi. The hut accommodates 36 guests and is open to the public from early June to mid-October on a full-service basis, and on a caretaker basis for the rest of the year. Pets are not permitted in the hut.

Crawford Notch Hostel (AMC)

Located at the head of historic Crawford Notch in the heart of the White Mountain National Forest, the Crawford Notch Hostel provides low-cost overnight accommodations for hikers and other visitors. The hostel, consisting of buildings that were once part of the Crawford House grand hotel complex, is located on NH 302 about 20 mi. west of North Conway and 10 mi. east of Twin Mountain village. The nearby Crawford Notch Depot Visitor Center is also operated by the AMC during the summer hiking season.

The main hostel building, known as the Shapleigh studio (since it was once the studio of a well-known White Mountain artist named Shapleigh), includes a natural history library; a meeting room for small groups; a small store that stocks last-minute hiker supplies and souvenir items; toilet facilities and showers; and a complete kitchen with stove, refrigerator, and sinks. It is heated in fall, winter, and spring. These amenities make it an excellent choice for families and small groups, and a convenient base to begin or end any hut experience. There is a caretaker in residence. Two adjacent cabins, heated by propane, each accommodate twelve persons. Winter workshops in snowshoeing, backcountry skiing, and ice climbing are regularly conducted with the hostel as a base. Operating as a traditional hostel, the Shapleigh building is open to the public from 6:00–10:00 A.M. and from 4:00–9:30 P.M. Overnight lodging is available year-round, and AMC members receive a discount. Reservations are encouraged, and may be made through the Pinkham Notch Visitor Center Reservation Office (603-466-2727).

The Depot Visitor Center, the former train station renovated by the AMC in 1984, houses educational displays, an information desk, and a small store that stocks last-minute hiker supplies and souvenir items. It is also a major stop and transfer point for the AMC hiker shuttle bus, which operates during the summer and early fall, and serves as a depot for the excursion trains that run on the Crawford Notch line during the tourist season.

The AMC's Crawford Notch property includes a major parking area for trailheads on the west side of the highway, including the Mount Willard Trail and the A-Z Trail. Parking next to the Depot Visitor Center is limited to 30 minutes. Parking for hostel overnight guests is located between the main building and the cabins. Parking for the Crawford Path is available in the USFS lot (recreational permit required) located just off Mt. Clinton Rd. near its junction with US 302.

CAMPING

Pemigewasset Wilderness

Wilderness regulations, intended to protect Wilderness resources and promote opportunities for challenge and solitude, prohibit use of motorized equipment or mechanical means of transportation of any sort. Camping and wood or charcoal fires are not allowed within 200 ft. of any trail except at designated campsites. Camping is prohibited within 200 ft. of the Wilderness Trail and the East Branch of the Pemigewasset River (including islands) from the Wilderness boundary up to the Thoreau Falls Trail junction, the Thoreau Falls Trail from the Wilderness Trail junction to the East Branch crossing, and the Bondcliff Trail from the Wilderness Trail crossing up to the second crossing of Black Brook. Camping and fires are also prohibited within a quarter-mile of 13 Falls Campsite, Thoreau Falls, the site of the former Desolation Shelter, Galehead Hut, Garfield Ridge Campsite, and Guyot Campsite (the last three facilities are outside, but less than a quarter-mile from, the Wilderness boundary). Hiking and camping group size must be no larger than 10 people. Camping and fires are also prohibited above treeline (where trees are less than 8 ft. tall), except in winter, when camping is permitted above treeline in places where snow cover is at least two feet deep, but not on any frozen body of water.

Forest Protection Areas

The WMNF has established a number of Forest Protection Areas (FPAs)—formerly known as Restricted Use Areas—where camping and wood or charcoal fires are prohibited throughout the year. The specific areas are under continual review, and areas are added to or subtracted from the list in order to provide the greatest amount of protection to areas subject to damage by excessive camping, while imposing the lowest level of restrictions possible. A general list of FPAs in this section follows, but since there are often major changes from year to year, one should obtain current information on FPAs from the WMNF.

(1) No camping is permitted above treeline (where trees are less than 8 ft. tall), except in winter, and then only in places where there is at least two feet of snow cover on the ground—but not on any frozen body of water. The point where the restricted area begins is marked on most trails with small signs, but the absence of such signs should not be construed as proof of the legality of a site.

(2) No camping is permitted within a quarter-mile of any trailhead, picnic area, or any facility for overnight accommodation such as a hut,

cabin, shelter, tentsite, or campground, except as designated at the facility itself. In the area covered by Section 3, camping is also forbidden within a quarter-mile of Garfield Pond and within 200 ft. of Black Pond.

(3) No camping is permitted within 200 ft. of certain trails, except at designated sites. In 1997, designated trails included those portions of the Old Bridle Path, Falling Waters Trail, and Liberty Spring Trail that are not in Franconia Notch State Park (where trailside camping is absolutely prohibited). No camping is permitted within a quarter-mile of the Wilderness Trail (Lincoln Woods Trail) or the East Branch of the Pemigewasset River (including islands) from the Kancamagus Highway to the Wilderness boundary near the Franconia Brook Trail junction, or along Franconia Brook from its confluence with the East Branch to the second island (including islands). The one usual exception to this rule, the Franconia Brook Campsite, has been closed for rehabilitation.

(4) No camping is permitted on WMNF land within a quarter-mile of certain roads (camping on private roadside land is illegal except by permission of the landowner). In 1997, these roads included US 302 west of Bartlett NH, the Zealand Rd., the Kancamagus Highway, the south branch of the Gale River Rd. (FR 92) from US 3 to the Garfield Trail trailhead, and the Haystack Rd. (FR 304) from US 3 to the North Twin Trail trailhead.

Franconia Notch State Park

Camping and fires are prohibited in Franconia Notch State Park, except at Lafayette Place Campground (fee charged).

Established Trailside Campsites

Camp 16 Campsite (WMNF), located at the junction of the Wilderness and Bondcliff trails, has been closed, and camping here is prohibited.

13 Falls Tentsite (AMC), located at the junction of the Franconia Brook, Lincoln Brook, and Twin Brook trails, has nine tent pads. The former shelter has been removed.

Franconia Brook Campsite (WMNF), located on the Wilderness Trail 2.8 mi. from the Kancamagus Highway, was closed for rehabilitation in 1997, and camping is not permitted at this site unless the WMNF decides to officially reopen it at some future date. Present plans call for a new campsite to be constructed on the other side of the East Branch just off the East Branch Truck Road, near the Wilderness boundary and approximately opposite the former site.

Guyot Campsite (AMC), located on a spur path that diverges from the Bondcliff Trail between its junction with the Twinway and the summit of Mt. Bond, has an open log shelter accommodating twelve, with six tent platforms in addition. There is a fine spring that is reliable in summer but may not always flow in the cold seasons. A caretaker is in charge during the summer months, and there is a fee.

Liberty Spring Tentsite (AMC), located near a fine spring on the Liberty Spring Trail 0.3 mi. below its junction with the Franconia Ridge Trail, has ten tent platforms. A caretaker is in charge during the summer months, and there is a fee. The former shelter was removed in 1970.

Garfield Ridge Campsite (AMC), located near a fine spring on a short spur path from the Garfield Ridge Trail 0.4 mi. east of Mt. Garfield, has seven four-person tent platforms and one twelve-person shelter. A caretaker is in charge during the summer months, and there is a fee.

Ethan Pond Campsite (AMC) is located near the shore of Ethan Pond, about 2.8 mi. from the Willey House Station. There is a shelter (capacity eight) and five tent platforms (capacity twenty). Water (which is not fit to drink without treatment) may be obtained where the side path crosses the inlet brook. A caretaker is in charge during the summer months, and there is a fee.

Trails on Franconia Ridge and the West Slopes

Trails on Garfield Ridge and the North Slopes

Trails on the Twin–Zealand Range

List of Trails	Map	Page
Twinway	2:G6–G7	163
North Twin Spur	2:G6	166
North Twin Trail	2:G6	166
Zeacliff Trail	2:G7	167
Zealand Trail	2:G7	168

Trails on Mount Hale and the Sugarloaves

List of Trails	Map	Page
Lend-a-Hand Trail	2:G7–G6	168
Hale Brook Trail	2:G7–G6	169
Sugarloaf Trail	2:F6	169
Trestle Trail	2:F6	170

Trails on the Willey Range

List of Trails	Map	Page
Around-the-Lake Trail	2:G8–G7	171
Mount Willard Trail	2:G8	171
Avalon Trail	2:G8–G7	172
A–Z Trail	2:G7	173
Ethan Pond Trail	2:H8–G7	173
Kedron Flume Trail	2:G8	174
Willey Range Trail	2:G8–G7	175
Mount Tom Spur	2:G7	176

Trails in the Arethusa Falls Region

List of Trails	Map	Page
Arethusa Falls Trail	2:H8	176
Bemis Brook Trail	2:H8	177
Arethusa–Ripley Falls Trail	2:H8	177
Frankenstein Cliff Trail	2:H8	178

Trails in the Pemigewasset Wilderness

THE TRAILS

Franconia Ridge Trail (AMC)

This trail follows the backbone of the ridge that runs south from Mt. Lafayette, beginning on the summit of Lafayette at the junction of the Garfield Ridge and Greenleaf trails; passing over Mt. Lincoln, Little Haystack Mtn., Mt. Liberty, and Mt. Flume; and ending at a junction with the Flume Slide Trail and the Osseo Trail just south of Mt. Flume. Much work has been done to define and stabilize the trail and to reduce erosion; hikers are urged to stay on the trail to save the thin alpine soils and fragile vegetation. From Mt. Lafayette to the Liberty Spring Trail this trail is part of the Appalachian Trail.

Caution: The portion of the Franconia Ridge above treeline from Lafayette to Little Haystack does not involve any unusually difficult or hazardous climbing, but it is almost constantly exposed to the full force of any storms and is dangerous in bad weather or high winds. In particular, due to the sharpness, narrowness, and complete exposure to weather of the ridgecrest on Lafayette, Lincoln, and Little Haystack, the danger from lightning is unusually great, and this portion of the ridge should be avoided when electrical storms appear to be brewing.

The following description of the path is in the southbound direction (away from Mt. Lafayette). See below for a description of the path in the reverse direction.

Leaving the summit of Mt. Lafayette, the trail descends at a moderate grade to the first sag, where it passes through a small scrub patch that might provide some shelter in bad weather. It then climbs across a prominent hump, descends to another sag, and climbs again to the summit of Mt. Lincoln at 1.0 mi. From there it descends sharply, keeping mostly just to the east of the crest of the knife-edged ridge between Mt. Lincoln and Little Haystack Mtn., which has steep slopes on both sides. At the base of this knife-edge section, the ridge becomes nearly level and much broader, and the trail continues on the ridgecrest in the open to the junction with the Falling Waters Trail on the right at 1.7 mi., just under the summit rock of Little Haystack Mtn.

The Franconia Ridge Trail continues to the south end of the Little Haystack summit ridge, enters the scrub and descends steeply over ledges for a short distance, then moderates and follows the long, fairly gradual ridge to a junction with the Liberty Spring Trail on the right at 3.5 mi. There is water at Liberty Spring Campsite, 0.3 mi. down this trail. The Franconia Ridge Trail ascends to the rocky summit of Mt. Liberty at 3.8 mi., reaching the summit from the east, then makes a hairpin turn and descends to the east just a few yards south of its ascent route. The descent is steep at first, then moderates. The trail passes through two small sags and ascends to the open summit of Mt. Flume, then descends along the edge of the west-facing cliff (use extra caution in windy or slippery conditions) and enters the woods. It ends 0.1 mi. south of the summit of Flume in a little col, at the junction with the Osseo Trail straight ahead and the Flume Slide Trail on the right.

Franconia Ridge Trail (map 2:H5)
Distances from Mt. Lafayette summit (5260')

   to Mt. Lincoln summit (5089'): 1.0 mi., 300 ft., 40 min.

   to Falling Waters Trail (4760'): 1.7 mi., 350 ft., 1 hr.

   to Liberty Spring Trail (4260'): 3.5 mi., 550 ft., 2 hr.

   to Mt. Liberty summit (4459'): 3.8 mi., 750 ft., 2 hr. 15 min.

   to Mt. Flume summit (4328'): 4.9 mi., 1200 ft., 3 hr. 5 min.

   to Flume Slide Trail/Osseo Trail junction (4240'): 5.0 mi. (8.0 km.), 1200 ft., 3 hr. 5 min.

Franconia Ridge Trail (AMC) [in reverse]

The trail begins 0.1 mi. south of the summit of Mt. Flume in a little col, at the junction with the Osseo Trail and the Flume Slide Trail. It climbs out of the scrub and ascends along the edge of the west-facing cliff (use extra caution in windy or slippery conditions). From Mt. Flume it descends across a lesser knob, crosses two small sags, and climbs at a progressively steepening grade to the open summit of Mt. Liberty at 1.2 mi., reaching the summit from the east, then makes a hairpin turn and descends to the east just a few yards north of its ascent route. It then continues to descend across ledges into the woods and passes a junction with the Liberty Spring Trail on the left at 1.5 mi. There is water at Liberty Spring Campsite, 0.3 mi. down this trail. The trail continues down and then up the long, gradual ridge, becoming rather steep over ledges as it approaches the treeline on Little Haystack. At 3.4 mi. it reaches the junction with the Falling Waters Trail on the left, just under the summit rock of Little Haystack Mtn.

From Little Haystack the trail follows a broad, nearly level ridgecrest in the open to the foot of Mt. Lincoln, then ascends sharply, keeping mostly just to the east of the crest of the knife-edged ridge between Mt. Lincoln and Little Haystack Mtn., which has steep slopes on both sides. After passing over the summit of Mt. Lincoln at 4.1 mi., the trail descends to a sag, climbs across a prominent hump, then descends to another sag, where it passes through a small scrub patch that might provide some shelter in bad weather. The trail then climbs at a moderate grade to the summit of Mt. Lafayette, where it meets the Greenleaf Trail on the left (west) and the Garfield Ridge Trail, which continues straight ahead along the north ridge.

Franconia Ridge Trail (map 2:H5)

Distances from Flume Slide Trail/Osseo Trail junction (4240')

   to Mt. Flume summit (4328'): 0.1 mi., 100 ft., 5 min.

   to Mt. Liberty summit (4459'): 1.2 mi., 650 ft., 55 min.

   to Liberty Spring Trail (4260'): 1.5 mi., 650 ft., 1 hr. 5 min.

   to Falling Waters Trail (4760'): 3.4 mi., 1350 ft., 2 hr. 25 min.

   to Mt. Lincoln summit (5089'): 4.1 mi., 1750 ft., 2 hr. 55 min.

   to Mt. Lafayette summit (5260'): 5.0 mi. (8.0 km.), 2200 ft., 3 hr. 35 min.

Flume Slide Trail (AMC)

This trail runs from the Liberty Spring Trail, 0.6 mi. from its junction with the Cascade Brook and Whitehouse trails, to the Franconia Ridge Trail 0.1 mi. south of the summit of Mt. Flume. It is an extremely steep, rough trail, with polished rock slabs that are extremely slippery when wet (and they are nearly always wet, due to the many seep springs on these steep slopes). It is not recommended for descent, and its use is discouraged in wet weather when the ledges are more than ordinarily dangerous. Views from the trail itself are very limited, as it ascends a part of the old slide that is almost completely overgrown. The route over the slide is marked by paint on the ledges.

The trail leaves the Liberty Spring Trail on an old logging road that contours to the right (south). Soon the trail swings left off the logging road in a more easterly direction and begins a gradual ascent on the southwest shoulder of Mt. Liberty, with occasional slight descents. At 0.3 mi. it crosses a small brook, and about 0.1 mi. farther on it crosses a large brook on stepping-stones. After rising from the brook bed, the trail climbs gradually, crossing several more small brooks. At 1.5 mi. the trail crosses a small brook, bears right after 40 yd., then turns left in another 20 yd., avoiding a beaten path straight ahead. At 1.9 mi. it crosses Flume Brook for the first time and follows it closely, making several more crossings of the main brook and its branches. In this region the trail should be followed carefully; in general it keeps close to the brook. As the trail ascends, it leaves the remnants of the brook behind, and slide gravel becomes more prominent underfoot. At 2.6 mi. there is a restricted view up to the summit crags of Mt. Flume. Now the climbing begins in earnest, and the first ledges are soon reached. While on the slide be careful not to dislodge stones that might endanger climbers below, and beware of rockfall from above. After struggling up the smooth, wet ledges with occasional outlooks, the trail turns left at 3.1 mi. and continues on a steep, rocky, rooty path through the woods to the main ridgecrest, where the Franconia Ridge Trail leads left (north) and the Osseo Trail leads right (south). A few steps before this junction is reached, a beaten path leads 30 yd. right (south) to a small crag with an excellent view.

Flume Slide Trail (map 2:H4–H5)

Distances from Liberty Spring Trail (1800')

to foot of slide (2850'): 2.6 mi., 1050 ft., 1 hr. 50 min.

to Franconia Ridge Trail (4240'): 3.3 mi. (5.3 km.), 2450 ft., 2 hr. 55 min.

Liberty Spring Trail (AMC)

This trail climbs past Liberty Spring Campsite to the Franconia Ridge Trail 0.3 mi. north of Mt. Liberty. It begins on the Franconia Notch bike path just north of the bridge over the Pemigewasset River, near the site of the former Whitehouse Bridge parking area (parking no longer available); the Cascade Brook Trail (Section 5) begins just south of this bridge. This trailhead is reached from the hikers' parking lot on US 3 just north of the Flume Visitor Center by the Whitehouse Trail or from the Basin parking areas by the paved bike path. The trail ascends steadily and rather steeply at times, but the footing, while not smooth, is always reasonably good. This trail is part of the Appalachian Trail.

From the bike path, the trail climbs moderately northeast through hardwood growth. At 0.4 mi. it turns sharp right, joining the old main logging road from the former Whitehouse mill, and soon levels off. At 0.6 mi. the Flume Slide Trail leaves right (south). The Liberty Spring Trail bears left, ascending gradually, and crosses a fairly large brook at 1.1 mi. It then climbs moderately, turns sharp left off the logging road at 1.4 mi., then turns sharp right at 2.2 mi. and climbs more steeply by switchbacks. In places the footing is rough. At 2.6 mi. the trail reaches Liberty Spring Campsite (3800 ft.) on the left and the spring (last sure water) on the right. The path then ascends fairly steeply through conifers and ends in 0.3 mi. at the Franconia Ridge Trail; turn left (north) for Mt. Lafayette, right (south) for Mt. Liberty.

Liberty Spring Trail (map 2:H4–H5)

Distances from Whitehouse Trail (1400')

> *to* sharp left turn (2350'): 1.4 mi., 950 ft., 1 hr. 10 min.

> *to* Liberty Spring Campsite (3870'): 2.6 mi., 2450 ft., 2 hr. 30 min.

> *to* Franconia Ridge Trail (4260'): 2.9 mi. (4.7 km.), 2850 ft., 2 hr. 55 min.

> *to* Mt. Liberty summit (4459') via Franconia Ridge Trail: 3.2 mi. (5.1 km.), 3050 ft., 3 hr. 10 min.

Whitehouse Trail (AMC)

This trail connects the hikers' parking lot off US 3 just north of the Flume Visitor Center with the Liberty Spring Trail and the Cascade Brook Trail (Section 5), near the former parking area site at Whitehouse Bridge (where parking is no longer available). Thus it is the usual route to these trails for hikers who arrive in the area by automobile.

The trail leaves the parking lot and runs north parallel to the main highway, passing over a minor ridge. It descends to the bike path at 0.6 mi. and follows it to the junction with the Cascade Brook Trail, which diverges left just before (south of) the bridge over the Pemigewasset River. The Whitehouse Trail continues across the bridge and officially ends in another 50 yd. where the Liberty Spring Trail diverges right off the bike path.

Whitehouse Trail (map 2:H4)

Distance from Flume hikers' parking area (1400')

> *to* Liberty Spring Trail (1400'): 0.8 mi. (1.3 km.), 100 ft. (rev. 100 ft.), 25 min.

Falling Waters Trail (AMC)

This trail begins at the Lafayette Place parking lots (located on each side of the Franconia Notch Parkway) and climbs to the Franconia Ridge Trail at the summit of Little Haystack Mtn., passing numerous waterfalls in its lower part. It is steep and rough in parts and better for ascent than descent, but not normally dangerous unless there is ice on the ledgy sections near the brook.

The trail leaves the parking lot on the east side of the parkway (reached from the west side by a paved path 0.1 mi. long) near the hiker information booth, in common with the Old Bridle Path, and passes through a clearing into the woods. In 0.2 mi. it turns sharp right from the Old Bridle Path and immediately crosses Walker Brook on a bridge, then leads away from the brook heading southeast and east. At 0.7 mi. it crosses Dry Brook (use care if the water is high), turns left and follows up the south bank to a beautiful cascade known as Stairs Falls. Above the falls the trail passes beneath Sawteeth Ledges and crosses the brook to the north bank just below Swiftwater Falls, which descend 60 ft. in a shady glen. Continuing on the north bank, the trail climbs on graded switchbacks for a short distance to an old logging road that rises gradually in the narrow gorge of Dry Brook. The trail leaves the old road at a steep embankment, ascends in graded sections to Cloudland Falls (80 ft.), and climbs steeply to a viewpoint overlooking the head of the falls and out over the valley toward Mt. Moosilauke on the skyline.

At the head of Cloudland Falls are two small (25 ft.) falls practically facing each other. The one to the south, which emerges from the woods, is on the branch of Dry Brook that runs down from Little Haystack, while the other is on the Mt. Lincoln branch. The trail continues steeply on the north bank of the Mt. Lincoln branch, soon crosses to the south bank, crosses back to the north side, climbs to and follows an old logging road, and recrosses to the south bank at 1.6 mi. Here it swings to the right, away from the brook, and angles uphill on an old logging road. After a view (cut) to the west, the trail takes the left fork of the old road, then diverges to the left off the road and ascends the ridge via a series of switchbacks.

At the south end of the last switchback, at 2.8 mi., a side trail leads south downhill about 100 yd. to the northeast corner of Shining Rock, where there are fine views north and west over Franconia Notch. This steep granite ledge, more than 200 ft. high and nearly 800 ft. long, is usually covered with water from springs in the woods above and, seen from the mountains across the notch, shines like a mirror in the sunlight. *Caution:* Climbing Shining Rock without rock-climbing equipment and training is extremely dangerous. This steep ledge is wet and very slippery; several accidents involving serious injuries have occurred here to hikers who tried to scramble up the rock.

From the Shining Rock spur junction, the main trail continues north for a short distance, then turns right and climbs in a nearly straight line to the summit of Little Haystack.

Falling Waters Trail (map 2:H4–H5)

Distances from Lafayette Place parking area (1780')

to Dry Brook (2000'): 0.7 mi., 200 ft., 25 min.

to highest crossing of Dry Brook (2860'): 1.6 mi., 1100 ft., 1 hr. 20 min.

to Shining Rock side path (4130'): 2.8 mi., 2350 ft., 2 hr. 35 min.

to Franconia Ridge Trail (4760'): 3.2 mi. (5.1 km.), 3000 ft., 3 hr. 5 min.

Old Bridle Path (AMC)

This trail runs from the Lafayette Place parking lots (located on each side of the Franconia Notch Parkway) to Greenleaf Hut, where it joins the Greenleaf Trail. It affords fine views, particularly down into and across Walker Ravine, from many outlooks in the upper half of the trail. For much of its length it follows the route of a former bridle path.

The trail leaves the parking lot on the east side of the parkway (reached from the west side by a paved path 0.1 mi. long) near the hiker information booth, in common with the Falling Waters Trail, and passes through a clearing into the woods. In 0.2 mi. the Falling Waters Trail turns sharp right and immediately crosses Walker Brook on a bridge, while the Old Bridle Path continues along the brook for 50 yd., then swings left away from the brook and starts to climb at a moderate grade. At 1.1 mi. it enters the WMNF (sign) and soon comes to the edge of the bank high above Walker Brook, then swings away again. At 1.6 mi. it makes a sharp left turn with rock steps at the edge of the ravine, where there is a glimpse of Mt. Lincoln through the trees, then turns right and soon gains the ridge. At 1.9 mi. the first of the spectacular outlooks from the brink of the ravine is reached, and several more are passed in the next 0.1 mi. The trail then begins to ascend the steep part of the ridge, sometimes called Agony Ridge (a name originated by hut people who had to pack heavy loads up this steep section). At 2.4 mi. there is an unmarked side path that diverges right, passes two fine outlooks, and rejoins the main trail 40 yd. above the lower junction. Still climbing, the main trail passes a view to Cannon Mtn., Kinsman Mtn., and Mt. Moosilauke from a grassy spot, then crosses a small sag through a patch of dead trees and soon reaches Greenleaf Hut.

Old Bridle Path (map 2:H4–H5)

Distances from Lafayette Place parking area (1780')

  to sharp turn with rock steps (3020'): 1.6 mi., 1250 ft., 1 hr. 25 min.

  to Greenleaf Hut (4220'): 2.9 mi. (4.7 km.), 2450 ft., 2 hr. 40 min.

  to Mt. Lafayette summit (5260') via Greenleaf Trail: 4.0 mi. (6.4 km.), 3600 ft., 3 hr. 50 min.

Greenleaf Trail (AMC)

This trail runs from the Cannon Mtn. Tramway parking lot on the west side of the Franconia Notch Parkway to Greenleaf Hut, where the Old Bridle Path joins, and thence to the summit of Mt. Lafayette, where it ends at the junction of the Franconia Ridge and Garfield Ridge trails. Until it reaches the hut, the trail is almost completely in the woods with few views, except when it traverses Eagle Pass, a wild, narrow cleft between Eagle Cliff and the west buttress of Mt. Lafayette that has many interesting cliff and rock formations.

From the parking lot, the trail follows a sidewalk through the parkway underpass, turns left and follows the northbound ramp for 25 yd., then turns right across a ditch into the woods (sign). It runs roughly parallel to the parkway, crosses the gravel outwash of a slide at 0.7 mi., then climbs moderately by numerous switchbacks to Eagle Pass at 1.5 mi. The path leads east nearly on the level through the pass, crosses a small overgrown gravel slide, then swings more to the south and rises by long switchbacks, angling up a northwest shoulder over loose stones that are slippery in wet weather. It finally reaches the top of the shoulder and continues a short distance to reach Greenleaf Hut at 2.7 mi.

At the hut, the Old Bridle Path enters on the right from Lafayette Place. The Greenleaf Trail heads toward Lafayette, enters the scrub, and dips slightly, passing south of the Eagle Lakes, two picturesque shallow tarns (though the upper lake is rapidly becoming a bog). The trail rises, passing over several minor knobs, and at 3.2 mi. swings left after passing an open, sandy area on the right. It soon climbs above the scrub into the open and ascends at a moderate grade, sometimes on rock steps between stone walls. At 3.6 mi. the trail bears left around a ledge on the right side of the trail from which a remarkable spring issues, very small but fairly reliable. Now the trail turns right and soon reaches the summit of Mt. Lafayette. Here the Garfield Ridge Trail leads north and then northeast to Mt. Garfield, Garfield Ridge Campsite, Galehead Hut, and the Twin Range. To the south the Franconia Ridge Trail leads to Liberty Spring Campsite and the Franconia Notch Parkway via the Liberty Spring Trail, or to the Kancamagus Highway via the Osseo Trail.

Greenleaf Trail (map 2:G4–H5)

Distances from Cannon Mtn. Tramway parking area (1980')

   to Eagle Pass (2980'): 1.5 mi., 1000 ft., 1 hr. 15 min.

   to Greenleaf Hut (4220'): 2.7 mi., 2250 ft., 2 hr. 25 min.

   to Mt. Lafayette summit (5260'): 3.8 mi. (6.1 km.), 3300 ft., 3 hr. 35 min.

Skookumchuck Trail (WMNF)

This is an attractive and less frequently used route from the Franconia Notch area to the north ridge of Mt. Lafayette, 0.8 mi. below the summit. It begins on US 3 at a parking lot that also serves the north end of the Franconia Notch bike path, located 0.3 mi. south of the junction of US 3 and NH 141 and just north of the point where US 3 divides at its northern junction with I-93 and the Franconia Notch Parkway.

Leaving the parking lot, the trail runs south, leading gradually away from the highway and crossing a grassy logging road three times. At 1.1 mi. it reaches the old route at the edge of Skookumchuck Brook and follows the brook upstream. At 1.8 mi. it crosses a small tributary on a rock bridge, climbs steeply away from the brook on rock steps, then continues up the valley well above the brook at a moderate grade through a fine stand of birch. At 2.5 mi. it passes a small brook (unreliable) and continues to a shoulder at 3.6 mi., where there is a glimpse ahead to Lafayette's north peak. After a short gradual descent, the trail angles to the north at mostly easy grades, then emerges above treeline just before reaching its junction with the Garfield Ridge Trail.

Skookumchuck Trail (map 2:G4–G5)

Distances from US 3 (1700')

> *to* Garfield Ridge Trail (4680'): 4.3 mi. (6.9 km.), 3000 ft., 3 hr. 40 min.

> *to* Mt. Lafayette summit (5260') via Garfield Ridge Trail: 5.1 mi. (8.2 km.), 3550 ft., 4 hr. 20 min.

Garfield Ridge Trail (AMC)

This trail runs from the junction with the Franconia Ridge and Greenleaf trails at the summit of Mt. Lafayette to the Twinway near Galehead Hut, traversing the high ridge that joins the Franconia Range to South Twin Mtn. and passing near the summit of Mt. Garfield on the way. The footway is rough, and there are numerous minor gains and losses of elevation, so the trail is more difficult than one might gather from a glance at the map. Extra time should be allowed, particularly by those carrying heavy packs.

The following description of the path is in the northbound direction (away from Mt. Lafayette). See below for a description of the path in the reverse direction.

The trail leaves the summit of Mt. Lafayette and runs north along the ridge over the north peak to a junction on the left with the Skookumchuck Trail on a shoulder at 0.8 mi. Swinging northeast, the Garfield Ridge Trail then drops steeply to timberline and continues to descend at a moderate grade near the crest of the ridge to a sag at 1.7 mi. From here the trail passes over a series of knobs (one of which has a short side path on the right that leads to a fine outlook over the Pemigewasset Wilderness) on a large wooded hump. It descends the rough end of the hump to a tangled col at 2.5 mi., then climbs gradually toward Mt. Garfield. At 3.0 mi., near the foot of Garfield's cone, it passes to the right (south) of Garfield Pond, then climbs steeply, with many rock steps, to its high point on Mt. Garfield at 3.5 mi.; the bare summit and its old fire tower foundation, with magnificent views, is 60 yd. to the right (south) over open ledges. The trail then descends steeply, bearing right at 3.7 mi. at the junction where the Garfield Trail enters on the left from US 3. At 3.9 mi., where there is a small brook beside the trail, a side path runs left 200 yd. to the AMC Garfield Ridge Campsite, passing a fine outlook over the Franconia Brook valley on the way. The main trail continues to descend, crosses a small brook, and reaches a major col at 4.4 mi., where the Franconia Brook Trail leaves right and descends to 13 Falls. From this junction the Garfield Ridge Trail runs along the bumpy ridge, sometimes north and sometimes south of the crest, with many ups and downs. After passing a good outlook to Owl's Head Mtn. and descending a steep pitch, it reaches the junction where the Gale River Trail enters from the left at 6.0 mi. The Garfield Ridge Trail now contours around the steep slope of Galehead Mtn., then turns right and climbs to a junction with the Twinway and the Frost Trail 40 yd. from Galehead Hut; turn right for the hut.

Garfield Ridge Trail (map 2:H5–G6)

Distances from Mt. Lafayette summit (5260')

to Skookumchuck Trail (4680'): 0.8 mi., 0 ft., 25 min.

to high point on Mt. Garfield (4460'): 3.5 mi., 1200 ft., 2 hr. 20 min.

to Garfield Ridge Campsite spur path (3900'): 3.9 mi., 1200 ft., 2 hr. 35 min.

to Franconia Brook Trail (3420'): 4.4 mi., 1200 ft., 2 hr. 50 min.

to Gale River Trail (3390'): 6.0 mi., 1500 ft., 3 hr. 45 min.

to Galehead Hut (3780'): 6.6 mi. (10.7 km.), 1900 ft., 4 hr. 15 min.

Garfield Ridge Trail (AMC) [in reverse]

From its junction with the Twinway and the Frost Trail 40 yd. from Galehead Hut, the Garfield Ridge Trail descends moderately, then swings left and contours around the steep slope of Galehead Mtn. to the junction where the Gale River Trail enters from the right at 0.6 mi. From there the Garfield Ridge Trail climbs a steep pitch to a good outlook to Owl's Head Mtn., then runs along the bumpy ridge, sometimes north and sometimes south of the crest, with many ups and downs, to a major col at 2.2 mi. where the Franconia Brook Trail leaves left and descends to 13 Falls. From this junction the Garfield Ridge Trail ascends moderately, crosses a small brook, and soon becomes much steeper. At 2.7 mi., where there is a small brook beside the trail, a side path runs right 200 yd. to the AMC Garfield Ridge Campsite, passing a fine outlook over the Franconia Brook valley on the way. The main trail continues to climb steeply past a junction at 2.9 mi. where the Garfield Trail enters on the right from US 3, and then reaches its high point on Mt. Garfield at 3.1 mi.; the bare summit and its old fire tower foundation, with magnificent views, is 60 yd. left (south) over open ledges. The trail then descends steeply, with many rock steps, and passes to the left (south) of Garfield Pond at 3.6 mi., near the foot of Garfield's cone. After descending gradually to a tangled col at 4.1 mi., it ascends the rough end of a large wooded hump and passes over a series of knobs (one of which has a short side path on the left that leads to a fine outlook over the Pemigewasset Wilderness). It reaches a sag at 4.9 mi., ascends near the crest of the ridge at a moderate grade, then climbs steeply past the timberline to a junction on the right with the Skookumchuck Trail on a shoulder at 5.9 mi. It then follows the crest of the ridge over the north peak of Mt. Lafayette to the main summit, where the Greenleaf Trail enters on the right and the Franconia Ridge Trail continues straight ahead.

Garfield Ridge Trail (map 2:H5–G6)

Distances from Galehead Hut (3780')

    to Gale River Trail (3390'): 0.6 mi., 0 ft., 20 min.

    to Franconia Brook Trail (3420'): 2.2 mi., 350 ft., 1 hr. 15 min.

    to Garfield Ridge Campsite spur path (3900'): 2.7 mi., 850 ft., 1 hr. 45 min.

    to high point on Mt. Garfield (4460'): 3.1 mi., 1400 ft., 2 hr. 15 min.

    to Skookumchuck Trail (4680'): 5.9 mi., 2850 ft., 4 hr. 25 min.

    to Mt. Lafayette summit (5260'): 6.6 mi. (10.7 km.), 3450 ft., 5 hr.

Garfield Trail (WMNF)

This trail runs from the Gale River Loop Rd. (FR 92) to the Garfield Ridge Trail 0.2 mi. east of the summit of Mt. Garfield, which is bare rock with magnificent views. Most of the way the trail follows an old road used for access to the former fire tower, and its grades are easy to moderate all the way to Garfield except for the short steep pitch on the Garfield Ridge Trail just below the summit. The trailhead is reached by leaving US 3 at a small picnic area 0.3 mi. south of its intersection with Trudeau Rd.; this intersection, often called Five Corners, has signs for Trudeau Rd. and for the Ammonoosuc District Ranger Station (which will be closed at some future date). Avoiding a right fork, follow the Gale River Loop Rd. south for 1.2 mi., then swing left and cross a bridge to a parking lot on the right. (Straight ahead on this road it is 1.6 mi. to the trailhead for the Gale River Trail.) This trail lies within the watershed of a municipal water supply, and hikers and campers should take care not to pollute any of the streams in this watershed.

    The trail begins at the parking lot, climbing an embankment and following the top of the north bank of the South Branch of the Gale River through fine woods with many large hemlocks. At 0.7 mi. it descends and swings to the right toward the river, meets the old fire tower access road, and turns left on it. The trail now climbs slowly away from the river heading generally south. It crosses Thompson and Spruce brooks and a snowmobile trail (which has bridges across the two brooks that flow close by on either side of the main trail in this area, potentially useful for avoiding some of these brook crossings in high-water conditions). The Garfield Trail then recrosses Spruce Brook at 1.2 mi.

At 2.8 mi. the trail crosses a ridge (once completely burned over and known as Burnt Knoll) and descends slightly. There is a fine birch forest in this vicinity that has grown up in the old burned area, particularly below the trail; above the trail the growth is mostly coniferous, indicating that the trail may follow the approximate upper boundary of the old burn. Soon the trail resumes its moderate ascent by several sweeping switchbacks in the mostly coniferous woods above the old burned area, and reaches a blowdown patch at 4.1 mi. Here it turns sharp left and climbs easily through an area of large conifers and then around the east side of the cone of Mt. Garfield to a junction with the Garfield Ridge Trail, which enters from the left, ascending from Garfield Ridge Campsite. The summit of Garfield is reached in 0.2 mi. by turning right and following the steep, rocky section of the Garfield Ridge Trail to its high point, then scrambling over the ledges on the left for another 60 yd. to the foundation of the old fire tower.

Garfield Trail (map 2:G5)

Distances from Gale River Loop Rd. (FR 92) (1500')

   to Garfield Ridge Trail (4180'): 4.8 mi. (7.7 km.), 2700 ft., 3 hr. 45 min.

   to Mt. Garfield summit (4500') via Garfield Ridge Trail: 5.0 mi. (8.0 km.), 3000 ft., 4 hr.

   to Garfield Ridge Campsite (3900') via Garfield Ridge Trail: 5.0 mi. (8.1 km.), 2700 ft., 3 hr. 50 min.

Gale River Trail (WMNF)

This trail runs from the Gale River Loop Rd. (FR 92) to the Garfield Ridge Trail 0.6 mi. west of Galehead Hut. The trailhead is reached by leaving US 3 at its intersection with Trudeau Rd.; this intersection, often called Five Corners, has signs for Trudeau Rd. and for the Ammonoosuc District Ranger Station (which will be closed at some future date). Follow the Gale River Rd. (FR 25) southeast, bearing left at 0.6 mi., then turn sharp right at 1.3 mi. on the Gale River Loop Rd. and continue to the parking area on the left at 1.6 mi. (Straight ahead on the road it is 1.6 mi. from here to the Garfield Trail parking lot.) This trail lies within the watershed of a municipal water supply, and hikers and campers should take care not to pollute any of the streams in this watershed.

The trail enters the woods, soon descends a bank and crosses a tributary brook, then turns right on an old logging road that climbs easily along the west side of the North Branch of the Gale River, some distance away from the stream. At 1.4 mi. it comes to the edge of the stream, crosses it on a bridge at 1.7 mi., and becomes somewhat rougher, with several bypasses of muddy sections and washouts. The trail passes through an old logging-camp site, crosses a major tributary, and recrosses to the west side of the North Branch at 2.5 mi. on stepping-stones (difficult only in very high water). After passing the gravel outwash of an overgrown slide, the trail emerges at 3.1 mi. on a gravel bank above the stream at the base of a slide, where there are fine views up the valley and toward the Twins. The trail now becomes significantly steeper and rougher, and ends with a fairly steep climb to the Garfield Ridge Trail.

Gale River Trail (map 2:G5–G6)

Distances from Gale River Loop Rd. (FR 92) (1600')

   to Garfield Ridge Trail (3390'): 4.0 mi. (6.4 km.), 1800 ft., 2 hr. 55 min.

   to Galehead Hut (3780') via Garfield Ridge Trail: 4.6 mi. (7.4 km.), 2200 ft., 3 hr. 25 min.

Frost Trail (AMC)

This short trail leads from Galehead Hut to the summit of Galehead Mtn. Leaving the hut clearing, it descends into a sag, then turns sharp right at a junction where the Twin Brook Trail enters left. After a short distance, the Frost Trail ascends a steep pitch, at the top of which a side path leads left 30 yd. to an excellent outlook over the Twin Brook valley. The main trail continues at a moderate grade to the rather flat summit, where there is a restricted view of Mt. Garfield and the Franconia Ridge.

Frost Trail (map 2:G6)

Distance from Galehead Hut (3780')

   to Galehead Mtn. summit (4024'): 0.5 mi. (0.8 km.), 250 ft., 25 min.

Twinway (AMC)

This trail extends from Galehead Hut to a junction with the Zealand Trail and the Ethan Pond Trail 0.2 mi. beyond Zealand Falls Hut, forming a very important ridgecrest link along the north edge of the Pemigewasset Wilderness that connects the mountains of the western part of the region—the Franconia Range, Garfield, and the Twins—to the Bonds, the Zealand-Hale region, the Willey Range, and the northern parts of the Pemigewasset Wilderness. It offers magnificent views from the summits of South Twin Mtn. and Mt. Guyot and from the outlook at Zeacliff, and connecting trails lead to a number of other superb outlooks. For its entire length it is part of the Appalachian Trail.

The following description of the path is in the eastbound direction (from Galehead Hut to Zealand Falls Hut). See below for a description of the path in the reverse direction.

From the junction of the Frost and Garfield Ridge trails 40 yd. from Galehead Hut, the Twinway passes over a ledgy hump with an outlook to the right, descends to a sag, then climbs steadily and steeply up the cone of South Twin to the south knob of the summit at 0.8 mi. Here the North Twin Spur begins, running straight ahead 40 yd. to the north knob and then on to North Twin, while the Twinway turns right (south) and descends along the ridge toward Mt. Guyot, with easy to moderate grades after an initial steep pitch below the summit. At 1.8 mi. the trail crosses a ledgy hump with views ahead to Guyot and Carrigain and back to South Twin. It descends easily to the main col between South Twin and Guyot, then climbs out of the scrub to open rocks on the side of Guyot and passes the junction with the Bondcliff Trail on the right at 2.8 mi. Guyot Campsite is 0.8 mi. from this junction via the Bondcliff Trail and a spur path.

The Twinway now turns left and ascends in the open to the flat summit of Guyot at 2.9 mi., and, re-entering the woods, descends at a moderate grade on the long ridge toward Zealand Mtn., reaching the col at 3.9 mi. It then climbs rather steeply, and at 4.1 mi., a few yards before reaching the height-of-land, passes a small cairn marking a side path on the left that runs nearly level 0.1 mi. to the true summit of Zealand Mtn. The main trail continues down the ridge, passes a ledge overlooking Zeacliff Pond at 5.1 mi., then descends a rather steep pitch with a ladder, and in a sag at 5.3 mi. passes a side path that leads off to the right and reaches the shore of Zeacliff Pond in 0.1 mi. The main trail ascends over a number of ledgy humps, passing the junction right with the Zeacliff Trail at 5.7 mi. It soon reaches a loop side path that leads to the right over the magnificent Zeacliff outlook and rejoins the main trail 50 yd. east of its point of departure. Here the Twinway turns left and descends moderately through a fine forest of birches. At 6.9 mi. the trail crosses two branches of Whitewall Brook on ledges, and the Lend-a-Hand Trail immediately enters on the left. The Twinway passes Zealand Falls Hut at 7.0 mi., descends steeply on rock steps for a short distance, passing a side path right to a viewpoint for Zealand Falls, then crosses the outlet of Zealand Pond and reaches the grade of the old logging railroad. Here the Zealand Trail turns left and the Ethan Pond Trail turns right, both on the railroad grade.

Twinway (map 2:G6–G7)

Distances from Galehead Hut (3780')

to South Twin summit (4902'): 0.8 mi., 1150 ft., 1 hr.

to Bondcliff Trail (4508'): 2.8 mi., 1350 ft., 2 hr. 5 min.

to Zealand Mtn. summit spur (4250'): 4.1 mi., 1650 ft., 2 hr. 55 min.

to Zeacliff Trail (3740'): 5.7 mi., 1750 ft., 3 hr. 45 min.

to Zealand Falls Hut (2630'): 7.0 mi., 1750 ft., 4 hr. 25 min.

to Ethan Pond Trail/Zealand Trail junction (2460'): 7.2 mi. (11.6 km.), 1750 ft., 4 hr. 30 min.

Twinway (AMC) [in reverse]

From the junction of the Zealand and Ethan Pond trails, the Twinway crosses the outlet of Zealand Pond, then climbs steeply on rock steps to Zealand Falls Hut, passing a side path left to a viewpoint for Zealand Falls. It then ascends moderately, passing a junction on the right with the Lend-a-Hand Trail just before it crosses two branches of Whitewall Brook on ledges, and continues to climb steadily through a fine forest of birches toward the crest of Zealand Ridge. At 1.4 mi., where the trail levels off and swings right, a loop side path continues straight ahead, passing over the magnificent Zeacliff outlook and rejoining the main trail 50 yd. west of its point of departure. The Twinway passes a junction with the Zeacliff Trail on the left, then ascends over several ledgy humps and crosses a sag at 1.9 mi., where a side path leads off to the left and reaches the shore of Zeacliff Pond in 0.1 mi. The main trail ascends a rather steep pitch with a ladder to a ledge overlooking the pond, then continues along the crest of the ridge over several wooded knobs. At 3.1 mi., just after crossing the height-of-land on the last of these knobs, it reaches a small cairn marking a side path on the right that runs nearly level 0.1 mi. to the true summit of Zealand Mtn. The main trail descends sharply to a col, then climbs moderately up the long ridge to Mt. Guyot, breaking into the open just as it reaches that summit. It then descends a short distance over open rocks to the junction with the Bondcliff Trail on the left at 4.4 mi. Guyot Campsite is 0.8 mi. from this junction via the Bondcliff Trail and a spur path.

From this junction the Twinway swings right and descends into the scrub, passes through the main col between Guyot and South Twin, and then begins the long, fairly gradual climb toward South Twin. At 5.5 mi. the trail crosses a ledgy hump with views ahead to South Twin and back to Guyot and Carrigain. After ascending a short steep pitch up the cone of South Twin, it reaches the south knob of the summit at 6.4 mi. Here the North Twin Spur begins, turning right and running 40 yd. to the north knob and then on to North Twin, while the Twinway turns left (west) and begins a steady steep descent toward Galehead Hut. At the bottom of this descent it crosses a small sag, passes over a ledgy hump with an outlook left, and soon reaches a junction 40 yd. from the hut, where the Garfield Ridge Trail enters on the right and the Frost Trail continues straight ahead to the hut.

Twinway (map 2:G6–G7)

Distances from Ethan Pond Trail/Zealand Trail junction (2460')

  to Zealand Falls Hut (2630'): 0.2 mi., 150 ft., 10 min.

  to Zeacliff Trail (3740'): 1.5 mi., 1250 ft., 1 hr. 25 min.

  to Zealand Mtn. summit spur (4250'): 3.1 mi., 1850 ft., 2 hr. 30 min.

  to Bondcliff Trail (4508'): 4.4 mi., 2400 ft., 3 hr. 25 min.

  to South Twin summit (4902'): 6.4 mi., 2950 ft., 4 hr. 40 min.

  to Galehead Hut (3780'): 7.2 mi. (11.6 km.), 3000 ft., 5 hr. 5 min.

North Twin Spur (AMC)

This trail connects the Twinway on the summit of South Twin with the North Twin Trail on the summit of North Twin. It leaves the Twinway at the south knob of South Twin, crosses the north knob in 40 yd., and descends moderately to the fern-filled col at 0.8 mi. Then it ascends to the summit of North Twin, where the North Twin Trail continues straight ahead and a spur path leads left 60 yd. to a fine outlook.

North Twin Spur (map 2:G6)

Distance from South Twin Mtn. summit (4902')

  to North Twin Mtn. summit (4761'): 1.3 mi. (2.0 km.), 300 ft. (rev. 450 ft.), 50 min.

North Twin Trail (WMNF)

This trail ascends to the summit of North Twin from Haystack Rd. (FR 304), which begins on US 3 about 2.3 mi. west of Twin Mountain village, just west of a large WMNF boundary sign, and runs south 2.5 mi. to a parking area just past its crossing of the Little River. *Caution:* The three crossings of the Little River on this trail are very difficult or impassable at high water; the third is the least difficult, and the first two may be avoided by staying on the east bank and bush-whacking along the river. This trail is in the watershed of a municipal water supply, and hikers and campers should take care not to pollute the streams.

The trail leaves the parking area and crosses the river three times, ascending easily on an old railroad grade with occasional bypasses. After the third crossing, at 1.9 mi., the trail begins to climb away from the river and railroad grade, crossing and recrossing a tributary brook. The long, steady climb continues, and at 3.5 mi. the trail becomes quite steep, reaching the ledgy end of the ridge at 4.0 mi. The trail now climbs easily, passes a superb outlook ledge at 4.2 mi., and reaches the summit of North Twin at 4.3 mi. The North Twin Spur continues straight ahead to South Twin, and a side path leads right 60 yd. to a fine outlook.

North Twin Trail (map 2:G6)
Distances from Haystack Rd. (1800')

   to third crossing of Little River (2350'): 1.9 mi., 550 ft., 1 hr. 15 min.

   to North Twin summit (4761'): 4.3 mi. (7.0 km.), 2950 ft., 3 hr. 40 min.

Zeacliff Trail (AMC)

This trail runs from the Ethan Pond Trail 1.3 mi. south of its junction with Zealand Pond to the Twinway 0.1 mi. west of the Zeacliff outlook. It is an attractive trail, much less frequently used than most trails in this area, but extremely steep and rough in parts and not recommended for hikers with heavy packs. Practically all of it is in the Pemigewasset Wilderness.

The trail leaves the Ethan Pond Trail and descends west over open talus, then drops very steeply to cross Whitewall Brook at 0.2 mi. It then climbs very steeply, up an old slide at first. The grade eases up at 0.6 mi., and soon the trail reaches the top of the ridge, where it ascends gradually through a beautiful birch forest, then swings left and angles up to a rock face at 1.1 mi. The main trail turns right here and ascends steeply to the right of the rock face, while a rough and somewhat obscure loop path runs under the rock face, then swings right, passes an outlook toward Carrigain Notch, and rejoins the main trail. Above this point the trail ascends steeply to the ridgecrest and the Twinway. To reach the Zeacliff outlook, turn right at this junction.

Zeacliff Trail (map 2:G7)
Distance from Ethan Pond Trail (2448')

   to Twinway (3740'): 1.4 mi. (2.3 km.), 1500 ft. (rev. 200 ft.), 1 hr. 25 min.

Zealand Trail (WMNF)

The Zealand Trail runs from the end of Zealand Rd. to a junction with the Ethan Pond Trail and the Twinway just below Zealand Falls Hut. It is reached by following Zealand Rd. (FR 16), which leaves US 302 at Zealand Campground about 2.3 mi. east of Twin Mountain village, to a parking area on the left 3.5 mi. from US 302, just before a gate. Zealand Rd. is closed to public vehicular use from mid-November to mid-May, and at those times hikers and skiers must not park at the gate or along the highway, but must use the parking area across US 302 0.2 mi. east of Zealand Rd. The Zealand Trail is relatively easy, following an old railroad grade much of the way, and passing through an area of beaver swamps, meadows, and ponds. All major brook crossings have bridges, but the trip can be a very wet one in wet weather, and some of the bridges occasionally float away in floods.

Leaving the parking area, the trail follows the railroad grade, then a bypass that is somewhat rough. It then returns to the grade and approaches Zealand River at 0.8 mi., near some ledges in the stream. Here it diverges right from the grade and continues on the west bank, then makes the first of several brook crossings at 1.5 mi. The trail now passes through an area of beaver activity, staying mostly on the railroad grade, and at 2.3 mi. the A–Z Trail enters from the left. The Zealand Trail crosses the outlet brook and skirts Zealand Pond, ending at 2.5 mi. where the Ethan Pond Trail continues straight ahead on the old railroad grade and the Twinway turns right to Zealand Falls Hut, 0.2 mi. away.

Zealand Trail (map 2:G7)

Distances from end of Zealand Rd. (2000')

  to A–Z Trail (2450'): 2.3 mi., 450 ft., 1 hr. 25 min.

  to Ethan Pond Trail/Twinway junction (2460'): 2.5 mi. (4.1 km.), 450 ft., 1 hr. 30 min.

  to Zealand Falls Hut (2630') via Twinway: 2.8 mi. (4.5 km.), 650 ft., 1 hr. 45 min.

Lend-a-Hand Trail (AMC)

This trail connects Zealand Falls Hut with the summit of Mt. Hale, which offers good views. The grade is fairly easy but the footing is rather rough for a good part of its distance, particularly for those trying to balance heavy packs, since there are a great many log bridges across a very wet section. The trail takes its name from a journal for charitable organizations that was edited by

Edward Everett Hale, the Boston pastor and author for whom Mt. Hale was named.

This trail diverges right (north) from the Twinway 0.1 mi. above Zealand Falls Hut and climbs steadily, crossing a small brook three times. After about 0.5 mi. the grade becomes easy in a long section with numerous log bridges, where small brooks flow in and through the trail. At 1.5 mi. the trail enters a scrubby, ledgy area and ascends moderately. In a rocky area at 1.9 mi. a ledge 15 yd. right of the trail offers a good outlook toward Carrigain Notch. At 2.4 mi. the trail climbs another rocky pitch and continues in dense conifers to the summit clearing, where the Hale Brook Trail leaves east (right). Many of the rocks around the former fire tower site are reputed to be strongly magnetic.

Lend-a-Hand Trail (map 2:G7–G6)
Distance from Twinway (2730')

   to Mt. Hale summit (4052'): 2.7 mi. (4.3 km.), 1300 ft., 2 hr.

Hale Brook Trail (WMNF)

This trail climbs from Zealand Rd. (FR 16), at a parking area 2.5 mi. from US 302, to the bare summit of Mt. Hale, where there are good views over trees that have been steadily reclaiming the formerly bare summit in the more than 30 years since the fire tower was removed. The trail is relatively easy, with moderate grades and good footing, and passes through a very fine birch forest much of the way.

The trail leaves the parking area, crosses a cross-country ski trail, then ascends steadily to cross Hale Brook at 0.8 mi. It continues the steady climb, then swings left at 1.1 mi. and ascends gradually across the steep slope above Hale Brook, recrossing the brook in its rocky bed at 1.3 mi. Now the trail ascends by several switchbacks, crossing a small brook at 1.7 mi. Still ascending and curving gradually to the right, it enters the conifers and attains the summit from the east.

Hale Brook Trail (map 2:G7–G6)
Distance from Zealand Rd. (1770')

   to Mt. Hale summit (4054'): 2.2 mi. (3.5 km.), 2300 ft., 2 hr. 15 min.

Sugarloaf Trail (WMNF)

This trail ascends both North Sugarloaf and Middle Sugarloaf from Zealand Rd. (FR 16), just south of the bridge over the Zealand River 1.0 mi. from US 302.

Parking is just north of the bridge. These two little peaks offer excellent views from their open, ledgy summits for a relatively small effort.

Leaving the road, the Sugarloaf Trail follows the river for 0.2 mi., coinciding with the Trestle Trail, then swings left as the Trestle Trail continues straight ahead along the river. After this junction the Sugarloaf Trail immediately crosses a snowmobile trail and a dirt road and climbs gradually, passing a few large boulders, where it turns sharp right (arrow). At 0.7 mi. it makes an abrupt ascent toward the col between North and Middle Sugarloaf. In this col, at 0.9 mi., the trail divides. The left branch turns sharp right after about 0.2 mi. and climbs to the summit of Middle Sugarloaf at 0.5 mi. from the col, becoming very steep in the last ledgy section, which includes a small ladder. The right branch descends slightly and then climbs to the summit of North Sugarloaf at 0.3 mi. from the col.

Sugarloaf Trail (map 2:F6)
Distances from Zealand Rd. (1644')

to Middle Sugarloaf (2539'): 1.4 mi. (2.3 km.), 900 ft., 1 hr. 10 min.

to North North Sugarloaf (2310'): 1.2 mi. (1.9 km.), 700 ft., 55 min.

for round-trip to both summits: 3.4 mi. (5.5 km.), 1000 ft., 2 hr. 10 min.

Trestle Trail (WMNF)

This short loop trail begins and ends at the bridge over the Zealand River on Zealand Rd. (FR 16), 1.0 mi. from US 302. (Parking is at the north end of the bridge.) An information leaflet is usually available at the trailhead. The trail leaves the road at the south end of the bridge and follows the river, coinciding with the Sugarloaf Trail for 0.2 mi. After the Sugarloaf Trail diverges left, the Trestle Trail leads away from the river, crosses a snowmobile trail, then turns sharp right at a large boulder and joins and follows the snowmobile trail for a short distance. Then the trail turns sharp right on an old railroad grade, crosses Zealand River on a bridge at 0.6 mi., and soon enters Sugarloaf II Campground. After following the campground road for 0.1 mi., it re-enters the woods and returns to Zealand Rd. at the north end of the bridge.

Trestle Trail (map 2:F6)
Distance from Zealand Rd. (1644')

for complete loop: 1.0 mi. (1.6 km.), 100 ft., 35 min.

Around-the-Lake Trail (AMC)

This trail provides an easy, scenic loop hike around Ammonoosuc Lake, a small, secluded alpine tarn located near the AMC Crawford Notch Hostel and almost hidden unexpectedly close to the other more conspicuous and well-known Crawford Notch attractions. This short loop walk can be combined with other walks in the area or explored by itself for its natural beauty and its many historical reminders of the Crawford House, which epitomized the grand hotel era of the 19th century.

The trail starts opposite the hostel at the turnaround and follows an old paved road downhill in a northerly direction. It turns left onto an old drive (sign), then bears right into the woods on an old grassy road. It then bears left onto a blazed trail, enters the WMNF, and reaches the loop junction at 0.3 mi. Taking the left (west) branch, the path crosses a brook on a plank bridge, dips past Merrill Spring (which often flows in winter), and runs along the west shore of the lake. At 0.6 mi. the Red Bench Trail, a spur path 0.3 mi. long, departs on the left (north) and runs parallel to the railroad, ascending gradually, then crosses the tracks diagonally and leads to a bench with an exceptional view of the Southern Presidentials. From the junction with this spur, the Around-the-Lake Trail bears right, passing the Down to the Lake Spur, a side path to a view of the Gateway of Crawford Notch, the deep cleft between Mts. Webster and Willard, from the north shore of the lake at the site of the former hotel's boat dock. The trail swings around the northeast shore, crosses a small dam and field at the outlet, follows an old road across a bridge and uphill away from the lake, and finally bears right into the woods back to the loop junction.

Around-the-Lake Trail (map 2:G8–G7)
Distances from Crawford Notch Hostel (1900')

   for complete loop around Ammonoosuc Lake: 1.2 mi. (1.9 km.), 100 ft., 40 min.

   for complete loop including Red Bench viewpoint: 1.8 mi. (2.9 km.), 150 ft., 1 hr.

Mount Willard Trail (NHDP)

This path runs from the AMC's Crawford Depot information center, on the west side of US 302 across from Saco Lake, to the ledges above the cliffs overlooking Crawford Notch. The upper part was formerly a carriage road, and the trail has easy grades, good footing, and magnificent views from the ledges, offering perhaps the finest views in the White Mtns. for the amount of effort required.

From Crawford Depot this trail coincides with the Avalon Trail for 0.1 mi., where it diverges to the left and runs on the level, then soon turns right to begin the ascent. In another 100 yd. the trail bears right, bypassing to the west a severely washed-out portion of the old carriage road. At 0.5 mi. the trail passes to the left of Centennial Pool, then bears left and at 0.7 mi. rejoins the old carriage road, which it follows the rest of the way. At 1.5 mi. a rough spur path 0.2 mi. long leads left to the head of Hitchcock Flume and an outlook, while the main trail continues to the ledges just east of the true summit.

Mount Willard Trail (map 2:G8)

Distance from Crawford Depot (1900')

   to Mt. Willard summit (2800'): 1.6 mi. (2.6 km.), 900 ft., 1 hr. 15 min.

Avalon Trail (AMC)

This trail runs from the AMC's Crawford Depot information center on the west side of US 302 to the Willey Range Trail 90 yd. north of the summit of Mt. Field, passing a short spur path to the fine outlook on Mt. Avalon along the way. Some parts of this trail are moderately steep and rough.

After 0.1 mi. from Crawford Depot the Mount Willard Trail leaves left, and the Avalon Trail ascends gradually and soon crosses a brook. Just beyond this crossing a loop path diverges left, passes by Beecher and Pearl cascades, and shortly rejoins the main trail. The Avalon Trail continues at an easy grade, recrosses the brook at 0.8 mi., and begins a moderate ascent. At 1.3 mi. the A–Z Trail to Zealand Falls Hut diverges right. The Avalon Trail soon begins to climb rather steeply, and at 1.8 mi., in the small col just below Mt. Avalon's summit, a short side path diverges left and climbs steeply 100 yd. to this fine viewpoint. The main trail passes through a flat, ledgy area, then climbs steadily, with restricted views to the northeast, to the Willey Range Trail. For the summit of Mt. Field go left (south) 90 yd.

Avalon Trail (map 2:G8–G7)

Distances from Crawford Depot (1900')

   to A–Z Trail (2700'): 1.3 mi., 800 ft., 1 hr. 5 min.

   to Mt. Avalon spur path (3350'): 1.8 mi., 1450 ft., 1 hr. 40 min.

   to Willey Range Trail (4280'): 2.8 mi. (4.5 km.), 2400 ft., 2 hr. 35 min.

A–Z Trail (AMC)

This trail runs to the Zealand Trail from the Avalon Trail 1.3 mi. from Crawford Depot, crossing the Willey Range at the Field-Tom col, and thus provides a route between Zealand Falls Hut and US 302 at the high point of Crawford Notch and access to the north end of the Willey Range from either starting point.

The A–Z Trail diverges right from the Avalon Trail and soon descends to cross a steep-walled gully, then climbs steadily, angling up along the side of the brook valley that has its head at the Field-Tom col. At 0.6 mi. the trail crosses the brook and soon begins to climb more steeply, reaching the height-of-land at 1.0 mi., where the Mount Tom Spur diverges right. The trail starts to descend gradually, and in 80 yd. the Willey Range Trail enters on the left. The trail now descends more steeply until it crosses Mt. Field Brook at 1.6 mi., then continues its descent at easy to moderate grades, passing through a logged area and crossing several small brooks. It reaches the Zealand Trail 2.3 mi. from the end of Zealand Rd.; Zealand Falls Hut is 0.5 mi. left via the Zealand Trail and Twinway.

A–Z Trail (map 2:G7)

Distances from Avalon Trail (2700')

  to Willey Range Trail (3700'): 1.0 mi., 1000 ft., 1 hr.

  to Zealand Trail (2450'): 3.7 mi. (6.0 km.), 1000 ft. (rev. 1250 ft.), 2 hr. 25 min.

  to Zealand Falls Hut (2630') via Zealand Trail and Twinway: 4.2 mi. (6.8 km.), 1200 ft., 2 hr. 40 min.

Ethan Pond Trail (AMC)

This trail begins at the Willey House Station site in a parking area just below the railroad tracks, reached by a paved road 0.3 mi. long that leaves the west side of US 302 directly opposite the Webster Cliff Trail, about 1 mi. south of the Willey House site. It ends at the junction of the Zealand Trail and the Twinway, 0.2 mi. below Zealand Falls Hut. It is part of the Appalachian Trail.

The trail crosses the tracks and ascends on an old logging road, and in 0.2 mi. the Arethusa–Ripley Falls Trail diverges left. The Ethan Pond Trail climbs steadily, then becomes more gradual, and at 1.3 mi. the Kedron Flume Trail enters on the right. At 1.6 mi. the Willey Range Trail leaves straight ahead, and the Ethan Pond Trail turns left and climbs steadily to the height-of-land at 2.1 mi., passing from Crawford Notch State Park into the WMNF. It enters and follows an old logging road down to a point close to the southeast corner of Ethan Pond, which however is not visible from the trail. This pond is named for its discoverer, Ethan Allen Crawford. Here, at 2.6 mi. from Willey House Station, a side trail on the right leads past the inlet of Ethan Pond, where there is a view of the Twin Range over the pond, then reaches Ethan Pond Campsite in 250 yd.

The Ethan Pond Trail now descends gradually through boggy terrain with occasional views. At 4.4 mi. it bears right, merging into a spur of the old Zealand Valley railroad and following it to the main line at 4.6 mi., where the Shoal Pond Trail enters from the left. At 4.9 mi. the Ethan Pond Trail crosses the North Fork on a wooden bridge, and at 5.1 mi. the Thoreau Falls Trail diverges left to continue down the North Fork. The Ethan Pond Trail follows the old railroad grade on a gradual curve into Zealand Notch, with its steep, fire-scarred walls. As the trail crosses the talus slopes of Whitewall Mtn. it comes into the open with fine views, and at 5.9 mi., in the middle of this section, the Zeacliff Trail diverges left. The Ethan Pond Trail soon re-enters the woods and continues on the remains of the railroad grade (which is badly washed out in places) to the junction with the Zealand Trail and the Twinway. For Zealand Falls Hut turn sharp left onto the Twinway and follow it for 0.2 mi.

Ethan Pond Trail (map 2:H8–G7)

Distances from Willey House Station site (1440')

to Willey Range Trail (2680'): 1.6 mi., 1250 ft., 1 hr. 25 min.

to side trail to Ethan Pond Campsite (2860'): 2.6 mi., 1450 ft., 2 hr.

to Shoal Pond Trail (2500'): 4.6 mi., 1450 ft. (rev. 400 ft.), 3 hr.

to Thoreau Falls Trail (2460'): 5.1 mi., 1450 ft. (rev. 50 ft.), 3 hr. 15 min.

to Zeacliff Trail (2448'): 5.9 mi., 1450 ft., 3 hr. 40 min.

to Zealand Trail/Twinway junction (2450'): 7.2 mi. (11.6 km.), 1500 ft., 4 hr. 20 min.

to Zealand Falls Hut (2630') via Twinway: 7.4 mi. (11.9 km.), 1600 ft., 4 hr. 30 min.

Kedron Flume Trail (AMC)

This trail runs from the Willey House site on US 302 to the Ethan Pond Trail 0.3 mi. south of its junction with the Willey Range Trail, passing Kedron Flume, an interesting cascade. As far as Kedron Flume, the trail has easy to moderate grades with good footing, but past the flume it is very steep and rough.

Leaving US 302 south of the buildings at the Willey House site, the trail passes through a picnic area and enters the woods. At 0.4 mi. it crosses the railroad tracks, where there is a fine view of Mt. Willey. At 1.0 mi., after a short descent, it crosses Kedron Brook. Above is an interesting flume and below is a waterfall where there is an excellent outlook; use care on slippery rocks. Above here the trail makes a very steep and rough climb, following a small brook part of the way, then becomes easier as it approaches the Ethan Pond Trail.

Kedron Flume Trail (map 2:G8)

Distances from Willey House site (1300')

   to Kedron Flume (1900'): 1.0 mi., 600 ft., 50 min.

   to Ethan Pond Trail (2450'): 1.3 mi. (2.1 km.), 1150 ft., 1 hr. 15 min.

Willey Range Trail (AMC)

This trail begins on the Ethan Pond Trail 1.6 mi. from the Willey House Station site, then runs over the summits of Mt. Willey and Mt. Field to the A–Z Trail in the Field-Tom col. In combination with the Ethan Pond, A–Z, and Avalon trails, it makes possible various trips over the Willey Range to or from the Willey House Station site, Crawford Depot, and Zealand Falls Hut. The section on the south slope of Mt. Willey is very steep and rough.

This trail continues straight ahead where the Ethan Pond Trail turns left, crosses Kedron Brook in 100 yd., and at 0.2 mi. turns sharp left and crosses a smaller brook. At 0.4 mi. it crosses another small brook, then climbs a very steep and rough slope with several ladders, offering occasional outlooks. The best view is from the east outlook, just before the summit of Mt. Willey, reached by an unsigned side path that leaves on the right 40 yd. below the summit cairn. The main trail reaches the summit at 1.1 mi. and circles around to the south outlook, which affords a sweeping view over the northeastern part of the Pemigewasset Wilderness. It then descends gradually, keeping mostly to the west side of the ridge and losing only 300 ft. in altitude at its low point, then climbs to the summit of Mt. Field at 2.5 mi. About 90 yd. north of this summit the Avalon Trail diverges right, and the Willey Range Trail climbs over a small knob and descends gradually northwest to the A–Z Trail just below the Field-Tom col at 3.4 mi. Turn left for Zealand Falls Hut, or right for the Mount Tom Spur, Crawford Depot, and US 302.

Willey Range Trail (map 2:G8–G7)

Distances from Ethan Pond Trail (2680')

   to Mt. Willey summit (4285'): 1.1 mi., 1600 ft., 1 hr. 20 min.

   to Mt. Field summit (4340'): 2.5 mi., 1950 ft. (rev. 300 ft.), 2 hr. 15 min.

   to A–Z Trail (3700'): 3.4 mi. (5.6 km.), 1950 ft. (rev. 650 ft.), 2 hr. 40 min.

Mount Tom Spur (AMC)

This short trail runs from the A–Z Trail to the summit of Mt. Tom. It leaves the A–Z Trail at the height-of-land, 80 yd. east of the Willey Range Trail junction, and climbs at a moderate grade to a false summit, where it swings left and reaches the true summit in another 60 yd. A blowdown patch near the summit will permit interesting views for a few years.

Mount Tom Spur (map 2:G7)

Distance from A–Z Trail (3700')

   to Mt. Tom summit (4051'): 0.6 mi. (0.9 km.), 350 ft., 30 min.

Arethusa Falls Trail (NHDP)

This trail is the direct route to Arethusa Falls, which are more than 200 ft. high, the highest in New Hampshire. It begins at the Arethusa Falls parking lot, located on a spur road off the west side of US 302, 3.4 mi. south of the Willey House site in Crawford Notch State Park. (There is plenty of parking space in the lot just off US 302 if the upper lot spaces are full.) The trail crosses the railroad and leads left (south) for 50 yd., then turns right into the woods. It soon passes a spur path left to some cascades, then follows old roads above the north bank of Bemis Brook. The Bemis Brook Trail, which diverges left at 0.1 mi. and rejoins at 0.5 mi., provides an attractive but rougher alternative route closer to the brook. At 0.8 mi. another spur leads left to cascades, and at 1.2 mi. the main trail crosses Bemis Brook on the Robert Joyce Memorial Bridge and soon reaches Arethusa Falls, where it ends at its junction with the Arethusa–Ripley Falls Trail.

Arethusa Falls Trail (map 2:H8)

Distance from Arethusa Falls parking area (1240')

   to Arethusa Falls (2000'): 1.3 mi. (2.1 km.), 750 ft., 1 hr.

Bemis Brook Trail (NHDP)

This is a slightly longer and somewhat rougher alternative route to the lower part of the Arethusa Falls Trail, running closer to Bemis Brook. It departs to the left from the Arethusa Falls Trail 0.1 mi. from its start at the railroad, angles toward the brook, and then follows close to the brook, passing spur paths leading left to Fawn Pool, Coliseum Falls, and Bemis Brook Falls. It then climbs steeply up the bank to rejoin the Arethusa Falls Trail.

Bemis Brook Trail (map 2:H8)

Distance from leaving Arethusa Falls Trail (1300')

   to rejoining Arethusa Falls Trail (1700'): 0.5 mi. (0.7 km.), 400 ft., 25 min.

Arethusa–Ripley Falls Trail (AMC/NHDP)

These two spectacular waterfalls in Crawford Notch are connected by a trail that starts at the upper end of the Arethusa Falls Trail, just below the falls. It immediately crosses the brook (may be difficult at high water—when falls viewing is best) and angles up the side of the valley away from the falls on a graded path, then doubles back on the south side of a smaller brook, which it soon crosses. Becoming rougher, it leads northeast across several small watercourses to the plateau behind Frankenstein Cliff. Turning east, the trail passes a southeast outlook and then the junction on the right with the Frankenstein Cliff Trail at 1.3 mi., and again heads north across the plateau. With various views of Mt. Webster, Crawford Notch, and Mt. Willey, the trail drops gradually and then more steeply on switchbacks to a spur path left to the top of Ripley Falls, which are about 100 ft. high. In dry weather, the water flow is rather low. The rocks just off the path near the falls are slippery and should be avoided. After crossing Avalanche Brook at the foot of the falls at 2.5 mi., the path rises gradually to the east with fairly rough footing to join the Ethan Pond Trail 0.2 mi. above the Willey House Station site, which is reached by continuing straight ahead.

Arethusa–Ripley Falls Trail (map 2:H8)

Distances from Arethusa Falls (2000')

   to Frankenstein Cliff Trail (2420'): 1.3 mi., 400 ft., 50 min.

   to Ripley Falls (1750'): 2.5 mi., 500 ft. (rev. 750 ft.), 1 hr. 30 min.

   to Ethan Pond Trail (1600'): 2.8 mi. (4.5 km.), 550 ft. (rev. 200 ft.), 1 hr. 30 min.

   to Willey House Station site (1440') via Ethan Pond Trail: 3.0 mi. (4.8 km.), 550 ft. (rev. 150 ft.), 1 hr. 40 min.

Frankenstein Cliff Trail (NHDP)

This trail provides access to Frankenstein Cliff, a prominent bluff that juts out from the tableland south of Mt. Willey and affords excellent views of the lower part of Crawford Notch. It begins at a spur road (prominently signed for Arethusa Falls) off the west side of US 302, 3.4 mi. south of the Willey House site in Crawford Notch State Park. There is plenty of parking space in the lot just off US 302 if the upper lot spaces are full.

Leaving the upper parking area, the trail runs below and roughly parallel to the railroad grade with many minor ups and downs. At 0.1 mi. a green-blazed shortcut path 0.1 mi. long leading from the lower parking lot enters on the right. At 0.6 mi. the trail reaches the junction with a former route coming up directly from US 302, where the present trail turns sharp left and passes under the Frankenstein railroad trestle near the south abutment. (Trespassing on the railroad right of way, including the use of its bed as a footway, is extremely dangerous and is prohibited; the tracks are now actively used by excursion trains from May through October.) The trail ascends by switchbacks and over stone step-like formations through the woods beneath the cliffs and up to the ridge, climbing rather steeply in places. It then passes through open hardwood forest, crossing a streambed where there is usually water, then continues through a fine forest of spruce and balsam to an outlook similar to that on Mt. Willard, with a view south along the notch, at 1.3 mi.

Leaving the outlook, the trail ascends gradually through a fine stand of spruce in a west-northwest direction, skirting the top of the cliffs, with views of the valley and Mt. Bemis, and passing just south of the summit of a small knob. At one point there is a view of Arethusa Falls far up at the head of the valley. Near the height-of-land the trail levels off, then descends the ridge for a short distance and winds gradually downward to meet the Arethusa–Ripley Falls Trail.

Frankenstein Cliff Trail (map 2:H8)

Distances from the Arethusa Falls parking area (1240')

   to Frankenstein Cliff outlook (2150'): 1.3 mi., 900 ft., 1 hr. 5 min.

   to Arethusa–Ripley Falls Trail (2420'): 2.1 mi. (3.4 km.), 1300 ft. (rev. 100 ft.), 1 hr. 45 min.

Wilderness Trail (WMNF)

The Wilderness Trail stretches for 8.9 mi. along the East Branch of the Pemigewasset River, from the Kancamagus Highway (NH 112) to Stillwater Junction, forming the central artery from which numerous trails diverge and lead to various parts of the Pemigewasset Wilderness and to the adjoining mountains. For most of its length, the trail follows the bed of a logging railroad that last operated in 1948. It begins at a large parking area (Lincoln Woods) just east of the highway bridge over the East Branch, 4.1 mi. from the information center at the I-93 exit in Lincoln and about 0.3 mi. beyond the Hancock Campground. This trail receives extremely heavy use, particularly in the few miles nearest the highway, and camping is strictly regulated. Details concerning such restrictions can be obtained at the Lincoln Woods Information Center, located next to the parking area, or from other USFS sources.

The USFS has renamed the segment of this trail between the Kancamagus Highway and the Pemigewasset Wilderness boundary near Franconia Brook as the Lincoln Woods Trail, in an attempt to emphasize which part of the trail runs within the officially designated Wilderness and which part lies outside of it. However, since the name of Wilderness Trail for the entire trail is very firmly established among the hiking public, and thus it seems unlikely that popular usage will also change, this guide will continue to refer to the entire trail from the Kancamagus Highway to Stillwater Junction as the Wilderness Trail in the hope of minimizing confusion.

East Branch Truck Road. A gravel road, commonly referred to as the East Branch Truck Road (FR 87), closely follows the east and south bank of the East Branch opposite the Wilderness Trail; its south end is crossed by the Wilderness (Lincoln Woods) Trail just past the end of the steps descending from the information center. Though it has been maintained in the past primarily to give access to official vehicles for administrative purposes rather than for hiking, this road is available to the public for pedestrian use only and provides an interesting, far less crowded access route to the upper part of the East Branch, running close to the attractive river at many points. Current plans call for a campsite to be constructed just off the road near the Wilderness boundary to replace the Franconia Brook Campsite, which was closed in 1997. Above the Wilderness boundary (roughly opposite the mouth of Franconia Brook) it is no longer used by vehicles and the roadway has become almost completely covered with grass. The road ends at a junction with the Cedar Brook Trail (see Section 4) about 0.5 mi. from that trail's junction with the Wilderness Trail near the suspension bridge above the Bondcliff Trail junction. A sign ("East Side Trail") was placed in 1997 at its point of divergence from the Cedar Brook Trail; if this sign were missing, it would be fairly difficult for a hiker who wishes to follow it toward the Kancamagus Highway to identify it at this end. Also, hikers wishing to cross the East

Branch at any point other than on one of the two suspension bridges (the one near the start of the Wilderness Trail or the one 5.4 mi. from the start) must ford the brook, which will probably involve at least some easy swimming in the most favorable conditions but will undoubtedly prove dangerous or impossible at high water or in cold seasons. The distance from the Lincoln Woods parking lot to the Wilderness boundary is 2.8 mi.; to the Cedar Brook Trail, 5.1 mi.; and to the Wilderness Trail at the suspension bridge, 5.6 mi.

Leaving the parking lot, the Wilderness (Lincoln Woods) Trail runs across the porch of the information center and descends a wooden stairway, crosses the East Branch on a suspension bridge, then turns right and follows the railroad bed, climbing almost imperceptibly. At 1.4 mi. the Osseo Trail diverges left. Soon the Wilderness Trail comes close to the river's edge, and a fine view upstream to Mt. Bond can be obtained from the rocks just off the trail. At 2.6 mi. the Black Pond Trail leaves left. The Franconia Brook Campsite (currently closed to all camping) is situated on the left at 2.8 mi.; current plans call for a new campsite to be constructed on the opposite side of the East Branch. Just before the bridge across Franconia Brook, a side trail leads north up the west bank 0.4 mi. to Franconia Falls, where the brook falls over broad ledges with many fine cascades and pools. As of 1998, hikers wishing to visit Franconia Falls must obtain permits (whose number will be limited) at the Lincoln Woods information center.

The Wilderness Trail crosses Franconia Brook on a footbridge, and in about 50 yd., at 2.9 mi., the Franconia Brook Trail climbs the bank on the left (north). Here the Wilderness Trail enters the Pemigewasset Wilderness. From this junction the trail bears right and continues to swing to the east. It crosses a brook at 3.9 mi. and reaches the Camp 16 clearing (where camping is no longer permitted) at 4.7 mi. Here the Bondcliff Trail diverges left (north), and the Wilderness Trail crosses Black Brook on a bridge to the left of the old railroad bridge. This bridge, the last railroad trestle of the East Branch line still standing, is the subject of a thorny administrative debate, since it is both a non-conforming artificial structure in Wilderness, which by law must be removed and an important historical artifact, which by law must be preserved. At 5.4 mi. the Wilderness Trail crosses to the south bank of the East Branch on a 180-ft. suspension bridge. On the far side, the Cedar Brook Trail (see Section 4) branches to the right (southwest).

Continuing upstream from the bridge, the Wilderness Trail now skirts the end of the long north ridge of Mt. Hancock, and just after crossing a small slide it reaches North Fork Junction at 6.3 mi., where the Thoreau Falls Trail diverges left (north) and the Wilderness Trail continues straight ahead. At 7.2 mi. the trail diverges from the railroad grade (which crossed the river here), crosses Crystal Brook, and soon rejoins the grade, which has crossed back to this bank. After passing through the clearing of Camp 18, the trail leaves the railroad for the last time at 8.0 mi., following a path along the bank that crosses a low, piney ridge and then descends to cross the Carrigain Branch (which may be difficult at high water) at 8.7 mi. Soon it reaches Stillwater Junction, coming into the junction at a right angle to the stream. Here the Carrigain Notch Trail (Section 4) leads right (southeast) to the Sawyer River Rd., while the Shoal Pond Trail crosses the stream directly ahead at an old dam (no bridge). (Avoid the path angling left down to the stream, which is an abandoned section of the Wilderness Trail.) Desolation Shelter, formerly located on the Carrigain Notch Trail 0.6 mi. from Stillwater Junction, was removed in 1997, and no camping is allowed within a quarter-mile of its site.

Wilderness Trail (map 2:I5–H7)

Distances from Kancamagus Highway (1160')

   to Franconia Brook Trail (1440'): 2.9 mi., 300 ft., 1 hr. 35 min.

   to Bondcliff Trail (1600'): 4.7 mi., 450 ft., 2 hr. 35 min.

   to Cedar Brook Trail (1640'): 5.4 mi., 500 ft., 2 hr. 55 min.

   to Thoreau Falls Trail (1743'): 6.3 mi., 600 ft., 3 hr. 25 min.

   to Stillwater Junction (2050'): 8.9 mi. (14.3 km.), 900 ft., 4 hr. 55 min.

Osseo Trail (AMC)

This trail connects the lower end of the Wilderness Trail with the south end of the Franconia Ridge, near the summit of Mt. Flume. It begins on the west side of the Wilderness Trail, 1.4 mi. north of the parking area on the Kancamagus Highway. It heads west, following a brook in a flat area, then climbs the bank to the right and soon enters a section of an old incline logging railroad grade at one of its switchbacks. It continues up the valley on this grade and then on old logging roads not far above the brook. At 2.1 mi. it turns right and climbs by switchbacks to the top of the ridge above the valley to the north, then ascends the ridge—winding about at first, then climbing by zigzags as the ridge steepens. At the top of this section are several wooden staircases, and at 3.2 mi. a side path (sign) leads right to a "downlook" with a very fine view of Mt. Bond.

Soon the trail reaches the top of the ridge, and its grade becomes easy until it reaches the crest of the Franconia Ridge in an unusually flat area at 3.7 mi. The trail turns sharp right here and ascends near the crest of a narrow ridge to a junction with the Flume Slide Trail on the left and the Franconia Ridge Trail straight ahead.

Osseo Trail (map 2:I6–H5)
Distance from Wilderness Trail (1300')

> *to* Flume Slide Trail/Franconia Ridge Trail junction (4220'): 4.1 mi. (6.6 km.), 2900 ft., 3 hr. 30 min.

Distance from Kancamagus Highway (1160')

> *to* Mt. Flume summit (4328') via Wilderness (Lincoln Woods) Trail, Osseo Trail, and Franconia Ridge Trail: 5.6 mi. (9.0 km.), 3150 ft., 4 hr. 25 min.

Black Pond Trail (WMNF)

This short, easy spur trail leaves the Wilderness Trail 2.6 mi. from the Kancamagus Highway and ends at Black Pond, where there is an interesting view of the lower ridges of Mt. Bond from the western shore. Diverging left (west) from the Wilderness Trail, it first follows a former logging railroad spur, then leaves it on the left after 150 yd. and skirts the north shore of an old ice pond, which is in sight but not actually reached. Beyond the boggy pond it joins an old logging road, crosses the Camp 7 clearing (now overgrown by raspberries), and approaches Birch Island Brook, then bears slightly right away from it up a moderate incline. At 0.5 mi. it makes a short but sharp descent to cross the outlet brook from Black Pond, then recrosses it at a boggy spot. Soon it crosses the outlet brook for the third time and follows it to Black Pond, then skirts the southwest side of the pond and ends at the viewpoint.

Black Pond Trail (map 2:H6)
Distance from Wilderness Trail (1410')

> *to* Black Pond (1590'): 0.8 mi. (1.4 km.), 200 ft., 30 min.

Franconia Brook Trail (WMNF)

This trail runs from the Wilderness Trail 2.9 mi. from the Kancamagus Highway to the Garfield Ridge Trail 0.9 mi. east of the summit of Mt. Garfield, thus connecting the Pemigewasset East Branch valley with the Franconia-Garfield ridgecrest. Practically the entire trail is in the Pemigewasset Wilderness.

It diverges north from the Wilderness Trail at a point about 50 yd. beyond of the footbridge across Franconia Brook, at the boundary of the Pemigewasset Wilderness, and climbs up a steep bank to an old railroad grade, which it follows. It crosses Camp 9 Brook twice, and at 1.0 mi. swings right off the railroad grade to bypass a section flooded by an enthusiastic beaver colony. The trail crosses Camp 9 Brook again, turns sharp left back along the brook (avoid the beaten path leading ahead into the swamp) and climbs its bank, and soon rejoins the railroad grade, turning sharp right on it and continuing to the junction with the Lincoln Brook Trail, which diverges left (west) at 1.7 mi.

The Franconia Brook Trail next passes to the left of several small open swamps, with occasional short sections made wet by beaver activity. It continues to ascend gradually on the old railroad grade, crossing Hellgate Brook at 2.6 mi., Redrock Brook at 3.6 mi., and Twin Brook at 4.7 mi., and passing through clearings at the sites of Camps 10, 12, and 13. At 5.2 mi. it reaches 13 Falls, a series of beautiful waterfalls and cascades, and turns right, leaving the old railroad grade on an old logging road. In 100 yd. the Lincoln Brook Trail re-enters from the left (west), and in quick succession a spur path leads right to 13 Falls Campsite and the Twin Brook Trail branches off to the right. The Franconia Brook Trail continues on an old logging road and crosses a branch of Franconia Brook at 6.2 mi., then climbs somewhat more steeply along old logging roads, often rather rough and muddy, to the top of the ridge, where it ends at the Garfield Ridge Trail in the deep col east of Mt. Garfield. Garfield Ridge Campsite is 0.6 mi. to the left (west) by the Garfield Ridge Trail and spur path; Galehead Hut is 2.2 mi. to the right.

Franconia Brook Trail (map 2:H6–G5)
Distances from Wilderness Trail (1440')

   to Lincoln Brook Trail, south junction (1760'): 1.7 mi., 300 ft., 1 hr.

   to 13 Falls Campsite (2196'): 5.2 mi., 750 ft., 3 hr.

   to Garfield Ridge Trail (3420'): 7.4 mi. (11.9 km.), 2000 ft., 4 hr. 40 min.

Lincoln Brook Trail (WMNF)

This trail begins and ends on the Franconia Brook Trail, and together these two trails make a complete circuit around the base of Owl's Head Mtn. The south junction is 1.7 mi. north of the Wilderness Trail, and the north junction is near 13 Falls Campsite, 5.2 mi. from the Wilderness Trail. *Caution:* Several of the brook crossings on this trail may be very difficult at high water. The entire trail is in the Pemigewasset Wilderness.

Turning left (west) off the Franconia Brook Trail, the Lincoln Brook Trail leads southwest through the woods above an area flooded by beavers to join an old railroad bed just before the crossing of Franconia Brook at 0.5 mi. In another 0.4 mi. it crosses Lincoln Brook from the north to the south side.

These crossings, which may be particularly difficult at high water, can be avoided by bushwhacking along the west banks of Franconia and Lincoln brooks from Franconia Brook Falls, following old logging roads part of the way. Another possible route involves bushwhacking due north from the end of the Black Pond Trail; this route rises easily through open woods, then descends a rather steep bank just before reaching the Lincoln Brook Trail. The Franconia Brook route merely requires one to follow the brook bank, while the Black Pond route requires some careful use of map and compass—although it is fairly easy to navigate going north toward Owl's Head (where it is relatively hard to miss the Lincoln Brook Trail entirely), it is somewhat more difficult to return to the pond (which is easily missed unless one follows the bearing very carefully).

Beyond the Lincoln Brook crossing, the Lincoln Brook Trail follows the brook upstream on a long northward curve. It crosses a small brook at 2.2 mi., then the larger Liberty Brook at 2.8 mi. Soon it enters the Camp 11 clearing, climbs left to avoid a mudhole, rejoins the road, and crosses Lincoln Brook (sometimes difficult) to the east side at 3.0 mi. At 3.4 mi. it traverses the base of an old slide from Owl's Head (the principal access route to that remote summit), then crosses Lincoln Brook again at 4.3 mi. and continues north, crossing a divide into the Franconia Brook drainage with some glimpses of the northern Franconia Range behind (west) and Mt. Garfield to the north. Parts of the trail through and north of the divide may be rough and, in some seasons, quite wet. From the divide the trail descends to cross a west branch of Franconia Brook at 6.6 mi., then turns sharp right and follows a logging road down the north bank of this tributary past cascades and pools. It then swings to the right off the old road, passes waterfalls, crosses the main stream just above the confluence with the western tributary, and rejoins the Franconia Brook Trail near 13 Falls Campsite.

Lincoln Brook Trail (map 2:H6–H5)

Distances from Franconia Brook Trail, south junction (1760')

   to Owl's Head slide (2560'): 3.4 mi., 800 ft., 2 hr. 10 min.

   to height-of-land (3200'): 4.8 mi., 1450 ft., 3 hr. 10 min.

   to Franconia Brook Trail near 13 Falls Campsite (2180'): 6.9 mi. (11.1 km.), 1450 ft. (rev. 1000 ft.), 4 hr. 10 min.

Owl's Head Path

This unofficial, unmaintained path ascends the slide on the west side of this remote mountain, starting from the Lincoln Brook Trail at a small cairn 3.4 mi. from its south junction with the Franconia Brook Trail and 0.4 mi. beyond the second crossing of Lincoln Brook. (Note: Hikers often mistake Liberty Brook for Lincoln Brook, and thus think they have already passed the Owl's Head slide path when they arrive at the Lincoln Brook crossing that is about 0.2 mi. beyond Liberty Brook but still 0.4 mi. before the Owl's Head path. At the slide, the main brook is nearby on the west and the steep mountainside rises immediately to the east.) The slide is very steep and rough, and though considerably overgrown it is still potentially dangerous because of loose rock and smooth ledges, especially when wet. Great care should be taken both ascending and descending. Hikers who find the slide unappealing may be able to bushwhack up or down the steep slope to the north, parallel to the slide, through mostly open woods. Since Owl's Head signs are apparently highly prized souvenirs, both the junction with the Lincoln Brook Trail and the summit usually lack such identification.

There is no well-defined path on the slide, but several routes are usually marked by cairns of varying size and visibility. In general, it is easier to ascend on the south side, which is mostly ledge with good holds for hands and feet, and descend on the north side, which is mostly loose gravel. (In other words, it is usually better to keep to the right.) At the top of the slide, 0.3 mi. and 700 ft. above the Lincoln Brook Trail, just before the trail enters the woods there is a small spring spurting from the rock like a fountain, which unfortunately is not completely reliable. From here a well-trodden, unmaintained path climbs rather steeply up to the ridge, which is reached at 0.8 mi., then swings left and runs near the crest with minor ups and downs until it finally climbs a short pitch and abruptly reaches a tiny clearing at the wooded summit. Above the slide, the path is sometimes blocked for short distances by blowdowns; be careful to return to the path after passing these obstructions. Excellent views are sometimes obtained from the summit area by ambitious tree-climbers, since if this summit were not densely wooded it would afford one of the finest views in the mountains, due to its strategic location in the center of the great horseshoe formed by the ridge running from the Franconias to the Bonds.

Owl's Head Path (map 2:H5)

Distance from Lincoln Brook Trail (2560')

   to Owl's Head summit (4025'): 1.0 mi. (1.5 km.), 1500 ft., 1 hr. 15 min.

Distance from Kancamagus Highway (1160')

 to Owl's Head (4025') via Wilderness Trail, Franconia Brook Trail, Lincoln Brook Trail, and Owl's Head slide path: 9.0 mi. (14.4 km.), 2850 ft., 5 hr. 55 min.

Twin Brook Trail (AMC)

This trail connects 13 Falls Campsite to Galehead Hut, running almost entirely within the Pemigewasset Wilderness. It diverges from the Franconia Brook Trail near the campsite and rises gradually east-northeast, soon entering beautiful birch woods. At the start, take care to follow the blazes at sharp bends, avoiding several old logging roads. After 0.4 mi. the trail swings to the northeast and heads up the valley of Twin Brook, keeping to the left (west) of the brook, which is occasionally audible but not visible. After traversing four distinct minor ridges of Galehead Mtn. in the next mile, the trail eventually climbs more steeply to its terminus on the Frost Trail 0.1 mi. from Galehead Hut. For the hut, make a right turn onto the Frost Trail.

Twin Brook Trail (map 2:H5–G6)
Distances from 13 Falls Campsite (2196')

 to Frost Trail (3850'): 2.6 mi. (4.1 km.), 1650 ft., 2 hr. 5 min.

 to Galehead Hut (3870') via Frost Trail: 2.7 mi. (4.3 km.), 1650 ft., 2 hr. 10 min.

Bondcliff Trail (AMC)

This trail begins on the Wilderness Trail at Camp 16, 4.7 mi. from the Kancamagus Highway, ascends over Bondcliff and Mt. Bond, and ends at the Twinway just west of the summit of Mt. Guyot. It connects the Pemigewasset Wilderness with the high summits of the Twin Range, and the entire trail is in the Pemigewasset Wilderness except for a short segment at the north end. The long section on Bondcliff and one shorter section on Guyot are above treeline, with great exposure to the weather. The views from this trail are unsurpassed in the White Mtns.

 Leaving the Wilderness Trail at Camp 16, the Bondcliff Trail runs level for 100 yd., then turns sharp left just before a phantom crossing of Black Brook and climbs a bank to an old logging road. Soon it enters a relocated section (this relocation has eliminated four crossings of Black Brook). At 1.1 mi. it rejoins the logging road along the brook and ascends easily, though parts of the road are severely eroded. It then crosses the brook four times; the second crossing, at 1.9 mi., provides the last sure water. At the third crossing, at 2.5 mi., the trail turns right, crosses the brook bed (often dry), climbs a steep slope on rock steps, then swings left to another old logging road and crosses a gravel bank where one can look almost straight up to the summit of Bondcliff. In a short distance it makes the last brook crossing in a steep, south-facing ravine; if the brook is dry here, water can often be found a short distance farther up in the streambed. The trail winds up a small, prow-shaped, "hanging" ridge that protrudes into the main ravine, then at 3.2 mi. swings left and begins a long sidehill ascent up the steep slope on a logging road, heading back to the southwest. At 4.1 mi. the trail reaches the crest of Bondcliff's south ridge, swings north, and ascends the ridge to a short, rather difficult scramble up a ledge. Soon it breaks out of the scrub and climbs along the edge of the cliffs, with spectacular views, reaching the summit of Bondcliff at 4.4 mi. *Caution:* The trail runs above treeline for about a mile and is potentially dangerous in bad weather, particularly high winds. When visibility is poor, stay well to the east of the edge of the precipices.

The trail now descends the open ridge into a long, flat col, then ascends the steep slope of Mt. Bond, re-entering scrubby woods about halfway up. At 5.6 mi. the trail passes just west of the summit of Mt. Bond, which commands a magnificent unrestricted view of the surrounding wilderness and mountains. The trail descends north, crossing a minor knob, then drops down rather steeply past the spur path to West Bond at 6.1 mi., and leaves the Pemigewasset Wilderness. It reaches the Bond-Guyot col at 6.3 mi., where a spur path descends right (east) 0.2 mi. and 250 ft. to Guyot Campsite and its spring. The Bondcliff Trail then ascends to the bare south summit of Mt. Guyot and continues in the open 0.2 mi. to its junction with the Twinway 0.1 mi. west of the higher, but less open, north summit of Guyot. Go straight ahead here for the Twins and Galehead Hut, or turn right for Zealand Mtn. and Zealand Falls Hut.

Bondcliff Trail (map 2:H6)
Distances from Wilderness Trail (1600')

   to Bondcliff summit (4265'): 4.4 mi., 2650 ft., 3 hr. 30 min.

   to Mt. Bond summit (4698'): 5.6 mi., 3100 ft. (rev 200 ft.), 4 hr. 20 min.

   to Guyot Campsite spur (4360'): 6.3 mi., 3150 ft. (rev. 350 ft.), 4 hr. 45 min.

   to Twinway (4508'): 6.9 mi. (11.1 km.), 3350 ft., 5 hr. 15 min.

West Bond Spur (AMC)

This short path provides access to the sharp rocky summit of the West Peak of Mt. Bond, which is perched high above the deep valleys of an extensive wilderness area, commanding magnificent views. The entire trail is in the Pemigewasset Wilderness. It leaves the Bondcliff Trail 0.6 mi. north of the summit of Mt. Bond and 0.2 mi. south of the spur to Guyot Campsite, descends moderately for 0.3 mi. to the col at the foot of West Bond, and ascends moderately for a short distance. It then climbs the steep cone to the summit, which is the most easterly of several small peaks on a ridge running east and west.

West Bond Spur (map 2:H6)

Distance from Bondcliff Trail (4500')

> *to* West Bond summit (4540'): 0.5 mi. (0.8 km.), 200 ft. (rev. 150 ft.), 20 min.

Thoreau Falls Trail (WMNF)

This trail runs from the Wilderness Trail at North Fork Junction, 6.3 mi. from the Kancamagus Highway, past Thoreau Falls to the Ethan Pond Trail roughly halfway between Ethan Pond Campsite and Zealand Falls Hut. Much of it follows an old railroad grade, but there are a few rather steep and rough sections. Practically the entire trail is in the Pemigewasset Wilderness.

The trail diverges left (north) from the Wilderness Trail on a railroad bed, which it leaves after 0.4 mi. to cross the East Branch of the Pemigewasset on a 60-ft. bridge, then the trail returns to the railroad bed and follows it along the North Fork. At 2.1 mi. the trail leaves the railroad grade for good and soon turns right and climbs, using a bypass that avoids two former crossings of the North Fork. Rejoining the old route at 2.9 mi., it follows a logging road, then leaves it on the left at 3.6 mi. and soon becomes rougher and steeper, reaching a ledge next to the North Fork at 4.0 mi. The trail approaches Thoreau Falls and climbs steeply on a rough footpath to the right of the falls, which are beautiful when there is a good flow of water. It crosses the North Fork at the top of the falls at 5.0 mi., where there is a fine view up to Mts. Bond and Guyot. (In high water there may be a better brook crossing just upstream from the trail.) Leaving the stream, the trail soon ends at the Ethan Pond Trail, about 0.2 mi. west of the latter's bridge over the North Fork. Turn left for Zealand Falls Hut or right for Ethan Pond Shelter.

Thoreau Falls Trail (map 2:H6–G7)

Distance from Wilderness Trail (1743')

to Ethan Pond Trail (2460'): 5.1 mi. (8.2 km.), 700 ft., 2 hr. 55 min.

Shoal Pond Trail (AMC)

This trail runs from its junction with the Wilderness Trail and the Carrigain Notch Trail (see Section 4) at Stillwater Junction to the Ethan Pond Trail between Zealand Falls Hut and Ethan Pond Campsite. Practically the entire trail is in the Pemigewasset Wilderness.

At Stillwater Junction, the trail leads across the East Branch on the foundation of an old dam (no bridge; may be difficult in moderate water and dangerous in high water), turns left on a railroad bed and almost immediately leaves it on the right, then soon bears right onto another railroad bed. Leaving the railroad temporarily, the trail crosses Shoal Pond Brook at 0.6 mi.; this crossing may be difficult if the water is high. The trail regains the railroad bed and passes a spur path on the right at 1.0 mi. that leads to a pleasant pool in the brook. At 1.2 mi. it bears left off the railroad bed and follows logging roads, crossing Shoal Pond Brook from west to east at 1.4 mi. and recrossing the brook at 2.4 mi. At 3.2 mi. the trail crosses the brook for the last time, from west to east, and soon reaches Shoal Pond. Because of bogginess caused by beaver activity, the trail runs a short distance to the east of the pond, keeping away from its immediate vicinity, but a short side path at 3.3 mi. leads to the south shore of the pond and a view of Zealand Notch. At 3.7 mi. the trail passes the junction with its abandoned east fork and continues to the Ethan Pond Trail.

Shoal Pond Trail (map 2:H7–G7)

Distances from Stillwater Junction (2050')

to Shoal Pond (2550'): 3.3 mi., 500 ft., 1 hr. 55 min.

to Ethan Pond Trail (2500'): 4.0 mi. (6.4 km.), 500 ft., 2 hr. 15 min.

Section 4

The Carrigain and Moat Regions

This section covers the eastern portion of the central region of the White Mtns. (that part not included in Section 3), consisting of the areas bounded on the north by US 302, on the east by NH 16, and on the south by the Kancamagus Highway (NH 112); at its western edge it includes all areas and trails south and east of the Wilderness Trail. For a more precise description of the western boundary of Section 4, see the first paragraph of Section 3. Section 4 includes Mt. Carrigain and Mt. Hancock, the lesser mountains that surround them, and the lower but interesting mountains that rise to the east between the Saco and Swift rivers, principally Mt. Tremont and the Moat Range. The area is covered by the AMC Crawford Notch–Sandwich Range map (map #3).

Important access roads in this area include the Kancamagus Highway (NH 112), connecting I-93 and US 3 in Lincoln to NH 16 in Conway. It is a regular state highway that is paved and well maintained, open in winter except during the worst storms. Bear Notch Rd. runs 9.3 mi. from US 302 at the crossroads in Bartlett village to the Kancamagus Highway in Albany Intervale about 13 mi. west of Conway. It is paved, but not plowed in winter except for the 2-mi. section immediately north of the Kancamagus Highway. North of Bear Notch it closely follows the line of an old railroad, and excellent outlooks have been cleared. The gravel Sawyer River Rd. (FR 34) begins on US 302 0.1 mi. north of the major bridge over Sawyer River, 1.6 mi. north of the Sawyer Rock picnic area or 7.9 mi. south of the Willey House site in Crawford Notch State Park. There may not be a road sign except for a brown post with "FR 34" on it, and it is usually closed by a locked gate during the snow season. (Note: A flood in 1996 created a major washout on the Sawyer River Rd., and the road has been closed since then. The USFS plans to repair and reopen it when funding for this project can be arranged, but until this occurs hikers using the trails that begin on this road will be required to walk in from US 302.)

The Appalachian Trail does not pass through this section.

GEOGRAPHY

Mt. Carrigain (4700 ft.) is the central and highest point of a mass of jumbled ridges that divides the watershed of the East Branch of the Pemigewasset River from that of the Saco River and its tributary, the Swift River. It was named for Philip Carrigain, New Hampshire secretary of state from 1805 to 1810. Carrigain made a map of the whole state in 1816, which included an early attempt to portray the White Mtn. region that can best be described as imaginative. He was one of the party that named Mts. Adams, Jefferson, Madison, and Monroe from the summit of Mt. Washington in 1820. The view from the observation tower on Mt. Carrigain takes in a wide area and includes most of the important peaks of the White Mtns., making this peak one of the competitors for the title of the finest viewpoint in the White Mtns. The view from **Signal Ridge,** Carrigain's south-easterly spur, is also magnificent. The northeasterly spur, **Vose Spur** (3862 ft.), forms the west wall of the deep cleft of **Carrigain Notch,** facing Mt. Lowell on the east. Vose Spur has no trails, and therefore the climb up its steep slopes through dense woods (or across the mostly pathless scrubby ridge from the summit of Carrigain) is one of the most challenging bushwhack ascents in the White Mtns.

Mt. Hancock rises to the west of Mt. Carrigain. It is a long ridge with several summits, of which the most important are the **North Peak** (4420 ft.) and the **South Peak** (4319 ft.). Both peaks are wooded to the top, but there is an excellent outlook ledge near the summit of the North Peak and a good but restricted outlook from the South Peak. At one time this was one of the most inaccessible mountains in the White Mtns., remote and trailless with slopes devastated by logging, but it is now routinely ascended via the Hancock Loop Trail.

The ridge between Mt. Carrigain and Mt. Hancock has no trail, and travel along it is extremely difficult; the line along this ridge shown on many maps is part of the Lincoln-Livermore town boundary. **Carrigain Pond,** a beautiful and remote mountain pond that is one of the higher sources of the Pemigewasset River, lies just north of the ridge between Carrigain and Hancock at an elevation of about 3200 ft. **The Captain** (3540 ft.), located only 0.3 mi. from Carrigain Pond, is a striking little peak, a miniature Half Dome with sheer cliffs overlooking the Sawyer River valley; however, it is well hidden at the end of this isolated valley and can be seen from only a few viewpoints, most notably the summit of Mt. Tremont.

Mt. Lowell (3740 ft.), **Mt. Anderson** (3740 ft.), **Mt. Nancy** (3926 ft.), and **Mt. Bemis** (3725 ft.) are a group of peaks northeast of Carrigain Notch that rise along the ridge that forms the watershed divide between the Saco and the East

Branch of the Pemigewasset. None of these peaks is reached by an officially maintained trail. The region is remarkable for its four picturesque ponds— **Nancy Pond, Norcross Pond, Little Norcross Pond,** and **Duck Pond**—which lie at the unusually high altitude of about 3100 ft. There is also a stand of virgin spruce just south of Nancy Pond on the north slopes of Duck Pond Mtn., said to be one of the two largest remaining areas of virgin forest in the state, though the hurricane of 1938 did great damage, felling many of the older trees. In October 1964, the USFS established in this region the 460-acre **Nancy Brook Scenic Area,** to be maintained as nearly as possible in an undisturbed condition.

Mt. Tremont (3371 ft.) is the highest of several lesser peaks that rise in the region around Sawyer Pond, east of Bear Notch Rd. Tremont lies south of the big bend in the Saco River above Bartlett; it is a narrow ridge that runs north and south, with three conspicuous summits of which the southernmost is the highest. Still farther south is a high shoulder, **Owl's Cliff** (2940 ft.). The main summit of Tremont has spectacular views to the south, west, and north; Owl's Cliff has a fine outlook to the south. Southwest of both Mt. Tremont and Sawyer Pond is **Green's Cliff** (2926 ft.), with cliffs on its south and east faces; it is very prominent from the overlooks on the eastern half of the Kancamagus Highway. Ledges near its summit provide interesting views, but there is no trail. **Sawyer Pond,** which lies in a steep-walled basin on the southwest side of Mt. Tremont, and **Church Pond,** which lies in a flat area north of the Kancamagus Highway and southeast of Green's Cliff, are attractive objectives reached by relatively short, easy trails.

Bear Notch, crossed by the scenic Bear Notch Rd. from Bartlett village to the Kancamagus Highway in Albany Intervale, lies between Bartlett Haystack and Bear Mtn. The **WMNF Bartlett Experimental Forest** occupies a large area on the north slopes of these mountains. **Bartlett Haystack** (2980 ft.), an aptly named mountain that was sometimes called Mt. Silver Spring in the days when hazy elegance was preferred to plain and effective description, is another interesting peak with no trails that rises east of Mt. Tremont. A ledge just a few feet west of the summit, shaped like the prow of a ship, affords a magnificent view to the south, west, and north. Bartlett Haystack is a relatively easy bushwhack from Haystacks Rd. (FR 44), and is one of the more rewarding objectives available to experienced hikers who wish to begin to acquire the skills of off-trail navigation by map and compass. The USGS Bartlett 7.5' quad, now available in provisional format, is very useful for the ascent of this peak (previous maps were highly inaccurate in their location of FR 44). Leave FR 44 at any convenient point less than 0.5 mi. from its junction with the Bear Notch Rd. near the height-of-land in Bear

Notch, climb roughly northwest to the crest of the peak's east ridge, then follow the ridgecrest to the summit. (Although a compass bearing is useful for confirmation of the proper direction, you should follow the ridgecrest, heading for the highest ground you can find rather than attempting to follow a precise compass bearing. This route illustrates one of the complexities of off-trail navigation in the Whites: in this case the mountain will lead you to its summit if you let it, while an attempt to follow a precise bearing on the ascent can pull you off the ridgecrest and into steep, difficult terrain. The compass is essential to the off-trail navigator, but following a bearing is often more difficult than following a feature of terrain—a ridge or a brook, for example—using the compass to confirm the correct approximate direction.) For the descent (which, as is often the case, may involve more sophisticated navigation than the ascent), you can follow the ridge you ascended east down to FR 44, or you can descend into the brook valley just to the north of this ridge and follow the brook out to the road (a somewhat easier route to navigate, as again the compass bearing is not necessary once the brook is reached and confirmed to be heading in the approximate correct direction). It is also possible to descend somewhat more to the south, more directly toward Bear Notch, but take care not to leave the ridge too quickly, because the slope directly below the summit on the south is steep and rough.

Moat Mtn. is a long ridge that rises impressively to the west of the Saco River nearly opposite North Conway. The whole ridge was burned over many decades ago, and all the major summits are still bare, with magnificent views; there are also numerous scattered outlooks along the wooded parts of the ridge. There has been some uncertainty about the names of the summits in the range, but in this guide the peaks are called **North Moat Mtn.** (3196 ft.), **Middle Moat Mtn.** (2805 ft.), and **South Moat Mtn.** (2770 ft.). The peak at the apex of the **Red Ridge** (2785 ft.) has sometimes also been called Middle Moat. From North Moat a ridge runs west to **Big Attitash Mtn.** (2910 ft.), sometimes called West Moat, then the ridge passes over the lesser summits of Big Attitash and swings southwest to **Table Mtn.** (2675 ft.), which has fine views to the south from several open ledges just below the summit. Next the ridge swings west again to the trailless **Bear Mtn.** (3220 ft.), which forms the east side of Bear Notch. South of Bear Mtn. and very close to the Kancamagus Highway are the picturesque **Rocky Gorge** on the Saco River and nearby **Falls Pond,** a small scenic body of water reached by a short, easy trail from the highway. An **unnamed rocky southern spur of the Moat group,** which affords excellent views, is ascended by the Boulder Loop Trail—a moderately strenuous nature trail with numbered stations keyed to an information leaflet. On the east side of the Moat Range are

White Horse Ledge (1450 ft.) and **Cathedral Ledge** (1159 ft.), two detached bluffs that present impressive cliffs to the Saco valley. An auto road ascends to the summit of Cathedral Ledge. Farther to the north, **Little Attitash Mtn.** (2504 ft.) is a trailless peak on a long, curving ridge that extends northeast from Big Attitash to end in **Humphrey's Ledge** (1510 ft.). **Pitman's Arch,** a shallow cave in the face of Humphrey's Ledge, was once reached by a toll path that is now completely overgrown. **Diana's Baths** is a set of very scenic cascades where Lucy Brook runs over ledges and through large potholes, located on the Moat Mtn. Trail near West Side Rd.

CAMPING
Pemigewasset Wilderness

Wilderness regulations, intended to protect Wilderness resources and promote opportunities for challenge and solitude, prohibit use of motorized equipment or mechanical means of transportation of any sort. Camping and wood or charcoal fires are not allowed within 200 ft. of any trail except at designated campsites. Camping is prohibited within 200 ft. of the Wilderness Trail and the East Branch of the Pemigewasset River (including islands) from the Wilderness boundary up to the Thoreau Falls Trail junction, the Thoreau Falls Trail from the Wilderness Trail junction to the East Branch crossing, and the Bondcliff Trail from the Wilderness Trail crossing up to the second crossing of Black Brook. Camping and fires are also prohibited within a quarter-mile of 13 Falls Campsite, Thoreau Falls, the site of the former Desolation Shelter, Galehead Hut, Garfield Ridge Campsite, and Guyot Campsite (the last three facilities are outside, but less than a quarter-mile from, the Wilderness boundary). Hiking and camping group size must be no larger than 10 people. Camping and fires are also prohibited above treeline (where trees are less than 8 ft. tall), except in winter, when camping is permitted above treeline in places where snow cover is at least two feet deep, but not on any frozen body of water.

Forest Protection Areas

The WMNF has established a number of Forest Protection Areas (FPAs)—formerly known as Restricted Use Areas—where camping and wood or charcoal fires are prohibited throughout the year. The specific areas are under continual review, and areas are added to or subtracted from the list in order to provide the greatest amount of protection to areas subject to damage by excessive camping, while imposing the lowest level of restrictions possible. A general list of FPAs in this section follows, but since there are often major changes from year to year, one should obtain current information on FPAs from the WMNF.

(1) No camping is permitted above treeline (where trees are less than 8 ft. tall), except in winter, and then only in places where there is at least two feet of snow cover on the ground—but not on any frozen body of water. The point where the restricted area begins is marked on most trails with small signs, but the absence of such signs should not be construed as proof of the legality of a site.

(2) No camping is permitted within a quarter-mile of any trailhead, picnic area, or any facility for overnight accommodation such as a hut, cabin, shelter, tentsite, or campground, except as designated at the facility itself. In the area covered by Section 4, camping and fires are also prohibited within a quarter-mile of the Big and Little Sawyer Ponds, Diana's Baths (located on the Moat Mountain Trail), and the site of the former Desolation Shelter. Camping is also not permitted in the Bartlett Experimental Forest.

(3) No camping is permitted within 200 ft. of certain trails. In 1997, designated trails included the Sawyer Pond Trail from the end of the quarter-mile FPA along the Sawyer River Rd. to the beginning of the quarter-mile FPA around Sawyer Pond, and the Cedar Brook Trail between its junctions with the Hancock Notch and Hancock Loop trails.

(4) No camping is permitted on WMNF land within a quarter-mile of certain roads (camping on private roadside land is illegal except by permission of the landowner). In 1997, these roads included US 302 west of Bartlett NH, the Sawyer River Rd., the Kancamagus Highway, the Bear Notch Rd., and the Dugway Rd. from the Kancamagus Highway to the picnic area.

Established Trailside Campsites

Desolation Shelter (AMC) has been removed. It was formerly located on the Carrigain Notch Trail beside Carrigain Branch, 0.6 mi. southeast of Stillwater Junction and the Wilderness Trail. The shelter was dismantled in 1997, and camping is prohibited within a quarter-mile of the site.

Sawyer Pond Campsite (WMNF) is located on Sawyer Pond, reached by the Sawyer Pond Trail. There are five tent platforms on the northwest side of the pond, and a shelter that accommodates eight.

Trails in the Mount Carrigain Region

Trails in the Mount Hancock Region

Trails in the Mount Tremont Region

Trails in the Moat Mountain Region

THE TRAILS

Signal Ridge Trail (WMNF)

This trail ascends to the summit of Mt. Carrigain by way of Signal Ridge, start-ing from Sawyer River Rd. (FR 34) 2.0 mi. from its junction with US 302, which is 1.6 mi. north of the Sawyer Rock Picnic Area. (*Note:* As of the fall of 1997 the Sawyer River Rd. was closed to vehicles due to a major washout, and hikers will have to walk in from US 302 until the road can be repaired at an indefinite future date.) The trail begins on the right just before the bridge over Whiteface Brook; there is a parking lot on the left, just beyond the bridge. A crossing of Whiteface Brook less than 0.2 mi. from the road may be difficult at high water; at such times it may be best to avoid the crossing by bushwhacking up the south bank of the brook from the parking lot. The trail climbs moderately for most of its distance, using old roads that once provided access to the firewarden's cabin. The views from the observation tower on the summit and from Signal Ridge are magnificent. The loop back to Sawyer River Rd. via the Desolation and Carri-gain Notch trails is interesting but much longer, rougher, and more strenuous.

Leaving the road, the Signal Ridge Trail soon reaches and follows an old logging road that crosses Whiteface Brook at 0.2 mi., then follows the south bank of the attractive brook, passing small cascades and pools. At 0.8 mi. it begins to climb steadily away from the brook, then levels and crosses a flat divide. At 1.4 mi. Carrigain Brook Rd. (FR 86), a grass-grown logging road, crosses the trail at a right angle. (This road is not passable by vehicles, but it can be followed south 1.6 mi. to Sawyer River Rd. about 0.3 mi. before the gate at the end of that road. However, there is a difficult brook crossing just before Sawyer River Rd. is reached, and the road is becoming overgrown.) At 1.7 mi. the Carrigain Notch Trail diverges right toward the site of the former Desolation Shelter and the Pemigewasset Wilderness, and the Signal Ridge Trail soon cross-es Carrigain Brook, which may be difficult at high water. The trail passes an area of beaver activity, crosses a brook, and begins to ascend, gradually at first. At 2.4 mi. it turns sharp left where an old road continues straight up the valley. The trail angles up the end of a ridge, turns right to climb, then makes another sharp left turn (arrow) at the site of an old camp and angles up again.

At 2.8 mi. the Signal Ridge Trail turns sharp right into a birch-lined straight section 1.0 mi. long that rises steadily at an angle up the steep side of the valley, with occasional views to the cliffs of Mt. Lowell across Carrigain Notch. At the end of this section, the trail turns sharp left and zigzags up the nose of Signal Ridge through several areas that were damaged by the windstorm of December 1980, reaching the high point of the bare crest of the ridge at 4.5 mi. Views are excellent, particularly to the cliffs of Mt. Lowell across Carrigain Notch. The trail descends slightly, then angles left around to the south slope of the summit cone, climbing gradually to the site of the old firewarden's cabin, where there is a well (water unsafe to drink without treatment). Bearing left from the small clearing, the trail soon swings right and climbs steeply to the small sag between Carrigain's two summit knobs, then turns right and soon reaches the summit. Here the Desolation Trail enters from the Pemigewasset Wilderness.

Signal Ridge Trail (map 3:I8–H7)

Distances from Sawyer River Rd.(1480')

   to Carrigain Notch Trail (1900'): 1.7 mi., 400 ft., 1 hr. 5 min.

   to Signal Ridge (4420'): 4.5 mi., 2950 ft., 3 hr. 45 min.

   to Mt. Carrigain summit (4700'): 5.0 mi. (8.1 km.), 3250 ft., 4 hr. 10 min.

Distance from US 302 (897')

   to Mt. Carrigain summit (4700'): 7.0 mi. (11.3 km.), 3900 ft., 5 hr. 25 min.

Carrigain Notch Trail (AMC)

This trail begins on the Signal Ridge Trail at a point 1.7 mi. from Sawyer River Rd., runs through Carrigain Notch and past the site of the former Desolation Shelter, and ends at Stillwater Junction where it meets the Wilderness and Shoal Pond trails (see Section 3). The section of this trail northwest of Carrigain Notch lies within the Pemigewasset Wilderness.

It diverges right (north) from the Signal Ridge Trail and crosses Carrigain Brook in 60 yd.; care is required to find the trail on the opposite bank at this crossing, going either way. Continuing on logging roads at easy grades, it passes through an area of beaver activity, then several stony areas, and at 1.6 mi. turns left off the road to bypass a muddy section. Here, just off to the right of the trail, there is a view of the ledges of Vose Spur, which form the west side of Carrigain Notch. Soon returning to the road, the trail climbs more steeply, and at 2.3 mi. reaches its height-of-land well up on the west wall of the notch and enters the Pemigewasset Wilderness. Very soon it strikes and follows an old logging road on the north side of the notch, descending moderately. At 3.1 mi. it turns left off the logging road and follows a path through the woods that avoids the wet sections of the old road while continuing to use some of the dry parts. At 4.1 mi. the trail enters an old railroad grade and turns sharp left on it; the Nancy Pond Trail follows the grade to the right from this point. At 4.9 mi. the trail bears left off the railroad grade, then soon turns sharp right where the Desolation Trail continues straight across the brook. At 5.1 mi. it passes the site of Desolation Shelter (camping now forbidden within a quarter-mile of this site), then bears to the right, away from the Carrigain Branch, and reaches Stillwater Junction on the East Branch; here the Wilderness Trail turns sharp left, and the Shoal Pond Trail turns right and immediately crosses the East Branch of the Pemigewasset.

Carrigain Notch Trail (map 3:I8–H7)

Distances from Signal Ridge Trail (1900')

  to Carrigain Notch (2637'): 2.3 mi., 750 ft., 1 hr. 30 min.

  to Nancy Pond Trail (2140'): 4.1 mi., 750 ft. (rev. 500 ft.), 2 hr. 30 min.

  to site of former Desolation Shelter (2160'): 5.1 mi., 750 ft., 3 hr.

  to Stillwater Junction (2050'): 5.7 mi. (9.2 km.), 750 ft. (rev. 100 ft.), 3 hr. 20 min.

Desolation Trail (AMC)

This trail ascends to the summit of Mt. Carrigain from the Carrigain Notch Trail about 0.2 mi. southeast of the site of the former Desolation Shelter. The upper part of the trail is very steep and rough and requires great care, particularly on the descent or with heavy packs; substantial extra time may be required in either direction. Practically all of the trail is in the Pemigewasset Wilderness.

The trail leaves the Carrigain Notch Trail at a sharp turn near the edge of a tributary of the Carrigain Branch and crosses the brook. It follows a railroad grade for 60 yd., then diverges left and climbs moderately, at times on old logging roads. It climbs into a fine stand of birches and merges into an unusually straight old logging road on the west side of the ridgecrest. (For a long section of this road, there is old telephone wire at the left edge of the trail that hikers need to watch for, as it may trip an unwary individual.) The old road crosses to the east side of the ridge, deteriorates, and ends at 1.3 mi. The trail crosses a short section of slippery rock blocks and continues through an area where many rock steps have been built, then swings directly up the slope into virgin woods and climbs a very steep and rough section. The grade gradually eases up and the footing slowly improves as the trail reaches the crest of the steep ridge. At 1.8 mi. the trail abruptly reaches the top of the steep section, swings left, and angles around the cone at an easy grade until it reaches and climbs the last short steep pitch to the summit observation tower, where it meets the Signal Ridge Trail.

Desolation Trail (map 3:H7)

Distances from Carrigain Notch Trail (2180')

   to upper end of old logging road (3530'): 1.3 mi., 1350 ft., 1 hr. 20 min.

   to Mt. Carrigain summit (4700'): 1.9 mi. (3.1 km.), 2500 ft., 2 hr. 10 min.

Nancy Pond Trail (Camp Pasquaney/WMNF)

This trail begins on the west side of US 302, 2.8 mi. north of the Sawyer Rock picnic area and 6.7 mi. south of the Willey House site in Crawford Notch State Park. It passes Nancy Cascades and Nancy and Norcross ponds, and ends on the Carrigain Notch Trail 1.0 mi. east of the site of the former Desolation Shelter (where camping is now forbidden). The section of the trail west of Norcross Pond lies within the Pemigewasset Wilderness. Deep snow or ice may remain in the shady ravine above Nancy Cascades quite late in the spring.

Leaving US 302, the trail follows an assortment of paths and old roads but is well marked with yellow paint and signs. It first follows a logging road for 250 yd., diverges left and crosses a small brook, then joins a logging road along Halfway Brook, and soon turns right off the road and crosses Halfway Brook. It enters the Nancy Pond Scenic Area, and then a woods road joins from the right (descending, bear right here). The trail continues to the WMNF boundary, marked by a large pile of red-painted stones, at 0.8 mi. Here it enters and follows an old logging road along Nancy Brook, crossing the brook on the rocks at 1.6 mi. (may be difficult at high water). It continues upstream on the road and passes the remains of the Lucy mill at 1.8 mi. Above here the old road virtually disappears, and the trail ascends through a rough area of landslides, recrosses Nancy Brook, and soon reaches the foot of Nancy Cascades at 2.4 mi., where the stream falls over a high, steep ledge into a beautiful pool.

The trail turns sharp left at the pool and ascends the steep slope by switchbacks, providing another outlook at the middle of the cascades, and passes near the top of the cascades, which are several hundred feet high, at 2.8 mi. From the top of the cascades, the trail winds through the moss-carpeted virgin spruce forest past a small overgrown tarn to the northeast shore of Nancy Pond (4 acres in area) at 3.4 mi. Continuing along the north shore, the trail crosses the swamp at the upper end, then passes over the almost imperceptible height-of-land that divides Saco from Pemigewasset drainage and reaches Little Norcross Pond. Skirting the north shore, it then climbs over another small rise to Norcross Pond (7 acres in area). Again hugging the north shore, and crossing into the Pemigewasset Wilderness, it enters a logging road 25 yd. before reaching the ledgy natural dam at the west end of Norcross Pond at 4.3 mi. (In the reverse direction, turn right off the logging road 25 yd. from the ledgy dam and follow a path along the shore of the pond.) At the ledges there is a commanding outlook to Mt. Bond and the Twin Range, with the Franconias in the distance.

After crossing the stream at the outlet of Norcross Pond, the Nancy Pond Trail descends gradually west on a logging road, passing a spring (iron pipe) on the south side of the trail at 5.5 mi. At 6.0 mi. the trail veers right, crosses Norcross Brook (may be difficult in high water), then shortly reaches an old railroad bed and swings left onto it. At 6.4 mi. it crosses Anderson Brook (may be difficult in high water), then passes along the south side of the Camp 19 clearing. At 6.8 mi. it turns left off the railroad grade and crosses the East Branch of the Pemigewasset River on a bridge, just a short distance below the point where the East Branch begins at the confluence of Norcross and Anderson brooks. On the other side, it follows another railroad grade, bearing right at a fork. It then crosses Notch Brook and ends 25 yd. beyond, where the Carrigain Notch Trail enters sharp left from Sawyer River Rd. and continues straight ahead on the railroad grade to the site of the former Desolation Shelter and Stillwater Junction.

Nancy Pond Trail (map 3:H8–H7)

Distances from US 302 (940')

> *to* foot of Nancy Cascades (2400'): 2.4 mi., 1450 ft., 1 hr. 55 min.
>
> *to* Nancy Pond (3100'): 3.5 mi., 2150 ft., 2 hr. 50 min.
>
> *to* Norcross Pond outlet (3120'): 4.3 mi., 2150 ft., 3 hr. 15 min.
>
> *to* Carrigain Notch Trail (2140'): 7.1 mi. (11.4 km.), 2150 ft. (rev. 1000 ft.), 4 hr. 40 min.
>
> *to* Stillwater Junction (2050') via Carrigain Notch Trail: 8.7 mi. (14.0 km.), 2150 ft. (rev. 100 ft.), 5 hr. 25 min.

Cedar Brook Trail (WMNF)

This trail runs from the Hancock Notch Trail, 1.7 mi. from the Kancamagus Highway, to the Wilderness Trail at the east end of the suspension bridge, 5.4 mi. from the Kancamagus Highway. In combination with the Hancock Notch and Hancock Loop trails, the southern portion of this trail affords the most direct route to Mt. Hancock. The five crossings of the North Fork of the Hancock Branch between the Hancock Notch Trail and the Hancock Loop Trail are difficult in high water, but the first two are easily bypassed and the others can be avoided by bushwhacking along the east bank to the Hancock Loop Trail (which makes a sixth crossing soon after its divergence from the Cedar Brook Trail).

Leaving the Hancock Notch Trail, the Cedar Brook Trail immediately crosses a small brook and climbs moderately on an old logging road for about 0.2 mi., then crosses the North Fork of the Hancock Branch five times in 0.4 mi. The first two crossings are only 40 yd. apart and can be avoided by following a well-beaten path on the near bank. The beginning of the Hancock Loop Trail is reached on the right at 0.7 mi., 150 yd. beyond the fifth crossing.

The Cedar Brook Trail soon passes into the Pemigewasset Wilderness, climbing moderately on a somewhat rough footway that occasionally must be carefully distinguished from miscellaneous brooks and muddy abandoned routes of the trail. It reaches the height-of-land between Mt. Hancock and Mt. Hitchcock at 1.4 mi. and descends on logging roads, swinging out to the west then back to the northeast side of the valley, crossing several brooks. It reaches the site of Camp 24A (sign) at 2.9 mi., then continues to descend on old roads, and at 4.1 mi. it drops down a bank to the old logging railroad at the edge of Cedar Brook and turns sharp right on the railroad grade. Soon it passes through the extensive clearings of Camp 24 and continues down toward the East Branch of the Pemigewasset. At 5.5 mi. an old grass-grown road enters on the left; this road, commonly known as the East Branch Truck Road (FR 87), follows the south and east banks of the East Branch to the Wilderness Trail parking lot, but it is no longer used by vehicles within the Wilderness, and it is somewhat overgrown near this junction so it would be rather hard to identify without the sign ("East Side Trail") that was placed here in 1997. The Cedar Brook Trail swings to the east, paralleling the East Branch, and joins the Wilderness Trail at the east end of the suspension bridge.

Cedar Brook Trail (map 3:I6–H6)
Distances from Hancock Notch Trail (2520')

to Hancock Loop Trail (2720'): 0.7 mi., 200 ft., 25 min.

to height-of-land (3100'): 1.4 mi., 600 ft., 1 hr.

to Camp 24A (2400'): 2.9 mi., 600 ft. (rev. 700 ft.), 1 hr. 45 min.

to Camp 24 (1940'): 4.3 mi., 600 ft. (rev. 450 ft.), 2 hr. 25 min.

to Wilderness Trail (1640'): 6.1 mi. (9.7 km.), 600 ft. (rev. 300 ft.), 3 hr. 20 min.

Hancock Notch Trail (WMNF)

This trail begins at the Kancamagus Highway at the hairpin turn, passes through Hancock Notch between Mt. Hancock and Mt. Huntington, then descends along the Sawyer River to the Sawyer River Trail. At the Kancamagus Highway terminus, parking is available at the Hancock Overlook just above the trailhead. With the Cedar Brook and Hancock Loop trails, this trail provides the easiest and most popular route to Mt. Hancock. From the Kancamagus Highway to the Cedar Brook Trail, the Hancock Notch Trail is heavily used, wide, and easily followed; from the Cedar Brook Trail to the Sawyer River Trail, it is often wet and rough, and in places requires care to follow.

Leaving the Kancamagus Highway, the trail follows an old railroad bed, crossing a brook at 0.6 mi. and gradually approaching the North Fork of the Hancock Branch. It stays on the same side of the North Fork, swinging right slightly uphill to enter a logging road at the point where the railroad grade crossed the river; take care not to follow the remains of the railroad grade across the river here. The trail follows the logging road at an easy grade, then descends slightly, crosses two brooks in less than 0.1 mi., and soon reaches the junction with the Cedar Brook Trail at 1.7 mi. (For Mt. Hancock, turn left on this trail across a small brook.)

The Hancock Notch Trail now rises somewhat more steeply for about 0.8 mi. to the notch, which is flat and very wet. East of the notch it passes through a dense stand of spruce on a rougher footway, descending quite rapidly at times. The grade soon moderates and the trail crosses to the north side of Sawyer River at 3.4 mi., then back to the south side at 4.0 mi. Soon the trail diverges from the river, passes by a beaver pond, and follows logging roads across a south branch of the river. Continuing to descend easily, it crosses Sawyer River twice more, at 5.3 mi. and 5.8 mi. (both crossings may be difficult at high water), and follows newer logging roads to its end at the Sawyer River Trail in Hayshed Field, an overgrown clearing 1.2 mi. from Sawyer River Rd.

Hancock Notch Trail (map 3:I6–I7)

Distances from Kancamagus Highway (2129')

> *to* Cedar Brook Trail (2520'): 1.8 mi., 400 ft., 1 hr. 5 min.
>
> *to* Hancock Notch (2800'): 2.5 mi., 700 ft., 1 hr. 35 min.
>
> *to* Sawyer River Trail (1780'): 6.7 mi. (10.8 km.), 700 ft. (rev. 1000 ft.), 3 hr. 40 min.

Hancock Loop Trail (AMC)

This trail makes a loop over both the major summits of Mt. Hancock. It is steep and rough but well trodden and easy to follow, though the part on the ridge between the peaks is subject to blowdowns. It is most easily reached from the hairpin turn on the Kancamagus Highway by following the Hancock Notch and Cedar Brook trails for 2.5 mi. There are five brook crossings on the Cedar Brook Trail that may be difficult at high water.

Leaving the Cedar Brook Trail on the right (east), 150 yd. north of the fifth crossing of the North Branch of the Hancock Branch, the trail follows an old logging road and soon recrosses the main brook, then passes over a steep, rocky brook bed and a wet area. Keeping south of the main brook, some distance away from it and considerably higher, the trail continues its gradual ascent and reaches the loop junction at 1.1 mi. from the start. From this point the circuit over the two main summits of Mt. Hancock can be made in either direction, so for convenience of description the trail is divided into three segments: North Link, Ridge Link, and South Link.

The *North Link* diverges left from the logging road at the loop junction and descends moderately at an angle. Soon it crosses a flat gravel area, usually dry but often with water flowing into it from the brook bed above and disappearing into the sand, where the foot of the Arrow Slide is visible about 50 yd. to the left. The trail then climbs roughly parallel to the slide, first at a moderate grade angling across the hillside, then straight up, very steep and rough. Near the top, the trail veers left and becomes less steep. At the wooded summit of North Hancock, a side path leads left 40 yd. to a fine view south to the Sandwich Range and Osceola, while the Ridge Link turns right.

The *South Link* continues along the logging road from the loop junction for another 0.1 mi., then swings right up the mountainside. The climb to South Hancock is unrelievedly steep, crossing numerous old logging roads. (These are some of the roads that are so prominent as light green lines across the dark slope when seen from other peaks.) At the summit, the Ridge Link enters on the left (north), and a short path descends straight ahead (east) to a viewpoint overlooking the Sawyer River valley.

The *Ridge Link* connects the summits of North and South Hancock. From the summit of North Hancock, it starts almost due north and curves to the right (east, then south), traversing the generally broad, bumpy ridge with several minor ups and downs, then climbs the final narrow section of ridge to the south peak at 1.4 mi., where the South Link enters on the right (west).

Hancock Loop Trail (map 3:I6–I7)

Distances from Cedar Brook Trail (2720')

to loop junction (3320'): 1.1 mi., 600 ft., 50 min.

to North Hancock (4420') via North Link: 1.8 mi., 1750 ft., 1 hr. 45 min.

to South Hancock (4319') via South Link: 1.6 mi., 1600 ft., 1 hr. 35 min.

Distances of loop over both summits

from Cedar Brook Trail (2720') in either direction: 4.8 mi. (7.7 km.), 2050 ft., 3 hr. 25 min.

from Kancamagus Highway (2129'): 9.8 mi. (15.7 km.), 2650 ft., 6 hr. 15 min.

Sawyer River Trail (WMNF)

This trail leads from Sawyer River Rd. (FR 34), at the end of the section open to public vehicular use about 4.0 mi. from US 302, to the Kancamagus Highway 3.1 mi. west of the Sabbaday Falls parking area and 0.6 mi. east of Lily Pond. Almost all the way it follows the bed of an old logging railroad at easy grades. (*Note:* As of the fall of 1997 Sawyer River Rd. was closed to vehicles due to a major washout, and hikers will have to walk in from US 302 until the road can be repaired at an indefinite future date.)

The trail follows the gravel road past the gate, and in 100 yd. the Sawyer Pond Trail turns left to cross Sawyer River on a footbridge. The Sawyer River Trail continues, taking the left of two gated gravel roads at a fork, crosses Sawyer River on the logging road bridge, and diverges right onto the old railroad grade 100 yd. beyond the bridge. (The gravel road can be followed 1.1 mi. to the junction of the Sawyer River Trail and Hancock Notch Trail at Hayshed Field, where it enters the Sawyer River Trail at a right angle; there are excellent views of Mt. Tremont and Mt. Carrigain from this road.) The railroad grade continues along the Sawyer River for 0.7 mi., then begins to swing to the south. It crosses a washed-out area and two brooks, and reaches the overgrown clearing called Hayshed Field at 1.2 mi., where the Hancock Notch Trail turns sharp right and the gravel road described above enters on the left. The Sawyer River Trail follows the old railroad bed across an imperceptible divide in the flat region west of Green's Cliff, passing several beaver swamps, and crosses Meadow Brook on a bridge at 2.5 mi. It follows the west bank of this stream for some distance, passing a junction where the Nanamocomuck (X-C) Ski Trail enters on the left at 3.2 mi., then swings southwest. The ski trail diverges right just before the Sawyer River Trail crosses the Swift River (which can be very difficult in high water) at 3.5 mi. The trail now ascends easily upstream along the river, passing a fine cascade and pool, then climbs up the bank, bearing left twice, to the Kancamagus Highway.

Sawyer River Trail (map 3:I8–I7)

Distances from Sawyer River Rd. (1610')

> *to* Hancock Notch Trail (1780'): 1.2 mi., 150 ft., 40 min.
>
> *to* Kancamagus Highway (1806'): 3.8 mi. (6.1 km.), 350 ft. (rev. 150 ft.), 2 hr. 5 min.

Church Pond Loop Trail (WMNF)

This loop trail provides an interesting short, level walk to Church Pond. It passes through an extensive, very flat and poorly drained region of pine and spruce swamps, providing access to a kind of terrain and forest that trails in the White Mtns. seldom visit. It is a very wet trip at times; the brook crossings can be quite difficult at high water. The trail begins in Passaconaway Campground just off the Kancamagus Highway, at the far end of the west loop road near Site 19. Parking at the trailhead is limited and the campground is closed much of the year, so it may be necessary to use the Downes Brook Trail parking lot on the south side of the highway.

The path descends slightly and crosses Downes Brook and the Swift River in rapid succession. Both these crossings may be difficult and will often require wading. The trail exits from the Swift River by a small rocky wash a bit upstream from where it enters the stream, then turns right and enters the woods. This part of the trail, with its dense, fast-growing stream-side vegetation, may require considerable care to follow. At 0.3 mi. the loop junction is reached; it is 0.8 mi. to the pond by the left-hand path (which is much drier), or 1.4 mi. by the right-hand path (which has very muddy sections). The Nanamocomuck (X-C) Ski Trail uses the first part of each branch.

From the loop junction, the walk is described in the clockwise direction. Taking the left-hand branch, the trail follows an old logging road for 0.4 mi. to the junction where the ski trail diverges left, then soon bears left and becomes a footpath, crosses a boggy area on log bridges, and at 1.1 mi. emerges on a knoll overlooking Church Pond, where there are fine views. Here the trail turns sharp right and runs above the shore of the pond for about 250 yd., then turns right again and starts back to the loop junction, first traversing a very muddy area, then running mostly on relatively high ground, repeatedly bearing right. The ski trail enters on the left 0.2 mi. before the loop junction.

Church Pond Loop Trail (map 3:J8–I8)

Distance from Passaconaway Campground (1251')

 for complete loop: 2.8 mi. (4.5 km.), 50 ft., 1 hr. 25 min.

Sawyer Pond Trail (WMNF)

This trail (which has easy grades throughout its length) begins at a new parking area on the Kancamagus Highway 0.6 mi. east of Passaconaway Campground and 1.4 mi. west of Bear Notch Rd. After passing Sawyer Pond and its campsite, the trail ends at Sawyer River Rd. (FR 34), near the gate that marks the end of public vehicular access at 4.0 mi. (*Note:* As of the fall of 1997 this road was closed to vehicles due to a major washout, and hikers will have to walk in from US 302 until the road can be repaired at an indefinite future date.) *Caution:* The crossing of the Swift River near the Kancamagus Highway usually requires wading and can be dangerous at high water.

From the Kancamagus Highway, the trail passes through a clearing, angles right to the bank of Swift River, and fords the stream to a sand bar. It soon enters the woods, where the Nanamocomuck (X-C) Ski Trail joins on the right, and runs through a beautiful pine grove. At 0.7 mi. the ski trail diverges on the left, and at 1.1 mi. the Brunel Trail diverges right. At 1.7 mi. the Sawyer Pond Trail crosses a new gravel logging road, then skirts the west slope of Birch Hill, descends gently, and crosses a grass-grown logging road (used and marked as a snowmobile trail) diagonally at 2.6 mi. It then comes close to a small brook, bears left away from it, passes over a flat divide, and descends to Sawyer Pond. As the pond is approached, there are a number of conflicting side paths; use care to stay on the correct path. At a point 15 yd. from the pond (where there are good views up to Mt. Tremont and Owl's Cliff), the trail turns left, crosses the outlet brook at 4.5 mi., and passes near the tent platforms of the Sawyer Pond campsite. In another 0.1 mi. it passes a side path that leads right 0.2 mi. to the shelter. It then descends gradually on an old logging road, and at 5.7 mi. turns sharp left off the road and recrosses the Sawyer Pond outlet brook on a bridge. From there it runs to the bank of Sawyer River, turns right to cross the river on a footbridge, then turns right again on the gravel extension of Sawyer River Rd. and continues about 100 yd. to the gate.

Sawyer Pond Trail (map 3:J8–I8)

Distances from Kancamagus Highway (1237')

   to Brunel Trail (1330'): 1.1 mi., 100 ft., 35 min.

   to Sawyer Pond (1940'): 4.5 mi., 900 ft. (rev. 200 ft.), 2 hr. 40 min.

   to Sawyer River Rd. (1610'): 6.0 mi. (9.7 km.), 900 ft. (rev 350 ft.), 3 hr. 25 min.

Rob Brook Trail (WMNF)

This nearly level trail follows old roads and a logging railroad grade through an area of attractive ponds and swamps, with some good views and much beaver activity (which may cause flooding of some trail sections). It parallels the Rob Brook Rd. (FR 35), beginning and ending on that road, which leaves Bear Notch Rd. about 0.8 mi. north of the Kancamagus Highway, opposite the trailhead of the Lower Nanamocomuck (X-C) Ski Trail. It is far more interesting and scenic but somewhat more difficult than the parallel section of road, traversing kinds of terrain not often visited by trails in the White Mtns. Most of the trail is dry, but some brook crossings (including several made on beaver dams) are extremely difficult at high water and wet (requiring wading in a significant depth of water) even in normal conditions.

   At the start it follows Rob Brook Rd., coinciding with the Upper Nanamocomuck (X-C) Ski Trail for the first mile. It diverges off the road to the right 0.2 mi. from Bear Notch Rd., then crosses back over Rob Brook Rd. at 0.7 mi. and descends easily on an old road. It crosses an area of open bogs on a boardwalk with a glimpse of Mt. Carrigain on the right and Mt. Chocorua on the left, then takes the right branch at a fork where the Upper Nanamocomuck Ski Trail continues straight. At 1.3 mi. the Rob Brook Trail reaches an old railroad grade and turns sharp right onto it. Soon it joins Rob Brook and crosses it five times. At the third crossing, which is made at a long beaver dam (usually requiring wading), there is a fine view of Mt. Tremont and Owl's Cliff. The Rob Brook Trail then continues on the railroad grade until it reaches the Rob Brook Rd., which at this point is also the route of the Brunel Trail. To the right, following this road, it is 0.3 mi. to the point where the Brunel Trail turns off the road and 2.9 mi. to the Bear Notch Rd.

Rob Brook Trail (map 3:I9–I8)

Distance from Bear Notch Rd. (1338')

   to Rob Brook Rd./Brunel Trail (1320'): 2.8 mi. (4.5 km.), 100 ft. (rev. 100 ft.), 1 hr. 25 min.

Brunel Trail (WMNF)

This trail runs from the Sawyer Pond Trail 1.1 mi. north of the Kancamagus Highway to the summit of Mt. Tremont. However, the most frequently used approach to this trail is the WMNF Rob Brook Rd. (FR 35), which leaves Bear Notch Rd. about 0.8 mi. north of the Kancamagus Highway. Rob Brook Rd. is closed to public vehicular travel, but it provides the easiest route to the point where the Brunel Trail departs from it, 2.6 mi. from Bear Notch Rd. The remainder of the Brunel Trail south of this point to the Kancamagus Highway is seldom used, largely because the ford of the Swift River near the start of the Sawyer Pond Trail is frequently difficult. The Rob Brook Trail provides a much more attractive alternative to this road walk but is apt to make a hiker's boots rather soggy. Parts of the Brunel Trail are very steep and rough; since the footway may be obscure in some areas, the yellow blazes must be followed with care. The views to the west from Mt. Tremont, and to the south from Owl's Cliff, are excellent.

The trail diverges right (northeast) from the Sawyer Pond Trail, and in 0.3 mi. it enters the extension of Rob Brook Rd., turns right, and follows this road past the junction with the Rob Brook Trail on the right at 0.9 mi. to the Albany-Bartlett town line (sign) at 1.2 mi., where the trail (sign) turns left off the road. This point is 2.6 mi. from Bear Notch Rd. via Rob Brook Rd.

Leaving Rob Brook Rd., the Brunel Trail passes through a stand of large conifers, and at 2.1 mi. it reaches and follows the edge of a logged area (follow blazes carefully). At 2.5 mi. it crosses a small brook and soon passes several large boulders that announce the approach to the east end of Owl's Cliff. At 2.8 mi. the trail swings left and climbs a very steep section, then turns sharp right (arrow). The grade moderates and finally becomes easy as the height-of-land is reached. At 3.1 mi. (1.9 mi. from Rob Brook Rd.) a spur path (sign) diverges left and climbs to a point just below the summit of Owl's Cliff, then descends slightly to a fine outlook ledge (use caution if wet or icy) 0.2 mi. from the main trail. From the junction, the Brunel Trail descends at a moderate grade into the sag, passes through a section where the footway is obscure (watch carefully for blazes), and then ascends very steeply; sections running straight up the slope alternate with old logging roads angling to the left. At 3.9 mi. (2.7 mi. from Rob Brook Rd.), the trail reaches the summit ledges of Mt. Tremont, where the Mount Tremont Trail enters from the north.

Brunel Trail (map 3:I8)

Distances from Sawyer Pond Trail (1330')

> *to* departure from Rob Brook Rd. at Albany-Bartlett town line (1330'): 1.2 mi., 0 ft., 40 min.

to Owl's Cliff spur (2800'): 3.1 mi., 1500 ft., 2 hr. 20 min.

to Mt. Tremont summit (3371'): 3.9 mi. (6.3 km.), 2300 ft. (rev. 250 ft.), 3 hr. 5 min.

Distances from Bear Notch Rd. (1338')

to departure from Rob Brook Rd. at Albany-Bartlett town line (1330') via Rob Brook Rd.: 2.6 mi., 100 ft. (rev. 100 ft.), 1 hr. 20 min.

to Mt. Tremont summit: 5.3 mi. (8.5 km.), 2400 ft. (rev. 250 ft.), 3 hr. 50 min.

Mount Tremont Trail (PEAOC)

This trail begins on the south side of US 302, 0.5 mi. west of the Sawyer Rock picnic area and 0.1 mi. west of the bridge over Stony Brook, and climbs to the summit of Mt. Tremont, where there are fine views.

Leaving US 302, it soon reaches and follows the west side of Stony Brook. At 0.7 mi. it swings right and climbs steadily for 0.3 mi. to the top of the ridge (watch for a sharp right turn up a steep bank). It then levels off and crosses a recent logging road. For the next a quarter-mile there is still some lingering evidence of the extensive blowdown caused by the windstorm of December 1980; the trail is almost straight and thus will continue in the original line after bypassing a bad spot.

At 1.5 mi. the trail crosses a branch of Stony Brook after a slight descent, then zigzags up the steep northeast side of the mountain at a moderate grade, crossing a rather sharp boundary between birch woods and virgin conifers at 2.4 mi. Reaching the ridge top, it passes an outlook on the right and continues to the ledgy summit.

Mount Tremont Trail (map 3:I8)
Distance from US 302 (820')

to Mt. Tremont summit (3371'): 2.8 mi. (4.6 km.), (2600 ft.), 2 hr. 40 min.

Lovequist Loop (WMNF)

This short, easy loop path provides access to scenic little Falls Pond from the popular Rocky Gorge Picnic Area, which is located on the Kancamagus Highway 8.4 mi. west of NH 16 and 3.4 mi. east of its junction with the Bear Notch Rd. From the parking area at Rocky Gorge, follow the paved walkway and the bridge across the gorge. About 50 yd. past the bridge the loop junction is reached; the section of the loop on the east shore of the pond is also part of the Lower Nanamocomuck (X-C) Ski Trail. Turning left, to follow the loop in a clockwise direction, the trails coincide for about 100 yd., then the pond loop turns right at the south end of the pond and swings around its west shore. After traveling 0.4 mi. from the ski trail junction, the pond loop rejoins the ski trail at the north end of the pond and returns to the loop junction near the bridge across the Swift River.

Lovequist Loop (3:I9)

Distance from Rocky Falls Picnic Area (1120')

  for complete loop: 1.0 mi. (1.6 km.), 50 ft., 30 min.

Boulder Loop Trail (WMNF)

This is a loop trail to ledges on a southwest spur of the Moat Range, starting from the north side of Dugway Rd. just west of the entrance to the WMNF Covered Bridge Campground. (The covered bridge is closed to vehicles from November to May, requiring a short extra walk at these times for hikers approaching this trailhead from the Kancamagus Highway.) It offers excellent views for a relatively modest effort, though it does involve about 1000 ft. of climbing. An interpretive leaflet, keyed to numbered stations along the trail, can be obtained at the Saco Ranger District Office on the Kancamagus Highway near NH 16, and is sometimes also available at the trailhead.

    The trail leaves Dugway Rd. and reaches the loop junction at 0.2 mi. From here the loop is described in the clockwise direction. Taking the left-hand branch, the trail shortly passes a large boulder (left), where it turns right and climbs moderately past an outlook to Chocorua, then soon turns sharp left. At 1.3 mi., at the main trail's high point, a spur path leads right (south) 0.1 mi. to ledges that afford a fine view of Mt. Passaconaway, Mt. Chocorua, and Middle Sister. The main trail continues around the ledges and descends toward Big Brook, then turns right below the ledges, crosses a stream, and passes an overhanging boulder (left) at 2.3 mi. It then returns to the loop junction at 2.6 mi., 0.2 mi. from Dugway Rd.

Boulder Loop Trail (map 3:I10)

Distances from Dugway Rd. (860')

  to loop junction (910'): 0.2 mi., 50 ft., 10 min.

  to spur path to ledges (1750'): 1.3 mi., 900 ft., 1 hr. 10 min.

  for complete loop including spur to ledges: 3.1 mi. (5.0 km.), 950 ft., 2 hr.

Moat Mountain Trail (WMNF)

This trail traverses the main ridge of Moat Mtn., providing magnificent views from numerous outlooks. Parts of the ridge are very exposed to weather, particularly the section that crosses Middle Moat and South Moat. The south terminus of the trail is located on Dugway Rd. At the lights in Conway village, turn north (directly opposite NH 153) onto Passaconaway Rd., which becomes West Side Rd. Go left at a fork, then left on Still Rd., which becomes Dugway Rd. The Moat Mountain Trail leaves Dugway Rd. about 3.5 mi. from Conway (sign). Dugway Rd. continues and joins the Kancamagus Highway near Blackberry Crossing Campground (but the covered bridge on Dugway Rd. near its junction with the Kancamagus Highway is closed to vehicles from November to May). The northeast terminus of the trail is reached from Conway village via Passaconaway Rd. and West Side Rd., or from North Conway (at a point just north of the Eastern Slope Inn) by following River Rd. west across the Saco River to West Side Rd. Once on West Side Rd., drive north to a point 0.7 mi. north of the road to Cathedral Ledge (2.2 mi. from the junction of NH 16 and River Rd. in North Conway), then turn left onto a gravel road that runs between farm fields, and park along the roadside.

Starting from the northeast terminus, continue on foot on the gravel road 0.5 mi. to the clearing just below mill site at Diana's Baths, a series of scenic cascades where Lucy Brook runs over ledges and through large potholes. The main path leaves the upper end of the clearing, close to the baths, by a logging road that follows the north bank of Lucy Brook to a fork (sign) at 1.1 mi. Here the Red Ridge Trail turns left across the brook, eventually rejoining the Moat Mountain Trail at the apex of Red Ridge, making possible a fine loop hike. The Moat Mountain Trail crosses Lucy Brook at 1.3 mi. and follows the south bank, then at 2.3 mi. turns abruptly left uphill, away from the stream (last sure water), at the point where the Attitash Trail continues straight ahead along the stream toward Big Attitash Mtn. The Moat Mountain Trail ascends through the woods, and at 2.7 mi. begins to pass over ledgy areas, reaching the first good outlook at 3.5 mi. It reaches a shoulder at 3.9 mi. and runs nearly level through a patch of larger trees, then climbs fairly steeply through decreasing scrub and increasing bare ledge to the summit of North Moat at 4.2 mi., where there is an unobstructed view in all directions.

From the summit of North Moat the trail descends sharply to the base of the cone, then easily along a shoulder with occasional views. At the end of the shoulder it drops steeply, passing over several ledges that require some scrambling, then moderates and continues to a col in a fine spruce forest. Ascending again, it passes the junction with the Red Ridge Trail left (east) at 5.3 mi., just below several large rocks that provide good views. The trail descends to the major col on the ridge, then climbs up to low scrub followed by open ledges with continuous views, and passes east of the summit of Middle Moat (which can be reached in 80 yd. over open ledges) at 6.3 mi. The trail descends to a minor col with a patch of woods that would provide some shelter in a storm, then ascends to the summit of South Moat at 6.9 mi.

The trail then descends into scrub and gradually increasing numbers of beautiful red pines, with views decreasing in frequency. At 7.5 mi. the trail passes an outlook to Mt. Chocorua (on the ascent from the south terminus, this is the first good outlook reached), and the trail becomes steep with rough footing. Below this section the grade eases considerably, and at 8.3 mi. the trail becomes a well-defined logging road with easy grades and footing. At 8.9 mi. it passes the red-painted WMNF boundary and goes straight at a crossroads, then turns right where another road enters from the left (in the reverse direction, bear left at an arrow 0.2 mi. from Dugway Rd.). Then the trail passes through a farmyard to reach Dugway Rd.

Moat Mountain Trail (map 3:I11–J10)

Distances from West Side Rd. (550')

> *to* Red Ridge Trail, lower junction (750'): 1.1 mi., 200 ft., 40 min.

> *to* Attitash Trail (1080'): 2.3 mi., 550 ft., 1 hr. 25 min.

> *to* North Moat summit (3196'): 4.2 mi., 2650 ft., 3 hr. 25 min.

> *to* Red Ridge Trail, upper junction (2760'): 5.3 mi., 2800 ft., 4 hr. 5 min.

> *to* Middle Moat summit area (2800'): 6.3 mi., 3150 ft., 4 hr. 45 min.

> *to* South Moat summit (2770'): 6.9 mi., 3250 ft., 5 hr. 5 min.

> *to* Dugway Rd. (620'): 9.2 mi. (14.8 km.), 3250 ft., 6 hr. 15 min.

Distances from Dugway Rd. (620')

> *to* South Moat summit (2770'): 2.3 mi., 2150 ft., 2 hr. 15 min.

> *to* Middle Moat summit area (2800'): 2.9 mi., 2300 ft., 2 hr. 35 min.

> *to* Red Ridge Trail, upper junction (2760'): 3.8 mi., 2600 ft., 3 hr. 10 min.

> *to* North Moat summit (3196'): 5.0 mi., 3200 ft., 4 hr. 5 min.

> *to* Attitash Trail (1080'): 6.8 mi., 3200 ft., 5 hr.

> *to* Red Ridge Trail, lower junction (750'): 8.1 mi., 3200 ft., 5 hr. 40 min.

> *to* West Side Rd. (550'): 9.2 mi. (14.8 km.), 3200 ft., 6 hr. 10 min.

Red Ridge Trail (WMNF)

This trail ascends Red Ridge, with magnificent views, leaving the Moat Mountain Trail 1.1 mi. from West Side Rd. and rejoining it at the unnamed peak at the apex of Red Ridge, 1.1 mi. south of the summit of North Moat. With the Moat Mountain Trail, it provides a very attractive loop over the open summit of North Moat.

This trail branches left (south) from the Moat Mountain Trail and immediately crosses Lucy Brook, a difficult crossing in high water. It ascends generally south at a gentle grade, crossing an area of active logging where it must be followed with care. The Red Ridge Link leaves on the left for White Horse Ledge at 0.8 mi., and the Red Ridge Trail generally descends gradually until it crosses the gravel Red Ridge Rd. (FR 379) at 1.5 mi. The trail now enters the WMNF, approaches Moat Brook and follows it, then crosses it at 2.0 mi. and zigzags upward, climbing to a gravel bank where there are good views. Continuing upward rather steeply, it ascends a steep ledge by means of an eroded trap dike and soon attains the crest of Red Ridge, where the grade moderates. Passing alternately through scrub and over ledges with good views, it reaches the bottom of an extensive open ledge section with magnificent views at 3.0 mi. At 3.4 mi. it re-enters scrub and soon rejoins the Moat Mountain Trail at the foot of several little rock knobs on the top of a small peak on the main ridgecrest between North Moat and Middle Moat.

Red Ridge Trail (map 3:I10)

Distances from Moat Mountain Trail, lower junction (750')

   to Red Ridge Link (950'): 0.8 mi., 200 ft., 30 min.

   to crossing of Moat Brook (1160'): 2.0 mi., 500 ft. (rev. 100 ft.), 1 hr. 15 min.

   to Moat Mountain Trail, upper junction (2760'): 3.6 mi. (5.7 km.), 2100 ft., 2 hr. 50 min.

Red Ridge Link (NHDP)

This short path links the Red Ridge Trail with the White Horse Ledge Trail, connecting the trails on Moat Mtn. with those on White Horse and Cathedral ledges. It leaves the Red Ridge Trail on the left (east) 0.8 mi. from the Moat Mountain Trail, just past the top of a small rise. It ascends through open hemlock forest and then younger growth at a moderate grade, turning sharp left, then sharp right 60 yd. farther, at the tops of two wooded ledges. These turns may be difficult to see, particularly descending, if the trail blazes are faded. It ends at the White Horse Ledge Trail 0.2 mi. below the summit ledges.

Red Ridge Link (map 3:I10)

Distance from Red Ridge Trail (950')

   to White Horse Ledge Trail (1370'): 0.4 mi. (0.7 km.), 400 ft., 25 min.

Attitash Trail (WMNF)

This trail runs from Bear Notch Rd., 2.7 mi. south of its junction with US 302 in Bartlett village, to the Moat Mountain Trail 2.3 mi. west of West Side Rd. The trail is well trodden from Bear Notch Rd. to the ledges of Table Mtn., where there are good views from an area burned by a small forest fire in October 1984. Except for these ledges, the trail is in the woods all the way, and between Table Mtn. and West Moat it is very lightly used and may require some care to follow.

Leaving the small parking area on Bear Notch Rd., the trail follows a grass-grown gravel logging road that crosses a major branch of Louisville Brook in about 120 yd. At 0.3 mi. the trail bears right on an older road as the gravel road bears left into a clearcut area. At 0.6 mi. the trail comes to the edge of Louisville Brook at a small, ledgy cascade, and follows near the brook. In less than 0.1 mi. it turns left (arrow) at a logging road fork and ascends moderately to the col between Bear Mtn. and Table Mtn. at 1.3 mi. Here it turns sharp left and climbs more steeply, soon reaching the edge of the burned area, and crosses two ledges with excellent views to the south and southwest. At 1.9 mi. it reaches its high point on Table Mtn., and passes somewhat south of the summit, with views available a short distance to the right from the edge of the south cliff.

From this point the trail appears to be used more by moose than by humans, and has at times been difficult to follow in some sections, although currently it is well cleared. It descends into a col at 2.5 mi., where there is a brook (unreliable), passes a ledgy spot with a glimpse of Mt. Carrigain, and soon climbs a very steep pitch to the main ridge of Big Attitash. From here the trail runs on the ridge top or a bit to its north side until it passes very close to the summit of Big Attitash at 4.7 mi. Then it descends, rather steeply at times, into the valley of Lucy Brook, which is crossed seven times. The first crossing, at 5.9 mi., may be dry; some of the lower crossings may be difficult in high water. The trail follows an old logging road along the brook, and at some of the crossings (which are mostly marked with arrows) care must be used to pick up the trail on the opposite bank. At 7.2 mi. it reaches the junction with the Moat Mountain Trail, which can be followed to the right to North Moat or straight ahead to Diana's Baths and West Side Rd.

Attitash Trail (map 3:I9–I10)

Distances from Bear Notch Rd. (1260')

    to high point on Table Mtn. (2680'): 1.9 mi., 1400 ft., 1 hr. 40 min.

    to Big Attitash Mtn. summit (2910'): 4.7 mi., 2300 ft. (rev. 200 ft.), 3 hr. 30 min.

    to Moat Mountain Trail (1080'): 7.2 mi. (11.6 km.), 2300 ft. (rev. 1850 ft.), 4 hr. 45 min.

Paths on White Horse Ledge and Cathedral Ledge (NHDP)

These two bluffs on an eastern spur of the Moat Range afford interesting views and are reached by trails from Echo Lake State Park. Cathedral Ledge is also ascended by an automobile road. The cliffs on both bluffs are very popular with rock climbers but cannot be safely ascended without proper equipment and training. The two principal trails are the White Horse Ledge Trail and the Bryce Path. The Bryce Path is named for James Bryce (later Viscount Bryce), a British statesman and author of many books on the theory of government, who wrote *The American Commonwealth,* an important study of the US government from a British perspective. This trail, which originally consisted of the path up the slope between the two cliffs and the branches to both summits, was laid out by Bryce in 1907 when he was British ambassador to the US Construction on private land between Echo Lake and the foot of White Horse Ledge has compelled a major relocation of the southern part of the White Horse Ledge Trail. For the sake of simplicity, and in order to describe the trails in the sequence in which they are usually followed, the two trails are described here as a single loop trail over White Horse Ledge, with a spur path to Cathedral Ledge. In recent years the part of the loop that runs south from White Horse Ledge and then back down to the loop junction has been somewhat difficult to follow in general, and the path has been obliterated in the section that runs along the new golf course; its future is in doubt, as the golf course management discourages its use during the golf season. For these reasons, the use of the southern section of the White Horse Ledge Trail between the loop junction and the Red Ridge Link is not recommended to the average hiker. It may be used, however, by experienced hikers who are willing to seek out their own route in the narrow strip of land between the golf course and the interesting jumbled boulders at the foot of the cliff.

    There are two routes available from public roads to the loop junction:

(1) Leave NH 16 in North Conway just north of the Eastern Slope Inn and take River Rd., which runs west across the Saco River. Turn left at 1.0 mi., then right at 1.4 mi., following signs for Echo Lake State Park, and reach the park gate at 1.5 mi. If the park is closed, parking is available on an old segment of road to the left, and the park road can be followed from the gate to the trailhead (signs). From here the path descends 60 yd. nearly to the edge of Echo Lake, then bears left and runs along the lake, some distance away but mostly in sight of it. At 0.4 mi. the trail to the ledges turns sharp left, while the Echo Lake Trail continues around the lake and returns to the trailhead at the parking area in another 0.5 mi.; it is poorly marked and its footway is not always well defined, particularly in the vicinity of the main beach, but its route along the shore is fairly obvious, and there are good views of the cliffs from the east shore. From its junction with the Echo Lake Trail, the trail to the ledges runs almost perfectly straight through attractive woods, crossing two unsigned but fairly well beaten paths, and reaches a crossroads, which is the loop junction, at 0.7 mi.

(2) This route is shorter (saving a bit less than 0.5 mi. and about 10 min. each way) and avoids park admission fees, but is less attractive. It has sometimes been called the Bryce Link. Continue straight at 1.0 mi. from NH 16 instead of turning left for Echo Lake State Park, then turn left onto Cathedral Ledge Rd. at 1.5 mi. from NH 16. Follow this road (which ends in 1.8 mi. just below the summit of Cathedral Ledge) for 0.3 mi., then turn left and follow a rough dirt road 0.1 mi. to a parking area. Continue on the dirt road on foot 0.2 mi. to the loop junction at the crossroads.

At the crossroads, where there is a fine view of the impressive slabs of White Horse Ledge, one road leads south into a clearing with a cabin near its high point. Facing this road, access route 1 is on your left, access route 2 is behind you, and on your right is the Bryce Path, which ascends to the sag between the two summits and gives access to either. The road you are facing is the beginning of the south part of the White Horse Ledge loop, which runs from the loop junction along the east side of White Horse Ledge and then climbs its south ridge to the Red Ridge Link junction near the summit of White Horse Ledge. This part of the loop is much less heavily used than the north part, and the footway is much less apparent and even obliterated in one section, so it is not well suited for inexperienced hikers. In addition, its use is discouraged by the neighboring private landowner. The loop is therefore described in the counter-clockwise direction. However, the road and the part of the loop path that continues from its end can be followed south 0.2 mi. to the point where the rock climbers' path to the base of White Horse Ledge leaves on the right; the steep slab, whose base is 80 yd. from this junction, is worth a visit, but its ascent is a technical climb that must be left to properly trained and equipped rock climbers.

From the loop junction, the Bryce Path passes near the foundation of an old sugar-house and the cabin in the clearing, then reaches a wooded rock slab and climbs directly uphill fairly steeply with rough footing for about 0.1 mi. It then bears right and runs almost level to a junction at 0.3 mi. from the loop junction.

Here the path to Cathedral Ledge continues almost straight across a flat, wooded upland for 0.2 mi., then turns sharp right and climbs rather steeply to a ⊤ intersection, where it turns left and reaches the turnaround at the top of the Cathedral Ledge Rd. in another 40 yd. A right at the ⊤ leads to the south outlook in 80 yd. (The summit area is interlaced with countless beaten paths.) The true summit is a wooded ledge, but there are several fine viewpoints from the rim of the summit area, including the fenced east outlook at the top of the main cliff.

The path to White Horse Ledge turns left uphill from the junction with the path to Cathedral Ledge. It turns right at a group of large boulders and climbs steeply for a short distance, then swings left and climbs moderately, and at 0.5 mi. from the loop junction it reaches an open ledge that provides the best view from the loop over White Horse Ledge. It continues to climb, soon returning to the woods, and reaches the summit area, bearing left and then swinging right to reach the highest ledge, where there is a fine view of Moat Mtn., at 0.9 mi. Swinging to the right off the ledge back into the woods, it descends northwest and then west, then turns sharp left where the Red Ridge Link enters on the right at 1.0 mi. From here the trail must be followed with care and may not be passable. It descends by switchbacks, then swings around the south end of White Horse Ledge, and at 1.7 mi. it turns sharp left with a gravel road visible straight ahead through the trees. For a while it runs near a line of WMNF boundary blazes, turns sharp right where a pile of red-painted rocks (a WMNF boundary marker) lies ahead, and then follows a narrow strip of woods between a golf course and the boulders at the foot of White Horse Ledge. In this region the trail is not well defined, and hikers must stay within the boundary of the WMNF (well marked with red paint blazes) and take care not to trespass on the golf course when it is in use. This may require scrambling on and around the boulders at the base of the cliff. At 2.5 mi. the rock climbers' path to the base of White Horse Ledge enters on the left. From here the trail continues to the cabin clearing and the loop junction at the crossroads.

White Horse Ledge Trail and Bryce Path (map 3:I11–I10)

Distances from Echo Lake parking area (490')

    to loop junction (570'): 0.7 mi., 100 ft., 20 min.

    to White Horse Ledge/Cathedral Ledge fork (850'): 1.0 mi., 350 ft., 40 min.

    to White Horse Ledge (1450'): 1.6 mi., 950 ft., 1 hr. 15 min.

    to loop junction (570'): 3.5 mi., 950 ft. (rev. 950 ft.), 2 hr. 15 min.

    for complete loop: 4.2 mi. (6.7 km.), 1050 ft., 2 hr. 40 min.

Distances from Echo Lake parking area (490')

    to Cathedral Ledge (1159') via Cathedral Ledge branch: 1.4 mi., 700 ft., 1 hr.

    for White Horse Ledge and Cathedral Ledge (returning to trail fork from each): 4.0 mi. (6.4 km.), 1300 ft., 2 hr. 40 min.

Section 5

Cannon and Kinsman

This section covers the trails on Kinsman Mtn., Cannon Mtn., and the lower peaks in the same range, principally Mt. Wolf, the Cannon Balls, and Mt. Pemigewasset. It also covers trails on several smaller mountains to the west and north, including Bald Mtn. and Artist's Bluff, Cooley Hill, and Mt. Agassiz. It is bounded on the east by I-93, US 3, and the Franconia Notch Parkway, and on the south by NH 112 (Lost River Rd.). The entire section is covered by the AMC Moosilauke–Kinsman map (map #4). In addition, all the trails in this section except the Cobble Hill and Jericho Road trails are also shown on the AMC Franconia–Pemigewasset map (map #2).

A paved bike path runs the entire length of the notch from the parking area at the Flume to the Skookumchuck Trail and is available for pedestrian use, though those on foot should be careful not to unnecessarily impede bicycle traffic. Information regarding trails and other facilities is available during the summer and fall tourist season at the Flume Visitor Center at the south end of the park, and throughout the year (except for the late fall and early spring "off-seasons") at the Cannon Mtn. Tramway. The New Hampshire Department of Parks (NHDP) maintains an information booth during the summer and on fall weekends at the Lafayette Place trailhead parking area to provide information about weather, trail conditions, facilities, and regulations. Concord Trailways has bus service from Boston at Logan Airport and South Station to Lincoln and Franconia, which may operate only on weekends. In the summer, connections to trailheads may be made by using the AMC hiker shuttle bus.

In this section, the Appalachian Trail follows the Kinsman Ridge Trail from Kinsman Notch to Kinsman Junction (near Kinsman Pond), the Fishin' Jimmy Trail from Kinsman Junction to Lonesome Lake Hut, and the Cascade Brook Trail from Lonesome Lake Hut to a trail junction near the former Whitehouse Bridge site, which is reached by the Whitehouse Trail from the hikers' parking area just north of the Flume Visitor Center or by the bike path from the Basin parking lots.

GEOGRAPHY

The heart of this region is the **Cannon-Kinsman Range.** The northern half of the range is a high, well-defined ridge, of which Cannon Mtn. and the two peaks of Kinsman Mtn. are the most important summits. The southern half of the range is broad, with only one significant summit, Mt. Wolf.

At the north end of the range is **Cannon Mtn.** (4100 ft.). This dome-shaped mountain is famous for its magnificent profile, the **Old Man of the Mountain,** and for its imposing east cliff. The mountain, also sometimes known as Profile Mtn., takes its officially recognized name from a natural stone table resting on a boulder that resembles a cannon when seen from Profile Clearing. The Great Stone Face (the name by which the Old Man was immortalized in a story by Nathaniel Hawthorne) is formed by three ledges at the north end of the east cliff that are not in a vertical line and only appear to be a profile when viewed from the vicinity of Profile Lake. For many years state park personnel have protected the Old Man from the otherwise inexorable forces of ice and gravity by filling cracks with cement and maintaining a system of cables and turnbuckles. Cannon Mtn. has a major ski area operated by the state of New Hampshire, with an aerial tramway (the successor to the first such passenger tramway in North America) that extends from a valley station (1970 ft.) just off the parkway to a mountain station (4000 ft.) just below the main summit. The tramway is operated throughout the year for tourists and for skiers in the winter. Hiking is not permitted on ski trails.

On the ridge southwest of Cannon Mtn. are three humps called the **Cannon Balls** (east to west: 3769 ft., 3660 ft., and 3693 ft.). All are wooded, but the highest, the northeast Cannon Ball, has several good outlooks. **Bridal Veil Falls,** one of the more attractive falls in the White Mtns., is located on Coppermine Brook in the ravine between Cannon Mtn. and the Cannon Balls on the northwest side of the ridge. **Lonesome Lake** (2740 ft.) is located on the high plateau that forms the floor of the ravine south of the ridge between Cannon Mtn. and the Cannon Balls. Trails completely encircle the lake, which has excellent views from its shores. The whole area around the lake is in Franconia Notch State Park, and camping is not permitted.

Kinsman Mtn. rises to the south of the Cannon Balls, and its two peaks are the highest points on the ridge. **North Kinsman** (4293 ft.) is wooded, and its true summit is actually a pointed boulder in the woods beside the trail, but ledges just to the east of the summit command magnificent views. The view of Mt. Lafayette and Mt. Lincoln across Franconia Notch is particularly impressive. **South Kinsman** (4358 ft.) has a broad, flat summit with two knobs of nearly equal height. The USGS Lincoln quad puts the summit elevation on the north knob, which is just off the main trail, but the south knob bears the cairn and is preferred by most hikers. Views are fine, but one must wander around the summit plateau to obtain the best outlooks. Kinsman Mtn. shelters two very beautiful small ponds: **Kinsman Pond** under the east cliffs of North Kinsman, and **Harrington Pond** under the bluff at the end of South Kinsman's south ridge.

Two spurs of the Kinsman group are especially notable. On the west, **Bald Peak** (2470 ft.) is a flat, ledgy knob with good views, reached by a short spur path from the Mount Kinsman Trail. On the east, lying below the massive southeast ridge of South Kinsman, is **Mt. Pemigewasset** (2557 ft.), with its famous natural rock profile, the **Indian Head;** the ledgy summit affords excellent views and its ascent requires only a modest effort.

South of Kinsman Mtn., only **Mt. Wolf** has much claim to prominence. Its summit bears a ledge with an excellent view to the east and northeast. Although lacking in impressive peaks, the southern part of the range does have several interesting aquatic attractions, including **Lost River, Gordon Pond, Gordon Falls, Georgiana Falls,** and **Harvard Falls. The Lost River Reservation,** property of the Society for the Protection of New Hampshire Forests (SPNHF), lies about 6 mi. west of North Woodstock on NH 112 (Lost River Rd.). Here Lost River, one of the tributaries of Moosilauke Brook, flows for nearly 0.5 mi. through a series of caves and large potholes, for the most part underground. At one place it falls 20 ft. within one of the caves, and at another, known as Paradise Falls, it falls 30 ft. in the open. Trails, walks, and ladders make the caves accessible. In order to protect the forest and caves, the SPNHF began to acquire the surrounding land in 1911, and it now owns about 770 acres bordering the highway on both sides for nearly 2.5 mi. The SPNHF maintains a nature garden containing more than 300 indigenous plants and an Ecology Trail that circles the inner parking lot area and provides information at numbered and marked sites described in a brochure provided by the SPNHF. The reservation is open from May through October; an admission fee is charged.

This section also includes several scattered peaks and trails. Just northeast of Cannon Mtn. are **Bald Mtn.** (2340 ft.) and **Artist's Bluff** (2340 ft.), two small but very interesting peaks at the north end of Franconia Notch that offer excellent views for little exertion. Bald Mtn. is a striking miniature mountain with a bold, bare, rocky cone, while Artist's Bluff is a wooded dome that bears the fine cliff for which it is named on its southeast face. **Mt. Agassiz** (2369 ft.), between the villages of Franconia and Bethlehem, is reached by a paved road 0.8 mi. long (formerly an auto toll road) that leaves NH 142 1.0 mi. south of its junction with

US 302 in Bethlehem village. There is an excellent and extensive view from the summit. The former restaurant and observation tower are now a private residence, so hikers, who are currently welcome to enjoy the views from the summit (on foot only), should exercise great care to respect the rights of the property owner by staying away from all buildings. **Cooley Hill** (2485 ft.) is a wooded, viewless peak, but a trail built to its former fire tower has survived the loss of its principal reason for existence.

HUTS
Lonesome Lake Hut (AMC)

Lonesome Lake Hut, at about 2760 ft., is located on the southwest shore of Lonesome Lake, with superb views of the Franconia Range. The hut was built in 1964, replacing cabins on the northeast shore. It accommodates 48 guests and is open to the public from mid-May to mid-October (on a caretaker basis in May, September, and October). Pets are not permitted in the hut. The hut can be reached by the Lonesome Lake Trail or the Whitehouse and Cascade Brook trails from the Franconia Notch Parkway, by the Fishin' Jimmy Trail from Kinsman Junction, or by the Dodge Cutoff from the Hi-Cannon Trail. Camping is not permitted around the hut or the lake, or anywhere else in Franconia Notch State Park except at Lafayette Campground. For schedules and information contact the Reservation Office, Pinkham Notch Visitor Center, PO Box 298, Gorham, NH 03581 (603-466-2727) or www.outdoors.org.

CAMPING
Forest Protection Areas

The WMNF has established a number of Forest Protection Areas (FPAs)—formerly known as Restricted Use Areas—where camping and wood or charcoal fires are prohibited throughout the year. The specific areas are under continual review, and areas are added to or subtracted from the list in order to provide the greatest amount of protection to areas subject to damage by excessive camping, while imposing the lowest level of restrictions possible. A general list of FPAs in this section follows, but since there are often major changes from year to year, one should obtain current information on FPAs from the WMNF.

(1) No camping is permitted above treeline (where trees are less than 8 ft. tall), except in winter, and then only in places where there is at least

two feet of snow cover on the ground—but not on any frozen body of water. The point where the restricted area begins is marked on most trails with small signs, but the absence of such signs should not be construed as proof of the legality of a site.

(2) No camping is permitted within a quarter-mile of any trailhead, picnic area, or any facility for overnight accommodation such as a hut, cabin, shelter, tentsite, or campground, except as designated at the facility itself. In this section, camping is also forbidden within 200 ft. of the Woodsville water supply dam on the Wild Ammonoosuc River.

Franconia Notch State Park

No camping is permitted in Franconia Notch State Park except at Lafayette Campground (fee charged). In this section, the areas included in the park consist mostly of the northeast slopes of Cannon Mtn. and the regions surrounding Lonesome Lake and extending east from the lake to the Franconia Notch Parkway.

Established Trailside Campsites

Eliza Brook Shelter (AMC) is located on the Kinsman Ridge Trail at its crossing of Eliza Brook, between Mt. Wolf and Mt. Kinsman.

Kinsman Pond Campsite (AMC), with a shelter and three tent platforms, is located on Kinsman Pond near Kinsman Junction, where the Kinsman Ridge, Kinsman Pond, and Fishin' Jimmy trails meet. There is a caretaker in the summer and a fee is charged. Water is available from the pond but is not potable without treatment.

Coppermine Shelter (WMNF) is located on the Coppermine Trail just west of Bridal Veil Falls.

Trail on Main Ridge

Trails on West Side of Franconia Notch

Trails on the Southeast Side of the Range

Trails on the West Side of the Range

Trails West of NH 116

THE TRAILS

Kinsman Ridge Trail (AMC)

This trail follows the crest of the main ridge from the height-of-land on NH 112 in Kinsman Notch to the Cannon Mtn. Tramway parking lot just off the Franconia Notch Parkway (look for the trail sign on a post in the lot and park nearby). At the south end, the trail leaves NH 112 just to the north of the height-of-land, 0.5 mi. north of the Lost River entrance and almost directly opposite the parking area at the north terminus of the Beaver Brook Trail. From NH 112 to Kinsman Junction, it is part of the Appalachian Trail. For much of its length it is a more difficult route than one might infer from the map—footing is often rough and there are many minor ups and downs. Hikers with heavy packs should allow considerable extra time for many parts of the trail. There is little water on or near several long sections of the trail, and none that a cautious hiker will drink without treatment.

The following description of the path is in the northbound direction (from Kinsman Notch to the Cannon Mtn. Tramway parking lot). See below for a description of the path in the reverse direction.

The trail leaves NH 112 and climbs a steep sidehill bearing gradually away from the road for 0.1 mi., then swings right and climbs very steeply northeast through a part of the SPNHF Lost River Reservation. At 0.4 mi. the grade relaxes, and the trail soon crosses a swampy sag on log bridges and reaches a junction on the right at 0.6 mi. with the Dilly Trail from Lost River. At 0.9 mi. the Kinsman Ridge Trail crosses the summit of a wooded knob and descends steeply by zigzags, soon passes a small stream (unreliable), and follows the ridge over several minor humps. At 2.4 mi. it passes the first of two good outlooks to the east, then crosses a larger wooded hump and descends past a boulder to the right of the trail that offers a view of Mt. Wolf ahead. At 3.3 mi. it reaches its low point south of Mt. Wolf, crossing a stagnant brook in a ravine, then ascends 30 yd. to the junction where the Gordon Pond Trail enters on the right, 0.3 mi. from Gordon Pond.

The trail now climbs by short, steep sections alternating with easy sections, crossing a small brook (reliable water) at 3.9 mi., and ascends to a point just below the summit of the west knob of Mt. Wolf. Then it descends slightly into a shallow sag and climbs to a point near the summit of the east knob of Mt. Wolf at 4.6 mi., where it makes a sharp left turn. Here a side path leads to the right 60 yd. to the summit of the east knob, where there is a fine view of the Franconias and the peaks to the east and southeast. The main trail then descends the east side of Wolf's north ridge at a moderate grade, but with a rough footway and numerous short ascents interspersed through the descent. At 6.0 mi. the trail turns left, runs almost level, and meets the Reel Brook Trail, which enters left at 6.5 mi., just south of the col between Mt. Wolf and Kinsman Mtn. (this was the original Kinsman Notch). The Kinsman Ridge Trail continues along the ridge top, crosses under power lines at 7.0 mi., and descends to the bank of Eliza Brook at 7.5 mi., where a side path runs left 55 yd. to Eliza Brook Shelter.

The Kinsman Ridge Trail crosses Eliza Brook and in 50 yd. intersects a grass-grown gravel logging road and follows it to the left. (Watch carefully for the point where the trail turns off this road, going in either direction.) The trail follows the road for 0.3 mi., then turns left off it and follows a very scenic section of Eliza Brook, with several attractive cascades and pools. At 8.6 mi. the trail recrosses Eliza Brook and soon climbs rather steeply to cross the bog at the east end of Harrington Pond on log bridges. Here, at 8.9 mi., there is an interesting view of the shoulder of South Kinsman rising above the beautiful pond. (*Note:* The section of the trail between Harrington Pond and South Kinsman may require much extra time, particularly for those with heavy packs, and is also somewhat exposed to weather.) The trail continues at a moderate grade for 0.3 mi., then climbs a steep pitch, crosses a minor hump and a blowdown patch, then struggles up a very steep and rough pitch to an outlook where the climbing becomes somewhat easier. It continues to the bare south knob of South Kinsman's summit, which is very exposed to the weather, at 9.9 mi.

From here the Kinsman Ridge Trail crosses a scrub-filled sag, passes 15 yd. to the west of the north knob of South Kinsman at 10.0 mi., and descends relatively easily to the col between South and North Kinsman at 10.5 mi. The trail then climbs steadily to a side path (sign) that leads to the right at 10.9 mi.; this side path runs 25 yd. to a fine outlook to the Franconias and continues another 70 yd. to a ledge that looks directly down on Kinsman Pond. The true summit of North Kinsman is a pointed boulder on the right (east) side of the main trail, 30 yd. north of the outlook spur. The Kinsman Ridge Trail now descends steeply to the junction with the Mount Kinsman Trail on the left at 11.3 mi., then continues to Kinsman Junction at 11.5 mi. Here the Fishin' Jimmy Trail continues the Appalachian Trail to Lonesome Lake, and the Kinsman Pond Trail bears right, leading in 0.1 mi. to Kinsman Pond and Kinsman Pond Shelter.

The Kinsman Ridge Trail turns sharp left at Kinsman Junction, and soon rises abruptly 100 ft. to a hump (3812 ft.) on the ridge. It then continues over the Cannon Balls, the three humps that make up the ridge leading to Cannon Mtn. After passing near the top of the first (west) Cannon Ball at 12.5 mi., it descends sharply to a deep ravine where a small, sluggish brook usually contains some water. The trail circles to the north of the second (middle) Cannon Ball and enters the next col with very little descent. After passing several scattered viewpoints while climbing over the third (northeast) Cannon Ball at 13.7 mi., it descends to the junction at 13.9 mi. with the Lonesome Lake Trail, which leads southeast 1.0 mi. to Lonesome Lake Hut (water can be found 0.2 mi. down this trail).

In a few yards the trail reaches the low point in Coppermine Col, at the base of Cannon Mtn., then climbs a very steep and rough slope among huge boulders. At 14.3 mi. the Hi-Cannon Trail enters right, and the Kinsman Ridge Trail swings left and climbs gradually to the gravel Rim Trail at 14.7 mi., where it encounters the maze of trails in the summit area. The true summit, with its observation platform and lookout tower, is reached in 120 yd. by following the gravel path straight ahead from this junction; a path continues from the tower down to the Cannon Mtn. Tramway summit station.

The Kinsman Ridge Trail bears right at the junction and coincides with the Rim Trail for about 0.2 mi. around the edge of the summit plateau, affording excellent views, then turns sharp right downhill (sign) as the Rim Trail continues on toward the tramway terminal. Descending the semi-open east flank of the main peak over rocks and ledges, then through scrub, it crosses a moist sag and ascends slightly to the east summit. At the point where it makes a right-angle turn left (north), a side trail turns sharp right and runs out upon the ledges to the southeast, where there is a magnificent view across the notch to the Franconia Range. The main trail descends steeply by switchbacks on a rough and rocky footway with many ledges that are slippery when wet, then improves somewhat in the lower half. Finally it emerges in a small clearing and follows service roads to its end at the Cannon Mtn. Tramway parking lot.

Kinsman Ridge Trail (map 4:I3–G4)

Distances from NH 112 in Kinsman Notch (1870')

   to Dilly Trail (2450'): 0.6 mi., 600 ft., 35 min.

   to Gordon Pond Trail (2800'): 3.3 mi., 1450 ft., 2 hr. 25 min.

   to Reel Brook Trail (2600'): 6.5 mi., 2200 ft., 4 hr. 20 min.

   to Eliza Brook Shelter spur (2400'): 7.5 mi., 2250 ft., 4 hr. 55 min.

   to Harrington Pond (3400'): 8.9 mi., 3250 ft., 6 hr. 5 min.

   to South Kinsman summit (4358'): 10.0 mi., 4200 ft., 7 hr. 5 min.

   to North Kinsman summit (4293'): 10.9 mi., 4500 ft., 7 hr. 40 min.

   to Mount Kinsman Trail (3900'): 11.3 mi., 4500 ft., 7 hr. 55 min.

   to Kinsman Junction (3750'): 11.5 mi., 4500 ft., 8 hr.

   to Lonesome Lake Trail (3400'): 13.9 mi., 5200 ft., 9 hr. 35 min.

   to Hi-Cannon Trail (3850'): 14.3 mi., 5650 ft., 10 hr.

   to Rim Trail junction near Cannon Mtn. summit (4050'): 14.7 mi., 5850 ft., 10 hr. 55 min.

to side path to ledges (3800'): 15.4 mi., 5900 ft., 10 hr. 40 min.

to Cannon Mtn. Tramway parking area (1980'): 16.9 mi. (27.1 km.), 5900 ft., 11 hr. 25 min.

Kinsman Ridge Trail (AMC) [in reverse]

From the Cannon Mtn. Tramway parking area near the main buildings, the trail turns left and follows a gravel road to a picnic area (sign) for 150 yd., then turns right and follows the left edge of a ski trail for 80 yd. to the bottom of a steep slope. Turning left (signs) into the woods, the trail climbs moderately and then steeply by switchbacks, becoming steeper and rockier with ledges that are slippery when wet as it ascends. In a level area at 1.5 mi., a side path runs straight ahead out upon the ledges to the southwest, where there is a magnificent view across the notch to the Franconia Range. Here the main trail turns sharp right (west) to cross over the east summit and pass through a moist sag, after which it climbs rather steeply up through rocks and scrub to the gravel Rim Trail at 2.0 mi. It turns left here (right leads to the tramway terminal) and coincides with the Rim Trail for 0.2 mi., affording excellent views. Then the Kinsman Ridge Trail continues straight ahead on an ordinary dirt footpath at the point where the gravel path turns sharp right to reach the summit observation platform and lookout tower in 120 yd. and then continues to the tramway summit station.

From this junction with the tourist paths, the Kinsman Ridge Trail descends gradually to the junction at 2.5 mi. with the Hi-Cannon Trail, which continues straight where the Kinsman Ridge Trail turns right and soon drops very steeply down a rough path among huge boulders to Coppermine Col. It then climbs for a few yards to the junction on the left at 3.0 mi. with the Lonesome Lake Trail, which leads southeast 1.0 mi. to Lonesome Lake Hut (water can be found 0.2 mi. down this trail). The Kinsman Ridge Trail now begins the traverse of the Cannon Balls, the three humps that make up the ridge leading to Kinsman Mtn. It ascends a rather steep and rough section above the Lonesome Lake Trail junction and passes several scattered viewpoints while climbing over the first (northeast) Cannon Ball at 3.2 mi., then descends to a col. The trail circles to the north of the second (middle) Cannon Ball and descends moderately to a deep ravine where a small, sluggish brook usually contains some water, then ascends sharply and passes near the top of the third (west) Cannon Ball at 4.4 mi. After crossing another hump (3812 ft.) and dropping to a flat region, it reaches Kinsman Junction at 5.4 mi. Here the Fishin' Jimmy Trail (a part of the Appalachian Trail) enters on the left from Lonesome Lake, and the Kinsman Pond Trail runs straight ahead, leading in 0.1 mi. to Kinsman Pond and Kinsman Pond Shelter.

From Kinsman Junction the Kinsman Ridge Trail (now part of the Appalachian Trail for the rest of its length) turns right and climbs up ledges to the junction where the Mount Kinsman Trail enters on the right at 5.6 mi., then continues to climb steeply to the summit of North Kinsman at 6.0 mi. Here a side path (sign) leads to the left 25 yd. to a fine outlook to the Franconias and continues another 70 yd. to a ledge that looks directly down on Kinsman Pond. The true summit of North Kinsman is a pointed boulder on the left (east) side of the main trail, 30 yd. north of the outlook spur. The main trail descends steadily to the col between North and South Kinsman at 6.4 mi., then ascends relatively easily and passes 15 yd. to the west of the north knob of South Kinsman's summit at 6.9 mi.

The Kinsman Ridge Trail then crosses a scrub-filled sag to the bare south knob of South Kinsman, which is very exposed to the weather, at 7.0 mi. (*Note:* The section of the trail between South Kinsman and Harrington Pond may require much extra time, particularly for those with heavy packs, and is also somewhat exposed to weather.) From South Kinsman the trail descends moderately, then drops down a very steep and rough pitch, crosses a blowdown patch and a minor hump, then descends another steep pitch. It continues to descend at a moderate grade for 0.3 mi., then crosses the bog at the east end of Harrington Pond on log bridges. Here, at 8.0 mi., there is an interesting view of the shoulder of South Kinsman rising above the beautiful pond. The trail resumes a rather steep descent, then crosses Eliza Brook at 8.3 mi. and follows a very scenic section of the brook, with several attractive cascades and pools. At 9.1 mi. the trail intersects a grass-grown gravel logging road and follows it to the right. (Watch carefully for the point where the trail turns off this road, going in either direction.) The trail follows the road for 0.3 mi., then turns right off it and in 50 yd. recrosses Eliza Brook, reaching a junction at 9.4 mi. where a side path runs right 55 yd. to Eliza Brook Shelter.

From here the Kinsman Ridge Trail ascends to the crest of the north ridge of Mt. Wolf, crosses under power lines at 9.9 mi., and follows the ridge top to the Reel Brook Trail, which enters right at 10.4 mi., just south of the col between Mt. Wolf and Kinsman Mtn. (this was the original Kinsman Notch). The main trail now runs almost level, then swings right and ascends the east side of Wolf's north ridge at a moderate grade, but with a rough footway and numerous short descents interspersed throughout the ascent, to a point near the summit of the east knob of Mt. Wolf at 12.3 mi., where it makes a sharp right turn. Here a side path leads left 60 yd. to the summit of the east knob, where there is a fine view of the Franconias and the peaks to the east and southeast. The main trail descends slightly into a shallow sag, then ascends slightly to a point just below the summit of the west knob of Mt. Wolf. Here it turns left, descending by short, steep sections alternating with easy sections across a small brook (reliable water) at 13.0 mi. to the junction with the Gordon Pond Trail on the left at 13.6 mi., 0.3 mi. from Gordon Pond.

The Kinsman Ridge Trail descends another 30 yd. to its low point south of Mt. Wolf, crosses a stagnant brook in a ravine, then ascends moderately past a boulder to the left of the trail that offers a view back to Mt. Wolf. It soon runs to the left of the summit of a large wooded hump, passes two good outlooks to the east, and follows the ridgecrest over several minor humps, finally ascending steeply by zigzags to the summit of a wooded knob at 16.0 mi. The trail now descends moderately to a junction with the Dilly Trail from Lost River on the left at 16.2 mi. The Kinsman Ridge Trail soon crosses a swampy sag on log bridges and begins a very steep descent southwest through a part of the SPNHF Lost River Reservation toward Kinsman Notch, swinging to the left with NH 112 visible below on the right for the last part of the descent.

Kinsman Ridge Trail (map 4:I3–G4)

Distances from Cannon Mtn. Tramway parking area (1980')

  to side path to ledges (3800'): 1.5 mi., 1800 ft., 1 hr. 40 min.

  to Rim Trail junction near tramway terminal (4050'): 2.0 mi., 2100 ft., 2 hr. 5 min.

  to Hi-Cannon Trail (3850'): 2.5 mi., 2100 ft., 2 hr. 20 min.

  to Lonesome Lake Trail (3400'): 3.0 mi., 2100 ft., 2 hr. 35 min.

  to Kinsman Junction (3750'): 5.4 mi., 3150 ft., 4 hr. 15 min.

  to Mount Kinsman Trail (3900'): 5.6 mi., 3300 ft., 4 hr. 25 min.

  to North Kinsman summit (4293'): 6.0 mi., 3700 ft., 4 hr. 50 min.

  to South Kinsman summit (4358'): 6.9 mi., 4050 ft., 5 hr. 30 min.

  to Harrington Pond (3400'): 8.0 mi., 4050 ft., 6 hr.

  to Eliza Brook Shelter spur (2400'): 9.4 mi., 4050 ft., 6 hr. 45 min.

  to Reel Brook Trail (2600'): 10.4 mi., 4300 ft., 7 hr. 20 min.

  to Gordon Pond Trail (2800'): 13.6 mi., 5250 ft., 9 hr. 25 min.

  to Dilly Trail (2450'): 16.2 mi., 5750 ft., 11 hr.

  to NH 112 in Kinsman Notch (1870'): 16.9 mi. (27.1 km.), 5750 ft., 11 hr. 20 min.

Bald Mountain–Artist's Bluff Path (NHDP)

Artist's Bluff and the summit of Bald Mtn. provide fine views for very little effort. The trail begins and ends on NH 18 just west of its junction with the Franconia Notch Parkway, north of Echo Lake. The west trailhead is located at the edge of the large parking lot for the Roland Peabody Memorial Slope section of the Cannon Mtn. Ski Area, on the north side of NH 18 about 0.4 mi. from the parkway. This parking lot is closed when the ski area is not open, and cars must be parked just off the highway. The east trailhead (no parking—the nearest parking is at the beach parking lot or the west trailhead) is on NH 18 opposite the Echo Lake beach.

Cross the Peabody Slopes parking lot to the trail sign. The trail follows an old carriage road and reaches the top of the ridge at 0.3 mi. At this point a spur path diverges left and climbs the rocky cone of Bald Mtn., reaching the top in another 0.1 mi. About 25 yd. beyond the junction with the trail to Bald Mtn., the main trail turns right from the old road and runs over the wooded hump that bears the Artist's Bluff cliff on its east end, then descends to the top of a steep, gravelly gully at 0.7 mi., where a path whose sign has been repeatedly pilfered leads left 50 yd. to the top of Artist's Bluff. The main trail continues down the gully to NH 18.

Bald Mountain–Artist's Bluff Path (map 4:G4)

Distances from Peabody Slopes parking area (2000')

to fork in trail (2180'): 0.3 mi., 200 ft., 15 min.

to Bald Mtn. (2340') via spur path: 0.4 mi., 350 ft., 25 min.

to Echo Lake beach (1960') direct via Artist's Bluff: 0.9 mi. (1.4 km.), 350 ft. 40 min.

to Echo Lake beach (1960') via Bald Mtn. and Artist's Bluff: 1.2 mi. (1.9 km.), 500 ft., 50 min.

for complete loop, including Bald Mtn.: 1.5 mi. (2.4 km.), 550 ft., 1 hr.

Lonesome Lake Trail (AMC)

This trail begins on the west side of the Franconia Notch Parkway, at the picnic area at the end of the south parking lot at Lafayette Campground, and runs past Lonesome Lake to the Kinsman Ridge Trail at Coppermine Col. It follows the route of an old bridle path much of the way to Lonesome Lake, with excellent footing and easy to moderate grades; beyond the lake it is of average difficulty.

The trail leaves the parking lot at a large trail sign, crosses the Pemigewasset on a footbridge and then crosses the Pemi Trail, and follows a yellow-blazed path through the campground, climbing at a moderate grade. At 0.3 mi. a bridge crosses a small brook at a sharp left turn in the trail, and at 0.4 mi. the Hi-Cannon Trail leaves right. From this point the trail ascends by three long switchbacks, then descends slightly to a junction at 1.2 mi. near the shore of Lonesome Lake, where the old bridle path ends; here the Cascade Brook Trail enters left and the Dodge Cutoff diverges right. A few steps ahead there is a fine view of North and South Kinsman rising from the far side of the lake. For the shortest route to Lonesome Lake Hut follow the Cascade Brook and Fishin' Jimmy trails. The Lonesome Lake Trail becomes a footpath that continues along the north shore, coinciding with the Around-Lonesome-Lake Trail, which diverges left after 0.2 mi. and leads to Lonesome Lake Hut in another 0.3 mi. The Lonesome Lake Trail continues northwest, soon begins to rise more steeply, and ends at the Kinsman Ridge Trail in Coppermine Col, 0.8 mi. southwest of the summit of Cannon Mtn.

Lonesome Lake Trail (map 4:H4)

Distances from Lafayette Campground west side parking area (1770')

   to Hi-Cannon Trail (2040'): 0.4 mi., 250 ft., 20 min.

   to Cascade Brook Trail/Dodge Cutoff (2740'): 1.2 mi., 950 ft., 1 hr. 5 min.

   to Kinsman Ridge Trail (3400'): 2.3 mi. (3.6 km.), 1650 ft., 2 hr.

   to Lonesome Lake Hut (2740') via Cascade Brook Trail and Fishin' Jimmy Trail: 1.6 mi. (2.6 km.), 950 ft., 1 hr. 15 min.

Around-Lonesome-Lake Trail (AMC)

This trail, composed mostly of portions of other trails, encircles Lonesome Lake and affords fine views, especially of the Franconia Range. The part on the west shore of the lake is subject to flooding in wet seasons, though log bridges cross most of the boggy places.

Starting at the junction of the Dodge Cutoff and the Lonesome Lake and Cascade Brook trails, this trail follows the Cascade Brook Trail south along the east shore. It then turns west and, following the Fishin' Jimmy Trail, crosses the outlet of the lake and continues across the open beach area as the Fishin' Jimmy Trail bears left to ascend to the hut. The trail continues north through the bogs along the west side of the lake (the only section not shared with another trail), crosses several inlet brooks, and meets the Lonesome Lake Trail shortly after entering the woods. Here it turns right on the Lonesome Lake Trail and continues to the junction with Dodge Cutoff and the Cascade Brook Trail, completing the circuit.

Around-Lonesome-Lake Trail (map 4:H4)

Distance from any starting point (2740')

   for complete loop: 0.8 mi. (1.2 km.), 0 ft., 25 min.

Hi-Cannon Trail (NHDP)

This trail begins at the Lonesome Lake Trail 0.4 mi. from the parking area at Lafayette Campground, and ends on the Kinsman Ridge Trail 0.4 mi. south of the summit of Cannon Mtn. It is steep near Cliff House, somewhat rough at times, and potentially dangerous if there is ice on the ledges above Cliff House. It passes several fine viewpoints, particularly the ledges overlooking Lonesome Lake.

   The trail diverges right (west) from the Lonesome Lake Trail and begins to ascend gradually by switchbacks. Watch carefully for a sharp right switchback at 0.1 mi., where an old logging road continues straight and rejoins the Lonesome Lake Trail. At 0.8 mi. the Dodge Cutoff from Lonesome Lake enters on the left at the top of a ridge. At 1.2 mi. there is a fine outlook to the area around Lafayette Campground and across Franconia Notch, and 100 yd. farther the trail passes Cliff House (right)—a natural rock shelter—and ascends a ladder. It then passes along a cliff edge with three fine outlooks over Lonesome Lake in the next 0.2 mi. (use caution on the ledges, as cliffs drop off sharply from them). Then the trail ascends moderately to the top of the ridge, turns right, and at 2.0 mi. ends at its junction with the Kinsman Ridge Trail. For the summit of Cannon Mtn. follow the Kinsman Ridge Trail straight uphill for 0.4 mi.

Hi-Cannon Trail (map 4:H4)

Distances from Lonesome Lake Trail (2040')

   to Dodge Cutoff (2960'): 0.8 mi., 900 ft., 50 min.

   to Kinsman Ridge Trail (3850'): 2.0 mi. (3.2 km.), 1800 ft., 1 hr. 55 min.

Distance from Lafayette Place (1770')

   to Cannon Mtn. summit (4100') via Lonesome Lake, Hi-Cannon, and Kinsman Ridge trails: 2.8 mi., 2350 ft., 2 hr. 35 min.

Dodge Cutoff (NHDP)

This short link between the Lonesome Lake and Hi-Cannon trails provides a shortcut between Lonesome Lake and Cannon Mtn. It was named in honor of Joe Dodge, a legendary, highly respected and cherished White Mtn. character who was best known as the longtime manager of the AMC hut system.

It begins at the junction of the Lonesome Lake and Cascade Brook trails on the east shore of the lake, 0.3 mi. from Lonesome Lake Hut. After climbing over a low ridge and crossing a moist sag, it ascends by switchbacks, rather steeply for a while, to the Hi-Cannon Trail 0.8 mi. above the junction of the Lonesome Lake and Hi-Cannon trails and 1.5 mi. below the summit of Cannon Mtn.

Dodge Cutoff (map 4:H4)

Distance from Lonesome Lake Trail (2740')

   to Hi-Cannon Trail (2960'): 0.3 mi. (0.5 km.), 200 ft., 15 min.

Distance from Lafayette Campground (1770')

   to summit of Cannon Mtn. (4100') via Lonesome Lake Trail, Dodge Cutoff, Hi-Cannon Trail, and Kinsman Ridge Trail: 3.0 mi. (4.8 km.), 2350 ft., 2 hr. 40 min.

Pemi Trail (NHDP)

This trail extends from Profile Lake to the hikers' parking lot just north of the Flume Visitor Center, providing pedestrians a fairly easy footpath that is an alternative route to the bike path along the central part of Franconia Notch. The markings are not always obvious and signs are not always present at intersections with roads and the bike path, so following it requires a bit of care, particularly at points where it diverges from these other routes. It has incorporated almost all of the former Profile Lake Trail, a name now applied to a short paved tourist path.

The Pemi Trail leaves the southwest corner of the Old Man parking area on the west side of the Franconia Notch Parkway, ascends granite steps into the woods, and turns sharp left. It skirts the west shore of Profile Lake, crossing numerous unmarked paths used by rock climbers. At 0.7 mi. it enters the bike path, follows it right for 50 yd., then turns left and re-enters the woods. It runs close to the parkway, then crosses the Pemigewasset on a bridge at 1.2 mi. and recrosses on another bridge at 1.9 mi. In another 100 yd. it crosses the bike path and bears right onto a gravel road that leads into Lafayette Campground just below the headquarters buildings.

It continues south on the campground road that follows most closely along the west bank of the river, crosses the Lonesome Lake Trail, and enters the woods between campsites 67 and 68. It continues for 1.7 mi. fairly close to the river until it intersects the Basin-Cascades Trail, 50 yd. west of the Basin.

It turns left here onto the Basin-Cascades Trail, then in 20 yd. it diverges to the right off the Basin-Cascades Trail; in another 40 yd. it turns left (sign), then right, and descends easily along the river, passing some cascades, and at 4.3 mi. crosses Cascade Brook on a bridge. The trail soon begins to swing away from the river, then joins the Cascade Brook Trail and follows it to the left, crossing Cascade Brook on a bridge and then passing under both lanes of I-93 to the bike path. From there it follows the Whitehouse Trail to the hikers' parking lot just north of the Flume.

Pemi Trail (map 4:H4)

Distances from Old Man parking area on west side of parkway (1960')

    to Lafayette Campground (1770'): 2.0 mi., 0 ft. (rev. 200 ft.), 1 hr.

    to the Basin-Cascades Trail (1520'): 3.9 mi., 0 ft. (rev. 250 ft.), 1 hr. 55 min.

    to Cascade Brook Trail (1520'): 4.7 mi., 0 ft., 2 hr. 20 min.

    to Whitehouse Trail (1400') via Cascade Brook Trail: 4.9 mi., 0 ft. (rev. 100 ft.), 2 hr. 25 min.

    to Flume hikers' parking lot (1400') via Whitehouse Trail: 5.6 mi. (9.0 km.), 100 ft. (rev. 100 ft.), 2 hr. 50 min.

Basin-Cascades Trail (NHDP)

This trail starts at the Basin (parking areas on either side of Franconia Notch Parkway) and ascends along the beautiful lower half of Cascade Brook to the Cascade Brook Trail. The brook is extremely scenic and trail grades are mostly moderate, but the footing is often fairly rough. From the parking areas on either side of the parkway, follow the tourist paths past the Basin and on to the west bank of the Pemigewasset, about 0.2 mi. from either starting point, where the trailhead is situated at the western edge of the maze of paths that surrounds the Basin.

From the trailhead (sign) at the junction with the Pemi Trail, the path angles toward Cascade Brook and climbs along the brook past cascades, small falls, and ledges with views of the Franconia Range across the notch, reached by numerous unmarked side paths. At 0.4 mi. the trail passes a rough side path (no sign) that leads down to a good view of Kinsman Falls, and 50 yd. farther up, as the main trail comes out on the bank of the brook, a ledge on the left provides a viewpoint at the top of these falls. In another 100 yd. the trail crosses Cascade Brook (no bridge; may be difficult in high water) and continues along the brook with more cascades and pools. It passes Rocky Glen Falls at 0.9 mi., then swings sharp left up through a small box canyon and soon ends at the Cascade Brook Trail on the south bank of the brook. For a good view of Rocky Glen Falls from above, return cautiously about 60 yd. down the brook bank.

Basin-Cascades Trail (map 4:H4)
Distance from trailhead near the Basin (1520')

   to Cascade Brook Trail (2084'): 1.0 mi. (1.5 km.), 550 ft., 45 min.

Cascade Brook Trail (AMC)

This trail, a link in the Appalachian Trail, leads to Lonesome Lake from the bike path at the former Whitehouse Bridge site, just south of the bike path's bridge over the Pemigewasset (the Liberty Spring Trail begins just north of the bridge). There is no parking at the Whitehouse Bridge site, which is reached in 0.8 mi. from the hikers' parking area just north of the Flume Visitor Center via the Whitehouse Trail (see Section 3) or in 0.7 mi. via the bike path from the Basin parking lot on the northbound side of the parkway. It is a relatively easy trail, but the crossing of Cascade Brook may be difficult at high water.

   From the junction with the bike path, the trail crosses under the parkway (coinciding with the Pemi Trail), then turns right at the edge of the parkway clearing and enters the woods, and after 0.2 mi. the Pemi Trail leaves on the right. The Cascade Brook Trail climbs at a moderate grade, crosses Whitehouse Brook at 0.4 mi., and continues generally northwest, reaching a junction at 1.5 mi. at the edge of Cascade Brook, where the Basin-Cascades Trail enters right. For a good view of Rocky Glen Falls from above, walk cautiously about 60 yd. down the brook bank. The Cascade Brook Trail immediately crosses Cascade Brook on the rocks (may be difficult) and continues to climb along the northeast bank. At 2.0 mi. the Kinsman Pond Trail diverges left and crosses the brook, and from this point the Cascade Brook Trail follows an old logging road, becoming rougher and rockier, to the junction with Fishin' Jimmy Trail at the outlet of Lonesome Lake at 2.8 mi. From here Lonesome Lake Hut is 150 yd. to the left. The Cascade Brook Trail continues along the east side of the lake and ends at a junction with the Lonesome Lake Trail and the Dodge Cutoff at 3.1 mi.

Cascade Brook Trail (map 4:H4)

Distances from Whitehouse Trail junction (1400')

   to Basin-Cascades Trail (2084'): 1.5 mi., 700 ft., 1 hr. 5 min.

   to Kinsman Pond Trail (2294'): 2.0 mi., 900 ft., 1 hr. 25 min.

   to Fishin' Jimmy Trail (2740'): 2.8 mi., 1350 ft., 2 hr. 5 min.

   to Lonesome Lake Trail and Dodge Cutoff (2740'): 3.1 mi. (5.0 km.), 1350
   ft., 2 hr. 15 min.

Fishin' Jimmy Trail (AMC)

This trail, a link in the Appalachian Trail, leads from Lonesome Lake to the
Kinsman Ridge Trail at Kinsman Junction, near Kinsman Pond. Parts of it are
steep and rough, with wooden steps on ledges. It received its peculiar name from
a well-known local character called Fishin' Jimmy—his real name was James
Whitcher—who lived in the Franconia area and was featured in a story by Annie
Trumbull Slosson, once a popular New England author.

   Diverging from the Cascade Brook Trail at the south end of Lonesome
Lake, this trail crosses the outlet brook, passes the junction with the Around-
Lonesome-Lake Trail near the beach at the southwest corner of the lake, and
reaches Lonesome Lake Hut at 0.1 mi. It runs around the lower end of a ridge
coming down from the Middle Cannon Ball, making several ascents and
descents and passing over a ledgy ridgecrest at 0.6 mi. It then crosses several
small brooks, with the last reliable water source in a small mossy, ledgy brook
at 1.1 mi., and soon begins to climb, at times steeply but with occasional minor
descents as well. At 1.7 mi. it curls around a large boulder on the left and passes through a fairly flat area. At 1.9 mi. it reaches the top of the serious climbing
and ascends gradually to Kinsman Junction and the Kinsman Ridge Trail at 2.0
mi., 0.1 mi. north of Kinsman Pond Shelter on the Kinsman Pond Trail.

Fishin' Jimmy Trail (map 4:H4)

Distances from Cascade Brook Trail (2740')

   to Lonesome Lake Hut (2740'): 0.1 mi., 0 ft., 5 min.

   to Kinsman Junction (3750'): 2.0 mi. (3.3 km.), 1200 ft. (rev. 200 ft.), 1 hr.
   35 min.

Kinsman Pond Trail (AMC)

This trail leads to Kinsman Pond and Kinsman Junction from the Cascade Brook Trail, 2.0 mi. from its beginning on the bike path at the Whitehouse Bridge site, which is reached by following the Whitehouse Trail (Section 3) 0.8 mi. north from the hikers' parking lot just north of the Flume Visitor Center. The upper part of this trail is wet, steep, rocky, and very rough, and at times it shares the footway with small brooks, making rocks slippery; it may also be difficult to follow for short stretches.

Leaving the Cascade Brook Trail, this trail immediately crosses to the southwest side of the brook and proceeds west on old logging roads. Soon it crosses a small brook and begins to rise moderately, following a brook past several small but attractive cascades and passing into virgin forest. The trail is very rough and eroded in parts, but the brook and the dense boreal forest are beautiful. At 1.3 mi. the trail crosses the brook and soon runs in its bed for 0.1 mi. At 1.6 mi. the grade becomes easy, and the trail crosses the outlet brook from the pond at 1.9 mi., passes a water source left (sign), and reaches the foot of the pond at 2.1 mi. It climbs up and down on the ledgy east shore of the pond, with the impressive bulk of North Kinsman rising from the opposite shore, and passes Kinsman Pond Shelter (which accommodates 12) and then several tentsites. Water in this area is unsafe to drink unless treated. Kinsman Junction, where the Kinsman Pond Trail meets the Kinsman Ridge and Fishin' Jimmy trails, is 0.1 mi. beyond the shelter.

Kinsman Pond Trail (map 4:H4)

Distance from Cascade Brook Trail (2294')

   to Kinsman Junction (3750'): 2.5 mi. (4.0 km.), 1500 ft., 2 hr.

Mount Pemigewasset Trail (NHDP)

This trail runs from the Flume Visitor Center parking area to the summit of Mt. Pemigewasset (Indian Head), where excellent views can be obtained with modest effort. Grades and footing are mostly easy. The trail reaches the vertical summit cliffs very abruptly, so care should be exercised, particularly with small children or in slippery conditions.

The trail follows the bike path north from the parking lot for 150 yd., turns left on a gravel path and passes under old US 3 in a tunnel, then turns left and crosses a brook on a bridge. It goes over a small rise, then turns sharp right and ascends under both lanes of the Franconia Notch Parkway. It enters the woods at 0.4 mi. and crosses several small brooks on log bridges, then turns right and then left along a small brook, climbing moderately. At 1.3 mi. it squeezes around a large boulder and swings left uphill, climbing a bit more steeply to the ridge-crest, which it follows to the left (south). It passes the junction with the Indian Head Trail on the right at 1.7 mi. and reaches the summit ledges at 1.8 mi. At the true summit, which is just beyond the first ledges and a bit to the left, there is a fine northeast view.

Mount Pemigewasset Trail (map 4:H4)
Distance from Flume Visitor Center parking area (1400')

> *to* Mt. Pemigewasset summit (2557'): 1.8 mi. (2.9 km.), 1150 ft., 1 hr. 30 min.

Indian Head Trail (AMC)

This trail runs to the summit of Mt. Pemigewasset (Indian Head), where open ledges afford excellent views. It begins on the west side of US 3 south of the Indian Head Resort at a small parking area, reached by a short gravel road marked with a "Trailhead Parking" sign. This trail is not nearly as heavily used as the Mount Pemigewasset Trail.

The trail leaves the parking area and crosses a small field. It turns left and accompanies a small brook under the parkway, then ascends by easy grades through hardwoods on an old logging road along the brook. At 1.1 mi. it turns to the right onto another old woods road, then soon leaves it and climbs moderate-ly, circling well around under the south side of the cliffs that form the Indian Head. It then ascends steeply for a short distance, and at 1.8 mi., just below the summit ledges, it joins the Mount Pemigewasset Trail and follows it to the right to the summit.

Indian Head Trail (map 4:I4–H4)
Distance from US 3 (1000')

> *to* Mt. Pemigewasset summit (2557'): 1.9 mi. (3.0 km.), 1550 ft., 1 hr. 45 min.

Georgiana Falls Path

Georgiana Falls are a series of cascades on Harvard Brook that end in a pool. Above Georgiana Falls there are more cascades terminating in the more impos-ing Harvard Falls about 0.4 mi. farther up the brook. These falls are also known as Upper and Lower Georgiana Falls, nomenclature which may in fact be more historically correct. The path is on private land and not officially maintained. It begins about 2.5 mi. north of North Woodstock on Hanson Farm Rd., which leaves the west side of US 3 opposite the Longhorn Restaurant, crosses Hanson Brook on a bridge, and reaches a parking area at about 0.1 mi. at the end of the pavement.

Follow a dirt road through a tunnel under the northbound lanes of I-93, then bear right, then left, through the tunnel under the southbound lanes. At 0.5 mi., where the road bears right, the trail (blazed red) turns left into the woods and follows the north side of Harvard Brook, reaching the base of Georgiana Falls at 0.7 mi. and continuing up the brook on sloping rocks beside the falls. Above these falls the trail is neither maintained nor marked; it re-enters the woods and follows a steep, sometimes slippery path to Harvard Falls and views of the Pemigewasset Valley and Loon Mtn.

Georgiana Falls Path (map 4:I4)

Distances from Hanson Farm Rd. (900')

to Georgiana Falls (1150'): 0.7 mi., 250 ft., 30 min.

to Harvard Falls (1650'): 1.2 mi. (1.9 km.), 750 ft., 1 hr.

Gordon Pond Trail (WMNF)

This trail runs from NH 112 1.7 mi. west of its junction with US 3 in North Woodstock to the Kinsman Ridge Trail south of Mt. Wolf, passing Gordon Falls and Gordon Pond. The trailhead on NH 112 (where the WMNF trail sign may be missing) is located at a private driveway opposite Govoni's Restaurant and Agassiz Basin (see Section 6); there are signs here for the restaurant and Agassiz Basin in the summer but not at other times. Park just west of the buildings.

This trail follows the driveway between the buildings on the north side of NH 112 ("No Trespassing" signs do not apply to hikers who stay on the trail), and at 0.1 mi. it turns right at a crossroads and follows an old railroad grade. At 0.6 mi. it reaches the power lines, turns left and follows the power line clearing, then turns right and crosses under the lines into the woods, rejoining the old railroad grade at 1.0 mi. and following it to the left. At 1.3 mi., turn left off the railroad grade where another road enters on the right. (In the opposite direction, bear right here; there may be an arrow pointing to the wrong branch.) At 1.8 mi. the trail approaches Gordon Pond Brook and a logging road crosses the brook, but the trail remains on the southwest bank and swings to the northwest to recross the power lines at 2.0 mi. The trail finally crosses Gordon Pond Brook (may be difficult at high water) at 2.2 mi. and continues along the north bank, crossing a tributary at 2.8 mi., then swings left to recross the main brook on a snowmobile bridge at 3.5 mi. It continues on an old road, becoming somewhat steeper, and crosses a minor ridge to the southerly branch of Gordon Pond Brook where it passes Gordon Fall. Crossing the brook on a ledge at the top of the fall at 3.9 mi., it soon recrosses, passes a very wet section of trail, then crosses Gordon Pond Brook at 4.6 mi. Just before it recrosses the main brook at 4.7 mi., unsigned paths lead right to the shore of the pond, where there is an interesting view of the steep face of Mt. Wolf. The main trail does not come within sight of the pond, but continues at a level grade, bears left where an unsigned path enters right, and climbs easily to the Kinsman Ridge Trail.

Gordon Pond Trail (map 4:I4–I3)

Distances from NH 112 (900')

> *to* Gordon Fall (2300'): 3.9 mi., 1400 ft., 2 hr. 40 min.

> *to* Kinsman Ridge Trail (2800'): 5.0 mi. (8.0 km.), 1900 ft., 3 hr. 25 min.

Dilly Trail (SPNHF)

This short but challenging trail runs from Lost River Reservation to the Kinsman Ridge Trail 0.6 mi. from NH 112. It is extremely steep and rough but offers an interesting outlook across the valley. Its trailhead, shared with the Ecology Trail, is on a parking area access road directly across from a gazebo. In 25 yd. from the road the Ecology Trail leaves on the left, and the Dilly Trail soon begins to ascend by short switchbacks a very steep, badly eroded gully with very loose footing, requiring caution, particularly when descending. At 0.4 mi., where the trail reaches the top rim of the steep slope, a side path leads sharp right 40 yd. to a fine outlook from the rim. The main trail turns sharp left, and continues at moderate grades to the Kinsman Ridge Trail.

Dilly Trail (map 4:I3)

Distances from Lost River Reservation parking lot (1820')

> *to* lookout over Lost River (2400'): 0.4 mi., 600 ft., 30 min.

> *to* Kinsman Ridge Trail (2450'): 0.5 mi. (0.8 km.), 650 ft., 35 min.

Coppermine Trail (WMNF)

This trail to Bridal Veil Falls begins on Coppermine Rd., which leaves the east side of NH 116 3.4 mi. south of NH 18 in Franconia (and 1.0 mi. south of the

Franconia Airport) or 7.7 mi. north of NH 112 at Bungay Corner. Park near NH 116 and follow the road. At 0.4 mi. the trail bears left on an older road (hiker logo sign and yellow blazes). At 1.0 mi. the trail joins Coppermine Brook and follows along the north side, climbing at easy to moderate grades, then crosses to the south side on a bridge at 2.3 mi., passes the WMNF Coppermine Shelter, and ends at the base of Bridal Veil Falls.

Coppermine Trail (map 4:G3–H4)
Distance from NH 116 (994')

   to Bridal Veil Falls (2100'): 2.5 mi. (4.0 km.), 1100 ft., 1 hr. 50 min.

Mount Kinsman Trail (WMNF)

This trail climbs to the Kinsman Ridge Trail 0.4 mi. north of North Kinsman from the east side of NH 116 at the Franconia-Easton town line, about 4 mi. south of NH 18 in Franconia village and 2.0 mi. north of the Easton town hall. There is a sign for the town line a few yards north of the trail, but none for the trail itself, which follows a logging road at a prominent gate opposite a house. The trail climbs at moderate grades and is well trodden but sparsely marked, and some care is frequently required to follow it, particularly in the lower section where there are many intersecting woods roads.

From the gate it follows a logging road that soon swings right, then bears right at a fork (arrow). Ascending easily, at times level, it passes a sugar-house left at 0.6 mi. and enters the WMNF at 1.1 mi., where a short loop path left bypasses a wet section of road. The road, now distinctly older and steeper, crosses a substantial brook at 1.5 mi. near the site of the former Kinsman Cabin. At 1.8 mi. it crosses a small brook that falls over a mossy ledge to the left of the trail, then at 2.1 mi. crosses Flume Brook. Just over Flume Brook, a side path on the right descends close to the brook bank for 150 yd. to small, steep-walled Kinsman Flume, a classic eroded dike with an overhanging boulder at the top that presents a reasonable facsimile of a profile. The main trail continues on the road for another 70 yd., then turns sharp left at the point where a spur path 0.2 mi. long diverges sharp right and makes an easy ascent to Bald Peak, a bare ledgy dome with fine views that crowns a western spur of Kinsman Mtn.

The axe-blazed trail now joins and follows Flume Brook, winding up the mountainside at easy to moderate grades, with good footing except for short, scattered steep pitches with rough footing. It crosses several small brooks and at 3.2 mi. climbs a ledge by means of two short ladders. Soon it swings right and angles upward, then swings left and climbs straight up to the ridge top, where it meets the Kinsman Ridge Trail. For North and South Kinsman, turn right; for Kinsman Pond and Kinsman Junction, turn left.

Mount Kinsman Trail (map 4:G3–H4)

Distances from NH 116 (1030')

    to Bald Peak spur trail (2350'): 2.1 mi., 1300 ft., 1 hr. 40 min.

    to Kinsman Ridge Trail (3900'): 3.7 mi. (5.9 km.), 2900 ft., 3 hr. 20 min.

Reel Brook Trail (WMNF)

This lightly used trail ascends to the Kinsman Ridge Trail in the col between Mt. Wolf and South Kinsman (the original Kinsman Notch), 1.0 mi. south of Eliza Brook Shelter. It begins on a gravel road that leaves NH 116 3.7 mi. north of the junction with NH 112 at Bungay Corner and 1.1 mi. south of the Easton town hall. The road, which is not plowed in winter, is passable for cars to a fork (hiker logo on post) at 0.6 mi. from NH 116, where the left branch leads to an open field (parking). The grades on this trail are moderate, but the footing is often very muddy.

    The trail enters the woods (sign) and follows a logging road southeast, parallel to but some distance northwest of Reel Brook, crossing several small brooks. At 1.2 mi. the road bears right and descends, and very shortly the trail diverges left, crosses a small brook, and turns left onto a wide logging road at 1.3 mi. (In the opposite direction, this turn, though usually marked by an arrow, could easily be missed; be sure to turn sharp right off the wide logging road 100 yd. after leaving the power line clearing.) In 100 yd. the trail enters the power line clearing, crosses it on a diagonal (avoid a path diverging left up along the lines), and re-enters the woods. The old road crosses a tributary, then Reel Brook itself twice, and enters a newer logging road that descends from the left just before the third and last crossing of Reel Brook at 1.9 mi. Here the trail turns right and follows the logging road away from the brook. The road is periodically bulldozed for maintenance access to the power lines, and as a result it is often very muddy, with numerous loose stones; when such conditions prevail, care must be taken, especially descending. It climbs moderately to a fork at 2.4 mi., where the main road swings left to the power lines, while the trail, with improved footing, forks right on another old logging road. In another 100 yd. the trail diverges right off this road, which swings left. From here the trail climbs gradually to the junction with the Kinsman Ridge Trail on the ridgecrest.

Reel Brook Trail (map 4:H3)

Distance from road fork near field (1400')

   to Kinsman Ridge Trail (2600'): 2.9 mi. (4.7 km.), 1200 ft., 2 hr. 5 min.

Jericho Road Trail (WMNF)

This trail ascends to the site of the Cooley Hill fire tower from a point just north of the height-of-land on the west side of NH 116, 1.9 mi. north of its junction with NH 112 at Bungay Corner, starting on a gated gravel logging road (FR 480). It was originally constructed as a horse trail and mostly follows logging roads of varying ages. There are no views, but some sections, particularly in the upper half, are quite pleasant for walking.

    The trail follows the gravel road uphill, swings to the right (north), and then continues straight (marked by a hiker logo and arrow) on an older road (FR 480A) at 0.3 mi., where a newer branch road bears right. After passing through a log yard at 1.3 mi., the road crosses a ditch where the newer section ends abruptly. The trail swings around the west side of a hump and descends into a sag, where it comes to a WMNF boundary corner distinctively marked with a pile of red-painted stones at 2.3 mi. Here the trail turns right off the road and, marked by flagging and axe blazes, continues to descend gradually, then climbs moderately. At 2.6 mi. it comes out on another old road that ascends from the right, and turns sharp left and follows the road up the crest of the ridge to a small wooded ledge near the concrete piers of the old fire tower. The trailless true summit of Cooley Hill is about 100 yd. north of the tower remains; from the end of the official hiking trail an unofficial trail-bike track continues down the northwest side of the mountain.

Jericho Road Trail (map 4:H3)

Distance from NH 116 (1385')

   to Cooley Hill (2480'): 3.2 mi. (5.2 km.), 1250 ft. (rev. 150 ft.), 2 hr. 15 min.

Cobble Hill Trail (WMNF)

This trail begins on NH 112 at a point 0.1 mi. west of the Woodsville Reservoir, and follows a gated gravel road (FR 310) and older woods roads along the west side of Dearth Brook to the WMNF boundary at the height-of-land between Cobble Hill and Moody Ledge. There are no views, but there is a small cascade in the brook on the right about 100 yd. from NH 112 that is interesting when there is a good flow of water. At 0.7 mi. from NH 112 the abandoned South Landaff Rd. leaves left, leading in about 2 mi. to an extensive area of old ruined farms where there are many interesting stone walls, cellar holes, and other remnants of the hill farm culture that once flourished in this part of New England. This culture declined severely during the second half of the 19th century and mostly died out in the first decades of the 20th century, and was the subject—or at least the setting—of much of Robert Frost's poetry. The old road continues north of the height-of-land for another 1.4 mi. down across private land to Mill Brook Rd. south of Landaff Center village, passing through woods much disrupted by logging.

Cobble Hill Trail (map 4:H2)
Distance from NH 112 (1017')

   to WMNF boundary (1800'): 2.1 mi. (3.4 km.), 800 ft., 1 hr. 25 min.

Section 6

The Moosilauke Region

This section covers Mt. Moosilauke and several lower ranges and peaks, including the Benton Range and the Stinson-Carr-Kineo area. It is bounded on the north by NH 112, on the east by US 3 (and I-93), and on the south by NH 25 from Plymouth to Woodsville. It is covered by the AMC Moosilauke–Kinsman map (map #4).

Many of the trails on the east side of Moosilauke begin at a trailhead at the end of Ravine Lodge Rd., the access road to the Dartmouth Outing Club (DOC) Ravine Lodge (which is now open to the public). The road (not plowed in the winter) leaves NH 118 on the north, 5.8 mi. east of its northerly junction with NH 25 and 7.2 mi. west of its junction with NH 112. From NH 118 it is 1.6 mi. to the turnaround at the end of the road, where the trails begin.

In this section the Appalachian Trail (AT), maintained by the DOC, leaves NH 25 on the Town Line Trail, runs along North and South Rd. and Sanatorium Rd. for short distances, then follows the Glencliff Trail and Moosilauke Carriage Road to the summit of Mt. Moosilauke and descends on the Beaver Brook Trail to Kinsman Notch.

GEOGRAPHY

Mt. Moosilauke (4802 ft.) is the farthest west of White Mtn. peaks over 4000 ft. and the dominating peak of the region between Franconia Notch and the Connecticut River. There is disagreement whether the name should be pronounced to rhyme with "rock" or with "rocky"; at one time Moosilauke was commonly corrupted to "Moosehillock," but the name actually means "a bald place" and has no reference to large, antlered beasts. The bare summit, once the site of a stone lodge called the Tip-Top House, commands an extremely fine view over ridge after ridge of the White Mtns. to the east, and across the Connecticut valley to the west. It has several minor summits, the most important being the **South Peak** (4523 ft.), an excellent viewpoint which provides fine views that are denied to the main summit into **Tunnel Ravine,** the deep ravine that lies between

Moosilauke and its trailless western neighbor, **Mt. Clough** (3561 ft.). To the north are two prominent wooded humps, the trailless **Mt. Blue** (4529 ft.), and **Mt. Jim** (4172 ft.), which form the ridge that encloses **Jobildunk Ravine,** a glacial cirque on the east side of the mountain, through which the headwaters of the **Baker River** flow from their source in a bog that was once **Deer Lake.** The summit of Moosilauke is very exposed to weather, and there is no longer any shelter near the summit. *A Trail Guide to Mount Moosilauke,* containing much information on the human and natural history of the mountain, has been published by the Environmental Studies Division of the DOC.

The **Benton Range,** which rises to the west of Mt. Clough, is composed of **Black Mtn.** (2830 ft.), **Sugarloaf Mtn.** (2609 ft.), **the Hogsback** (2810 ft.), **Jeffers Mtn.** (2994 ft.), **Blueberry Mtn.** (2662 ft.), and **Owls Head** (1967 ft.). Of these peaks, all but Jeffers provide excellent views, though only Black, Sugarloaf, and Blueberry have trails.

Stinson Mtn. (2900 ft.), **Carr Mtn.** (3453 ft.), **Rattlesnake Mtn.** (1594 ft.), and trailless **Mt. Kineo** (3313 ft.) rise in the angle formed by the Pemigewasset and Baker rivers. Stinson Mtn. and Carr Mtn. offer good views from summits that once bore fire towers. In the northern part of the area is the site of the village of Peeling, a hill community that was the original settlement in the town of Woodstock but was deserted about the time of the Civil War. Most of the area has grown up, and only traces of the village remain. Those interested in visiting this region should contact the Pemigewasset Ranger District office in Plymouth for information.

Agassiz Basin is an interesting series of potholes on Moosilauke Brook next to NH 112, 1.6 mi. west of North Woodstock. The basin is next to Govoni's Restaurant, and there are signs during the summer season. Two bridges cross the gorge, connected by a short path on the south bank; the upper one reaches NH 112 on the porch of the restaurant. The entire loop is about 250 yd. long.

CAMPING

Forest Protection Areas

The WMNF has established a number of Forest Protection Areas (FPAs)—formerly known as Restricted Use Areas—where camping and wood or charcoal fires are prohibited throughout the year. The specific areas are under continual review, and areas are added to or subtracted from the list in order to provide the greatest amount of protection to areas subject to damage by excessive camping, while imposing the lowest level of restrictions possible. A general list of FPAs in this section follows, but since there are often major changes from year to year, one should obtain current information on FPAs from the WMNF.

(1) No camping is permitted above treeline (where trees are less than 8 ft. tall), except in winter, and then only in places where there is at least two feet of snow cover on the ground—but not on any frozen body of water. The point where the restricted area begins is marked on most trails with small signs, but the absence of such signs should not be construed as proof of the legality of a site.

(2) No camping is permitted within a quarter-mile of any trailhead, picnic area, or any facility for overnight accommodation such as a hut, cabin, shelter, tentsite, or campground, except as designated at the facility itself. In the area covered by Section 6, camping is also prohibited on the islands on Long Pond and within one-quarter mile of the site of the former Beaver Brook Shelter (not at the new shelter), the Jackman Brook Overlook on NH 118, and Stinson Lake Rd. where it crosses Brown Brook.

(3) No camping is permitted within 200 ft. of certain trails. In 1997, designated trails included the entire Appalachian Trail from NH 25 in Glencliff to the summit of Mt. Moosilauke.

Dartmouth College Land

No camping or fires are permitted on Dartmouth College land, which lies east and south of the summit of Moosilauke, roughly bounded by a line starting just south of Hurricane Mtn. and following the ridgecrest over South Peak, Mt. Moosilauke, Mt. Blue, Mt. Jim, and Mt. Waternomee, and then south from Waternomee to NH 118.

Established Trailside Campsites

Jeffers Brook Shelter (DOC) is located just off the Town Line Trail, which is a part of the Appalachian Trail.

Beaver Brook Shelter (DOC)—a newly constructed shelter that replaces an older one in a different location—is located on the Beaver Brook Trail (a part of the Appalachian Trail), 1.5 mi. from NH 112 in Kinsman Notch. Camping is prohibited at the former shelter site.

Three Ponds Shelter (WMNF) is located on a knoll above the middle pond on a side trail from the Three Ponds Trail.

Trails on Mount Moosilauke

Trails on the Benton Range

Trails of the Stinson-Carr-Kineo Region

THE TRAILS

Beaver Brook Trail (DOC)

This trail, which climbs to the summit of Moosilauke from NH 112 at a small parking area near the height-of-land in Kinsman Notch, is a link in the Appalachian Trail. It passes the beautiful Beaver Brook Cascades, but the section along the cascades is extremely steep and rough, making this trail the most arduous route to Moosilauke in spite of its relatively short distance. *Caution:* In icy conditions this part of the trail may be dangerous. The upper part of the trail has recently been completely relocated and now coincides with the Benton Trail for the last 0.4 mi. to Moosilauke's summit. As a result it now ascends Moosilauke's open north ridge, where it is much more exposed to weather than the former route (which was quite well sheltered); consequently this part may be dangerous in bad weather. A new Beaver Brook Shelter has been constructed at a site 1.5 mi. from NH 112; the old shelter has been dismantled, and camping at the site is forbidden.

Leaving NH 112 almost directly opposite the Kinsman Ridge Trail, this trail crosses a bridge over Beaver Brook, swings to the left, and recrosses the brook on a bridge. The trail soon begins the climb along Beaver Brook, rising very steeply past Beaver Brook Cascades with many rock steps, wooden steps, and hand rungs. At 1.1 mi. the cascades end, and the trail bears left along a tributary and becomes progressively easier, following old logging roads. At 1.5 mi. it passes a side path that leads right in 80 yd. to Beaver Brook Shelter (DOC). Here there is an excellent view to the northeast, and a small stream 60 yd. farther along provides water (may not be reliable). The main trail continues to climb, and at a junction in a flat area at 1.9 mi. the Asquam-Ridge Trail turns sharp left. Here the Beaver Brook Trail bears right and ascends easily toward the edge of Jobildunk Ravine. The old trail skirted the edge of this ravine, but the new trail turns sharp right uphill on the relocated route at 2.5 mi., then immediately turns sharp left and climbs fairly steeply to a point high up on the side of the highest knob of Mt. Blue. It then descends to a col, climbs over another knob with several restricted outlooks, descends to a second col, and climbs to the junction with the Benton Trail just below treeline, at 3.4 mi. From this point the two trails coincide, soon reaching treeline and ascending the open, very exposed ridgecrest to the summit.

Beaver Brook Trail (map 4:I3)

Distances from NH 112 (1870')

> *to* Beaver Brook Shelter (3750'): 1.5 mi., 1900 ft., 1 hr. 40 min.
>
> *to* Asquam-Ridge Trail (4050'): 1.9 mi., 2200 ft., 2 hr. 5 min.
>
> *to* Benton Trail (4550'): 3.4 mi., 2850 ft. (rev. 150 ft.), 3 hr. 10 min.
>
> *to* Mt. Moosilauke summit (4802'): 3.8 mi. (6.1 km.), 3100 ft., 3 hr. 25 min.

Tunnel Brook Trail (WMNF)

This trail runs between Tunnel Brook Rd. (FR 147) and North and South Rd. (FR 19) through the deep valley (the "tunnel") between Mt. Moosilauke and Mt. Clough. To reach the north trailhead, follow the road that leaves NH 112 at a point 0.5 mi. east of its eastern junction with NH 116, go straight (south) at a hairpin turn at 1.4 mi., and continue to the trailhead at the end of the maintained section, 3.8 mi. from NH 112. The south trailhead is located on North and South Rd., 0.4 mi. north of the point where it leaves Sanatorium Rd. 1.0 mi. from NH 25 in Glencliff. The central portion is subject to disruption by beaver activity, and, though the trail is currently well maintained and clear, short sections could become very wet or obscure. There are good views of beaver ponds and the slides on Mt. Clough, and grades are mostly easy.

Leaving the parking area at the end of Tunnel Brook Rd., the trail continues south on an old logging road, crosses Tunnel Brook at 0.8 mi., recrosses at 1.3 mi., and soon reaches an outlook to Slide Pond and the slides on Mt. Clough. At 1.6 mi. it recrosses Tunnel Brook on a beaver dam at the southeast corner of Slide Pond, and at 1.9 mi. it reaches an open spot on the shore of Mud Pond, with a view up to the South Peak of Moosilauke. Soon it crosses the outwash from a slide and begins to descend on a logging road along Slide Brook, passing a reservoir at 3.3 mi. and crossing and recrossing the brook. Care should be taken not to pollute Slide Brook, the water supply for the New Hampshire Home for the Elderly in Glencliff. At 4.2 mi. the trail crosses Jeffers Brook, passes a camp, and ends at North and South Rd.

Tunnel Brook Trail (map 4:I2)

Distances from end of Tunnel Brook Rd. (1880')

> *to* Mud Pond (2280'): 1.9 mi., 400 ft., 1 hr. 10 min.
>
> *to* North and South Rd. (1393'): 4.4 mi. (7.1 km.), 400 ft. (rev. 900 ft.), 2 hr. 25 min.

Benton Trail (WMNF)

This trail climbs to the summit of Mt. Moosilauke from Tunnel Brook Rd. (FR 147). To reach the trailhead, follow the road that leaves NH 112 at a point 0.5 mi. east of its eastern junction with NH 116, go straight (south) at a hairpin turn at 1.4 mi., then continue to the trailhead 3.0 mi. from NH 112. The trail follows the route of an old bridle path with moderate grades and good footing, making this a very pleasant and fairly easy route to the magnificent views from Moosilauke's summit, though the brook crossing at about 0.2 mi. from the start is difficult when the water level is high. For the last 0.3 mi. the Benton Trail ascends the open north ridge of Moosilauke, where it is greatly exposed to the elements, so this section may be dangerous in bad weather.

The trail descends slightly from the parking lot to an old logging road, follows the road along Tunnel Brook for 0.2 mi., then crosses the brook (may be difficult at high water) and bears right on an old logging road, ascending the wooded spur that forms the south wall of Little Tunnel Ravine. At 1.3 mi. there is a splendid view to the left into the ravine. The trail passes a spring (sign) on the right at 2.2 mi., then soon turns sharp right and climbs at moderate grades through a beautiful evergreen forest to treeline. The Beaver Brook Trail (a part of the Appalachian Trail) enters from the left at 3.2 mi. just before the Benton Trail breaks out from the scrubby trees, and the two trails together ascend the bare north ridge, marked by cairns, to the summit.

Benton Trail (map 4:I2–I3)

Distances from Tunnel Brook Rd. (1700')

> *to* Little Tunnel Ravine outlook (2800'): 1.3 mi., 1100 ft., 1 hr. 10 min.
>
> *to* Beaver Brook Trail junction (4550'): 3.2 mi., 2850 ft., 3 hr.
>
> *to* Mt. Moosilauke summit (4802'): 3.6 mi. (5.7 km.), 3100 ft., 3 hr. 20 min.

Glencliff Trail (DOC)

This trail runs from Sanatorium Rd., 1.2 mi. from its junction with NH 25 in Glencliff village, to the Moosilauke Carriage Road in a sag just north of Moosilauke's South Peak. It is part of the Appalachian Trail. There is only one steep section, and the footing is generally good.

The trail leaves the road, passes a gate and enters a pasture, and soon crosses a small brook on a bridge. It joins a farm road (descending, bear left), then crosses a brook, follows a cart track along the left edge of a field, and enters the woods at 0.4 mi., where the Hurricane Trail immediately diverges right (east). The Glencliff Trail ascends moderately on a logging road that gradually fades away, crosses several small brooks, and passes a restricted outlook from a blowdown patch at 2.0 mi. Soon the trail swings right, going straight up the slope, and at 2.5 mi. it becomes quite steep. At the top of the ridge it levels and reaches the junction with a spur path (sign) that leads right 0.2 mi. to the open summit of South Peak. In a few more steps it enters the Moosilauke Carriage Road; for the summit, turn left.

Glencliff Trail (map 4:J2–I2)

Distances from Sanatorium Rd. (1480')

  to Moosilauke Carriage Road (4460'): 3.0 mi. (4.8 km.), 3000 ft., 3 hr.

  to Mt. Moosilauke summit (4802') via Moosilauke Carriage Road: 3.9 mi. (6.3 km.), 3300 ft., 3 hr. 35 min.

Town Line Trail (DOC)

This trail, a short link in the Appalachian Trail constructed mainly to eliminate a road walk for AT hikers, runs from the northeast side of NH 25, just southeast of the Warren-Benton town line (parking 100 yd. farther southeast on the southwest side of NH 25), to the North and South Rd. 0.1 mi. north of the point where it leaves Sanatorium Rd. 1.0 mi. from NH 25 in Glencliff. In times of high water the crossing of Oliverian Brook next to NH 25 is dangerous, and in such conditions hikers traveling between Mt. Moosilauke and points to the south on the Appalachian Trail should follow Sanatorium Rd. and NH 25 rather than attempting to use this trail.

   The trail crosses Oliverian Brook (fairly difficult even at moderate water levels) and follows the bank of the brook downstream, then swings left away from the brook, climbs moderately over a narrow ridgecrest, and continues across low ridges and shallow sags. At 0.9 mi. the trail crosses a good-sized brook on a bridge, and in another 90 yd. a side path leaves left and runs north 0.1 mi. to Jeffers Brook Shelter. The main trail soon reaches the bank of Jeffers Brook and continues to North and South Rd.

Town Line Trail (map 4:J2)

Distance from NH 25 (1000')

   to North and South Rd. (1330'): 1.1 mi. (1.8 km.), 400 ft. (rev. 50 ft.), 45 min.

Hurricane Trail (DOC)

This trail runs around the lower south end of Moosilauke, making possible a number of loop trips by linking the low end of the Glencliff Trail, the lower part of the Moosilauke Carriage Road, and the complex of trails that leave Ravine Lodge Rd. East of the Moosilauke Carriage Road, the Hurricane Trail is level and clear; some parts to the west are moderately steep and rough.

The Hurricane Trail continues straight where the Gorge Brook Trail turns right, 0.2 mi. from Ravine Lodge Rd. It crosses Gorge Brook on a log bridge and descends to the bank of Baker River, where it picks up a logging road and follows it on a long curve away from the river. At 1.0 mi. it reaches the Moosilauke Carriage Road and turns left (downhill). The two trails coincide for 0.3 mi., crossing Big Brook on a bridge, then the Hurricane Trail turns right (west) off the Carriage Road and follows a logging road into a small, moist clearing. Here it turns sharp left, follows Little Brook for a while, and climbs to the height-of-land at 2.6 mi. It continues nearly level for 0.2 mi., passing north of the little hump called Hurricane Mtn., then descends, rather steeply at times, to the Glencliff Trail 0.4 mi. from Sanatorium Rd.

Hurricane Trail (map 4:I3–I2)
Distances from Gorge Brook Trail (2460')

  to Moosilauke Carriage Road, upper junction (2380'): 1.0 mi., 50 ft. (rev. 100 ft.), 30 min.

  to Glencliff Trail (1680'): 4.3 mi. (6.9 km.), 900 ft. (rev. 1600 ft.), 2 hr. 35 min.

Moosilauke Carriage Road (WMNF/DOC)

This former carriage road climbs to the summit of Moosilauke from Breezy Point, the site of the Moosilauke Inn. The road to Breezy Point leaves NH 118 2.5 mi. north of its junction with NH 25 (which is 1.0 mi. north of Warren village). Follow the road for 1.6 mi., just past the driveway to the inn, and park where the road descends slightly (sign). Grades are easy to moderate and the footing is in general very good; marking is light in the first part, after which the trail becomes unmistakable. The upper part is above treeline and greatly exposed to the elements, and can be dangerous in bad weather. The lower part, up to a barricade at 4.1 mi., receives heavy snowmobile use in winter.

Continuing on the dirt road, the trail crosses Merrill Brook on a bridge, then enters a clearing at 0.3 mi., where it passes straight through and continues on a logging road with DOC markings. The Hurricane Trail enters left at 1.3 mi., and the two trails cross Big Brook together on a bridge. The Hurricane Trail diverges right to Ravine Lodge Rd. after another 0.2 mi., and the old carriage road begins to climb by a series of switchbacks through a beautiful mature hardwood forest, with easy to moderate grades and excellent footing. At 3.0 mi. the recently relocated Snapper Trail enters right. The next section of the road has been widened and improved, eliminating what was formerly a washed-out section with poor footing. At 4.1 mi. the old road is blocked by a row of boulders to prevent further vehicular use. At 4.2 mi. the Glencliff Trail enters from the left; a few steps along the Glencliff Trail, a spur trail leads left 0.2 mi. to South Peak, a fine viewpoint. The old road, now part of the Appalachian Trail, continues along the ridge, with a narrow fringe of trees on each side, passing to the left of a viewpoint that overlooks the ravine of Gorge Brook. At 4.9 mi. it reaches treeline and ascends the windswept ridge to the summit.

Moosilauke Carriage Road (map 4:J2–I3)

Distances from Breezy Point trailhead (1720')

to Snapper Trail (3360'): 3.0 mi., 1650 ft., 2 hr. 20 min.

to Glencliff Trail (4460'): 4.2 mi., 2750 ft., 3 hr. 30 min.

to Mt. Moosilauke summit (4802'): 5.1 mi. (8.3 km.), 3100 ft., 4 hr. 5 min.

Gorge Brook Trail (DOC)

This trail runs from the end of Ravine Lodge Rd. to the summit of Moosilauke. The upper part has been completely relocated, making the trail substantially longer but eliminating the steep grades and rough footing of the former route. It is now a relatively easy trail that affords some interesting views as it climbs.

Leaving the turnaround at the end of Ravine Lodge Rd., it follows the gravel logging road for 100 yd., then turns left, descends to Baker River and crosses it on a footbridge, and immediately turns left at 0.2 mi. where the Asquam-Ridge Trail diverges right. At 0.3 mi., where the Hurricane Trail continues straight ahead, the Gorge Brook Trail turns sharp right uphill and follows Gorge Brook, then crosses it on a bridge at 0.6 mi. The recently relocated Snapper Trail diverges on the left just past this bridge, while the Gorge Brook Trail continues close to the brook and recrosses it at 1.3 mi. on another bridge. At 1.6 mi. it passes the memorial plaque for the Ross McKenney Forest; here the new route begins and swings well to the right of the former route. At 2.1 mi. it turns left onto an old logging road, passes a cleared outlook to the south, then turns left off the road and winds uphill at moderate grades, passing more outlooks to the south and east. At 3.3 mi. it reaches a shoulder covered with low scrub that affords a view to the summit ahead and soon breaks into the open on the grassy ridgecrest. It continues to the base of the summit rocks, then clambers up the last rocky 50 yd. to the summit.

On the descent, though the trails are fairly well signed, the maze of beaten paths (including several abandoned trails) in this area might prove confusing in poor visibility. From the summit the Gorge Brook Trail descends eastward down the rocks and then runs southeast along a grassy shoulder until it reaches the scrub.

Gorge Brook Trail (map 4:J3–I3)

Distances from Ravine Lodge Rd. (2460')

to Snapper Trail (2620'): 0.6 mi., 250 ft. (rev. 100 ft.), 25 min.

to McKenney Forest plaque (3350'): 1.6 mi., 1000 ft., 1 hr. 15 min.

to Mt. Moosilauke summit (4802'): 3.7 mi. (6.0 km.), 2450 ft., 3 hr. 5 min.

Snapper Trail (DOC)

This trail was originally cut as a downhill ski trail, but it has been almost completely relocated recently and now features less steep grades and drier footing than before. It runs from the Gorge Brook Trail 0.6 mi. from Ravine Lodge Rd. to the Moosilauke Carriage Road 2.1 mi. below the summit of Moosilauke. It makes possible a number of loop hikes from Ravine Lodge Rd.; particularly attractive is the circuit over the summit of Moosilauke that combines the Snapper Trail–Moosilauke Carriage Road route with the Gorge Brook Trail—these two routes are now approximately equal in distance and difficulty.

Leaving the Gorge Brook Trail just after its first crossing of Gorge Brook, it ascends northwest along a tributary and crosses it at 0.3 mi. It swings left, then right, crosses another tributary, then angles up the slope in a southwest direction at a moderate grade. At 0.9 mi. it crosses the old trail route and continues to its junction with the Moosilauke Carriage Road.

Snapper Trail (map 4:J3–J2)

Distance from Gorge Brook Trail (2620')

to Moosilauke Carriage Road (3360'): 1.1 mi. (1.8 km.), 750 ft., 55 min.

Distance from Ravine Lodge Rd. (2460')

to Mt. Moosilauke summit (4802') via Gorge Brook Trail, Snapper Trail, and Moosilauke Carriage Road: 3.8 mi. (6.1 km.), 2450 ft., 3 hr. 5 min.

Asquam-Ridge Trail (DOC)

This trail runs from the Gorge Brook Trail 0.2 mi. from Ravine Lodge Rd. to the Beaver Brook Trail on top of the Blue Ridge, providing a long but rather easy route to Moosilauke's summit.

It leaves the Gorge Brook Trail just across the Baker River footbridge, where it turns sharp right and follows the west bank of the river. At 0.5 mi. it merges with a logging road that comes in from the right; this road ascends 0.5 mi. from the end of Ravine Lodge Rd. and crosses the river on a bridge before it reaches this intersection. The Asquam-Ridge Trail continues along the river, then crosses it on a footbridge at 1.5 mi. and turns sharp right to ascend gradually away from the river. At 1.9 mi. the trail turns sharp left where the Al Merrill Loop from Ravine Lodge Rd. enters straight ahead, and then follows another logging road very gradually upward. Eventually it encounters some steeper pitches, passes a few yards left of the wooded summit of Mt. Jim, then descends easily to the Beaver Brook Trail.

Asquam-Ridge Trail (map 4:J3–I3)

Distances from Gorge Brook Trail (2360')

   to Beaver Brook Trail (4050'): 3.9 mi. (6.4 km.), 1700 ft., 2 hr. 50 min.

   to Mt. Moosilauke summit (4802') via Beaver Brook Trail: 5.8 mi. (9.3 km.), 2600 ft., 4 hr. 10 min.

Al Merrill Loop (DOC)

This trail follows logging roads for its entire length from the end of Ravine Lodge Rd. to the Asquam-Ridge Trail and, while it was originally intended mostly as a ski trail, it is also excellent for hiking. Up to the height-of-land (just past the fine 10th Mountain Division memorial outlook), it provides easy grades and footing, affording a hike of less than 5 mi. while rising only about 900 feet to a fine viewpoint. A loop hike that is a bit longer with slightly rougher footing can be made by continuing to the junction with the Asquam-Ridge Trail and following that trail back to the starting point. This loop is perhaps a bit easier in the opposite direction (up by the Asquam-Ridge Trail, down by the Al Merrill Loop).

Leaving the turnaround at the end of Ravine Lodge Rd., this trail continues on the gravel logging road past the junction where the Gorge Brook Trail diverges from the road on the left. It takes the right fork of the road at 0.1 mi., where the left fork leads to a bridge across the stream and continues to join the Asquam-Ridge Trail. It continues past a spur path that leads left to John Rand

Cabin (not open to the public) at 0.5 mi., and climbs to a fork in a clearing at 1.2 mi. where it bears left as a dead-end ski trail goes to the right. Still ascending easily, at 2.4 mi. it reaches the 10th Mountain Division memorial outlook, where there is a fine view up to the summit of Moosilauke. Soon it crosses the height-of-land and descends with somewhat less easy footing to the junction where it enters the Asquam-Ridge Trail at a switchback; left (downhill) leads down toward Ravine Lodge Rd., while right (uphill) leads toward Mt. Jim and the summit of Moosilauke.

Al Merrill Loop (map 4:J3–I3)

Distances from Ravine Lodge Rd. (2460')

   to 10th Mountain Division outlook (3350'): 2.4 mi., 900 ft., 1 hr. 40 min.

   to Asquam-Ridge Trail (3000'): 3.2 mi. (5.2 km.), 950 ft. (rev. 400 ft.), 2 hr. 5 min.

   for complete loop via Asquam-Ridge Trail: 5.1 mi. (8.2 km.), 1050 ft., 3 hr. 10 min.

Blueberry Mountain Trail (WMNF)

This trail crosses the ridge of Blueberry Mtn., affording interesting views from scattered ledges on both sides of the crest. The east terminus is reached by following Sanatorium Rd. for 1.0 mi. from NH 25 in Glencliff, then turning left (north) on North and South Rd. and following it for 0.8 mi. to a small parking area on the left. The west terminus is reached by taking Lime Kiln Rd. from NH 25 in East Haverhill, 5.2 mi. north of Glencliff and 0.4 mi. north of a power line crossing where there is an interesting view of the Benton Range to the north. Keep straight ahead at a junction at 1.4 mi. where Lime Kiln Rd. turns left, and continue to the trail sign on a side road that leaves left at 2.4 mi. Parking is available in a field on the right 0.1 mi. up this road, just before a gate that one should not drive past even if it is open. The western section of the trail is not being maintained at the present time, but trail-bike traffic has kept the footway fairly easy to follow for experienced hikers.

Starting at North and South Rd., the trail follows a relatively new logging road for 0.2 mi., then turns sharp right up a short, steep bank and follows old logging roads, crossing a newer grassy road at 0.4 mi. It enters coniferous woods and begins to ascend ledges with restricted views, then turns sharp right at 1.2 mi. and continues to climb. Soon it reaches ledges that are more open, with outlooks to the east and south, including an unusual and interesting view into the slide-scarred ravine of Slide Brook on Moosilauke. At 1.7 mi. it reaches the crest of the main ridge, where a side path leads right (north) 0.1 mi. to the ledges of the true summit, which offers good views.

The trail (official maintenance temporarily suspended from here on) then descends gradually through scrubby trees and ledges with limited views, passing to the left of a boggy depression and crossing a small moist glen, then turns sharp right at a cairn capped with a shark-fin rock and soon reaches a fine view of Black Mtn., Sugarloaf, and the Hogsback. Other views to Sugarloaf and to the Connecticut Valley are passed as the trail descends on ledges. The trail drops below the ledges, passes through a short area of moss-carpeted coniferous woods, and enters the upper end of a system of logging roads that it follows the rest of the way. It crosses many small brooks and one rather wet stretch. At 3.2 mi., after leaving an extensive section of birch woods, it crosses a stone wall and enters a region of abandoned farms where many stone walls and cellar holes remain, and mint that escaped from a farm garden many decades ago still grows among the corduroy logs in the old road. At 4.0 mi. the trail enters a fairly new gravel road and turns sharp left on it, crossing the WMNF boundary in 125 yd. (This junction is not well marked and hikers following this trail in the eastbound direction need to watch carefully for the sharp right turn.) The newer road leads past a sawmill and a gate, passes a field with a good view up to Sugarloaf, and ends on the branch road from Lime Kiln Rd. just after passing a small sugar-house.

Blueberry Mountain Trail (map 4:I2–I1)
Distances from North and South Rd. (1558')

> *to* ridgecrest near Blueberry Mtn. summit (2600'): 1.7 mi., 1050 ft., 1 hr. 25 min.
>
> *to* branch road from Lime Kiln Rd. (1176'): 4.5 mi. (7.3 km.), 1050 ft. (rev. 1400 ft.), 2 hr. 45 min.

Black Mountain Trail (WMNF)

This trail ascends Black Mtn. from the north, using old logging roads and the old tractor road to the former fire tower. It is a fairly easy way to ascend this attractive small mountain, but is much less interesting and only slightly easier than the Chippewa Trail. From the four-way intersection on NH 116 in Benton village, 2.9 mi. west of the western junction of NH 112 and NH 116, follow Howe Hill Rd., which runs uphill approximately south. At 0.8 mi. the road swings west and becomes gravel, and is marked with a USFS signpost as FR 76. Depending on the condition of the road, it may be possible to drive to a small parking space 1.4 mi.

from NH 116 (bear left where a snowmobile trail leaves on the right at 1.3 mi.); since the road often becomes rough and muddy well before the parking area, it may be better to park lower down and walk part or all of this 0.7-mi. road section.

From the parking area, the trail follows the road, bearing slightly left in a log yard, then takes the right branch at a fork and winds uphill, passing near several logged areas. At 1.7 mi. the Chippewa Trail joins from the right, and the open, ledgy ridgecrest at the old fire tower site is another 40 yd. ahead. There are good views from the ridgecrest both east and west of the tower site; Tipping Rock, where there are more good views, is 50 yd. to the east.

Black Mountain Trail (map 4:H2–I1)
Distance from marked parking space on FR 76 (1630')

   to Black Mtn. summit (2830'): 1.7 mi. (2.7 km.), 1200 ft., 1 hr. 25 min.

Chippewa Trail (WMNF)

This very scenic trail ascends Black Mtn. from Lime Kiln Rd., which leaves NH 25 in East Haverhill, 5.2 mi. north of Glencliff and 0.4 mi. north of a power line crossing. Bear left at a major fork at 1.4 mi. and continue to the trailhead at a point 3.1 mi. from NH 25. The trail, well blazed with yellow paint, begins on the right at a small parking area, marked with a hiker logo sign and a sign reading "Haverhill Heritage Trail 13: Lime Kilns."

The trail descends a short, fairly steep pitch, crosses a small brook and then a somewhat larger one, then climbs the bank to a logging road and turns right on it; the Lime Kilns are located to the left on this road (sign). In another 60 yd. the trail diverges left from this road on a much older road and begins the ascent of the mountain. At 0.6 mi. it passes to the left of a cellar hole in an overgrown pasture and, after passing through a shallow sag, begins to climb more steeply. It passes a WMNF boundary sign and then turns sharp left just before a rock outcrop on the ridgecrest, continuing to climb among ledges in woods dominated by red pines. At 1.1 mi. the main trail turns sharp left where a side path leads right 25 yd. to a ledge that affords fine views south and west. In this area the blue blazes of a property line must not be confused with trail blazes. After 1.3 mi. the trail climbs mostly on ledges past excellent outlooks scattered along the way until it reaches a knob with an interesting view of the summit rocks ahead, then crosses a shallow, moist sag and reaches the junction with the Black Mountain Trail from Benton village. The open ridgecrest at the old fire tower site is 40 yd. to the right, with good outlook points on the ridgecrest both east and west of the tower site. Tipping Rock, on a ledge with good views, is 50 yd. east of the tower site.

Chippewa Trail (map 4:I1)

Distance from parking area off Lime Kiln Rd. (1320')

   to Black Mtn. summit (2830'): 1.8 mi. (2.9 km.), 1550 ft., 1 hr. 40 min.

Sugarloaf Trail

This trail ascends Sugarloaf Mtn., an interesting small mountain that offers a number of good viewpoints. The trail is not officially maintained and may be dangerous on the ledges, particularly in wet or icy conditions, and the ladders may not be safe to climb. To reach the trail, follow Lime Kiln Rd. north from NH 25 in East Haverhill, 5.2 mi. north of Glencliff and 0.4 mi. north of a power line crossing where there is an interesting view of the Benton Range to the north, including an excellent view of Sugarloaf. Go straight ahead at the junction at 1.4 mi. and continue 0.8 mi. to a gated road on the left, where cars must be parked (do not block the gate or other roads).

   Follow the gated road, then turn right at a garage in 0.1 mi. and follow a dirt road past an automobile junkyard. The trail leaves the road on the right (sign) 0.7 mi. from the gate, just beyond a small brook. It crosses an old apple orchard, now mostly overgrown, then passes through a shallow, moist sag and begins to climb at moderate to steep grades. At 1.4 mi. it reaches a very steep ledge that is climbed by two ladders (use great caution), then turns sharp right and ascends near the edge of the cliff, with good outlooks. It then zigzags up rocks with increasing views until it reaches a bare ledge where trail marking currently ends, about 60 yd. below the true summit. There are a number of other good outlooks that can be reached by exploring scattered ledges separated by rather thick woods.

Sugarloaf Trail (map 4:I1)

Distances from gate next to side road off Lime Kiln Rd. (1150')

   to beginning of trail (1280'): 0.7 mi., 150 ft., 25 min.

   to Sugarloaf Mtn. summit (2609'): 1.9 mi. (3.1 km.), 1450 ft., 1 hr. 40 min.

Stinson Mountain Trail (WMNF)

The fire tower on this small, relatively easy mountain has been dismantled, but fine views are still available in every direction except southwest, and metamorphosed strata make the summit ledge geologically interesting. The trail is reached by following Stinson Lake Rd. north from NH 25 in Rumney. At the foot of the lake, 5.0

mi. from NH 25 and 0.1 mi. south of the Stinson Lake General Store and Post Office, turn right uphill for 0.8 mi., then turn right again on the old Doe Town Rd. to a parking lot at 0.3 mi. on the left.

The trail leaves the parking lot and soon enters and follows an old farm road between stone walls. After passing a cellar hole on the left side of the trail, it becomes steeper, and at 0.9 mi. it bears left, joining a logging road that comes up from the right. At 1.1 mi., the trail takes the right fork at a junction; left is the old tractor road to the summit, longer and less pleasant. The trail climbs by switchbacks and rejoins the old tractor road just below the summit (note the left turn here for the descent). From the summit a spur path leads southwest about 80 yd. to a view over Stinson Lake.

Stinson Mountain Trail (map 4:K3)
Distance from parking lot (1495')

   to Stinson Mtn. summit (2900'): 1.8 mi. (2.9 km.), 1400 ft., 1 hr. 35 min.

Rattlesnake Mountain Trail (WMNF)

This trail has been radically changed by the elimination of its eastern half and the construction of a new loop trail over the ledges of Rattlesnake Mtn., which afford fine views over the Baker River valley, so that now it provides excellent views for a very modest effort. It begins on Buffalo Rd., the road along the north bank of Baker River, 2.5 mi. west from the crossroads in Rumney village; or, from NH 25, 6.4 mi. west of the West Plymouth traffic circle, follow Sand Hill Rd. across Baker River, then turn right after 0.3 mi. and follow Buffalo Rd. 1.2 mi. to a small parking area just before the Nathan Clifford Birthplace historical marker.

The trail follows a logging road that soon becomes rather steep, then levels out on the ridgecrest and passes the west end of the summit loop on the right at 0.8 mi. In another 80 yd. the east end of the summit loop turns right off the old road and ascends over ledges with many fine views, reaching the summit at 1.3 mi. It descends and then turns sharp right at the base of the summit ledge, and returns over a rocky knob to the old road at 1.7 mi. Turn left here to return to the parking area.

Rattlesnake Mountain Trail (map 4:L2)
Distances from Buffalo Rd. (630')

   to Rattlesnake Mtn. summit (1594'): 1.3 mi., 950 ft., 1 hr. 10 min.

   for complete loop: 2.5 mi. (4.0 km.), 1000 ft., 1 hr. 45 min.

Carr Mountain Trail (WMNF)

This trail provides access to the summit of Carr Mtn., where several rounded rock knobs provide good views. It begins on the Three Ponds Trail 0.5 mi. from the new parking area on Stinson Lake Rd., ascends to the ridgecrest where a short spur trail leads to the summit of Carr Mtn., and descends to the old Warren-Wentworth highway 0.1 mi. south of the former state fish hatchery. Maintenance has been suspended on the western half of the trail, and this section can be recommended only for hikers with extensive experience in following obscure trails (although it is easier to follow on the descent than ascent).

The trail diverges sharp left (south) from the Three Ponds Trail and descends to cross Sucker Brook at 0.2 mi. on flat ledges that are submerged when water flow is above average, then crosses an old road on the south bank of the brook. (The Sucker Brook crossing is difficult at high water, and the trail section between Three Ponds Trail and the brook receives little use and may be overgrown and obscure. Most use of the Carr Mountain Trail is by local residents who enter the trail from Stinson Lake Rd. by this old road along the south bank of Sucker Brook. This is private land, however, and the landowner objects strongly to hikers' cars being parked in this area rather than at the official trailhead parking lot. The brook crossing can also be avoided by following the Three Ponds Trail to its bridge over Sucker Brook, then returning back southeast along the brook on the old logging road to the Carr Mountain Trail. This route is about 0.8 mi. longer than the direct trail route.)

Once across Sucker Brook, the trail climbs easily to meet its former route (an old woods road) and continues a moderate ascent. It swings sharp right at 1.4 mi. and then swings back to the left at 1.7 mi., then winds upward near the crest of a ridge close to a small brook. Higher up it approaches and then crosses a very small mossy brook, then zigzags upward and soon comes close to the crest of the main ridge. The ascent becomes gradual through dense, moist coniferous woods, and at 2.9 mi. a side path turns left to the summit area. The best view is probably from the top of the first knob encountered on the left side of this spur, which ends in about 70 yd. at the remnants of the former fire tower.

The main trail (no longer maintained and often difficult to follow) descends, reaching a small brook that it crosses several times, then enters logging roads that gradually become more and more discernible. At 4.8 mi. it turns sharp left in a tiny clearing onto a much newer woods road (a very obscure spot in the ascent); leading right from this junction (straight ahead, ascending) is an obscure footpath that runs 0.2 mi. to Waternomee Falls. At 5.6 mi. the road passes a house and becomes a clear gravel road that continues to the old Warren-Wentworth highway opposite a small cemetery, near the old fish hatchery.

Carr Mountain Trail (map 4:K3–K2)

Distances from Three Ponds Trail (1450')

    to Carr Mtn. summit side path (3420'): 2.9 mi., 2100 ft., 2 hr. 30 min.

    to old Warren-Wentworth highway (700'): 6.5 mi. (10.5 km.), 2100 ft. (rev. 2700 ft.), 4 hr. 20 min.

Three Ponds Trail (WMNF)

This trail starts on Stinson Lake Rd. at a new parking lot 6.9 mi. north of NH 25 and 1.8 mi. north of the Stinson Lake General Store and Post Office. It passes the attractive ponds with several interesting outlooks to Mts. Carr and Kineo, crosses a low ridge, and descends to the gravel road used by the Hubbard Brook Trail 0.2 mi. from NH 118. This gravel road leaves NH 118 4.4 mi. northeast of the junction of NH 118 and NH 25, which is about 1 mi. north of Warren village. The western part of this trail, between the ponds and NH 118, has received little maintenance in recent years and may be very difficult to follow; it is not recommended for inexperienced hikers.

    Leaving the parking lot, it passes junctions with the Mount Kineo Trail right at 0.1 mi. and the Carr Mountain Trail left at 0.5 mi. At 1.0 mi. it crosses Sucker Brook on a bridge and continues upstream along the brook, crossing it three more times without bridges; all of these crossings may be difficult at high water. At 2.2 mi., a side path diverges right on the shore of the middle pond, passes Three Ponds Shelter on a knoll overlooking the pond, and rejoins the main trail. At 2.5 mi. the Donkey Hill Cutoff continues straight, while the Three Ponds Trail turns left across a brook on a beaver dam, picks up a logging road, and follows it to a point 80 yd. from the upper pond. Here the road continues to the edge of the pond, but the trail turns sharp left and starts to ascend. From here on it is much less heavily used and likely to be obscure, and must be followed with great care. The trail enters a logging road, leaves it on a bypass around the swamp at Foxglove Pond, and crosses Brown Brook for the first of three times at 3.8 mi. The trail climbs to the height-of-land at 5.1 mi., then descends, makes a hairpin turn right, and enters a system of logging roads, following them to the Hubbard Brook Trail 0.2 mi. east of NH 118.

Three Ponds Trail (map 4:K3–J3)

Distances from Stinson Lake Rd. (1310')

    to Three Ponds Shelter (1750'): 2.3 mi., 450 ft., 1 hr. 20 min.

    to height-of-land (2380'): 5.1 mi., 1100 ft., 3 hr. 5 min.

to Hubbard Brook Trail (1430'): 7.2 mi. (11.7 km.), 1100 ft. (rev. 950 ft.), 4 hr. 10 min.

Donkey Hill Cutoff (WMNF)

This trail links the Three Ponds Trail 2.5 mi. from the Stinson Lake Rd. parking area to the Mount Kineo Trail 1.7 mi. from the parking area, making possible a loop hike. It crosses several small ridges and follows the edge of an extensive beaver swamp for much of its distance.

Donkey Hill Cutoff (map 4:K3)

Distance from Three Ponds Trail (1730')

to Mount Kineo Trail (1680'): 1.1 mi. (1.8 km.), 50 ft. (rev. 100 ft.), 35 min.

Mount Kineo Trail (WMNF)

This trail begins on the Three Ponds Trail 0.1 mi. from the new parking lot on Stinson Lake Rd., crosses the ridge of Mt. Kineo almost a mile east of the true summit, and descends to a spur road off Hubbard Brook Rd. (FR 22) 6.3 mi. from US 3 in West Thornton. The part of this trail south of the ridgecrest is an attractive woods walk.

Leaving the Three Ponds Trail, it proceeds north over several minor ups and downs and enters the old route of the trail (a logging road along Brown Brook) at 1.0 mi. The trail climbs along the attractive brook, and at 1.6 mi., where the Donkey Hill Cutoff diverges left, the Mount Kineo Trail crosses the brook on ledges (difficult in high water). It runs northwest along the edge of a large swamp, then at 2.3 mi. it swings right, away from the swamp, crosses several small brooks, and eventually climbs east, alternately angling up on old logging roads and climbing straight up on steep, rough sections. At 3.9 mi. it crosses the ridge in a small col, then descends to an old logging road, which it follows through several extremely muddy stretches to a gravel spur road passable by cars, about 0.5 mi. from its junction with Hubbard Brook Rd. (sign).

Mount Kineo Trail (map 4:K3–J3)

Distances from Three Ponds Trail (1340')

to Donkey Hill Cutoff (1680'): 1.6 mi., 350 ft., 1 hr.

to height-of-land (2850'): 3.9 mi., 1500 ft., 2 hr. 45 min.

to Hubbard Brook Rd. spur (1930'): 5.1 mi. (8.2 km.), 1500 ft. (rev. 900 ft.), 3 hr. 20 min.

Hubbard Brook Trail (WMNF)

This trail leaves Hubbard Brook Rd. (FR 22) at a hairpin turn across Hubbard Brook, 7.6 mi. from US 3 in West Thornton, and runs to NH 118, 4.4 mi. northeast of the junction with NH 25 (this junction is 1.0 mi. north of Warren village). Its only significant attractions are several beaver ponds, and it has received little maintenance in recent years and may be very difficult to follow; it is not recommended for inexperienced hikers.

Leaving the road, it soon passes a beaver pond where the trail might be subject to disruption, but by following the northeast bank the trail will be found where it enters the woods just above the north end of the pond. It crosses a low height-of-land at 0.9 mi. and descends on an assortment of logging roads and paths, crosses a beaver dam between two ponds, and enters a gravel logging road at 2.0 mi. ("HB" is blazed into a tree at the junction) that passes the Three Ponds Trail on the left at 2.3 mi. and continues to NH 118.

Hubbard Brook Trail (map 4:J3)
Distance from Hubbard Brook Rd. (1860')

   to NH 118 (1430'): 2.5 mi. (4.1 km.), 100 ft. (rev. 550 ft.), 1 hr. 20 min.

Peaked Hill Pond Trail (WMNF)

This trail follows a logging road to Peaked Hill Pond from US 3, north of exit 29 of I-93, at the 93 Motel. The trail is easy, and there are pleasant views from the shore of the pond, which is partly private property. From US 3, follow the road west under I-93, then turn right at 0.4 mi. and park just before a steel gate at 0.6 mi. The road ascends gradually, and at 0.5 mi. from the gate a woods road bears to the right off the road to bypass an old pasture, then returns to the main road and follows it to the right. It bears left at 0.9 mi. and skirts a logging clearing at 1.4 mi. At 1.5 mi. it leaves the road on the right and runs to the shore of the pond, where blazes end.

Peaked Hill Pond Trail (map 4:K4)
Distance from gate (820')

   to Peaked Hill Pond (1200'): 1.7 mi. (2.8 km.), 400 ft., 1 hr. 5 min.

Section 7

The Waterville Valley and Squam Lake Regions

This section covers the mountains that surround the valley of the Mad River, commonly called the Waterville Valley, including Mt. Tecumseh, Mt. Osceola, Mt. Tripyramid, Sandwich Mtn., and their subordinate peaks. It also covers the lower ranges to the south and southwest, including the mountains in the vicinity of Squam Lake: the Squam Range, the Rattlesnakes, and Red Hill. This region is bounded on the west by the Pemigewasset River (and I-93, which follows the river fairly closely), on the north by the Kancamagus Highway (NH 112), and on the south by NH 25. This is the western part of a larger mountainous region bounded on the east by NH 16; it extends nearly 30 mi. from Lincoln to Conway without being crossed from north to south by any road. This western part of the larger region consists of a jumble of relatively disorganized shorter ridges and isolated peaks, while the eastern part (covered in Section 8, Chocorua and the Eastern Sandwich Range) is dominated by the prominent and well-defined ridgecrest of the eastern Sandwich Range formed by Mts. Whiteface, Passaconaway, Paugus, and Chocorua. This division of the larger region into two sections places Mt. Tripyramid and Sandwich Mtn. in Section 7 and Mt. Whiteface and the Sleeper Ridge in Section 8, although all these mountains have traditionally been considered part of the Sandwich Range (while the rest of the mountains covered in Section 7 have not customarily been considered as belonging to the Sandwich Range). At the boundary between Section 7 and Section 8, the only points of contact between trails are at the junction of the Mt. Tripyramid Trail (Section 7) with the Kate Sleeper Trail (Section 8), and at the junction of the Flat Mountain Pond Trail (Section 7) with the McCrillis Trail (Section 8).

Almost the entire section is covered by the AMC Crawford Notch–Sandwich Range map (map #3). On Red Hill, the Red Hill Trail and the southern end of the Eagle Cliff Trail are not covered by any of the AMC maps, but are shown on the USGS Center Sandwich and Center Harbor quads. The southern part of the Squam Range (Mt. Livermore and points to the south) is covered better by the AMC Moosilauke–Kinsman map (map #4), but this map does not extend all the way to the southern ends of the Crawford-Ridgepole Trail and the Old Highway. The area containing these trails is shown on the USGS Holderness quad, though the Crawford-Ridgepole Trail up to the southeast summit of Cotton Mtn. is not shown, and the Old Highway is shown but not titled. The Squam Lakes Association (SLA), which maintains most of the trails on Squam Range, publishes Bradford Washburn's detailed map of the Squam Range (scale 1:15,000) and a trail guide to the paths they maintain, both of which can be ordered from the SLA, PO Box 204, Holderness NH 03245 (603-968-7336). The Washburn map, although offering much greater detail than the AMC maps, omits the same areas. However, the SLA trail guide has a map that, while not nearly as detailed as the AMC maps, covers Red Hill and the south end of the Squam Range to an extent that will probably be adequate for the great majority of hikers.

GEOGRAPHY

Waterville Valley, the town, must be carefully distinguished from **the Waterville Valley** (the valley of the Mad River); a significant part of the Waterville Valley lies in the town of Thornton, while the town of Waterville Valley includes the summits of Mts. Whiteface and Passaconaway, which are not considered part of the Waterville Valley by even the broadest definition. Therefore some features are in the Waterville Valley but not in Waterville Valley, and vice versa. The potential for confusion has been encouraged by certain recreational and tourist-oriented businesses that are technically located in the towns of Thornton or Campton, but within the area traditionally considered the Waterville Valley, and who wish to use the well-known name of Waterville Valley. In fact, the original name of the town was plain Waterville; it was changed to Waterville Valley in 1967 to share in the publicity that the major ski area of that name had generated. *The Waterville Valley,* by Nathaniel Goodrich (who participated in the scouting and building of many White Mtn. trails and also was the first person to suggest the creation of a Four Thousand Footer Club), recounts the history of the Waterville Valley from its first settlers up to a time just before the modern major tourist development started, and gives a fascinating picture not only of this particular place when it was a rustic backwater known only to a few people—who, however, loved it passionately—but of a period of history and a way of life that, among other things, produced a large portion of the hiking trails that we enjoy today.

From I-93 near Campton, **NH 49 (Mad River Rd.)** runs northeast beside the Mad River for more than 11 mi. into the center of Waterville Valley, passing a group of lodges and condominiums and ending near the Waterville Valley library, the Golf and Tennis Club, the ski-touring center, and the Snows Mtn. Ski Area. At 10.6 mi. from I-93, **Tripoli Rd. (FR 30)** turns sharp left, passes the road to the Mt. Tecumseh Ski Area at 1.3 mi., and soon after that begins to follow the West Branch of the Mad River northwest to the height-of-land west of Waterville Valley (Thornton Gap, 2300 ft., the pass between Mts. Osceola and Tecumseh). It then continues westward to its end at NH 175 (East Side Rd.) and I-93 near Woodstock. The road is gravel except for paved sections on each end, and much of it is narrow and winding; drive slowly and with caution. This road has not been plowed during the winter (except from NH 49 to the junction with the side road to the Livermore Rd. parking area) and is usually gated from late fall through the spring; there is also a gate at the height-of-land, which may be closed to prevent use of the road by through traffic when the gates at the ends are open. There is a town road that runs from Waterville Valley at the town library about 0.8 mi. west to Tripoli Rd. at a point north of the ski area, crossing a bridge over the West Branch of Mad River just before it reaches Tripoli Rd. **Livermore Rd. (FR 53)** and its trailhead parking area are reached from Tripoli Rd. by following this road a short distance across the bridge to a fork where Livermore Rd. bears left and the road to Waterville Valley village turns right.

Mt. Tecumseh (4003 ft.), named for the Shawnee leader, is the highest and northernmost summit of the ridges that form the west wall of the Waterville Valley, beneath which the **Mad River** flows. **Thornton Gap,** at the head of the northwestern branch of the Mad River, separates Mt. Tecumseh from Mt. Osceola to the northeast; to the west, southwest, and south, several ridges run out from Tecumseh toward Woodstock and Thornton. On the end of the south ridge, the fine rocky peak of **Welch Mtn.** (2605 ft.) overlooks the Campton meadows and forms the impressive northwest wall of the narrow south gateway to the upper Waterville Valley. The views from Welch's open summit are excellent. **Dickey Mtn.** (2734 ft.) is close to Welch on the northwest, with its best views available from a fine open ledge 0.2 mi. north of its summit.

Mt. Osceola (4340 ft.), the highest peak in the region, lies north of the valley. It was named for the great chief of the Seminole people. It is a narrow, steep-sided ridge with a number of slides in its valleys, and is particularly impressive when seen from the outlooks along the western half of the Kancamagus Highway. Although there is no longer a fire tower on its summit, it still commands magnificent views. Osceola has two subordinate peaks, the **East Peak** (4156 ft.)

and the trailless **West Peak** (4114 ft.). Continuing the ridge of Osceola to the west is trailless **Scar Ridge** (3774 ft.), which runs northwest parallel to the Han-cock Branch and the Kancamagus Highway and ends with a group of lower peaks above Lincoln village, of which the most important is **Loon Mtn.** (3065 ft.), which can be ascended via the major ski area on its north slope. At the far west end of the Loon group is **Russell Crag** (1926 ft.), rising directly above I-93 just north of the Tripoli Rd. exit, with interesting ledges but no trails; north of the crag is **Russell Pond,** with a WMNF campground reached by a paved side road (closed in winter) off Tripoli Rd. To the east of Osceola is **Mad River Notch,** in which the Greeley Ponds are located, and across that notch is **Mt. Kancamagus** (3763 ft.), a trailless mass of rounded, wooded ridges named for a Penacook chieftain.

Mt. Tripyramid is the rugged and very picturesque mountain that forms the east wall of the Waterville Valley and also overlooks Albany Intervale, which lies to the north and east. It was named by the illustrious cartographer Arnold Guyot for the three pyramidal peaks that cap the narrow, steep-sided ridge. **North Peak** (4180 ft.) affords a sweeping view to the north that is gradually becoming overgrown. **Middle Peak** (4140 ft.), the most nearly symmetrical pyramid of the three, provides a view toward Passaconaway and Chocorua from the summit; two fine outlooks over the Waterville Valley toward Tecumseh and Osceola lie to the west of the trail near the summit. **South Peak** (4100 ft.) is viewless. From South Peak, the high, rolling **Sleeper Ridge** (covered in Section 8) connects Tripyramid with Mt. Whiteface and the eastern part of the Sandwich Range. A major east spur of Tripyramid is called the **Fool Killer** (3548 ft.) because it blends into the main mass so well, when viewed from a distance, that incautious parties attempting to climb Tripyramid from the east before the con-struction of the trails often found themselves on top of the Fool Killer instead, separated from their goal by a long, scrubby ridge with deep valleys on either side from which the ascent to the summits of Tripyramid would require a lengthy and very difficult battle with the dense, wind-wracked small trees.

Tripyramid is best known for its slides, great scars that are visible from long distances. The **North Slide,** which occurred during heavy rains in August 1885, is located on the northwest slope of North Peak. This slide exposed a great deal of bedrock that is geologically interesting, and is ascended mainly on steep ledges. The **South Slide,** located on the southwest face of the South Peak, fell in 1869 and is mostly gravel. Two smaller slides descend into the valley of Sabba-day Brook from the east face of Middle Peak. Tripyramid is steep and rugged, and all routes to its summits have at least one rough section; consequently the mountain is more difficult to climb than a casual assessment of the altitude, distance, and elevation gain might suggest.

Sabbaday Falls, a picturesque small waterfall and pool formed by an eroded trap rock dike, is reached from Sabbaday Falls Picnic Area on the Kancamagus Highway by a gravel pathway section of the Sabbaday Brook Trail.

Sandwich Mtn. (3980 ft.), sometimes called Sandwich Dome, is the westernmost major summit of the Sandwich Range; its western ridge forms the south wall of the Waterville Valley. It looks over the lower Mad River to the west, and Sandwich Notch separates it from the Campton and Holderness mountains on the south and southwest. Sandwich Mtn. was once called **Black Mtn.**, a name that has also been applied to its southwest spur (3500 ft.), which is ledgy with many fine outlooks, and to a nubble (2732 ft.) at the end of this spur. According to the USGS, it is the nubble that is currently officially entitled to the name of Black Mtn., but the southwest spur is also commonly referred to as Black Mtn. To the northeast, a high pass separates Sandwich Mtn. from the long ridge of the **Flat Mtn.** (3334 ft.) in Waterville; **Pond Brook** has cut a deep ravine between its east shoulder and the rounded **Flat Mtn.** (2940 ft.) in Sandwich. The **Flat Mtn. Ponds** (2320 ft.) lie east of Sandwich Mtn. and west of Mt. Whiteface, between the two Flat Mtns.; originally two separate ponds, they have been united by the dam at their south end, making one larger pond. The area is still recovering from lumbering begun in 1920 and an extensive fire in 1923. In the flat region south of Sandwich Mtn. lie a number of attractive ponds, including **Guinea Pond** and **Black Mtn. Pond.** South of these ponds is **Mt. Israel** (2630 ft.), which provides a fine panorama of the Sandwich Range from its north ledge and offers great rewards for the modest effort required to reach it.

Jennings Peak (3460 ft.) and **Noon Peak** (2976 ft.) form a ridge running north from Sandwich Mtn. toward Waterville Valley. Sandwich Mtn. has fine views north over the valley, but the views from the cliffs that drop from the summit of Jennings Peak into the valley of Smarts Brook are even better. **Acteon Ridge** runs from Jennings Peak to the west over sharp, bare **Sachem Peak** (2860 ft.) and ends in the open rocky humps of **Bald Knob** (2300 ft.), which faces Welch Mtn. across the Mad River Valley and forms the other half of the gateway; this ridge is occasionally traversed, although there is no path.

Sandwich Notch is crossed by the **Sandwich Notch Rd.,** a rough, interesting gravel road that passes through a former farming region which has almost completely reverted to forest and is now a part of the WMNF. The road, which runs northwest from Center Sandwich to NH 49 between Campton and Waterville Valley, is sound but narrow, steep and rough, and very slow going; it is maintained this way to protect it from becoming an attractive route for through traffic. Unlike other White Mtn. notches, Sandwich Notch is a complex notch, made up of two distinct mountain passes: the one on the south (1470 ft.), between Mt. Israel and the eastern end of the Squam Range, separates the watershed of the Bearcamp River (a Saco tributary) from the valley of the Beebe River (a Pemigewasset tributary); the one on the north (1770 ft.), between Sandwich Mtn. and Campton Mtn., separates the valley of the Beebe River from the Waterville Valley—the valley of the Mad River (another Pemigewasset tributary). **Beede Falls (Cow Cave),** in the Sandwich town park 3.4 mi. from Center Sandwich, is worth a visit; this is also a Bearcamp River Trail trailhead. From NH 113 in Center Sandwich, take the road northwest from the village and keep left at 2.6 mi. where the right-hand road leads to Mead Base (Explorer Scout camp), the trailhead for the Wentworth Trail to Mt. Israel; the new Bearcamp River Trail passes through this trailhead. The road continues past trailheads for the Crawford-Ridgepole Trail at 3.9 mi., the Guinea Pond Trail at 5.7 mi., and the Algonquin Trail at 7.3 mi., and ends at NH 49 at 11.0 mi.

The **Squam Range** begins at Sandwich Notch across from Mt. Israel and runs roughly southwest toward Holderness. This area is almost entirely private property, open to day hikers by the gracious permission of the landowners, but camping is not permitted. Its peaks, from northeast to southwest, are an **unnamed knob** (2218 ft.), **Mt. Doublehead** (2158 ft.), **Mt. Squam** (2223 ft.), **Mt. Percival** (2212 ft.), a knob sometimes called the **Sawtooth** (2260 ft.) that is the actual high point of the range, **Mt. Morgan** (2220 ft.), **Mt. Webster** (2076 ft.), **Mt. Livermore** (1500 ft.), and **Cotton Mtn.** (1270 ft.). The Crawford-Ridgepole Trail crosses over or near all of these summits except for Cotton Mtn., and several trails ascend the ridge from NH 113; curiously, the Sawtooth, the high point of the range, is bypassed by the trail. By far the most popular hike on the range, often fairly crowded, is the loop over Mts. Morgan and Percival, which offer superb views south over the lake and hill country and north to the higher mountains; the rest of the range is lightly visited and the trails, including the Crawford-Ridgepole Trail, often require some care to follow, though the rewards of pleasant walks to several excellent viewpoints are great.

The **Rattlesnakes—West Rattlesnake** (1260 ft.) and **East Rattlesnake** (1289 ft.)—are a pair of hills that rise just across the highway from Mt. Morgan and Percival and offer excellent lake views for little effort. West Rattlesnake has fine views to the south and west from its southwest cliff. East Rattlesnake has a more limited but still excellent view over Squam Lake. **Five Finger Point,** which lies southeast of the Rattlesnakes and has a perimeter trail connected to the Rattlesnakes' trail network, offers attractive lakeside walking on undeveloped rocky shores.

Red Hill (2030 ft.) and its ledgy northern spur, **Eagle Cliff** (1410 ft.), rise between Squam Lake and Lake Winnipesaukee. The summit of Red Hill (which has a fire tower) offers excellent views in all directions for very modest effort; Eagle Cliff offers interesting but much less extensive views and a somewhat more challenging trail to ascend.

There are a number of public and quasi-public reservations in this region that offer the opportunity for pleasant walking; some have trails. The newly created **Bearcamp River Trail** from Sandwich Notch to South Tamworth, nearly 17 mi. long, offers a variety of walks through woods, farmlands, and wetlands along or near the Bearcamp River, linking several reservations and parcels of land protected by conservation easements. The **Alice Bemis Thompson Wildlife Refuge** offers a loop path 2 mi. long through interesting wetlands drained by Atwood Brook, which flows into Bearcamp Pond, with views of the Sandwich Range.

CAMPING

Sandwich Range Wilderness

Wilderness regulations, intended to protect Wilderness resources and promote opportunities for challenge and solitude, prohibit use of motorized equipment or mechanical means of transportation of any sort. Camping and wood or charcoal fires are not allowed within 200 ft. of any trail except at designated campsites. Hiking and camping group size must be no larger than 10 people. Camping and fires are also prohibited above treeline (where trees are less than 8 ft. tall) except in winter, when camping is permitted above treeline in places where snow cover is at least two feet deep, but not on any frozen body of water. Many shelters have been removed, and the remaining ones will be dismantled when major maintenance is required; one should not count on using any of these shelters.

Squam Lakes Region

The trails described in this guide on the Squam Range, the Rattlesnakes, and Red Hill are almost entirely on private land, and while the owners welcome hikers for day use, camping is not allowed.

Forest Protection Areas

The WMNF has established a number of Forest Protection Areas (FPAs)—formerly known as Restricted Use Areas—where camping and wood or charcoal fires are prohibited throughout the year. The specific areas are under continual review, and areas are added to or subtracted from the list in order to provide the greatest amount of protection to areas subject to damage by excessive camping, while imposing the lowest level of restrictions possible. A general list of FPAs in this section follows, but since there are often major changes from year to year, one should obtain current information on FPAs from the WMNF.

(1) No camping is permitted above treeline (where trees are less than 8 ft. tall), except in winter, and then only in places where there is at least two feet of snow cover on the ground—but not on any frozen body of water. The point where the above-treeline restricted area begins is marked on most trails with small signs, but the absence of such signs should not be construed as proof of the legality of a site.

(2) No camping is permitted within a quarter-mile of any trailhead, picnic area, or any facility for overnight accommodation such as a hut, cabin, shelter, tentsite, or campground, except as designated at the facility itself. In the area covered by Section 7, camping is also forbidden within a quarter-mile of Sabbaday Falls and at any point within the Greeley Ponds Scenic Area.

(3) No camping is permitted within a quarter-mile of Smarts Brook (along which the Smarts Brook Trail runs) from NH 49 to the Beaver Pond.

(4) No camping is permitted on WMNF land within a quarter-mile of certain roads (camping on private roadside land is illegal except by permission of the landowner). In 1997, these roads included the Kancamagus Highway, NH 49 (Mad River Rd.), and the Hix Mtn. Rd. for the first quarter-mile east from the Tripoli Rd. Camping is permitted along the Tripoli Rd., but not within 200 ft. of any trail or along the half-mile section east of the crossing of the West Branch of Mad River (BM 1949)—an area where the stream runs close by the north side of the road.

Established Trailside Campsites

Flat Mtn. Pond Shelter (WMNF) is located on the shore of Flat Mtn. Pond on the Flat Mountain Pond Trail.

Black Mtn. Pond Shelter (WMNF), formerly located on the shore of Black Mtn. Pond on the Black Mountain Pond Trail, has been removed. Tent camping is permitted in the area.

Trails on Mount Tecumseh and Vicinity

Shorter Trails near Waterville Valley

Trails on Mount Osceola and Scar Ridge

Trails on Mount Tripyramid

Trails on Sandwich Mountain

Trails on Mount Israel

Trails in the Squam Lake Area

THE TRAILS

Mount Tecumseh Trail (WMNF)

This trail ascends Mt. Tecumseh, starting at the Waterville Valley Ski Area at the top edge of the parking area well to the right of the main lodge (as you face it). It climbs the east slope of Tecumseh, then descends the northwest ridge to a new parking area just off Tripoli Rd. (FR 30), 1.2 mi. west of the Mount Osceola Trail parking lot and 0.1 mi. east of the former trailhead. The eastern part of the trail was relocated in 1991 to eliminate the former sections that used the ski slopes.

Starting at a trail sign at the edge of the ski area parking lot, the trail follows the south side of Tecumseh Brook for 0.3 mi., then crosses the brook and follows a new section of trail along a small ridge above the north side. At 1.1 mi.

the trail drops down and recrosses the brook, then climbs to intersect the former route, an old logging road, about 20 yd. from the edge of the ski slope; good views can be obtained by following the old trail left to the edge of the open slope. The main trail turns right and follows the old road, angling upward along the south side of the Tecumseh Brook valley, then climbs to the main ridgecrest south of Tecumseh, where it turns right in a flat area. Here, at 2.2 mi., the Sosman Trail from the top of the ski area enters from the left. In another 120 yd. the Sosman Trail forks left to ascend the summit from the west. The Mount Tecumseh Trail swings right, descends slightly to circle the base of the steep cone, and finally climbs steeply to reach the summit from the north at 2.5 mi. The summit offers good views over and between trees, particularly to Mt. Osceola and Mt. Tripyramid. The trail junctions at the summit have not usually been well signed; the Mount Tecumseh Trail leaves north (about 15° magnetic) for the ski area and west-northwest (about 310° magnetic) for Tripoli Rd., while the Sosman Trail runs almost due south (about 190° magnetic) along the ridgecrest, then turns sharp right (west) off the ridge and descends.

From the summit of Tecumseh, the Mount Tecumseh Trail descends west, then swings northwest past an excellent outlook and down to a shallow saddle. It ascends to the summit of the west ridge at 3.2 mi., passes over numerous knobs, then descends to another saddle at 4.2 mi. Here it turns right and angles down the north slope of the ridge on an old logging road. Near the bottom of the slope it turns right, crosses Eastman Brook (difficult at high water), and ends at Tripoli Rd.

Mount Tecumseh Trail (map 3:J6)
Distances from Mt. Tecumseh ski area parking lot (1840')

   to Mt. Tecumseh summit (4003'): 2.5 mi., 2200 ft., 2 hr. 20 min.

   to Tripoli Rd. (1820'): 5.6 mi. (9.0 km.), 2400 ft. (rev. 2400 ft.), 4 hr.

Sosman Trail (WVAIA)

This trail connects the summit of Tecumseh with the top of the ski slopes. It leaves the summit of Tecumseh along the ridge to the south (sign may be absent), then turns to the west and switchbacks with rough footing down the slope and around the rocky nose of the ridge. It turns to the right onto the Mount Tecumseh Trail at 0.2 mi., then after 120 yd. it diverges right and follows the ridge south, passing over a rocky hump with an interesting view of Tecumseh's summit cone and several outlooks to the west, as well as an outlook to the northeast with a carved wooden bench in a small clearing. Finally it comes out on a ledge at the top of the ski area. From here it is about 1.8 mi. to the base lodge via ski trails. To find the trail at the top of the ski area, where there is no sign, ascend in a rocky area where the ledge has been fractured into flat plates, marked by a large cairn, and follow a beaten path that turns sharp left beneath two large black pipes; beyond this point the trail is easy to follow.

Sosman Trail (map 3:J6)

Distances from summit of Mt. Tecumseh (4003')

>   *to* top of ski area (3850'): 0.8 mi. (1.3 km.), 100 ft. (rev. 250 ft.), 25 min.

>   *to* ski area base lodge (1840') via ski trails: 2.6 mi. (4.2 km.), 100 ft. (rev. 2000 ft.), 1 hr. 20 min.

Welch-Dickey Loop Trail (WVAIA)

This loop trail affords excellent views for a modest effort. On the south ledges of Welch Mtn. it runs through the southernmost of the four stands of jack pine *(Pinus banksiana)* that occur in New Hampshire; this is a tree that commonly occurs much farther north and benefits from fires because it releases its seeds most readily after its cones have been scorched (when, presumably, most of its competitors have been killed by the fire). The section that ascends Welch Mtn. is often one of the first trails to be clear of snow in the spring. However, some of the ledges may be slippery when wet and dangerous in icy conditions, and so must be ascended with caution. From NH 49, about 4.5 mi. from its junction with NH 175, turn left onto Upper Mad River Rd., which runs northwest across the Mad River. In 0.7 mi. turn right on Orris Rd. ("Welch Mountain" sign) and follow this road for 0.6 mi., then take a short fork to the right into a small parking area, where the trail begins.

In 15 yd. from the parking area, the trail forks. This description follows the counter-clockwise direction, first taking the right-hand fork leading toward Welch Mtn. This branch soon crosses a brook and follows its east side for about 0.5 mi., then turns sharp right and angles up southward to reach the large, flat open ledges on the south ridge of Welch Mtn. at 1.3 mi. from the start. Then the trail climbs, steeply at times, over open ledges interspersed with jack pines and dwarf birches to the ledgy summit of Welch Mtn. at 1.9 mi.

From here the loop drops steeply to a wooded notch, then rises, working to the left around a high rock slab. Just above this slab a branch trail leads right 0.2 mi. to the north outlook from an open ledge. The main loop continues over the summit of Dickey Mtn. at 2.4 mi. and descends another prominent ridge to the southwest, with many outlook ledges, entering the woods to stay at the base of a particularly interesting ledge with an impressive drop-off at 3.2 mi. It continues to descend, then turns left onto a logging road with a cellar hole on the right, and soon reaches the loop junction and the parking lot.

Welch-Dickey Loop Trail (map 3:K5)

Distances from Orris Rd. parking area (1060')

> *to* Welch Mtn. summit (2605') via Welch branch: 1.9 mi., 1550 ft., 1 hr. 45 min.

> *to* Dickey Mtn. summit (2734') via Dickey branch: 2.1 mi., 1650 ft., 1 hr. 55 min.

> *for* complete loop: 4.4 mi. (7.0 km.), 1800 ft., 3 hr. 5 min.

Short Walks (WVAIA)

A system of local trails is maintained in the Waterville Valley. Trail information and a map, "Hiking Trails of the Waterville Valley," may be obtained at the service station on Tripoli Rd. opposite the Waterville Campground or at the Jugtown store. These trails often intersect or coincide with ski-touring trails (marked in black and yellow) that may have the same name as a hiking trail but follow a somewhat different route. A separate map of the ski-touring trails is available locally. Comments on some of the most interesting paths follow.

The *Fletcher's Cascade Trail* (1.2 mi.), to the beautiful Fletcher's Cascades, leaves the Drake's Brook Trail 0.4 mi. from NH 49.

The *Cascade Path* (2.3 mi.) runs from the Finish Line Restaurant parking lot to a series of beautiful waterfalls on Cascade Brook at about 1.7 mi., then joins and follows a gravel logging road to the Livermore Trail at 2.3 mi. from the Livermore Rd. parking area. The *Norway Rapids Trail* (0.5 mi.) runs from the Cascade Path at 1.2 mi. to the Livermore Trail at 1.8 mi.; its crossing of Avalanche Brook is difficult even in moderate water. The *Boulder Path* (1.0 mi.) begins on the Livermore Trail at 0.5 mi., leads past the Big Boulder in Slide Brook that is visible from the trail, and runs to the Snow's Mtn. ski area parking lot. The *Big Pines Path* (0.2 mi.) leaves the Livermore Trail at 0.6 mi.

The *Greeley Ledge Trail* (0.2 mi.) leaves the top of the Snow's Mtn. ski area, passes Greeley Ledges, and ends on the Snow's Mountain Trail at 0.7 mi. The *Elephant Rock Trail* (0.3 mi.) begins on the Cascade Path at 0.5 mi. and runs past Elephant Rock to the top of the Snow's Mtn. ski area and the Greeley Ledge Trail.

The Scaur, a rock outlook between Mad River and Slide Brook with views north, south, and west, may be reached by the steep *Scaur Trail* (0.6 mi.) from the Greeley Ponds Trail 0.7 mi. from the Livermore Trail (with a potentially difficult stream crossing at the start), or by the easier *Kettles Path* (0.9 mi.), which leaves the Livermore Trail at 0.9 mi. and joins the Scaur Trail at the foot of the final 0.2 mi. climb to the outlook.

On a shoulder of the East Peak of Osceola are the large Davis Boulders and Goodrich Rock (one of the largest glacial erratics in New Hampshire), reached by the *Goodrich Rock Trail* (0.8 mi.) from the Greeley Ponds Trail 0.9 mi. from the Livermore Trail. The rock itself is ascended by a steep ladder—use caution.

The Flume, an attractive small gorge in the headwaters of Flume Brook (not to be confused with the Franconia Notch Flume), is reached by the *Flume Trail* (1.3 mi.), which leaves the Greeley Ponds Trail 1.2 mi. from the Livermore Trail.

Snows Mountain Trail (WVAIA)

This trail follows the route of the former Woodbury Trail to the shoulder of Snows Mtn., ascends the ridge south and east to the summit, and then descends the west slope of the mountain back to Waterville. *Note:* Due to blowdown from recent storms, compounded by uncertainty concerning projected residential and ski trail construction, this trail has not received full maintenance; some sections, particularly on the south loop (beyond the summit outlook spur path), may be difficult to follow.

The trail leaves the Finish Line Restaurant parking lot, crosses under the chair lift, and crosses the brown bridge at the north end of the tennis courts. It turns left on a paved road, then right onto a ski slope. It ascends under the chair lift, then turns to the right into the woods (arrow) at 0.3 mi. and climbs for another 0.3 mi., then levels off. At 0.7 mi. the Greeley Ledge Trail leaves left to Greeley Ledges and the top of the ski slopes. At 1.2 mi. the Snows Mountain Trail reaches the end of the old Woodbury Trail section and turns right, climbing gradually to Snows Mtn. Outlook, which offers a restricted view to the west. The ascent continues, passing a large boulder with a northeast view, and the trail levels out for a while, then climbs to a high point of the ridge. At 2.0 mi. a side trail leads left 0.1 mi. to a ledge at the summit with a view south to Sandwich Mtn. The Snows Mountain Trail turns sharp right and descends, passing additional viewpoints to the south and west, and continues gradually down the west slope of the mountain to Upper Greeley Hill Rd. It then descends past the swimming pool back to the starting point.

Snows Mountain Trail (map 3:J6–J7)

Distances from Finish Line Restaurant (1520')

   to Snows Mtn. summit spur (2780'): 2.0 mi., 1300 ft., 1 hr. 40 min.

   for complete loop: 3.9 mi. (6.3 km.), 1300 ft., 2 hr. 35 min.

Mount Osceola Trail (WMNF)

This trail begins at a parking area on Tripoli Rd. (FR 30), just west of the height-of-land in Thornton Gap 7.0 mi. from I-93, climbs over Mt. Osceola and East Osceola, and descends to the Greeley Ponds Trail at the height-of-land in Mad River Notch, 1.3 mi. south of the Kancamagus Highway. At the height-of-land on Tripoli Rd. there is a gate that is sometimes closed in spring and fall, so it may not be possible to reach the parking lot from the Waterville Valley side in a vehicle at such times. The trail from Thornton Gap to the summit of Osceola is relatively easy, with moderate grades and reasonably good footing, but the section between East Osceola and Greeley Ponds Trail is extremely steep and rough.

   The trail leaves Tripoli Rd. and climbs moderately with somewhat rocky footing, going east across the south slope of Breadtray Ridge. At 1.3 mi. it begins to climb by switchbacks toward the ridge top, and at 2.3 mi. it crosses a small brook (unreliable) on a log bridge. The trail resumes its switchbacks, gains the summit ridge and turns right, and soon reaches the summit ledge at 3.2 mi., with excellent views. A good outlook to the north can be obtained from a small ledge on a short side path, which begins at the older fire tower site that is located in the woods just to the west of the open ledge.

   The trail then turns left and descends from the summit, alternating flat stretches with steep, rocky descents. Just before reaching the main pass between Osceola and East Osceola, it descends a steep chimney, which can be avoided by a detour to the left (north). The trail crosses the pass at 3.8 mi. and climbs moderately with steep pitches past a fine outlook on the left, reaching the summit of East Osceola (marked by a small cairn) at 4.2 mi. The trail then crosses a lower knob and descends steeply, then moderately, to a shoulder. At the top of a gully there is an outlook 25 yd. to the left on a side path. The main trail descends the steep, loose gully, then goes diagonally across a small, rocky slide with good views. It continues to descend very steeply past a sloping rock face, where it turns left. At 4.9 mi. it turns sharp left, with an abandoned route of the trail straight ahead, and descends moderately under the impressive cliffs of Osceola's north spur to the Greeley Ponds Trail.

Mount Osceola Trail (map 3:J6–I6)

Distances from Tripoli Rd. (2280')

> *to* Mt. Osceola summit (4340'): 3.2 mi., 2050 ft., 2 hr. 40 min.

> *to* Mt. Osceola, East Peak (4156'): 4.2 mi., 2400 ft. (rev. 550 ft.), 3 hr. 20 min.

> *to* Greeley Ponds Trail (2300'): 5.7 mi. (9.2 km.), 2400 ft. (rev. 1850 ft.), 4 hr. 5 min.

Greeley Ponds Trail (WMNF)

This trail diverges from the Livermore Trail about 0.3 mi. from the parking area on Livermore Rd. (FR 53), leads past the Greeley Ponds and through Mad River Notch, and ends at the Kancamagus Highway 4.5 mi. east of the Lincoln Woods (Wilderness Trail) parking lot. The trail is crossed many times by a ski-touring trail marked with blue diamonds. Grades are easy, and the ponds are beautiful.

The trail leaves the Livermore Trail sharp left just after the first bridge beyond the Depot Camp clearing, and follows an old truck road past the Scaur Trail right at 0.7 mi. and the Goodrich Rock Trail left at 0.9 mi. The truck road ends at 1.1 mi., where the trail crosses Mad River on Knight's Bridge. At 1.2 mi. the Flume Trail diverges right, and the trail soon crosses Flume Brook on a bridge and passes the site of an old logging camp. It continues across several small brooks and enters the Greeley Ponds Scenic Area at 2.6 mi., soon crosses Mad River, and reaches the lower Greeley Pond at 2.9 mi., then the upper pond at 3.4 mi. Here an unmarked path crosses the upper pond outlet brook to a fine view on a small beach. The main trail ascends easily to Mad River Notch, passing the Mount Osceola Trail left at the height-of-land at 3.8 mi., and descends over numerous brooks (all the difficult crossings are bridged) to the Kancamagus Highway.

Greeley Ponds Trail (map 3:J6–I6)

Distances from Livermore Trail (1580')

> *to* lower Greeley Pond (2180'): 2.9 mi., 600 ft., 1 hr. 45 min.

> *to* Mount Osceola Trail (2300'): 3.8 mi., 700 ft., 2 hr. 15 min.

> *to* Kancamagus Highway (1940'): 5.1 mi. (8.2 km.), 700 ft. (rev. 350 ft.), 2 hr. 55 min.

East Pond Trail (WMNF)

This trail passes scenic East Pond and climbs across the notch between Mt. Osceola and Scar Ridge, reaching an elevation of 3100 ft. The southern trailhead is at a parking lot about 100 yd. up a gravel side road that leaves Tripoli Rd. (FR 30) 5.1 mi. east of its intersection with I-93. The northern trailhead is on the Kancamagus Highway at the bridge over the Hancock Branch, 3.7 mi. east of the Lincoln Woods (Wilderness Trail) parking lot.

From the southern trailhead, this trail follows the gravel road past a gate and continues straight on an older road where the gravel road swings right. At 0.4 mi., near the site of the old Tripoli Mill, the Little East Pond Trail turns left on an old railroad grade, while the East Pond Trail continues ahead on a logging road. At 0.8 mi. it crosses East Pond Brook, and at 1.4 mi., near the point where the East Pond Loop leaves left for Little East Pond, a side path leads right 40 yd. to the south shore of East Pond.

The trail swings to the left away from the pond and climbs moderately on old logging roads to the height-of-land at 2.2 mi., then descends steadily on logging roads, crossing Cheney Brook at 3.1 mi. and Pine Brook at 4.3 mi. Just after the latter crossing (which may be difficult at high water) the trail reaches an old logging railroad spur and follows it almost all the way to the Kancamagus Highway.

East Pond Trail (map 3:J5–I6)

Distances from Tripoli Rd. (1800')

> *to* East Pond (2600'): 1.4 mi., 800 ft., 1 hr. 5 min.

> *to* height-of-land (3100'): 2.2 mi., 1300 ft., 1 hr. 45 min.

> *to* Kancamagus Highway (1760'): 5.1 mi. (8.2 km.), 1300 ft. (rev. 1350 ft.), 3 hr. 15 min.

Little East Pond Trail (WMNF)

This trail leaves the East Pond Trail left (northwest) 0.4 mi. from Tripoli Rd. and follows an old railroad grade slightly uphill, crossing Clear Brook at 0.7 mi. Soon after that it bears sharp right from the end of the railroad grade and climbs at a moderate grade to Little East Pond, where the East Pond Loop enters on the right.

Little East Pond Trail (map 3:J6–I5)

Distance from East Pond Trail (1980')

> *to* Little East Pond (2596'): 1.7 mi. (2.8 km.), 600 ft., 1 hr. 10 min.

East Pond Loop (WMNF)

This trail runs between East Pond and Little East Pond, going up and down over several minor ridges at easy grades, making possible a loop trip that visits both ponds.

East Pond Loop (map 3:I6–I5)

Distance from East Pond (2600')

> *to* Little East Pond (2596'): 1.5 mi. (2.5 km.), 200 ft. (rev. 200 ft.), 50 min.

Distance from Tripoli Rd. (1800')

> *for* complete loop to both ponds: 5.0 mi. (8.1 km.), 1000 ft., 3 hr.

Livermore Trail (WMNF)

This trail begins at a parking area at the beginning of Livermore Rd. near Waterville Valley and climbs through Livermore Pass (2900 ft.) to the Kancamagus Highway across from Lily Pond. It once connected Waterville Valley to the Sawyer River logging railroad, which led to the now deserted village of Livermore on Sawyer River. (The present Sawyer River Trail was a part of this Waterville-Livermore route.) The Livermore Trail consists of logging roads of various ages and conditions; the part through Livermore Pass is muddy and can be difficult to follow. The gravel southern section, from Tripoli Rd. to Flume Brook Camp, is also called Livermore Rd. (FR 53).

From the parking area on Livermore Rd., the trail follows the gated gravel road across a bridge over a branch of Mad River. The Greeley Ponds Trail, another gravel road, diverges sharp left at 0.3 mi., 40 yd. past the bridge. Soon the Livermore Trail crosses the main branch of Mad River on another bridge. In the next 2.0 mi. several of the WVAIA local paths intersect the trail: the Boulder Path diverges right at 0.5 mi. from the parking area; the Big Pines Path diverges left at 0.7 mi.; the Kettles Path diverges left at 0.9 mi.; the Norway Rapids Trail diverges right at 1.8 mi.; and the Cascade Path diverges right at 2.1 mi. across a major logging road bridge.

At 2.6 mi. the Livermore Trail passes the south end of the Mount Tripyramid Trail, which leads to the right across Avalanche Brook and provides access to the Tripyramid peaks via the South Slide. After passing the site of Avalanche Camp to the left of the trail at 3.1 mi., where the road becomes more grassgrown, the trail reaches a hairpin turn to the left at 3.6 mi., where the northern part of the Mount Tripyramid Trail diverges right toward the peaks via the difficult North Slide. At 3.8 mi. the Scaur Ridge Trail diverges right, offering a longer but safer and easier route to the summit of North Tripyramid. After climbing steadily for some distance, the trail crosses a branch of Flume Brook at 4.8 mi. and soon passes the clearing of Flume Brook Camp on the right of the trail, becoming wet and muddy at times.

At 5.0 mi. the gravel road ends in a clearing. The Livermore Trail bears slightly right on an older road (sign) and is rough, often very wet and muddy, and sparsely marked, and must be followed with care, particularly at junctions with cross-country skiing trails. It climbs gradually into the very flat Livermore Pass at 5.6 mi. and descends from the pass, slowly at first. It runs in a dry brook bed for a while, then descends rather steeply, angling down the wall of a deep, wooded gorge; at 5.9 mi. it crosses the brook bed at the bottom of the gorge. The trail descends moderately, crossing several brooks, then bears left off the logging road at 6.7 mi. near an old logging camp located on the right and crosses a moist area to a clearing at 7.1 mi. Here it turns right and follows a grassy gravel logging road, passing several restricted but interesting views, and reaches the Kancamagus Highway east of Kancamagus Pass across from Lily Pond.

Livermore Trail (map 3:J6–I7)

Distances from Livermore Rd. parking area (1580')

to south end, Mount Tripyramid Trail (2000'): 2.6 mi., 400 ft., 1 hr. 30 min.

to north end, Mount Tripyramid Trail (2400'): 3.6 mi., 800 ft., 2 hr. 10 min.

to crossing of branch of Flume Brook (2780'): 4.8 mi., 1200 ft., 3 hr.

to Kancamagus Highway (2060'): 7.7 mi. (12.4 km.), 1300 ft. (rev. 700 ft.), 4 hr. 30 min.

Mount Tripyramid Trail (WVAIA)

This trail makes a loop over the three summits of Tripyramid from the Livermore Trail, and is usually done from north to south in order to ascend the steep rock slabs of the North Slide and descend the loose gravel of the South Slide. Descent of the North Slide is more difficult than ascent and may be particularly daunting to hikers who have difficulty or lack experience on steep rock, while ascent of the South Slide can be very frustrating due to constant backsliding on the loose gravel. *Caution:* The steep rock slabs of the North Slide are difficult, and they are dangerous in wet or icy conditions. At all times—but particularly in adverse conditions, or for the descent—the Scaur Ridge Trail is a much easier and safer route than the North Slide. The North Slide lies mostly in deep shade in seasons when the sun is low, so ice may form early in the fall and remain late in the spring. The loose footing on the South Slide may also be hazardous when wet or icy. Allow plenty of time for the steep, rough trip over the Tripyramids via the slides. This trail is almost entirely within the Sandwich Range Wilderness.

The north end of the loop leaves the Livermore Trail at a hairpin turn 3.6 mi. from the Livermore Rd. parking area (0.5 mi. beyond the Avalanche Camp clearing). The trail descends sharply for 50 yd. to cross Avalanche Brook (last reliable water), then ascends at a moderate grade, occasionally requiring some care to follow, and reaches the gravel outwash of the North Slide at about 0.5 mi. from the Livermore Trail. It now becomes extremely steep, climbing about 1200 ft. in 0.5 mi. Follow paint blazes (often faint and sparse) on the rocks. Soon the trail reaches the first slabs and views become steadily more extensive. Higher up, the trail ascends the right-hand track of the slide almost to its top, then turns sharp left into the woods at a cairn, and in 0.1 mi. the Pine Bend Brook Trail enters from the left 20 yd. below the summit of North Peak.

The Mount Tripyramid Trail and the Pine Bend Brook Trail now coincide. They cross over the summit of North Peak and descend at a moderate grade toward Middle Peak. Just north of the saddle between the North and Middle peaks, the Sabbaday Brook Trail enters left from the Kancamagus Highway, and the Pine Bend Brook Trail ends. The Mount Tripyramid Trail crosses the saddle and makes a steep ascent of the cone of Middle Peak. There are two outlooks to the right of the trail near the true summit, which is a few yards left at the high point of the trail. The trail descends into the saddle between Middle and South peaks, then climbs moderately to the wooded summit of South Peak. From this summit the trail starts to descend steeply, and soon reaches the top of the South Slide. In another 60 yd. the Kate Sleeper Trail (Section 8) to Mt. Whiteface diverges left at a sign. The descent to the foot of the slide at 3.0 mi. is steep, with loose gravel footing becoming more prevalent as one descends. From a small open area at the bottom of the slide, the trail turns right and follows logging roads, crossing several small brooks; Cold Brook, the first sure water, is crossed at 4.1 mi. Continuing on old roads, the trail eventually crosses Avalanche Brook and ends in another 25 yd. on the Livermore Trail, 2.6 mi. from the Livermore Rd. parking area.

Mount Tripyramid Trail (map 3:J7)
Distances from Livermore Trail (2400')

   to summit of North Peak (4180'): 1.2 mi., 1800 ft., 1 hr. 30 min.

   to Sabbaday Brook Trail (3850'): 1.7 mi., 1800 ft. (rev. 350 ft.), 1 hr. 45 min.

to summit of Middle Peak (4140'): 2.0 mi., 2100 ft., 2 hr. 5 min.

to summit of South Peak (4100'): 2.4 mi., 2200 ft. (rev. 150 ft.), 2 hr. 20 min.

to Kate Sleeper Trail (3850'): 2.6 mi., 2200 ft. (rev. 250 ft.), 2 hr. 25 min.

to Livermore Trail (2000'): 4.9 mi. (7.9 km.), 2200 ft. (rev. 1850 ft.), 3 hr. 35 min.

Distance from Livermore Rd. parking area (1580')

for complete loop over Mt. Tripyramid via Livermore and Mount Tripyramid trails: 11.0 mi. (17.7 km.), 3000 ft., 7 hr.

Scaur Ridge Trail (WMNF)

This trail runs from the Livermore Trail to the Pine Bend Brook Trail, affording an easier, safer alternative route to the North Slide. It is almost entirely within the Sandwich Range Wilderness.

It diverges right (east) from the Livermore Trail at a point 3.8 mi. from the Livermore Rd. parking area. Following an old logging road at a moderate grade, it crosses a small brook at 0.9 mi., then soon bears left off the road. Now climbing somewhat more steeply, it turns right at 1.1 mi., then swings left and enters the Pine Bend Brook Trail at the top of a narrow ridge at 1.2 mi. The summit of North Tripyramid is 0.8 mi. to the right via the Pine Bend Brook Trail.

Scaur Ridge Trail (map 3:J7)
Distance from Livermore Trail (2500')

to Pine Bend Brook Trail (3440'): 1.2 mi. (1.9 km.), 950 ft., 1 hr. 5 min.

Distance from Livermore Rd. parking area (1580')

for complete loop over Mt. Tripyramid via Livermore, Scaur Ridge, and Mount Tripyramid trails: 12.1 mi., 3000 ft., 7 hr. 35 min.

Pine Bend Brook Trail (WMNF)

This trail ascends North Tripyramid from the Kancamagus Highway 1.0 mi. west of the Sabbaday Falls Picnic Area. Parts of it are steep and rough. The upper part of the trail is in the Sandwich Range Wilderness.

The trail leaves the highway and soon turns sharp right onto the grade of the old Swift River logging railroad, follows it for 0.1 mi., then turns sharp left off the railroad grade and follows Pine Bend Brook southwest on an old logging road, making three crossings of the brook. The second crossing is at the confluence with a tributary where the crossing may appear to involve several small brooks instead of a single large one. After the third crossing, at 1.3 mi., the trail begins to swing more to the west and crosses several small tributaries. It then passes over a minor divide to a westerly branch of Pine Bend Brook, which it crosses and recrosses (last sure water), and enters the Sandwich Range Wilderness at 2.1 mi. After crossing the brook bed again in a rocky section at 2.2 mi., the trail becomes rough and steep as it ascends along the north bank of the brook valley, then recrosses the brook bed and angles steeply with very poor footing up an even steeper slope. Soon it reaches and ascends a minor easterly ridge, with much less difficult climbing. Shortly after reaching this ridge, there is a good view out to Mt. Washington and the cliffs of Mt. Lowell.

Eventually the trail reaches the ridge running from Tripyramid north to Scaur Peak, crosses it and descends slightly to the west side, then turns left and continues almost level to the junction on the right at 3.2 mi. with the Scaur Ridge Trail. Rising gradually on the very narrow wooded ridge, the Pine Bend Brook Trail provides occasional glimpses of the North Slide, then descends slightly. Soon it attacks the final steep, rough, and rocky climb to North Peak. The Mount Tripyramid Trail enters from the North Slide on the right 20 yd. below this summit. (There are good views from the top of the slide, 0.1 mi. from this junction via the Mount Tripyramid Trail.) The two trails then coincide, passing the summit of North Peak and descending at a moderate grade to the junction with the Sabbaday Brook Trail just north of the saddle between North and Middle peaks.

Pine Bend Brook Trail (map 3:J8–J7)

Distances from Kancamagus Highway (1370')

   to Scaur Ridge Trail (3440'): 3.2 mi., 2050 ft., 2 hr. 40 min.

   to summit of North Peak (4180'): 4.0 mi., 2800 ft., 3 hr. 25 min.

   to Sabbaday Brook Trail (3850'): 4.5 mi. (7.2 km.), 2800 ft. (rev. 350 ft.), 3 hr. 40 min.

Sabbaday Brook Trail (WMNF)

This trail begins at the Sabbaday Falls Picnic Area and ascends to the saddle between North Tripyramid and Middle Tripyramid. There are numerous brook crossings, some of which may be difficult at high water. Except for the very steep, rough section just below the main ridgecrest, grades are easy to moderate and the footing is mostly good. The upper part of the trail is in the Sandwich Range Wilderness.

From the parking area follow a gravel tourist path along the brook. A side path bears left and passes several viewpoints over Sabbaday Falls, rejoining at 0.3 mi. where the gravel path ends, and from there the trail continues on an old logging road with easy grades. At 0.7 mi. the trail makes the first of three crossings of Sabbaday Brook in 0.2 mi. (All three may be difficult in high water, but the first two can be avoided by bushwhacking along the west bank, since they are only 0.1 mi. apart.) The trail follows the old logging road on the east bank of Sabbaday Brook for nearly 2.0 mi., entering the Sandwich Range Wilderness at 1.7 mi. (about halfway through this section), and then at 2.8 mi. it turns sharp right, descends briefly, and makes a fourth crossing of the brook. Above this point both the brook and trail swing to the west, then northwest, up the narrow valley between Tripyramid and the Fool Killer, climbing more steadily and crossing the brook twice more. The trail passes the base of a small slide on the Fool Killer at 3.7 mi., crosses the brook for the seventh and last time (last water) at the head of the ravine at 4.1 mi., then swings back to the south and soon re-enters the old route of the trail above the slide on the east slope of Tripyramid. Here it turns sharp right and climbs steeply up slabs and broken rock, then becomes less steep but remains rough, with many rocks and roots. Finally it levels off and meets the Pine Bend Brook Trail and the Mount Tripyramid Trail just north of the saddle between North and Middle Tripyramid; turn right for North Peak (0.5 mi.) or left for Middle Peak (0.3 mi.).

Sabbaday Brook Trail (map 3:J8–J7)
Distances from Sabbaday Falls Picnic Area (1320')

   to fourth crossing of Sabbaday Brook (2100'): 2.8 mi., 800 ft., 1 hr. 50 min.

   to Pine Bend Brook Trail/Mount Tripyramid Trail (3850'): 4.9 mi. (7.9 km.), 2550 ft., 3 hr. 45 min.

Sandwich Mountain Trail (WMNF)

This trail runs to the summit of Sandwich Mtn. from a parking lot just off NH 49, 0.4 mi. southwest of its junction with Tripoli Rd. There are fine views from the trail at several different elevation levels. The upper part of the trail is in the Sandwich Range Wilderness.

The trail leaves the southwest corner of the parking lot, skirts left around a power station, and crosses Drakes Brook. If the brook is very high and the crossing difficult, it is possible to reach the trail on the other side of the brook by bushwhacking up the west bank from where Drakes Brook crosses NH 49 just south of the parking lot. The trail turns east soon after crossing the brook and climbs steeply to the summit of the narrow ridgecrest of Noon Peak at 1.7 mi. It then follows a curving, gradual ridge covered with beautiful mosses and passes several outlooks. There is a spring (unreliable) on the right (west) side of the trail, which soon skirts the east slope of Jennings Peak. The Drakes Brook Trail enters on the left at 2.7 mi., and at 2.8 mi. a spur path leads right 0.2 mi. to the ledgy summit of Jennings Peak, which commands impressive views. The trail then enters the Sandwich Range Wilderness. The Smarts Brook Trail enters on the right at 3.3 mi., and the Sandwich Mountain Trail ascends moderately toward the summit of Sandwich Mtn. About 90 yd. below the summit the Algonquin Trail enters on the right, and 15 yd. below the summit the Bennett Street Trail enters on the right.

Sandwich Mountain Trail (map 3:J6–K7)
Distances from parking area off NH 49 (1400')

    to Drakes Brook Trail, upper junction (3240'): 2.7 mi., 1850 ft., 2 hr. 15 min.

    to Sandwich Mtn. summit (3980'): 3.9 mi. (6.3 km.), 2600 ft., 3 hr. 15 min.

Drakes Brook Trail (WMNF)

This trail leaves the same parking lot off NH 49 as the Sandwich Mountain Trail and rejoins that trail near Jennings Peak, providing an alternate route for ascent or descent of Sandwich Mtn. as well as access to Fletcher's Cascades.

    The trail leaves east from the north side of the parking lot and follows a logging road for 0.4 mi. At this point the trail to Fletcher's Cascades continues up the road, and the Drakes Brook Trail diverges right and crosses Drakes Brook (difficult at high water). The trail follows an old logging road, climbing away from the brook and returning to its bank several times. At 2.6 mi. it leaves the logging road and climbs by switchbacks up the west side of the ravine to join the Sandwich Mountain Trail north of Jennings Peak, about 1.2 mi. from the summit of Sandwich Mtn.

Drakes Brook Trail (map 3:J6–K6)
Distances from parking area off NH 49 (1400')

    to Sandwich Mountain Trail (3240'): 3.2 mi. (5.2 km.), 1850 ft., 2 hr. 35 min.

    to Sandwich Mtn. summit (3980') via Sandwich Mountain Trail: 4.4 mi. (7.1 km.), 2600 ft., 3 hr. 30 min.

Smarts Brook Trail (WMNF)

This trail follows the valley of Smarts Brook from NH 49 to the Sandwich Mountain Trail in the sag south of Jennings Peak. The valley is wild and pleasant, and the trail is relatively easy. The upper part of the trail is in the Sandwich Range Wilderness.

The trail leaves the east side of NH 49 from the south end of a parking area just northeast of the Smarts Brook bridge, crosses the brook on the highway bridge, and immediately turns left. It climbs a short distance to a logging road, which it follows left, then soon joins a better road and follows it past a swimming hole in the brook on the left. At 1.3 mi. the Tri-Town (X-C ski) Trail enters from the right. Here an interesting but faintly marked loop side path turns sharp left and crosses the brook on a bridge, then turns right, follows the brook, recrosses it, and rejoins the main trail at 1.6 mi. The main trail passes the Beaver Pond at 1.5 mi., then follows an older road when the newer road diverges right. In a short distance farther it continues straight ahead at the junction with the loop and the Tri-Town Trail. It enters the Sandwich Range Wilderness, crosses a tributary at 2.6 mi., and at 3.7 mi. passes several large boulders. It then crosses the brook and passes several more very large boulders in the next 0.4 mi. Soon it turns left and climbs by a long switchback to the ridge top, where it meets the Sandwich Mountain Trail.

Smarts Brook Trail (map 3:K6)

Distances from parking area on NH 49 (900')

   to pools in Smarts Brook (1100'): 1.1 mi., 200 ft., 40 min.

   to Sandwich Mountain Trail (3416'): 5.1 mi. (8.2 km.), 2300 ft., 3 hr. 40 min.

   to Sandwich Mtn. summit (3980') via Sandwich Mountain Trail: 5.7 mi. (9.2 km.), 3100 ft., 4 hr. 25 min.

Bennett Street Trail (WODC)

This trail runs to the summit of Sandwich Mtn. from the Flat Mountain Pond Trail at a point 0.3 mi. past Jose's bridge and 0.5 mi. from the parking area on Bennett St. (which is 2.2 mi. from NH 113A; for trailhead access directions see Flat Mountain Pond Trail p. 294). Its blue blazes should be followed with care. The upper part of the trail is in the Sandwich Range Wilderness.

From the parking area, go west on the Flat Mountain Pond Trail past the gate and Jose's bridge to a small clearing, where the Bennett Street Trail begins, turning right. It follows a logging road along the southwest bank of Pond Brook, crossing several small streams, and at 0.6 mi. from the Flat Mountain Pond Trail the Gleason Trail diverges left. The Bennett Street Trail soon passes a waterfall with a swimming hole, then bears away from Pond Brook and follows a tributary, crossing it twice. At 1.6 mi. it crosses the Flat Mountain Pond Trail, which at this point is an old railroad grade. The Bennett Street Trail ascends the bank above the grade, soon entering the Sandwich Range Wilderness. It climbs steadily, and at 2.3 mi. turns sharp right onto an old logging road. At 2.9 mi. it turns left off the logging road and at 3.5 mi. the Gleason Trail rejoins on the left. The trail soon turns left onto another old road at a point where there is an unreliable spring on a side path right, and shortly passes a spur path left (sign) to another unreliable spring. It then climbs to a junction with the Sandwich Mountain Trail; the summit is 15 yd. to the right.

Bennett Street Trail (map 3:K7)

Distances from Flat Mountain Pond Trail (1200')

   to crossing of Flat Mountain Pond Trail (1850'): 1.6 mi., 650 ft., 1 hr. 10 min.

   to upper junction with Gleason Trail (3600'): 3.5 mi., 2400 ft., 2 hr. 55 min.

   to Sandwich Mtn. summit (3960'): 4.0 mi. (6.4 km.), 2800 ft., 3 hr. 25 min.

Distance from Bennett St. parking area (1060')

   to Sandwich Mtn. summit (3980') via Flat Mountain Pond and Bennett Street trails: 4.5 mi. (7.2 km.), 2900 ft., 3 hr. 40 min.

Gleason Trail (AMC)

This trail begins and ends on the Bennett Street Trail, providing an alternative route to the summit of Sandwich Mtn. that is 0.7 mi. shorter, but consequently steeper and rougher. The yellow blazes must be followed with care. The trail is rather steep, and footing may be poor when the trail is wet. The upper part of the trail is in the Sandwich Range Wilderness.

   It diverges left from the Bennett Street Trail at 0.6 mi. (1.1 mi. from the Bennett St. parking area) and ascends across a ledgy brook to cross the Flat Mountain Pond Trail (an old railroad grade) at 0.5 mi. The trail enters the Sandwich Range Wilderness, soon turns left and climbs through a beautiful hardwood forest, then approaches a brook and turns right without crossing it at 1.0 mi. Soon the trail turns left onto a logging road, follows it for 40 yd., then turns off the road to the right. It continues rather steeply to the ridge top at 1.5 mi. and then levels off. It then ascends moderately to its upper junction with the Bennett Street Trail, 0.5 mi. below the summit of Sandwich Mtn.

Gleason Trail (map 3:K7)

Distance from Bennett Street Trail, lower junction (1400')

   to Bennett Street Trail, upper junction (3600'): 2.2 mi. (3.6 km.), 2200 ft., 2 hr. 10 min.

Distance from Bennett St. parking area (1060')

   to summit of Sandwich Mtn. (3980') via Flat Mountain Pond, Bennett Street, Gleason, and Bennett Street trails: 3.8 mi. (6.1 km.), 2900 ft., 3 hr. 20 min.

Flat Mountain Pond Trail (WMNF)

This trail, with easy grades and footing for most of its distance, begins on White-face Intervale Rd. at a point 0.3 mi. north of its intersection with Bennett St., ascends to the Flat Mtn. Ponds, then descends to Bennett St. at a new parking area 2.2 mi. from NH 113A. To reach these trailheads, take Whiteface Intervale Rd., which leaves NH 113A about 3 mi. north of the western junction of NH 113 and NH 113A, where NH 113A bends from north-south to east-west. Bennett St. turns left from Whiteface Intervale Rd. 0.1 mi. from NH 113A, continues straight past a junction at 1.7 mi., where it becomes rougher, and is gated at 2.2 mi. at a parking lot 0.2 east of Jose's (rhymes with "doses") bridge. The upper section of the Flat Mountain Pond Trail east of Flat Mtn. Ponds is in the Sandwich Range Wilderness.

The trail leaves Whiteface Intervale Rd. just before the bridge over White-face River on a gated logging road, crosses a beaver pond outlet with good views, bears left at a fork, and turns sharp right off the road at 0.6 mi. Soon it reaches an older, grassy logging road and follows it left for 60 yd., then leaves this road to the right and passes an outlook to Mt. Whiteface at 0.9 mi. It ascends easily along a small ridge, then descends rather abruptly to Whiteface River. It crosses the river on a bridge at 1.6 mi., entering the Sandwich Range Wilderness, and immediately picks up the older route of the trail, a logging road that it follows to the left upstream along the east bank. At 1.7 mi. the McCrillis Trail turns sharp right up the bank, and the Flat Mountain Pond Trail continues to ascend along the river at comfortable grades, crossing a major branch at 3.1 mi. (difficult at high water). Continuing the ascent, it passes over a small hump and descends to the edge of Flat Mtn. Pond at 4.2 mi., where it enters the old Beebe River logging railroad grade. It follows the grade to a fork at the edge of the major inlet brook; the trail follows the left fork across the stream, while the right fork runs to the edge of a swampy area. Continuing along the shore of the long, narrow pond, the main trail soon diverges right on a rough footway to circle around an area in which the grade has been flooded. It passes a boulder with a view of Mt. Whiteface, and returns to the grade at the south end of the pond at 5.3 mi., leaving the Sandwich Range Wilderness. Here, 70 yd. straight ahead on a spur path, is the Flat Mtn. Pond Shelter, worth visiting just for the view across the pond. The main trail turns right on the railroad grade and descends gradually into the valley of Pond Brook.

At 6.3 mi. the grade makes a hairpin turn to the left at an old beaver pond, soon crosses a small brook, passes a logging camp site, and crosses the brook twice more. At 7.6 mi. the trail crosses a major tributary and swings left, and at 7.7 mi. the Bennett Street Trail crosses. After a wet section where the railroad ties remain, the Gleason Trail crosses at 8.2 mi. (junction signed for the Gleason Trail only). Either the Bennett Street Trail or the Gleason Trail can be used as an attractive shortcut to Jose's bridge and the Bennett St. parking area. At 9.2 mi. the Guinea Pond Trail continues ahead on the railroad grade, while the Flat Mountain Pond Trail turns left on a logging road, passes a gate, goes through a small clearing where the Bennett Street Trail enters on the left, and passes a second gate just before reaching the parking area 0.2 mi. past Jose's bridge.

Flat Mountain Pond Trail (map 3:K8–K7)

Distances from Whiteface Intervale Rd. (968')

  to McCrillis Trail (1500'): 1.7 mi., 550 ft., 1 hr. 10 min.

  to Flat Mtn. Pond Shelter spur path (2320'): 5.3 mi., 1350 ft., 3 hr. 20 min.

  to Guinea Pond Trail (1560'): 9.2 mi., 1350 ft. (rev. 750 ft.), 5 hr. 15 min.

  to Bennett St. parking area (1060'): 10.3 mi. (16.6 km.), 1350 ft. (rev. 500 ft.), 5 hr. 50 min.

Algonquin Trail (SLA)

This trail ascends Sandwich Dome from Sandwich Notch Rd., and has many extensive views from open ledges on the southwest shoulder, sometimes called Black Mtn. The trail is steep and rough, with a few rock scrambles that can be avoided by side paths. The upper part of the trail is in the Sandwich Range Wilderness.

The trail leaves the north side of Sandwich Notch Rd. 1.5 mi. north of the power line along the Beebe River and 3.7 mi. south of NH 49. It follows an old logging road across a brook and past a small meadow, and at 0.9 mi., in a small clearing, turns left off the road (watch carefully for yellow blazes). Soon it begins to climb steeply, then moderates and passes through a ledgy area with two small brooks, then climbs steeply again to a small pass at 2.1 mi., where it enters the Sandwich Range Wilderness. Here it turns right, descends slightly, then attacks the west end of the ridge, climbing steeply with two rock pitches, both of which can be avoided by paths to the right, former bypasses that have now become the established route of the trail; at the second, good views are missed unless one walks back to the ledges on the former route of the trail. The grade moderates, and at 2.8 mi. (elevation 3300 ft.) the Black Mountain Pond Trail enters on the right. The Algonquin Trail continues to ascend moderately past several viewpoints, then descends steeply for a short distance into a sag at 3.5 mi. and ascends moderately again to the Sandwich Mountain Trail 90 yd. below the summit.

Algonquin Trail (map 3:K6–K7)

Distances from Sandwich Notch Rd. (1420')

> *to* Sandwich Range Wilderness boundary (2600'): 2.1 mi., 1200 ft., 1 hr. 40 min.

> *to* Black Mountain Pond Trail (3300'): 2.8 mi., 1900 ft., 2 hr. 20 min.

> *to* Sandwich Mountain Trail (3950'): 4.5 mi. (7.3 km.), 2550 ft., 3 hr. 30 min.

Black Mountain Pond Trail (SLA)

This trail runs from the Guinea Pond Trail, 1.6 mi. from Sandwich Notch Rd., past Black Mtn. Pond to the Algonquin Trail 1.8 mi. below the summit of Sandwich Mtn. Sections of the trail below Black Mtn. Pond are wet, and the part from the pond to the ridge is very steep and rough. The former Black Mtn. Pond Shelter has been removed. Most of the trail is in the Sandwich Range Wilderness.

This trail leaves the north side of the Guinea Pond Trail almost directly opposite the Mead Trail, crosses Beebe River (may be difficult at high water) and continues generally north to the west bank of Beebe River (which has turned north) and recrosses it. At 0.8 mi. it crosses an overgrown gravel road that crosses the brook on the left side of the trail, and enters the Sandwich Range Wilderness. At 1.9 mi. a side path leads left to Mary Cary Falls. The main trail continues to ascend easily, and at 2.4 mi. it reaches the west edge of Black Mtn. Pond at the site of the former shelter. (The shelter site and the area to the west are not within the Sandwich Range Wilderness.) The trail winds around in the woods near the pond, passing through a small stand of virgin spruce, then turns right and crosses a beaver dam with a small pond on the left, and begins the steep climb. About halfway up, it reaches the first of several outlook ledges with good views south; views to the west increase as the trail works around toward the west end of the shoulder. At 3.3 mi. it passes a boulder cave, turns sharp right, and continues to meet the Algonquin Trail at an elevation of 3300 ft.

Black Mountain Pond Trail (map 3:K7–K6)

Distances from Guinea Pond Trail (1580')

   to Black Mtn. Pond (2220'): 2.4 mi., 650 ft., 1 hr. 30 min.

   to Algonquin Trail (3300'): 3.5 mi. (5.6 km.), 1700 ft., 2 hr. 35 min.

Guinea Pond Trail (WMNF)

This trail runs east from Sandwich Notch Rd. 5.7 mi. from Center Sandwich, just south of the bridge over Beebe River, to the Flat Mountain Pond Trail 1.1 mi. from the Bennett St. parking area. It follows a gated road to the old railroad grade in a power line clearing, then follows the grade along Beebe River past numerous ponds and swamps. At 1.2 mi. it passes a second gate, and soon the trail turns right, then left, on a old road in order to bypass a flooded section of the grade. Soon the trail runs through the woods to bypass a flooded section of the road, then rejoins the railroad grade and reaches the junctions with the Mead Trail on the right at 1.6 mi. and the Black Mountain Pond Trail on the left 10 yd. farther on. Continuing east, the trail crosses a brook twice; in high water, follow a beaten path along the south bank. The trail crosses another brook, and at 1.8 mi. a side path runs left 0.2 mi. to the shore of Guinea Pond. At 2.8 mi. the trail crosses a branch of Cold River on a bridge and continues on the grade to the junction with the Flat Mountain Pond Trail, which enters right from Jose's bridge and follows the railroad grade ahead to Flat Mtn. Pond.

Guinea Pond Trail (map 3:K6–K7)

Distances from Sandwich Notch Rd. (1320')

   to Mead Trail/Black Mountain Pond Trail (1580'): 1.6 mi., 250 ft., 55 min.

   to Flat Mountain Pond Trail (1560'): 4.0 mi. (6.4 km.), 350 ft. (rev. 100 ft.), 2 hr. 10 min.

Mead Trail (SLA)

This trail ascends to the summit of Mt. Israel, where there are outstanding views (particularly to the higher peaks of the Sandwich Range close by on the north), from the Guinea Pond Trail 1.6 mi. from Sandwich Notch Rd.

It leaves the Guinea Pond Trail and crosses a small ridge, a sag, and the power lines; then it ascends along the ravine of a small brook, crossing it at 0.9 mi. It continues to ascend past a small spring (unreliable) to the Wentworth Trail; the summit ledge, with fine views, is 70 yd. left.

Mead Trail (map 3:K7)

Distance from Guinea Pond Trail (1580')

   to Wentworth Trail (2610'): 1.7 mi. (2.8 km.), 1050 ft., 1 hr. 25 min.

Wentworth Trail (SLA)

This trail ascends Mt. Israel from Mead Base (Explorer Scout camp), located on a side road off Sandwich Notch Rd. 2.6 mi. from Center Sandwich, and affords splendid views of the Lakes Region and the Sandwich Range. Park in the field below the camp buildings.

The trail, blazed in yellow, enters the woods at the left rear of the main camp building (sign) and leads directly uphill, following an old cart path through an opening in a stone wall 0.3 mi. above the camp. It turns right and angles up the hillside above the wall, turns left, then turns right again at a brook bed at 0.8 mi. Soon it begins to switchback up the slope, and at 1.5 mi. it passes a rock face right and a fine outlook 10 yd. on the left across Squam Lake and Lake Winnipesaukee. The trail reaches the ridge 100 yd. farther up and climbing becomes easier, soon becoming almost level in a dense, shady coniferous forest. Then the trail turns right at a ledge (good view north) near the summit of the west knob and continues along the ridge to the junction on the left with the Mead Trail; the summit is a ledge 70 yd. past the junction. Some cairns lead about 100 yd. northeast from the summit to ledges with more views to the north and east.

Wentworth Trail (map 3:L7–K7)

Distance from Mead Base (930')

   to Mt. Israel summit (2630'): 2.1 mi. (3.5 km.), 1700 ft., 1 hr. 55 min.

Crawford-Ridgepole Trail (SLA)

This trail follows the backbone of the Squam Range from Sandwich Notch Rd. to the south knob of Cotton Mtn. Except for the very popular segment between Mt. Percival and Mt. Morgan, the trail is used infrequently, despite fine views in the Squam-Doublehead section.

The trail starts on the Sandwich Notch Rd. 0.5 mi. beyond Beede Falls (Cow Cave) and 2.0 mi. south of the power line along the Beebe River. From the road (sign) it ascends steeply, passes southeast of the summit of an unnamed wooded peak (2218 ft.), and continues along the ridge across a saddle to Doublehead Mtn. (2158 ft.), where there is a good view north just before the summit of East Doublehead. At 1.9 mi., 100 yd. beyond the summit of East Doublehead, the trail bears right and descends where the Doublehead Trail diverges left to NH 113. There is a very fine viewpoint, well worth the side trip, on the Doublehead Trail 0.1 mi. from this junction. After passing over West Doublehead, where there is an outlook to the north, the Crawford-Ridgepole Trail continues along the ridge, much of the way over ledges which are slippery when wet. It crosses the east summit of Mt. Squam (2223 ft.), where there is a fine view, at 3.0 mi. The trail continues to the Mount Percival Trail and Mt. Percival's excellent views at 4.4 mi., passes just west of the actual high point of the range (sometimes called the Sawtooth, it can be reached by a short but thick bushwhack and has a good view), and continues to a junction with the Mount Morgan Trail at 5.2 mi. Here the Mount Morgan Trail leads to the right 90 yd. to a fork; the left branch (almost straight ahead) leads another 50 yd. to a cliff-top viewpoint, while the right branch leads 50 yd. to the true summit of Mt. Morgan, where there is an interesting view north.

From this junction the Crawford-Ridgepole Trail and the Mount Morgan Trail coincide, descending a set of steps. Shortly a spur path branches right, ascends a ladder, and climbs about 100 yd. through a boulder cave to the cliff-top viewpoint. The main trail descends to a junction at 5.6 mi. where the Mount Morgan Trail continues its descent to NH 113, while the Crawford-Ridgepole Trail turns right for Mt. Webster. At 7.2 mi. a spur path leads left 50 yd. to the summit of Mt. Webster, and at 7.5 mi. an unmarked spur leads left a few steps to the beautiful east outlook.

The trail continues past the junction with the Old Mountain Road at 9.6 mi., and continues to the summit of Mt. Livermore (view) at 10.0 mi. Coinciding with the Prescott Trail, it descends west from Mt. Livermore along a stone wall, then turns left on an old carriage road and descends by switchbacks. At 10.3 mi. the Prescott Trail branches left; the Crawford-Ridgepole Trail crosses two tiny streams near a low pass, then climbs through a rocky area in a beautiful hemlock grove to a south spur of Cotton Mtn. Here the Crawford-Ridgepole Trail ends, since the Science Center of New Hampshire has closed the former connector to its trails because it requires an admission fee for use of its trails. From the spur of Cotton Mtn., descent can be made by following the yellow blazes of the former Cotton Mountain Trail down to the edge of the large gravel pit and thence to NH 113 near the Old Highway trailhead. This old trail has been somewhat disrupted by logging but can be followed downhill fairly readily, though ascent by this route is not recommended.

Crawford-Ridgepole Trail (maps 3/4:L6/USGS Holderness quad)

Distances from Sandwich Notch Rd. (1220')

- *to* East Doublehead summit (2158'): 1.9 mi., 1150 ft. (rev. 200 ft.), 1 hr. 30 min.

- *to* Mt. Squam, east summit (2223'): 3.0 mi., 1450 ft. (rev. 250 ft.), 2 hr. 15 min.

- *to* Mt. Percival summit (2212'): 4.4 mi., 1700 ft. (rev. 250 ft.), 3 hr. 5 min.

- *to* upper junction with Mount Morgan Trail (2200'): 5.2 mi., 1800 ft. (rev. 100 ft.), 3 hr. 30 min.

- *to* Mt. Livermore summit (1500'): 10.0 mi., 2300 ft. (rev. 1000 ft.), 6 hr. 10 min.

- *to* spur of Cotton Mtn. (1210'): 11.3 mi. (18.1 km.), 2600 ft. (rev. 600 ft.), 6 hr. 55 min.

Doublehead Trail (SLA)

This trail provides access to a ledge high on Doublehead Mtn. that provides one of the finest views in the Squam Range. It begins on NH 113 at a point 3.5 mi. southwest of Center Sandwich, following a gravel road (part of the old Holderness–Center Sandwich highway) that diverges right (west) at an angle past an old cemetery and a residence. Most vehicles should park near NH 113, taking care not to block any roads.

Continue on the old highway. The trail proper leaves the old highway on the right 1.0 mi. from NH 113 and follows a logging road that bears to the right through a clearing. At 1.5 mi. the trail turns left onto a skidder road and enters an overgrown logged area where the footway is poorly defined and blazes must be followed with care. In another 100 yd. the trail turns sharp right (arrow) across a small brook, follows another skidder road, and joins a small brook. At the top of a steep pitch it turns sharp left and soon crosses a stone wall, where it re-enters mature woods. It ascends steeply up the valley of a small brook, then swings right and climbs to a ledge at 2.3 mi. with excellent views to the south. It then turns left off the ledge and climbs to the Crawford-Ridgepole Trail 80 yd. west of the summit of East Doublehead.

Doublehead Trail (map 3:L6)

Distance from NH 113 (720')

> *to* Crawford-Ridgepole Trail (2120'): 2.4 mi. (3.9 km.), 1450 ft., 1 hr. 55 min.

Mount Percival Trail (SLA)

This trail provides access to the fine views and interesting boulder caves on Mt. Percival, and in combination with the Mount Morgan and Crawford-Ridgepole trails offers one of the most popular and scenic loop hikes on the southern fringe of the White Mtns. It begins on the north side of NH 113, 0.3 mi. northeast of the Mount Morgan Trail parking area (which is usually the best place to park).

It follows a logging road past a gate to an old clearing, then bears left into the woods, passes a stone wall, bears left through another old clearing (arrow), and passes several more stone walls. After a short ascent, the trail turns right (east) and traverses the south slope of Mt. Percival for 0.1 mi. The trail becomes steep at 1.6 mi., climbing past a fine view of Squam Lake to the summit, where it joins the Crawford-Ridgepole Trail. Just below the summit a side path diverges left and ascends very roughly and strenuously through a boulder cave, then rejoins the main path just below the summit.

Mount Percival Trail (map 3:L6)

Distances from NH 113 (800')

> *to* Mt. Percival summit (2212'): 1.9 mi. (3.1 km.), 1450 ft., 1 hr. 40 min.
>
> *for* loop over Mts. Percival and Morgan via Mount Percival,
> Crawford–Ridgepole, and Mount Morgan trails: 4.8 mi. (7.7 km.), 1550 ft., 3 hr. 10 min.

Mount Morgan Trail (SLA)

This trail leaves the west side of NH 113, 0.5 mi. northeast of its junction with Pinehurst Rd. (the road that leads to Rockywold and Deephaven camps). From a small clearing (parking), the trail follows a logging road, turning left off it almost immediately. The trail bears right at a fork and soon begins the steeper ascent of the southeast slope of the mountain. At 1.7 mi. the Crawford-Ridgepole Trail enters left from Mt. Webster, and the two trails coincide, passing a spur path that branches left, ascends a ladder, and climbs about 100 yd. through a boulder cave to the cliff-top viewpoint. After climbing a set of steps, the trails soon reach a junction where the Crawford-Ridgepole Trail diverges right for Mt. Percival. Here the Mount Morgan Trail leads left to the cliff-top viewpoint; partway along, a short spur leaves it on the right and runs to the true summit.

Mount Morgan Trail (map 3:L6)

Distance from NH 113 (800')

    to Mt. Morgan summit (2220'): 2.1 mi. (3.4 km.), 1450 ft., 1 hr. 30 min.

Old Highway (SLA)

This trail, used for access to the lower ends of the Prescott Trail and Old Mountain Road, continues straight where NH 113 turns right 1.3 mi. northeast of Holderness and 0.2 mi. beyond a gravel pit where parking is available on the shoulder of NH 113. A century ago, the old road followed by this trail was part of the main highway between Holderness and Center Sandwich. It leaves NH 113 at the same point as a paved driveway. The Prescott Trail diverges left (north) at the height-of-land at 0.9 mi., 100 yd. beyond the Prescott Cemetery, and the Old Mountain Road diverges left at an acute angle at 1.1 mi. and runs near the edge of a large field. The Old Highway continues past a sugar-house to a locked gate at the edge of a paved road that runs to NH 113 (no parking here).

Old Highway (map 4:L6/USGS Holderness quad)

Distances from NH 113 (585')

    to Prescott Trail (900'): 0.9 mi., 300 ft., 35 min.

    to paved road (750'): 1.4 mi. (2.2 km.), 300 ft. (rev. 150 ft.), 50 min.

Prescott Trail (SLA)

This trail to Mt. Livermore (1500 ft.) turns left off the Old Highway at the height-of-land 0.9 mi. from NH 113, 100 yd. beyond the Prescott Cemetery. It follows a logging road for 0.2 mi., turns sharp left off it and ascends gradually, then turns right uphill at 0.3 mi. The trail now climbs by switchbacks over a low ridge and descends gradually to the Crawford-Ridgepole Trail, which enters left at 1.0 mi. From this point the two trails ascend together via switchbacks. Just below the summit they turn sharp right and ascend steeply to the summit, where there is a view over Squam Lake.

Descending, the Crawford-Ridgepole Trail heading south and the Prescott Trail leave the summit together, turn sharp right (west) and descend along an old stone wall, then turn left onto an old bridle trail. After 0.4 mi. the Crawford-Ridgepole Trail leaves on the right.

Prescott Trail (map 4:L6)

Distances from Old Highway Trail (900')

> *to* Crawford-Ridgepole Trail (1200'): 1.0 mi., 300 ft., 40 min.

> *to* summit of Mt. Livermore (1500'): 1.4 mi. (2.2 km.), 600 ft., 1 hr.

Distance from NH 113 (585')

> *for* loop over Mt. Livermore (1500') via Old Highway, Prescott Trail, Craw-
> ford–Ridgepole Trail, Old Mountain Road, and Old Highway: 4.5 mi.
> (7.2 km.), 1000 ft., 2 hr. 45 min.

Old Mountain Road (SLA-Webster)

This trail leaves the Old Highway Trail 1.1 mi. from its western end at NH 113, and ascends on an old road to the Crawford-Ridgepole Trail at the low point between Mt. Livermore and Mt. Webster. The old road continues on from here descending to the north, but this section is not an official trail.

Old Mountain Road (map 4:L6)

Distance from Old Highway (800')

> *to* Crawford-Ridgepole Trail (1300'): 0.7 mi. (1.1 km.), 500 ft., 35 min.

Rattlesnake Paths (SLA)

The *Old Bridle Path* is the easiest route to the West Rattlesnake outlooks. A very short and easy route to an excellent viewpoint, it receives very heavy use. It leaves NH 113 between Center Sandwich and Holderness, 0.5 mi. northeast of the junction with Pinehurst Rd. (the road to Rockywold and Deephaven camps) and about 70 yd. southwest of the entrance to the Mount Morgan Trail (where there is a small parking area). It follows an old cart road 0.9 mi. (40 min.) to the cliffs near the summit. Descending, this trail begins slightly northwest of the summit cliffs.

The *Ramsey Trail* is a much steeper route to West Rattlesnake. It leaves Pinehurst Rd. 0.7 mi. from NH 113 and 90 yd. east of the entrance to Rockywold and Deephaven camps, along with the Undercut Trail (sign), which has another entrance almost opposite the camp entrance. In 0.1 mi. there is a crossroads, where the Ramsey Trail takes a sharp right and climbs steeply 0.4 mi. to a point just north of the summit cliffs, joining the Old Bridle Path (no sign at top). Left at the crossroads is the alternate route 0.1 mi. to Pinehurst Rd.; the *Undercut Trail* continues straight ahead from the crossroads and runs 0.9 mi. (follow markings very carefully) to NH 113 0.1 mi. west of the Old Bridle Path parking area.

The *Pasture Trail* leads to West Rattlesnake from Pinehurst Rd. 0.9 mi. from NH 113. Park in the small area to the right before the first gate. The trailhead is 100 yd. east of the gate. Start on a road to the left, then turn right past Pinehurst Farm buildings. At 0.2 mi. the East Rattlesnake and Five Finger Point trails diverge right, and in 15 yd. the Pasture Trail bears left where the Col Trail continues straight ahead. The cliffs are reached at 0.6 mi. from the gate after a moderate ascent.

The *Col Trail* continues straight where the Pasture Trail bears left 0.2 mi. from the gate on Pinehurst Rd. In 0.3 mi. it joins the Ridge Trail, follows it right for 30 yd., then turns left (sign, "Saddle"), passes over the height-of-land, and descends (follow with care) to the edge of a beaver swamp. It enters an old road and turns left, then bears right and reaches a gravel road 0.7 mi. from the Ridge Trail junction. This trailhead is reached in 0.2 mi. from NH 113 at a point 0.3 mi. east of the Holderness-Sandwich town line.

The *Ridge Trail* connects West and East Rattlesnake. It begins just northeast of the cliffs of West Rattlesnake and descends gradually. At 0.4 mi. the Col Trail comes in from the right, and just beyond leaves again to the left. The Ridge Trail ascends, and the East Rattlesnake Trail enters right at 0.8 mi. The Ridge Trail reaches the outlook ledge at 0.9 mi. and continues to the summit and the Butterworth Trail at 1.0 mi.

The *East Rattlesnake Trail* branches right from the Pasture Trail 0.2 mi. from the gate. In 25 yd. the Five Finger Point Trail continues straight ahead. The East Rattlesnake Trail turns left and ascends steadily 0.4 mi. to the Ridge Trail, 0.1 mi. west of the East Rattlesnake outlook. The *Five Finger Point Trail* runs on a slight downgrade for 0.7 mi. to a loop path 1.3 mi. long that circles around the edge of Five Finger Point, with several interesting viewpoints and attractive small beaches where swimming is permitted (no lifeguards).

The *Butterworth Trail* leads to East Rattlesnake from Metcalf Rd., which leaves NH 113 0.7 mi. east of the Holderness-Sandwich town line. The trail leaves Metcalf Rd. on the right 0.5 mi. from NH 113 and climbs moderately 0.7 mi. to the summit. The East Rattlesnake viewpoint is 0.1 mi. farther via the Ridge Trail.

Red Hill Trail (SLA)

In Center Harbor at the junction of NH 25 and NH 25B, go northwest on Bean Rd. for 1.4 mi., turn right (east) and follow Sibley Rd. (sign for fire lookout) for 1.1 mi., then turn left and continue 0.1 mi. and park on the side of the road. The trail, an old jeep road, soon makes a sharp right turn uphill and crosses a brook. At 0.4 mi. it swings left around a cellar hole and enters the old firewarden's road to the summit. At 1.0 mi. there is a piped spring left. The Eagle Cliff Trail enters on the left just before the fire tower and firewarden's cabin on the summit of Red Hill.

Red Hill Trail (USGS Center Sandwich and Center Harbor quads)
Distance from parking area (680')

    to Red Hill summit (2030'): 1.7 mi. (2.7 km.), 1350 ft., 1 hr. 30 min.

Eagle Cliff Trail (SLA)

This trail ascends Red Hill via Eagle Cliff, which has fine views but may be hazardous in wet or icy conditions. From the junction of NH 25 and NH 25B in Center Harbor, follow Bean Rd. for 5.2 mi. to a turnout at the edge of Squam Lake, about 0.3 mi. north of the Moultonborough-Sandwich town line. The trail is well marked but there is no trail sign at the beginning, which is difficult to see from the road: it is a path through a ditch in a thicket, 200 yd. south of the lakeside turnout, 50 yd. north of a high hedge, and directly opposite a "Traffic Turning and Entering" sign.

The trail climbs through an overgrown field and enters the woods. It ascends on a well-beaten path, becoming steep and rough as it gets well up on the ledge, and reaches the main viewpoint on Eagle Cliff at 0.6 mi. From the upper ledge, the trail enters the woods and continues along the ridge toward the fire tower on Red Hill. It crosses a knoll and descends sharply to a small pass at 1.0 mi., where the Teedie Trail enters right.

Teedie Trail. This path descends in 0.6 mi. to a gravel driveway next to a private tennis court on Bean Rd. at the Moultonborough-Sandwich town line, about 0.3 mi. south of the beginning of the Eagle Cliff Trail. It should be considered as a way of avoiding the descent over the Eagle Cliff ledges in adverse conditions.

The Eagle Cliff Trail crosses another knoll and ascends steadily through a mixture of young growth in cutover areas and mature woods, and about a quarter-mile below the summit it enters an area burned over by a fire set by an arsonist in April 1990. It finally levels out and meets the Red Hill Trail just below the summit of Red Hill. Descending, it diverges right from the Red Hill Trail (jeep road) just below the firewarden's cabin (sign).

Eagle Cliff Trail (map 3:L7/USGS Center Sandwich quad)

Distances from Bean Rd. (580')

> *to* Eagle Cliff viewpoint (1270'): 0.6 mi., 700 ft., 40 min.
>
> *to* Red Hill fire tower (2030'): 2.6 mi. (4.1 km.), 1650 ft. (rev. 200 ft.), 2 hr. 10 min.

Bearcamp River Trail (Sandwich Land Trust Committee)

This new trail, which runs for 17 mi. along the Bearcamp River from Sandwich Notch to Hell's Gate (a rocky gorge in South Tamworth), has been constructed through the efforts of countless volunteers. Since 1987, the Sandwich Land Trust Committee has raised funds and stimulated community interest toward protecting more than 3000 acres of undeveloped land in the Bearcamp Valley. The Bearcamp River Trail crosses six conservation areas, ten privately managed tree farms, and several historic sites.

The Bearcamp River, a tributary of the Saco River, flows from Sandwich Notch and its surrounding mountains down to Ossipee Lake. It was named by Israel Gilman and his companions in the 1760s when their provisions were ransacked by a black bear during a hunting trip along the river.

The trail, blazed in yellow, may be hiked in its entirety or in smaller segments. Camping is not permitted. The trail is described from Sandwich Notch toward Tamworth (roughly west to east) and is broken into sections suitable for shorter hikes. Many sections are ideal for young families due to the trail's consistently gentle grade. Mileages given in each section are for that section only; a list of cumulative mileages will be found at the end of the last section. The trail loses about 300 ft. in the first 0.6-mi. segment from Beede Falls to Mead Base as the stream descends rapidly from the mountain pass, but thereafter it passes along terrain that is flat or gently rolling, following the river on its leisurely downhill course through swamps and meadows. Since there is no significant elevation gain—there is actually a slight net loss—in the greatest part of its length, elevation gain figures are omitted from the list of cumulative mileages.

Section 1: Beede Falls to Mount Israel Road

The western terminus of this section (and the entire trail) is at Sandwich Town Park, located on Sandwich Notch Rd. 3.2 miles from NH 113 in Center Sandwich or 7.5 miles from NH 49 west of Waterville Valley. This rough dirt road is not suitable for all vehicles and is not maintained for winter travel. The eastern terminus of this section is located on Mt. Israel Rd., which turns right (north) from Sandwich Notch Rd. just northwest of Center Sandwich village; follow Mt. Israel Rd. about 1 mi. north to a point about 100 yd. beyond the bridge over the Bearcamp River, where a logging road turns right (cars may be parked on the left here). Within this section is another possible starting point at Mead Wilderness Base Camp (Explorer Scout camp), where parking is available; take the road that bears right from Sandwich Notch Rd. (sign) 2.6 mi. northwest of Center Sandwich village and park in the field below the camp buildings.

The yellow-blazed trail descends gradually to the Bearcamp River at Beede Falls. The shallow pool at the foot of this beautiful cascade is a popular swimming hole in the summer. Cross the river and descend along its northern bank, then bear left away from the river, and at 0.2 mi. pass Cow Cave (left), where legend says a lost cow safely spent a winter. Cross a small stream and bear right onto a grassy road, then pass a picnic area with restrooms (left) opposite an open field. At 0.6 mi., turn right (south) onto a gravel road at Mead Base. (The Wentworth Trail leaves from here to ascend Mt. Israel.) After following the road for 0.3 mi., turn left onto Cook Farm Rd., an unsigned gravel road opposite Cook Farm (arrow).

Cook Farm is part of a 300-acre conservation program that resulted from a cooperative venture between the owners, the town of Sandwich, and the New Hampshire Land Conservation Investment Program. Once a glacial lake, Cook Farm is now a mountain intervale and one of the last undeveloped pockets of farm land in the White Mtns.

The trail heads east along Cook Farm Rd. through open fields with views of Mt. Israel to the left, then swings right at a gravel pit and winds through the pit area (arrows); be careful to avoid any farm machinery. The trail turns hard right (arrow), then left (sign) onto an old road, and re-enters the woods near an old shack off to the right. Almost immediately to the left are the graves of Israel Gilman, pioneer and Revolutionary War veteran, and his unnamed Indian friend. Soon the old road narrows to a trail, crosses several stone walls and a stagnant stream, then swings left along the north bank of the Bearcamp River. Cross a beautifully constructed log bridge over the river at 1.7 mi. and descend gradually along its south bank, passing a series of fine cascades and waterfalls, then swing right away from the river and ascend (sign). The trail crosses several seasonal streams and, at 2.5 mi., turns left onto Dale Rd. (signs/arrows), a gravel country road. It passes several houses on the left and then, at 3.2 mi., turns left (north) onto the paved Mt. Israel Rd. (arrows). Follow this road 0.6 mi. to the little bridge that crosses the Bearcamp River and continue 100 yd. to the parking place at 3.9 mi.

Section 2: Mount Israel Road to NH 113

The western end of this section is located on Mt. Israel Rd., which turns right (north) from Sandwich Notch Rd. just northwest of Center Sandwich village; follow Mt. Israel Rd. about 1 mi. to a point about 100 yd. beyond the bridge over the Bearcamp River, where a logging road turns right (cars may be parked on the left here). The eastern end is on NH 113 about 2 mi. east of Center Sandwich village, about 100 yd. west of the crossroads where NH 113 meets Middle Rd. and Top of the World Rd. and turns fairly abruptly left (north). In the middle of this section the trail crosses Upper Rd., which leaves NH 113 on the north about 1 mi. east of Center Sandwich village; the trail crossing is about 1 mi. north of NH 113 at the junction with Plummer Mill Rd., and cars may be parked on Upper Rd. where the trail leaves east on a logging road.

From Mt. Israel Rd. 100 yd. north of the Bearcamp River bridge, the trail follows the logging road on the right (arrows/sign). This is the White Sylvania Trust land, which encompasses 530 acres near the banks of the Bearcamp River. Ascend gradually on the logging road, swing left at a clearing (right), cross a tributary brook, then descend gradually to a loading area in a clearing. Bear left here onto a trail where a skidder road surrounded by red boundary blazes leaves to the left. The trail passes through a wet area next to a beaver bog lying to the right, then skirts to the right of a recently logged area and swings left to run along the north bank of the Bearcamp River in a hemlock gorge. It crosses a tributary stream next to a small series of waterfalls, then crosses the river on flat rocks at 1.1 mi., bears left, and ascends away from the river. It swings right at a stone wall, then swings left, eventually merging with an old woods road along stone walls. At 1.4 mi., it turns left onto the gravel Elm Hill Rd. and descends (arrows/trail sign). At 1.8 mi., it turns right at a T intersection onto Plummer Mill Rd. (arrows) and descends along the Bearcamp River. It passes an old grist mill site with waterfalls and then a small electrical generator in the river to the left. At 2.4 mi. the trail crosses Upper Rd. at a T intersection.

The trail then enters the woods on a logging road, bears right up a small hill on a trail (trail guide right), and follows undulating grades in a hemlock forest past glacial erratics (right) and an open marsh (left). It crosses several small streams and stone walls, then at 3.4 mi. it swings right along the south bank of the Bearcamp River with views back to Mt. Israel (left). It passes several bird feeders, and bears right away from the river briefly before returning to the south bank near several small cascades and pools. It then bears right again along a long stone wall, passes several boundary stakes, and swings right onto an old woods road (double blazes) at 4.2 mi. Then it turns left onto a trail next to a stone wall, bears right at a small stream, merges left onto an old woods road, bears right at a fork, and reaches NH 113 on the north side of Ainger Hill at 4.7 mi.

Section 3: NH 113 to Bearcamp Pond

This section departs from the Bearcamp River to circle a huge marsh that lies between Middle Rd. and Bearcamp Pond. There are several fine views from Top of the World Rd. The western end of this section is on NH 113 about 2 mi. east of Center Sandwich village, about 100 yd. west of the crossroads where NH 113 meets Middle Rd. and Top of the World Rd. and turns fairly abruptly left (north). The eastern end is at the Bearcamp Pond Public Access (boat launch area), just off Bearcamp Pond Rd., which leaves NH 25 a short distance north of East Sandwich village. The central part of the section can be reached at a variety of points via Vittum Hill Rd., which leaves NH 25 at East Sandwich village.

From NH 113, follow an old logging road in a partially logged area (the trail sign is on the right). The trail turns right onto an old woods road, then bears right at a fork and passes through a partially cleared area, descending gradually through the woods. At 0.3 mi., it turns right (south) onto the gravel Top of the World Rd. and ascends gradually. There are fine views toward the Ossipee Mtns. and Bearcamp Pond to the left. The trail passes a white house on the right signed "Top of the World", then 0.3 mile beyond the house turns left onto a grassy road through a stone wall (arrows/sign). It descends gradually through a small clearing, bears right at a fork onto an old woods road, then bears left onto a trail at a double blaze. It crosses a brook on beaver dams and ascends gradually on an old woods road, passing several stone walls. At 1.6 mi. it turns right onto an old road, then takes another right onto a similar road through a stone wall (arrows). At 1.9 mi. it turns right onto Partridge Hill Rd. (arrows), then at 2.3 mi. turns left onto the paved Vittum Hill Rd. (arrows).

The trail now follows Vittum Hill Rd. to the east for about a mile with no trail markings. At 3.3 mi., just past the Vittum Hill Cemetery and parking area (right), the trail turns left onto the Vittum Hill Spur (signs) and descends on an old woods road marked with yellow circles. It bears right at a fork, turns left onto an old woods road, then turns right onto an old grassy road (arrows). It passes a stone wall (left), crosses a small stream, and bears right at a fork in a small logging clearing and loading area. It bears right in a partially logged area, turns left onto a dirt driveway (arrow), then turns right onto a trail along the south shore of Bearcamp Pond. This 90-acre pond contains extensive marshes and bogs on the northwest shore and is largely undeveloped except on the southern shore. This section of the trail ends at the parking lot for the public boat launch area at 4.0 mi.

Section 4: Bearcamp Pond to Hell's Gate

Caution: The first part of this section is the most challenging part of the trail. It involves fording the Bearcamp River and two mouths of the Cold River. These crossings may be dangerous or completely impassable in high water. There may be tree limbs and debris in the water that cannot always be seen from the river banks. *Do not attempt these crossings if you have any doubt as to their safety.* In addition, the mile of trail from the ford of the Bearcamp River to NH 113 is marked only with ribbons and may be difficult to follow. Allow plenty of extra time to navigate this part and return to the last marker if there is any doubt as to the location of the route.

The western end of this section is at the Bearcamp Pond Public Access (boat launch area) just off Bearcamp Pond Rd., which leaves NH 25 a short distance north of East Sandwich village. The eastern end of the section is at Bartlett Mill Bridge on NH 25 in South Tamworth, just north of the blinking light. In the middle of the section the trail crosses NH 113 at a bridge over the Bearcamp River located just north of the western junction of NH 113 with NH 25; parking is available beside the bridge.

The trail leaves the boat launch area, follows a path along the south shore of the pond, and bears right into the parking lot of the public beach. It then follows the dirt road leading out of the parking lot, and in about 100 yd. it turns left onto an unmarked gravel road. After another 0.2 mi., it turns right onto an old woods road opposite a small white house and ascends gradually, then crosses a brook on a bridge (trail sign on the right) near a beaver dam. After crossing a stagnant stream and passing through a logging clearing, it bears left into the woods on a trail (double blazes) and descends gradually, then swings right along the south bank of the Bearcamp River past several wet areas. At 1.0 mi. it swings right (double blaze) and runs across a wet area. At 1.7 mi. it fords the Bearcamp River. *Do not make this crossing if the water is high and the crossing dangerous—turn back to Bearcamp Pond.* On the far side of the river, the trail emerges from a path marked with ribbons to an open field with views of the Sandwich Range. Follow the ribbons along the southern edge of the open field. In 0.2 mi. from the Bearcamp River crossing, the trail fords the first mouth of the Cold River, then the deeper second mouth. It then turns right and follows the east bank of the Cold River south to ribbons near some old farm implements at the southwest corner of a hay field. The trail then swings left (east) and follows ribbons along the southern edge of the hay field near the north bank of the Bearcamp River. It enters a marsh (yellow ribbons) on a path along the river and emerges at a second hayfield, and continues east along its southern edge until the southeast corner is reached. The trail bears right into the brush along the north bank of the river onto a narrow tongue of land, then crosses a minor tributary brook on a fallen log. Bear right (south), then left (east) along the north bank of the river. At 2.7 mi., the trail passes under the NH 113 bridge at Perkins Farm, a 300-acre conservation property collectively managed by the Perkins family, the town of Tamworth, and the Community School.

The trail now heads east, following the southern edge of the field along the north bank of the river. It enters the brush on a path marked by ribbons, then follows a blazed trail into the woods and swings left back along the river. It crosses a brook that may be deep at times of high water, bears left away from the river, then turns right onto a grassy road where the Perkins Trail from Jackman Pond enters on the left at 3.3 mi. This grassy road returns to the river bank and passes riffles and pools, and also several marker signs. It soon narrows to a trail and bears left away from the river. The trail then swings right onto an old road and passes a stone wall in a white pine grove. It crosses an old bridge over a stagnant stream and enters the Hackett Hill conservation land (boundary marker on right), a 200-acre forest now owned and managed by the New Hampshire Fish and Game Department. The trail passes old stone walls and cellar holes, and ends at Bartlett Mill Bridge at 4.4 mi.

The large white house nearby was once the Barlett Mill School, named for the mill that harnessed the waterpower of the river. Below the bridge, the rocks narrow to form a gorge called Hell's Gate. Lumber from throughout the Bearcamp River Valley was stacked during the winter in the mill pond above the gorge, then in the spring it was driven down the river to the Saco River mills. Log drivers once rode logs through the gorge to break up logjams; today, kayakers run the gorge every spring.

Bearcamp River Trail (map 3:L7–L9)

Distances from Sandwich Notch Rd. (1200')

to Beede Falls (1200'): 0.1 mi., 5 min.

to Mead Wilderness Base Camp/Wentworth Trail (930'): 0.6 mi., 15 min.

to Cook Farm Rd. (891'): 0.9 mi., 30 min.

to Dale Rd. (850'): 2.5 mi., 1 hr. 15 min.

to Mt. Israel Rd. (787'): 3.2 mi., 1 hr. 35 min.

to Elm Hill Rd. (850'): 5.3 mi., 2 hr. 40 min.

to Plummer Mill Rd. (730'): 5.6 mi., 2 hr. 50 min.

to Upper Rd. (790'): 6.2 mi., 3 hr. 5 min.

to NH 113 on north side of Ainger Hill (680'): 8.6 mi., 4 hr. 20 min.

to Top of the World Rd. (770'): 8.9 mi., 4 hr. 30 min.

to Partridge Hill Rd. (750'): 10.5 mi., 5 hr. 15 min.

to Vittum Hill Rd. at junction with Partridge Hill Rd. (720'): 10.9 mi., 5 hr. 30 min.

to Vittum Hill Cemetery (720'): 11.9 mi., 5 hr. 55 min.

to Bearcamp Pond Public Access (600'): 12.6 mi., 6 hr. 20 min.

to ford of Bearcamp River (590'): 14.4 mi., 7 hr. 15 min.

to fords of Cold River (590'): 14.6 mi., 7 hr. 20 min.

to NH 113 at Perkins Farm near NH 25 (580'): 15.4 mi., 7 hr. 40 min.

to Perkins Trail (580'): 15.8 mi., 7 hr. 55 min.

to Bartlett Mill Bridge near Hell's Gate (550'): 16.9 mi., 8 hr. 30 min.

Mount Chocorua and the Eastern Sandwich Range

This section covers trails on Mts. Chocorua, Paugus, Passaconaway, and White-face, and on their subsidiary peaks and ridges. The region is bounded on the north by the Kancamagus Highway (NH 112), on the east by NH 16, on the south by NH 25, and on the west by Section 7 (Waterville Valley and Squam Lakes Region). This division places Mt. Tripyramid in Section 7 and Mt. Whiteface and the Sleeper Ridge in Section 8. At the boundary between Section 8 and Section 7, the only points of contact between trails are at the junction of the Mt. Tripyramid Trail (Section 7) with the Kate Sleeper Trail (Section 8), and at the junction of the Flat Mountain Pond Trail (Section 7) with the McCrillis Trail (Section 8). The entire section is covered by the AMC Crawford Notch–Sandwich Range map (map #3). The Chocorua Mountain Club (CMC), Wonalancet Outdoor Club (WODC), and the WMNF maintain most of the trails in this area. The CMC marks its trails with yellow paint and signs, while the WODC trails have blue paint and signs. The WODC publishes a contour map of the Sandwich Range Wilderness and the surrounding area, with short trail descriptions on the back, which covers most of Section 8 except for the east slopes of Mt. Chocorua; it can be obtained from the WODC, Wonalancet, NH 03897. The CMC publishes a contour map of the Chocorua-Paugus region (12th ed., 1994) that includes a peak-identifying panorama of the view from the summit of Chocorua; it can be obtained from the CMC, Chocorua, NH 03817.

GEOGRAPHY

The **Sandwich Range** and the jumbled collection of ridges that rise to the west compose a mass of mountains that extend about 30 mi. from Conway on the Saco River to Campton on the Pemigewasset, with summits just over 4000 ft. high rising abruptly about 3000 ft. from the lake country to the south. Although the Sandwich Range is not outstanding for its elevation—the North Peak of Mt.

Tripyramid, at 4140 ft., is its highest point—the mountains are nevertheless quite rugged, and their viewpoints offer interesting combinations of mountain, forest, and lake scenery.

Mt. Chocorua (3500 ft.), the picturesque rocky cone at the east end of the range, is reputedly one of the most frequently photographed mountains in the world—and certainly one of the most frequently ascended peaks in the White Mtns. It has a substantial network of trails; several trails are very heavily used, but it is usually possible to avoid crowds (until the summit is reached) by taking less popular trails. The Piper Trail, Champney Falls Trail, and Liberty Trail are probably the most popular. Confusion sometimes occurs from the fact that several trails are considered to extend all the way to the summit, although they converge below the summit, which is reached by only one path. Thus a given segment of trail may bear several names at once—at least according to trail signs—although in this guide one trail is usually considered to end where two merge, and only two trails (the Piper Trail and the Brook Trail) are described as reaching the summit. In descending from the summit, go 50 yd. southwest on the only marked path, down a small gully to the first junction. The trails on the open rocks are marked with paint, and junctions are signed with WMNF signs or paint, or both. Camping on the upper slopes of Chocorua—a Forest Protection Area—is severely restricted to prevent damage to the mountain's natural qualities.

Caution: The extensive areas of open ledge that make Chocorua so attractive also pose a very real danger. Many of the trails have ledgy sections that are dangerous when wet or icy, and the summit and upper ledges are severely exposed to lightning during electrical storms. Despite its comparatively modest elevation, Chocorua is one of the most dangerous peaks in the White Mtns. in a thunderstorm. The safety of any untreated water source in this heavily used area is very doubtful. Although Chocorua is relatively low compared to other major White Mtn. peaks, its trailheads are also located at low elevations, resulting in a substantial amount of elevation gain that makes Chocorua as strenuous a trip as many much higher peaks.

Three Sisters, which forms the northern ridge of Mt. Chocorua, is nearly as high and also has bare summits. **First Sister** (3354 ft.) is the highest of the three rocky knobs, and **Middle Sister** (3340 ft.) bears the remains of an old stone fire tower. **White Ledge** (2010 ft.) is a bluff just east of the Three Sisters, with a ledgy top from which there is a good view east. The rocky south shoulder of Chocorua is called **Bald Mtn.** (2140 ft.). On the northwest side of the mountain is **Champney Falls,** named for Benjamin Champney (1817–1907), pioneer White Mountain artist. These falls are beautiful when there is a good flow of water but meager in dry seasons.

Mt. Paugus (3198 ft.), a low but rugged and shaggy mountain once aptly called "Old Shag," was named by Lucy Larcom for the Pequawket chief who led the Abenaki forces at the battle of Lovewell's Pond. Because of its lumpy shape and scarred sides it has been given many different names; it may hold the record for having had the most different names—both common and unusual—of any peak in the White Mtns., including Bald Mtn., Moose Mtn., Ragged Mtn., Deer Mtn., Hunchback, Middle Mtn., and Frog Mtn. All trails end at an overgrown ledge 0.3 mi. south of the wooded true summit, which is not reached by any trail; good views can be obtained by descending a short distance down the west side of this ledge. **Paugus Pass** (2220 ft.) is the lowest pass on the ridge that connects Mt. Paugus with Mt. Passaconaway and the Wonalancet Range on the west.

Mt. Passaconaway (4043 ft.) is a graceful peak named for the great and legendary sachem of the Penacooks (his name is thought to mean "Child of the Bear") who ruled at the time the first Europeans settled in New England. The mountain is densely wooded, but there is a restricted view toward Mt. Whiteface from the true summit, and a ledge on the Walden Trail a short distance from the summit offers a fine outlook to the east and north. A side path diverges from the Walden Trail between the summit and the east outlook and descends steeply 0.3 mi. to the splendid, secluded north outlook. A major ridge extends southeast to Paugus Pass over the two subpeaks that give the mountain its characteristic step-like profile when viewed from the lake country to the south. The first subpeak bears the unofficial name of **Nanamocomuck Peak** (3340 ft.) after the eldest son of Passaconaway. **Square Ledge** (2620 ft.) is a bold, rocky promontory that is a northeast spur of Nanamocomuck Peak. From the farther subpeak, which is sometimes called **Mt. Hedgehog** (3140 ft.), the Wonalancet Range runs south, consisting of **Hibbard Mtn.** (2940 ft.) and **Mt. Wonalancet** (2780 ft.); both peaks are wooded but have good outlook ledges. Wonalancet is named for a Penacook sachem who was a son of Passaconaway and succeeded him as senior chieftain.

Another **Hedgehog Mtn.** (2532 ft.) is located north of Mt. Passaconaway. This small but rugged mountain rises between Downes and Oliverian brooks and commands fine views over the Swift River Valley and up to Passaconaway; the best views are from ledges near the summit and on the east shoulder. **Potash Mtn.** (2700 ft.) lies to the west of Hedgehog, between Downes and Sabbaday brooks. The summit is open and ledgy and affords excellent views of the surrounding mountains and valleys in all directions.

Mt. Whiteface (4020 ft.) doubtless received its name from the precipitous ledges south of its south summit. The true summit of the mountain is wooded, but the slightly lower south summit, 0.3 mi. south of the true summit, affords magnificent views from the bare ledge at the top of the precipices. Two lesser ridges run south on either side of the cliffs, while the backbone of the mountain runs north, then northeast, connecting it with Mt. Passaconaway. Sleeper Ridge on the northwest connects Whiteface to Mt. Tripyramid.

East of Mt. Whiteface lies the **Bowl,** a secluded valley encircled by the main ridge of Mt. Whiteface and the south ridge of Mt. Passaconaway. This area was never logged, due to the efforts of many local people, of whom Kate Sleeper Walden was probably the most active and influential. The representative of the Kennett lumber interests in negotiating the sale of this land to the WMNF in a virgin state was Louis Tainter, whose ashes rest in a crypt cut into the ledge at the south summit of Mt. Whiteface. The Bowl was preserved for many decades as a special natural and research area, and is now included within the Sandwich Range Wilderness.

West of Whiteface the range sprawls; one major ridge continues northwest over the high, rolling **Sleeper Ridge**—composed of **West Sleeper** (3881 ft.) and **East Sleeper** (3840 ft.)—to Tripyramid, then ends at **Livermore Pass,** the high notch (2900 ft.) between Tripyramid and Mt. Kancamagus that is crossed by the Livermore Trail. Though Sleeper Ridge could have been named quite aptly for the sleepy appearance of its two rounded, rather gently sloping domes, it is actually named for Katherine Sleeper Walden, a civic-minded local innkeeper whose efforts in trail-building (she founded the WODC), conservation, and public improvements were so energetic and pervasive that she earned the sobriquet of "matriarch of Wonalancet and the WODC." She is memorialized by two natural features (Sleeper Ridge and Mt. Katherine) and a trail (the Kate Sleeper Trail). The Walden Trail memorializes her husband, Arthur Walden, founder of the famous Chinook husky kennels in Wonalancet. West of the high Livermore Pass lies the mountain mass composed of peaks such as Kancamagus, Osceola, Scar Ridge, and Tecumseh; these have not been traditionally regarded as part of the Sandwich Range, although connected with it. Another major ridge runs southwest over Sandwich Dome and soon loses its definition as it descends across the Sandwich Notch Rd. to the Campton mountains and toward the Squam Range. Everything west of the Tripyramid–Sleeper Ridge col is covered in Section 7.

There are a number of public and quasi-public reservations in this region that offer the opportunity for pleasant walking; some have trails. Of particular note is **Hemenway State Forest,** where fine views of the Sandwich Range can be obtained from the fire tower on **Great Hill** (1300 ft.), which is reached by old roads that leave Great Hill Rd. at its junction with Hemenway Rd. There is also a network of short trails in this area maintained by the Tamworth Outing Club;

most of these trails are multi-use, primarily maintained for cross-country skiing. The area can be reached from Tamworth village at the eastern junction of NH 113 and NH 113A by taking the road that leads west from the crossroads and bearing right (northwest) onto Great Hill Rd.

Note: Confusion in finding trailheads on the southern side of the Sandwich Range sometimes results from the rather erratic behavior of NH 113 and NH 113A, the alternate routes between North Sandwich and Tamworth. Both roads change direction frequently, making directional designations almost meaningless, and NH 113 unites with and then diverges from NH 25 between its two junctions with NH 113A. It is therefore necessary to follow very carefully access directions for trailheads on the southeast slopes of the Sandwich Range—in particular, it is easy to end up on the wrong section of NH 113.

Whiteface Intervale Rd. leaves NH 113A about 3.0 mi. north of the western junction of NH 113 and NH 113A, where NH 113A bends from north-south to east-west. **Bennett St.** turns left from Whiteface Intervale Rd. 0.1 mi. from NH 113A, and continues straight past a junction at 1.7 mi., where it becomes rougher; it is gated at 2.2 mi. at a parking lot 0.2 east of Jose's (rhymes with "doses") bridge.

Ferncroft Rd. leaves NH 113A at Wonalancet village, at a right-angle turn in the main highway; at 0.5 mi. from NH 113A a gravel road (FR 337) turns right and reaches a parking area and kiosk in 0.1 mi. No parking is permitted on Ferncroft Rd. beyond this gravel road.

Fowler's Mill Rd. runs between NH 16 (at the bridge that crosses the south end of Chocorua Lake, about 1.5 mi. north of Chocorua village) and NH 113A (3.3 mi. north of the eastern junction of NH 113 and NH 113A in Tamworth, and just north of the bridge over Paugus Brook). **Paugus Mill Rd.** (FR 68) branches north (sign) from Fowler's Mill Rd. 1.2 mi. east of NH 113A, and runs to a parking area at 0.8 mi., beyond which the road is closed to vehicles.

CAMPING
Sandwich Range Wilderness

Wilderness regulations, intended to protect Wilderness resources and promote opportunities for challenge and solitude, prohibit use of motorized equipment or mechanical means of transportation of any sort. Camping and wood or charcoal fires are not allowed within 200 ft. of any trail except at designated campsites. Hiking and camping group size must be no larger than 10 people. Camping and fires are also prohibited above treeline (where trees are less than 8 ft. tall) except in winter, when camping is permitted above treeline in places where snow cover is at least two feet deep, but not on any frozen body of water. Many shelters have been removed, and the remaining ones will be dismantled when major maintenance is required; one should not count on using any of these shelters.

Forest Protection Areas

The WMNF has established a number of Forest Protection Areas (FPAs)—formerly known as Restricted Use Areas—where camping and wood or charcoal fires are prohibited throughout the year. The specific areas are under continual review, and areas are added to or subtracted from the list in order to provide the greatest amount of protection to areas subject to damage by excessive camping, while imposing the lowest level of restrictions possible. A general list of FPAs in this section follows, but since there are often major changes from year to year, one should obtain current information on FPAs from the WMNF.

(1) No camping is permitted above treeline (where trees are less than 8 ft. tall), except in winter, and then only in places where there is at least two feet of snow cover on the ground—but not on any frozen body of water. The point where the above-treeline restricted area begins is marked on most trails with small signs, but the absence of such signs should not be construed as proof of the legality of a site.

(2) No camping is permitted within a quarter-mile of any trailhead, picnic area, or any facility for overnight accommodation such as a hut, cabin, shelter, tentsite, or campground, except as designated at the facility itself. In the area covered by Section 8, camping is also forbidden within a quarter-mile of Champney Falls and at any point within the Mt. Chocorua Scenic Area, except at Jim Liberty Cabin (which may be locked, with reservations required) and Camp Penacook.

(3) No camping is permitted within 200 ft. of certain trails. In 1997, designated trails included the Champney Falls Trail from the edge of the Kancamagus Highway FPA to the edge of the Champney Falls FPA.

(4) No camping is permitted on WMNF land within a quarter-mile of certain roads (camping on private roadside land is illegal except by permission of the landowner). In 1997, these roads included the Kancamagus Highway.

Established Trailside Campsites

Camp Penacook (WMNF), located on a spur path off the Piper Trail on Mt. Chocorua, is an open shelter that accommodates six to eight, with a tent platform that also accommodates six to eight. There is water nearby.

Jim Liberty Cabin (WMNF) is located on a ledgy hump 0.5 mi. below the summit of Mt. Chocorua. The USFS intends to keep Jim Liberty Cabin locked and open to the public by reservation only and with a substantial fee, but the lock on the cabin has been repeatedly vandalized, so hikers interested in using the cabin should check with the WMNF Saco Ranger District office (603-447-5448) for its current status. The water source is scanty in dry weather.

Old Shag Camp (CMC) on Mt. Paugus has been removed.

Camp Rich (WODC) is on the southwest side of Mt. Passaconaway on the Dicey's Mill Trail at about 3500 ft. elevation. It is an open log shelter for eight. Wilderness policies will probably require its eventual removal.

Camp Shehadi (WODC) is an open shelter for six at the junction of the Rollins and Kate Sleeper trails, 0.1 mi. north of the south summit of Mt. Whiteface. The nearest reliable water is 0.8 mi. down the Downes Brook Trail. Wilderness policies will probably require its eventual removal, and at present it is in poor condition and probably unfit for human habitation.

Camp Heermance (WODC) is an open shelter accommodating six in a partially sheltered spot near the south summit of Mt. Whiteface, about 20 yd. north of an unreliable spring near the top of the Blueberry Ledge Trail. The nearest reliable water is 0.9 mi. down the Rollins and Kate Sleeper trails. The original shelter at this site was built in 1912. Wilderness policies will probably require its eventual removal, and at present it is in poor condition and probably unfit for human habitation.

Trails on or near Mount Chocorua

List of Trails	Map	Page
Champney Falls Trail	3:J9	321
White Ledge Loop Trail	3:J10	322
Carter Ledge Trail	3:J10–J9	323
Middle Sister Trail	3:J10–J9	323
Piper Trail	3:J10–J9	324
Nickerson Ledge Trail	3:J10	325
Weetamoo Trail	3:J10–J9	325
Hammond Trail	3:J10–J9	326

Trails between Mount Chocorua and Mount Paugus

Trails on Mount Paugus

Trails to Paugus Pass and Vicinity

Trails on Mount Passaconaway and Its Ridges

Trails on Mount Potash and Hedgehog Mountain

List of Trails	Map	Page
UNH Trail	3:J8	340
Mount Potash Trail	3:J8	341

Trails on Mount Whiteface and Vicinity

List of Trails	Map	Page
Rollins Trail	3:J8	341
Blueberry Ledge Trail	3:K8–J8	342
Blueberry Ledge Cutoff	3:K8	343
Tom Wiggin Trail	3:J8	344
McCrillis Trail	3:K8–J8	344
McCrillis Path	3:K8	345
Downes Brook Trail	3:J8	346
Kate Sleeper Trail	3:J7–J8	347
Shorter Paths in the Ferncroft Area	3:K8	348

THE TRAILS

Champney Falls Trail (WMNF)

This heavily used trail runs from the Kancamagus Highway, at a point 11.5 mi. from NH 16 in Conway, to the Piper Trail in the flat saddle between Chocorua and the Three Sisters. Champney Falls is attractive, particularly when there is a good flow of water, and the trail has moderate grades all the way.

Leaving the parking area, the trail soon crosses Twin Brook on a footbridge, turns right, passes the junction at 0.1 mi. where the Bolles Trail diverges right, and proceeds south with easy grades, mostly on an old logging road, to Champney Brook. There it swings right to avoid an abandoned section of trail along the brook. At 1.4 mi. a loop path 0.4 mi. long diverges left to Pitcher Falls and Champney Falls. *Caution:* Many of the ledges in the area around the falls are very slippery; there have been many serious accidents in this vicinity. The main trail passes a restricted outlook to the north, and the loop path rejoins it at 1.7 mi. The steady ascent continues. At 2.4 mi. the trail reaches the first of several switchbacks, and at 3.0 mi. the Middle Sister Cutoff diverges left toward Middle Sister.

Middle Sister Cutoff (WMNF). This short trail leads from the Champney Falls Trail to the col between Middle Sister and First Sister, giving access to the fine views from the old tower site on Middle Sister. Leaving the Champney Falls Trail, it follows an old road past an outlook ledge, then swings to the right onto open ledges and soon reaches the Middle Sister Trail; total distance: 0.3 mi. (15 min.).

Soon after this junction the Champney Falls Trail reaches the ledgy saddle—where there is an outlook on a side path to the right—then passes the junction on the left with the Middle Sister Trail, and in another 80 yd. ends at its junction with the Piper Trail, 0.6 mi. from the summit of Chocorua.

Champney Falls Trail (map 3:J9)

Distances from Kancamagus Highway (1260')

    to Champney Falls loop, lower end (1780'): 1.4 mi., 500 ft., 55 min.

    to Piper Trail (3200'): 3.2 mi., 1950 ft., 2 hr. 35 min.

    to Mt. Chocorua summit (3500') via Piper Trail: 3.8 mi. (6.1 km.), 2250 ft., 3 hr.

White Ledge Loop Trail (WMNF)

This loop trail to White Ledge has two entrance routes. The main access route is from White Ledge Campground; the alternative access route leaves NH 16 opposite Pine Knoll Camp, about 0.5 mi. northeast of White Ledge Campground, and follows an old town road 0.5 mi. to the east branch of the trail, reaching it at a point 0.6 mi. from the campground.

The main trail diverges right from the main campground road and reaches the loop junction at 0.3 mi. The loop is described here in a counter-clockwise direction. Taking the east branch to the right across a small brook, the trail runs past the junction with the alternative access route at 0.6 mi., then soon bears left in an open area and climbs steadily to the height-of-land east of the main bluff of White Ledge at 1.3 mi. The trail now descends gradually, and at 2.0 mi. it turns sharp left in an overgrown pasture and climbs moderately up the east end of White Ledge to the summit at 2.7 mi., where there is a good view east. The trail descends past an outlook to Mt. Chocorua, then turns sharp left at 3.7 mi. and reaches the loop junction at 4.1 mi.

White Ledge Loop Trail (map 3:J10)

Distances from White Ledge Campground (740')

    to loop junction (800'): 0.3 mi., 50 ft., 10 min.

to White Ledge summit (2010') via east branch: 2.7 mi., 1400 ft., 2 hr. 5 min.

to White Ledge summit (2010') via west branch: 1.7 mi., 1300 ft., 1 hr. 30 min.

for complete loop: 4.4 mi. (7.1 km.), 1400 ft., 2 hr. 55 min.

Carter Ledge Trail (WMNF)

This trail provides an attractive route to Middle Sister from White Ledge Campground or (via Nickerson Ledge Trail) from the Piper Trail. Carter Ledge, an interesting objective in its own right, is a fine open ledge with views of Chocorua and one of the three colonies of jack pine *(Pinus banksiana)* that exist in the White Mtns. The trailhead is located on the left branch of the campground road; park in the parking lot at the campground picnic area.

The trail diverges west from the left branch road 0.1 mi. south of the main fork. It climbs moderately to the long southeast ridge of Carter Ledge, passing the junction at 1.0 mi. where the Middle Sister Trail diverges to the right. The Carter Ledge Trail then continues to the junction with the Nickerson Ledge Trail, which enters on the left at 2.0 mi. Soon the Carter Ledge Trail ascends a steep, gravelly slope, turns right at an outlook to Mt. Chocorua, passes through the jack pine stand and reaches the summit of the ledge at 2.5 mi. It passes through a sag, then works its way up the ledgy slope of Third Sister—steeply at times, with ledges that can be dangerous in wet or icy conditions—and reaches the Middle Sister Trail 0.3 mi. northeast of Middle Sister.

Carter Ledge Trail (map 3:J10–J9)
Distances from White Ledge Campground (740')

to Middle Sister Trail, lower junction (1100'): 1.0 mi., 350 ft., 40 min.

to Nickerson Ledge Trail (1740'): 2.0 mi., 1000 ft., 1 hr. 30 min.

to Middle Sister Trail, upper junction (3240'): 3.7 mi. (6.0 km.), 2600 ft., 3 hr. 10 min.

Middle Sister Trail (WMNF)

This trail begins on the Carter Ledge Trail 1.1 mi. from the WMNF White Ledge Campground, climbs over the Three Sisters, and ends at the Champney Falls Trail in the saddle between the Sisters and Chocorua. It provides good views.

Leaving the Carter Ledge Trail, this trail ascends through mixed hardwoods and softwoods and crosses Hobbs Brook at 1.3 mi., then skirts an area severely damaged by the December 1980 windstorm. At 1.8 mi. it joins the former route of the trail and climbs more steeply to the col between the Three Sisters ridge and Blue Mtn. at 2.4 mi., where the trail turns sharp left and ascends the northeast spur of the Third Sister, with several good outlooks. At 3.3 mi. the Carter Ledge Trail enters on the left, and the Middle Sister Trail crosses the ledgy summit of Third Sister and a small dip beyond, then reaches the summit of the Middle Sister at 3.6 mi. The trail continues across ledges marked by paint, passes the Middle Sister Cutoff right, and continues ahead over First Sister to its terminus on the Champney Falls Trail. From here it is 80 yd. (left) to the Piper Trail, then 0.6 mi. to the summit of Mt. Chocorua.

Middle Sister Trail (map 3:J10–J9)

Distances from Carter Ledge Trail (1100')

  to Middle Sister summit (3340'): 3.6 mi., 2250 ft., 3 hr.

  to Champney Falls Trail (3200'): 4.1 mi. (6.6 km.), 2400 ft. (rev. 300 ft.), 3 hr. 20 min.

Piper Trail (WMNF)

This heavily used trail to Chocorua from NH 16, first blazed by Joshua Piper, begins behind Davies Campground and General Store. It is one of the most heavily used trails in the White Mountains. To reach the trailhead, pay the parking fee at the store ($2 for day parking or $3 for overnight in 1997), then drive in on the dirt road to the right (signs) for 0.2 mi. to the new parking area.

The trail, running first on a newly constructed section, enters the woods, swings right across a stream and follows it for 0.3 mi., then turns first sharp left, then right to join a woods road that is the old route of the trail. (The section of the old route leading back from here to NH 16 is not open to the public.) The trail follows the logging road across the WMNF boundary at 0.5 mi., where there is a trail register. The Weetamoo Trail diverges left at 0.6 mi., and the Nickerson Ledge Trail diverges right at 1.2 mi. After crossing Chocorua River (a small brook at this point) at 1.8 mi., the trail ascends moderately past a cleared outlook that affords a view up to Carter Ledge, then climbs up a series of switchbacks with stone steps and paving. At 2.8 mi. a spur path diverges left 0.2 mi. to Camp Penacook (open shelter, tent platform, water). The main trail turns sharp right at this junction and ascends, with more stone steps and paving, soon reaching open ledges with spectacular views to the north, east, and south. The Champney Falls Trail enters right at 3.6 mi., and in another 0.2 mi. the West Side Trail (part of the original Liberty Trail bridle path) enters on the right. The Piper Trail, marked with yellow paint, continues over open ledges to the junction with the Brook Trail, then swings left and climbs the rock gully to the summit.

Piper Trail (map 3:J10–J9)

Distances from new WMNF parking area off NH 16 (780')

 to Nickerson Ledge Trail (1320'): 1.2 mi., 550 ft., 55 min.

 to Chocorua River crossing (1540'): 1.8 mi., 750 ft., 1 hr. 15 min.

 to Camp Penacook spur trail (2500'): 2.8 mi., 1700 ft., 2 hr. 15 min.

 to Champney Falls Trail (3200'): 3.6 mi., 2400 ft., 3 hr.

 to Mt. Chocorua summit (3500'): 4.3 mi. (6.9 km.), 2700 ft., 3 hr. 30 min.

Nickerson Ledge Trail (WMNF)

This trail connects the Piper Trail with the Carter Ledge Trail and Middle Sister, making possible loop hikes that include the attractive ledges on the northeast part of the mountain. It leaves the Piper Trail 1.2 mi. from the parking lot off NH 16 and climbs rather steeply 0.2 mi. to Nickerson Ledge, which has a restricted view of the summit of Chocorua, then continues with a gradual ascent to the Carter Ledge Trail 2.0 mi. above White Ledge Campground.

Nickerson Ledge Trail (map 3:J10)

Distance from Piper Trail (1320')

 to Carter Ledge Trail (1740'): 0.8 mi. (1.3 km.), 400 ft., 35 min.

Weetamoo Trail (CMC)

This trail connects the lower part of the Piper Trail, 0.6 mi. from the parking lot off NH 16, with the Hammond Trail well up on Bald Mtn., and gives access to the open ledges of the south ridge of Chocorua from the Piper Trail.

 The trail diverges left from the Piper Trail and crosses Chocorua River at 0.4 mi., then leaves the river and runs through a logged area. It crosses a small brook (last sure water) at 1.0 mi., then passes an outlook to Chocorua and reaches Weetamoo Rock, an immense boulder, at 1.7 mi. The trail ends at the Hammond Trail, 2.0 mi. from the summit of Mt. Chocorua via the Hammond Trail, the Liberty Trail, and the Brook Trail.

Weetamoo Trail (map 3:J10–J9)

Distance from Piper Trail (960')

 to Hammond Trail (2100'): 1.9 mi., 1150 ft., 1 hr. 30 min.

Hammond Trail (CMC)

This trail provides a route up Bald Mtn., the ledgy south ridge of Mt. Chocorua. The trailhead is on Scott Rd., a dirt road (not plowed in winter) that leaves NH 16 on the left (west) directly opposite a large boulder, 3.0 mi. north of the junction with NH 113 in Chocorua village; parking is on the right 0.4 mi. from NH 16.

The trail leaves the parking area, crosses Stony Brook, passes the WMNF boundary, then recrosses Stony Brook. At 0.8 mi. the trail crosses a logging road, then climbs steadily to the crest of Bald Mtn. at 1.9 mi. It crosses a sag, then ascends along the ridge. At 2.1 mi. the Weetamoo Trail enters on the right, and the Hammond Trail passes over several humps to its end at the junction with the Liberty Trail, 1.1 mi. from the summit of Mt. Chocorua via the Liberty Trail and the Brook Trail.

Hammond Trail (map 3:J10–J9)

Distances from parking area on Scott Rd. (600')

  to Bald Mtn. (2140'): 1.9 mi., 1550 ft., 1 hr. 45 min.

  to Liberty Trail (2540'): 3.0 mi. (4.8 km.), 2000 ft., 2 hr. 30 min.

Liberty Trail (WMNF)

This is the easiest route to Chocorua from the southwest (and probably the easiest of all the routes on the mountain). It begins at the parking area just before the gate on Paugus Mill Rd. (FR 68). This is a very old path that was improved somewhat by James Liberty in 1887, and further developed as a toll bridle path by David Knowles and Newell Forrest in 1892. Knowles built the two-story Peak House in 1892, which was blown down in September 1915. The stone stable was rebuilt by the CMC in 1924 and named the Jim Liberty Shelter. This lasted until 1932, when the spring winds blew off the roof, and in 1934 the WMNF replaced it with an enclosed cabin with bunks. This cabin has been kept locked at times recently, and hikers should check with the Saco Ranger District office if they plan to use it.

The Liberty Trail follows a gated side road that branches right just before the gate on the main road (which continues to the Bolles and Brook trails), and ascends at a steady, moderate grade, mostly along the route of the former bridle path. It crosses Durrell Brook at 1.1 mi. and at 2.7 mi. it reaches the ridge top, where the Hammond Trail enters right. The Liberty Trail crosses a hump, descends into the sag beyond, then climbs to Jim Liberty Cabin at 3.3 mi., where a red-blazed side path leads right 0.1 mi. to a mediocre water source. The Liberty Trail swings to the left (west) at the foot of a ledge and follows the old bridle path, which was blasted out of the rock in many places. It circles around the southwest side of the cone, ascending moderately, and meets the Brook Trail on a ledge at 3.6 mi. The summit of Mt. Chocorua is 0.2 mi. farther via the Brook Trail; it can be avoided during bad weather by following the West Side Trail, which diverges to the left 35 yd. beyond the Brook Trail junction and runs north around the west side of the summit cone to the Piper Trail.

Liberty Trail (map 3:K9–J9)
Distances from Paugus Mill Rd. parking area (900')

> *to* Hammond Trail (2540'): 2.7 mi., 1650 ft., 2 hr. 10 min.

> *to* Jim Liberty Cabin (2980'): 3.3 mi., 2100 ft., 2 hr. 40 min.

> *to* Brook Trail (3200'): 3.6 mi., 2300 ft., 2 hr. 55 min.

> *to* Mt. Chocorua summit (3500') via Brook Trail: 3.9 mi. (6.2 km.), 2600 ft., 3 hr. 15 min.

West Side Trail (WMNF)

This trail runs from the Piper Trail 0.4 mi. north of the summit of Chocorua to the ledge where the Liberty and Brook trails join. It has easy grades and is well sheltered, and affords a route for avoiding the summit rocks in bad weather. It leaves the Piper Trail in a flat area north of the summit and circles the west side of the cone to the Brook Trail, 35 yd. above its junction with the Liberty Trail.

West Side Trail (map 3:J9)
Distance from Piper Trail (3200')

> *to* Brook Trail (3200'): 0.5 mi. (0.7 km.), 50 ft. (rev. 50 ft.), 15 min.

Brook Trail (CMC)

This trail runs from the parking area at the end of Paugus Mill Rd. (FR 68) to the summit of Chocorua. It was cut by the country people to avoid paying a toll on the Liberty Trail. High up, it ascends steep ledges with excellent views; it is much more scenic but also more difficult than the Liberty Trail, and potentially dangerous in wet or icy conditions. An excellent loop trip can be made by ascending the Brook Trail and descending the Liberty Trail.

From the parking area on Paugus Mill Rd., continue north on the gravel road (FR 68) past the gate. After 0.1 mi. the Bolles Trail diverges left, and at 0.4

mi., just before the bridge over Claybank Brook, the Brook Trail diverges to the right off the gravel road. It follows the south bank of the brook, passes a junction on the left with the Bickford Trail at 0.9 mi., and climbs well above the brook. At 1.8 mi. the trail returns to the brook at a tiny waterfall, then finally crosses it at 2.5 mi. The trail steepens, and the first ledge is reached at 3.0 mi.; just beyond here, the Bee Line Trail now enters from the left. From here the trail climbs the steep, open ledges of Farlow Ridge, where it is marked with cairns and yellow paint. At 3.4 mi. the Liberty Trail joins from the right on a ledge. In about 35 yd. from this junction the West Side Trail, a bad-weather summit bypass, turns left (north), and the Brook Trail climbs steeply east over the ledges, then swings left (northeast) to the junction where the Piper Trail enters left (sign). The two trails climb east to the summit through a small gully.

Brook Trail (map 3:K9–J9)

Distances from Paugus Mill Rd. parking area (900')

   to Bickford Trail (1140'): 0.9 mi., 250 ft., 35 min.

   to Claybank Brook crossing (1900'): 2.5 mi., 1000 ft., 1 hr. 45 min.

   to Bee Line Trail (2600'): 3.0 mi., 1700 ft., 2 hr. 20 min.

   to Liberty Trail (3200'): 3.4 mi., 2300 ft., 2 hr. 50 min.

   to Mt. Chocorua summit (3500'): 3.6 mi. (5.9 km.), 2600 ft., 3 hr. 5 min.

Bee Line Trail (CMC)

This trail runs from the Old Paugus Trail on the south ridge of Mt. Paugus to the Brook Trail on the upper west ledges of Mt. Chocorua, linking the two summits almost by a "bee line." It crosses the Bolles Trail well south of the height-of-land in the valley between the mountains, at a point 2.0 mi. north of the Paugus Mill Rd. parking area and 3.8 mi. south of the Champney Falls Trail parking area on the Kancamagus Highway (NH 112). The upper end of the Chocorua section of this trail is now located 0.4 mi. below its former upper terminus; the former section of the Bee Line Trail above this point has been abandoned due to erosion and poor footing that resulted from the trail's steepness. Although the trail was originally designed to provide a direct route between the two summits, nowadays it is most frequently used to ascend to or descend from one of the peaks rather than as a connector between them—that is, from the middle to either end rather than from one end to the other—so it will be described in that manner. Most of the Paugus branch is in the Sandwich Range Wilderness, and the upper part of the Chocorua branch is in the Mt. Chocorua Forest Protection Area.

Chocorua Branch. The trail leaves the Bolles Trail and ascends gradually on an old logging road along the bank of a small brook that originates high on the western slope of Chocorua. After crossing this brook at 0.7 mi. and 1.1 mi., the trail enters the Mt. Chocorua Forest Protection Area (signs). It ascends moderately away from the brook, becoming gradually steeper as it enters a mixed softwood forest. At 1.4 mi. the trail bears right off the former route and traverses the wooded slope, climbing moderately, until it reaches its junction with the Brook Trail at 1.7 mi., just above its lowest semi-open ledge. From here it is 0.4 mi. to the junction with the Liberty Trail and 0.6 mi. to the summit of Chocorua.

Paugus Branch. Leaving the Bolles Trail, the Bee Line Trail soon crosses Paugus Brook, enters the Sandwich Range Wilderness, and runs over a narrow ridge. At 0.2 mi. the Bee Line Cutoff departs left (southeast), providing a shortcut to Paugus Mill Rd. The Bee Line Trail crosses a small brook and climbs by increasingly steep grades up the side of the mountain, making some use of old lumber roads, to the Old Paugus Trail near the top of the ridge, 1.1 mi. from the Bolles Trail and 0.7 mi. below the junction with the Lawrence Trail on the ledge near the summit of Paugus.

Bee Line Trail (map 3:J9)

Distances from Bolles Trail (1300')

> *to* Brook Trail (2600') via Chocorua Branch: 1.7 mi. (2.7 km.), 1300 ft., 1 hr. 30 min.

> *to* Old Paugus Trail (2350') via Paugus Branch: 1.1 mi. (1.8 km.), 1100 ft., 1 hr. 5 min.

Distances from Paugus Mill Rd. parking area (900')

> *to* Mt. Chocorua summit (3500') via Bolles Trail, Bee Line Trail, and Brook Trail: 4.3 mi. (6.9 km.), 2600 ft., 3 hr. 25 min.

> *to* ledge near Mt. Paugus summit (3100') via Bolles Trail, Bee Line Trail, and Old Paugus Trail: 3.8 mi. (6.1 km.), 2250 ft., 3 hr.

Bee Line Cutoff (CMC)

This trail provides a shortcut to the Bee Line Trail to Mt. Paugus from the Paugus Mill Rd. parking area. It is almost entirely within the Sandwich Range Wilderness. It diverges northwest from the Bolles Trail 1.2 mi. from the parking area and follows an old lumber road. At 0.2 mi. it bears right, crosses a brook, and continues to the Bee Line Trail, 0.2 mi. west of the junction of the Bee Line and Bolles trails.

Bee Line Cutoff (map 3:J9)
Distance from Bolles Trail (1100')

   to Bee Line Trail (1300'): 0.6 mi. (1.0 km.), 200 ft., 25 min.

Bolles Trail (WMNF)

This trail connects the Paugus Mill Rd. (FR 68) parking lot with the Champney Falls Trail parking lot on the Kancamagus Highway, passing between Mt. Chocorua and Mt. Paugus and using old logging roads most of the way. It is named for Frank Bolles, who reopened a very old road approximately along the route of this trail in 1892 and called it the "Lost Trail." South of the height-of-land, the majority of the trail is in or near the Sandwich Range Wilderness.

   The Bolles Trail diverges from the Brook Trail (which here is the gravel logging road extension of Paugus Mill Rd.) 0.1 mi. north of the Paugus Mill Rd. parking lot. At 0.2 mi. it crosses Paugus Brook (may be difficult at high water), and at 0.5 mi. the Old Paugus Trail and Bickford Trail enter left. In 90 yd. the Bickford Trail diverges right. Soon the Bolles Trail passes the huge Paugus Mill sawdust pile (left), and at 1.1 mi. the Bee Line Cutoff diverges left. The Bolles Trail now crosses two branches of Paugus Brook on snowmobile bridges. At 2.0 mi. the Bee Line Trail crosses, and at 2.6 mi. the Bolles Trail recrosses Paugus Brook, turns right in an old logging camp site, and soon begins to climb more steeply through a sandy area to the height-of-land at 3.7 mi. The trail then descends steeply to Twin Brook, crosses it eleven times, and reaches the Champney Falls Trail 0.1 mi. south of its trailhead parking lot on the Kancamagus Highway.

Bolles Trail (map 3:J9)
Distances from Brook Trail (940')

   to Bickford Trail/Old Paugus Trail (1000'): 0.5 mi., 50 ft., 15 min.

   to Bee Line Trail (1300'): 1.9 mi., 350 ft., 1 hr. 10 min.

   to Kancamagus Highway (1260'): 5.7 mi. (9.2 km.), 1300 ft. (rev. 1000 ft.), 3 hr. 30 min.

Bickford Trail (WODC)

This trail runs from NH 113A 1.1 mi. east of Wonalancet to the lower part of the Brook Trail, offering a walking route from Wonalancet to the Old Paugus, Bolles, and Brook trails to Mt. Paugus and Mt. Chocorua. The trail's blue blazes must be followed with care due to lack of an obvious footway.

The trail leaves NH 113A and ascends easily on an old logging road, passes behind two camps, and descends easily to a field with a private home at 0.7 mi. Turning left at the horse corral, it re-enters the woods at the east edge of the field, soon enters the WMNF, climbs moderately to a ridge top, and descends on the other side. The Old Paugus Trail enters left 20 yd. west of Whitin Brook, and the two trails cross the brook and meet the Bolles Trail at 2.0 mi. The Bickford Trail turns left (north) on the Bolles Trail for 90 yd., then turns right (east), crosses Paugus Brook (may be difficult), and soon reaches a logging road (which can be followed to the right to the Paugus Mill Rd. parking area). The Bickford Trail turns left and follows the road for about 0.1 mi., then turns right (turns marked with arrows), descends easily, and crosses Claybank Brook to the Brook Trail, where the Bickford Trail ends.

Bickford Trail (map 3:K9–J9)

Distances from NH 113A (1170')

> *to* Bolles Trail (1000'): 2.0 mi., 500 ft. (rev. 700 ft.), 1 hr. 15 min.
>
> *to* Brook Trail (1140'): 2.7 mi. (4.3 km.), 650 ft., 1 hr. 40 min.

Old Paugus Trail (CMC)

This trail runs to the south knob of Mt. Paugus from the Bolles Trail 0.7 mi. from the Paugus Mill Rd. parking area. It is almost entirely within the Sandwich Range Wilderness. Portions of the trail are very steep and rough, with poor footing, and may be dangerous in wet or icy conditions.

This trail leaves the Bolles Trail along with the Bickford Trail and the two trails cross Whitin Brook together, then the Bickford Trail diverges left 20 yd. beyond the brook. The Old Paugus Trail continues along Whitin Brook, crosses it at 0.7 mi., then turns right at 1.0 mi. as the Whitin Brook Trail continues straight ahead along the brook. The trail now climbs steeply, passes a junction left with the Big Rock Cave Trail at 1.3 mi., climbs a steep gully, then swings right along the base of a rock face and climbs steadily through a spruce forest to the junction right with the Bee Line Trail at 2.1 mi. It ascends sharply, passes an outlook on the right (sign), then eases up and passes the site of the former Old Shag Camp. Soon it crosses a small brook and climbs to the south knob. Here the Old Paugus Trail ends and the Lawrence Trail continues ahead. An interesting view can be obtained by descending the southwest side of the ledge a short distance.

Old Paugus Trail (map 3:J9)

Distances from Bolles Trail (1000')

to Bee Line Trail (2350'): 2.1 mi., 1350 ft., 1 hr. 45 min.

to Lawrence Trail (3100'): 2.8 mi. (4.5 km.), 2150 ft., 2 hr. 30 min.

Whitin Brook Trail (CMC)

This trail runs from the Old Paugus Trail to the Cabin Trail and gives access to points in the vicinity of Paugus Pass from the Paugus Mill Rd. parking area. It must be followed with care, particularly at the crossings of Whitin Brook. It is almost entirely within the Sandwich Range Wilderness.

The trail continues along Whitin Brook where the Old Paugus Trail turns right, upslope, 1.0 mi. above the junction of the Old Paugus and Bolles trails. In 0.2 mi. the Big Rock Cave Trail crosses, then the Whitin Brook Trail crosses the brook three times. After the last crossing, at 0.7 mi., the trail swings left away from the brook and climbs through spruce woods to the Cabin Trail, 0.4 mi. south of its junction with the Lawrence Trail.

Whitin Brook Trail (map 3:J9–J8)

Distance from Old Paugus Trail (1550')

to Cabin Trail (2150'): 1.6 mi. (2.5 km.), 600 ft., 1 hr. 5 min.

Big Rock Cave Trail (WODC)

This trail runs from the Cabin Trail 0.3 mi. from NH 113A over the flat ridge of Mt. Mexico to the Whitin Brook and Old Paugus trails. It provides easy access to Big Rock Cave, an interesting boulder cave that invites exploration.

Diverging right from the Cabin Trail, the Big Rock Cave Trail ascends moderately on a recently used logging road that fades away to a trail, reaching the very flat summit of Mt. Mexico at 1.1 mi. and entering the Sandwich Range Wilderness. From here it descends moderately, then steeply, and passes Big Rock Cave (right) at 1.6 mi. It then crosses Whitin Brook (may be difficult at high water) and the Whitin Brook Trail at 1.7 mi., and climbs to its end at the Old Paugus Trail.

Big Rock Cave Trail (map 3:K8–J9)

Distances from Cabin Trail (1200')

to Big Rock Cave (1700'): 1.6 mi., 800 ft. (rev. 300 ft.), 1 hr. 10 min.

to Old Paugus Trail (1720'): 2.1 mi. (3.4 km.), 900 ft. (rev. 100 ft.), 1 hr. 30 min.

Cabin Trail (WODC)

This trail runs from NH 113A 0.5 mi. east of Wonalancet to the Lawrence Trail 0.3 mi. east of Paugus Pass. It starts on a driveway and passes a house, and at 0.3 mi. the Big Rock Cave Trail diverges right. The Cabin Trail ascends easily on a logging road over several small brooks, passing into the Sandwich Range Wilderness just before reaching the height-of-land at 2.2 mi., where the Whitin Brook Trail enters from the right. The Cabin Trail stays to the east side of Whitin Ridge, passes an outlook to Mt. Paugus, and ends at the Lawrence Trail.

Cabin Trail (map 3:K8–J8)

Distances from NH 113A (1060')

 to Whitin Brook Trail (2150'): 2.2 mi., 1100 ft., 1 hr. 40 min.

 to Lawrence Trail (2260'): 2.7 mi. (4.3 km.), 1300 ft. (rev. 100 ft.), 2 hr.

Lawrence Trail (WODC)

This trail runs from the junction of the Old Mast Road and the Walden and Square Ledge trails, 2.0 mi. from the Ferncroft Rd. parking area (via the Old Mast Road), to the junction with the Old Paugus Trail on the south knob of Mt. Paugus. Sections of it are extremely steep and rough, with poor footing. It is entirely within the Sandwich Range Wilderness.

 The trail leaves the multiple junction at the north end of the Old Mast Road and descends slightly into Paugus Pass at 0.3 mi., where it is joined on the left (north) by the Oliverian Brook Trail from the Kancamagus Highway and on the right (south) by the Kelley Trail from Ferncroft. The Lawrence Trail climbs to a knob at 0.6 mi. where the Cabin Trail enters from the right. The Lawrence Trail next descends to the southeast side of the ridge at the base of the Overhang and passes along the face of high, wooded cliffs, then ascends a very steep and rough slope to an outlook to Mt. Paugus at 0.9 mi. The trail then descends steeply into a hollow and crosses two small brooks. It climbs steeply again, crosses another brook, and continues at a moderate grade to the south knob of Mt. Paugus, where the Old Paugus Trail continues ahead. An interesting view can be obtained by descending the southwest side of the ledge a short distance.

Lawrence Trail (map 3:J8–J9)

Distance from Old Mast Road (2350')

 to Old Paugus Trail (3100'): 2.1 mi. (3.4 km.), 1100 ft. (rev. 350 ft.), 1 hr. 35 min.

Kelley Trail (WODC)

This trail runs from the Ferncroft Rd. parking area through an interesting ravine to a junction with the Lawrence and Oliverian Brook trails at Paugus Pass. The upper part of the trail is rough, with poor footing and numerous slippery rocks.

For a short time during the retreat of the last continental glacier this ravine was the outlet of glacial Lake Albany, which occupied the Albany Intervale, the broad valley to the north of the eastern Sandwich Range. This lake was contained by an ice dam at the east end, and until enough ice had melted from the ice dam to allow the melt-water to pass out by the present route of the Swift River, the water was forced through Paugus Pass and down this ravine in a torrential stream, which left evidence of significant carving by large and powerful waterfalls that the present small stream could not possibly have caused.

The trail leaves the Ferncroft Rd. parking area and follows a gated gravel logging road (FR 337), coinciding with the Old Mast Road and bearing left at a fork where the Gordon Path follows the road that runs straight ahead. After passing the junction with Wonalancet Range Trail on the left at 0.1 mi., the trails cross Spring Brook on a wooden bridge, and at 0.3 mi. the Kelley Trail turns off the Old Mast Road to the right and follows a woods road to a grassy logging road (FR 337) at 0.5 mi. Here the trail turns right and descends along this road 0.1 mi. to meet its former route at a culvert, where it turns left and ascends along the brook. Soon the trail begins to climb above the brook, then returns to the brook at the top of a small cascade. It now crosses the brook (or its dry bed) five times, then climbs steeply out of a small box ravine—one of the remnants of the outflow of glacial Lake Albany—and soon reaches Paugus Pass, just inside the Sandwich Range Wilderness.

Kelley Trail (map 3:K8–J8)

Distance from Ferncroft Rd. parking area (1140')

> *to* Lawrence Trail and Oliverian Brook Trail (2220'): 2.3 mi. (3.7 km.),
>   1100 ft., 1 hr. 40 min.

Oliverian Brook Trail (WMNF)

This trail runs from the Kancamagus Highway to the Lawrence and Kelley trails at Paugus Pass. It begins at a new parking lot 0.1 mi. in from the Kancamagus Highway on a gravel road that begins on the south side of the highway 1.0 mi. west of the Bear Notch Rd. intersection. Much of the trail, particularly south of the Passaconaway Cutoff, is wet, though recent relocations have improved the situation. The upper part of the trail is in the Sandwich Range Wilderness.

The trail follows the gravel road beyond the gate for 0.1 mi., turns sharp left on a cross-country ski trail that it follows for another 0.1 mi., then turns sharp right on the old route of the trail. It crosses an old railroad bed and a recent logging road, then joins an old railroad grade along the west side of Oliverian Brook and follows it for nearly 0.5 mi. At 1.1 mi. it turns left off the railroad grade, and at 1.9 mi. the Passaconaway Cutoff diverges right (southwest). The Oliverian Brook Trail continues south and crosses a major tributary at 2.2 mi., then the main brook at 2.7 mi., where it enters the Sandwich Range Wilderness. The trail now follows a relocated section on higher ground away from the brook to the east, then descends slightly to reach the junction with the Square Ledge Branch Trail, which leaves on the right and immediately crosses Oliverian Brook at 3.3 mi. The trail then rejoins the original route, crosses Oliverian Brook on a bridge, and continues to ascend along the brook to the multiple trail junction in Paugus Pass.

Oliverian Brook Trail (map 3:J8)

Distances from Kancamagus Highway (1240')

to Passaconaway Cutoff (1500'): 1.9 mi., 250 ft., 1 hr. 5 min.

to Square Ledge Branch Trail (1840'): 3.3 mi., 600 ft., 1 hr. 55 min.

to Paugus Pass (2220'): 4.4 mi. (7.1 km.), 1000 ft., 2 hr. 40 min.

Old Mast Road (WODC)

This trail, which has easy grades and good footing throughout, runs from the Ferncroft Rd. parking area to the junction with the Walden, Square Ledge, and Lawrence trails 0.3 mi. west of Paugus Pass. The original road was reputedly built for hauling out the tallest timbers as masts for the British navy.

Leaving the parking area along with the Kelley Trail, the Old Mast Road follows the left-hand road at the first fork, where the Gordon Path follows the road that continues straight ahead. At 0.1 mi. the Wonalancet Range Trail diverges left, just before the bridge over Spring Brook, and at 0.3 mi. the Kelley Trail diverges right. Soon the Old Mast Road passes the WMNF boundary, then at 0.9 mi. it crosses an overgrown logging road and soon enters another old road and follows it for 0.1 mi. The trail continues to climb, then levels, passes to the right of a small brook, and ends at the multiple trail junction, which lies just inside the Sandwich Range Wilderness.

Old Mast Road (map 3:K8–J8)
Distance from Ferncroft parking area (1140')

> *to* Lawrence Trail/Walden Trail/Square Ledge Trail (2350'): 2.0 mi. (3.2 km.), 1200 ft., 1 hr. 35 min.

Dicey's Mill Trail (WODC)

This trail ascends Mt. Passaconaway from the Ferncroft Rd. parking area, with moderate grades and good footing. It was the first trail to be built on the mountain. Most of it is in the Sandwich Range Wilderness.

From the parking area, return to Ferncroft Rd. and turn right, following the gravel road past Squirrel Bridge, where the Blueberry Ledge Trail turns left. Pass a gate (not intended to keep out hikers) and a house in a large clearing, and continue on the road, which becomes a logging road as it enters the woods. About 40 yd. before the trail enters the WMNF and Sandwich Range Wilderness at 0.8 mi., a marked path left crosses Wonalancet River to the Blueberry Ledge Cutoff on the opposite bank. Soon the trail swings right and steepens, then the grade becomes easy again and continues to the junction on the left with the Tom Wiggin Trail at 1.9 mi. At 2.3 mi. the Dicey's Mill Trail crosses the river at the site of Dicey's Mill—there are some remains of the old mill hidden in the woods nearby. Across the stream the trail passes a large boulder and begins a long ascent, angling up the side of a ridge, following an old logging road at a moderate grade through hardwoods with occasional glimpses of the steep-sided Wonalancet Range rising on the opposite side of the valley. At the ridge top, at 3.7 mi., the Rollins Trail from Mt. Whiteface enters on the left. The Dicey's Mill Trail then climbs through a rough, wet section, crosses a small brook, and reaches the junction at 3.9 mi. where the East Loop bears right.

East Loop. This very short trail begins on the Dicey's Mill Trail near the small brook just below Camp Rich, and runs nearly level for 0.2 mi. (5 min.) until it ends with a short, sharp descent to the Walden Trail at the point where that trail turns right at the base of its steep climb to the summit of Mt. Passaconaway. It is entirely within the Sandwich Range Wilderness. Signs have often been missing in the past, and without them its junction with the Walden Trail may escape notice.

From the East Loop junction the Dicey's Mill Trail bears left, passes Camp Rich (25 yd. left on a side trail), and climbs via wide switchbacks, steeply at times, to meet the Walden Trail. The summit and south outlook are 40 yd. right on a spur path, while the Walden Trail leads ahead 90 yd. to the east outlook.

Dicey's Mill Trail (map 3:K8–J8)

Distances from Ferncroft Rd. parking area (1140')

> *to* Tom Wiggin Trail (1950'): 1.9 mi., 850 ft., 1 hr. 25 min.
>
> *to* Rollins Trail (3300'): 3.7 mi., 2200 ft., 2 hr. 55 min.
>
> *to* Mt. Passaconaway summit (4043'): 4.6 mi. (7.3 km.), 2950 ft., 3 hr. 45 min.

Walden Trail (WODC)

This trail ascends Mt. Passaconaway from the junction of the Old Mast Road and the Square Ledge and Lawrence trails via the southeast ridge. It is a more interesting but longer and rougher route to Mt. Passaconaway from Ferncroft Rd. (via the Old Mast Road) than the direct Dicey's Mill Trail. It is entirely within the Sandwich Range Wilderness. It was named for Arthur Walden, founder of the Chinook Kennels in Wonalancet and a widely known handler and breeder of husky sled dogs.

The trail runs northwest from the Old Mast Road up a very steep slope with poor footing, where much work has been done—and much more is planned—to rectify the erosion problems created by the steep grade. At the top of the shoulder the grade eases and the trail crosses a minor knob and a sag, then climbs again and passes a side path that leads right 20 yd. to an outlook to the east and northeast, including Mts. Paugus and Chocorua. At 0.7 mi. it passes a side trail to the left (south) that leads about 100 yd. to a fine viewpoint to the south. Within a short distance after this spur path, the main trail passes just to the south of the large boulder that is the true summit of Mt. Hedgehog, and at 0.9 mi. the Wonalancet Range Trail enters left. The Walden Trail now descends steeply past an outlook to Mt. Washington to a col, follows along a brook bed (possible water) for 50 yd., then climbs very steeply again over the next subpeak, locally called Nanamocomuck Peak in honor of the eldest son of Passaconaway. It then descends easily to a col, then climbs gradually to the junction right with the Square Ledge Trail at 2.1 mi. The trail now starts to angle upward around the south face of the mountain, and at 2.2 mi. the East Loop continues straight where the Walden Trail swings right and climbs steeply to a south outlook, then reaches the excellent east outlook. The junction with the Dicey's Mill Trail is 90 yd. beyond the outlook, and the true summit is 40 yd. left from that junction. Between the east outlook and the Dicey's Mill Trail a side path descends right 0.3 mi. to a fine north outlook.

Walden Trail (map 3:J8)
Distances from Old Mast Road (2350')

   to Wonalancet Range Trail (3100'): 0.9 mi., 800 ft., 50 min.

   to Square Ledge Trail (3300'): 2.1 mi., 1350 ft. (rev. 350 ft.), 1 hr. 45 min.

   to Mt. Passaconaway summit (4043'): 2.8 mi. (4.5 km.), 2100 ft., 2 hr. 25 min.

Wonalancet Range Trail (WODC)

This trail ascends from the Old Mast Road, 0.1 mi. from the Ferncroft Rd. parking area, over the Wonalancet Range to the Walden Trail 0.2 mi. west of Mt. Hedgehog. There are good views from ledges on the way, and the trail offers an attractive but significantly longer and rougher alternative to the Dicey's Mill Trail, the most direct route to Mt. Passaconaway from Ferncroft. Most of this trail is within the Sandwich Range Wilderness.

   The trail diverges left from the Old Mast Road just before the bridge over Spring Brook, and crosses a logging road on a steep bank, entering the Sandwich Range Wilderness. It runs through a flat area, then passes a logged area, crossing an old logging road at 0.7 mi. At 1.4 mi. it passes a shortcut trail that climbs 0.4 mi. to rejoin the main trail 0.4 mi. north of the summit of Mt. Wonalancet, avoiding ledges that provide good views but are slippery when wet or icy. The main trail turns left and starts to climb steeply, soon crossing a fine outlook ledge, then swings around to the south edge of Mt. Wonalancet and makes a hairpin turn north to pass over the flat summit at 1.8 mi. The trail passes the upper end of the shortcut in a sag at 2.2 mi., then climbs past a short spur on the right, which leads to an outlook to the south, and continues to ascend past an outlook to the west to the inconsequential summit of Mt. Hibbard at 2.7 mi. The trail continues to ascend moderately, then descends slightly to the junction with the Walden Trail.

Wonalancet Range Trail (map 3:K8–J8)
Distances from Old Mast Road (1140')

   to Mt. Wonalancet summit (2780'): 1.8 mi., 1650 ft., 1 hr. 45 min.

   to Walden Trail (3100'): 3.2 mi. (5.1 km.), 2150 ft. (rev. 200 ft.), 2 hr. 40 min.

Passaconaway Cutoff (WMNF)

This trail provides the shortest route to Mt. Passaconaway from the north, running from the Oliverian Brook Trail, 1.9 mi. from its parking lot off the Kancamagus Highway, to the Square Ledge Trail (and thence to the summit via the

Walden Trail). Leaving the Oliverian Brook Trail, the cutoff follows an old logging road, crosses a brook at 0.5 mi., then runs above the brook to the junction with the Square Ledge Trail west of Square Ledge.

Passaconaway Cutoff (map 3:J8)

Distance from Oliverian Brook Trail (1500')

   to Square Ledge Trail (2550'): 1.7 mi. (2.8 km.), 1050 ft., 1 hr. 25 min.

Distance from Kancamagus Highway (1240')

   to Mt. Passaconaway summit (4043') via Oliverian Brook, Square Ledge, and Walden trails: 5.1 mi. (8.2 km.), 2800 ft., 3 hr. 55 min.

Square Ledge Trail (WODC)

This trail begins at the junction of the Old Mast Road and the Walden and Lawrence trails, climbs over Square Ledge, and ascends to the Walden Trail just below the summit cone of Mt. Passaconaway. It is entirely within the Sandwich Range Wilderness. In some recent years peregrine falcons have nested on the cliff of Square Ledge, so access to the principal Square Ledge viewpoint may be restricted during the nesting season (April 1 to August 1).

From the junction at its southern end, it descends from the height-of-land, crossing two small brooks, and at 1.1 mi., just before the second brook, the Square Ledge Branch Trail diverges right (east) to join the Oliverian Brook Trail. A short distance farther, the main trail makes a sharp turn left (west) to ascend the ledge. It bears east for a short distance, then climbs very steeply to the shoulder. At 1.5 mi., at a sharp left turn, a spur leads right 20 yd. to Square Ledge outlook, where there is a fine view across the valley. Leaving the ledge, the trail ascends to the wooded summit of the knob above the ledge. Near this summit a short side path leads left to views of Mt. Passaconaway and the Paugus Pass area. The main trail descends from this knob to the junction with the Passaconaway Cutoff on the right at 2.1 mi. Here the Square Ledge Trail turns sharp left, crosses a dip, passes through an old logging camp site, and crosses a small slide. It then becomes steep as it climbs to the Walden Trail.

Square Ledge Trail (map 3:J8)

Distances from Old Mast Road/Lawrence Trail/Walden Trail (2350')

   to Square Ledge (2550'): 1.5 mi., 750 ft. (rev. 550 ft.), 1 hr. 10 min.

   to Passaconaway Cutoff (2550'): 2.1 mi., 850 ft. (rev. 100 ft.), 1 hr. 30 min.

   to Walden Trail (3300'): 2.8 mi. (4.2 km.), 1600 ft., 2 hr. 10 min.

Square Ledge Branch Trail (WMNF)

This short trail begins on the Oliverian Brook Trail 3.3 mi. from the Kancamagus Highway, immediately crosses Oliverian Brook, and runs to the Square Ledge Trail below the steep section that ascends the ledge. It is most frequently used to make a loop over Square Ledge from the Kancamagus Highway.

Square Ledge Branch Trail (map 3:J8)

Distance from Oliverian Brook Trail (1840')

   to Square Ledge Trail (2000'): 0.5 mi. (0.8 km.), 150 ft., 20 min.

UNH Trail (WMNF)

This loop trail to the ledges of Hedgehog Mtn. offers fine views from several viewpoints for a modest effort. It begins at the new Downes Brook Trail parking lot, at the end of a gravel road that leaves the south side of the Kancamagus Highway opposite the WMNF Passaconaway Campground. It was named for the University of New Hampshire Forestry Camp, formerly located nearby.

   The trail leaves the Downes Brook Trail on the left 60 yd. from the edge of the parking lot and follows an old railroad grade 0.2 mi. to the loop junction; here the west branch of the loop turns right uphill, while the east branch continues straight on the old railroad grade. From this point the loop will be described in the clockwise direction (east branch to summit, then west branch back), although the loop is equally good in the opposite direction.

   From the loop junction, the east branch continues on the railroad grade, then bears off it on the right at 0.4 mi. and follows a logging road, climbing moderately. It crosses a small brook at 1.6 mi. from the parking lot, shortly swings left to a view north and east, then bears right to reach the east ledges at 2.0 mi., where there are fine views south and east. The trail then runs along the top of the cliffs on the south face and enters the woods under the steep, ledgy south side of the main peak. It then bears gradually toward the north onto the west slope of the main peak of Hedgehog Mtn., which it climbs in a short series of switchbacks, reaching the summit at 2.9 mi. The trail then descends steadily and makes a left turn at 3.7 mi., where a side path leads 60 yd. right to Allen's Ledge. Here the "lower perch" viewpoint offers a wide, unrestricted view to the east and northeast. The main trail descends to a logging road, turns right on it, and follows it to the loop junction.

UNH Trail (map 3:J8)

Distances from parking lot off Kancamagus Highway (1250')

   to east ledges (2300'): 2.0 mi., 1100 ft., 1 hr. 35 min.

   to Hedgehog Mtn. summit (2532'): 2.9 mi., 1450 ft., 2 hr. 10 min.

   for complete loop: 4.8 mi. (7.7 km.), 1450 ft., 3 hr. 10 min.

Mount Potash Trail (WMNF)

This trail ascends to the open ledges of Potash Mtn., providing excellent views for relatively little effort. It begins on Downes Brook Trail, 0.3 mi. from the new parking lot on the road that leaves the Kancamagus Highway almost directly opposite the entrance to the Passaconaway Campground.

The trail turns sharp right off the Downes Brook Trail and heads generally southwest. After crossing Downes Brook (may be difficult) at 0.1 mi., the trail turns sharp left and soon crosses a gravel logging road. It enters a beautiful hemlock forest, and at 0.9 mi. it turns sharp left and climbs, swinging left off the old route of the trail at 1.2 mi., then swinging right to rejoin the old route, which it now follows to the left. It crosses a southeast outlook and ascends moderately on scattered ledges, then at 1.6 mi. leaves the old route again and angles up the east side of the mountain, circling clockwise around the cone to avoid the steepest ledges while affording excellent views up the valley of Downes Brook. The trail finally gains the summit from the south.

Mount Potash Trail (map 3:J8)

Distance from Downes Brook Trail (1300')

   to Potash Mtn. summit (2700'): 1.9 mi. (3.1 km.), 1400 ft., 1 hr. 40 min.

Rollins Trail (WODC)

This trail runs along the high ridge that connects Mt. Whiteface to Mt. Passaconaway. It begins at a junction with the Blueberry Ledge and McCrillis trails on the open ledges of the south knob of Mt. Whiteface and ends on the Dicey's Mill Trail 0.2 mi. below Camp Rich. On the ridge of Mt. Whiteface some sections are steep and rough. It is entirely within the Sandwich Range Wilderness.

Leaving the south ledges, the Rollins Trail passes over a wooded ledge with a glimpse ahead to the true summit, then descends sharply into the steep, narrow col between the true summit and the open south summit of Whiteface, passing the junction on the left at 0.1 mi. with the Kate Sleeper Trail at Camp Shehadi (which is expected to be removed in the near future). From this col it climbs north rather steeply, then runs along the ridgecrest to the true summit (no marking) of Mt. Whiteface at 0.3 mi. It continues along the narrow ridge, with outlooks to the east across the Bowl, descending gradually with occasional steep pitches to the deep pass between Whiteface and Passaconaway. The trail then angles slightly upward around the south face of Passaconaway to meet the Dicey's Mill Trail.

Rollins Trail (map 3:J8)

Distance from Blueberry Ledge Trail/McCrillis Trail junction (3990')

   to Dicey's Mill Trail (3300'): 2.5 mi. (4.0 km.), 200 ft. (rev. 900 ft.), 1 hr. 20 min.

Blueberry Ledge Trail (WODC)

This trail, which was opened in 1899, ascends Mt. Whiteface from the Ferncroft Rd. parking area, ending at a junction with the McCrillis and Rollins trails on the wide ledges of the lower south summit. The trail is very scenic, but the upper part is steep and requires some rock scrambling. Though rock steps have been drilled out in the ledges at some difficult spots, the wooden steps that were also installed on the steepest ledge on this trail have been removed. This trail is still one of the more challenging climbs in the White Mtns. It is particularly difficult on the descent, and even more difficult when wet, and dangerous in icy conditions. Most of the trail is within the Sandwich Range Wilderness.

From the parking area, return to Ferncroft Rd. and follow it to Squirrel Bridge at 0.3 mi., where the Dicey's Mill Trail continues straight ahead. The Blueberry Ledge Trail turns left across the bridge and follows a private gravel road, avoiding driveways, then diverges left into the woods where the road curves right to the last house. Here, at 0.5 mi., the Pasture Path to Mt. Katherine leaves left. In 0.1 mi. the trail joins an old road, and soon the Blueberry Ledge Cutoff diverges right to follow the bank of Wonalancet River. The trail crosses into the WMNF and the Sandwich Range Wilderness, and at 0.9 mi. it continues straight where the McCrillis Path to Whiteface Intervale Rd.—not to be confused with the McCrillis Trail to Mt. Whiteface—follows the old road sharp left. The Blueberry Ledge Trail now passes through a flat area, then ascends moderately, At 1.6 mi. reaches the bottom of the ledges (where views are very limited) and climbs to the top of the ledges, where there is a view of the Ossipee Range. The Blueberry Ledge Cutoff rejoins on the right at a large cairn at 2.0 mi., and the Blueberry Ledge Trail re-enters the woods.

The trail climbs gently through open hardwoods, then rises steeply past Wonalancet Outlook to the top of the ridge. It drops slightly into a hollow, then ascends slightly to a junction with the Tom Wiggin Trail on the right at 3.2 mi. Now the trail climbs moderately, then swings sharp right at an outlook at 3.6 mi., where it abruptly approaches the edge of a steep cliff and may be dangerous if slippery. Just beyond here it climbs a steep ledge, then continues to scramble up the steep, rough, rocky ridge, with several excellent viewpoints. At the top of the ridge it passes a spur path leading to the right to Camp Heermance. The McCrillis Trail enters from the left, just north of the ledges of the lower south summit; here the Rollins Trail continues north to the true summit of Mt. Whiteface and on toward Mt. Passaconaway.

Blueberry Ledge Trail (map 3:K8–J8)
Distances from Ferncroft Rd. parking area (1140')

> *to* Blueberry Ledge Cutoff, upper junction (2150'): 2.0 mi., 1000 ft., 1 hr. 30 min.

> *to* south summit ledges of Mt. Whiteface (3990'): 3.9 mi. (6.3 km.), 2850 ft., 3 hr. 25 min.

Blueberry Ledge Cutoff (WODC)

This trail begins and ends on the Blueberry Ledge Trail, providing a walk along the Wonalancet River as an alternative to the viewless ledges. It is equal in distance but somewhat rougher than the parallel section of the Blueberry Ledge Trail. The upper part of the trail is in the Sandwich Range Wilderness.

It leaves the Blueberry Ledge Trail 0.6 mi. from the Ferncroft Rd. parking area, and descends slightly to the river bank. At 0.3 mi. the Dicey's Mill Trail runs on the opposite bank quite near the river; an old logging road comes across the river from the Dicey's Mill Trail at this point, and the Blueberry Ledge Cutoff follows this road upstream into the Sandwich Range Wilderness. The trail soon climbs a small ridge and returns to the bank high above the brook. It swings away from the brook again, meets and follows a small tributary, then swings right and climbs steeply to the bottom of the upper ledge. Marked by cairns and paint, it climbs to meet the Blueberry Ledge Trail at the top of the ledge at a large cairn.

Blueberry Ledge Cutoff (map 3:K8)
Distance from Blueberry Ledge Trail, lower junction (1300')

> *to* Blueberry Ledge Trail, upper junction (2150'): 1.4 mi. (2.3 km.), 850 ft., 1 hr. 10 min.

Tom Wiggin Trail (WODC)

This steep, rough trail, cut by Thomas Wiggin in 1895 and nicknamed the "Fire Escape," connects the Dicey's Mill Trail 1.9 mi. from the Ferncroft Rd. parking area with the Blueberry Ledge Trail just below the upper ledges. It lies entirely within the Sandwich Range Wilderness.

Leaving the Dicey's Mill Trail, it crosses Wonalancet River (may be difficult at high water), bears left and ascends a little knoll, crosses a small brook, and bears right. It tends to angle to the right as it climbs steeply up the mountainside. Eventually it reaches the Blueberry Ledge Trail just north of a small hollow.

Tom Wiggin Trail (map 3:J8)
Distance from Dicey's Mill Trail (1950')

   to Blueberry Ledge Trail (3350'): 1.1 mi. (1.8 km.), 1450 ft., 1 hr. 15 min.

McCrillis Trail (WMNF)

This trail ascends Mt. Whiteface—ending at the lower south summit—from the Flat Mountain Pond Trail (see Section 7), 1.7 mi. from Whiteface Intervale Rd. It is fairly steep and rough, but unlike the Blueberry Ledge Trail does not require rock scrambling (except for one ledge at the top that can be tricky in wet or icy conditions) and is more sheltered in bad weather. It is entirely within the Sandwich Range Wilderness. Be careful not to confuse this trail with the McCrillis Path, which runs from Whiteface Intervale Rd. to the Blueberry Ledge Trail.

Leaving the Flat Mountain Pond Trail on the east bank of Whiteface River, it ascends a bank, then runs east nearly on the level to intersect the former route, an old logging road, at 0.4 mi. Turning left on this road, it climbs moderately, passes through a wet area, and at 2.0 mi. begins to climb steeply. At 2.6 mi. it passes the first of several outlooks, some of which provide good views out onto the "white face." The trail re-enters the woods, climbs steeply again, and finally climbs along the edge of the southwest ledges (use caution) to a junction with the Rollins and Blueberry Ledge trails just north of the ledges of the lower south summit. The true summit is 0.3 mi. farther north via the Rollins Trail. (To descend on this trail, walk southwest from the highest rock of the south ledges along the southeast edge of the ledges. Once the first markings are found, it is easily followed.)

McCrillis Trail (map 3:K8–J8)

Distances from Flat Mountain Pond Trail (1500')

> *to* base of steep climb (2600'): 2.0 mi., 1100 ft., 1 hr. 35 min.
>
> *to* Blueberry Ledge Trail/Rollins Trail (3990'): 3.2 mi. (5.1 km.), 2500 ft., 2 hr. 50 min.

Distance from Whiteface Intervale Rd. (968')

> *to* Blueberry Ledge Trail/Rollins Trail (3990') via Flat Mountain Pond and McCrillis trails: 4.9 mi. (7.9 km.), 3050 ft., 4 hr.

McCrillis Path (WODC)

This trail follows old roads with mostly easy grades from the Blueberry Ledge Trail, 0.9 mi. from the Ferncroft Rd. parking area, to the trailhead for the Flat Mountain Pond Trail on Whiteface Intervale Rd. Be careful not to confuse it with the McCrillis Trail to Mt. Whiteface. The eastern part of this trail gives access to a network of minor trails via the Tilton Spring Path, and passes through the remains of old farms that can be explored. Use of this trail west of the cellar hole at 0.8 mi., particularly as a part of a through route between Ferncroft and White-face Intervale, is not recommended; the western section is not officially maintained (although it is historically a public right of way) and may be overgrown or difficult to follow in places, since it runs mostly through private property with numerous unmarked intersecting logging roads. At present it is much easier to follow from east to west (Ferncroft to Whiteface Intervale).

The trail leaves the Blueberry Ledge Trail on the left and climbs to the height-of-land, following the old road that was once the main highway between Wonalancet and Whiteface Intervale. Tilton Spring Path leaves left at 0.2 mi., and there is a small cellar hole on the right at 0.8 mi. Beyond this point the trail may be overgrown and obscure. It leaves the Sandwich Range Wilderness and enters an area of recent logging activity at 1.1 mi. A branch road enters on the right at 1.3 mi., just across Tewksberry Brook (eastbound, bear right across brook). At 2.1 mi. the road reaches the edge of a very wet open meadow (markings end at a faded old sign 30 yd. back from there). Turn right on a gravel road and follow it to a gravel pit, bear left, turn left on another gravel road at an intersection, and reach the Whiteface Intervale Rd. just east of Whiteface Auto Body. Parking is not permitted in this area. The trailhead for the Flat Mountain Pond Trail is 0.6 mi. to the right (west, then south).

McCrillis Path (map 3:K8)

Distances from Blueberry Ledge Trail (1400')

  to cellar hole (1350'): 0.8 mi., 50 ft. (rev. 100 ft.), 25 min.

  to Flat Mountain Pond Trail trailhead (968'): 2.9 mi. (4.7 km.), 50 ft. (rev. 500 ft.), 1 hr. 30 min.

Downes Brook Trail (WMNF)

This trail provides a route to the south summit ledges or the true summit of Mt. Whiteface in combination with the Kate Sleeper Trail and the Rollins Trail. (The trail segment between the Kate Sleeper Trail junction and the col between the summits of Mt. Whiteface, formerly a part of the Downes Brook Trail, is now part of the Kate Sleeper Trail.) The Downes Brook Trail begins at a new parking area 0.1 mi. from the Kancamagus Highway on a gravel road that leaves on the south side of the highway almost directly opposite Passaconaway Campground. The trail crosses Downes Brook ten times, and several crossings may range from difficult to impassable at high water.

Leaving the parking area, the trail follows the edge of a gravel pit, and the UNH Trail diverges left on an old railroad grade in 60 yd. The Downes Brook Trail turns right, enters the woods, then turns left and follows an old logging road that runs along Downes Brook, at first some distance away and later mostly along the bank. At 0.3 mi. the Mount Potash Trail diverges right, and at 0.7 mi. the Downes Brook Trail makes the first of four crossings of Downes Brook in a span of 0.6 mi. At 2.3 mi. it crosses an extensive gravel outwash, crosses the main brook twice more, and passes through an old logging camp at 3.0 mi. After three more crossings, there are views of the slides on the steep slope of Mt. Whiteface across the valley, and the trail crosses the brook for the last time in the flat pass between Sleeper Ridge and Mt. Whiteface. Here, at 5.2 mi., with a swampy area visible straight ahead, it ends at the junction with the Kate Sleeper Trail. To reach Mt. Whiteface, turn left on the Kate Sleeper Trail, which climbs moderately to the little col between the true summit and the bare south summit of Mt. Whiteface at 6.0 mi. where Camp Shehadi (expected to be removed) is located. To the left from this junction, the Rollins Trail climbs over the true summit of Whiteface at 0.2 mi. and continues toward Mt. Passaconaway; to the right it climbs a short, steep pitch and soon ends at the junction with the McCrillis and Blueberry Ledge trails at the edge of the broad, open ledges of the south summit.

Downes Brook Trail (map 3:J8)

Distances from Kancamagus Highway (1250')

> *to* Sleeper Trail junction (3400'): 5.2 mi. (8.4 km.), 2150 ft., 3 hr. 40 min.
>
> *to* Rollins Trail junction (3900') via Kate Sleeper Trail: 6.0 mi. (9.7 km.), 2650 ft., 4 hr. 20 min.

Kate Sleeper Trail (WODC)

This trail connects Mt. Tripyramid with Mt. Whiteface and the eastern peaks of the Sandwich Range. It begins at the little col between the summits of Mt. Whiteface and runs over the high, double-domed Sleeper Ridge to the Mount Tripyramid Trail high on the South Slide. A section of trail between Mt. Whiteface and the junction of the Downes Brook and Kate Sleeper trails, formerly part of the Downes Brook Trail, has been annexed to the Kate Sleeper Trail in order to restore the historic extent of this trail. It is entirely within the Sandwich Range Wilderness. The only sure water on or near the Kate Sleeper Trail is on the Downes Brook Trail just north of the junction between the two trails in the sag between Whiteface and the Sleepers.

The trail leaves the col between the summits of Mt. Whiteface and descends at a moderate grade 0.8 mi. to its junction with the Downes Brook Trail. The Kate Sleeper Trail then skirts to the north of a swampy area and soon begins to ascend the East Sleeper; there are occasional glimpses to the east and north through the trees. Passing left (southwest) of the top of East Sleeper at 1.6 mi.—where a side path (sign) leads right 0.1 mi. to this viewless summit—the trail descends into the col between the Sleepers, then climbs to a point 30 yd. south of the summit of West Sleeper at 2.6 mi. After descending again and traversing a bit below the Tripyramid col, the trail bears west and contours along South Tripyramid until it enters the South Slide on the smaller eastern slide. Small cairns and blue blazes mark the winding route on the slide, as the trail climbs very steeply on loose gravel about 100 yd., then re-enters the brush on the opposite side. After running about 50 yd. through this brushy area the trail enters the larger western slide, where it meets the Mount Tripyramid Trail. To locate the beginning of the trail on the Tripyramid slide, look for a small sign at the extreme eastern edge of the western slide, 60 yd. below its top.

Kate Sleeper Trail (map 3:J7–J8)

Distances from Rollins Trail junction (3900')

   to Downes Brook Trail (3400'): 0.8 mi., 0 ft. (rev. 500 ft.), 25 min.

   to Mount Tripyramid Trail (3850'): 3.3 mi. (5.3 km.), 900 ft. (rev. 450 ft.), 2 hr. 5 min.

Shorter Paths in the Ferncroft Area (WODC)

These trails are often not as well beaten as the more important paths, and signs and other markings are frequently sparse or absent, so they must be followed with great care. They also frequently cross private property, and landowner rights and privacy must be respected.

The *Brook Path* (2.1 mi.) leaves NH 113A opposite the Cabin Trail trailhead and follows the north bank of Wonalancet River for 0.9 mi., then crosses on a bridge and follows the south bank for another 0.9 mi. to Old Locke Rd., which it follows to NH 113A just south of the bridge across Wonalancet River. The *Gordon Path* (1.2 mi.) begins at the Ferncroft Rd. parking area, taking the right fork (almost straight ahead) where the Old Mast Road and Kelley Trail bear left; after 0.2 mi. it turns to the right off this road and runs across a branch of Spring Brook to a gravel driveway that comes out onto NH 113A, at a point 0.1 mi. east of its junction with Ferncroft Rd. and 0.3 mi. west of the trailhead for the Cabin and Big Rock Cave trails. The *Pasture Path* (1.1 mi.) diverges from the Blueberry Ledge Trail 0.5 mi. from the Ferncroft Rd. parking area; it leads past Tilton Spring at 0.6 mi., where it passes through an intersection with the Tilton Spring Path (right) and the Red Path (left), then continues to the summit of Mt. Katherine, a broad ledge with restricted views. The *Red Path* (0.7 mi.) runs from the site of the former Wonalancet post office (on Ferncroft Rd. just west of its junction with NH 113A) to Tilton Spring, where it meets the Tilton Spring Path and the Red Path. The *Tilton Spring Path* (0.9 mi.) runs from Tilton Spring to the McCrillis Path at a point 0.2 mi. from the Blueberry Ledge Trail.

The Carter and Baldface Ranges

This section covers the Carter-Moriah Range and the Baldface Range, along with the broad valley of the Wild River that lies between these two high ranges as well as the lower mountains on the long subsidiary ridges that extend south from them. In the Carter-Moriah Range the major peaks are Wildcat Mtn., Carter Dome, Mt. Hight, South Carter Mtn., Middle Carter Mtn., Mt. Moriah, and Shelburne Moriah Mtn.; in the Baldface Range, the major peaks are North Baldface, South Baldface, West Royce Mtn., and East Royce Mtn.; and in the southern part, the major peaks are Black Mtn., North and South Doublehead, Kearsarge North, Black Cap, Peaked Mtn., and Middle Mtn. The area is bounded on the west by NH 16, on the north by US 2, and on the east and south by ME 113/NH 113 (which crosses the state line several times). Many trails in this section coincide with or intersect cross-country ski or snowmobile trails, and care often must be taken to distinguish the hiking trails from the others. The entire area is covered by the AMC Carter Range–Evans Notch map (map #5).

In this section the Appalachian Trail begins at NH 16 opposite Pinkham Notch Visitor Center and follows the Lost Pond, Wildcat Ridge, Nineteen-Mile Brook, Carter-Moriah, Kenduskeag, and Rattle River trails to US 2 east of Gorham. It crosses the summits of Wildcat Mtn., Carter Dome, Mt. Hight, South Carter Mtn., Middle Carter Mtn., and North Carter Mtn., and passes near the summit of Mt. Moriah.

GEOGRAPHY

The **Carter-Moriah Range** would be a great deal more prominent among White Mtn. ranges were it not for those neighbors that rise 1500 ft. higher across Pinkham Notch. On a ridge about 10 mi. long there are eight significant peaks over 4000 ft. and wild, dramatic Carter Notch. Mt. Hight, which remains bare after having been swept by fire in 1903, commands the finest views in the range, while those from Shelburne Moriah Mtn., Carter Dome, and Mt. Moriah are also excellent, and there are several fine outlooks in various directions along the trails. To the east the range overlooks the broad, forested valley of the Wild River and the rocky peaks of the Baldface group, and far beyond lies the Atlantic Ocean, which reflects the sun on the southeast horizon behind Sebago Lake on clear mid-mornings.

Wildcat Mtn. rises at the south end of the range. Of its numerous summits, the highest is the one nearest to Carter Notch; its five most prominent summits are designated, from east to west, **A Peak** (4422 ft.), **B Peak** (4330 ft.), **C Peak** (4298 ft.), **D Peak** (4062 ft.), and **E Peak** (4046 ft.). The mountain is heavily wooded, but there are magnificent outlook ledges on the Wildcat Ridge Trail west of E Peak, a lookout platform with extensive views on D Peak near the top of the Wildcat Ski Area, a good view east to the Baldface area from C Peak, and fine views straight down into Carter Notch from A Peak.

Carter Notch, the deep cleft between Carter Dome and Wildcat Mtn., includes some of the finest scenery in this region, particularly the two small, beautiful **Carter Lakes** that lie in the secluded hollow in the deepest part of the notch. The actual pass (3388 ft.) in the main ridge connecting Carter Dome to Wildcat Mtn. is north of the lakes and 100 ft. higher than them, while the **Rampart,** a barrier of rocks that have fallen from the cliffs above on both Wildcat and Carter Dome, stretches across the floor of the notch, so that the lakes are totally enclosed by natural walls and their outlet brook on the south side is forced to run underground. Above the lakes the impressive wooded cliffs of Wildcat Mtn. rise vertically nearly 1000 ft. to the west, and to the east Carter Dome also rises steeply, with the immense boulder called **Pulpit Rock** jutting out above the notch. A rough trail leaves the Wildcat River Trail about 100 yd. south of Carter Notch Hut and runs east over the Rampart's huge rocks, where there is a good view toward Jackson, and the many boulder caves among the fallen rocks, where ice sometimes remains through the summer, invite exploration (use caution).

Carter Dome (4832 ft.) once bore a fire tower on its flat, scrub-fringed top. There are excellent views in most directions from open areas in the vicinity of the summit. **Mt. Hight** (4675 ft.) is a bare rock peak with the best views in the range. **South Carter Mtn.** (4430 ft.) is wooded with no views. **Middle Carter Mtn.** (4610 ft.) is wooded, but there are good outlooks from various points along its ridgecrest, including an excellent view of the Presidentials 70 yd. north of the summit. **North Carter Mtn.** (4530 ft.) has views from its summit and from ledges along the ridge north and south of the summit; the best views are east to the Baldface Range. **Imp Mtn.** (3730 ft.) is a trailless north spur of North Carter. **Imp Profile** (3165 ft.) is an interesting cliff on a west spur of North Carter. The profile, which is named for its imagined resemblance to the grotesquely misshapen face of a part-human wood sprite, is best seen from the Pinkham B (Dolly Copp) Rd. at the monument marking the site of the Dolly Copp house.

Mt. Moriah (4049 ft.) has fine views in all directions from its ledgy summit block. **Mt. Surprise** (2194 ft.) is a northwest spur of Moriah that offers restricted views. **Mt. Evans** (1443 ft.) is a low north spur of the Moriah group that affords fine views for comparatively little effort of Mt. Washington and the Northern Peaks and good views up and down the Androscoggin River and across to the Mahoosuc Range. **Shelburne Moriah Mtn.** (3735 ft.) offers magnificent views—surpassed in this range only by Mt. Hight—from acres of flat ledges at the summit and outlooks on its southwest ridge.

The **Baldface-Royce Range** extends southwest from Evans Notch, between the **Wild River** and the **Cold River.** The summits are relatively low, but so are the valleys; thus the mountains rise impressively high above their bases. The highest peaks in the range are **North Baldface** (3610 ft.) and **South Baldface** (3570 ft.). Their upper slopes were swept by fire in 1903 and the resulting great expanses of open ledge make the circuit over these peaks one of the finest trips in the White Mtns. With **Eagle Crag** (3030 ft.), a northeast buttress, these peaks enclose a cirque-like valley on their east. To the southwest are **Sable Mtn.** (3519 ft.) and **Chandler Mtn.** (3335 ft.), both wooded and trailless, and to the southeast is **Eastman Mtn.** (2939 ft.), which affords fine views from its ledgy summit.

A ridge descends northeast from Eagle Crag over **Mt. Meader** (2782 ft.), which has ledgy outlooks, to the **Basin Rim,** where there are fine views from the brink of a cliff, then ascends to the Royces. **West Royce Mtn.** (3210 ft.), with good views to the east and southeast from a ledge near the summit, is located in New Hampshire, and **East Royce Mtn.** (3114 ft.), with good views in nearly all directions, is in Maine; the state line crosses slightly to the east of the col between them.

A number of lower mountains rise from the ridges that extend south from the main ranges. **Spruce Mtn.** (2270 ft.), which is trailless, and **Eagle Mtn.** (1613 ft.), which has a path and views from the summit, are small peaks on a south ridge of Wildcat Mtn. **Black Mtn.** (3304 ft.), which lies across Perkins Notch from Carter Dome, is a long ridge with a multitude of bumps, of which seven have traditionally been considered summits—though which seven bumps should be counted as summits has never been entirely clear. The highest summit is densely wooded and trailless. Good views can be obtained from the southernmost summit, the **Knoll** (2010 ft.), which is part of the Black Mtn. Ski Area, and from a knob (2757 ft.) in the middle of the ridge that is reached by the Black Mountain Ski Trail. **North Doublehead** (3053 ft.), with a cabin on the summit and good views east and west from outlooks near the summit, and **South Doublehead** (2939 ft.), with good views from several ledges, form a small, sharp ridge southeast of Black Mtn. Southwest of Doublehead is the low range composed of **Thorn Mtn.** (2282 ft.) and **Tin Mtn.** (2031 ft.). Tin Mtn. is said to have been the site of the first discovery of tin ore in the United States, but the old mines are filled with water and cannot be easily reached. The former hiking trail on Thorn Mtn. has been closed, but the summit affords excellent views and (in season) blueberries; it can be ascended via the trails of the abandoned ski area on its north slope, an easy if not very attractive route (due largely to debris remaining from the former ski development) reached by following Thorn Mtn. Rd. to the gap between Thorn Mtn. and Middle Mtn. East of Doublehead lie the valleys of the **East Branch of the Saco** and **Slippery Brook.** In the valley of Slippery Brook is **Mountain Pond,** a crescent-shaped body of water about three-quarters of a mile long by half a mile wide, entirely surrounded by woods and overlooked by South Baldface, Mt. Shaw, and Doublehead.

Kearsarge North (3268 ft.), sometimes called Mt. Pequawket, rises above Intervale. The summit bears an abandoned fire tower that is in good condition, and the views are magnificent in all directions; this is one of the finest viewpoints in the White Mtns. **Bartlett Mtn.** (2661 ft.) is a shoulder extending westward toward Intervale; it has no official trails, but has a number of ledges that invite exploration. There is a range of trailless hills extending northeast from Kearsarge North, of which the most prominent is **Mt. Shaw** (2585 ft.).

Running south from Kearsarge North are the **Green Hills of Conway: Hurricane Mtn.** (2100 ft.), **Black Cap** (2369 ft.), **Peaked Mtn.** (1739 ft.), **Middle Mtn.** (1857 ft.), **Cranmore Mtn.** (1690 ft.), and **Rattlesnake Mtn.** (1590 ft.). The summits of Black Cap, Peaked Mtn., Cranmore Mtn., and Middle Mtn. afford excellent views, and there are several other good viewpoints. Except for Hurricane Mtn., these peaks are included within the Green Hills Preserve, a tract of 2822 acres of hilly terrain with numerous streams and cascades and a beaver pond, as well as numerous rare and endangered plants and a beautiful high-elevation stand of red pine on Peaked Mtn. and Middle Mtn.. This reservation, which was established in 1990 through the generosity of the Anna B. Stearns Foundation, individuals, businesses, and other foundations, is owned and managed by the Nature Conservancy, a private organization that maintains the preserve for the benefit of the public. The trail system has been improved and expanded so that all the major peaks except Rattlesnake Mtn. are reached by well-maintained paths. Visitors are requested to park their vehicles only at designated sites. To protect this resource for the enjoyment of all, removal of rocks, minerals, plants, or artifacts from the preserve is forbidden. Information and a trail map can be obtained from the Green Hills Preserve headquarters, PO Box 310, North Conway, NH 03860 (603-356-8833); information is also posted at several kiosks along the trails (mentioned in trail descriptions) which have detailed maps on display and often have a supply of trail maps, but hikers would be well advised not to count on obtaining trail maps from this source.

HUTS

Carter Notch Hut (AMC)

The AMC constructed this stone hut in 1914. It is located at an elevation of 3288 ft., about 60 yd. south of the smaller lake, at the southern terminus of the Nineteen-Mile Brook Trail and the northern terminus of the Wildcat River Trail. The hut, with two bunkhouses, accommodates 40 guests. Pets are not permitted in the hut. It is currently open on a caretaker basis throughout the year, with no full-service season.

For current information and schedule, contact the Reservation Office, Pinkham Notch Visitor Center, Box 298, Gorham, NH 03581 (603-466-2727) or www.outdoors.org.

CAMPING

Forest Protection Areas

The WMNF has established a number of Forest Protection Areas (FPAs)—formerly known as Restricted Use Areas—where camping and wood or charcoal fires are prohibited throughout the year. The specific areas are under continual review, and areas are added to or subtracted from the list in order to provide the greatest amount of protection to areas subject to damage by excessive camping, while imposing the lowest level of restrictions possible. A general list of FPAs in this section follows, but since there are often major changes from year to year, one should obtain current information on FPAs from the WMNF.

(1) No camping is permitted above treeline (where trees are less than 8 ft. tall) except in winter, and then only where there is at least two feet of snow cover on the ground—but not on any frozen body of water. The point where the above-treeline restricted area begins is marked on most trails with small signs, but the absence of such signs should not be construed as proof of the legality of a site.

(2) No camping is permitted within a quarter-mile of any trailhead, picnic area, or any facility for overnight accommodation such as a hut, cabin, shelter, tentsite, or campground, except as designated at the facility itself. In the area covered by Section 9, camping is also forbidden within a quarter-mile of Zeta Pass or the summit of Carter Dome.

(3) No camping is permitted within 200 ft. of certain trails. In 1997, designated trails included the first mile of the Wild River Trail south of Wild River Campground.

(4) No camping is permitted on WMNF land within a quarter-mile of certain roads (camping on private roadside land is illegal except by permission of the landowner). In 1997, these roads included Wild River Rd. (FR 12) and NH 16 north of Glen Ellis Falls.

Established Trailside Campsites

Imp Campsite (AMC) is located on a spur path from the Carter-Moriah Trail between Moriah and North Carter. There is a shelter and five tentsites. In summer there is a caretaker and a fee is charged. Water is available in a nearby brook.

Rattle River Shelter (WMNF) is located on the Rattle River Trail 1.7 mi. from US 2.

Spruce Brook Shelter (WMNF) is located on the Wild River Trail about 3.2 mi. from Wild River Campground.

Perkins Notch Shelter (WMNF) is located on the southeast side of Wild River, just south of the No-Ketchum Pond, with bunk space for six.

Blue Brook Shelter (WMNF) is located on the Black Angel Trail (and a branch trail connecting to the Basin Trail) 0.3 mi. west of Rim Junction.

Baldface Shelter (WMNF) is located on the Baldface Circle Trail, just below the ledges on South Baldface. The water source near the shelter is not reliable.

Province Pond Shelter (WMNF) is located on the Province Brook Trail at Province Pond.

Mountain Pond Shelter (WMNF) is located on the Mountain Pond Loop Trail at Mountain Pond.

Doublehead Cabin (WMNF) is located at the summit of North Doublehead, with bunks for eight. The cabin is kept locked and reservations for its use must be made with the Saco Ranger District office (603-447-5448). There is no water nearby.

Black Mtn. Cabin (WMNF) is located on the Black Mountain Ski Trail (which is also used for hiking) near the central summit of Black Mtn. It has bunks for eight. The cabin is kept locked and reservations for its use must be made with the Saco Ranger District office (603-447-5448). There is a spring (unreliable water source in summer, usually frozen in winter) near the cabin.

Trails on Ridge and West Slopes of Carter Range

List of Trails	**Map**	**Page**
Wildcat Ridge Trail	5:G9–F10	357
Lost Pond Trail	5:F9–G9	359
Square Ledge Trail	5:F9–F10	359
Thompson Falls Trail	5:F10	360
Carter-Moriah Trail	5:E10–F10	360
Nineteen-Mile Brook Trail	5:F10	365
Carter Dome Trail	5:F10	365
Imp Trail	5:F10	366
North Carter Trail	5:F10	367
Stony Brook Trail	5:E10–F11	367

Trails on the Ridge and North Slopes of Moriah Group

List of Trails	**Map**	**Page**
Kenduskeag Trail	5:E11–E12	368
Rattle River Trail	5:E11	368
Mount Evans Trail	5:E11	369
Shelburne Trail	5:E12–F12	370

Trails of the Wild River Valley

List of Trails	**Map**	**Page**
Wild River Trail	5:F12–G10	370
Hastings Trail	5:E13–E12	372
Highwater Trail	5:E13–F11	372
Burnt Mill Brook Trail	5:F12	373
Moriah Brook Trail	5:F12–F11	373
Black Angel Trail	5:F12–F10	374

Trails on East Side of Baldface-Royce Range

Trails in the East Branch Region

Trails on the Southern Ridges of the Carter Range

Trails on Mount Doublehead

Trails of the Kearsarge North Region

Trails of the Green Hills of Conway Range

THE TRAILS

Wildcat Ridge Trail (AMC)

This trail climbs up to and across the numerous summits on the long ridge of Wildcat Mtn., then descends to the Nineteen-Mile Brook Trail 0.3 mi. north of Carter Notch Hut. The trail officially begins at the Glen Ellis Falls parking lot on NH 16 south of Pinkham Notch Visitor Center, but this end is more commonly reached by following the Lost Pond Trail from Pinkham Notch Visitor Center in order to avoid the often difficult and sometimes dangerous crossing of the Ellis River. From the Lost Pond Trail junction to Carter Notch, this trail is a part of the Appalachian Trail. The sections from the Lost Pond Trail junction to E Peak and from A Peak to Carter Notch are very steep and rough, and there are several ups and downs and other steep, rough sections along the rest of the trail that make it more difficult and time-consuming than one might infer from a casual glance at the map or the distance summary. *Caution:* The section between NH 16 and E Peak may be dangerous when wet or icy, and hikers with heavy packs should allow substantial extra time.

The trail starts on the east side of NH 16 opposite the parking area for Glen Ellis Falls, and leads east across the Ellis River (may be very difficult) to a target. At 0.1 mi. the Lost Pond Trail enters on the left, and the trail shortly begins the very steep climb up the end of the ridge (use care on all ledge areas), crossing two open ledges, both with fine views of Mt. Washington across Pinkham Notch. At 0.9 mi. it passes a level, open ledge with fine views south, marked by a rock with "Sarge's Crag" engraved on it. The trail dips slightly, then resumes the climb. At 1.2 mi. a side path (sign) leads left to a spring, and at 1.5 mi. the main trail climbs to the top of a steep ledge with a superb view of the southeast face of Mt. Washington. The trail continues to climb over several knobs and passes 3 yd. left of the summit of E Peak at 1.9 mi., then descends to the summit station of the Wildcat Ski Area in the col at 2.1 mi. From here the easiest ski trails (those farthest to the north) descend to the Wildcat Ski Area base lodge in 2.6 mi.

The trail next climbs steeply to the summit of D Peak, where there is an observation tower; an easier trail maintained by the ski area parallels this segment to the west. The Wildcat Ridge Trail then descends into Wildcat Col, the deepest col on the main ridge, at 2.5 mi. Here it passes over a small hogback and through a second sag, then begins the climb to C Peak over several "steps"— fairly steep climbs interspersed with level sections. There is a good outlook east from C Peak at 3.3 mi., followed by a significant descent into a col and a climb to B Peak, then a descent to a shallower col and an easy climb to A Peak at 4.2 mi. As the trail turns left near this summit there is a spur path that leads right 20 yd. to a spectacular view into Carter Notch. The actual summit of Wildcat Mtn. is a rock in the scrub just off the spur path within a few yards of this outlook. The trail now descends rather steeply to the Nineteen-Mile Brook Trail at the height-of-land in Carter Notch, crossing a large recent landslide track about halfway down. For Carter Notch Hut, turn right (south).

Wildcat Ridge Trail (map 5:G9–F10)

Distances from Glen Ellis Falls parking area (1960')

   to summit of E Peak (4030'): 1.9 mi., 2150 ft. (rev. 100 ft.), 2 hr.

   to Wildcat Col (3770'): 2.5 mi., 2250 ft. (rev. 400 ft.), 2 hr. 25 min.

   to summit of C Peak (4298'): 3.3 mi., 2800 ft., 3 hr. 5 min.

   to summit of A Peak (4422'): 4.2 mi., 3150 ft. (rev. 200 ft.), 3 hr. 40 min.

to Nineteen-Mile Brook Trail (3388'): 4.9 mi. (7.9 km.), 3150 ft. (rev. 1050 ft.), 4 hr.

Lost Pond Trail (AMC)

This short link trail runs from Pinkham Notch Camp to the lower end of the Wildcat Ridge Trail, avoiding the difficult and sometimes dangerous crossing of the Ellis River at the beginning of the Wildcat Ridge Trail. It is part of the Appalachian Trail.

It leaves NH 16 opposite Pinkham Notch Camp, crosses a bridge over the Ellis River, and turns south at the end of the bridge, where the Square Ledge Trail leaves on the left. The Lost Pond Trail follows the east bank of the Ellis River, which is soon joined from the opposite side by the larger Cutler River. The trail then leaves the river bank and climbs at a moderate grade to Lost Pond at 0.5 mi. It follows the east shore with good views, descends slightly, and ends at the Wildcat Ridge Trail.

Lost Pond Trail (map 5:F9–G9)

Distance from NH 16 opposite Pinkham Notch Visitor Center (2030')

to Wildcat Ridge Trail (1980'): 0.9 mi. (1.5 km.), 100 ft. (rev. 100 ft.), 30 min.

Square Ledge Trail (AMC)

This short trail (with blue blazes) leads to an excellent outlook from a ledge that rises from the floor of Pinkham Notch on the side of Wildcat Mtn. The trail diverges left where the Lost Pond Trail turns south 20 yd. beyond the east end of the footbridge across Ellis River. It climbs moderately, and after 80 yd. a spur path leads left 50 yd. to a ledge signed "Ladies' Lookout," which, though overgrown, offers a fine view of Pinkham Notch Camp. The trail bears right, then swings to the east and crosses the Square Ledge Loop Ski Trail. It then rises moderately, passes Hangover Rock, and ascends to the base of Square Ledge. It swings around to the east side of the ledge, then climbs steeply via a V-slot about 50 yd. to an outlook that offers excellent views of Pinkham Notch and Mt. Washington.

Square Ledge Trail (map 5:F9–F10)

Distance from Lost Pond Trail (2020')

to Square Ledge (2500'): 0.5 mi. (0.8 km.), 500 ft., 30 min.

Thompson Falls Trail (WMNF)

This trail runs from the Wildcat Ski Area to Thompson Falls, a series of cascades on a brook flowing from Wildcat Mtn. Except in wet seasons, the brook is apt to be rather low.

From the Wildcat Ski Area parking area, cross the bridge to the east side, turn left and follow the Nature Trail north; continue ahead where a branch leaves on the left at 0.1 mi. and also where a loop leaves on the right and then rejoins. Leaving the Nature Trail, the trail to the falls crosses a small stream and a maintenance road, then leads up the south side of the brook to the foot of the first fall at 0.6 mi. It crosses to the north side above the fall, bears right, and continues up the brook for another 0.1 mi.

Thompson Falls Trail (map 5:F10)

Distance from Wildcat Ski Area (1930')

   to end of trail (2100'): 0.7 mi. (1.1 km.), 200 ft., 25 min.

Carter-Moriah Trail (AMC)

This trail runs 13.8 mi. from Gorham to Carter Notch, following the crest of the Carter Range. To reach the trailhead at Gorham, follow US 2 east from Gorham 0.5 mi., take a sharp right onto Bangor Rd. just past the bridge and railroad track, and follow this paved road about 0.5 mi. to the turnaround at its end. Park only on the left side of the road, opposite the homes. (On foot from Gorham, follow the road that leaves the east side of NH 16 just south of the railroad tracks. Bear right in 0.1 mi. on Mill St., and in 0.1 mi. more a path left leads across the Peabody River on a footbridge. Turn right here and follow the road to its end, where the trail enters the woods on the left.) From the Kenduskeag Trail junction near the summit of Mt. Moriah to Carter Notch, the Carter-Moriah Trail is part of the Appalachian Trail. Water is very scarce on many parts of this trail, since it runs mostly on or near the crest of the ridge.

The following description of the path is in the southbound direction (from Gorham to Carter Notch). See below for a description of the path in the reverse direction.

Part I. Gorham to Mount Moriah

The trail follows a logging road up a steep bank, then climbs moderately through second-growth woods past a clear-cut. It bears right, then left along the edge of another clear-cut, and ascends through open hardwoods above the more recently logged area. At 2.0 mi. a ledge to the right affords good views, and the trail soon passes to the right of the insignificant summit of Mt. Surprise and its tiny box canyon. From here the trail descends slightly, then ascends gradually at first, but soon becomes steeper as it climbs over ledges that have excellent views. The trail stays near the ridge top but winds from side to side, occasionally dipping below the crest. At 4.2 mi. there is a glimpse of Moriah's summit ahead, and at 4.5 mi. a spur path leads right 50 yd. to the ledgy summit of Mt. Moriah, which affords excellent views.

Part II. Mount Moriah to North Carter

From the junction with the Mt. Moriah summit spur path, two routes descend the ledges of the Moriah summit block. The right-hand one is probably easier, but both are rock scrambles and are dangerous when icy (in which case it may be better to bushwhack down through the woods). By either route, it is less than 100 yd. to the junction where the Kenduskeag Trail turns left, then shortly right, toward Shelburne Moriah Mtn. Here the Carter-Moriah Trail turns right (southwest). From this junction south it is part of the Appalachian Trail and has white blazes. It follows the ridgecrest south through woods and over an open knob, then descends moderately to excellent outlooks from the top of the south cliffs, and reaches the deep col between Moriah and the Carters at 5.9 mi. Here the Moriah Brook Trail enters left and the Carter-Moriah Trail turns right and follows a boardwalk. In 40 yd. the Stony Brook Trail enters straight ahead, and the Carter-Moriah Trail turns left. It continues with several minor ups and downs and crosses some ledges. At 6.6 mi. a spur trail descends right 0.2 mi. to Imp Campsite, which has a shelter, tent platforms, and water. The main trail crosses a small brook and passes through a wet area, ascending on the plateau south of Imp Mtn., and at 7.7 mi. begins a steep and rough climb to North Carter Mtn., reaching its summit at 8.2 mi.

Part III. North Carter to Zeta Pass

The path continues south, passes a fine outlook, and winds along the crest of the ridge. At 8.5 mi. the North Carter Trail enters right, and the trail continues over numerous ledgy humps and boggy depressions. The best views in this area are from the ledgy knob called Mt. Lethe, a few steps to the left of the trail. A good outlook to the Presidentials is passed 70 yd. before the trail reaches the wooded summit of Middle Carter Mtn. (sign) at 9.1 mi. The trail descends easily and passes an open area with a view west, then ascends a short, steep ledge and descends to the col between Middle and South Carter at 10.0 mi. It then ascends to a point 10 yd. left (east) of the summit of South Carter (sign) at 10.4 mi. and descends gradually, with occasional steeper sections, to Zeta Pass, where it makes a short ascent to the junction with the Carter Dome Trail on the right at 11.2 mi. Water may occasionally be available in a small stream (usually dry in mid-summer) that is reached by a side path from the Carter Dome Trail 80 yd. below this junction.

Part IV. Zeta Pass to Carter Notch

The two trails climb easily to the south for 0.2 mi., then the Carter Dome Trail continues ahead and the Carter-Moriah Trail turns left and climbs steeply up to the summit of Mt. Hight at 11.8 mi. At this bare summit, which commands the best views in the range, the trail makes a very sharp right turn; great care must be exercised to stay on the trail if visibility is poor, particularly going north, since a beaten path which soon peters out continues north from the summit. (Compass bearings from the summit are: southbound, 240° magnetic; northbound, 290° magnetic.) The trail passes through a shallow sag and the Carter Dome Trail re-enters from the right at 12.2 mi. In another 25 yd. the Black Angel Trail enters on the left, and the Carter-Moriah Trail climbs steadily to the summit of Carter Dome at 12.6 mi., where the Rainbow Trail enters on the left. The trail then descends moderately, passing a side path at 13.1 mi. that leads to the right 60 yd. to a fine spring. At 13.5 mi. a side path leads 30 yd. to the left to an excellent outlook over Carter Notch. Soon the trail begins to descend very steeply to Carter Notch, ending on the Nineteen-Mile Brook Trail at the shore of the larger Carter Lake. Carter Notch Hut is 0.1 mi. to the left.

Carter-Moriah Trail (map 5:E10–F10)

Distances from Bangor Rd. (800')

> *to* Mt. Moriah summit (4049'): 4.5 mi., 3400 ft., 3 hr. 50 min.
>
> *to* Moriah Brook and Stony Brook trails (3127'): 5.9 mi., 3450 ft., 4 hr. 40 min.
>
> *to* Imp Shelter spur trail (3200'): 6.6 mi., 3600 ft., 5 hr. 5 min.
>
> *to* North Carter Trail (4470'): 8.5 mi., 4950 ft., 6 hr. 45 min.
>
> *to* Middle Carter summit (4610'): 9.1 mi., 5150 ft., 7 hr. 10 min.
>
> *to* South Carter summit (4430'): 10.4 mi., 5400 ft., 7 hr. 55 min.
>
> *to* Zeta Pass (3890'): 11.2 mi., 5400 ft., 8 hr. 20 min.
>
> *to* Mt. Hight summit (4675'): 11.8 mi., 6200 ft., 9 hr.
>
> *to* Black Angel Trail (4600'): 12.2 mi., 6250 ft., 9 hr. 15 min.
>
> *to* Carter Dome summit (4832'): 12.6 mi., 6500 ft., 9 hr. 35 min.
>
> *to* Nineteen-Mile Brook Trail (3300'): 13.8 mi. (22.2 km.), 6500 ft., 10 hr. 10 min.

Carter-Moriah Trail (AMC) [in reverse]

Part I. Carter Notch to Zeta Pass

The trail begins on the Nineteen-Mile Brook Trail at the shore of the larger Carter Lake, 0.1 mi. north of Carter Notch Hut. It climbs very steeply at first, then moderates, and at 0.3 mi. a side path leads 30 yd. to the right to an excellent outlook over Carter Notch. The trail continues to climb at a moderate grade, passing a side path at 0.7 mi. that leads to the left 60 yd. to a fine spring, and at 1.2 mi. it reaches the summit of Carter Dome, where the Rainbow Trail enters on the right. The Carter-Moriah Trail descends steadily, and at 1.6 mi. the Black Angel Trail enters on the right. In another 25 yd., as the Carter Dome Trail continues straight ahead, the Carter-Moriah Trail bears right, passes through a shallow sag, and ascends moderately to the summit of Mt. Hight at 2.0 mi. At this bare summit, which commands the best views in the range, the trail makes a very sharp left turn; great care must be exercised to stay on the trail if visibility is poor, particularly going north, since a beaten path which soon peters out continues north from the summit. (Compass bearings from the summit are: northbound, 290° magnetic; southbound, 240° magnetic.) The trail descends steeply and rejoins the Carter Dome Trail at 2.4 mi., and the two trails continue to Zeta Pass at 2.6 mi., where the Carter Dome Trail turns left and descends toward NH 16. Water may occasionally be available in a small stream (usually dry in midsummer) that is reached by a side path from the Carter Dome Trail 80 yd. below this junction.

Part II. Zeta Pass to North Carter

From the junction with the Carter Dome Trail in Zeta Pass, the trail descends slightly to the actual low point of the pass, then ascends gradually, with occasional steeper sections, to a point 10 yd. right (east) of the summit of South Carter (sign) at 3.4 mi. It descends to the col between Middle and South Carter at 3.8 mi., then ascends easily, descending a short, steep ledge and passing an open area with a view west. It reaches the wooded summit of Middle Carter Mtn. (sign) at 4.7 mi. There is a good outlook to the Presidentials 70 yd. farther along the trail. The trail now descends over numerous ledgy humps and boggy depressions. The best views in this area are from the ledgy knob called Mt. Lethe, a few steps to the right of the trail. At 5.3 mi. the North Carter Trail enters on the left, and the Carter-Moriah Trail winds along the crest of the ridge past a fine outlook, reaching the summit of North Carter at 5.6 mi.

Part III. North Carter to Mount Moriah

The Carter-Moriah Trail makes a steep and rough descent (difficult for those with heavy packs) from North Carter, and at 6.1 mi. the grade becomes moderate to easy as the trail descends on the plateau south of Imp Mtn., passing through a wet area and crossing a small brook. At 7.2 mi. a spur trail descends to the left 0.2 mi. to Imp Campsite, which has a shelter, tent platforms, and water. The main trail crosses some ledges and continues with several minor ups and downs to the deep col between the Carters and Moriah at 7.9 mi. Here the Stony Brook Trail enters on the left, where the Carter-Moriah Trail turns sharp right on a boardwalk, and in 40 yd. the Moriah Brook Trail enters on the right. Here the Carter-Moriah Trail turns left and starts to climb up the ledgy ridge of Mt. Moriah, soon reaching excellent outlooks from the top of the south cliffs. It continues to climb moderately up ledges to a shoulder, then follows the ridgecrest north through woods and over an open knob to a junction at 9.3 mi., where the Kenduskeag Trail (continuing the Appalachian Trail north) goes straight and shortly turns right toward Shelburne Moriah Mtn. At this junction the Carter-Moriah Trail turns left, and two routes ascend the ledges of the Moriah summit block. The left-hand one is probably easier, but both are rock scrambles and are dangerous when icy (in which case it may be better to bushwhack through the woods). By either route, it is less than 100 yd. to the junction with the spur path that leads left 50 yd. to the ledgy summit of Mt. Moriah, which affords excellent views.

Part IV. Mount Moriah to Gorham

The trail descends moderately, staying near the ridge top but winding from side to side, occasionally dipping below the crest. It then becomes steeper and climbs down over ledges that have excellent views. After a fairly level section below the ledges and a slight ascent, it passes to the left of the insignificant summit of Mt. Surprise and its tiny box canyon at 11.8 mi. and descends again, passing the last open ledge, which is just to the left of the trail. Soon it enters second-growth woods in a fairly recently logged area and descends on logging roads. It follows the right edge of a clear-cut and then bears right, and continues on logging roads until it finally descends a steep bank to the end of Bangor Rd.

Carter-Moriah Trail (map 5:E10–F10)

Distances from Nineteen-Mile Brook Trail (3300')

to Carter Dome summit (4832'): 1.2 mi., 1550 ft., 1 hr. 25 min.

to Black Angel Trail (4600'): 1.6 mi., 1550 ft., 1 hr. 35 min.

to Mt. Hight summit (4675'): 2.0 mi., 1700 ft., 1 hr. 50 min.

to Zeta Pass (3890'): 2.6 mi., 1700 ft., 2 hr. 10 min.

to South Carter summit (4430'): 3.4 mi., 2250 ft., 2 hr. 50 min.

to Middle Carter summit (4610'): 4.7 mi., 2700 ft., 3 hr. 40 min.

to North Carter Trail (4470'): 5.3 mi., 2800 ft., 4 hr. 5 min.

to Imp Shelter spur trail (3200'): 7.2 mi., 2800 ft., 5 hr.

to Moriah Brook and Stony Brook trails (3127'): 7.9 mi., 2850 ft., 5 hr. 25 min.

to Mt. Moriah summit (4049'): 9.3 mi., 3800 ft., 6 hr. 35 min.

to Bangor Rd. (800'): 13.8 mi. (22.2 km.), 3950 ft., 8 hr. 55 min.

Nineteen-Mile Brook Trail (WMNF)

This trail runs from NH 16 about 1 mi. north of the Mt. Washington Auto Rd. to Carter Notch Hut and is the easiest route to the hut. Sections of the trail close to the brook bank sometimes become dangerously icy in the cold seasons.

Leaving NH 16, the trail follows the northeast bank of Nineteen-Mile Brook on the remains of an old road. At 1.2 mi. the main trail passes a dam in the brook, and at 1.9 mi. the Carter Dome Trail diverges left for Zeta Pass. Here the Nineteen-Mile Brook Trail crosses a tributary on a footbridge, and at 2.2 mi. it crosses another brook at a small cascade, also on a footbridge. At 3.1 mi. the trail crosses a small brook and begins to ascend more steeply to the height-of-land at 3.6 mi., where the Wildcat Ridge Trail diverges right (west). The Nineteen-Mile Brook Trail then drops steeply to the larger Carter Lake, passes the Carter-Moriah Trail left at 3.8 mi., crosses between the lakes, and reaches Carter Notch Hut and the junction with the Wildcat River Trail.

Nineteen-Mile Brook Trail (map 5:F10)

Distances from NH 16 (1487')

to Carter Dome Trail (2322'): 1.9 mi., 850 ft., 1 hr. 25 min.

to Wildcat Ridge Trail (3388'): 3.6 mi., 1900 ft., 2 hr. 45 min.

to Carter Notch Hut (3300'): 3.8 mi. (6.2 km.), 1900 ft. (rev. 100 ft.), 2 hr. 50 min.

Carter Dome Trail (WMNF)

This trail runs from the Nineteen-Mile Brook Trail 1.9 mi. from NH 16 to Zeta Pass and the summit of Carter Dome, following the route of an old road that served the long-dismantled fire tower that once stood on Carter Dome. Grades are steady and moderate all the way.

Leaving the Nineteen-Mile Brook Trail, it follows a tributary brook, crossing it at 0.5 mi. and recrossing at 0.8 mi. at a small, attractive cascade. Here it swings left, then in 50 yd. turns sharp right and ascends by a series of seven switchbacks, passing a good spring left at 1.1 mi. and an unreliable water source located on a spur path that leads right (sign) 80 yd. below the junction with the Carter-Moriah Trail at Zeta Pass at 1.9 mi. The Carter Dome Trail coincides with the Carter-Moriah Trail to the right (south), then at 2.1 mi. the Carter-Moriah Trail—which offers excellent views but is steep and exposed to weather—turns left to climb to the bare summit of Mt. Hight, while the Carter Dome Trail continues its steady, sheltered ascent. At 2.7 mi. the Carter-Moriah Trail re-enters from the left, the Black Angel Trail enters from the left in another 25 yd., and the Carter Dome and Carter-Moriah trails coincide to the junction with the Rainbow Trail at the summit of Carter Dome.

Carter Dome Trail (map 5:F10)

Distances from Nineteen-Mile Brook Trail (2322')

to Zeta Pass (3890'): 1.9 mi., 1550 ft., 1 hr. 45 min.

to Carter Dome summit (4832'): 3.1 mi. (5.0 km.), 2500 ft., 2 hr. 50 min.

Imp Trail (WMNF)

This trail makes a loop over the cliff that bears the Imp Profile, providing fine views. The ends of the loop are 0.3 mi. apart on NH 16, with the north end about 2.6 mi. north of the Mt. Washington Auto Rd. and 5.4 mi. south of Gorham.

The north branch of the trail heads east up the south side of the Imp Brook valley, through a pleasant stand of hemlocks, then crosses the brook at 0.8 mi. (difficult at high water). It angles north up to a ridge and follows its crest, nearly level for some distance. The trail then angles more steeply up the north side of the ridge and continues nearly to the bottom of a ravine northeast of the Imp Profile cliff, where it turns right and then climbs steeply, swinging to the left, to reach the Imp viewpoint at 2.2 mi.

From the cliff, the trail skirts the edge of the Imp Brook ravine and crosses a large brook in 0.3 mi. Becoming gradual but somewhat rough, it continues generally south, ascending and then descending to the junction with the North Carter Trail on the left at 3.1 mi., then passes the site of an old logging camp. Here the Imp Trail turns right and descends a logging road generally southwest, then, just before reaching Cowboy Brook, turns northwest. After another 0.8 mi. it crosses a brook and follows an old logging road north downhill to cross a small brook, then immediately crosses a larger brook. It turns sharp left, runs about level for 75 yd., and ends at NH 16.

Imp Trail (map 5:F10)

Distances from northern terminus on NH 16 (1270')

 to viewpoint (3165'): 2.2 mi., 1900 ft., 2 hr. 5 min.

 to North Carter Trail (3250'): 3.1 mi., 2100 ft. (rev. 100 ft.), 2 hr. 35 min.

 to southern terminus on NH 16 (1270'): 6.3 mi. (10.1 km.), 2100 ft. (rev. 2000 ft.), 4 hr. 10 min.

North Carter Trail (WMNF)

This trail leaves the south branch of the Imp Trail 3.1 mi. from NH 16, just above an old logging camp site. It follows an old logging road, and at 0.3 mi. turns to the right onto another old road. At 0.5 mi. it turns sharp left off the old road and climbs more steeply to the Carter-Moriah Trail 0.3 mi. south of the summit of North Carter.

North Carter Trail (map 5:F10)

Distance from Imp Trail (3250')

 to Carter-Moriah Trail (4470'): 1.2 mi. (1.9 km.), 1200 ft., 1 hr. 10 min.

Stony Brook Trail (WMNF)

This trail begins at a new parking area just off NH 16 on a paved road that leaves the highway just south of the bridge over the Peabody River, about 2 mi. south of Gorham. The trail ends in the col between North Carter and Moriah and provides the best access to the beautiful south ledges of Mt. Moriah. The lower part of the trail has been relocated onto WMNF land to avoid an area of private home construction on the former route.

From NH 16 the trail crosses Stony Brook on a footbridge and follows the brook upstream for 0.8 mi., then recrosses the brook and rejoins the old route, a logging road that becomes less and less obvious. It ascends moderately, and at 2.3 mi. the trail crosses Stony Brook at a pleasant small cascade and pool and begins to climb more steeply. At 3.1 mi. it crosses a small brook on a mossy ledge and climbs steadily to the ridge and the Carter-Moriah Trail.

Stony Brook Trail (map 5:E10–F11)
Distance from NH 16 (930')

>   *to* Carter-Moriah Trail (3127'): 3.6 mi. (5.8 km.), 2200 ft., 2 hr. 55 min.

Kenduskeag Trail (WMNF)

This trail runs from the Carter-Moriah Trail near the summit of Mt. Moriah to the Shelburne Trail in the col between Shelburne Moriah Mtn. and Howe Peak, 4.5 mi. south of US 2. The ledges of Shelburne Moriah afford excellent views. The name of the trail is an Abenaki word meaning "a pleasant walk." From Mt. Moriah to the Rattle River Trail junction it is part of the Appalachian Trail.

From the trail junction below the summit ledges of Mt. Moriah, the Kenduskeag Trail turns sharp right in 15 yd. and runs over a lesser summit, then descends steeply past an outlook, moderates, and continues the descent to the junction with the Rattle River Trail at 1.4 mi. The trail now climbs over a section of knobs and ledges, with fine views, to the flat, ledgy summit of Shelburne Moriah Mtn. at 2.7 mi. The upper part of this section of trail is very exposed to weather—in fact, more so than any other part of the Carter-Moriah Range. The trail descends steadily to a sharp, narrow col at 3.3 mi., then climbs over two knolls with views, and ends at the Shelburne Trail.

Kenduskeag Trail (map 5:E11–E12)
Distances from Carter-Moriah Trail (4000')

>   *to* Rattle River Trail (3300'): 1.4 mi., 100 ft. (rev. 800 ft.), 45 min.

>   *to* Shelburne Moriah Mtn. summit (3735'): 2.7 mi., 650 ft. (rev. 100 ft.), 1 hr. 40 min.

>   *to* Shelburne Trail (2750'): 4.1 mi. (6.5 km.), 750 ft. (rev. 1100 ft.), 2 hr. 25 min.

Rattle River Trail (WMNF)

This trail runs from US 2 to the Kenduskeag Trail in the Moriah–Shelburne Moriah col. The trailhead is on US 2 near the east end of the bridge over Rattle River, about 300 yd. east of the North Rd. intersection and 3.5 mi. east of the eastern junction of US 2 and NH 16 in Gorham. This trail is a part of the Appalachian Trail.

From US 2 the trail leads generally south, following a logging road on the east side of the stream. A snowmobile trail enters on the right at 0.3 mi., the trails enter the WMNF, and the snowmobile trail leaves on the left at 0.6 mi., just before the Rattle River Trail crosses a tributary brook. At 1.7 mi. it passes the WMNF Rattle River Shelter (left) and soon crosses Rattle River (may be difficult at high water), then crosses back over its westerly branch. At 3.2 mi. it again crosses the river and starts to climb steadily. It passes a small cascade to the left of the trail at 3.7 mi., and soon bears away from the brook and climbs steeply to the ridge top, where it meets the Kenduskeag Trail.

Rattle River Trail (map 5:E11)

Distances from US 2 (760')

to Rattle River Shelter (1250'): 1.7 mi., 500 ft., 1 hr. 5 min.

to Kenduskeag Trail (3300'): 4.3 mi. (6.9 km.), 2550 ft., 3 hr. 25 min.

Mount Evans Trail (AMC)

This short path ascends little Mt. Evans, beginning on US 2 2.5 mi. east of the eastern junction with NH 16 0.1 mi. west of the sign for Shadow Pool and 0.8 mi. west of the Rattle River Trail parking area. For a modest effort, its ledges afford fine views of Mt. Washington and the Northern Peaks and good views up and down the Androscoggin River and across to the Mahoosuc Range. It begins on private property, on a road that is posted against vehicular entry.

Follow a dirt logging road (marked by a trail sign) uphill under power lines to a small clearing made for lumber operations at 0.1 mi. Continue straight ahead here on a less used road into the woods, and in another 0.1 mi. the trail crosses a small stream, narrows to a footpath, and turns left onto the crest of a narrow ridge. It follows the ridgecrest south, ascending by switchbacks when the ridgecrest broadens. As the trail approaches the summit, just after passing an overhanging rock outcrop, a faint unsigned path leads left to a narrow viewpoint to the Mahoosuc Range and the valley below. In a few more steps, the trail crosses a large ledge with views of the Presidentials, then passes through a flat area and turns left, continuing to a ledge with views of the Mahoosucs and a large boulder that is, perhaps, the actual summit.

Mount Evans Trail (map 5:E11)

Distance from US 2 (800')

to Mt. Evans summit (1443'): 0.7 mi. (1.1 km.), 650 ft., 40 min.

Shelburne Trail (WMNF)

This trail begins on FR 95 1.0 mi. from US 2 near the Maine–New Hampshire border, passes through the col between Shelburne Moriah Mtn. and Howe Peak, and descends to Wild River Rd. For the north terminus, leave US 2 about 9 mi. east of Gorham, at the west end of an abandoned wayside area just west of the Maine–New Hampshire border; go about 0.1 mi. into this area, and take FR 95 (a rough gravel road) right for 0.9 mi. to a gate. At the Wild River end, the trail leaves Wild River Rd. (FR 12) 0.6 mi. north of Wild River Campground and fords the river, which can be difficult even at moderate water levels. For this reason the Wild River end of the trail is often approached via the Wild River Trail, the Moriah Brook Trail bridge, and the Highwater Trail.

The trail follows the continuation of FR 95 past the gate (follow the trail with care in this area of active logging). At 2.1 mi., 0.2 mi. after the first bridge, it turns left off the main road (sign) onto an older logging road and begins to climb. At 3.9 mi. the trail crosses a very small stream twice and shortly reaches the height-of-land, where it meets the eastern terminus of the Kenduskeag Trail at 4.0 mi. (For Shelburne Moriah Mtn., follow this trail to the right.) The Shelburne Trail continues over the height-of-land and descends steadily, crossing a brook and entering an old logging road. It then turns sharp left at 6.3 mi. onto another logging road, which it follows east down the valley of Bull Brook, soon crossing a branch of the brook. At 7.0 mi. the Highwater Trail enters from the right (southwest) and leaves on the left (northeast) 10 yd. farther on. This junction may be poorly signed. To avoid the Wild River crossing, follow the Highwater Trail south to the Moriah Brook Trail bridge. The Shelburne Trail continues straight across a dry channel and fords Wild River to Wild River Rd.

Shelburne Trail (map 5:E12–F12)

Distances from gate on FR 95 (900')

> *to* Kenduskeag Trail (2750'): 4.0 mi., 1850 ft., 2 hr. 55 min.
>
> *to* Wild River Rd. (1079'): 7.2 mi. (11.6 km.), 1850 ft. (rev. 1700 ft.), 4 hr. 35 min.

Wild River Trail (WMNF)

This trail begins at a parking area near the end of Wild River Rd. (FR 12) and just outside of Wild River Campground, a trailhead shared with the Basin Trail. It runs along the Wild River valley to Perkins Notch, then descends to the Wildcat River Trail between Carter Notch Rd. and Carter Notch. Wild River Rd.

leaves ME 113 just south of the bridge over Evans Brook at Hastings and runs 5.7 mi. to the campground, where there is a parking area on the left just before the campground entrance. All the river crossings (except the one made on Spider Bridge) and those of Spruce Brook and Red Brook may be difficult at moderate water levels and dangerous at high water.

The trail, relocated at the start to avoid passing through the campground, immediately crosses Wild River Rd., then a small stream, and follows the bank of Wild River. At 0.2 mi. it joins and follows the old logging railroad bed that extends from the end of Wild River Rd. and runs generally southwest along the southeast bank of Wild River. At 0.3 mi. the Moriah Brook Trail leaves on the right to cross the river on a bridge, and at 1.0 mi. the trail narrows. At 2.6 mi. the Black Angel Trail enters from the left and coincides with the Wild River Trail as both trails turn west and cross to the northwest side of Wild River on Spider Bridge. Just across the bridge, the Highwater Trail from Hastings enters from the right and ends, and the Wild River and Black Angel trails turn left onto an old railroad grade. In 0.1 mi. the Black Angel Trail diverges to the right for Carter Dome. The Wild River Trail continues generally southwest, passes Spruce Brook Shelter (right), then crosses Spruce Brook at 3.5 mi. At 4.4 mi. it crosses Red Brook, then leaves the old railroad bed and bears right. At 4.8 mi. the Eagle Link leaves on the left for Eagle Crag, and at 5.7 mi. the trail crosses to the south bank of Wild River. At 6.3 mi. the East Branch Trail leaves on the left and the Wild River Trail crosses the Wild River to the north bank, then recrosses for the last time at 6.7 mi.

Soon the trail skirts the south side of No-Ketchum Pond, passes the WMNF Perkins Notch Shelter at 7.0 mi., heads more west, and begins a gradual climb into Perkins Notch. At 7.8 mi. the Rainbow Trail leaves right for Carter Dome, and at 8.5 mi., at the Carroll–Coos county line (sign), the Bog Brook Trail leaves left for Carter Notch Rd. From this junction the trail descends gradually and ends at the Wildcat River Trail.

Wild River Trail (map 5:F12–G10)
Distances from Wild River Campground trailhead parking area (1150')

to Moriah Brook Trail (1170'): 0.3 mi., 0 ft., 10 min.

to Spider Bridge (1495'): 2.7 mi., 350 ft., 1 hr. 30 min.

to Eagle Link (2150'): 4.8 mi., 1000 ft., 2 hr. 55 min.

to East Branch Trail (2400'): 6.3 mi., 1250 ft., 3 hr. 45 min.

to Perkins Notch Shelter (2570'): 7.0 mi., 1400 ft., 4 hr. 10 min.

to Rainbow Trail (2590'): 7.8 mi., 1450 ft., 4 hr. 40 min.

to Bog Brook Trail (2417'): 8.5 mi., 1450 ft. (rev. 150 ft.), 5 hr.

to Wildcat River Trail (2320'): 9.6 mi. (15.5 km.), 1550 ft. (rev. 200 ft.), 5 hr. 35 min.

Hastings Trail (WMNF)

This trail starts at a parking lot at the junction of ME 113 and Wild River Rd. (FR 12) about 100 yd. south of the Evans Brook bridge, at the deserted logging village of Hastings. It follows logging roads to its terminus on US 2, 60 yd. inside the east end of an abandoned wayside area immediately west of the Maine–New Hampshire border, about 9.2 mi. east of Gorham and 2.0 mi. west of Gilead ME.

From Wild River Rd. it crosses Wild River on a 180-ft. suspension footbridge. On the west bank the Highwater Trail leaves left, heading up the northwest side of the river. The Hastings Trail enters the woods on a logging road running generally north. After passing the remains of an old telephone line, it ascends gradually on an old, narrow logging road. At 2.0 mi. it descends (right) onto an old, broad logging road marked as a snowmobile trail, then turns right again at 2.3 mi. onto a private dirt road that it follows to the old wayside area.

Hastings Trail (map 5:E13–E12)
Distance from Hastings (830')

to abandoned wayside area (710'): 2.8 mi. (4.5 km.), 300 ft. (rev. 400 ft.), 1 hr. 35 min.

Highwater Trail (WMNF)

This trail runs along the northwest side of Wild River from Hastings on ME 113 to the Wild River Trail at the west end of Spider Bridge, providing a means of avoiding unbridged crossings of the Wild River, which are frequently very difficult. Most of the way it follows old logging roads with easy grades, close to the river, but it is often not blazed or signed clearly at intersections.

It leaves the Hastings Trail left (south) at the west end of the suspension bridge over the Wild River across from the parking lot at Hastings. At 0.7 mi. it bears right on an old logging road that angles somewhat away from the river. The trail crosses into New Hampshire and continues up the river, then enters FR 52 and follows it for a while, passing the site of a logging bridge that formerly crossed Wild River at 2.3 mi. to connect with the Wild River Rd. Heading generally southwest, it crosses Martins Brook at 4.0 mi. At 5.3 mi. it enters the Shelburne Trail, turns right and follows it for 10 yd., then turns left off it (no signs) and soon crosses Bull Brook on a bridge. At 6.7 mi. it reaches the footbridge where the Moriah Brook Trail crosses Wild River, 0.3 mi. above Wild River Campground. It joins the Moriah Brook Trail, then the trails turn sharp right after 0.1 mi., and at 7.0 mi. the Highwater Trail turns left off the Moriah Brook Trail and crosses Moriah Brook (difficult in high water). The trail continues on top of a steep bank, where there is a restricted view across the valley, then crosses or follows several logging roads, each for a short distance. It crosses Cypress Brook at 9.5 mi. and soon ends near Spider Bridge at its junction with the coinciding Black Angel and Wild River trails.

Highwater Trail (map 5:E13–F11)

Distances from Hastings Trail (830')

> *to* FR 52 bridge (950'): 2.3 mi., 100 ft., 1 hr. 10 min.
>
> *to* Shelburne Trail (1090'): 5.3 mi., 250 ft., 2 hr. 45 min.
>
> *to* Moriah Brook Trail (1170'): 6.7 mi., 350 ft., 3 hr. 30 min.
>
> *to* Wild River Trail/Black Angel Trail (1495'): 9.6 mi. (15.4 km.), 950 ft. (rev. 300 ft.), 5 hr. 15 min.

Burnt Mill Brook Trail (WMNF)

This trail ascends from Wild River Rd. (FR 12), 2.7 mi. south of ME 113, to the Royce Trail in the col between East Royce Mtn. and West Royce Mtn. From Wild River Rd. the trail ascends south on logging roads, passing a cascade to the left of the trail at 0.6 mi. At 1.4 mi. it begins to climb more steeply, crosses Burnt Mill Brook at 1.7 mi., and ascends to the col between the Royces, where it meets the Royce Trail.

Burnt Mill Brook Trail (map 5:F12)

Distance from Wild River Rd. (966')

> *to* Royce Trail (2600'): 2.0 mi. (3.2 km.), 1650 ft., 1 hr. 50 min.

Moriah Brook Trail (WMNF)

This trail ascends to the col between Mt. Moriah and North Carter from the Wild River Trail 0.3 mi. south of Wild River Campground. It is an attractive trail, passing Moriah Gorge, traversing beautiful birch woods that have grown up after fires, and providing fine views up to the impressive south cliffs of Moriah.

The trail leaves to the right from the Wild River Trail and in 75 yd. crosses the Wild River on a suspension footbridge, where the Highwater Trail joins on the right. The trail turns left and follows the river bank about 0.1 mi., then turns sharp right and generally follows the course of the former lumber railroad up the north bank of Moriah Brook. At 0.4 mi. the Highwater Trail leaves left. At 1.4 mi. the Moriah Brook Trail crosses Moriah Brook (may be difficult at high water); the gorge downstream from this crossing merits exploration. The trail follows the south bank of the brook, then recrosses at 2.8 mi., and in another 0.4 mi. passes some attractive cascades and pools, crosses a ledge, then crosses a branch of Moriah Brook just above the confluence with the main brook. The trail continues through birch woods and crosses the main brook four more times, the last crossing in a boulder area below a small cascade at 5.0 mi. The trail becomes rather wet as it winds through almost pure stands of white birch below the impressive south cliffs of Mt. Moriah, then climbs to the col and the Carter-Moriah Trail.

Moriah Brook Trail (map 5:F12–F11)
Distance from Wild River Trail (1170')

   to Carter-Moriah Trail (3127'): 5.5 mi. (8.8 km.), 1950 ft., 3 hr. 45 min.

Black Angel Trail (WMNF)

This trail begins at Rim Junction—where the Basin and Basin Rim trails cross—and descends to cross the Wild River on Spider Bridge along with the Wild River Trail, then climbs to the Carter-Moriah Trail 0.4 mi. north of Carter Dome.

Leaving Rim Junction, it descends gradually southwest 0.5 mi. to Blue Brook Shelter, where a branch trail runs right (north) for 0.3 mi. to connect with the Basin Trail 0.3 mi. west of Rim Junction. From Blue Brook Shelter the Black Angel Trail crosses Blue Brook, ascends moderately west and passes through a col, then descends to an old logging road and follows it generally west for 1.4 mi. down the Cedar Brook valley, remaining on the north side of the stream and making several obvious shortcuts at curves. The trail then leaves the logging road, turns more north, and joins the Wild River Trail to cross Wild River on Spider Bridge at 2.8 mi. Just across the bridge the Highwater Trail leaves right for Hastings, and the Black Angel and Wild River trails continue ahead.

The Black Angel Trail diverges to the right in 0.1 mi. and rises slowly through open woods. About 1.5 mi. up from the Wild River the grade steepens;

at 5.2 mi. the trail crosses a north branch of Spruce Brook, and about 0.5 mi. beyond enters virgin timber. The grade lessens but the footing becomes rougher as the trail angles up the east slope of Mt. Hight, passing lookout points as it traverses a steep, ledgy section on its south-southeast slope, then swings southwest and ends at the Carter-Moriah Trail.

Black Angel Trail (map 5:F12–F10)
Distances from Rim Junction (1950')

    to Blue Brook Shelter (1800'): 0.5 mi., 150 ft., 15 min.

    to Spider Bridge (1495'): 2.8 mi., 500 ft. (rev. 800 ft.), 1 hr. 40 min.

    to Carter-Moriah Trail (4600'): 7.7 mi. (12.5 km.), 3600 ft., 5 hr. 40 min.

Basin Trail (WMNF)

This trail runs from the parking area just outside of Wild River Campground (also the trailhead for the Wild River Trail) to Basin Pond (0.7 mi. from NH 113, near Cold River Campground), crossing the ridge connecting Mt. Meader to West Royce somewhat north of its lowest point and giving easy access to the magnificent views along the brink of the cliffs.

Leaving the parking area, it follows an old lumber road. At 0.4 mi., where the road swings right, the trail continues straight ahead and soon approaches the southwest bank of Blue Brook, which it follows for about 0.8 mi. At 1.3 mi. it crosses the brook at the foot of a pretty cascade and then follows the northeast bank, passing opposite a very striking cliff to the south of the brook. The trail leaves Blue Brook, crosses another small brook, then climbs somewhat more steeply. At 2.0 mi. a side trail branches right 0.3 mi. to Blue Brook Shelter and the Black Angel Trail, and at 2.2 mi. the Basin Trail crosses the Basin Rim Trail and meets the Black Angel Trail at Rim Junction. The best viewpoint from the top of the cliff that overhangs the Basin is located 0.1 mi. south of this junction on the Basin Rim Trail.

The trail now descends very steeply along the south side and foot of the great cliff and crosses a wide, stony brook. At 3.0 mi. it passes the upper end of the Hermit Falls Loop, a loop path slightly longer than the main trail that leads right 0.1 mi. to Hermit Falls and then returns to the main trail 0.2 mi. below its point of departure. The Basin Trail descends to an old logging road and turns right on it, then runs across numerous small brooks, using segments of old roads, to the parking area.

Basin Trail (map 5:F12)

Distances from Wild River Campground hiker parking area (1150')

   to Rim Junction (1950'): 2.2 mi., 800 ft., 1 hr. 30 min.

   to Hermit Falls loop path, lower junction (730'): 3.2 mi., 800 ft. (rev. 1200 ft.), 2 hr.

   to Basin Pond parking area (670'): 4.5 mi. (7.2 km.), 800 ft. (rev. 50 ft.), 2 hr. 40 min.

Eagle Link (AMC)

This trail runs from the Wild River Trail 4.8 mi. southwest of Wild River Campground to the junction with the Baldface Circle and Meader Ridge trails 0.2 mi. south of Eagle Crag. It leaves the Wild River Trail and soon crosses two channels of Wild River (may be difficult at high water), then bears sharp right and ascends generally east at a moderate grade. It crosses a small brook at 1.2 mi., angles up through a birch forest on the north slope of North Baldface, and ends at the junction of the Baldface Circle and Meader Ridge trails.

Eagle Link (map 5:F11–F12)

Distance from Wild River Trail (2150')

   to Baldface Circle Trail/Meader Ridge Trail (2990'): 2.7 mi. (4.4 km.), 1000 ft. (rev. 150 ft.), 1 hr. 45 min.

Royce Trail (AMC)

This trail runs to the summit of West Royce Mtn. from the west side of ME 113, at a point opposite the Brickett Place about 0.3 mi. north of the access road to the WMNF Cold River Campground. Leaving ME 113, it follows a narrow road about 0.3 mi., then crosses Cold River and bears off the road to the right onto a blue-blazed footpath. The trail recrosses the river at 0.7 mi. and again at 1.4 mi. Then, after crossing the south branch of Mad River, it rises more steeply and soon passes Mad River Falls, where a side path leads left 25 yd. to a viewpoint. The trail becomes rather rough, with large boulders, and rises steeply under the imposing ledges for which East Royce is famous. At 2.7 mi. the Laughing Lion Trail enters right, and at a height-of-land at 2.9 mi., after a very steep ascent, the Royce Connector Trail branches right, leading to the East Royce Trail for East Royce.

   Royce Connector Trail (AMC). This short trail, 0.2 mi. (5 min.) long, links the Royce Trail and the East Royce Trail, permitting the ascent of either summit of Royce from either trail, and provides views from ledges along the way.

The Royce Trail bears left at this junction and descends somewhat, then climbs to the height-of-land between the Royces at 3.6 mi., where the Burnt Mill Brook Trail to Wild River Rd. bears right, while the Royce Trail turns abruptly left (west) and ascends the steep wall of the pass. It then continues by easy grades over ledges and through stunted spruce to the summit of West Royce, where it meets the Basin Rim Trail.

Royce Trail (map 5:F12)

Distances from ME 113 (600')

> *to* Mad River Falls (900'): 1.6 mi., 300 ft., 55 min.
>
> *to* Laughing Lion Trail (2400'): 2.7 mi., 1800 ft., 2 hr. 15 min.
>
> *to* Royce Connector Trail (2650'): 2.9 mi., 2050 ft., 2 hr. 30 min.
>
> *to* West Royce Mtn. summit (3210'): 4.3 mi. (7.0 km.), 2700 ft., 3 hr. 30 min.
>
> *to* East Royce Mtn. summit (3114') via Royce Connector and East Royce Trail: 3.6 mi. (5.8 km.), 2650 ft., 3 hr. 10 min.

East Royce Trail (AMC)

This trail climbs rather steeply to East Royce Mtn. from the west side of ME 113 just north of the height-of-land. Leaving the highway, it immediately crosses Evans Brook and ascends steeply, crossing several other brooks in the first 0.5 mi. At the final brook crossing at 1.0 mi., the Royce Connector Trail leaves on the left, leading in 0.2 mi. to the Royce Trail for West Royce. The East Royce Trail emerges on ledges at 1.1 mi. and passes a spur path that leads left to an outlook ledge with excellent views east into the Caribou–Speckled Mtn. Wilderness. The trail soon reaches a subsidiary summit with views to the south, turns right, and climbs to a broad open ledge with wide-ranging views, where the plainly marked trail ends. Here a faintly marked beaten path turns right (north), dropping down the steep edge of the ledge, and runs generally northeast over several more ledges, passing over the true summit of East Royce in 250 yd. and continuing another 180 yd. to a large open ledge with a beautiful outlook to the north and west.

East Royce Trail (map 5:F13–F12)

Distances from ME 113 (1420')

> *to* ledge at the end of the East Royce Trail (3070'): 1.3 mi. (2.2 km.), 1650 ft.,1 hr. 30 min.
>
> *to* East Royce Mtn. summit: 1.5 mi. (2.4 km.), 1700 ft., 1 hr. 35 min.

Laughing Lion Trail (CTA)

This trail begins on the west side of ME 113, just north of a roadside picnic area and about 2.3 mi. north of the road to Cold River Campground, and ends on the Royce Trail. It descends to Cold River and ascends west to a ridgecrest, which it follows north, alternating moderate and steep sections and providing occasional fine views down the valley, then swings west and levels off just before it ends at the Royce Trail.

Laughing Lion Trail (map 5:F13–F12)

Distance from ME 113 (1370')

> *to* Royce Trail (2400'): 1.1 mi. (1.8 km.), 1200 ft. (rev. 150 ft.), 1 hr. 10 min.

Basin Rim Trail (AMC)

This trail follows the ridge that runs from Mt. Meader, starting from the east knob at the junction with the Mount Meader and Meader Ridge trails and ending at the summit of West Royce Mtn., where it meets the Royce Trail. It has fine views, particularly at the top of the cliff that forms the wall of the Basin.

The trail leaves the east knob of Mt. Meader and descends north over the ledges. Just after crossing a small brook, it reaches a col, then ascends slightly along the east side of a prominent hump called Ragged Jacket. The trail soon descends steeply from ledge to ledge down the north slope to the lowest point of the ridge (1870 ft.), then rises gradually over ledges. It passes the best outlook over the Basin about 0.1 mi. before reaching Rim Junction at 1.4 mi., where the Basin Trail crosses and the Black Angel Trail also enters. At 1.5 mi. a short spur leads right to Basin Outlook, a restricted but interesting viewpoint at the edge of the cliffs on the east. In the next 0.3 mi. there are more good views east over the great cliff of the Basin Rim. Passing west of the prominent southeast knee of West Royce, the trail climbs, with only short intervening descents. At 2.6 mi. it climbs a very steep pitch to an outlook to the Carter-Moriah Range, then passes a small brook (unreliable), and ends at the summit of West Royce Mtn.

Basin Rim Trail (map 5:F12)

Distances from Mount Meader Trail/Meader Ridge Trail (2750')

> *to* Rim Junction (1950'): 1.4 mi., 200 ft. (rev. 1000 ft.), 50 min.

> *to* West Royce Mtn. summit (3210'): 3.9 mi. (6.3 km.), 1600 ft. (rev. 100 ft.), 2 hr. 45 min.

Mount Meader Trail (AMC)

This trail runs from the west side of NH 113, about 0.5 mi. north of the entrance to the Baldface Circle Trail, to a junction with the Meader Ridge and Basin Rim trails on the ridgecrest at an easterly knob of Mt. Meader.

From NH 113 it follows a logging road (do not block entrance) that stays on the north side of Mill Brook, and at 1.0 mi. it passes a side path left that runs 0.1 mi. to Brickett Falls. The trail soon turns left uphill off the logging road (sign), and at 2.1 mi. it begins a steep climb up the heel of the ridge, turning sharp left at the top of the heel at 2.5 mi. Coming out on open ledges with fine views at 2.9 mi., it soon reaches the east knob of Mt. Meader.

Mount Meader Trail (map 5:G12–F12)

Distance from NH 113 (520')

> *to* Meader Ridge Trail (2750'): 3.0 mi. (4.8 km.), 2250 ft., 2 hr. 40 min.

Meader Ridge Trail (AMC)

This trail runs along the ridgecrest from the junction with the Mount Meader and Basin Rim trails on the east knob of Mt. Meader to the junction with the Baldface Circle Trail and Eagle Link, 0.2 mi. south of Eagle Crag.

From the east knob of Mt. Meader, the trail descends slightly in a southwest direction and in 0.2 mi. passes just south of the true summit of Mt. Meader, which is reached by a short spur trail. Descending again, with a small intervening ascent, it passes several good viewpoints to the east. At 0.4 mi. a short side path (sign) leads west 100 yd. up to a large open ledge with fine views to the west. The Meader Ridge Trail passes the deepest col of the ridge at 0.6 mi., where it crosses an unreliable small brook; sometimes there is also water upstream a short distance in a swampy place called the Bear Traps. The trail then climbs to an intermediate peak at 1.2 mi. and descends to another col at 1.4 mi. Climbing again, it emerges from timberline at 1.9 mi., passes over the summit of Eagle Crag, and then descends slightly to meet the Baldface Circle Trail and Eagle Link.

Meader Ridge Trail (map 5:F12)

Distance from Mount Meader Trail/Basin Rim Trail (2750')

> *to* Baldface Circle Trail/Eagle Link (2990'): 2.0 mi. (3.2 km.), 550 ft. (rev. 300 ft.), 1 hr. 15 min.

Baldface Circle Trail (AMC)

This trail makes a loop over North and South Baldface from NH 113 at a new parking area 0.1 mi. north of the driveway to the AMC Cold River Camp. It is one of the most attractive trips in the White Mtns., with about 4 mi. of open and semi-open ledge providing long stretches of unobstructed views and equally great exposure to storms. This is a strenuous trip that should not be underestimated.

Leaving NH 113 about 60 yd. north of the parking area, the trail reaches Circle Junction at 0.7 mi., where a side path leads right (north) 0.1 mi. to Emerald Pool. From here, the trail is described in a clockwise direction—up South Baldface, over to North Baldface, and down from Eagle Crag—but the circuit in the reverse direction is equally fine.

From Circle Junction, the south branch follows an old road, then turns left (south), crosses a brook bed, and climbs past the junction with the Slippery Brook Trail on the left at 0.9 mi. to an old logging road that it follows for almost a mile. At 1.2 mi. a loop path 0.5 mi. long leads left to Chandler Gorge (a small flume with several pools and lesser cascades in a rocky bed) and rejoins the main trail 0.1 mi. above its departure point. The trail swings around the south side of Spruce Knoll and, at 2.5 mi., leaves the old road in a rocky area and soon reaches Last Chance Spring (unreliable) and South Baldface Shelter. In a short distance the trail comes out on the ledges and climbs very steeply in the open on rocks that are dangerous if wet or icy. At 3.0 mi. the trail reaches the crest of a rounded ridge and swings left, ascending near the crest toward a knob, becoming much less steep. On that knob, at 3.2 mi., the Baldface Knob Trail enters on the left (south). The Baldface Circle Trail then ascends to the summit of South Baldface at 3.7 mi.

Bearing right at the summit of South Baldface, it follows the broad ridge, descending into the shelter of mature conifers at 4.0 mi., then coming out on a semi-open knob at 4.2 mi. From here to North Baldface the trail runs mostly in the open, though there are several small cols where some shelter could be obtained in a storm. At 4.9 mi. it mounts the last steep pitch to the summit of North Baldface, then descends steeply to the broad, lumpy, ledgy ridge that runs toward Eagle Crag. At 5.8 mi. the Bicknell Ridge Trail leaves right, providing a scenic alternative route to NH 113.

At 6.1 mi. the trail reaches a multiple junction where the Eagle Link leaves left (west) for the Wild River valley, the Meader Ridge Trail continues straight ahead (north) for Eagle Crag and Mt. Meader, and the Baldface Circle Trail turns sharp right and descends on a steep and rough way over ledges for 0.2 mi. At the base of the ledges the trail swings left and, after a gradual section, descends moderately. At 6.9 mi. it crosses a very small brook (unreliable) with a ledgy, mossy bed and becomes less steep; at 7.3 mi. it enters an old logging road and follows it to the right. At 7.7 mi. the Eagle Cascade Link, 0.7 mi. long, leaves on the right, crosses the brook (use caution) above Eagle Cascade in 0.4 mi., and climbs to the Bicknell Ridge Trail. At 8.4 mi. the Bicknell Ridge Trail enters right just after crossing a branch of Charles Brook on flat ledges. The Baldface Circle Trail now angles left away from the brook, then returns to it and crosses it (may be difficult in high water) at 9.0 mi., just before reaching Circle Junction.

Baldface Circle Trail (map 5:G12)

Distances from NH 113 (520')

> *to* Circle Junction (720'): 0.7 mi., 200 ft., 25 min.
>
> *to* Slippery Brook Trail junction (800'): 0.9 mi., 300 ft., 35 min.
>
> *to* South Baldface Shelter (1950'): 2.5 mi., 1450 ft., 2 hr.
>
> *to* Baldface Knob Trail (3030'): 3.2 mi., 2500 ft., 2 hr. 50 min.
>
> *to* South Baldface summit (3570'): 3.7 mi., 3050 ft., 3 hr. 25 min.
>
> *to* North Baldface summit (3610'): 4.9 mi., 3500 ft. (rev. 400 ft.), 4 hr. 10 min.
>
> *to* Eagle Link/Meader Ridge Trail (2990'): 6.1 mi., 3600 ft. (rev. 700 ft.), 4 hr. 50 min.
>
> *to* Bicknell Ridge Trail, lower junction (970'): 8.4 mi., 3600 ft. (rev. 2000 ft.), 6 hr.
>
> *to* Circle Junction (720'): 9.1 mi., 3600 ft. (rev. 250 ft.), 6 hr. 20 min.
>
> *to* NH 113 (520'), for complete loop: 9.8 mi. (15.8 km.), 3600 ft. (rev. 200 ft.), 6 hr. 40 min.

Bicknell Ridge Trail (CTA)

This trail begins on the north branch of the Baldface Circle Trail 1.4 mi. from NH 113 and ends on the same trail 0.9 mi. north of North Baldface. Diverging from the Baldface Circle Trail, it immediately crosses a branch of Charles Brook and ascends gradually through second-growth hardwood. After about 1.0 mi., it turns more to the west, rises more rapidly along the south side of Bicknell Ridge, and, just before the first ledges, crosses a brook bed where there is usually water among the boulders. Soon the trail emerges on the open ledges, and the Eagle Cascade Link enters right from Eagle Cascade and the Baldface Circle Trail. Above this junction the trail mostly travels over broad, open ledges with excellent views, then reaches the ridge top, where it rejoins the Baldface Circle Trail.

Bicknell Ridge Trail (map 5:G12)

Distances from Baldface Circle Trail, lower junction (970')

> *to* Eagle Cascade Link (2020'): 1.4 mi., 1050 ft., 1 hr. 20 min.

> *to* Baldface Circle Trail, upper junction (3050'): 2.5 mi. (4.0 km.), 2100 ft., 2 hr. 20 min.

Baldface Knob Trail (WMNF)

This trail, in combination with the Slippery Brook Trail, provides an alternative route to South Baldface that avoids the steepest ledges on the Baldface Circle Trail. It begins at the Slippery Brook Trail in the col between Eastman Mtn. and South Baldface, opposite the beginning of the Eastman Mountain Trail, then climbs to Baldface Knob and continues along the open ridge to the Baldface Circle Trail on the shoulder below the summit of South Baldface.

Baldface Knob Trail (map 5:G12)

Distance from Slippery Brook Trail (2650')

> *to* Baldface Circle Trail (3030'): 0.7 mi. (1.1 km.), 450 ft. (rev. 50 ft.), 35 min.

Eastman Mountain Trail (CTA)

This trail ascends Eastman Mtn. from the Slippery Brook Trail at the height-of-land in the col between Eastman Mtn. and South Baldface, opposite the lower terminus of the Baldface Knob Trail. The trail first descends slightly, then rises at a moderate grade onto the north ridge, where outlook points provide fine views of South Baldface and Sable Mtn. It continues generally southeast to the summit, which has a rewarding view in all directions.

Eastman Mountain Trail (map 5:G12)

Distance from Slippery Brook Trail (2650')

> *to* Eastman Mtn. summit (2939'): 0.8 mi. (1.3 km.), 500 ft. (rev. 100 ft.), 40 min.

Slippery Brook Trail (WMNF)

This trail runs from the south branch of the Baldface Circle Trail 0.9 mi. from NH 113 through the col between South Baldface and Eastman Mtn. to Slippery Brook Rd. (FR 17, called Town Hall Rd. at its southern end), 7.0 mi. from NH 16A.

Leaving the Baldface Circle Trail, it ascends a small ridge and then descends, crossing a branch of Chandler Brook and a tributary before joining the older route on an old logging road. The trail ascends generally southwest through woods, first easily then moderately, and reaches the col between South Baldface and Eastman Mtn. at 2.6 mi., where the Baldface Knob Trail leaves right (north) for South Baldface and the Eastman Mountain Trail leaves left (south). The Slippery Brook Trail soon descends to Slippery Brook, which it crosses six times. After the last crossing, the trail runs along the east bank, crosses a logging road, and ends at Slippery Brook Rd., 200 yd. north of the gate. (In the reverse direction, it diverges left from the road north of the gate.)

Slippery Brook Trail (map 5:G12–G11)

Distances from Baldface Circle Trail (800')

> *to* Baldface Knob Trail/Eastman Mountain Trail (2650'): 2.6 mi., 1850 ft., ft., 2 hr. 15 min.

> *to* last crossing of Slippery Brook (2050'): 4.2 mi., 1850 ft. (rev. 600 ft.), 3 hr.

> *to* Slippery Brook Rd. (1610'): 6.6 mi. (10.6 km.), 1850 ft. (rev. 450 ft.), 4 hr. 15 min.

Mountain Pond Loop Trail (WMNF)

This trail begins on Slippery Brook Rd. (FR 17, called Town Hall Rd. at its southern end), 6.3 mi. from NH 16A. (In winter the road is plowed for about 3.5 mi., after which it receives heavy use by snowmobiles.) East of Mountain Pond the former route of the trail has been officially closed by the WMNF, and the cabin formerly located at the pond has been removed.

The trail runs 0.3 mi. from the road to a fork; bearing left, it reaches the Mountain Pond Shelter at 1.0 mi., then continues around the pond with occasional moderately rough footing. Just before returning to the fork, it crosses the pond's outlet brook, where at times of high water the crossing may be difficult and the trail hard to follow (but it is fairly easy to bushwhack along the south bank of the outlet brook back to the road and parking area).

Mountain Pond Loop Trail (map 5:G11)

Distance from Slippery Brook Rd. (1483')

> *for* complete loop around Mountain Pond (1509'): 2.7 mi. (4.3 km.), 50 ft., 1 hr. 25 min.

East Branch Trail (WMNF)

This trail begins on Slippery Brook Rd. (FR 17, called Town Hall Rd. at its southern end), 4.8 mi. from NH 16A and about 0.5 mi. southwest of the junction with East Branch Rd. (FR 38). It follows the East Branch of the Saco River, crossing East Branch Rd. and making three difficult crossings of the East Branch, then rejoins East Branch Rd. (which is passable for cars up to this point). It then ascends along the East Branch and crosses a height-of-land, finally ending on the Wild River Trail at the foot of the hill east of Perkins Notch, 0.3 mi. east of Perkins Notch Shelter. It is very muddy south of the height-of-land, at times difficult to follow, and the three crossings of the East Branch are hard at normal water levels and would be hazardous at high water (but can be avoided by starting at the upper road crossing).

Leaving Slippery Brook Rd., the trail descends to cross Slippery Brook, then enters and follows an old railroad bed on the east side of the East Branch. At 2.3 mi. it crosses East Branch Rd., then crosses the East Branch three times (difficult); the last crossing is at a stretch of still water, and 0.1 mi. farther it joins East Branch Rd. from the right at the point where the part of the road open to vehicles ends. Here also a road leaves left to connect with the Bald Land Trail (sign). The East Branch Trail then crosses Gulf Brook, leaves the railroad bed within 0.1 mi., and follows old logging roads. At 4.9 mi. the trail crosses Black Brook and shortly bears northwest away from the river, then climbs by easy grades to a divide between Black Mtn. and a prominent southwest spur of North Baldface at 7.2 mi. The logging road dwindles to a trail, passes through a patch of spruce, and descends to its junction with the Wild River Trail on the south bank of Wild River. In this section it is followed or paralleled by a snowmobile trail, which may be more obvious in some locations.

East Branch Trail (map 5:H11–G11)

Distances from Slippery Brook Rd. (1205')

   to crossing of East Branch Rd. (1650'): 2.3 mi., 450 ft., 1 hr. 25 min.

   to end of East Branch Rd. (1700'): 3.5 mi., 550 ft., 2 hr.

   to height-of-land (2590'): 7.2 mi., 1450 ft., 4 hr. 20 min.

   to Wild River Trail (2400'): 7.6 mi. (12.2 km.), 1450 ft. (rev. 200 ft.), 4 hr. 30 min.

Bald Land Trail (WMNF)

This trail follows an old roadway from Black Mtn. Rd. to the East Branch through the divide between Black Mtn. and North Doublehead. It is marked in parts as a cross-country ski trail and crosses several other ski trails, and is somewhat hard to follow because it is not well marked or signed as a hiking trail. The west trailhead is reached in 3.0 mi. from NH 16 in Jackson by following NH 16B to Dundee Rd., taking the latter past Black Mtn. Ski Area, then bearing left uphill on Black Mtn. Rd. to a small parking area on the right. The east trailhead is at the end of East Branch Rd. (FR 38), a branch of Slippery Brook Rd. (FR 17).

The trail passes a gate and follows the East Pasture (X-C Ski) Trail for 0.4 mi., then diverges right (sign), crosses Great Brook, and follows an old road with a stone wall on the right. At 0.8 mi. it turns right onto the main ski trail, which leads into an overgrown pasture with fine views of Doublehead Mtn., then bears left away from the pasture and soon rejoins the old ski trail that continued straight at the 0.8 mi. junction. At 1.2 mi. the trail bears left onto an old logging road (marked by orange tape) and ascends through an overgrown pasture. It bears left at an old ski trail (arrow) just before crossing the Bald Land Ski Trail at a double blue diamond marker. (If you miss the unsigned turn at 1.2 mi., you can continue up the Bald Land Ski Trail to the Scenic Vista Spur, then turn sharp left and follow the main ski trail just past the height-of-land to its intersection with the hiking trail at the double blue diamonds; turn right there.) Descend along the hiking trail, crossing a logging road (Woodland Ski Trail) at 2.0 mi., and continue to the East Branch Rd.

Bald Land Trail (map 5:G11)

Distance from Black Mtn. Rd. (1585')

> *to* East Branch Rd. (1730'): 2.1 mi. (3.4 km.), 700 ft. (rev. 550 ft.), 1 hr. 25 min.

Rainbow Trail (WMNF)

This trail climbs to the summit of Carter Dome from the Wild River Trail in Perkins Notch about 0.8 mi. west of the Perkins Notch Shelter near No-Ketchum Pond. After leaving the Wild River Trail, it passes through a sag, then ascends steadily on the southeast slope of Carter Dome. At 1.5 mi. it passes just east of the summit of a southerly knob and runs in the open with fine views, returns into the woods at a sag, then climbs moderately to the Carter-Moriah Trail at the summit of Carter Dome.

Rainbow Trail (map 5:G11–F10)
Distances from Wild River Trail (2590')

>   *to* south knob (4274'): 1.5 mi., 1700 ft., 1 hr. 35 min.

>   *to* Carter Dome summit (4832'): 2.5 mi. (4.0 km.), 2300 ft., 2 hr. 25 min.

Bog Brook Trail (WMNF)

This trail begins at a small parking area on Carter Notch Rd., about 3.0 mi. from NH 16B just west of its sharp turn at the crossing of Wildcat Brook. It ends on the Wild River Trail 1.5 mi. west of Perkins Notch Shelter. Some brook crossings may be difficult at high water, but they can be avoided by following the gravel logging road extension of Carter Notch Rd. (FR 233) to the point where the Bog Brook Trail crosses it.

The trail follows a dirt road (sign) past two camps and bears right off the road into the woods (marked here by blue diamonds) at a turnaround at the WMNF boundary. Running nearly level, it crosses Wildcat Brook, then another brook, and then the Wildcat River, a tributary of Wildcat Brook. In 60 yd. the Wildcat River Trail continues straight ahead, while the Bog Brook Trail diverges right. The trail now ascends moderately, crossing a gravel logging road (FR 233) that leads (to the left) back to Carter Notch Rd. The trail then follows Bog Brook through a wet area, crossing and recrossing the brook, to the Wild River Trail.

Bog Brook Trail (map 5:G10)
Distances from Carter Notch Rd. (1810')

>   *to* Wildcat River Trail (1790'): 0.7 mi., 50 ft. (rev. 50 ft.), 25 min.

>   *to* Wild River Trail (2417'): 2.8 mi. (4.5 km.), 700 ft., 1 hr. 45 min.

Wildcat River Trail (AMC)

This trail runs to Carter Notch Hut from the Bog Brook Trail just east of the Wildcat River crossing 0.7 mi. from Carter Notch Rd. Brook crossings may be difficult at high water, but the ones on the Bog Brook Trail can be avoided by following the gravel logging road extension of Carter Notch Rd. (FR 233) to the point where the Wildcat River Trail crosses it, just beyond the bridge over Wildcat River.

From the Bog Brook Trail junction, the trail follows the east bank of Wildcat River, crossing a gravel logging road (FR 233) that leads back (to the left) to Carter Notch Rd. At 1.0 mi. the trail crosses Bog Brook, and the Wild River Trail enters right at 1.9 mi. Soon the trail crosses Wildcat River, turns sharp right in 100 yd., and continues to ascend at a moderate grade. It climbs toward Carter Notch, passes a side trail right that leads to the rocks of the Rampart, and in 100 yd. more reaches Carter Notch Hut and the junction with the Nineteen-Mile Brook Trail.

Wildcat River Trail (map 5:G10–F10)

Distances from Bog Brook Trail (1790')

to Bog Brook crossing (2170'): 1.0 mi., 400 ft., 40 min.

to Wild River Trail (2320'): 1.9 mi., 550 ft., 1 hr. 15 min.

to Carter Notch Hut (3288'): 3.6 mi. (5.8 km.), 1500 ft., 2 hr. 35 min.

Hutmen's Trail (HA)

This trail crosses the flat ridge between Spruce Mtn. on the south and Wildcat Mtn. on the north, running from NH 16 at a point 4.2 mi. north of Jackson and 5.6 mi. south of Pinkham Notch Camp to Carter Notch Rd. about 2.7 mi. north of its junction with NH 16B and 0.3 mi. south of the Bog Brook Trail trailhead. The western section follows its traditional route as a hiking trail, while the middle and eastern sections follow logging roads that become cross-country ski trails during the winter. The Jackson Ski Touring Foundation, which maintains these ski trails, graciously permits hikers to use the trails in winter provided that they do not bring dogs and do not disrupt the ski tracks in any way. The trail affords several fine outlooks toward Mt. Washington, the northern part of the Montalban Ridge, and Wildcat Mtn.

Leaving NH 16, where there is a trail sign in the front yard of a house, the trail crosses a small field where new homes are being built, then bears left and begins to ascend the moderately steep west slope of Spruce Mtn. following the left side of a small brook. After 0.4 mi. the grade decreases and the trail bears left away from the brook, turns more north, and shortly crosses another small brook. The trail then runs nearly on the level through an area of mixed softwoods with recent logging activity, then bears right (east) and enters the WMNF at 0.6 mi. At 0.8 mi. the Dana Place (X-C Ski) Trail enters from the left and the trails coincide, soon passing south of a large logged area that provides fine views of Mt. Washington and the northern Montalban Ridge. At 1.1 mi., turn left onto a grassy logging road, the Marsh Brook (X-C Ski) Trail and follow it in a generally northeast direction along the flat ridgecrest. At 1.7 mi. a logging road on the left leads in 0.2 mi. to an outlook similar to the previous one. From here the trail descends gradually, and at 2.2 mi. it follows the Marsh Brook Trail straight ahead where the Dana Place Trail branches left toward the Hall's Ledge Trail.

Soon the trail enters a large clearing that affords expansive views of Carter Notch and Wildcat Mtn., where it swings to the right into the woods (marked by signs and blue diamonds), crosses Marsh Brook, and leaves the WMNF. It continues to descend, passing to the right of a dilapidated camp, to Carter Notch Rd.

Hutmen's Trail (map 5:G10)
Distances from NH 16 (1050')

   to Marsh Brook Trail (1750'): 1.1 mi., 750 ft., 55 min.

   to Carter Notch Rd. (1300'): 3.1 mi. (5.0 km.), 750 ft. (rev. 450 ft.), 1 hr. 55 min.

Hall's Ledge Trail (HA)

This trail starts on the east side of NH 16, just south of the bridge over the Ellis River and 5.2 mi. north of the covered bridge in Jackson. Use the Rocky Branch Trail parking lot, 0.1 mi. north of the NH 16 bridge. The trail ends on the Carter Notch Rd. 0.1 mi. north of the Bog Brook Trail parking area.

From NH 16, follow the river a short distance, then veer right uphill toward an overgrown field. Turn right, following cairns, then turn left uphill into woods and ascend to a high bank overlooking a brook. To this point the trail is marked with yellow blazes. It bears away from the brook and in about 0.1 mi. begins a short, steep ascent. From the top of this rise it runs generally north and northeast through fine woods with intervals of level stretches and slight rises, then ascends moderately through a section of spruce a short distance below the ledge. The ledge, on the left, is small and overgrown; at 1.7 mi., at the end of a straight, almost level stretch of about 100 yd., Mt. Washington, Boott Spur, and the Gulf of Slides may be seen from a cleared area. From here the trail coincides with the Hall's Ledge Ski Trail and the Wildcat Valley Ski Trail to Carter Notch Rd.

Hall's Ledge Trail (map 5:G10)
Distances from NH 16 (1150')

   to Hall's Ledge (2500'): 1.6 mi., 1350 ft., 1 hr. 30 min.

   to Carter Notch Rd. (1850'): 3.3 mi. (5.3 km.), 1350 ft. (rev. 600 ft.), 2 hr. 20 min.

Black Mountain Ski Trail (WMNF)

This trail to leads Black Mtn. Cabin and a nearby knob (2757 ft.) on the ridge of Black Mtn. that provides fine views of Mt. Washington, Carter Notch, and other peaks in its vicinity. To reach the trailhead, follow Carter Notch Rd. for 3.7 mi. from Wentworth Hall in Jackson, then turn right onto Melloon Rd. at the junction, where the WMNF trail is located. Follow Melloon Rd. (gravel) past the Jackson town dump and across Wildcat River, then bear left uphill, passing the Wildcat Valley Ski Trail (right). Continue to a parking area on the left 0.3 mi. from Carter Notch Rd., just before a private driveway with a chain gate. The road is plowed to this point in winter. Black Mtn. Cabin is kept locked and reservations for its use must be made with the Saco Ranger District office (603-447-5448). There is a spring (unreliable water source) near the cabin and the trail crosses several small streams (also unreliable).

The trail ascends the gravel driveway and turns to the right onto an old woods road (sign) just before reaching a brown house. It crosses several small brooks, enters the WMNF, then swings right and angles up the western slope of Black Mtn., ascending moderately at first and then more steeply. At 1.3 mi. the trail reaches Black Mtn. Cabin, where there is an interesting view northwest toward Mt. Washington. The direct route to the fine viewpoint on the nearby knob of Black Mtn. follows the main trail left (north) for 0.3 mi. to a spur path that leads left to the outlook. To make a scenic loop back to the cabin that is only 0.3 mi. longer than the direct route, follow the trail that leads left downhill from the spur path junction for 0.1 mi. Turn right here onto the Black Mountain Cutoff and ascend, crossing the ridgecrest in a beautiful softwood forest; then swing right and descend, emerging just to the south of the cabin on a path that leads to the left to a nearby spring.

Black Mountain Ski Trail (map 5:G10)

Distances from parking area on Melloon Rd. (1300')

to Black Mtn. Cabin (2450'): 1.3 mi., 1150 ft., 1 hr. 15 min.

to summit of knob (2757'): 1.6 mi. (2.6 km.), 1450 ft., 1 hr. 30 min.

Eagle Mountain Path

Eagle Mtn. is a small peak with a restricted but interesting view to Doublehead, Kearsarge North, and the Moat Range. It can be climbed from NH 16B, 0.8 mi. from Wentworth Hall in Jackson, by a path that starts in the parking lot behind the Eagle Mtn. House. The path is lightly used and marked, but its green spray-paint blazes can be followed easily by careful hikers. Start uphill on a dirt road, and soon, just before reaching the crest of the ridge, turn right and then bear to the left of a pump house. The road becomes older, then becomes a path, and ascends to an open swampy area. Cairns mark the way along the right side of the swamp and into the woods, where the climbing becomes steeper. After passing a large boulder on the right, the trail turns left uphill and climbs a steep and rough section by switchbacks, aiming for a small gap at the top right edge of the rock face. At the top of the rock face, it turns left and climbs up the right side of a ledge, then turns left toward a false summit. It then turns right where there is a good cleared view to the south on the left; the true summit (marked by a large cairn) is a few steps farther on.

Eagle Mountain Path (map 5:H10)

Distance from NH 16B (1000')

   to summit of Eagle Mtn. (1613'): 0.9 mi. (1.4 km.), 600 ft., 45 min.

Doublehead Ski Trail (WMNF)

This trail ascends North Doublehead from Dundee Rd. From NH 16 at the Jackson covered bridge follow NH 16A, then turn right on NH 16B at the Jackson Post Office. Go up a long hill, turn right again at the Black Mtn. Ski Area, then finally turn right onto Dundee Rd. and continue to the parking area on the east (left) side of the road 2.9 mi. from NH 16. The WMNF Doublehead Cabin, located on the summit, is kept locked, and reservations for its use must be made with the Saco Ranger District office (603-447-5448).

   The trail follows a private road for about 100 yd., then turns right, enters the woods, swings left, and becomes steeper. At 0.6 mi. it bears slightly left where the Old Path leaves right. The ski trail ascends by a zigzag route on the west slope of North Doublehead, terminating at the Doublehead Cabin on the summit. The nearest water is alongside the trail about halfway down. Beyond the cabin, a path leads in 30 yd. to a good view east, overlooking Mountain Pond, the mountains of the Baldface Range, and the hills and lakes of western Maine.

Doublehead Ski Trail (map 5:H11)

Distance from Dundee Rd. (1480')

   to North Doublehead summit (3053'): 1.8 mi. (2.9 km.), 1600 ft., 1 hr. 40 min.

Old Path (JCC)

This trail ascends to North Doublehead from the Doublehead Ski Trail, 0.6 mi. from Dundee Rd. It diverges right and passes a brook left in 50 yd., rises at a moderate grade for about 0.1 mi., then steepens somewhat until it reaches the height-of-land in the col between the peaks at 0.6 mi. Here the New Path enters right, and the Old Path turns left and ascends moderately, then more steeply, passing a side path that leads left somewhat downhill about 100 yd. to a splendid view west to Mt. Carrigain, Moat Mtn., and the Sandwich Range. In a short distance it reaches the summit of North Doublehead, the cabin (which is kept locked), and the Doublehead Ski Trail.

Old Path (map 5:H11)

Distance from Doublehead Ski Trail (1860')

> *to* North Doublehead summit (3053'): 0.9 mi. (1.4 km.), 1200 ft., 1 hr. 5 min.

New Path (JCC)

This trail ascends South Doublehead and continues to the col between South and North Doublehead, where it meets the Old Path. It starts on Dundee Rd., 3.4 mi. from NH 16 at the Jackson covered bridge and 0.5 mi. beyond the parking area for the Doublehead Ski Trail. It is marked with cairns, and is steep in its upper half.

The trail descends slightly as it leaves the road and in 60 yd. bears right, then left, and follows a logging road at a slight upgrade. At 0.3 mi. from Dundee Rd. bear left and in about 100 yd. descend slightly and cross a small brook. Proceed uphill for 100 yd. and bear right at a cairn. About 0.2 mi. from this point the trail crosses a small, almost flat, ledge, and crosses a smaller ledge a short distance beyond. From here it begins the steep climb to South Doublehead, approaching it from the southeast slope. It meets the ridgecrest at a point between two knobs. To the right, a spur path leads over two knobs with open ledges; the second provides the wider view. The New Path turns left and crosses the summit of South Doublehead; just before it starts to descend it bears right, and here a spur path leads to the left about 30 yd. to a superb outlook ranging from the Sandwich Range to Carter Notch. The New Path then descends slightly to meet the Old Path in the col to the north.

New Path (map 5:H11)

Distances from Dundee Rd. (1590')

> *to* South Doublehead (2939'): 1.2 mi., 1350 ft., 1 hr. 15 min.
>
> *to* Old Path (2700'): 1.4 mi. (2.3 km.), 1350 ft. (rev. 250 ft.), 1 hr. 25 min.

Mount Kearsarge North Trail (WMNF)

This trail ascends Kearsarge North from the north side of Hurricane Mtn. Rd., 1.5 mi. east of NH 16 near the state highway rest area at Intervale. It is a very popular and relatively easy trail to the magnificent views of Kearsarge North, but inexperienced hikers should not underestimate the total climb of 2600 ft., which is comparable to the ascent required for many much higher peaks.

Leaving the road, the trail runs level for a short distance, then climbs rather easily past a summer residence on an old road well up on the bank above a brook. At 1.1 mi. it passes several boulders and the old road starts to become rougher. It climbs steadily into a ledgy area, where there are views to Mt. Chocorua and Moat Mtn., crosses the crest of the ridge connecting Kearsarge North to Bartlett Mtn. at 2.4 mi., then swings right and ascends mostly along the north side of the ridge. At 2.9 mi. the trail makes a sharp right turn at a steep spot, then angles upward, circling to the left around to the west edge of the summit ledges, and climbs to the tower.

Mount Kearsarge North Trail (map 5:I11–H11)

Distances from Hurricane Mtn. Rd. (680')

   to boulders (1400'): 1.1 mi., 700 ft., 55 min.

   to crest of ridge (2750'): 2.4 mi., 2050 ft., 2 hr. 15 min.

   to Kearsarge North summit (3268'): 3.1 mi. (5.0 km.), 2600 ft., 2 hr. 50 min.

Weeks Brook Trail (WMNF)

This trail ascends Kearsarge North from the east, a somewhat rough and sparsely marked route that, for experienced hikers, provides an attractive, lightly used alternative to the Mount Kearsarge North Trail, the very popular trail that ascends this outstanding mountain from Hurricane Mtn. Rd. The lower part of the Weeks Brook Trail has been recently relocated to begin at a new trailhead on FR 317 0.1 mi. from South Chatham Rd.; FR 317 leaves South Chatham Rd. at a point 4.9 mi. from ME 113 in North Fryeburg ME and 0.4 mi. north of the east terminus of Hurricane Mtn. Rd. Following this trail may require considerable care, particularly in the part near the road and in the upper part.

From the parking area, this trail follows FR 317 uphill and crosses Weeks Brook on a bridge at 0.4 mi. The trail soon bears left (south), then at 0.6 mi. it turns to the right off FR 317 onto a gated USFS road, then quickly bears left off the road into a hemlock forest, following old logging roads marked by yellow blazes. In a large logging clearing at 1.5 mi., the trail re-enters the USFS road and follows it to the left for about 100 yd. Here the trail joins the former route, bearing right into the woods on a logging road. This road quickly becomes distinctly older and rougher and begins to climb gradually, then moderately, to Shingle Pond. At 3.1 mi. the trail makes its closest approach to the pond, which has been visible for some time. At 3.5 mi. the trail reaches Weeks Brook, then soon crosses on a ledge and follows the north bank of the attractive brook, crossing and recrossing a branch several times. The trail enters an open boggy area in the sag between Kearsarge and Rickers Knoll at 4.2 mi., and turns sharp left (south) at a sign. It makes a winding ascent (watch for arrows), first moderately, then steeply, and enters low scrub and blueberries, passing a fine view east. Here it turns sharp right and soon reaches a ledge with views south, from which the fire tower is visible. From here to the summit the trail may be somewhat obscure, but the direction is obvious (however, follow the trail with extreme care when descending).

Weeks Brook Trail (map 5:H12–H11)
Distances from trailhead on FR 317 (550')

> *to* Shingle Pond (1700'): 3.1 mi., 1150 ft., 2 hr. 10 min.

> *to* Kearsarge North summit (3268'): 5.1 mi. (8.2 km.), 2700 ft., 3 hr. 55 min.

Province Brook Trail (WMNF)

This trail provides an easy hike to Province Pond, where there is a WMNF shelter. North of the shelter the former route of the trail has been officially closed by the WMNF. The trail begins at the end of Peaked Hill Rd. (FR 450) 2.6 mi. from South Chatham Rd. Peaked Hill Rd. leaves South Chatham Rd. 4.4 mi. from ME 113 in North Fryeburg ME and 0.9 mi. north of the east end of Hurricane Mtn. Rd.

The trail leaves the north end of Peaked Hill Rd. and heads northwest up Province Brook on a logging road. After descending slightly and swinging north, it crosses Province Brook on a bridge shortly before reaching the south end of Province Pond on a grassy bank. Turn sharp right here (no sign) and follow a yellow-blazed path along the east shore of the pond to Province Pond Shelter on the north shore.

Province Brook Trail (map 5:H12)
Distance from north end of Peaked Hill Rd. (950')

> *to* Province Pond Shelter (1330'): 1.6 mi. (2.6 km.), 400 ft., 1 hr.

Hurricane Mountain Path

This unmarked and unmaintained path to the summit of Hurricane Mtn. leaves the north side of Hurricane Mtn. Rd. (no sign) 3.7 mi. east of NH 16 and 0.1 mi. west of the height-of-land, diagonally opposite the Black Cap Path. Follow an old road for about 0.3 mi., then bear right onto the trail and follow cairns that lead to open ledges and the north end of the wooded summit.

Hurricane Mountain Path (map 5:I12)

Distance from Hurricane Mtn. Rd. (1700')

   to Hurricane Mtn. summit (2100'): 0.5 mi. (0.8 km.), 400 ft., 25 min.

Black Cap Trail (AMC/NC)

This path provides a relatively easy ascent to the bare summit of Black Cap, the highest peak in the Green Hills Preserve, which affords the best views in the Green Hills range. It leaves the south side of steep, winding Hurricane Mtn. Rd. (which is closed to automobiles from November through mid-May) at a point 3.7 mi. from NH 16 at the Intervale scenic vista and rest area and 0.1 mi. west of the height-of-land, at a sign (park with care along the roadside). In winter the trail is used by snowmobiles up to the Black Cap Connector junction.

   The trail runs almost level through beautiful old-growth spruce woods, then ascends moderately through mixed hardwoods to an information kiosk at 0.5 mi. At 0.7 mi. the Cranmore Trail leaves right and runs 1.2 mi. to Cranmore Mtn., and at 0.8 mi. the Black Cap Connector diverges right to traverse the west side of Black Cap toward Peaked Mtn. and Pudding Pond. The Black Cap Path soon reaches ledges which become more open, with excellent views westward, as the summit nears. At the summit there are views in all directions (though not from any single spot); a spur path leads left (east) to a fine view to the east toward the hills of western Maine. A link trail descends to the right to meet the Black Cap Connector in 0.2 mi., which can be followed to the right 0.4 mi. back to the Black Cap Path, making an interesting short loop from the summit.

Black Cap Trail (map 5:I12)

Distance from Hurricane Mtn. Rd. (1700')

   to Black Cap summit (2369'): 1.1 mi. (1.8 km.), 650 ft., 55 min.

Cranmore Trail

This path provides access to the summit of Cranmore Mtn. and the Cranmore Mtn. Ski Area from Hurricane Mtn. Rd. Leaving the Black Cap Trail 0.7 mi.

from Hurricane Mtn. Rd., it descends gradually for 1.0 mi., then climbs over a small but steep knob and resumes its descent to the main col at 1.1 mi. Here it starts to ascend Cranmore Mtn., joining a service road coming up from the left after 30 yd. This service road climbs to the flat summit area, passing a radio tower and reaching the actual summit at the top of the chairlift. The Cranmore Ski Area base lodge can be reached in about 1.2 mi. with about 1100 ft. of descent via ski trails.

Cranmore Trail (map 5:I12–I11)
Distance from Black Cap Trail (2000')

    to summit of Cranmore Mtn. (1690'): 1.2 mi. (2.0 km.), 100 ft. (rev. 400 ft.), 40 min.

Black Cap Connector (AMC/NC)

This trail traverses the west slope of the Green Hills and connects Peaked Mtn. and Middle Mtn. with Black Cap and Cranmore Mtn. It begins on the coinciding Middle Mountain and Peaked Mountain trails 0.7 mi. from their Thompson Rd. trailhead and ends on the Black Cap Trail just south of its junction with the Cranmore Trail, 0.8 mi. from Hurricane Mtn. Rd. It follows old logging roads, and the northern half is multiple use, open to mountain bikes and snowmobiles.

    This trail coincides with the Peaked Mountain Trail on an old road for 0.5 mi. to an information kiosk, where the Peaked Mountain Trail turns uphill to the right toward Peaked Mtn. and a path (an old route of the trail) turns downhill to the left to return to Thompson Rd. at a point where parking is forbidden. The Black Cap Connector continues straight from this junction, then swings right (east) and ascends the valley of Artist Brook between Peaked Mtn. and Cranmore Mtn. After crossing several small streams, it passes a junction on the right at 0.9 mi. with the Peaked Mountain Connector Trail, which climbs steeply 0.1 mi. to the Peaked Mtn. Trail at the lower ledges. The main trail now climbs for about a mile to a ridgecrest, where it descends briefly and then climbs again to the junction with the Mason Brook Snowmobile Trail at a snow fence at 2.1 mi. (The Mason Brook Snowmobile Trail descends 3.3 mi. to East Conway Rd. and may be used by hikers, though it is not signed and not maintained for hiking.) From here on the trail is open to multiple uses. It continues to ascend by several switchbacks and swings gradually northward, occasionally descending into gullies. At 3.6 mi. a short link path diverges right and reaches the Black Cap Trail at the summit of Black Cap in 0.2 mi., and at 4.0 mi. the Black Cap Connector ends at its junction with the Black Cap Trail.

Black Cap Connector (map 5:I11–I12)

Distances from Middle Mountain Trail junction (700')

> *to* Mason Brook Snowmobile Trail (1700'): 2.1 mi., 1200 ft. (rev. 200 ft.), 1 hr. 40 min.

> *to* Black Cap Trail (2100'): 4.0 mi. (6.4 km.), 1600 ft., 2 hr. 50 min.

Peaked Mountain Trail (AMC/NC)

This trail offers an unusually great variety of scenic vistas and natural features, including fine open stands of red and pitch pine, for relatively little effort. The sharp, rocky knoll of Peaked Mtn., bare except for a few small pines, affords excellent views toward Mt. Washington, the Saco Valley, and nearby mountains. From NH 16 in North Conway, take Artist's Falls Rd. (across from the Millbrook House) for 0.4 mi., then turn right and follow Thompson Rd. for 0.3 mi. to the Pudding Pond Trail parking area, just before the power line crossing. Parking is forbidden at the former trailhead at the upper end of Thompson Rd., near the small reservoir, although the old section of path remains and can be used by walking up the road 0.6 mi. from the official parking area. There is an interesting small flume in the brook where it is crossed by this old path about 25 yd. from Thompson Rd.

The Peaked Mountain Trail, coinciding with the Pudding Pond and Middle Mountain trails, follows an old road parallel to the power lines for 0.2 mi. to an information kiosk. Here the Pudding Pond Trail diverges to the right, while the Peaked Mountain and Middle Mountain trails turn left, cross under the power lines, swing around a snow fence to enter the woods, and ascend gradually on an old road. At 0.7 mi., at the boundary of the Green Hills Preserve, the Middle Mountain Trail continues straight uphill, while the Peaked Mountain Trail, now coinciding with the Black Cap Connector, turns left onto another old road. It first ascends, then descends gradually to another information kiosk at 1.2 mi. Here the old route of the Peaked Mountain Trail (blue blazes) descends 0.3 mi. to Thompson Rd. at a point where parking is forbidden, while the Black Cap Connector continues straight ahead for Black Cap and Hurricane Mtn. Rd.

At this junction the Peaked Mountain Trail (blue blazes) turns right and ascends moderately past a former trail junction on the right to a junction on the left at 1.5 mi. with a short link trail that descends steeply 0.1 mi. to the Black Cap Connector. Here the main trail turns sharp right and ascends scattered ledges into stands of red pine with increasing views to the west and north. At 1.8 mi. a spur path descends to the right about 100 yd. to an outlook west toward the Moats and

Mt. Chocorua. The main trail bears left, and at 1.9 mi. the Middle Mountain Connector leaves on the right and descends 0.3 mi. on several switchbacks to the Middle Mountain Trail. The Peaked Mountain Trail swings left and ascends the final ledges to the summit, a pointed, grassy knoll with views east, south, and west.

Peaked Mountain Trail (map 5:I11)

Distance from Thompson Rd. parking area (550')

  to Peaked Mtn. summit (1739'): 2.1 mi. (3.4 km.), 1200 ft., 1 hr. 40 min.

Middle Mountain Trail (AMC/NC)

This trail provides access to a fine southern outlook from Middle Mtn., and passes through a scenic hemlock ravine with several cascades in its middle section that are interesting when there is a good flow of water. The trailhead is the same as for the Peaked Mountain Trail (above).

   This trail coincides with the Peaked Mountain and Pudding Pond trails for 0.2 mi. to the information kiosk, then turns left and continues along with the Peaked Mountain Trail, crossing straight under the power lines, swinging around a snow fence into the woods, and ascending gradually on an old road to the Green Hills Preserve boundary at 0.7 mi. Here the Peaked Mountain Trail and Black Cap Connector leave on the left, while the Middle Mountain Trail continues to ascend straight ahead on the old road, reaching the cascades in 0.5 mi. After a short steep climb the grade eases, and soon the Middle Mountain Connector leaves on the left and ascends by switchbacks 0.3 mi. to the Peaked Mountain Trail at a point 0.2 mi. below the summit of Peaked Mtn. At this junction the main trail bears right and crosses a small brook, turning south then gradually swinging to the west, angling up scattered ledges with increasing views to the south and west. The trail then bears right (sign), ascends moderately to a small ridgecrest, then swings left and descends slightly before the final ascent to the pine grove at the summit.

Middle Mountain Trail (map 5:I11)

Distance from Thompson Rd. parking area (550')

  to summit of Middle Mtn. (1857'): 2.1 mi. (3.4 km.), 1300 ft., 1 hr. 40 min.

Pudding Pond Trail (NC)

This trail provides a very easy and scenic 2.0-mi. nature walk to a beaver pond and its surrounding woodlands, particularly suited for families with small children. It passes several beaver dams and lodges, a variety of ecosystems, and numerous bird habitats, including a nesting area for the great blue heron. The trailhead is the same as for the Peaked Mountain Trail (above).

It leaves the trailhead and follows the old road parallel to the power lines for 0.2 mi. to the information kiosk, where the Peaked Mountain and Middle Mountain trails diverge left. The Pudding Pond Trail turns right on an old road and descends gradually, passing several unmarked junctions with old roads and the junction on the left (may not be signed) with the section of the loop that returns from the pond. At 0.5 mi., just before a bridge over the outlet brook, an unmarked spur path continues across the bridge to the end of Locust Lane, where very limited parking is available. The main trail does not cross this bridge, but leads to the left (south) along the east bank of the brook past several unmarked paths to viewpoints for two beaver dams with lodges. At 0.9 mi. a side path to the right runs to an outlook over the pond—a good place for viewing birds and other wildlife. At 1.1 mi. the trail turns sharp left away from the pond and returns to the loop junction at 1.6 mi., from which the route used to reach the pond can be retraced to the starting point.

Pudding Pond Trail (map 5:I11)
Distance from Thompson Rd. parking area (550')

> *for* complete loop around Pudding Pond (500'): 2.0 mi. (3.2 km.),
> 50 ft., 1 hr.

Speckled Mountain Region

This section covers the mountains and trails in the region east of Evans Notch and the valleys of Evans Brook and Cold River that lead up to Evans Notch from the north and south respectively. The section is bounded on the west by ME 113/NH 113, the highway that runs through Evans Notch from Chatham NH to Gilead ME, and on the north by US 2. Except for a sliver of land near North Chatham NH, the entire section lies in Maine. Almost all the land in this section is within the WMNF, and most of its central portion is included in the Caribou–Speckled Mountain Wilderness, the newest designated Wilderness in the WMNF. The AMC Carter Range–Evans Notch map (map #5) covers the entire area. The Chatham Trails Association (CTA) publishes a detailed map of the trail system in the Cold River Valley.

The Appalachian Trail does not pass through this section.

GEOGRAPHY

The major part of this region is occupied by a jumbled mass of ridges with numerous ledges; although the peaks are not high, they offer a variety of fine walks. With the exception of a few trails off ME 113, this area probably receives less hiking traffic than any comparable section of the WMNF, allowing visitors to enjoy relative solitude on trails in an area that is quite rugged and scenic if not quite as spectacular as the Presidentials and Franconias.

Speckled Mtn. (2906 ft.) is the highest peak of the region, one of at least three mountains in Maine that have been known by this name, and its open summit ledges have excellent views in all directions. **Blueberry Mtn.** (1781 ft.) is a long, flat spur running southwest from Speckled Mtn. The top is mostly one big open ledge, where mature trees are slowly reclaiming what was once a burned-over summit with only sparse and stunted trees. Numerous open spaces afford excellent views, especially from the southwest ledges on the summit. In the valley between Blueberry Mtn. and the west ridge of Speckled Mtn., **Bickford Brook** passes two sets of flumes, falls, and boulders of unusual beauty. A long, ledgy ridge extends east from Speckled Mtn. to **Miles Notch,** running over **Dur-gin Mtn.** (2404 ft.), **Butters Mtn.** (2246 ft.), **Red Rock Mtn.** (2141 ft.), and **Miles Knob** (2090 ft.). The west ridge of Speckled Mtn., which descends toward ME 113, includes **Ames Mtn.** (2686 ft.) and **Spruce Hill** (2510 ft.).

Mt. Caribou (2850 ft.)—called "Calabo" in the Walling map of Oxford County (1853)—is the second highest peak in the area. It also has a bare, ledgy summit that affords excellent views. South of Caribou Mtn. is **Haystack Notch,** overlooked by the cliffs of **Haystack Mtn.** (2210 ft.). **Peabody Mtn.** (2462 ft.) is a wooded mountain that rises to the north of Caribou Mtn. **Albany Mtn.** (1930 ft.) has open ledges near its summit with excellent views in several directions. To the west of Albany Mtn. and **Albany Notch** are several small but interesting rugged mountains that have no trails but invite exploration, of which the most prominent is **Farwell Mtn.** (1865 ft.). **Round Pond** is an interesting mountain pond that lies east of Albany Mtn. and is easily visited from Crocker Pond Campground.

Deer Hill (1367 ft.), often called Big Deer, is located south of Speckled Mtn. and east of Cold River. The views from the east and south ledges are excellent. **Little Deer Hill** (1090 ft.), a lower hill west of Deer Hill that rises only about 600 ft. above the valley, gives fine views of the valley and the Baldfaces from its summit ledges. **Pine Hill** (1250 ft.) and **Lord Hill** (1257 ft.) rise southeast of Deer Hill, with scattered open ledges that afford interesting views. There are several short paths in the vicinity of AMC Cold River Camp which are not covered in this guide because they are not open to the public, though some are mentioned where they intersect other more important trails.

The Roost (1374 ft.) is a small hill near Hastings, with open ledges that afford fine views of the Wild River valley, the Evans Brook valley, and many mountains.

CAMPING
Caribou–Speckled Mountain Wilderness

Wilderness regulations, intended to protect Wilderness resources and promote opportunities for challenge and solitude, prohibit use of motorized equipment or mechanical means of transportation of any sort. Camping and wood or charcoal fires are not allowed within 200 ft. of any trail except at designated campsites. Hiking and camping group size must be no larger than 10 people. Camping and fires are also prohibited above treeline (where trees are less than 8 ft. tall) except in winter, when camping is permitted above treeline in places where snow cover is at least two feet deep, but not on any frozen body of water. Caribou Shelter has been dismantled.

Forest Protection Areas

The WMNF has established a number of Forest Protection Areas (FPAs)— formerly known as Restricted Use Areas—where camping and wood or charcoal fires are prohibited throughout the year. The specific areas are under continual review, and areas are added to or subtracted from the list in order to provide the greatest amount of protection to areas subject to damage by excessive camping, while imposing the lowest level of restrictions possible. A general list of FPAs in this section follows, but since there are often major changes from year to year, one should obtain current information on FPAs from the WMNF.

(1) No camping is permitted above treeline (where trees are less than 8 ft. tall), except in winter, and then only in places where there is at least two feet of snow cover on the ground—but not on any frozen body of water. The point where the restricted area begins is marked on most trails with small signs, but the absence of such signs should not be construed as proof of the legality of a site.

(2) No camping is permitted within a quarter-mile of any trailhead, picnic area, or any facility for overnight accommodation such as a hut, cabin, shelter, tentsite, or campground, except as designated at the facility itself. In this section, camping is also forbidden within one-quarter mile of ME/NH 113 for one-half mile in either direction from Hastings Campground.

Established Trailside Campsites

Caribou Shelter (WMNF), formerly located on the Caribou Trail northeast of the summit of Mt. Caribou, has been removed. The spring near the shelter site is not reliable.

Trails to the North and East of Speckled Mountain

List of Trails	Map	Page
Roost Trail	5:E13	402
Wheeler Brook Trail	5:E13	403
Caribou Trail	5:E13–E14	404
Mud Brook Trail	5:E13	404

Trails on Speckled Mountain

Trails South of Speckled Mountain

THE TRAILS

Roost Trail (WMNF)

This trail ascends to the Roost, a small mountain with fine views, from two trailheads about 0.7 mi. apart on the east side of ME 113. The north trailhead is located just north of a bridge over Evans Brook, 0.1 mi. north of the junction of ME 113 with Wild River Rd. at Hastings ME; the south trailhead is just south of another bridge over Evans Brook.

Leaving the north trailhead, the trail ascends a steep bank for 30 yd., then bears right (east) and ascends gradually along a wooded ridge. It crosses a small brook at 0.3 mi., then rises somewhat more steeply and emerges on a small rock ledge at the summit at 0.5 mi. Here a side trail descends 0.1 mi. west through woods to spacious open ledges, where the views are excellent. The main trail descends generally southeast from the summit at a moderate grade and crosses a small brook, then turns right (west) on an old road (no sign) and follows it past a cellar hole and an old clearing back to ME 113.

Roost Trail (map 5:E13)

Distances from ME 113, north trailhead (820')

> *to* the Roost (1374'): 0.5 mi., 550 ft., 30 min.

> *to* ME 113, south trailhead (850'): 1.2 mi. (2.0 km.), 550 ft. (rev. 500 ft.), 55 min.

Wheeler Brook Trail (WMNF)

The trailheads for this trail are on the south side of US 2, 2.3 mi. east of the junction of US 2 and ME 113, and on Little Lary Brook Rd. (FR 8) 1.6 mi. from its junction with ME 113, which is 9.2 mi. north of the road to Cold River Campground and 3.7 mi. south of the junction of US 2 and ME 113.

From US 2, the trail joins and follows the west side of Wheeler Brook, generally following old logging roads and crossing the brook four times. It turns left (arrow) at a logging road fork at 1.0 mi., just before the third crossing of the brook. The trail rises to its highest point, just over 2000 ft., at the crest of the northwest ridge of Peabody Mtn. (2462 ft.) at 2.1 mi. (There is no trail to the wooded summit of Peabody Mtn.) The trail then descends generally southwest, merges onto an old logging road that comes down from the left, and reaches Little Lary Brook Rd. Turn left on Little Lary Brook Rd. and continue about 100 yd. to a locked gate near the bridge over Little Lary Brook, 1.6 mi. from ME 113.

In the reverse direction, proceed along Little Lary Brook Rd. about 100 yd. from the locked gate, then turn right at the junction where FR 185 continues straight ahead. The trail leaves the left side of the road in another 0.3 mi.

Wheeler Brook Trail (map 5:E13)

Distance from US 2 (680')

> *to* gate on Little Lary Brook Rd. (1100'): 3.5 mi. (5.6 km.), 1350 ft. (rev. 900 ft.), 2 hr. 25 min.

Caribou Trail (WMNF)

This trail provides access to the attractive ledges of Caribou Mtn. Its west trail-head, which it now shares with the Mud Brook Trail, is located on the east side of ME 113 about 6 mi. north of the road to WMNF Cold River Campground and 4.6 mi. S of US 2. The east trailhead is on Bog Rd. (FR 6), which leaves the south side of US 2 1.3 mi. west of the West Bethel Post Office (there is current-ly a sign for "Pooh Corner Farm" at this junction, but no road sign) and leads 2.8 mi. to the trailhead where a gate ends public travel on the road.

From ME 113 the trail runs north. It crosses Morrison Brook at 0.4 mi. and follows the brook, crossing it several more times. The third crossing, at 2.0 mi., is at the head of Kees Falls, a 25-ft. waterfall. The trail levels off at the height-of-land as it crosses the col between Gammon Mtn. and Mt. Caribou at 2.9 mi. Soon the Mud Brook Trail leaves right to return to ME 113 via the summit of Mt. Caribou, passing the site of the former Caribou Shelter and Caribou Spring (unreliable) in 0.3 mi. The Caribou Trail continues ahead at the junction, descends more rapidly, then turns northeast toward the valley of Bog Brook, which lies east of Peabody Mtn. It then follows a succession of logging roads down this valley. At 4.8 mi. it bears left in a clearing, then bears left again on the extension of Bog Rd. (FR 6) and continues to the gate.

Caribou Trail (map 5:E13–E14)

Distances from ME 113 (960')

> *to* Mud Brook Trail (2420'): 3.0 mi., 1450 ft., 2 hr. 15 min.
>
> *to* Bog Rd. (860'): 5.5 mi. (8.9 km.), 1450 ft. (rev. 1550 ft.), 3 hr. 30 min.
>
> *to* Caribou Mtn. summit (2850') via Mud Brook Trail: 3.6 mi. (5.8 km.), 1900 ft., 2 hr. 45 min.

Mud Brook Trail (WMNF)

This trail begins on ME 113 at the same point as the Caribou Trail, about 6 mi. north of the road to WMNF Cold River Campground, then passes over the sum-mit of Mt. Caribou and ends at the Caribou Trail in the pass between Caribou Mtn. and Gammon Mtn. Despite the ominous name, the footing on the trail is generally dry and good.

From ME 113 the trail runs generally south, then turns east along the north side of Mud Brook, rising gradually. It crosses the headwaters of Mud Brook at 1.9 mi. and swings left (north) uphill, climbing more steeply. The trail crosses several smaller brooks and at 3.0 mi. comes out on a small bare knob with excellent views east. It turns left into the woods and makes a short descent into a small ravine, then emerges above timberline and crosses ledges to the summit of Mt. Caribou at 3.4 mi. It then descends north, passes Caribou Spring (unreliable) left at 3.6 mi. and the site of the former Caribou Shelter right 70 yd. farther, and meets the Caribou Trail in the pass.

Mud Brook Trail (map 5:E13)

Distances from ME 113 (960')

   to Mt. Caribou summit (2850'): 3.4 mi., 1900 ft., 2 hr. 40 min.

   to Caribou Trail (2420'): 3.9 mi. (6.3 km.), 1900 ft. (rev. 400 ft.), 2 hr. 55 min.

Haystack Notch Trail (WMNF)

This trail, with good footing and easy grades but some potentially difficult brook crossings, runs through Haystack Notch. Its west trailhead is on the east side of ME 113, 4.8 mi. north of the road to WMNF Cold River Campground. The east trailhead is on the Miles Notch Trail 0.2 mi. from that trail's north terminus, which is reached by following the road that leads south from US 2 opposite the West Bethel Post Office to a crossroads at 3.1 mi., then taking the road that runs right (west). Continue straight ahead at a junction just beyond a small cemetery. The road becomes rather rough after about 1 mi. from the crossroads, and it may not be possible for some cars to drive all the way to the trailhead, which is about 2.5 mi. from the crossroads.

   Leaving ME 113, the trail runs generally east along the east branch of Evans Brook, crossing it several times. The first crossing in particular may be difficult at high water. At 2.1 mi. it crosses through Haystack Notch and descends down the valley of the West Branch of the Pleasant River, making several crossings of that brook, some of which may also be difficult at high water. Eventually it merges into an old logging road and meets the Miles Notch Trail, where it ends.

Haystack Notch Trail (map 5:F13–E14)

Distances from ME 113 (1070')

   to Haystack Notch (1900'): 2.1 mi., 800 ft., 1 hr. 25 min.

   to Miles Notch Trail (919'): 5.4 mi. (8.7 km.), 800 ft. (rev. 1000 ft.), 3 hr. 5 min.

Albany Notch Trail (WMNF)

This trail passes through the notch west of Albany Mtn. Parts of its northern section still suffer from invasion by berry bushes as a result of the loss of the mature forest in the 1980 wind storm. The southern section, which is located mostly on old, rather overgrown logging roads, is poorly marked and requires much care to follow. Most use of this trail is on the north section, where it makes possible an attractive loop hike over Albany Mtn. in combination with the Albany Mountain Trail and the branch trail that runs from the height-of-land in Albany Notch to the base of the ledges on the Albany Mountain Trail.

To reach the north trailhead, follow the road that leads south from US 2 opposite the West Bethel Post Office, which becomes FR 7 when it enters the WMNF at 4.5 mi. At 5.8 mi., turn right on FR 18, following signs for Crocker Pond Campground. The trailhead is on the right in another 0.6 mi., just past the end of an extensive beaver swamp; the trail sign is hard to see from the road because it is located at the back of a small clearing where it is concealed from most angles by a large tree close to the road. The south trailhead is reached by leaving ME 5 at the west end of Keewaydin Lake, 2.4 mi. west of the East Stoneham Post Office and 0.7 mi. east of the Lovell-Stoneham town line, and following Bartlettboro Rd. north. Bear right on Birch Ave. at 0.4 mi. from ME 5 and continue to the trailhead, which is 1.0 mi. from ME 5. Park carefully to avoid blocking any roads; the road that the trail follows is passable in cars for at least another 0.2 mi., but parking is extremely limited.

Leaving the small clearing on FR 18, the trail follows an old logging road that becomes well defined after the first few yards. At 0.6 mi. it bears right at the junction where the Albany Mountain Trail diverges left (south). At 1.2 mi. the Albany Notch Trail enters the region damaged by blowdown, where berry bushes are often a nuisance, though the trail becomes markedly drier underfoot. Returning to mature woods at 1.4 mi., it starts to climb at a moderate grade to the left of a small brook, and at 1.7 mi. it reaches the junction where the branch trail leads left (east) 0.4 mi. to the Albany Mountain Trail at the base of the ledges.

The trail now descends moderately with a few steeper pitches just below the pass, and crosses a small brook several times. It then runs mostly on a very old road until it reaches a much newer logging road at 2.4 mi. and turns left on this road; if ascending from the south, turn sharp right off the road. This road is fairly easy to follow, but is rather wet and overgrown with tall grasses and other vegetation that permit little evidence of a footway. It passes junctions with a snowmobile trail on the left at 2.8 mi. and 3.1 mi.; at the second junction the road bears right and improves greatly, then crosses Meadow Brook on a snowmobile bridge at 3.6 mi. and continues to the trailhead.

Albany Notch Trail (map 5:F15–F14)

Distances from FR 18 (800')

   to Albany Mountain Trail (990'): 0.6 mi., 200 ft., 25 min.

   to branch trail junction in Albany Notch (1530'): 1.7 mi., 750 ft., 1 hr. 15 min.

   to trailhead on Birch Ave. (750'): 4.2 mi. (6.7 km.), 750 ft. (rev. 800 ft.), 2 hr. 30 min.

Albany Mountain Trail (WMNF)

This trail ascends the north slope of Albany Mtn. to an open ledge near its summit that affords a good view east and north. It begins on the Albany Notch Trail 0.6 mi. from FR 18.

Leaving the Albany Notch Trail, the Albany Mountain Trail soon turns left onto a skidder road and follows it for 20 yd., then bears right off it and continues to ascend moderately through woods where there has been some light to moderate wind damage and some salvage logging activity. At 0.6 mi. the trail turns right at the foot of a small mossy rock face, and climbs to the junction at 0.9 mi. where the branch trail leads right (west) 0.4 mi. to the Albany Notch Trail at the height-of-land in Albany Notch. Soon the trail passes a ledge with a good view of the Baldfaces and Mt. Washington and continues to the northeast outlook, where regular marking ends. The true summit, wooded and not reached by any well-defined trail, is about 100 yd. south. The summit area has other viewpoints not reached by the trail that repay efforts devoted to cautious exploration by experienced hikers. The best viewpoint on the mountain is about 0.1 mi. southwest of the true summit; a sketchy and incomplete line of cairns leads to it.

Albany Mountain Trail (map 5:F14)

Distance from Albany Notch Trail (990')

   to Albany Mtn. upper outlook (1900'): 1.3 mi. (2.1 km.), 900 ft., 1 hr. 5 min.

Albany Brook Trail (WMNF)

This short, easy trail follows the shore of Crocker Pond and then leads to attractive, secluded Round Pond. It begins at the turnaround at the end of the main road at Crocker Pond Campground (do not enter the actual camping area), reached by following the road that runs south from US 2 opposite the West

Bethel Post Office, which becomes FR 7 when it enters the WMNF at 4.5 mi. At 5.8 mi. turn right on FR 18, following signs 1.5 mi. to the campground entrance.

Leaving the turnaround, the trail descends to a small brook and follows the west shore of Crocker Pond for 0.2 mi., then joins and follows Albany Brook with gentle ups and downs. At 0.9 mi. it goes straight through a logging-road intersection with a clearing visible on the right, and soon reaches the north end of Round Pond.

Albany Brook Trail (map 5:F15)

Distance from Crocker Pond Campground (830')

   to Round Pond (800'): 1.0 mi. (1.6 km.), 100 ft. (rev. 100 ft.), 35 min.

Miles Notch Trail (WMNF)

This trail runs through Miles Notch, giving access to the east end of the ledgy ridge that culminates in Speckled Mtn. To reach its south terminus, near which the Great Brook Trail also begins, leave ME 5 in North Lovell ME on a road with signs for Evergreen Valley Ski Area and follow that road northwest for 1.8 mi., then turn right onto Hut Rd. just before the bridge over Great Brook and continue 1.5 mi. to the trailhead. To reach the north terminus, follow the road that leads south from US 2 opposite the West Bethel Post Office to a crossroads at 3.1 mi., then take the road that runs right (west) and continue straight ahead at a junction just beyond a small cemetery. The road becomes rather rough after about 1 mi. from the crossroads, and it may not be possible for some cars to drive all the way to the trailhead, which is about 2.5 mi. from the crossroads.

From the south terminus, the trail follows an old logging road generally north. At 0.3 mi. it bears left off the road (arrow), then climbs over a small ridge. At 1.2 mi. it enters another old logging road, which it follows it to the left for 0.2 mi., then bears to the right off the old road and soon crosses a branch of Beaver Brook. At 2.3 mi. it crosses Beaver Brook, passes over a steeper section, runs in the gully of a small brook, then turns left away from the brook and reaches Miles Notch at 2.9 mi. The trail now descends gradually, and at 3.2 mi. the Red Rock Trail leaves on the left for the summit of Speckled Mtn. The Miles Notch Trail then descends moderately, crossing Miles Brook repeatedly. At 5.4 mi. the Haystack Notch Trail enters on the left, and the Miles Notch Trail soon reaches its northern end.

Miles Notch Trail (map 5:F14–E14)

Distances from south terminus (470')

> *to* Red Rock Trail (1750'): 3.2 mi., 1500 ft. (rev. 200 ft.), 2 hr. 20 min.
>
> *to* north terminus (800'): 5.6 mi. (9.0 km.), 1500 ft. (rev. 950 ft.), 3 hr. 35 min.

Bickford Brook Trail (WMNF)

This trail ascends Speckled Mtn. from the Brickett Place on ME 113, 0.2 mi. north of the road to WMNF Cold River Campground. The trail enters the woods near the garage, then at 0.3 mi. turns to the right onto an old WMNF service road built for access to the former fire tower on Speckled Mtn. and follows this road for the next 2.5 mi. At 0.7 mi. the Blueberry Ridge Trail leaves on the right (east) for the lower end of the Bickford Slides and Blueberry Mtn.; this trail rejoins the Bickford Brook Trail 0.5 mi. below the summit of Speckled Mtn., affording the opportunity for a loop hike. At 0.9 mi. the Bickford Slides Loop enters on the right from the lower end of the Upper Slides, and at 1.1 mi. the spur path along the Upper Slides enters on the right. The Bickford Brook Trail soon swings away from the brook and winds up a southwest spur to the crest of the main west ridge of the Speckled Mtn. range, where the Spruce Hill Trail enters left at 3.1 mi. The Bickford Brook Trail then passes west and north of the summit of Ames Mtn. into the col between Ames Mtn. and Speckled Mtn., where the Blueberry Ridge Trail rejoins right at 3.8 mi. The Bickford Brook Trail then continues upward to the summit.

Bickford Brook Trail (map 5:F12–F13)

Distances from ME 113 (600')

> *to* Blueberry Ridge Trail, lower junction (950'): 0.7 mi., 350 ft., 30 min.
>
> *to* Spruce Hill Trail (2420'): 3.1 mi., 1800 ft., 2 hr. 25 min.
>
> *to* Blueberry Ridge Trail, upper junction (2590'): 3.8 mi., 2000 ft., 2 hr. 55 min.
>
> *to* Speckled Mtn. summit (2906'): 4.3 mi. (6.9 km.), 2300 ft., 3 hr. 20 min.

Blueberry Ridge Trail (CTA)

This trail begins and ends on the Bickford Brook Trail, leaving at a sign 0.7 mi. from its trailhead at the Brickett Place on ME 113 and rejoining 0.5 mi. below the summit of Speckled Mtn. (The upper part of the Blueberry Ridge Trail may also be reached from Shell Pond Rd. via the Stone House or White Cairn trails.) It descends toward Bickford Brook, and at 0.1 mi. the trail passes the lower end of the Bickford Slides Loop, which diverges to the left just before the main trail crosses Bickford Brook. Care should be taken to avoid (or else deliberately explore) numerous unofficial side paths from the Bickford Slides and over to the Bickford Brook Trail.

Bickford Slides Loop. This side path, 0.5 mi. long, leaves the Blueberry Ridge Trail just before it crosses Bickford Brook, at a point 0.1 mi. from its lower junction with the Bickford Brook Trail. At the same point a spur path descends along Bickford Brook 50 yd. to the Lower Slides. At a point 20 yd. from its beginning, the Bickford Slides Loop crosses Bickford Brook (may be difficult at high water) and climbs along it for 0.3 mi. to another junction near the base of the Upper Slides. Here the main path bears left across the brook at the base of the Upper Slides and in another 0.2 mi. rejoins the Bickford Brook Trail at a point 0.2 mi. above the lowest junction of these paths, while a spur path 0.3 mi. long continues up along the brook and the Upper Slides, then crosses the brook above the slides and rejoins the Bickford Brook Trail 0.3 mi. above the lowest junction of the paths.

From the junction with the Bickford Slides Loop and the spur path to the Lower Slides, the Blueberry Ridge Trail crosses Bickford Brook (may be difficult at high water) and ascends southeast to an open area just over the crest of Blueberry Ridge, where the White Cairn Trail enters right at 0.7 mi. An overlook loop 0.5 mi. long, with excellent views to the south, leaves the Blueberry Ridge Trail shortly after this junction and rejoins it shortly before the Stone House Trail enters on the right at 0.9 mi., a few steps past the high point of the trail on Blueberry Mtn. From the junction with the Stone House Trail, marked by signs and a large cairn, the Blueberry Ridge Trail bears left and descends to a spring (unreliable) a short distance from the trail on the left (north). Here it turns sharp right, and ascends over ledges marked by cairns and through occasional patches of woods, passing over several humps. The trail ends at the Bickford Brook Trail in the shallow pass at the head of the Rattlesnake Brook ravine, about 0.5 mi. below the summit of Speckled Mtn.

Blueberry Ridge Trail (map 5:F13)
Distances from Bickford Brook Trail, lower junction (950')

 to Stone House Trail (1750'): 0.9 mi., 900 ft., 55 min.

 to Bickford Brook Trail, upper junction (2590'): 3.1 mi., 1850 ft., 2 hr. 30 min.

Spruce Hill Trail (WMNF)

This trail begins on the east side of ME 113 3.0 mi. north of the road to WMNF Cold River Campground, opposite the start of the East Royce Trail, and ascends to the Bickford Brook Trail, with which it forms the shortest route to the summit of Speckled Mtn. It ascends moderately through woods, passing the Wilderness boundary sign at 0.6 mi. and affording restricted views of Evans Notch, to the summit of Spruce Hill at 1.5 mi. It then descends into a sag and climbs to meet the Bickford Brook Trail on the ridgecrest west of Ames Mtn.

Spruce Hill Trail (map 5:F13)

Distances from ME 113 (1450')

> *to* Bickford Brook Trail (2420'): 1.9 mi. (3.0 km.), 1050 ft. (rev. 200 ft.), 1 hr. 30 min.

> *to* Speckled Mtn. summit (2906') via Bickford Brook Trail: 3.1 mi., 1650 ft., 2 hr. 25 min.

Cold Brook Trail (WMNF)

This trail ascends Speckled Mtn. from a trailhead reached from ME 5 in North Lovell ME. Follow the road with signs for Evergreen Valley Ski Area for 1.9 mi. and take the first right (with an Evergreen Valley sign) just after the bridge over Great Brook, then continue to a gravel road on the right 2.2 mi. from ME 5. The WMNF sign is on the paved road, but it may be possible to drive 0.5 mi. on the rough gravel road to a parking area.

Beyond here the road becomes rougher, and in 0.7 mi. from the paved road it bears left past a gate. The next 1.0 mi. is on a muddy road that circles on contour to a cabin, the Duncan McIntosh House. Continuing ahead on the road, take the left fork, then the right. The trail descends to Cold Brook and crosses it at 1.9 mi., just above a fork. It then climbs and circles along the farther branch, passes west of Sugarloaf Mtn., and ascends the south side of Speckled Mtn., passing a junction left at 2.7 mi. with the "Link Trail" (not described in this guide) from the Evergreen Valley Ski Area. It emerges on semi-open ledges at 3.5 mi., passes two excellent south outlooks, and bears right to re-enter the woods at 4.4 mi. At 4.9 mi. it emerges on semi-open ledges again and soon reaches the junction with the Red Rock Trail right and the Bickford Brook Trail left, where it follows the latter trail left 30 yd. to the summit of Speckled Mtn.

Cold Brook Trail (map 5:F14–F13)

Distance from paved road (500')

   to Speckled Mtn. summit (2906'): 4.9 mi. (7.9 km.), 2500 ft., 3 hr. 40 min.

Red Rock Trail (WMNF)

This trail ascends to Speckled Mtn. from the Miles Notch Trail 0.3 mi. north of Miles Notch, 3.2 mi. from its southern trailhead and 2.4 mi. from its northern trailhead. It traverses the long eastern ridge of the Speckled Mtn. range, affording fine views of the surrounding mountains.

   It leaves the Miles Notch Trail, descends to cross Miles Brook in its deep ravine, then angles up the north slope of Miles Knob and gains the ridgecrest northwest of that summit. It descends to a col, then ascends, passing an obscure side path that leads left downhill to a spectacular viewpoint (dangerous if wet or icy) at the top of the sheer south cliff of Red Rock Mtn. The main trail continues to the ledgy summit of Red Rock Mtn. at 1.2 mi., where there is a view to the north, and follows the ridge, with several ups and downs, over Butters Mtn. at 2.5 mi. and then on to the next col to the west. Here, at 3.4 mi., the Great Brook Trail diverges left (east) and descends southeast to its trailhead, which is very close to the southern trailhead of the Miles Notch Trail. The Red Rock Trail swings southwest, crosses the summit of Durgin Mtn. at 4.4 mi., then runs generally southwest to the junction with the Cold Brook Trail and Bickford Brook Trail 30 yd. east of the summit of Speckled Mtn. There is a spring near the trail about 0.1 mi. east of the summit.

Red Rock Trail (map 5:F14–F13)

Distances from Miles Notch Trail (1750')

   to Great Brook Trail (2000'): 3.4 mi., 1000 ft. (rev. 750 ft.), 2 hr. 10 min.

   to Speckled Mtn. summit (2906'): 5.6 mi. (9.0 km.), 2100 ft. (rev. 200 ft.), 3 hr. 50 min.

Great Brook Trail (WMNF)

This trail ascends to the Red Rock Trail east of Speckled Mtn. To reach its trailhead, leave ME 5 in North Lovell ME on a road with signs for Evergreen Valley Ski Area and follow that road northwest for 1.8 mi. Turn right here just before the bridge over Great Brook onto Hut Rd., and continue 1.5 mi. to the trailhead, which is about 100 yd. past the southern trailhead for the Miles Notch Trail.

The trail continues up the gravel road and bears right onto FR 4 at 0.8 mi., just after crossing Great Brook on a bridge with a gate. At 1.8 mi. it turns left onto a grassy older road and follows Great Brook. At 3.0 mi. it crosses Great Brook, with some interesting cascades just above the crossing. The trail then bears left (arrow), becomes steeper, and continues along Great Brook to the ridgecrest, where it joins the Red Rock Trail in the col between Butters Mtn. and Durgin Mtn.

Great Brook Trail (map 5:F14–F13)

Distances from trailhead (500')

    to Red Rock Trail (2000'): 3.7 mi. (5.9 km.), 1500 ft., 2 hr. 35 min.

    to Speckled Mtn. summit (2906') via Red Rock Trail: 5.8 mi. (9.3 km.), 2600 ft. (rev. 200 ft.), 4 hr. 10 min.

Stone House Trail (CTA)

This trail ascends to the scenic ledges of Blueberry Mtn. from Shell Pond Rd. To reach the trailhead, leave NH 113 on the east side 0.7 mi. north of AMC Cold River Camp and follow Shell Pond Rd. 1.1 mi. to a padlocked steel gate that makes it necessary to park cars at that point.

The trail leaves the road on the left (north) 0.5 mi. beyond the gate, east of an open shed. It follows a logging road and approaches Rattlesnake Brook. At 0.2 mi. from Shell Pond Rd. it merges with a private road (descending, bear right at arrow) and immediately reaches the junction with a spur path that leads right 30 yd. to a bridge overlooking Rattlesnake Flume, a small, attractive gorge. The main trail soon swings right (arrow), and at 0.5 mi. another spur leads right 0.1 mi. to the exquisite Rattlesnake Pool, which lies at the foot of a small cascade. The main trail soon enters the WMNF, and at 1.2 mi. it swings left and begins to climb rather steeply straight up the slope, running generally northwest to the top of the ridge, where it ends at the Blueberry Ridge Trail only a few steps from the top of Blueberry Mtn. For Speckled Mtn., turn right on the Blueberry Ridge Trail.

Stone House Trail (map 5:G13–F13)

Distance from Shell Pond Rd. (600')

    to Blueberry Ridge Trail (1750'): 1.5 mi. (2.4 km.), 1150 ft., 1 hr. 20 min.

White Cairn Trail (CTA)

This trail provides access to the open ledges on Blueberry Mtn. and, with the Stone House Trail, makes an easy half-day circuit. It begins on Shell Pond Rd., which leaves NH 113 on the east side 0.7 mi. north of AMC Cold River Camp and runs 1.1 mi. to a padlocked steel gate that makes it necessary to park cars at that point.

The trail leaves Shell Pond Rd. at a small clearing 0.3 mi. beyond the gate. It follows old logging roads north and west to an upland meadow, passing into the WMNF at 0.3 mi. At 0.8 mi. it begins to climb steeply up the right (east) margin of the cliffs that are visible from the road, then turns sharp left and begins to climb on ledges. The grade soon moderates as the trail runs northwest along the crest of the cliffs to the west, with views to the south. At 1.2 mi. it passes a spring, then swings right (north) and passes another spring just before ending at the junction with the Blueberry Ledge Trail, 0.2 mi. west of the upper terminus of the Stone House Trail. A loop trail that leaves the Blueberry Ledge Trail near its junction with this trail provides a scenic alternate route to the Stone House Trail.

White Cairn Trail (map 5:F13)
Distance from Shell Pond Rd. (600')

   to Blueberry Ridge Trail (1750'): 1.4 mi. (2.3 km.), 1150 ft., 1 hr. 15 min.

Shell Pond Trail (WMNF)

This trail runs between Shell Pond Rd., at the locked gate 1.1 mi. from NH 113, and Deer Hill Rd. (FR 9), 3.5 mi. from NH 113. Shell Pond Rd. leaves NH 113 on the east side 0.7 mi. north of AMC Cold River Camp.

From the gate on Shell Pond Rd., continue east on the road. The White Cairn Trail leaves left at 0.3 mi. and the Stone House Trail leaves left at 0.5 mi. At 0.6 mi. the Shell Pond Trail passes the Stone House (left). Just beyond here the trail proper begins, following an old overgrown road. The trail crosses Rattlesnake Brook on a bridge at 1.1 mi., passes through a wet area, and turns left off the road at 1.3 mi. (may be poorly marked), where the old road leads straight to circle Shell Pond. (The trail itself does not come within sight of the pond, and the path that circles the pond passes over private property not open to the public.) This turn is marked by a sign for the Stone House Farm and a cairn (but no sign or arrow) for the trail. From here the trail ascends gradually to Deer Hill Rd.

Shell Pond Trail (map 5:G13)
Distance from gate on Shell Pond Rd. (600')

   to Deer Hill Rd. (850'): 1.8 mi. (2.9 km.), 250 ft., 1 hr.

Horseshoe Pond Trail (CTA)

This trail, blazed with bright yellow paint, starts from Deer Hill Rd. (FR 9) 4.7 mi. from NH 113 at a small parking area at a curve in the road, where the pond is visible; it ends on the Conant Trail.

From Deer Hill Rd., it descends moderately past the Styles grave, which is on the right of the trail and enclosed by a stone wall, then enters a recent logging road and turns right on it. In a few steps, the Horseshoe Pond Loop, 0.4 mi. long, leaves left for the northwest shore of Horseshoe Pond. The main trail continues on the logging road, then bears right on another logging road at 0.3 mi., and the Horseshoe Pond Loop rejoins on the left at an incipient apple orchard in another 100 yd. The trail ascends through the clear-cut resulting from the timber salvage operations after the 1980 wind storm, following cairns and overgrown skid roads back into the woods to the old trail, which continues to the Conant Trail between Lord Hill and Harndon Hill.

Horseshoe Pond Trail (map 5:G13)
Distance from Deer Hill Rd. (700')

   to Conant Trail (1100'): 1.1 mi. (1.8 km.), 500 ft. (rev. 100 ft), 50 min.

Conant Trail (CTA)

This loop path to Pine Hill and Lord Hill is an interesting and fairly easy walk with a number of good outlooks. It is frequently referred to (and may be signed as) the Pine-Lord-Harndon Trail, though it does not go particularly close to the summit of Harndon Hill; it should not be confused with the Conant Path, a short trail (not open to the public) near AMC Cold River Camp. It is reached by following Deer Hill Rd. (FR 9) and making a right turn 1.5 mi. from NH 113, then turning left almost immediately and parking near a dike.

The trail runs straight ahead along the dike across Colton Brook—Colton Dam is located several hundred yards to the right from here—and continues to the loop junction at 0.4 mi., where the path divides. From here the path is described in a counter-clockwise direction. The south branch turns right and follows a logging road (Hemp Hill Rd.) to a level spot at 1.0 mi. near the old Johnson cellar hole. Here it turns left on a logging road, then left again in a few steps. The trail turns left again at 1.2 mi. and ascends Pine Hill, rather steeply at times, passing a ledge with a fine view to the west at 1.4 mi. It reaches the west end of the summit ridge and continues to the most easterly knob, which has a good view north, at 2.0 mi. The trail zigzags down past logged areas, crosses Bradley Brook at 2.3

mi., and then climbs, crossing the logging road that provides access to the mine on Lord Hill and passing an outlook over Horseshoe Pond. It reaches ledges near the summit of Lord Hill at 3.0 mi., where the Mine Loop leaves on the left.

Mine Loop. This path is 1.0 mi. long, 0.1 mi. shorter than the section of Conant Trail it bypasses. Except for the one critical turn mentioned below, it is fairly easy to follow. From the junction with the Conant Trail near the summit of Lord Hill, it climbs briefly to the ledge at the top of the old mica mine and then descends on a woods road, and at 0.1 mi. it passes a spur path that leads right 30 yd. to the mine. At 0.5 mi. it turns sharp left on a good logging road, then at 0.7 mi. it reaches a fork and turns sharp right back on the other branch of the road, which shows much less evidence of use. This turn is easily missed because it is difficult to mark adequately and the correct side road is less obvious than the main road. (The main road, continuing straight at this fork, crosses the Conant Trail between Pine Hill and Lord Hill and continues south toward Kezar Lake.) At a clearing the Mine Loop leaves the road on the right and descends 50 yd. to rejoin the Conant Trail 1.1 mi. from its trailhead.

From Lord Hill the Conant Trail descends to the junction with the Horseshoe Pond Trail on the right at 3.2 mi., where it bears left, then soon turns left and runs at a fairly level grade along the south side of Harndon Hill. It passes a cellar hole, and the Mine Loop rejoins on the left at 4.1 mi. At 4.5 mi. the road passes a gate, becomes wider, reaches the loop junction, and continues straight ahead across the dike to the trailhead.

Conant Trail (map 5:G13)
Distance from trailhead off Deer Hill Rd. (550')

   for complete loop: 5.2 mi. (8.3 km.), 1000 ft., 3 hr. 5 min.

Little Deer–Big Deer Trail (CTA)
This trail ascends Little Deer Hill and Big Deer Hill, providing a relatively easy trip that offers interesting views. The trail proper runs from the AMC Cold River Camp to Deer Hill Rd. (FR 9); members of the public who wish to use this trail are requested to park at the Baldface Circle Trail trailhead parking area and follow a newly cut path called the Deer Hill Connector, which runs south of Charles Brook for 0.3 mi. to a junction on the right with the Tea House Path (not open to the public) to Cold River Camp, then runs another 0.1 mi. to the dam on the Cold River near Cold River Camp. Here the trail from the AMC camp enters on the right; its junction with the Conant Path is a few steps to the right (neither of these trails is open to the public). The trail to the Deer Hills crosses Cold River on the

dam, soon passing a short spur path that leads left to the Leach Link Trail and then crossing the Leach Link Trail itself. The main trail climbs moderately past an outlook west, then bears left onto ledges and reaches the summit of Little Deer Hill at 1.3 mi. Here the Ledges Trail enters on the right. The main trail descends into a sag, then climbs to the summit of Big Deer Hill at 2.0 mi. It then descends the south ridge with several fine outlooks, turning left at 2.5 mi. where a connecting path to the Ledges Trail and Little Deer Hill leaves on the right. (This connecting path descends to a spur path at 0.6 mi., which leads right 0.2 mi. to the summit of Big Deer Hill, and then continues from the spur junction to end at the Ledges Trail at 0.8 mi.) Soon the main trail turns left again, then turns right onto an old logging road at 2.7 mi. Here a spur path follows the logging road left for a few steps, then descends in 0.2 mi. to Deer Hill Spring (also called Bubbling Spring), an interesting shallow pool with air bubbles rising through a small area of light-colored sand. The main trail descends from the junction to Deer Hill Rd.

Little Deer–Big Deer Trail (map 5:G12–G13)

Distances from ME 113 at the Baldface Circle Trail parking area (520')
via Deer Hill Connector

to Little Deer Hill summit (1090'): 1.3 mi., 550 ft., 55 min.

to Big Deer Hill summit (1367'): 2.0 mi., 1000 ft. (rev. 200 ft.), 1 hr. 30 min.

to Deer Hill Rd. (500'): 3.3 mi. (5.3 km.), 1000 ft. (rev. 850 ft.), 2 hr.

Ledges Trail (CTA)

This trail passes interesting ledges and a cave but is very steep and rough, dangerous in icy conditions, and not recommended for descent. It leaves the south end of the Leach Link Trail and climbs rather steeply with numerous outlooks. At 0.2 mi. the connecting path that leads in 0.8 mi. to the Little Deer–Big Deer Trail south of Big Deer diverges right, affording an alternate route to the summit of Little Deer via the spur path (0.2 mi. long) that leaves it 0.2 mi. from the Ledges Trail. At 0.4 mi. the Ledges Trail divides; the right branch, which is slightly longer, rejoins in about 100 yd. Just above the point where these branches rejoin, the spur path from the connecting path mentioned above enters on the right, and soon the Ledges Trail reaches the summit of Little Deer Hill.

Ledges Trail (map 5:G12)

Distance from Leach Link Trail (500')

to Little Deer Hill summit (1090'): 0.5 mi. (0.8 km.), 600 ft., 35 min.

Leach Link Trail (CTA)

This trail gives access to Little Deer Hill and Big Deer Hill from Shell Pond Rd., which leaves NH 113 on the east side 0.7 mi. north of AMC Cold River Camp. The trail leaves Shell Pond Rd. just east of the bridge over Cold River and at 0.4 mi. crosses Shell Pond Brook (may be difficult at high water). On the far bank the Shell Pond Brook Trail enters on the left; this is an alternate route from Shell Pond Rd., 0.5 mi. long, that makes the Shell Pond Brook crossing on a snow-mobile bridge (useful at high water). At 1.1 mi., bear left where a short spur path leads right to the Little Deer–Big Deer Trail, and then cross that trail in another 70 yd.; to the left the Little Deer–Big Deer Trail ascends Little Deer Hill, and to the right it leads to the dam at the AMC Cold River Camp. From here the Leach Link Trail continues along the river, ending at the Ledges Trail.

Leach Link Trail (map 5:G12)

Distance from Shell Pond Rd. (600')

　　to Ledges Trail (500'): 1.5 mi. (2.4 km.), 0 ft. (rev. 100 ft.), 45 min.

Section 11

Mahoosuc Range Area

This section includes the region along the Maine–New Hampshire border that lies east and north of the Androscoggin River, which runs south from Lake Umbagog near Errol to Gorham, then swings east from Gorham to Bethel ME. The region is bounded by NH 16 on the west, by US 2 on the south, and by ME/NH 26 on the northeast. The backbone of the region is the Mahoosuc Range, which rises from the east bank of the river above Berlin and Gorham, runs east at first, then gradually swings toward the north as it continues to its far end at Grafton Notch. This section covers the main Mahoosuc Range and all the trails on it, but does not cover some of the routes on eastern spurs of the range that lie wholly within Maine. Such mountains and routes are covered in the *AMC Maine Mountain Guide.* The most important peaks in the Mahoosuc Range are Old Speck Mtn., Mahoosuc Arm, Goose Eye Mtn., Mt. Carlo, Mt. Success, Cascade Mtn., and Mt. Hayes. The region is completely covered by the AMC North Country–Mahoosuc Range map (map #6).

In this section the Appalachian Trail begins at the trailhead of the Rattle River Trail (Section 9) on US 2. It follows the highway west 0.2 mi. to North Rd., then follows North Rd. for 0.5 mi., crossing the Androscoggin River, then turns left on Hogan Rd. for 0.2 mi. to the Centennial Trail. It then follows the Centennial Trail, the Mahoosuc Trail, and the Old Speck Trail to Grafton Notch, the eastern boundary of the area covered in this guide; the Baldpate Mountain Trail (see the *AMC Maine Mountain Guide*) continues the Appalachian Trail on the opposite side of Grafton Notch. In its course through the Mahoosucs, the Appalachian Trail crosses the summits of Cascade Mtn., Mt. Success, and Mt. Carlo, and passes near the summits of Mt. Hayes, Goose Eye Mtn., Mahoosuc Arm, and Old Speck Mtn.

GEOGRAPHY

The southern part of the **Mahoosuc Range** is a broad, ledgy, lumpy ridge, with numerous spurs extending south toward the Androscoggin valley. The main peaks, from west to east, are **Mt. Hayes** (2555 ft.), **Cascade Mtn.** (2631 ft.), **Bald Cap** (3065 ft.), and Bald Cap's two subsidiary peaks, **Bald Cap Peak** (2795 ft.) and **North Bald Cap** (2893 ft.); all three Bald Cap peaks are trailless. The northern part of the range is higher and narrower, with a well-defined ridgecrest and two long subsidiary ridges running southeast toward the Androscoggin and Bear rivers; the **Sunday River** flows between these subsidiary ridges. The main peaks, from southwest to northeast, are **Mt. Success** (3565 ft.), **Mt. Carlo** (3565 ft.), the three peaks of **Goose Eye Mtn.** (**West Peak,** the highest, 3870 ft., **East Peak,** 3790 ft., and **North Peak,** 3690 ft.), **Fulling Mill Mtn.** (**North Peak,** 3450 ft., and **South Peak,** 3395 ft.), **Mahoosuc Mtn.** (3470 ft.), **Mahoosuc Arm** (3765 ft.), and **Old Speck Mtn.** (4170 ft.). Old Speck is the third highest mountain in Maine; its name distinguishes it from the several other Speckled mountains (so called for their scattered open ledges) in the general area. Mt. Success is named for the unincorporated township in which it is located, and Mt. Carlo is named for a dog, the faithful companion of Eugene B. Cook. Cook was a pioneer White Mtn. trail-builder who made several early explorations of the Mahoosuc area, often accompanied by Lucia and Marian Pychowska, whose letters concerning their experiences in the White Mtns., including their exploratory adventures with Cook, have been published under the title of *Mountain Summers*. The origin of Goose Eye Mtn.'s peculiar name is in doubt; the most plausible explanation maintains that Canada geese in their flight south from the Rangeley Lakes appear almost to graze its summit, and it is, therefore, "goose high."

The views from Goose Eye, a striking rock peak, are among the best in the White Mtns., and most of the other peaks have fine views, either from the summits or from the numerous open ledges scattered throughout the range. There are several fine mountain ponds, including **Speck Pond** (one of the highest ponds in Maine), **Gentian Pond, Dream Lake,** and **Page Pond.** The most remarkable feature of the range is **Mahoosuc Notch,** where the trail winds around and under huge fragments of rock that have fallen from the cliffs of Mahoosuc Mtn. to the northwest; Fulling Mill Mtn. forms the southeast wall.

The **Alpine Cascades** on Cascade Brook, which flows from the northwest slope of Cascade Mtn., are an attractive sight except in dry seasons. They can be approached from the gravel road along the railroad tracks on the east side of the Androscoggin, probably best reached from NH 16 by crossing the river at the highway bridge just south of Berlin and following the road south along the railroad. Nearly opposite the Cascade Mill of the James River Co., a footpath diverges left across the tracks, then divides into three paths; the right branch leads about 100 yd. to the foot of Cascade Falls.

From the major peaks of the southern part of the range, ridges run toward the Androscoggin, bearing interesting smaller peaks. Among these mountains are **Middle Mtn.** (2010 ft.), **Mt. Crag** (1412 ft.), **Mt. Ingalls** (2242 ft.), **Mt. Cabot** (1512 ft.), and **Crow's Nest** (1287 ft.). There are also two interesting waterfalls on the south side of the range. **Dryad Fall** is reached by the Dryad Fall Trail. **Lary Flume** is a wild chasm that resembles the Ice Gulch and Devil's Hopyard, with many boulder caves and one fissure cave. There is no trail, but experienced bushwhackers have visited it by ascending along the brook that may be reached by following a compass course east where the Austin Brook Trail begins its last 0.5 mi. of ascent to Gentian Pond.

Success Pond Rd. runs from the east side of the Androscoggin River in Berlin to Success Pond in about 14 mi., and continues to ME 26 north of Grafton Notch. Over the years this has been perhaps the most difficult road in the White Mtns. for a person unfamiliar with the region to find; important landmarks disappeared or changed, and the first part of the road itself was moved with astounding but unpredictable regularity. However, it now appears that the situation may have become sufficiently stable to give cause for hope, though even at the best of times following it requires a good deal of care and often some trial and error. To find it, leave NH 16 just south of the city of Berlin, 4.5 mi. north of the eastern junction of US 2 and NH 16 in Gorham, and cross the Androscoggin on the Cleveland Bridge. At the east end of the bridge, the road (Unity St.) swings left and passes straight through a set of traffic lights in 0.7 mi. from NH 16. At 0.8 mi. the road bears right across railroad tracks and becomes Hutchins St. It turns sharp left at 1.6 mi. at Frank's Village Store and continues past the Crown Vantage mill yard. At 1.9 mi. from NH 16, where there has usually been a large sign reading "OHRV PARKING 1 MILE," the Success Pond Rd. begins on the right (east). It no longer winds among the huge wood piles of the mill yard, but one should still watch out for large trucks, especially those entering from the right. The first part of the road has frequently been difficult to distinguish from branch roads, but once past this area it is well defined—though it is often easy to take a dead-end branch road by mistake. The road is not generally open to public vehicular use in winter, and it can be very rough and muddy, particularly in spring and early summer before yearly maintenance is carried out. Trailheads are marked only with small AMC standard trail signs, often at old diverging logging roads with no well-defined parking area, so one must look for them carefully. The lower parts of the trails originating on this road have been disrupted frequently in the past by construction of new logging roads; great care is necessary to follow the blazes that mark the proper roads, ascending or descending.

North Rd. provides access to the trails on the south side of the Mahoosuc Range. This road leaves US 2 about 2.8 mi. east of its easterly junction with NH 16 in Gorham, and crosses the Androscoggin River on the Lead Mine Bridge; the Appalachian Trail follows this part of the road. North Rd. then swings east and runs along the north side of the river to rejoin US 2 just north of Bethel ME. Bridges connect North Rd. with US 2 at the villages of Shelburne NH and Gilead ME.

CAMPING

Except for the corridor of the Appalachian Trail on the ridgecrest, land in this section is owned by the state of Maine (mostly the higher-elevation lands along the Mahoosuc ridgecrest in Maine), and by the Crown Vantage Co. and other private interests. Hiking is permitted through their courtesy. No part of this section is included in the WMNF. Camping and wood fires are prohibited by state laws except at the five authorized campsites.

Trident Col Campsite (AMC) is located on a side path from the Mahoosuc Trail in Trident Col. There are sites for four tents. Water is available about 50 yd. below (west of) the site.

Gentian Pond Campsite (AMC) on Gentian Pond has a large shelter and four tent platforms.

Carlo Col Campsite (AMC), consisting of a shelter and four tent platforms, is located on the Carlo Col Trail 0.3 mi. below the Mahoosuc Trail at Carlo Col.

Full Goose Campsite (AMC), consisting of a shelter and four tent platforms, is located on the Mahoosuc Trail between Fulling Mill Mtn. and Goose Eye Mtn. There is a spring 30 yd. east of the shelter.

Speck Pond Campsite (AMC), located at Speck Pond on the Mahoosuc Trail, includes a shelter and six tent platforms.

Trail on Mahoosuc Range Crest

List of Trails	**Map**	**Page**
Mahoosuc Trail	6:E10–C13	424

Trails to Main Range from Success Pond Road

List of Trails	**Map**	**Page**
Success Trail	6:D12	430
Carlo Col Trail	6:C12–D12	430
Goose Eye Trail	6:C12–C13	431

THE TRAILS
Mahoosuc Trail (AMC/MDP)

This trail extends along the entire length of the Mahoosuc Range from Gorham NH to the summit of Old Speck. Beyond its junction with the Centennial Trail, the Mahoosuc Trail is a link in the Appalachian Trail. Camping is limited to the tentsites at Trident Col and to the four shelters: Gentian Pond, Carlo Col, Full Goose, and Speck Pond (all of which also have tentsites). These sites may have a caretaker, in which case a fee is charged. Some of these shelters are slated for removal but the tentsites will remain. Water is scarce, particularly in dry weather, and its purity is always in question. Do not be deceived by the relatively low elevations; this trail is among the most rugged of its kind in the White Mtns., a very strenuous trail—particularly for those with heavy packs—with numerous minor humps and cols, and many ledges, some of them quite steep, that are likely to be slippery when wet. Many parts of the trail may require significantly more time than that provided by the formula, particularly for backpackers, and Mahoosuc Notch may require several extra hours, depending in part on how much time one spends enjoying the spectacular scenery. Mahoosuc Notch is regarded by many who have hiked the entire length of the Appalachian Trail as its most difficult mile. *Caution:* Mahoosuc Notch can be hazardous in wet or icy conditions and can remain impassable due to unmelted snowdrifts through the end of May and perhaps even longer.

Part I. Gorham to Centennial Trail

To reach the trail, cross the Androscoggin River by the footbridge under the Boston & Maine Railroad bridge, 1.3 mi. north of the Gorham post office on NH 16. On the east bank, follow the road to the right (southeast) along the river for 0.4 mi., then cross the canal through the open upper level of the powerhouse (left of entrance). At the east end of the dam, keep straight ahead about 100 yd. to the woods, where the trail sign will be found. The trail is sparsely blazed in blue. Turn left and follow an old road north along the side of the canal for 0.1 mi., then turn right uphill on an old logging road. At 0.8 mi. from NH 16 the trail crosses a power line clearing, then bears right and reaches but does not cross a brook, following it closely for 100 yd. Avoid side paths from recent logging operations. The trail ascends at only a slight grade to a side path at 1.1 mi. that leads right 0.2 mi. to Mascot Pond, just below the cliffs seen prominently from Gorham. The Mahoosuc Trail crosses a woods road, then ascends the valley of a brook, which it crosses several times. At 2.5 mi. it passes a short spur (sign) that leads left to Popsy Spring, then climbs steeply and emerges on the southwest side of the flat, ledgy summit of Mt. Hayes. An unmarked footway leads a few yards right to the best viewpoint south over the valley. A cairn marks the true summit of Mt. Hayes at 3.1 mi. The trail descends on open ledges with good views north to the junction on the right with the Centennial Trail at 3.2 mi.

Part II. Centennial Trail to Gentian Pond

From here north, the Mahoosuc Trail is part of the Appalachian Trail, marked with white blazes. It descends north to the col between Mt. Hayes and Cascade Mtn. at 4.1 mi., where there is sometimes water. The trail then ascends Cascade Mtn. by a southwest ridge over ledges and large fallen rocks, emerging on the bare summit ledge at 5.1 mi. It turns back sharply into the woods, descending gradually with occasional slight ascents to the east end of the mountain, then enters a fine forest and descends rapidly beside cliffs and ledges to Trident Col at 6.3 mi., where a side path leads left 0.2 mi. to Trident Col Tentsite. Water is available about 50 yd. below (west of) the site. The bare ledges of the rocky cone to the east of Trident Col repay the effort required to scramble to its top; a route ascends between two large cairns near the tentsite side path.

The trail descends rather steeply to the southeast and runs along the side of the ridge at the base of the Trident, which is made up of the previously mentioned cone, the ledgy peak just west of Page Pond, and a somewhat less prominent peak between them. The trail crosses several small brooks, at least one of which usually has water. It follows a logging road for 0.1 mi., then turns left off the road at a sign and ascends to Page Pond at 7.3 mi. The trail passes the south end of the pond, crosses a beaver dam, and climbs gradually, then more steeply, to a short spur path at 7.9 mi. that leads left to a fine outlook from ledges near the summit of Wocket Ledge, a shoulder of Bald Cap. The main trail crosses the height-of-land and descends east, crosses the upper (west) branch of Peabody Brook, then climbs around the nose of a small ridge and descends gradually to the head of Dream Lake. The trail bears left here, then bears right to run around the north end of the lake, and crosses the inlet brook at 9.0 mi. Just beyond, the Peabody Brook Trail leaves on the right.

From this junction, the Mahoosuc Trail follows a lumber road left for 100 yd. It soon recrosses the inlet brook, passes over a slight divide into the watershed of Austin Brook, ascends through some swampy places, and descends to Moss Pond at 10.5 mi. It continues past the north shore of the pond and follows an old logging road down the outlet brook, then crosses the brook, turns abruptly right downhill from the logging road, and descends to Gentian Pond. It skirts the southwest shore of the pond, then drops to cross the outlet brook. A few yards beyond, at 11.2 mi., is Gentian Pond Campsite (shelter and tentsites), and here the Austin Brook Trail diverges right for North Rd. in Shelburne.

Part III. Gentian Pond to Carlo Col

From Gentian Pond Shelter the trail climbs to the top of the steep-sided hump whose ledges overlook the pond from the east, then descends moderately to a sag. It then starts up the west end of Mt. Success, climbing rather steeply at first to the lumpy ridge, and passes a small stream at 12.6 mi. in the col that lies under the main mass of Mt. Success. The trail now climbs rather steeply and roughly for about 0.5 mi. to the relatively flat upper part of the mountain, then ascends over open ledges with an outlook to the southwest, passes through a belt of high scrub, crosses an alpine meadow, and finally comes out on the summit of Mt. Success at 14.0 mi.

The trail turns sharp left here and descends through scrub, then forest, to the sag between Mt. Success and a northern subpeak, where the Success Trail enters left at 14.6 mi. The main trail climbs slightly, then descends moderately to the main col between Mt. Success and Mt. Carlo at 15.3 mi. The trail then rises over a low hump and descends to a lesser col, where it turns right, then left, passes the Maine–New Hampshire border signs, and ascends moderately again. At 16.4 mi. it drops sharply past a fine outlook ledge into the little box ravine called Carlo Col. The Carlo Col Trail from Success Pond Rd. enters left here; Carlo Col Campsite is located 0.3 mi. down the Carlo Col Trail, at the head of a small brook.

Part IV. Carlo Col to Mahoosuc Notch

From Carlo Col the trail climbs steadily to the bare southwest summit of Mt. Carlo at 16.8 mi., where there is an excellent view. It then passes a lower knob to the northeast, descends through a mountain meadow—where there is a fine view of Goose Eye ahead—and reaches the col at 17.4 mi. The trail turns more north and climbs steeply to a ledgy knoll below Goose Eye, then passes through a sag and climbs steeply again to the narrow ridge of the main peak of Goose Eye Mtn. at 18.2 mi. Use care on the ledges. Here, at the ridge top, the Goose Eye Trail branches sharp left, reaching the open summit and its spectacular views in 0.1 mi. and continuing to Success Pond Rd. From the ridge-top junction the Mahoosuc Trail turns sharp right (east) and follows the ridgecrest through mixed ledge and scrub to a col at 18.5 mi., where it meets the south branch of the Wright Trail to Bull Branch Rd. in Ketchum ME. The Mahoosuc Trail then climbs steeply through woods and open areas to the bare summit of the East Peak of Goose Eye Mtn. Here it turns sharp left (north) down the open ledges of the ridge and enters the scrub at the east side of the open part, meeting the north branch of the Wright Trail at 18.8 mi. Beyond the col the trail runs in the open nearly to the foot of the North Peak, except for two interesting box ravines, where there is often water. At the summit of the North Peak, at 19.8 mi., the trail turns sharp right (east) along the ridgecrest, then swings northeast down the steep slope, winding through several patches of scrub. At the foot of the steep slope it enters the woods and angles down the west face of the ridge to the col at 20.8 mi. Full Goose Campsite is located on a ledgy shelf near here; there is a spring 80 yd. to the right (east of the campsite). The trail then turns sharp left and ascends, coming into the open about 0.3 mi. below the summit of the South Peak of Fulling Mill Mtn., which is reached at 21.3 mi. Here the trail turns sharp left and runs through a meadow. It descends northwest through woods, first gradually, then steeply, to the head of Mahoosuc Notch at 22.3 mi. Here the Notch Trail to Success Pond Rd. diverges sharp left (southwest).

Part V. Mahoosuc Notch to Old Speck

From the head of Mahoosuc Notch the trail turns sharp right (northeast) and descends the length of the narrow notch along a rough footway, passing through a number of boulder caverns, some with narrow openings where progress will be slow and where ice remains into the summer. The trail is blazed on the rocks with white paint. *Caution:* Great care should be exercised in the notch because of the numerous slippery rocks and dangerous holes. The notch may be impassable through early June because of snow, even with snowshoes. Heavy backpacks will impede progress considerably.

At the lower end of the notch, at 23.4 mi., the trail bears left and ascends moderately but roughly under the east end of Mahoosuc Mtn. along the valley that leads to Notch 2, then crosses to the north side of the brook at 23.9 mi. The trail then winds upward among rocks and ledges on the very steep wooded slope of Mahoosuc Arm with a steep, rough footway. A little more than halfway up, it passes the head of a little flume, in which there is sometimes water. At 25.0 mi., a few yards past the top of the flat ledges near the summit of Mahoosuc Arm, the May Cutoff diverges left and leads 0.3 mi. over the true summit to the Speck Pond Trail. The Mahoosuc Trail swings right and wanders across the semi-open summit plateau for about 0.5 mi., then drops steeply to Speck Pond (3430 ft.), one of the highest ponds in Maine, bordered with thick woods. The trail crosses the outlet brook and continues around the east side of the pond to Speck Pond Campsite at 25.9 mi. (in summer, there is a caretaker and a fee for overnight camping). Here the Speck Pond Trail to Success Pond Rd. leaves on the left.

The trail then climbs to the southeast end of the next hump on the ridge, passes over it, and runs across the east face of a second small hump. In the gully beyond, a few yards east of the trail, there is an unreliable spring. The trail climbs on the west shoulder of Old Speck, reaching an open area where the footway is well defined on the crest. Near the top of the shoulder the trail bears right, re-enters the woods, and follows the wooded crest with blue blazes that mark the boundary of Grafton Notch State Park. The Old Speck Trail, which continues the Appalachian Trail north, diverges left to Grafton Notch at 27.0 mi., and the Mahoosuc Trail runs straight ahead to the summit of Old Speck and its observation tower, where the poorly marked East Spur Trail enters.

Mahoosuc Trail (map 6:E10–C13)

Distances from NH 16 in Gorham (800')

to Mt. Hayes summit (2555'): 3.1 mi., 1750 ft., 2 hr. 25 min.

to Centennial Trail (2550'): 3.3 mi., 1750 ft., 2 hr. 30 min.

to Cascade Mtn. summit (2631'): 5.1 mi., 2450 ft., 3 hr. 45 min.

to Trident Col (2000'): 6.3 mi., 2500 ft., 4 hr. 25 min.

to Page Pond (2220'): 7.3 mi., 2850 ft., 5 hr. 5 min.

to Wocket Ledge (2800'): 7.9 mi., 3450 ft., 5 hr. 40 min.

to Dream Lake, inlet brook crossing (2620'): 9.0 mi., 3650 ft., 6 hr. 20 min.

to Gentian Pond Campsite (2166'): 11.2 mi., 3850 ft., 7 hr. 30 min.

to Mt. Success summit (3565'): 14.0 mi., 5750 ft., 9 hr. 55 min.

to Success Trail (3170'): 14.6 mi., 5750 ft., 10 hr. 10 min.

to Carlo Col Trail (3170'): 16.4 mi., 6250 ft., 11 hr. 20 min.

to Mt. Carlo (3565'): 16.8 mi., 6650 ft., 11 hr. 45 min.

to Goose Eye Trail (3800'): 18.2 mi., 7350 ft., 12 hr. 45 min.

to Wright Trail, south jct. (3620'): 18.5 mi., 7350 ft., 12 hr. 55 min.

to Goose Eye Mtn., East Peak (3790'): 18.6 mi., 7500 ft., 13 hr. 5 min.

to Wright Trail, north jct. (3450'): 18.8 mi., 7500 ft., 15 hr. 50 min.

to Goose Eye Mtn., North Peak (3675'): 19.8 mi., 7800 ft., 13 hr. 50 min.

to Full Goose Campsite (3030'): 20.8 mi., 7800 ft., 14 hr. 20 min.

to Notch Trail (2460'): 22.3 mi., 8150 ft., 15 hr. 15 min.

to foot of Mahoosuc Notch (2150'): 23.4 mi., 8150 ft., 15 hr. 45 min.

to Mahoosuc Arm summit (3770'): 25.0 mi., 9750 ft., 17 hr. 25 min.

to Speck Pond Campsite (3400'): 25.9 mi., 9750 ft., 17 hr. 50 min.

to Old Speck Trail junction (4000'): 27.0 mi., 10,550 ft., 18 hr. 45 min.

to Old Speck Mtn. summit (4170'): 27.3 mi. (43.9 km.), 10,750 ft., 19 hr.

Distances from Old Speck Mtn. summit (4170')

to Old Speck Trail junction (4000'): 0.3 mi., 0 ft., 10 min.

to Speck Pond Campsite (3400'): 1.4 mi., 200 ft., 50 min.

to Mahoosuc Arm summit (3770'): 2.3 mi., 550 ft., 1 hr. 25 min.

to foot of Mahoosuc Notch (2150'): 3.9 mi., 550 ft., 2 hr. 15 min.

to Notch Trail (2460'): 5.0 mi., 850 ft., 2 hr. 55 min.

to Full Goose Campsite (3030'): 6.5 mi., 1800 ft., 4 hr. 10 min.

to Goose Eye Mtn., North Peak (3675'): 7.5 mi., 2450 ft., 5 hr.

to Wright Trail, north jct. (3450'): 8.5 mi., 2450 ft., 5 hr. 30 min.

to Goose Eye Mtn., East Peak (3790'): 8.7 mi., 2800 ft., 5 hr. 45 min.

to Wright Trail, south jct. (3620'): 8.8 mi., 2800 ft., 5 hr. 50 min.

to Goose Eye Trail (3800'): 9.1 mi., 3000 ft., 6 hr. 5 min.

to Mt. Carlo (3565'): 10.5 mi., 3450 ft., 7 hr.

to Carlo Col Trail (3170'): 10.9 mi., 3450 ft., 7 hr. 10 min.

to Success Trail (3170'): 12.7 mi., 3950 ft., 8 hr. 20 min.

to Mt. Success summit (3565'): 13.3 mi., 4350 ft., 8 hr. 50 min.

to Gentian Pond Campsite (2166'): 16.1 mi., 4850 ft., 10 hr. 30 min.

to Dream Lake, inlet brook crossing (2620'): 18.3 mi., 5500 ft., 11 hr. 55 min.

to Wocket Ledge (2800'): 19.4 mi., 5900 ft., 12 hr. 40 min.

to Page Pond (2220'): 20.0 mi., 5900 ft., 13 hr.

to Trident Col (2000'): 21.0 mi., 6050 ft., 13 hr. 30 min.

to Cascade Mtn. summit (2631'): 22.2 mi., 6700 ft., 14 hr. 25 min.

to Centennial Trail (2550'): 24.0 mi., 7300 ft., 15 hr. 40 min.

to Mt. Hayes summit (2555'): 24.2 mi., 7300 ft., 15 hr. 45 min.

to NH 16 in Gorham (800'): 27.3 mi. (43.9 km.), 7300 ft., 17 hr. 20 min.

Success Trail (AMC)

This trail ascends to the Mahoosuc Trail 0.6 mi. north of Mt. Success, starting on Success Pond Rd. 5.4 mi. from Hutchins St. in Berlin. The trail sign is easy to miss, and the lower part of the trail must be followed with care through logged areas. The trail follows a logging road, bears right at a fork (sign) at 0.2 mi., and passes straight through a clearing, entering the woods at a sign at 0.5 mi. Here the trail runs along the bank of an eroded roadbed, then begins to climb at a moderate grade along an old woods road. At 1.4 mi. the trail reaches the upper edge of an area of small second-growth trees, swings right, and ascends steeply along an eroded stream bed, where care must be taken due to slippery rocks. At 1.6 mi. a loop path 0.3 mi. long diverges right to a spectacular ledge outlook with fine views of the Presidentials and the mountains of the North Country. In a little more than 100 yd. the upper end of the loop path rejoins, and the main trail ascends to a ridgecrest, from which it descends to a brook (unreliable) at an old logging camp site. The trail soon enters a wet, boggy area, climbs over a small ridge, passes through another short boggy area, and then makes a short steep ascent to the Mahoosuc Trail at the main ridgecrest.

Success Trail (map 6:D12)

Distances from Success Pond Rd. (1610')

   to Mahoosuc Trail (3170'): 2.4 mi. (3.8 km.), 1550 ft., 2 hr.

   to Mt. Success summit (3565') via Mahoosuc Trail: 3.0 mi. (4.8 km.), 1950 ft., 2 hr. 30 min.

Carlo Col Trail (AMC)

This trail ascends to the Mahoosuc Trail at the small box ravine called Carlo Col. It leaves Success Pond Rd. in common with the Goose Eye Trail 8.1 mi. from Hutchins St. The lower part of the trail must be followed with care through logged areas.

From the road the two trails follow a broad logging road, and in 100 yd. the Goose Eye Trail diverges sharp left down an embankment, while the Carlo Col Trail continues straight ahead on the road, which it follows east for 0.8 mi. with little gain in elevation. Turning left off the road at a log yard, the trail immediately crosses the main brook (may be difficult at high water), continues near it for about 0.3 mi., then turns left away from the brook and follows a branch road with a steeper grade. It swings back to the south, crossing over the north and south branches of the main brook, and bends east up the rather steep south bank of the south branch. Avoiding several false crossings of this brook, it climbs to Carlo Col Campsite at 2.4 mi. (last water, perhaps for several miles). The trail continues up the dry ravine and ends at the Mahoosuc Trail at Carlo Col. There is a fine outlook ledge a short distance to the right (southwest) on the Mahoosuc Trail.

Carlo Col Trail (map 6:C12–D12)

Distance from Success Pond Rd. (1630')

> *to* Mahoosuc Trail (3170'): 2.7 mi. (4.3 km.), 1550 ft., 2 hr. 10 min.

Goose Eye Trail (AMC)

This trail ascends Goose Eye Mtn. from Success Pond Rd., starting in common with the Carlo Col Trail 8.1 mi. from Hutchins St. and reaching the Mahoosuc Trail 0.1 mi. beyond the summit. This is a generally easy trail to a very scenic summit, but there is one fairly difficult scramble up a ledge just below the summit. The lower part of the trail must be followed with care through logged areas.

From the road the two trails follow a broad logging road, and in 100 yd., where the Carlo Col Trail continues straight ahead, the Goose Eye Trail diverges sharp left down an embankment, then turns sharp right onto another old logging road. The Goose Eye Trail follows this logging road, crosses two brooks, and enters a more recent gravel road that comes in from the right (descending, bear right). In 100 yd. it diverges right (watch carefully for sign) from the gravel road, passes through a clear-cut area, and crosses a wet section. At 1.4 mi. it reaches the yellow-blazed Maine–New Hampshire state line. The trail angles up the south side of a ridge at a moderate grade through fine hardwoods, climbs more steeply uphill, then becomes gradual at the crest of the ridge; at 2.6 mi. there is a glimpse of the peak of Goose Eye ahead. The trail ascends moderately along the north side of the ridge, then climbs steeply, scrambling up a difficult ledge that may be dangerous if wet or icy. Soon it comes out on the open ledges below the summit. From the summit, which has magnificent views in all directions, the trail descends steeply and roughly over ledges 0.1 mi. to the Mahoosuc Trail, which turns right (southbound) and runs straight ahead at the junction (northbound).

Goose Eye Trail (map 6:C12–C13)

Distances from Success Pond Rd. (1630')

> *to* Goose Eye Mtn. summit (3870'): 3.1 mi., 2250 ft., 2 hr. 40 min.

> *to* Mahoosuc Trail (3800'): 3.2 mi. (5.2 km.), 2250 ft., 2 hr. 45 min.

Notch Trail (AMC)

This trail ascends to the southwest end of Mahoosuc Notch, providing the easiest access to that wild and beautiful place. It begins on a spur road that leaves Success Pond Rd. 10.9 mi. from Hutchins St. and runs 0.3 mi. to a small parking area.

The trail continues on the spur road across two bridges, then turns left (sign) onto an old logging road at 0.3 mi. It ascends easily along a slow-running brook with many signs of beaver activity, following logging roads much of the way with bypasses at some of the wetter spots. At the height-of-land it meets the Mahoosuc Trail; turn left to traverse the notch. Very soon after entering the Mahoosuc Trail, the valley, which has been an ordinary one, changes sharply to a chamber formation, and the high cliffs of the notch, which have not been visible at all on the Notch Trail, come into sight.

Notch Trail (map 6:C12–C13)

Distance from spur road off Success Pond Rd. (1650')

> *to* Mahoosuc Trail (2460'): 2.2 mi. (3.5 km.), 800 ft., 1 hr. 30 min.

Speck Pond Trail (AMC)

This trail ascends to Speck Pond from Success Pond Rd.; take the right fork of the road 11.4 mi. from Hutchins St. and continue 0.8 mi. to the trailhead.

The trail leaves the road, enters the woods, and follows the north side of a small brook for 1.4 mi. It then swings left away from the brook, climbs rather steeply at times, passes a relatively level section, then climbs rather steeply to the junction at 3.1 mi. with the May Cutoff, which diverges right.

May Cutoff (AMC). This short trail runs 0.3 mi. (10 min.) from the Speck Pond Trail to the Mahoosuc Trail with only minor ups and downs, crossing a hump that is probably the true summit of Mahoosuc Arm along the way.

The Speck Pond Trail continues over ledges, passes an excellent outlook over the pond and up to Old Speck, then descends steeply to the pond and reaches the campsite and the Mahoosuc Trail.

Speck Pond Trail (map 6:C12–C13)

Distance from branch of Success Pond Rd. (1700')

> *to* Speck Pond Campsite (3400'): 3.6 mi. (5.8 km.), 2050 ft. (rev. 350 ft.), 2 hr. 50 min.

Old Speck Trail (AMC)

This trail, part of the Appalachian Trail, ascends Old Speck Mtn. from a well-signed parking area on ME 26 at the height-of-land in Grafton Notch. From the north side of the parking lot follow the trail leading to the left; the right-hand trail goes to Baldpate Mtn. In 0.1 mi., the Eyebrow Trail leaves right to circle over the top of an 800-ft. cliff shaped like an eyebrow and rejoin the Old Speck Trail. The Old Speck Trail crosses a brook and soon begins to climb, following a series of switchbacks to approach the falls on Cascade Brook. Above the falls the trail, now heading more north, crosses the brook for the last time (last water), and at 1.1 mi. it passes the upper terminus of the Eyebrow Trail on the right. The main trail bears left and ascends gradually to the north ridge, where it bears more to the left and follows the ridge, which has occasional views southwest. High up, the trail turns southeast toward the summit, and at 3.1 mi. the Link Trail (no sign) diverges left. The Old Speck Trail swings more to the south and ascends to the Mahoosuc Trail, where it ends. The flat, wooded summit of Old Speck, where an observation tower affords fine views, is 0.3 mi. left (east); Speck Pond Shelter is 1.1 mi. to the right.

Old Speck Trail (map 6:B13–C13)
Distances from ME 26 (1500')

> *to* Eyebrow Trail, upper junction (2550'): 1.1 mi., 1050 ft., 1 hr. 5 min.
>
> *to* Link Trail (3600'): 3.1 mi., 2200 ft., 2 hr. 40 min.
>
> *to* Mahoosuc Trail (4000'): 3.5 mi. (5.6 km.), 2600 ft., 3 hr. 5 min.
>
> *to* Old Speck Mtn. summit (4170') via Mahoosuc Trail: 3.8 mi. (6.1 km.), 2800 ft., 3 hr. 20 min.

Link Trail

This trail, which is no longer officially maintained and may be obscure, descends very steeply from the Old Speck Trail, 3.1 mi. from ME 26, to the site of the former firewarden's cabin, giving access to the East Spur Trail, which provides an attractive but much more difficult loop to the summit. It is blazed in blue and fairly well beaten, but may not have signs at either end.

Link Trail (map 6:C13)
Distance from Old Speck Trail (3600')

> *to* East Spur Trail (3200'): 0.3 mi. (0.5 km.), 0 ft. (rev. 400 ft.), 10 min.

East Spur Trail

This trail, which is no longer officially maintained and may be obscure, ascends the east spur of Old Speck; it is much steeper and rougher than the Old Speck Trail and can be fairly hard to follow, but it has much better views. It is not recommended for inexperienced hikers or in bad weather. It begins at the site of the old firewarden's cabin, reached from the Old Speck Trail via the Link Trail. Both trails are marked here only by blue blazes on rocks, and one must avoid the abandoned firewarden's trail, which was once the route of the Appalachian Trail and can still be seen quite clearly running up and down the ravine. The East Spur Trail crosses the brook and ascends steeply, then angles upward around the nose of the ridge, passing through an extensive area of open ledge with good views. Returning to the woods, it passes to the left of a large pointed boulder and climbs up on ledges, some of which are quite steep and would be dangerous if wet or icy, with very fine views. It then swings left and climbs through scrub that still permits views, and ends at the north terminus of the Mahoosuc Trail in a small clearing 30 yd. north of the summit of Old Speck Mtn.

East Spur Trail (map 6:C13)

Distance from Link Trail (3200')

   to Old Speck summit (4170'): 1.0 mi. (1.6 km.), 1000 ft., 1 hr.

Eyebrow Trail (MDP/AMC)

This trail provides an alternative route to the lower part of the Old Speck Trail, passing along the edge of the cliff called the Eyebrow that overlooks Grafton Notch. The trail leaves the Old Speck Trail on the right 0.1 mi. from the parking area off ME 26. It turns right at the base of a rock face, crosses a rock slide (potentially dangerous if icy), then turns sharp left and ascends steadily, bearing right where a side path leaves straight ahead for an outlook. Soon the trail runs at a moderate grade along the top of the cliff, with good views, then descends to an outlook and runs mostly level until it ends at the Old Speck Trail.

Eyebrow Trail (map 6:B13)

Distance from Old Speck Trail, lower junction (1550')

   to Old Speck Trail, upper junction (2550'): 1.2 mi. (1.9 km.), 1100 ft., 1 hr. 10 min.

Wright Trail (MBPL)

This new trail provides access to Goose Eye Mtn. and the Mahoosuc Range via a scenic route from the east that begins in a place known as Ketchum, located on a branch of the Sunday River. The upper part of the trail has two separate branches that make possible a loop hike; the north branch passes through old-growth forest and a small glacial cirque, while the south branch follows a scenic ridge. To reach the trailhead, leave US 2 2.8 mi. north of Bethel ME and follow Sunday River Rd. At a fork at 2.2 mi. bear right onto Ketchum Rd. (no sign), and follow it past Artist Covered Bridge (left) at 3.8 mi. from US 2. At 6.5 mi., the road becomes gravel. At 7.8 mi. turn left across the two steel bridges, then take the first right, which is Bull Branch Rd. (no sign). At 9.3 mi. Goose Eye Brook is crossed on a bridge, and at 9.5 mi. from US 2 there is a small parking area on the left with signs.

The blue-blazed trail leaves the south side of the parking area and runs toward Goose Eye Brook, then follows its north side upstream past several large pools and a 30-ft. gorge. At 0.5 mi. it makes a left turn onto a woods road and follows it for 0.2 mi., then makes a right turn onto an older road. At 0.9 mi. it bears left off the road and descends gradually 100 yd. to Goose Eye Brook at its confluence with a tributary, where it bears right and follows the tributary for 0.1 mi., then turns sharp left and crosses it. From this point the trail roughly follows the north side of Goose Eye Brook until it reaches the junction of the two parts of the loop at 2.5 mi.

North Branch. The north branch continues a gradual ascent on an old logging road along Goose Eye Brook for 0.2 mi., crossing it twice, then bears right and climbs moderately up away from the floor of the small glacial cirque in which Goose Eye Brook originates. It passes beneath several large rock slabs, then at 3.0 mi. comes out on an open ledge from which the whole cirque is visible. The trail descends from this ledge, crosses Goose Eye Brook, and climbs a steep and rough slope with a number of wooden steps along Goose Eye Brook, crossing the stream six more times. Finally it reaches the ridgecrest and descends gradually for 100 yd. to the junction with the Mahoosuc Trail at 4.0 mi. For the south branch of the Wright Trail, follow the Mahoosuc Trail south for 0.3 mi., climbing steeply up the ledgy East Peak of Mt. Goose Eye and descending the other side of the peak to the junction in the col. From this point the West Peak (main summit) of Mt. Goose Eye can be reached in 0.4 mi. by following the Mahoosuc Trail (southbound) and the Goose Eye Trail.

South Branch. The south branch immediately crosses Goose Eye Brook and starts its climb, gradually at first and then moderately by switchbacks with rough sections and wooden steps, to the ridgecrest at 3.1 mi. At 3.4 mi., after a rough ascent, it reaches an open spot, then descends slightly back into the woods. It then resumes a rough ascent on ledges to an open knob with beautiful views at 3.6 mi. The trail continues along the ridge with several open areas and occasional minor descents to cross small sags, then finally climbs moderately to the Mahoosuc Trail in the small gap between the East Peak and the West Peak (main summit) of Mt. Goose Eye at 4.4 mi. The main summit can be reached in 0.4 mi. by following the Mahoosuc Trail to the left (southbound) and then the Goose Eye Trail. The upper end of the north branch of the Wright Trail is on the far side of the steep, ledgy East Peak, 0.3 mi. to the right (northbound) via the Mahoosuc Trail.

Wright Trail (map 6:C13)

Distances from parking area on Bull Branch Rd. (1240')

> *to* loop junction (1900'): 2.5 mi., 650 ft., 1 hr. 35 min.

> *to* Mahoosuc Trail (3450') via north branch: 4.0 mi. (6.4 km.), 2200 ft., 3 hr. 5 min.

> *to* Mahoosuc Trail (3620') via south branch: 4.4 mi. (7.1 km.), 2400 ft., 3 hr. 25 min.

> *for* complete loop with side trip to West Peak of Mt. Goose Eye via Mahoosuc Trail and Goose Eye Trail: 9.5 mi. (15.3 km.), 2800 ft., 6 hr. 10 min.

Centennial Trail (AMC)

This trail, a part of the Appalachian Trail, was constructed by the AMC in 1976, its centennial year. The trail begins on Hogan Rd., a dirt road that turns west from North Rd. north of its crossing of the Androscoggin River, just before it swings abruptly to the east. There is a small parking area 0.2 mi. from North Rd., and parking is also permitted at the junction of North Rd. and Hogan Rd.; in any case, do not block the road.

From the parking area on Hogan Rd., the trail runs generally northwest. After 50 yd. on an old road, it bears left up a steep bank into the woods, levels off, and reaches the first of many stone steps in 0.1 mi. The trail ascends rather steeply, then more gradually, with a limited view of the Androscoggin River. It turns left onto a woods road and crosses a brook at 0.7 mi. (last water). The trail then crosses a logging road and climbs past several restricted viewpoints, then descends to a sag in a birch grove at 1.6 mi. Climbing again, it soon turns sharp left and continues upward past ledges that provide increasingly open views. At

2.8 mi. the trail reaches an easterly summit of Mt. Hayes, where there is an excellent view of the Carter-Moriah Range and Northern Presidentials from open ledges. The trail descends slightly, then ascends across a series of open ledges to end at the Mahoosuc Trail at 3.1 mi. The summit of Mt. Hayes, with fine views, is 0.2 mi. left; the Appalachian Trail turns right (north) on the Mahoosuc Trail.

Centennial Trail (map 6:E11)
Distance from Hogan Rd. (750')

   to Mahoosuc Trail (2550'): 3.1 mi. (5.0 km.), 1800 ft., 2 hr. 25 min.

Peabody Brook Trail (AMC)

This trail ascends to the Mahoosuc Trail at Dream Lake from North Rd., 1.3 mi. east of US 2. Overnight parking is not permitted at the base of this trail.

   The trail follows a logging road between two houses and makes a right turn onto an old logging road at 0.5 mi. It continues north along the brook and bears right at a fork at 0.8 mi., soon becomes a footpath, and begins to ascend moderately. At 1.2 mi. a path leaves left and leads in 0.3 mi. to Giant Falls. The main trail rises more steeply, and at 1.5 mi. there is a glimpse of Mt. Washington and Mt. Adams through open trees. The trail climbs a short ladder just beyond here. At 2.1 mi. it crosses the east branch of the brook, then recrosses it at 2.4 mi. From here the trail climbs easily to Dream Lake and the junction on the right with the Dryad Fall Trail at 3.0 mi., and continues along the southeast shore of the lake to the Mahoosuc Trail.

Peabody Brook Trail (map 6:E11–D11)
Distance from North Rd. (750')

   to Mahoosuc Trail (2620'): 3.1 mi. (5.0 km.), 1900 ft., 2 hr. 30 min.

Austin Brook Trail (AMC)

This trail ascends to the Mahoosuc Trail at Gentian Pond from North Rd., 0.6 mi. west of Meadow Rd. (which crosses the Androscoggin at Shelburne village). There is limited parking on the south side of the road. The road that the first part of this trail follows is sometimes open to vehicle travel for 1.6 mi., but is usually closed by a locked gate. The trail passes through a turnstile on private land and follows the west side of Austin Brook, crossing the Yellow Trail at 0.4 mi. The Austin Brook Trail follows logging roads along the brook, then crosses it and reaches the gravel Mill Brook Rd., which is normally gated at North Rd., at 1.1

mi. (Austin Brook and Mill Brook are different names for the same stream.) Turn left on the logging road and continue past a brook crossing to the junction left with the Dryad Fall Trail at 1.9 mi. At 2.1 mi. the trail turns left onto an old logging road. At 3.1 mi. the trail crosses the brook that drains Gentian Pond and climbs rather steeply to the Mahoosuc Trail at Gentian Pond Shelter.

Austin Brook Trail (map 6:E12–D12)

Distance from North Rd. (700')

  to Gentian Pond Campsite (2166'): 3.5 mi. (5.7 km.), 1450 ft., 2 hr. 30 min.

Dryad Fall Trail (AMC)

This trail runs from the Austin Brook Trail to the Peabody Brook Trail near Dream Lake, passing Dryad Fall, one of the highest cascades in the mountains— particularly interesting for a few days after a rainstorm, since its several cascades fall at least 300 ft. over steep ledges. The trail is blazed in yellow.

    The trail leaves the Austin Brook Trail on the left 1.9 mi. from North Rd., just past the third brook crossing. (*Note:* Plans call for a relocation of this trail in the near future; it will probably leave the Austin Brook Trail about 0.5 mi. farther north in order to bypass an eroded section of the current trail.) It gradually ascends old logging roads, then drops down (right) to Dryad Brook, which it follows nearly to the base of the falls at 0.5 mi. *Caution:* Rocks in the vicinity of the falls are very slippery and hazardous. From here the trail climbs steeply northeast of the falls. At 0.6 mi. it turns right away from the falls, then turns left on an old road and comes back to the top of the falls. Here it turns left on another road and crosses Dryad Brook at 0.9 mi., then climbs at mostly moderate grades to the Peabody Brook Trail near Dream Lake 0.1 mi. east of the Mahoosuc Trail. (Descending, watch carefully for the junction where the trail turns down steeply to the right off the logging road above the falls.)

Dryad Fall Trail (map 6:D12–D11)

Distances from Austin Brook Trail (950')

  to Dryad Fall (1600'): 0.5 mi., 650 ft., 35 min.

  to Peabody Brook Trail (2620'): 1.8 mi. (2.9 km.), 1650 ft., 1 hr. 45 min.

Scudder Trail

This trail, blazed red and white, provides access to the ledges and summit of Mt. Ingalls (2242 ft.). It begins on Mill Brook Rd., a gated logging road that leaves

North Rd. about 50 yd. west of Meadow Rd. (the road that crosses the Androscoggin on a bridge from Shelburne village). It diverges (orange blazes, no sign) from Mill Brook Rd. on the second road on the right, 0.5 mi. from North Rd., crosses the Yellow Trail in 0.1 mi., and shortly enters an open area. Bearing left, the trail continues as a woods road to a sign on the right, where it follows another road that climbs to the Ingalls-Cabot col at 1.3 mi. The Scudder Trail turns sharp left at the col and soon comes out on a ledge on the west side of the ridge, with views over the Androscoggin valley. The trail climbs back eastward, passing the blue blazes of a Boise-Cascade Co. boundary in a ravine beneath a high cliff. The trail wanders back and forth, emerging on open ledges on both sides of the ridge, and finally circles an extensive ledge with views southwest. It then climbs 150 yd. to the wooded summit of Mt. Ingalls. A beaten path, axe-blazed with some white paint markings, leads down 0.1 mi. to Ray's Pond, a scenic mountain tarn.

Scudder Trail (map 6:E12–D12)

Distances from Mill Brook Rd. (770')

> *to* Ingalls-Cabot col (1330'): 1.3 mi., 550 ft., 55 min.

> *to* Mt. Ingalls summit (2242'): 2.7 mi. (4.4 km.), 1450 ft., 2 hr. 5 min.

Middle Mountain Path

This trail ascends Middle Mtn. (2010 ft.), an interesting peak that offers a few good views, but at present it is severely overgrown and can be recommended only for hikers who are experienced in following obscure trails and routes.

Follow Gates Brook Rd., a woods road that leaves North Rd. on the north just east of Gates Brook, 2.4 mi. from the western junction of North Rd. and US 2. Continue on this road past a trail on the right at 0.4 mi. that leads to Mt. Crag, then at 0.9 mi. take a left branch that leads up the ravine between First Mtn. and Middle Mtn., at one point making a sharp left turn up a blowdown-strewn gully. The trail, blazed yellow, should not be confused with large yellow boundary markings on the woods road and on the summit trail. Just before the height-of-land, the trail turns off the road right and climbs, steeply at first, along the ridge to the bare summit of Middle Mtn., where there are fine views.

Middle Mountain Path (map 6:E12–D11)

Distance from North Rd. (750')

> *to* Middle Mtn. summit (2010'): 1.7 mi. (2.7 km.), 1250 ft., 1 hr. 30 min.

Mount Crag

This small mountain (1412 ft.) is easily climbed and offers an excellent view up and down the Androscoggin valley. It has two trails.

(1) Take Gates Brook Rd., a woods road that leaves North Rd. on the north just east of Gates Brook, 2.4 mi. from the west junction of North Rd. and US 2. An unnamed trail leaves this road 0.4 mi. from North Rd., on the right, and climbs steeply 0.3 mi. to the Yellow Trail a few steps below the summit.

(2) *The Yellow Trail.* This attractive trail gives convenient access to the Austin Brook Trail and Mt. Crag from the Philbrook Farm Inn on North Rd. (For the shortest route to Mt. Crag via the Yellow Trail, follow the Austin Brook Trail 0.4 mi. in from North Rd., then go left on the Yellow Trail to Mt. Crag.) The Yellow Trail leads west from the north end of the access road behind the cottages connected with the inn. It coincides with the Red Trail to Mt. Cabot for 50 yd., then branches left and leads west on a practically level grade. It crosses in sequence several woods roads, the Scudder Trail, Mill Brook Rd., Austin Brook, and the Austin Brook Trail. After the Austin Brook Trail junction, at 1.0 mi., it heads generally northwest to the summit of Mt. Crag at 1.8 mi., going through an extensive lumbered area (but it is easy to follow).

Mount Cabot and Crow's Nest

This range runs south and southeast from Mt. Ingalls. Several trails, distinguished by color, start from the access road at the Philbrook Farm Inn on North Rd. in Shelburne. Hikers are permitted to park at the Inn but are requested to speak with the Inn management before leaving their vehicles. The path farthest to the east is the White Trail, which leads to Crow's Nest (1287 ft.). The Blue and Red trails both lead to the summit of Mt. Cabot (1512 ft.), making a loop trip possible. The Yellow Trail, described above, runs west to Mt. Crag and also provides access to Mt. Ingalls via the Scudder Trail.

The *White Trail* is best reached from the dirt road that starts immediately west of the fire pond east of the Philbrook Farm Inn. Follow this road to the first cottage, where the White Trail turns right by a large rock. Shortly the Wiggin Rock Trail (Orange Trail) leaves left, while the White Trail climbs east along an old logging road through a recently logged area (follow blazes carefully). Leaving the logging road right at 1.2 mi., it makes a short, steep ascent to the wooded summit of Crow's Nest at 1.3 mi. The trail ends a few yards farther at a limited viewpoint to the northeast.

The *Wiggin Rock Trail (Orange Trail)* climbs from its junction with the White Trail for 0.2 mi. to Wiggin Rock, a small ledge with a view southeast across the Androscoggin valley. Beyond the viewpoint, the trail drops steeply for another 0.2 mi. to the Blue Trail.

The *Blue Trail* starts from the gravel road immediately to the west of the Philbrook Farm Inn, follows a good woods road, and passes the Orange (Wiggin Rock) Trail on the right in 80 yd. Shortly before this road reaches an old reservoir, the Blue Trail turns right on a badly eroded road. The Blue Trail continues much of the way on logging roads at an easy grade to a boundary marker at 1.0 mi., beyond which the trail climbs more steeply to the summit of Mt. Cabot and the Red Trail at 1.3 mi. The summit is wooded, but a ledge on the right shortly before the summit gives a view east, and an orange-blazed trail from the summit leads left to an open ledge with views southwest.

The *Red Trail* bears left from the Blue Trail on the access road west of the Philbrook Farm Inn, coinciding for 90 yd. with the Yellow Trail, which then diverges left. The Red Trail continues on a series of logging roads, passes an orange-blazed trail to a viewpoint (Mary's Aerie) on the right at 0.6 mi., crosses a small brook, circles around, and finally climbs steeply to approach Mt. Cabot from the north. (See Blue Trail for description of views.)

Section 12

Northern New Hampshire

This section covers the entire section of New Hampshire that lies west of NH 16 and north of US 2. The Cherry-Dartmouth Range, which rises south of US 2 between Jefferson and Twin Mtn., is also included here. From the hiker's point of view, the heart of this section is the three principal ranges in the triangle formed by US 2, US 3, and NH 110; the corners of this triangle are located roughly at the towns of Lancaster, Groveton, and Gorham. This region is composed of the Pliny, Pilot, and Crescent ranges; the very similar Cherry-Dartmouth Range to the south should also be considered with this group. These are relatively compact mountain ranges, with officially maintained trail networks, on or adjacent to lands of the WMNF. North of NH 110 lies the North Country proper, a sparsely populated region with extensive woodlands owned mostly by large corporations and managed for lumber and pulpwood production. This region, so similar to the small adjacent corner of Vermont and the much vaster woodlands of northern Maine to the east, is on the southern edge of the great band of boreal forest that covers much of Ontario, Quebec, and the northern part of the Great Lakes Region in the United States. There are only a few trails to widely scattered natural features, and the region is far better known for hunting, fishing, and snowmobiling than for hiking. Even the southern part of the area covered in this section has a higher level of logging activity than in the main ranges of the White Mtns. to the south and east, along with hiking trails that frequently receive much less use and less intensive maintenance. This area can perhaps best be understood as a transitional zone between the main ranges, with their heavily used, intensively maintained trail systems that visit almost every significant feature, and the vast commercial woodlands of the north, where logging roads are the principal routes of travel both by wheel and on foot, and logging activity is visible almost everywhere.

Four relatively distinct ranges and trail networks are covered in this section, and they are treated in separate subsections: **(A) the Cherry-Dartmouth Range,** which includes the main peak of Cherry Mtn. and its fine northern crag, Owl's Head; **(B) the Crescent Range,** including Mt. Randolph, Mt. Crescent, Lookout Ledge, the Ice Gulch, and the rest of the Randolph Mountain Club

(RMC) trail system north of US 2; **(C) the Pilot-Pliny Range,** including Mt. Waumbek, Mt. Starr King, Mt. Weeks, Terrace Mtn., Mt. Cabot, the Bulge, the Horn, and the region of the headwaters of the Upper Ammonoosuc River to the east of Unknown Pond, whose most prominent features are Rogers Ledge and the Devils Hopyard; and **(D) the North Country proper,** whose principal points of interest are the Percy Peaks and Sugarloaf, Dixville Notch and Table Rock, the Diamond Peaks, and Magalloway Mtn. Subsection A is completely covered by the AMC Franconia–Pemigewasset map (map #2), subsections B and C (except for the trails on Mt. Prospect) are completely covered by the AMC North Country–Mahoosuc Range map (map #6), and subsection D requires USGS maps as indicated for each objective.

CAMPING

Substantial portions of subsections A, B, and C are included in the WMNF, and in such areas normal WMNF camping regulations apply. Most of the remaining forested areas in these subsections and in all of subsection D are private commercial woodlands or New Hampshire State Parks or State Forests. On state lands camping is usually restricted to official campgrounds, while on private lands camping requires the permission of the landowner, which normally cannot be obtained due to the owners' unwillingness to risk a devastating forest fire that might result from a single carelessly kindled campfire.

Forest Protection Areas

The WMNF has established a number of Forest Protection Areas (FPAs)—formerly known as Restricted Use Areas—where camping and wood or charcoal fires are prohibited throughout the year. The specific areas are under continual review, and areas are added to or subtracted from the list in order to provide the greatest amount of protection to areas subject to damage by excessive camping, while imposing the lowest level of restrictions possible. A general list of FPAs in this section follows, but since there are often major changes from year to year, one should obtain current information on FPAs from the WMNF.

(1) No camping is permitted above treeline (where trees are less than 8 ft. tall), except in winter, and then only in places where there is at least two feet of snow cover on the ground—but not on any frozen body of water. The point where the restricted area begins is marked on most trails with small signs, but the absence of such signs should not be construed as proof of the legality of a site.

(2) No camping is permitted within a quarter-mile of any trailhead, picnic area, or any facility for overnight accommodation such as a hut, cabin, shelter, tentsite, or campground, except as designated at the facility itself. In this section, camping is also forbidden at the South Pond Recreation Area.

Established Trailside Campsites

Cabot Firewarden's Cabin (WMNF) is located on the Mount Cabot Trail just south of the cleared south summit of Mt. Cabot where the fire tower used to stand. It has bunks for about eight people. The nearest reliable water source is Bunnell Brook, at the crossing 1.3 mi. below the cabin.

A. *Cherry-Dartmouth Range*

List of Trails	Map	Page
Cherry Mountain Trail	2:F6–F7	446
Owl's Head Trail	2:E7	447
Martha's Mile	2:E7–E6	448

B. *Crescent Range*

List of Trails	Map	Page
Boy Mountain Path	6:E8	450
Bee Line	6:E9	450
Short Paths in Randolph Village Area	6:E9	451
Vyron D. Lowe Trail	6:E9	451
Sargent Path	6:E9	452
Ledge Trail	6:E9	452
Pasture Path	6:E9	453
Notchway	6:E9	453
Mount Crescent Trail	6:E9	454
Crescent Ridge Trail	6:E9	455
Carlton Notch Trail	6:E9	455
Boothman Spring Cutoff	6:E9	456
Cook Path	6:E9–D9	456
Ice Gulch Path	6:E9–D9	457
Peboamauk Loop	6:E9	458

C. Pliny and Pilot Ranges

D. The North Country

A. CHERRY-DARTMOUTH RANGE

Though technically speaking this range is the western extension of the Presidential Range, in its terrain, the type and amount of use, as well as the nature of its trail system—in sum, its general flavor for hiking visitors—it is far more similar to its neighbors to the north than to the great mountains connected to it on the east. **Cherry Mtn.** is a prominent mountain located in the town of Carroll, west of the Presidential Range. The highest peak is **Mt. Martha** (3573 ft.), which has good outlooks from the summit area, although the former fire tower has been dismantled. A northern spur, **Owl's Head** (3258 ft.), has a spectacular view from a fine ledge just south of the wooded summit. The **Dartmouth Range** is a ridge with numerous humps running southwest to northeast between Cherry Mtn. and the Presidentials. The range is completely trailless; **Mt. Dartmouth** (3727 ft.) and **Mt. Deception** (3671 ft.) are the most important summits. **Cherry Mtn. Rd.** (FR 14), 6.9 mi. long, runs from US 302 about 0.8 mi. west of the Fabyan Motel to the junction of NH 115 and NH 115A, passing through the high notch that separates the two mountain masses. This area is covered by the AMC Franconia–Pemigewasset map (map #2).

The **Pondicherry Wildlife Refuge,** a fine 300-acre wild tract of pond and bog located mostly in Jefferson with a few acres in Whitefield, is a National Natural Landmark. It consists of **Big Cherry Pond** (about 90 acres) and **Little Cherry Pond** (about 25 acres). As "Great Ponds," these are in the custody of the state. Surrounding each are bands of open bog and bog-swamp forest belonging to the Audubon Society of New Hampshire. "Pondicherry" is the old name for Cherry Pond and nearby Cherry Mtn. The refuge is managed jointly by the New Hampshire Fish and Game Department and the Audubon Society. Fishing is allowed, but not hunting or trapping. At least 50 kinds of water birds and an unusual variety of mammals have been recorded in the refuge, and several uncommon species of both water and land birds nest there. Pondicherry is also interesting for its vegetation and its spectacular views of the Presidential Range. Best access is east from Whitefield Airport by following either the old Boston & Maine Railroad right of way, which is passable to cars, and then the tracks beyond, or by following the old Maine Central Railroad right of way off the road from the airport to NH 115.

THE TRAILS

Cherry Mountain Trail (WMNF)

This trail runs across the ridge of Cherry Mtn. just south of the summit (which is reached by a spur path). The west trailhead is at a newly constructed parking lot opposite Lennon Rd. on NH 115, 1.9 mi. from its junction with US 3; the east trailhead, which is far less frequently used, is on Cherry Mtn. Rd. (FR 14) (which is narrow—use care) just north of its height-of-land, 3.2 mi. from US 302 and 3.7 mi. from NH 115. The eastern part of the trail, from the height-of-land to Cherry Mtn. Rd., is heavily used by snowmobiles in winter.

Leaving NH 115 on a recently constructed logging road, the trail passes straight through a log yard at 0.3 mi., and continues straight ahead at 0.5 mi.

where another road diverges right. In 0.7 mi. it becomes a footpath on an old roadbed, climbing higher above the brook that it parallels, and passes a spring left at 1.3 mi. At 1.7 mi. the trail reaches the ridgecrest, and a spur path turns left and climbs 0.2 mi. to the summit of Mt. Martha, where it meets Martha's Mile.

From the junction with the summit spur, the Cherry Mountain Trail turns right and descends moderately on an old road with excellent footing in the upper part, and at 3.3 mi. it passes the junction on the right with the abandoned Black Brook Trail. The Cherry Mountain Trail continues down the slope on the old road, becoming muddy at times, and ends at Cherry Mtn. Rd.

Cherry Mountain Trail (map 2:F6–F7)
Distances from NH 115 (1650')

   to Mt. Martha summit spur trail (3370'): 1.7 mi., 1700 ft., 1 hr. 40 min.

   to Mt. Martha summit (3573') via spur trail: 1.9 mi., 1900 ft., 1 hr. 55 min.

   to Cherry Mtn. Rd. (2190'): 5.3 mi. (8.5 km.), 1900 ft. (rev. 1400 ft.), 3 hr. 35 min.

Owl's Head Trail (RMC)

This trail ascends to the fine outlook on Owl's Head. It begins on NH 115 at a parking lot with the Stanley Slide historical marker, 5.9 mi. from the junction with US 3 and 0.7 mi. from the junction with NH 115A. Logging operations have taken place over much of the lower slopes of this mountain in recent years, frequently disrupting the path to some extent; great care is often required in following the trail along skid roads and through second growth.

The trail descends gradually east, crosses a small stream, then at 0.1 mi. turns to the right (south) onto an old trail and ascends following a series of old stone walls. At 0.8 mi. the path descends into the trench made by the 1885 landslide and soon crosses Stanley Brook. It then turns to the left onto an old logging road, and ascends moderately steeply across a dirt road and through a region that has been recently logged. At the top of the logged area the trail turns sharp right into the overgrown track of the slide, where footing is slippery and poor. The trail climbs steeply to the ridge above the slide, entering a softwood forest, and follows the steep ridge to the summit of Owl's Head. Here Martha's Mile continues across the magnificent outlook ledge and on to Mt. Martha.

Owl's Head Trail (map 2:E7)
Distance from NH 115 (1250')

   to Owl's Head summit (3258'): 2.0 mi. (3.2 km.), 2000 ft., 2 hr.

Martha's Mile

Martha's Mile is a link trail between the summits of Mt. Martha and Owl's Head. It leaves the ledge at the summit of Owl's Head, swings north, then sharp left. It descends a very short steep pitch, then descends easily to a col and climbs moderately, with excellent footing, to the summit of Mt. Martha.

Martha's Mile (map 2:E7–E6)
Distance from Owl's Head (3258')

   to Mt. Martha summit (3573'): 0.8 mi. (1.3 km.), 450 ft. (rev. 100 ft.), 40 min.

B. CRESCENT RANGE

The Crescent Range lies north of US 2 and west of NH 16 in the towns of Jefferson, Randolph, and Berlin. This area is covered by the AMC North Country–Mahoosuc Range map (map #6). The chief summits, from southwest to northeast, are Mt. Randolph, Mt. Crescent, Black Crescent Mtn., Mt. Jericho, and Mt. Forist. **Mt. Crescent** (3251 ft.) derives its name from the shape of the ridge on which it is the highest summit. It is ascended by the Mount Crescent and Crescent Ridge trails. **Mt. Randolph** (3081 ft.) is the heavily wooded peak at the southern end of the Crescent Ridge, reached by the Crescent Ridge Trail. **Black Crescent Mtn.** (3264 ft.) lies to the north across the deep notch called **Hunter's Pass.** It is the highest peak in the range but has no trails; hikers with sufficient map and compass skills can ascend it fairly easily from the Bog Dam Rd. on the west, or by a much more difficult but more interesting route from the head of the Ice Gulch, climbing up a slide that affords excellent views. **Lookout Ledge** (2260 ft.) is a granite cliff on a knob of the southeast ridge of Mt. Randolph that affords one of the best views of the floor of King Ravine and its rock glacier, with moderate effort. It is reached by the Pasture Path, Ledge Trail, Sargent Path, Vyron D. Lowe Trail, and Crescent Ridge Trail. The ledge is on private property and no fires are permitted. **Boy (Bois) Mtn.** (2234 ft.) is a small peak at the west edge of the Crescent Range that offers an interesting view.

   Mt. Jericho (2487 ft.) lies at the northeast end of the Crescent Range, just west of Berlin NH. Like many northern mountains, its summit was burned over to bare rock by the forest fires of the early 1900s. Now partially overgrown, it still offers a fine view east to the Mahoosucs and an obstructed view of the Carter Range, the northern Presidentials, and the Tinker Brook valley. **Mt. Forist** (2068 ft.) has an impressive east cliff that rises abruptly from the edge of the city of Berlin. Locally known as Elephant Mtn. because of its shape as seen from Berlin, it was named for Merrill C. Forist, an early settler. (Note that the name of this mountain is misspelled on the USGS Berlin quad.) The summit is on the elephant's "head," and there is an outlook on its "rear end." There is no maintained hiking trail to the summit of either Mt. Jericho or Mt. Forist, but experienced hikers with map and compass skills may be able to make some use of old paths and more recent snowmobile trails while bushwhacking up these mountains; a snowmobile trail network generally to the north of the ridge line may help to provide access to these two mountains.

The **Ice Gulch,** one of the wildest and most beautiful places in the White Mtns., is a deep cut on the southeast slope of the Crescent Range, between Mt. Crescent and Black Crescent Mtn. The bed of the gulch is strewn with great boulders that lie in picturesque confusion, similar in many respects to those scattered over the floor of King Ravine. Among the boulders are many caves, some with perpetual ice. Springs and the melting ice form the headwaters of Moose Brook. Two paths lead to the gulch: the Cook Path to the head, and the Ice Gulch Path to the foot and from there up through the gulch. A short trail, the Peboamauk Loop, follows Moose Brook below the Ice Gulch, past **Peboamauk Fall** and several fine springs back to the Ice Gulch Path. The walk along the gulch itself is very strenuous with constant scrambling over wet, possibly icy, slippery rocks, requiring great care.

Most of the paths in this region are part of the Randolph Mountain Club (RMC) trail system. The town of Randolph consists of two sections: the lower section lies along Durand Rd. (the former US 2), in the Moose River valley, and the upper section is situated on Randolph Hill—a plateau extending southeast from the foot of Mt. Crescent, from which there are excellent views of the Northern Presidentials—reached by Mt. Crescent Rd. Lowe's Store and the Ravine House site are located in the lower section, and the Mt. Crescent House site is in the upper section. On the south slope of the hill, connecting the two sections of the town and providing access from various points to major mountain trails, is a well-developed network of paths maintained by the RMC. Some of these short and less important trails—those that are mainly connecting links to places in the town for local residents—are omitted from this guide, but they are described in detail, along with the other RMC trails that are covered in this guide, in the RMC guidebook *Randolph Paths* (1992). They also are shown on the RMC map of the Randolph valley and the Northern Peaks, which covers this area with somewhat more detail than the AMC map.

Active lumbering and residential developments on the south slopes may intrude on some of the following trails, many of which are partly or wholly on private land. Watch carefully for markers and signs; it may be useful to inquire locally for further information.

THE TRAILS

Boy Mountain Path

This path ascends Boy (Bois) Mtn. (2234 ft.), a small mountain, located east of Jefferson Highlands, with an open ledge near the summit that provides a fine and easily accessible view of the northern Presidential Range. It is maintained by the Carter–Bridgman family. There is no trail sign where it leaves US 2, 1.3 mi. east of the junction of US 2 and NH 115. Park on the terrace south of the highway, west of the branch road to Jefferson Notch, and not in the driveway to the Carter estate. Go up the dirt drive between the garden and the raspberry patch and pass between the house and barn. From this point (small sign) enter the woods to the right and ascend. At 0.2 mi. turn left (arrow) onto an old logging road, then at 0.4 mi. turn right onto an old path. The path passes a cement marker and climbs to the ledge near the summit.

Boy Mountain Path (map 6:E8)
Distance from US 2 (1575')

   to Boy Mtn. summit (2234'): 0.7 mi. (1.1 km.), 650 ft., 40 min.

Bee Line (RMC)

This path is an important connecting link between the Appalachia parking area, the Ravine House site, and the trails on Randolph Hill.

   Beginning on US 2 directly opposite the Appalachia parking area, the trail descends through an opening in the chain-link fence. It swings left, then right, and runs around the west shore of Durand Lake. It crosses Moose River on a bridge, then crosses Durand Rd. just west of the Ravine House site. The trail briefly ascends on a gravel drive, then bears right into the woods (sign), passes an excellent spring, and reaches a junction on the right with the Diagonal at 0.8 mi. From here, Mossy Glen can be reached in a short distance by following the Diagonal and then the Glenside downhill. The Bee Line crosses Carlton Brook on the Peeko Folsom Memorial Bridge, passes a junction on the right with the Burnbrae Path, and turns to the right onto a logging road, which it follows for 0.4 mi. Shortly after leaving this logging road, it turns to the left onto a dirt road and in 0.1 mi. meets the Pasture Path on Stearns Rd. at 1.5 mi. For the Mt. Crescent House site, follow Highacres Rd. straight ahead to Randolph Hill Rd.; the Mt. Crescent House site is a short distance to the right (east) via Randolph Hill Rd., and the Ice Gulch Path begins about 0.4 mi. east of that site. The various paths to Lookout Ledge and the Crescent Range, as well as the Cook Path to the Ice Gulch, can be reached by turning left on Randolph Hill Rd.

Bee Line (map 6:E9)

Distance from US 2 (1300')

    to Randolph Hill Rd. (1820'): 1.6 mi. (2.6 km.), 500 ft., 1 hr. 5 min.

Short Paths in Randolph Village Area

The Diagonal (RMC). This path begins on the Bee Line 0.4 mi. from the Ravine House site on Durand Rd. and runs northeast uphill, linking many of the paths on the lower part of Randolph Hill. From the Bee Line, it descends gradually to a junction with the Glenside, which continues straight ahead. The Diagonal turns sharp left here, crosses Carlton Brook, and begins a gentle to moderate ascent. It passes a junction on the right with the Burnbrae Path, then turns to the right onto a logging road and follows it for a short distance. At 0.5 mi. the trail crosses the EZ Way and its grade becomes level. It crosses the Wood Path at 0.9 mi. and continues to its end at 1.3 mi. at the Pasture Path, which it reaches a short distance west of Pasture Path Rd. Randolph Hill Rd. is a short distance north via the Short Circuit Path.

    Burnbrae Path (RMC). This path begins on Durand Rd. just east of Carlton Brook and the Randolph Public Library. It ascends, soon passing a junction on the left with the Glenside and then crossing the Diagonal. It ends at 0.5 mi. on the Bee Line just above the Bee Line's crossing of Carlton Brook.

    The Glenside (RMC). This extremely scenic short path leaves the Burnbrae Path 0.2 mi. north of Durand Rd. and follows Carlton Brook up through beautiful Mossy Glen. There are several short side paths and loops within Mossy Glen. The Glenside ends at 0.2 mi. on the Diagonal a short distance east of the junction of the Diagonal and Bee Line.

Vyron D. Lowe Trail (RMC)

This path ascends to Lookout Ledge from the vicinity of Lowe's Store and Cabins, near the west end of Durand Rd. Entering the woods north of Durand Rd. just east of Lowe's Cabins (sign), the trail parallels the road, then ascends, following or crossing a number of logging roads and passing through recently logged areas (watch carefully for signs and blazes). At 1.8 mi. it joins the Crescent Ridge Trail. Turn right (east) for Lookout Ledge.

Vyron D. Lowe Trail (map 6:E9)
Distance from Durand Rd. (1400').

   to Lookout Ledge (2260'): 1.9 mi. (3.0 km.), 850 ft., 1 hr. 25 min.

Sargent Path (RMC)

This is the most direct route to Lookout Ledge, as well as the steepest. The trail is little used but well blazed, and with care it can be readily followed. Leave Durand Rd. opposite a dark red cottage 0.8 mi. west of the Ravine House site and 1.0 mi. east of Randolph Spring. The path immediately bears left and rises steadily to the ledge, where it meets the Ledge and Crescent Ridge trails.

Sargent Path (map 6:E9)
Distance from Durand Rd. (1310')

   to Lookout Ledge (2260'): 0.8 mi. (1.3 km.), 950 ft., 55 min.

Ledge Trail (RMC)

Leading from the Ravine House site to Lookout Ledge, this trail forms a steep but direct route to the outlook. At the west end of the hotel site, look for a trail sign on the driveway. Follow blazes across a rocky slope above which the Eusden house is visible. The trail soon leaves the yard and, rising steadily northwest, climbs through deep and beautiful woods to the notch at 0.6 mi., where the Notchway diverges right for Randolph Hill. The Ledge Trail turns sharp left, steepens, and leaves the woods to follow an overgrown lumber road through second growth. It then bears off the road to the right and shortly intersects the Pasture Path on the right at 1.2 mi. The trail re-enters the woods and climbs steeply over some rocks, then descends slightly, passing the Eyrie (a small outlook), and continues a few yards more to its end at the Crescent Ridge Trail. Just below is Lookout Ledge.

Ledge Trail (map 6:E9)
Distance from Ravine House site (1800')

   to Lookout Ledge (2260'): 1.3 mi. (2.1 km.), 450 ft., 55 min.

Pasture Path (RMC)

This trail leads from Randolph Hill Rd. to the Ledge Trail. The Pasture Path begins at Randolph Hill Rd. about 0.1 mi. above Stearns Rd. and runs west through old pastures and woods, using parts of Stearns Rd., Glover Spring Rd., and High Acres Rd., and passing several local paths: the Diagonal, Wood Path, EZ Way, and Bee Line. At 1.2 mi., the path leaves High Acres Rd. below High Acres and passes through ancient forest, then light woods. Grassy Lane then diverges right at 1.4 mi. to Randolph Hill Rd., providing a shortcut 0.1 mi. long to the road (Grassy Lane affords the most direct route from the Mt. Crescent House site to Lookout Ledge via the upper part of the Pasture Path, although parking is not available at the intersection of Grassy Lane and Randolph Hill Rd.). The Pasture Path enters young second growth and turns sharp left onto a logging road at 1.9 mi. Soon it turns sharp right off the road where the Notchway continues straight ahead. The Pasture Path runs across several tributaries of Carlton Brook, then ascends to meet the Ledge Trail 0.2 mi. below Lookout Ledge.

Pasture Path (map 6:E9)
Distances from Randolph Hill Rd. (1575')

> *to* Ledge Trail (2070'): 2.7 mi. (4.4 km.), 500 ft., 1 hr. 35 min.
> *to* Lookout Ledge (2260') via Ledge Trail: 2.9 mi. (4.7 km.), 700 ft., 1 hr. 50 min.

Notchway (RMC)

This is a connecting path from the Ledge Trail 0.6 mi. from Durand Rd. to the Pasture Path 2.0 mi. west of the Mt. Crescent House site. The Notchway leaves the Ledge Trail at the notch and ascends slightly, then passes through a lumbered area, an old forest, and a swamp. It crosses two tributaries of Carlton Brook and climbs. Follow arrows to the left to a logging road and from there to the Pasture Path 0.9 mi. below Lookout Ledge.

Notchway (map 6:E9)
Distance from Ledge Trail (1800')

> *to* Pasture Path (1800'): 0.5 mi. (0.8 km.), 100 ft. (rev. 100 ft.), 20 min.

Mount Crescent Trail (RMC)

This trail begins at Randolph Hill Rd. about 0.3 mi. west of the Mt. Crescent House site, opposite the head of Grassy Lane. Do not park here; leave cars at the Mt. Crescent House site.

The trail coincides for 0.1 mi. with the Cook Path, which then branches right. The Mount Crescent Trail continues on the logging road for another 0.1 mi. to the junction with the Carlton Notch Trail, which continues straight ahead, while the Mount Crescent Trail turns right and begins to ascend the mountain. At 0.3 mi. from Randolph Hill Rd., the Jimtown logging road is crossed, the Boothman Spring Cutoff enters from the Mt. Crescent House site, and the main trail steepens. At 1.0 mi. it passes Castleview Loop, which leads left 80 yd. to Castleview Rock.

Castleview Loop (RMC). The Castleview Loop, 0.4 mi. long, diverges left from the Mount Crescent Trail 1.0 mi. from the Mt. Crescent House site. In a few feet a side trail leads left to Castleview Rock, an interesting boulder. The main trail descends gently through light woods, passing Castleview Ledge, which is named for its unique view of the Castellated Ridge of Mt. Jefferson. Entering thick forest, the loop then descends steeply, losing about 200 ft. of elevation, through raspberry bushes to its end at the Carlton Notch Trail near the Mt. Crescent Water Co. reservoir, 1.0 mi. from the Mt. Crescent House site.

At 1.4 mi. the Crescent Ridge Trail, an alternate route that rejoins at the north summit of Mt. Crescent, branches right. The Mount Crescent Trail climbs northwest, occasionally becoming steep and rough over ledges, to the south viewpoint. It then ascends to the south summit of Mt. Crescent, where there is a glimpse of the Northern Peaks. It then continues for 0.2 mi. to the north summit, also wooded, from which the Pliny and Pilot ranges can be seen across the broad valley of the Upper Ammonoosuc. The trail ends here, at the second junction with the Crescent Ridge Trail.

Mount Crescent Trail (map 6:E9)

Distances from Randolph Hill Rd. at Mt. Crescent House site (1800')

   to Crescent Ridge Trail, lower junction (2800'): 1.4 mi., 1000 ft., 1 hr. 10 min.

   to Crescent Ridge Trail, upper junction (3210'): 2.0 mi. (3.6 km.), 1400 ft., 1 hr. 40 min.

Crescent Ridge Trail (RMC)

This trail branches right from the Mount Crescent Trail 1.4 mi. from the Mt. Crescent House site on Randolph Hill Rd. and crosses the east flank of the mountain. From there it turns west and climbs steeply to the north outlook, where it again meets the Mount Crescent Trail at 0.6 mi. Continuing southwest, it descends gradually, crossing Carlton Brook at 1.3 mi., to Carlton Notch, where it passes a junction on the left with the Carlton Notch Trail at 1.6 mi. The Crescent Ridge Trail then ascends the ridge that rises west from Carlton Notch and passes Lafayette View, an outlook with an excellent view of King Ravine and Mts. Madison, Adams, and Jefferson. The trail then descends into the col between Mt. Randolph and the slightly higher unnamed peak north of it, crosses the headwaters of a branch of Carlton Brook, and climbs to the summit of Mt. Randolph. From here the trail descends steeply on an old lumber road, passing a junction on the right with the Vyron D. Lowe Trail, and continues to the Ledge Trail just above Lookout Ledge.

Crescent Ridge Trail (map 6:E9)

Distances from Mount Crescent Trail, lower junction (2800')

   to Mt. Crescent, north outlook (3250'): 0.6 mi., 450 ft., 30 min.

   to Carlton Notch Trail (2820'): 1.6 mi., 450 ft. (rev. 450 ft.), 1 hr.

   to Lafayette View (3050'): 2.3 mi., 650 ft., 1 hr. 30 min.

   to Mt. Randolph summit (3081'): 2.9 mi., 900 ft. (rev. 200 ft.), 1 hr. 55 min.

   to Lookout Ledge (2260'): 3.8 mi. (6.1 km.), 900 ft. (rev. 800 ft.), 2 hr. 20 min.

Carlton Notch Trail (RMC)

The Carlton Notch Trail leads from the Mount Crescent Trail to the Crescent Ridge Trail in Carlton Notch, the pass between Mt. Randolph and Mt. Crescent. The section of trail that formerly continued from the notch to the Pond of Safety has been abandoned.

   The trail starts on the Mount Crescent Trail 0.2 mi. from Randolph Hill Rd. and 0.1 mi. above its junction with the Cook Path. The Mount Crescent Trail turns right at this point, and the Carlton Notch Trail continues straight ahead. The trail rises gently on an old logging road, passing the Mt. Crescent Water Co. reservoir and the Castleview Loop (right) at 0.7 mi. from Randolph Hill Rd. (1.0 mi. from the Mt. Crescent House site). It then ascends moderately across Carlton Brook to Carlton Notch, where it ends at the Crescent Ridge Trail.

Carlton Notch Trail (map 6:E9)

Distance from Randolph Hill Rd. at Mt. Crescent House site (1800')

   to Carlton Notch (2820'): 2.0 mi. (3.2 km.), 1000 ft., 1 hr. 30 min.

Boothman Spring Cutoff (RMC)

This short path avoids the road walk on the way to the Cook Path and Mount Crescent Trail from the Mt. Crescent House site on Randolph Hill Rd., which is a good starting point with parking spaces. The trail is level throughout, leading from the old hotel driveway (sign), through a field, then into the woods. At 0.3 mi. it passes the excellent Boothman Spring, then at 0.5 mi. it crosses the Cook Path (to the Ice Gulch), then the Jimtown lumber road, and ends at the Mount Crescent Trail.

Boothman Spring Cutoff (map 6:E9)

Distance from Randolph Hill Rd. at the Mt. Crescent House site (1800')

   to Mount Crescent Trail (1900'): 0.6 mi. (0.9 km.), 100 ft., 20 min.

Cook Path (RMC)

This trail begins on Randolph Hill Rd. opposite Grassy Lane, about 0.3 mi. west of the Mt. Crescent House site. Do not leave cars here; park at the Mt. Crescent House site. The Boothman Spring Cutoff may be used to avoid the road walk at the start of the Cook Path.

    The trail coincides with the Mount Crescent Trail for about 0.1 mi., then branches right, passing an old trail, and at 0.3 mi. crosses the Boothman Spring Cutoff, which comes directly from the Mt. Crescent House site. The Cook Path ascends over a low ridge, passing through a recently logged area (watch carefully for blazes), and then descends easily to the head of Ice Gulch, where it ends. The Ice Gulch Path begins here and descends through the Ice Gulch.

Cook Path (map 6:E9–D9)

Distance from Randolph Hill Rd. at the Mt. Crescent House site (1800')

   to Ice Gulch Path (2460'): 2.8 mi. (4.5 km.), 950 ft. (rev. 300 ft.), 1 hr. 40 min.

Ice Gulch Path (RMC)

This path gives access to the wild, beautiful Ice Gulch from Randolph Hill Rd., starting at an old farm with a prominent sign, "Sky Meadows," located about 0.4 mi. east of the Mt. Crescent House site. It runs to the bottom of the Ice Gulch and then up through it. The following description assumes that the trip will be made in the traditional direction; that is, by following the Cook Path to the head of the gulch, then descending through it and returning to Randolph Hill Rd. via the Ice Gulch Path. However, many hikers will feel more comfortable ascending, rather than descending, the slippery rocks in the gulch, so the ascent via the Ice Gulch Path and return via the Cook Path should be seriously considered. Caution: The trip through the gulch itself is one of the most difficult and strenuous trail segments in the White Mtns., involving nearly constant scrambling over wet, slippery rocks, and it may take much more time than the standard formula allows. There is no way to exit from the ravine in the mile between the Vestibule and Fairy Spring; hikers must either retrace their steps to the end they started from or continue to the other end, and should take this fact into account when considering the suitability of this trip for their party or estimating the amount of time they should allow for it.

From the Cook Path at the head of the Ice Gulch, the descent is very steep for 0.1 mi. to the Vestibule, where there is an excellent spring. The steep descent continues generally southeast, with views toward Gorham and down the gulch. At the foot of the gulch the trail passes Fairy Spring. Just below this spring, at 0.9 mi., the Peboamauk Loop leaves on the left to follow the brook down to Peboamauk Fall. The Ice Gulch Path turns right here and climbs steeply for a short distance up the west bank of the ravine, then descends to the south across several wet areas to the "Marked Birch," where it bears right as the Peboamauk Loop rejoins on the left. The Ice Gulch Path runs southwest for about 2.0 mi., crossing three major brooks and a woods road, and ends on Randolph Hill Rd.

Ice Gulch Path (map 6:E9–D9)
Distances from head of Ice Gulch (2460')

to site of "Marked Birch" (1770'): 1.4 mi., 0 ft. (rev. 700 ft.), 45 min.

to Randolph Hill Rd. (1780'): 3.4 mi. (5.5 km.), 200 ft. (rev. 200 ft.), 1 hr. 50 min.

Distance from Randolph Hill Rd. at the Mt. Crescent House site (1800')

  for complete loop via Ice Gulch Path and Cook Path: 6.6 mi. (10.6 km.),
    1150 ft., 3 hr. 55 min.

Peboamauk Loop (RMC)

This path is an alternate route to the main Ice Gulch Path at the lower end of the gulch, longer and more strenuous but much more rewarding than the main route. It travels beside a pleasant stream and passes Peboamauk Fall, a fine cascade fed by the slowly melting ice in the gulch ("Peboamauk" means "Winter's Home"). On the descent, the path leaves the Ice Gulch Path on the left at the foot of the Ice Gulch just below Fairy Spring and descends steeply along Moose Brook for 0.4 mi. to Peboamauk Fall, then rises steeply to rejoin the Ice Gulch Path at the "Marked Birch."

Peboamauk Loop (map 6:E9)

Distance from Ice Gulch Path, upper junction (1860')

  to Ice Gulch Path, lower junction (1770'): 0.5 mi. (0.8 km.), 100 ft., 20 min.

C. PLINY AND PILOT RANGES

These two ranges are essentially one mountain mass, extending north and south between the Israel and Upper Ammonoosuc rivers, east of Lancaster. The **Pliny Range** forms the semicircular southern end of this mass; its chief summits are Mt. Starr King, Mt. Waumbek, and the three peaks of Mt. Weeks. Across **Willard Notch** from Mt. Weeks, the **Pilot Range** begins, including Terrace Mtn., Mt. Cabot, Mt. Mary, and Hutchins Mtn., which is often known as Mt. Pilot. A spur that extends northeast from Mt. Cabot carries the Bulge and the Horn. Mt. Cabot is the highest peak in the entire North Country. Two fire towers accessible by auto provide excellent views that may be helpful to hikers planning trips in this region. **Mt. Prospect** (2077 ft.) is located in Weeks State Park, the former estate of John W. Weeks (see Mt. Weeks below), reached by a paved road (small fee charged for vehicles) that leaves US 3 at its high point between Whitefield and Lancaster. There is now also a small trail network on this mountain. **Milan Hill** (1737 ft.) is located in Milan Hill State Park (campground) on NH 110B west of Milan village; its fire tower offers a panoramic view that includes the Mahoosucs and the mountains north of NH 110 as well as the region covered in this subsection. This entire subsection is covered by the AMC North

Country–Mahoosuc Range map (map #6); the USGS Pliny Range and Stark quads may also be useful.

Mt. Starr King (3907 ft.) was named for Thomas Starr King, a minister in Boston and San Francisco who was the author of *The White Hills,* one of the most important and influential books ever written about the White Mtns.; King Ravine on Mt. Adams and a peak in the Sierra Nevada of California are also named for him. New Hampshire's Mt. Starr King is located northeast of Jefferson village, from which it is reached by the Starr King Trail. The summit is wooded, but there is a fine cleared vista toward the Presidentials. **Mt. Waumbek** (4006 ft.) lies immediately east of Mt. Starr King and is also reached by the Starr King Trail, as well as being the southern terminus of the Kilkenny Ridge Trail. Formerly called Pliny Major, Mt. Waumbek is the highest point of the Pliny Range but has only a very restricted view to the east. **Mt. Weeks** is located northeast of Mt. Waumbek and has three distinct peaks—the **North Peak** (3901 ft.), the **Middle Peak** (3684 ft.), and the **South Peak** (3885 ft.)—all of which are wooded with no significant views and are traversed by the Kilkenny Ridge Trail. Formerly known as Round Mtn., it was renamed to honor John W. Weeks, who was the sponsor and chief proponent of the Weeks Act (1911), the piece of federal legislation that authorized the purchase of lands for national forests and thereby made possible the establishment of the WMNF.

The **Pilot Range** begins on the north side of Willard Notch with **Terrace Mtn.** (3655 ft.), a narrow ridge with several summits, named for its appearance when seen from the west. It is traversed by the Kilkenny Ridge Trail, and its principal summit affords an interesting if somewhat restricted view. **Mt. Cabot** (4170 ft.), the highest peak of the North Country, is located north of Terrace Mtn. across **Bunnell Notch.** Its true summit is wooded with no views, but good outlooks east and west have been cleared at the site of the former fire tower, 0.3 mi. southeast of the true summit, and there is an excellent vista from the ledges above Bunnell Notch. **The Bulge** (3950 ft.) and **the Horn** (3905 ft.) lie just north of Mt. Cabot. They are reached via the Kilkenny Ridge Trail, which follows the ridge that joins them to Mt. Cabot over the Bulge and then circles around the northwest side of the Horn, which is ascended by a spur path. The Bulge is a wooded hump with no views. The Horn is a fine sharp peak composed of a jumble of bare rocks that afford views in all directions; it is unquestionably one of the finest summits in the region.

Hutchins Mtn. (3730 ft.), sometimes also called Mt. Pilot, was named after Alpheus Hutchins, an early settler. It lies at the northwest end of the Pilot Range, separated from Mt. Cabot by **Mt. Mary** and several unnamed peaks. It has no regular trail but can be ascended by experienced bushwhackers by following a private logging road that leaves the road from Grange to Groveton via Lost Nation at a sharp turn near an old schoolhouse at the foot of the mountain (use care not to block any roads). The most frequently used route follows the logging road that runs up the southeast side of Cummings Brook into the basin below the summit, then ascends to the southwest ridge of Hutchins Mtn. and follows it to the summit. See the USGS Stark quad.

The wide valley east of the Pilot Range and north of the Crescent Range, drained by the headwaters of the Upper Ammonoosuc River, has been traditionally known to local residents as "**the Kilkenny,**" from the uninhabited township in which many of the peaks of the Pilot and Pliny ranges, including Mt. Waumbek and Mt. Cabot, are located. Ironically, most of the region usually called by the name of Kilkenny lies in the towns of Berlin, Randolph, Milan, and Stark, with very little in Kilkenny itself; though if the Pilot and Pliny ranges are included in the region (as is sometimes the case) the name of Kilkenny is then amply justified. It is a rather flat, densely forested region known well by loggers and those who love to hunt and fish, but not to nearly the same extent by hikers. Historically this region has been a major timber harvest area, and many of the features of interest reflect past and present logging activity both on private inholdings and on the National Forest lands, which are managed for multiple use. The trails in this region generally follow an extensive network of old, older, and ancient logging roads or railroad grades. Primary trails are usually blazed with yellow paint. The visual environment on the maintained trails has generally been screened from logging activity, but the longer view often includes vegetational diversity resulting from timber harvest and reforestation, and access roads may be in evidence. As a result of the variety of vegetation types, chances are excellent that one will see many kinds of native wildlife. The Kilkenny Ridge Trail links some of the main attractions of this area, including the Devil's Hopyard and Rogers Ledge. There are primitive campsites at Rogers Ledge and Unknown Pond. This is a backcountry area in which trails are normally maintained only once annually. It may be useful to check with the Androscoggin Ranger District office in Gorham (603-466-2713) for the current status of particular trails.

The center of this area is accessible by **York Pond Rd.** (FR 13) to the Berlin Fish Hatchery at York Pond, and by **Bog Dam Rd.** (FR 15), which makes a 15.5 mi. loop south of York Pond. Bog Dam Rd. follows in part the earlier Upper Ammonoosuc Trail and logging road network, passing the sites of several former logging camps. With the present Upper Ammonoosuc Trail and the Landing Camp Trail, it provides access to the site of Bog Dam, built to provide a "head" of water for the spring logging drives and later used as a town water supply. York Pond Rd. leaves NH 110 7.4 mi. northwest of its beginning at NH 16 in Berlin. There is a gate at the Berlin Fish Hatchery that is locked from 4 P.M. to 8 A.M. Hikers who plan to leave cars at the trailheads west of this gate should make prior arrangements in person at the gatehouse, or by phone with the hatchery (603-449-3412). Foot travel past the gate is not restricted.

The **South Pond Recreation Area** is a picnic and swimming area operated by the WMNF at South Pond, south of NH 110 in Stark; camping is not permitted here. This is the northern terminus of the Kilkenny Ridge Trail and the Devil's Hopyard Trail. The access road to South Pond Recreation Area has a gate 1.1 mi. from the trailhead in the picnic area; this gate is kept locked from 8 P.M. to 9 A.M. during the season when the beach and picnic area are open. At other times it is usually locked, but it is normally left open from Labor Day to the end of hunting season. Foot travel is always permitted. Check with the Androscoggin Ranger District office of the WMNF (603-466-2713) for details.

The **Devil's Hopyard** is a picturesque gorge on a brook that empties into South Pond. It resembles the Ice Gulch in Randolph but is shorter and narrower. **Rogers Ledge** (2965 ft.), one of the most interesting little-known mountains in the White Mtns., lies about 3.5 mi. northwest of York Pond. It was named in honor of Major Robert Rogers, leader of Rogers's Rangers in the French and Indian Wars. The entire southwest face of the mountain is a cliff, and the view from the top includes the Kilkenny area, the Pilot Range, the Mahoosucs, and the Presidential Range. It may be reached from South Pond by the Kilkenny Ridge Trail, or from the York Pond Fish Hatchery by the Mill Brook Trail and the Kilkenny Ridge Trail. **Unknown Pond,** which is reached by the Kilkenny Ridge Trail or the Unknown Pond Trail, is one of the jewels of the White Mtns.—a beautiful mountain tarn in a birch forest carpeted with dense ferns, offering a spectacular view up to the rugged and picturesque Horn from its shore. **Pond of Safety** is a small but attractive pond that lies just north of the Crescent Range and east of the Pliny Range in the town of Randolph. It derived its name from an incident that occurred during the American Revolution. Four local men who had joined the Continental Army were captured by the British and paroled on condition that they not participate further in the conflict. The Continental authorities felt that their parole papers were spurious and insisted that they return to their units. Since they feared severe punishment if they were recaptured by the British, they retired to this isolated region to hunt and fish, and remained out of reach until there was no further danger that they might be apprehended as deserters. Many years after the end of the war, having become respected citizens in the region, they were exonerated of the desertion charges and placed on the pension rolls. The pond has continued to be a place of refuge from the woes of civilization for fishermen, hunters, cross-country skiers, and snowmobilers, but unfortunately there is no longer a purely pedestrian trail to the pond. It may be reached from Bog Dam Rd. by the WMNF Pond of Safety Trail, which is a series of logging roads heavily used by snowmobiles in winter, and from Jefferson by Stag Hollow Rd., which is passable by four-wheel-drive vehicle.

THE TRAILS

Mount Prospect Auto Road (NHDP)

This road runs from US 3 between Lancaster and Whitefield to the summit of Mt. Prospect in Weeks State Park, where the picturesque fieldstone tower provides excellent views. It is usually open to vehicles (fee charged) daily from mid-June to Labor Day, and on weekends from Memorial Day to mid-June and from Labor Day to Columbus Day. At other times it is gated and open to pedestrian use (and to skiers in winter) only. Refer to the USGS Lancaster quad.

Leaving US 3 at the top of the hill between Whitefield and Lancaster, it ascends in a counter-clockwise direction, crossing the Around the Mountain Trail (of which this section is a part of the New Hampshire Heritage Trail, a path that is planned to extend the entire length of the state) in 0.1 mi. At 0.7 mi. the road passes a viewpoint to Blood Pond and Mountain Meadow Pond, and at 1.1 mi. it passes an excellent outlook to the Presidentials with a mountain identification sign. At 1.3 mi., at a hairpin turn to the left, the Old Carriage Road diverges on the right and descends along the north slope of the mountain, crossing the Around the Mountain Trail in 0.4 mi. and reaching Reed Rd. in 0.7 mi. The Auto Road continues to the summit and its buildings.

Mount Prospect Auto Road (USGS Lancaster quad)

Distance from US 3 (1430')

to Mt. Prospect summit (2077'): 1.6 mi. (2.6 km.), 650 ft., 1 hr. 10 min.

Around the Mountain Trail (NHDP)

This trail runs completely around the lower slopes of Mt. Prospect, providing a pleasant 3-mi. loop on interconnecting woods roads that is particularly useful as a cross-country ski route. It begins at the entrance gate to the Mt. Prospect Ski Area on US 3 0.2 mi. north of the lower end of the Mount Prospect Auto Road; it is described here in the counter-clockwise direction.

Leaving the ski area, the trail follows an old grassy road southward, marked by white blazes as part of the New Hampshire Heritage Trail. At 0.3 mi. it crosses the Mount Prospect Auto Rd., and at 0.4 mi. the New Hampshire Heritage Trail diverges right, while the Around the Mountain Trail swings left and ascends eastward. It passes a well (right) and an outlook to the south (right), then turns left (north) onto an old woods road bordered with stone walls. It bears left off the road and ascends to a semi-open outlook to the east near a stone wall. The trail continues to climb across a small stream and reaches its high point at 1.8 mi., then descends left (west). It crosses over several small streams and under maple-sugaring sap lines, then swings left past old building foundations (right) and at 2.6 mi. crosses the Old Carriage Road. (The summit of Mt. Prospect is 0.7 mi. to the left via the Old Carriage Road and the Auto Road. The New Hampshire Heritage Trail, which has followed the Old Carriage Road 0.3 mi. up from Reed Rd., now coincides with the Around the Mountain Trail for the rest of its distance.) Soon the Around the Mountain Trail swings left (south) and continues to the starting point at the ski area.

Around the Mountain Trail (USGS Lancaster quad)
Distance from Mt. Prospect Ski Area (1410')

    for complete loop: 3.0 mi. (4.8 km.), 300 ft., 1 hr. 40 min.

Kilkenny Ridge Trail (WMNF)

The Kilkenny Ridge Trail is a ridgecrest trail that runs from South Pond Recreation Area off NH 110 to the summit of Mt. Waumbek. From South Pond, it climbs over Rogers Ledge, descends to Unknown Pond, then circles to the northwest side of the Horn to gain the crest of the Pilot-Pliny ridge at the col between the Bulge and the Horn (the Horn is reached by a spur path). It then follows the backbone of the main ridge over the Bulge, Mt. Cabot, Terrace Mtn., and the three peaks of Weeks to its southern end on Mt. Waumbek. This trail was designed primarily to provide an extended route for backpackers interested in avoiding crowds of day-hikers, since, except for the section that coincides with the Mount Cabot Trail, use of those sections and features that are accessible to day-hikers is very light. The trail has generally easy to moderate grades and reaches several fine viewpoints—notably the Horn and Rogers Ledge—but has long stretches of woods-walking that are pleasant but lacking in significant views.

From the parking lot at South Pond, go right (south) toward the west shore to the sign for the Devil's Hopyard. At 0.7 mi. the Devil's Hopyard Trail diverges right (west) and the Kilkenny Ridge Trail continues straight ahead. It crosses two brooks on bridges and runs southeast and south following old logging roads. At 2.5 mi. the trail bears sharp right (west), crossing from one logging road to another, then resumes its generally southerly course, crossing the town boundary between Stark and Kilkenny at 3.2 mi. At 3.4 mi. the grade steepens along the crest of a narrowing ridge, and the trail ascends to a sharp left turn at 4.1 mi., with the summit of Rogers Ledge a few steps ahead. The best view is at the edge of the cliff, reached by a short spur on the right just before this turn. From the south-facing ledge the view includes the Presidential Range, the Androscoggin River valley, the Mahoosuc Range, the entire Kilkenny basin, and the northern shoulder of Mt. Cabot.

Descending from Rogers Ledge, the trail curves east around the foot of the ledge and passes a side path to a backcountry campsite at 4.6 mi., then continues to its junction with Mill Brook Trail at 4.7 mi. from South Pond. The trail continues west, passing a beaver pond called Kilback Pond at 5.3 mi., and at 6.0 mi. begins the steady ascent to the ridge east of Unknown Pond. It reaches the crest of the ridge at 6.4 mi. and descends to the pond at 6.8 mi., where it meets the Unknown Pond Trail.

The Kilkenny Ridge Trail follows the Unknown Pond Trail to the right for 100 yd., then turns sharp left off it and runs around the north shore of the pond. Crossing two small brooks, it swings north around the end of the ridge and begins the climb up the north slope of the Horn to the sag between the Bulge and the Horn at 8.5 mi. Here a side trail climbs to the left (east) 0.3 mi. and 250 ft. to the open rocks of the Horn, from which there are magnificent views. The Kilkenny Ridge Trail turns right (west) and ascends to the wooded summit of the Bulge, drops to the saddle, and climbs to the true summit of Mt. Cabot at 9.6 mi., where it joins the Mount Cabot Trail.

The two trails descend together past the lower but more open summit of Cabot and the cabin just below it, and continue to descend easily past the fine outlook from Bunnell Rock on the left as the trail makes a great curving 180° turn to the right. At 11.0 mi., where the Mount Cabot Trail turns sharp right and continues its descent to East Lancaster, the Kilkenny Ridge Trail bears slightly left and runs southeast with gentle ups and downs. At 11.3 mi. it meets the Bunnell Notch Trail, follows it to the left for 0.1 mi., and then leaves it on the right to begin the ascent of Terrace Mtn., climbing moderately to the partly overgrown clearing constructed for emergency helicopter landings in the event of a forest fire (called a "helspot") at the summit of the northern knob. It then continues along the ridge with many ups and downs over small peaks, passing an older and almost unrecognizable overgrown helspot on the way. At 13.3 mi., where a spur path continues straight 0.1 mi. to the interesting but restricted outlook at the summit of Terrace Mtn., the main trail turns sharp left and drops off the ridge, then begins a long circling descent to the York Pond Trail.

Crossing a small brook at its low point in Willard Notch, the trail ascends slightly to the York Pond Trail at 14.4 mi., follows it left (east) for 100 yd., then leaves it on the right and begins a rather long and winding ascent of North Weeks, reaching the summit at 15.7 mi., where there is a canister register maintained by the Four Thousand Footer Club. The trail descends at easy to moderate grades past a small spring (unreliable) at 16.0 mi. to a potential campsite in the main col at 16.5 mi. Ascending again, it passes over Middle Weeks at 17.1 mi. and crosses through a much shallower col to South Weeks at 18.1 mi. Here a short spur continues straight to another canister at the blowdown-infested summit, while the main trail turns left and descends to the col between Weeks and Waumbek at 18.7 mi. From here it swings to the west and ascends along the crest of the ridge, slowly gaining elevation in spite of occasional losses, then crosses the interesting, rather steep-sided east knob of Waumbek and continues another 0.2 mi. to the true summit, where it meets the Starr King Trail.

Kilkenny Ridge Trail (map 6:B8–D7)

Distances from South Pond Recreation Area (1120')

   to Rogers Ledge (2965'): 4.1 mi., 1850 ft., 3 hr.

   to Mill Brook Trail (2400'): 4.7 mi., 1850 ft. (rev. 550 ft.), 3 hr. 15 min.

   to Unknown Pond (3177'): 6.8 mi., 2750 ft. (rev. 150 ft.), 4 hr. 45 min.

   to the side trail to the Horn (3650'): 8.5 mi., 3250 ft., 5 hr. 55 min.

   to Mt. Cabot summit (4170'): 9.6 mi., 4000 ft. (rev. 250 ft.), 6 hr. 50 min.

   to departure from Mount Cabot Trail (3150'): 11.0 mi., 4050 ft. (rev. 1050 ft.), 7 hr. 30 min.

   to Terrace Mtn. summit spur (3540'): 13.3 mi., 4750 ft. (rev. 300 ft.), 9 hr.

   to York Pond Trail, west junction (2720'): 14.4 mi., 4750 ft. (rev. 800 ft.), 9 hr. 35 min.

   to North Weeks summit (3901'): 15.7 mi., 5950 ft., 10 hr. 50 min.

   to South Weeks summit (3885'): 18.1 mi., 6750 ft. (rev. 800 ft.), 12 hr. 25 min.

   to to Mt. Waumbek summit (4006'): 20.6 mi. (33.1 km.), 7350 ft. (rev. 500 ft.), 14 hr.

Devil's Hopyard Trail (WMNF)

This trail begins at the South Pond Recreation Area off NH 110 and provides access to the wild and beautiful Devil's Hopyard, a small gorge with cliffy walls and a boulder-strewn floor. At the start it coincides with the Kilkenny Ridge Trail, which leads south from the picnic area, skirting the west side of the pond, and crosses a brook in 0.6 mi. After another 60 yd., the Devil's Hopyard Trail diverges right (west) from the Kilkenny Ridge Trail (sign). At 0.8 mi. it recrosses the brook to the north side and soon enters the Hopyard. The small stream that drains the gorge is for the most part completely out of sight beneath moss-covered boulders, while ledges overhang the path. (Use caution where rocks are wet or covered with moss.) At 1.2 mi. the path rises steeply on the rocks at the west end of the Hopyard and ends at a cascade.

Devil's Hopyard Trail (map 6:B8)

Distance from South Pond (1120')

   to end of trail (1600'): 1.3 mi. (2.0 km.), 500 ft., 55 min.

Starr King Trail (RMC/WMNF)

This trail begins on a gravel road to several houses that leaves the north side of US 2 (trail sign) 0.2 mi. east of its junction with NH 115A. Go up the road, always bearing left to avoid driveways on the right, then bear right at 0.2 mi. where the road straight ahead (former route of trail, which may be used by pedestrians) is much rougher, and continue 100 yd. to a small parking lot on the left. If the parking lot cannot be reached by car (as when the access road is unplowed in winter), park in the lot for the Jefferson village swimming pool, just east of the junction of US 2 and NH 115A, and walk up the road; do not obstruct the roads by parking cars on them. The trail is generally fairly easy all the way up, with moderate grades and good footing.

From the parking area, ascend gradually on a grassy logging road for 100 yd., then turn left (arrow) and ascend another 100 yd. to meet the old route of the trail, a logging road on which the trail turns uphill to the right and soon passes the stone foundations of a springhouse (right). At 0.4 mi. the trail bears right at a fork (where the left branch is overgrown and will soon cease to be discernible) and ascends the broad southwest ridge of the mountain. At 1.4 mi. it angles left and runs north on a long traverse of the west flank of the mountain, passing a spring on the left (downhill side) of the trail at 2.1 mi. Swinging right and leaving the traverse at 2.5 mi., the trail climbs to the summit at 2.6 mi., then continues another 60 yd. to an excellent cleared vista south and west at the site of a former shelter. From the remains of the old cabin's fireplace, the trail enters the woods again, angling left, then swings right (east) and follows close to the crest of the ridge or slightly below it on one side or the other, dipping just below the col on the south and then rising to the summit of Mt. Waumbek, where it meets the south end of the Kilkenny Ridge Trail.

Starr King Trail (map 6:D7)

Distances from trailhead parking area (1650')

> *to* beginning of traverse (2900'): 1.4 mi., 1250 ft., 1 hr. 20 min.

> *to* Mt. Starr King summit (3907'): 2.6 mi., 2250 ft., 2 hr. 25 min.

> *to* Mt. Waumbek summit (4006'): 3.6 mi. (5.8 km.), 2500 ft. (rev. 150 ft.), 3 hr. 5 min.

Mount Cabot Trail (WMNF)

In addition to ascending Mt. Cabot, this trail provides access to the York Pond, Kilkenny Ridge, and Bunnell Notch trails. From the junction of US 2 and NH 116 just west of the village of Jefferson, go west 0.2 mi., then turn right (north) on North Rd. for 2.3 mi., then turn right again on Gore Rd. (which becomes Garland Rd. at a sharp left turn). At 4.0 mi. from US 2, turn right again on Pleasant Valley Rd., and at 4.8 mi. turn right on Arthur White Rd. and continue 0.4 mi. to the parking area (sign) about 50 yd. before the end of the road at "Heath's Gate"; do not block the road or the driveway. Any or all of the road signs at intersections may be missing, so the directions given above should be followed with care. The trail follows logging roads and the old tractor road to the former fire tower almost all the way, with steady moderate grades; footing is fair to good on the upper part, but the lower part has a severely eroded stretch of logging road.

From Heath's Gate, the Mount Cabot Trail follows a logging road through a cut-over area 0.4 mi. to the old Kilkenny logging railroad bed. Here the York Pond Trail to York Pond and the Berlin Fish Hatchery by way of Willard Notch goes right (southeast) along the railroad bed. The Mount Cabot Trail continues ahead on a recent road for another 0.4 mi., then the newer road ends and the trail becomes a footway on much older roads to the Bunnell Brook crossing at 2.2 mi. Just past the brook the Bunnell Notch Trail (sign) leaves on the right. After zigzagging up from the brook, the trail passes a junction at 2.5 mi. where it turns left as the Kilkenny Ridge Trail joins from the right. Soon the trail swings right (southeast) and ascends past a limited southwest outlook. In another 100 yd., after swinging to the left, the trail passes a spur path right (sign) at 2.9 mi. that leads a few steps to Bunnell Rock, a ledge at the cliff-top that offers an excellent vista to the south—probably the best view on the trail. From here the trail turns left (northeast) and climbs through evergreens, with two switchbacks, to the old fire-warden's cabin, now maintained by the Jefferson Boy Scouts and the Pinkerton Academy Outing Club. From the cabin the trail climbs a few steps to the open rocky area where the fire tower was formerly located (views), then passes through a shallow sag and climbs gradually to the true summit (sign). The Kilkenny Ridge Trail continues northward from here, leading over the Bulge and past a side trail to the Horn, then on to Unknown Pond, Rogers Ledge, and South Pond.

Mount Cabot Trail (map 6:D7–C8)
Distances from Heath's Gate (1510')

> *to* York Pond Trail (1640'): 0.4 mi., 150 ft., 15 min.
>
> *to* Bunnell Brook crossing (2650'): 2.2 mi., 1150 ft., 1 hr. 35 min.
>
> *to* outlook at Bunnell Rock (3350'): 2.9 mi., 1850 ft., 2 hr. 25 min.
>
> *to* cabin (4070'): 3.5 mi., 2550 ft., 3 hr.
>
> *to* Mt. Cabot summit (4170'): 3.9 mi. (6.2 km.), 2700 ft. (rev. 50 ft.), 3 hr. 15 min.

York Pond Trail (WMNF)

This trail leaves York Pond Rd. (FR 13) near its west end and follows old logging roads through Willard Notch and down to the old Kilkenny logging railroad bed, on which it continues to East Lancaster at Heath's Gate (see Mount Cabot Trail). It is blazed with yellow paint. The eastern and western ends are in generally excellent condition with good footing, but much of the central part of the trail from the Kilkenny Ridge Trail to the logging railroad bed is very wet and muddy.

From the fish hatchery gate at York Pond (see the warning above concerning the times this gate is locked), continue west 2.1 mi. on York Pond Rd. to a fenced raceway. The trailhead (sign) is on the road to the left. The entrance to the trail is gated, but foot travel is not restricted. The York Pond Trail follows a good gravel road for 0.2 mi., then bears left (arrow) where the Bunnell Notch Trail diverges right. In 100 yd. it crosses a small concrete dam, then continues up the south side of the brook, crossing two branches. At 0.9 mi. it begins to swing up a hardwood ridge, following a well-defined old logging road in excellent condition. At 2.4 mi. it reaches its highest point, just east of Willard Notch on a minor ridge from North Weeks. Descending slightly, it passes two junctions with the Kilkenny Ridge Trail 100 yd. apart; at the first, the Kilkenny Ridge Trail leads left (south) to Mt. Weeks and Mt. Waumbek, and at the second it leads right (north) to Terrace Mtn., Mt. Cabot, and South Pond. The York Pond Trail contours along the south side of the notch, rising and falling gently and remaining somewhat above the floor of the notch. It then descends gradually through several swampy areas and crosses a number of small streams, becoming very muddy at times, then crosses a fairly substantial branch of Garland Brook at 4.6 mi. and joins the old logging railroad grade, where the footing improves greatly. At 5.6 mi. it crosses the WMNF boundary and at 6.6 mi., just after crossing a stream on a culvert bridge, it bears right at a fork (the more obvious left branch is the Tekwood Rd., which continues down Garland Brook to Pleasant Valley Rd.). The trail continues on the old railroad grade in a northwesterly direction and joins the Mount Cabot Trail at 7.0 mi. Turn right (east) for Mt. Cabot or left (west) to reach the parking area at Heath's Gate (the former White's farm) in East Lancaster at 7.4 mi.

York Pond Trail (map 6:D8–D7)

Distances from York Pond Rd. trailhead (1670')

> *to* high point of trail (2750'): 2.4 mi., 1100 ft., 1 hr. 45 min.
>
> *to* WMNF boundary (1920'): 5.6 mi., 1100 ft. (rev. 800 ft.), 3 hr. 20 min.
>
> *to* Mount Cabot Trail (1640'): 7.0 mi., 1100 ft. (rev. 300 ft.), 4 hr. 5 min.
>
> *to* Heath's Gate (1510'): 7.4 mi. (11.9 km.), 1100 ft. (rev. 150 ft.), 4 hr. 15 min.

Bunnell Notch Trail (WMNF)

This trail connects the York Pond Rd. with the Kilkenny Ridge Trail in Bunnell Notch and the Mount Cabot Trail just above the crossing of Bunnell Brook. It has been reopened recently after having been abandoned around 1980, and although it can be followed fairly readily by experienced hikers, it is rough and somewhat wet, and not yet marked or signed in accordance with usual standards. Its future may perhaps still be in doubt, so hikers not skilled in following poorly marked trails might be well advised to check on its condition with the Androscoggin Ranger District office before attempting to use it. Its principal importance is that it makes possible a rather long but very attractive loop trip to Unknown Pond, the Horn, and Mt. Cabot.

Leaving the York Pond Trail 0.2 mi. from York Pond Rd., it follows logging roads through recently logged areas, climbing at a moderate grade up the valley of the headwaters of the West Branch of the Upper Ammonoosuc River, crossing the stream several times, until it reaches the height-of-land in Bunnell Notch. Here the Kilkenny Ridge Trail leaves on the left (south) for Terrace Mtn. and Mt. Waumbek, and in another 0.1 mi. it leaves on the right (north) for Mt. Cabot and South Pond. The Bunnell Notch Trail then descends moderately, crossing Bunnell Brook, to the Mount Cabot Trail a few yards above its Bunnell Brook crossing.

Bunnell Notch Trail (map 6:D8–D7)

Distances from York Pond Trail (1690')

   to Kilkenny Ridge Trail, east junction (3040'): 2.8 mi., 1350 ft., 2 hr. 5 min.

   to Mount Cabot Trail (2660'): 3.3 mi. (5.1 km.), 1350 ft. (rev. 400 ft.), 2 hr. 20 min.

Unknown Pond Trail (WMNF)

This trail connects York Pond Rd. with Mill Brook Rd. near the village of Stark, passing beautiful Unknown Pond and crossing the Kilkenny Ridge Trail. The south terminus is on York Pond Rd. 2.0 mi. west of the fish hatchery gate (sign) between a small pond and a beaver swamp (see the warning above concerning the locked gate at the fish hatchery). The north terminus is at a gate on Mill Brook Rd. (FR 11) 3.7 mi. south of NH 110. There is a sign (hiker symbol) on NH 110 at the beginning of Mill Brook Rd. and a sign ("Trail" with an arrow) at the gate. The trail continues on the forest road for 0.8 mi., then leaves it just east of a bridge across Mill Brook; there is a standard WMNF trail sign at this point. The gate is usually closed except in hunting season.

Leaving York Pond Rd., the trail reaches an old railroad grade at 0.2 mi. and, turning left on it, continues northwest. At about 2.5 mi. the trail begins a steeper ascent to Unknown Pond, which it reaches at 3.3 mi. Nearby there is a backcountry campsite with a pit toilet.

The Kilkenny Ridge Trail enters right (east) at the southeast corner of the pond and coincides with the Unknown Pond Trail for 100 yd. The two paths swing east around the pond through birch woods carpeted with ferns, passing a beautiful view up to the picturesque Horn rising over the pond. At the northeast corner of the pond, the Kilkenny Ridge Trail leaves left (west) toward Mt. Cabot and the Unknown Pond Trail goes north toward Mill Brook Rd. in Stark, crossing a moist area and descending moderately in beautiful birch woods for a mile. It then becomes more gradual, soon crossing the Kilkenny-Stark town line. It traverses the slope east of Mill Brook and enters the gravel Mill Brook Rd. (FR 11) in 2.2 mi. Turn right (northeast) and continue on the road to the gate.

Unknown Pond Trail (map 6:D8–C8)

Distances from York Pond Rd. trailhead (1640')

> *to* Unknown Pond (3177'): 3.3 mi., 1550 ft., 2 hr. 25 min.
>
> *to* Mill Brook Rd. (1755'): 5.5 mi., 1550 ft. (rev. 1400 ft.), 3 hr. 30 min.
>
> *to* WMNF gate (1630'): 6.3 mi. (10.2 km.), 1550 ft. (rev. 150 ft.), 3 hr. 55 min.

Mill Brook Trail (WMNF)

Formerly a through route from Stark village to York Pond, the north section of this trail, from the junction with the Kilkenny Range Trail at the height-of-land to Stark, has been abandoned by the WMNF, and beaver activity and logging have obliterated the old footway. The remaining part of the trail is important mostly because it provides the most convenient route from the south to the spectacular views from Rogers Ledge. It now begins near the main building of the Berlin Fish Hatchery on York Pond Rd. (FR 9). (The lower part of the trail may be difficult to locate; if so, ask at the hatchery for directions.)

From the trail sign on York Pond Rd., ascend gradually on a paved road for 0.2 mi., then follow a dirt road (sign) to the left of a fish hatchery building. After 100 yd., bear right off the dirt road (no sign) and go behind an old brown pumphouse on a concrete dam by a small pond, then turn left onto an old grassy woods road. The trail joins Cold Brook and ascends along it for about 1.3 mi., then diverges right (east) up a side stream. It crosses the Berlin-Milan town boundary at 1.7 mi. and the Milan-Kilkenny boundary at 2.7 mi. Just north of the height-of-land, the trail ends at the Kilkenny Ridge Trail. To the right (east) it is 0.6 mi. to Rogers Ledge; to the left (west) it is 2.1 mi. to Unknown Pond.

Mill Brook Trail (map 6:C8)

Distance from York Pond Rd. (1550')

> *to* Kilkenny Ridge Trail (2400'): 3.8 mi. (6.1 km.), 850 ft., 2 hr. 20 min.

Pond of Safety Trail (WMNF)

This trail, which follows logging roads that are mostly also used as snowmobile trails, leaves Bog Dam Rd. (FR 15) 7.9 mi. south of its eastern junction with York Pond Rd. (FR 13). The trail has been severely disrupted by heavy logging in a number of places and may be difficult to follow, since signs and arrows are often missing. Pond of Safety lies on private land within the WMNF proclamation boundary, and while it is an attractive mountain pond, there is no attractive walking route to it at the present time, though the Pond of Safety Trail still officially exists. During the summer season it can usually be reached by most vehicles via the extension of Stag Hollow Rd.

From Bog Dam Rd., the trail follows a good logging road (FR 236, which may be gated), crossing a branch of the Upper Ammonoosuc River at 0.1 mi. At 0.5 mi. it turns right onto the state snowmobile trail (which may be muddy) and follows it west toward Pond of Safety. There may be signs at this turn.

Rising gradually, the trail bears west and southwest on a good logging road to a junction at 1.7 mi., where the Pond of Safety Trail turns left (southeast). There are snowmobile trail signs and an obscure Forest Service arrow at this junction. Pass through a WMNF gate, then after 0.2 mi. merge to the right with a recent skidder road (very muddy, marked with red ribbons) and follow it uphill 0.1 mi. to a large logging clearing, then bear left and follow the main road at a fork. From here the trail, on an increasingly good logging road, crosses the low ridge and descends through several clearings, making several sweeping turns, then crosses a brook and meets Stag Hollow Rd., which leads 3.8 mi. to Ingerson Rd. near Jefferson. At this intersection, an unmarked road leads to the right (west) 0.2 mi. to a clearing from which a path on the right (north) descends to the boggy shore of the Pond of Safety.

Pond of Safety Trail (map 6:D9–E8)
Distance from Bog Dam Rd. (1730')

> *to* Pond of Safety (2190'): 3.2 mi. (5.1 km.), 550 ft. (rev. 100 ft.), 1 hr. 50 min.

Upper Ammonoosuc Trail (WMNF)

This trail, a remnant of a former 19-mi. through route from Jefferson to West Milan, crosses between the two sides of Bog Dam Rd. (FR 15); the east trailhead is 4.1 mi. south of its eastern junction with York Pond Rd., and the west trailhead is 5.3 mi. south of its western junction with York Pond Rd. The trail passes through areas flooded by beavers and has received little maintenance, so it may be quite difficult to follow and is not recommended for inexperienced hikers.

From the east trailhead, the trail leads generally southwest, crossing Bend Brook at 0.5 mi., and reaches the site of Bog Dam at 1.5 mi. There is a clearing here, and also a pool in the river, but the dam that formerly provided a "head" of water for river log-driving each spring is gone. At 1.7 mi. the Landing Camp Trail diverges left (east). At 1.9 mi. the trail fords the Upper Ammonoosuc River (wading often required) and at 2.3 mi. crosses Keenan Brook (no bridge). It then rises to the west trailhead on Bog Dam Rd.

Upper Ammonoosuc Trail (map 6:D9–D8)

Distances from Bog Dam Rd., east trailhead (1680')

> *to* Landing Camp Trail (1610'): 1.7 mi., 50 ft. (rev. 150 ft.), 50 min.
>
> *to* Bog Dam Rd., west trailhead (1730'): 2.8 mi. (4.4 km.), 150 ft., 1 hr. 30 min.

Landing Camp Trail (WMNF)

This trail links the Upper Ammonoosuc Trail with the southern part of Bog Dam Rd.; it is the remnant of an old trail that connected Bog Dam with Randolph through Hunter's Pass. It leaves the east side of Bog Dam Rd. 6.2 mi. south of its eastern junction with York Pond Rd. (The site of the former logging Camp 19 is located in this vicinity.) Descending gradually, the trail crosses two small streams and passes a clearing at the site of the former Camp 18 at 1.2 mi. It then crosses another small stream, rises over a knoll and descends briefly, then runs nearly level to its end on the Upper Ammonoosuc Trail.

Landing Camp Trail (map 6:D9)

Distance from Bog Dam Rd. (1820')

> *to* Upper Ammonoosuc Trail (1610'): 1.9 mi. (3.0 km.), 0 ft. (rev. 200 ft.), 55 min.

West Milan Trail (WMNF)

This trail runs between York Pond Rd. (FR 13), just west of the bridge over the Upper Ammonoosuc River 1.8 mi. from NH 110, and Spruceville Rd. (FR 460), at a gate 1.5 mi. south of its beginning on NH 110 just west of the junction of NH 110 and NH 110A in West Milan. Much of the first 0.8 mi. passes through private land logged in 1986; close attention to trail signs and paint blazes is advised. The trail follows a snowmobile trail most of the way.

From York Pond Rd. (sign), the trail follows a gravel road for 100 yd., then bears right at a clearing onto an old railroad grade. It soon crosses the Berlin-Milan town line, then crosses Fogg Brook on a snowmobile bridge at 0.8 mi., just after leaving the logged area. It continues and crosses Fifield Brook on a snowmobile bridge at 1.7 mi., then Higgins Brook on a similar bridge at 3.8 mi. The snowmobile trail bears left uphill 50 yd. after this crossing, but the West

Milan Trail continues straight (no sign) on the railroad grade. The snowmobile trail rejoins on the left at 4.2 mi., and, just beyond the point where an old logging road enters left (west) at 4.3 mi., the trail turns right onto another logging road (FR 460) and continues 100 yd. to a gate and another 50 yd. to the Spruceville Rd. trailhead.

West Milan Trail (map 6:C9)

Distance from York Pond Rd. trailhead (1170')

   to Spruceville Rd. (1000'): 4.5 mi. (7.2 km.), 0 ft. (rev. 150 ft.), 2 hr. 15 min.

D. THE NORTH COUNTRY

As C. F. Belcher comments (*Appalachia* XXXIII:37), referring to the Kilkenny region that lies to the south, "this area has built up a legend of isolation and mystery…even though for years it has been the intimate hunting and fishing preserve of those living nearby and a knowing few"—and, one might add, a source of income for the wood-products industries and their employees and suppliers. These remarks apply, with emphasis, to the true North Country, the region north of NH 110 and NH 110A between Groveton and Milan. The appearance of wilderness masks the active presence of logging operations, and the lack of marked and signed trails disguises the extensive network of roads and paths known very well to many local residents and others who enjoy the sense of being far from the crowds. To the south of this region, the mountain backcountry is mostly within the WMNF and has a well-developed trail system. In the great tracts of the North Country there are only a few hiking trails, even on mountains over 3000 ft., and most of these are not regularly maintained by any organization. Many experienced hikers will find pleasure in the area's remoteness, but those who expect to find their trails groomed and manicured are doomed to disappointment, and possibly to the inconvenience of getting lost. The scarcity of settlements and the confusing river drainages make inappropriate the usual advice about following a stream when lost; one must have a map and compass, know how to use them, and be prepared to traverse considerable distances on a compass course to the nearest road, possibly obstructed by swamps or logged areas with slash piles and dense second growth of blackberry, raspberry, and cherry. In general, camping and fires are prohibited throughout the region; due to the large amounts of drying slash in the extensive logged-over areas, the risk of a large forest fire is far greater than in the selectively logged areas to the south, and most landowners are intensely concerned about the possibility of a hiker or camper carelessly starting a major fire.

From the Presidential Range this vast wooded region extends more than 60 mi. north to the Canadian border. The North Country proper is about 30 mi. long from north to south and varies in width from 20 mi. at the southern end to less than 15 mi. at Pittsburg. Its natural boundaries are the Upper Ammonoosuc, Androscoggin, and Magalloway rivers on the south and east and the Connecticut River on the west. To the south of this region, below the line made by NH 110 and NH 110A between the towns of Groveton and Milan, the mountains are still relatively high—two just over 4000 ft.—and grouped compactly into ranges, like those farther south. Above this line lies the true North Country, a region very similar to the adjacent section of Maine. The mountains are lower—only about ten exceed 3500 ft.—and most have wooded summits. The noteworthy mountains, for example the Percy Peaks, Mt. Magalloway, and Rump Mtn., are scattered, separated by long stretches of less interesting terrain. Although the main backbone of the White Mtns.—the divide between the Connecticut River and the streams and lakes to the east—continues north through this country all the way to the Canadian border, it crosses for the most part a broad upland jumbled with medium-sized rounded mountains, with no outstanding summits directly on the divide. Except for Dixville Notch, there is little rugged mountain scenery, although there are several large lakes.

South of NH 110, good public roads are always within a reasonable distance, but there are only three main highways in this northern section. US 3 follows the Connecticut Valley to its uppermost headwaters on the Canadian border beyond the Connecticut Lakes; NH 145 is an alternate road between the towns of Colebrook and Pittsburg. On the east side of the state, NH 16, which continues as ME 16, accompanies the Androscoggin and Magalloway rivers north to the outlet of Lake Aziscohos, then swings east to the Rangeley Lakes. NH 26, the only east-west paved road north of NH 110, crosses from Errol to Colebrook through Dixville Notch. Even public secondary roads are few and short, although the paper companies have constructed an intricate system of good main-haul gravel roads. Many of these have gates or are restricted, and heavy log trucks have the right of way on all of them. These roads are not signed, and the lack of striking landmarks makes travel on them confusing for the inexperienced. Because this northern section is managed for the continuous production of timber, roads and trails may change radically from one year to the next. Visitors may well find it helpful to obtain specific information about current conditions in advance. Among official sources that may be of help are the New Hampshire Fish and Game District Chief and Conservation Officers; information on who these people are and how to contact them can be obtained from New

Hampshire Fish and Game in Concord. The chief landowners are: International Paper, Stratford NH and Augusta ME; Champion International, West Stewartstown NH; Boise Cascade, Woods Department, Rumford ME; Crown Vantage, Groveton NH and Berlin NH; and Diamond International, Groveton NH.

There are only a few trails in this region that are suitable for this guide. Many natural features, particularly ponds, are reached by woods roads passable to four-wheel-drive vehicles or by snowmobile trails, with limited appeal to pedestrian users; but many others, including most mountain summits, are simply pathless. Many trails, including several to fire towers that used to be operated in the North Country, have fallen into disuse or been abandoned, and can no longer be followed except by hikers with fairly sophisticated navigational skills. Whatever the reasons, over the past decade or so there has been a definite decline in the number of trails in this region that are suitable for and open to use by the general hiking public.

One exception to this trend is in the valley of **Nash Stream** north of NH 110 between Groveton and Stark, where a large tract of land has been purchased to be managed by the state of New Hampshire. While major benefits to hikers have yet to develop, there are certainly many enticing possibilities within this tract. Included in this recent purchase are the Percy Peaks and their trail, and most of the trail to Sugarloaf, but not its summit. The **Percy Peaks,** located northeast of Groveton, are the most conspicuous mountains in the northern view from Mt. Washington. The summit of the **North Peak** (3430 ft.) is bare, except for low scrub; that of the **South Peak** (3234 ft.) is wooded, but there are several good viewpoints. The trail described in this guide is on North Percy; there is no maintained trail to South Percy. **Sugarloaf Mtn.** (3710 ft.) rises east of North Stratford at the head of Nash Stream, and its bare rocky peak commands an extensive view, particularly of the Percy Peaks. **Blue Mtn.** (3730 ft.), a trailless peak in the same mountain mass, is the highest peak in New Hampshire outside the WMNF. (There are plans to rename Blue Mtn. for Vicki Bunnell, a local lawyer and judge who was murdered in 1997.) **Devil's Slide** (1590 ft.) is a small mountain with a sheer cliff that rises 600 ft. on the north edge of Stark village. There is no trail, but a very steep and rough ascent may be made up the west slope by cautious bushwhackers.

North of Berlin and east of the main divide lies a region of rivers and lakes of special interest to those who love fishing and canoeing. Among these waterways, which include **Lake Umbagog** and the Androscoggin, Magalloway, and Diamond rivers, there are a few hills from which the view is worth the visit. Much of this land is in private hands, with gates on the access roads. The chief landowners are Dartmouth College and Boise Cascade Corporation. Both are hospitable to hikers but do not usually permit vehicular traffic over their roads, which limits access to the region due to the considerable distances that are frequently involved. The Thirteen Mile Woods, along the Androscoggin River between Milan and Errol, is managed by a consortium of landowners and state agencies. This provides a scenic drive along the river, access to fishing and canoeing, and a public campground at Mollidgewock. The former firewarden's trail to **Signal Mtn.,** a small mountain west of Errol with an abandoned and unsafe fire tower that overlooks this region, has been devastated by logging and can no longer be recommended to the general hiker.

Far to the north of Hanover, above the headwaters of the Androscoggin River, lies the Second College Grant, given to Dartmouth College by the state in 1807 "for the assistance of indigent students." On this grant, between Errol NH and Wilsons Mills ME, the **Swift Diamond** and the **Dead Diamond** come together to form the **Diamond River,** which then enters the Magalloway River from the west. This in turn joins the Androscoggin River at Umbagog Lake. Branches of the Dead Diamond extend well up into the Connecticut Lakes region. (Refer to the USGS Wilsons Mills quad.) Immediately below the confluence of its two branches, the Diamond has carved a wild and beautiful gorge between the Diamond Peaks on the north and Mt. Dustan on the south.

This valley is served by Dartmouth's private logging road, open to pedestrians but not to vehicles without a permit. In the village of Wentworth Location NH, 8.7 mi. north of Errol or 0.5 mi. west of the Maine–New Hampshire state line, this gravel road leaves NH 16 on the west near a small cemetery. The College Grant gatehouse is reached in 1.0 mi. Hikers may leave their cars here, cross the Diamond on a logging bridge, and proceed up through the gorge. Good viewpoints are reached in about 0.5 mi., the Dartmouth Peaks Camp at 1.1 mi., and the Management Center at 1.5 mi. **Hellgate,** another scenic gorge, named because of the trouble river drivers had getting their logs through its narrow channel without jamming, is 12.5 mi. from the gatehouse. For hikers, the principal feature of interest is the path that runs from the Management Center to the fine ledges on the **Diamond Peaks** (2050 ft.). Other short paths to points of interest have also been opened. For further information, consult the gatekeeper in person or by telephone (603-482-3225), or write to the Director of Outdoor Programs, Dartmouth College, PO Box 9, Hanover, NH 03755.

Dixville Notch, the most spectacular spot in the North Country, lies between Sanguinary Mtn. (north) and Mt. Gloriette (south). With the Mohawk River flowing west and Clear Stream east, the notch itself is less than 2 mi. in length with a steep grade on each side, and is only wide enough to admit the highway. The cliff formations, composed of vertical strata, are impressively jagged. Just west of the notch is the Balsams, a hotel and resort complex that includes most of the land west of the notch on both sides of NH 26. The management maintains a number of summer and winter trails—and is actively increasing the network of available paths at the present time—including both cross-country ski and snowmobile trails and some paths that are suitable for horse travel and mountain biking, in addition to hiking opportunities. Part of their operation is the Wilderness Ski Area on the west slopes of Dixville Peak. The Balsams has a guide to paths in the notch, available in summer from the information booth on NH 26 just across from the hotel entrance road or from the outdoor recreation center to the rear of the hotel (in season). The New Hampshire Heritage Trail now passes through this region, traversing the summit of Dixville Peak and descending over Table Rock to the notch.

The mountains in the vicinity of Dixville Notch are relatively low and have no open summits. **Mt. Gloriette** (2630 ft.) forms the south side of the notch and bears the rock formations Table Rock, Old King, Third Cliff, and Profile Cliff. There were once paths to all of them, but only that to Table Rock is now maintained and signed, and hiking to the others is not encouraged because the terrain is very rough and it is easy to stray into dangerous areas. **Table Rock** (2510 ft.) is a cliff that juts out from the north side of Mt. Gloriette, south of the highway. Formed of vertical slabs, it is less than 10 ft. wide at its narrowest point and extends more than 100 ft. from the shoulder of the mountain. The view is spectacular and extensive. It can be climbed by a trail that begins and ends at points 0.5 mi. apart on NH 26 in the heart of the notch. The rock formation known as the Profile can be seen high up on the cliffs by looking south from the high point in the notch. On the north side of the road just west of the high point is **Lake Gloriette** (1846 ft.), an artificial lake on the grounds of the Balsams, formed from the headwaters of the Mohawk River.

Dixville Peak (3490 ft.) is the highest mountain in the vicinity of Dixville Notch, but it is wooded except for the cleared summit. It is accessible by snowmobile trails which have now been designated as part of the New Hampshire Heritage Trail; inquire at the Balsams information booth or outdoor recreation center. **Sanguinary Mtn.** (2710 ft.) forms the north wall of Dixville Notch and is named for the color of its cliffs at sunset. The Sanguinary Ridge Trail, which does not go to the summit, traverses the cliffs north of the notch, running between one trailhead at the hotel entrance road and another at a picnic area north of the highway 1 mi. east of the Balsams. A very short trail (sign) from the same picnic area leads to a small but attractive flume. A little farther east on the south side of the highway is a second picnic area from which a slightly longer trail leads to **Huntingdon Cascades.** There are no maintained trails to **Cave Mtn.** (3191 ft.). There was once a trail to **Mt. Abeniki** (2723 ft.), which is in the process of being restored.

Some 10 mi. above Colebrook, the Connecticut River Valley bends northeast and, just beyond the village of Beecher Falls VT, comes wholly within New Hampshire. Between its source near the Canadian line and the village of Pittsburg, the river passes through a chain of lakes of increasing size, numbered first to fourth in upstream order from the south. A high dam at Pittsburg created **Lake Francis**—the lowest lake in the series, below First Lake—and dams are responsible for the present size of both First and Second lakes. **First Lake** (5.5 mi. long and 2.5 mi. wide at its broadest) and Lake Francis are the largest bodies of water in New Hampshire north of the Presidential Range. US 3, the only major highway in the region, passes close to all of the lakes except **Fourth Lake,** crossing the river from west to east between **Second Lake** and **Third Lake,** and eventually entering Canada. Refer to USGS Second Lake, Indian Stream, and Moose Bog quads. Much of the land in the Connecticut Lakes Region is privately owned. While the owners do not discourage the use of their lands for hiking, they do request that these activities be limited to the daylight hours. Overnight camping and open fires are prohibited. Use of registered vehicles is limited to those roads that are not gated and not posted for road closure. Use of ATVs is prohibited at all times.

The town of Pittsburg is a notable historical curiosity, since it was once—in the minds of its residents, at least—an independent republic. Lying in a region that was claimed by both the United States and Canada until the Webster-Ashburton treaty of 1842 awarded it to the United States, the township was proclaimed by its residents as the Republic of Indian Stream in 1832; this tiny republic, which had its own written constitution, managed its own affairs for three years until trouble with the large, quarrelsome neighbor to the north led to its occupation by the large, quarrelsome neighbor to the south. This fascinating piece of New England frontier history is chronicled in *Indian Stream Republic,* a recently published book by Daniel Doan (who was best known as a writer of hiking trail guides).

Mt. Magalloway (3383 ft.), located east of First Connecticut Lake, overlooks the Middle Branch of the Dead Diamond River; it has the only existing mountain trail of any consequence in the Connecticut Lakes region. A fire tower (no longer operated most of the time) affords excellent views; there are also good views from a ledge near the summit. **Deer Mtn.** (2997 ft.) is located west of the Connecticut River, between Second and Third lakes. The former fire tower has been removed, eliminating the unique view, particularly over the wilderness lying north toward the Canadian border, that was once available from its summit. The upper part of the former firewarden's trail can probably still be followed, but it can be reached only by a rough bushwhack through second growth and slash, since the lower part of the trail has been obliterated by logging. **Fourth Connecticut Lake** (2670 ft.), a little mountain tarn northwest of Third Lake and just south of the Canadian border, is the ultimate source of the Connecticut River. Once considered as remote a spot as the mountains had to offer, it is located in a 78-acre reservation given by Champion International to the Nature Conservancy in 1990, and is now accessible from US 3 by a maintained trail.

   Rump Mtn. (3654 ft.) is located in Maine just east of the New Hampshire border, 7 mi. south of the Canadian line. Rump Mtn. was formerly known as Mt. Carmel, or Camel's Rump, from its appearance from the southwest; it can best be viewed from the far side of the dam on Second Connecticut Lake a few yards from US 3. This attractive but remote mountain has views of three states and Quebec province, and an unusual view of Bigelow Mtn. near Stratton ME; the dubious claim is sometimes made that in clear weather Katahdin may be visible. Rump Mtn. is on land now owned by the Boise Cascade Corporation. Although the company does not object to hikers crossing its lands, there may be restrictions on vehicle travel and camping is not permitted. It would probably be useful to contact the company's Woods Department in Rumford ME or its district forester in West Milan NH. The most convenient approach to Rump Mtn. is probably from the East Inlet Rd., ascending to the narrow east-west ridge near the state line and following this ridge to the summit ledge on the far eastern knob; but only hikers thoroughly experienced in wilderness navigation should consider this trip, since the route-finding is not easy and it is possible to wind up a very long way from the starting point. Refer to the USGS Rump Mtn. quad.

THE TRAILS

Percy Peaks Trail (WMNF)

This trail ascends North Percy Peak from Nash Stream Rd. Leaving NH 110 2.6 mi. east of Groveton, go north on Emerson Rd. 2.2 mi. until the paved road makes a prominent curve to the right (east); here the gravel Nash Stream Rd. turns left (north). Formerly owned and maintained by Diamond International, this road has usually been closed during the winter and almost always from spring thaw through Memorial Day weekend in the past. Follow the road for 2.7 mi. to a small parking area (sign) on the east side; the trail (sign) begins 50 yd. farther up, also on the east side of the road. Refer to the AMC North Country–Mahoosuc Range map (map #6) and the USGS Percy Peaks quad.

The current trail is a combination of the lower part of the former West Side Trail and the Notch Trail. The upper part of the former West Side Trail has been officially closed. This section of trail, one of the most spectacular and challenging in New England, was laid out by Robert and Miriam Underhill, both noted rock climbers who delighted in finding short but challenging routes to good viewpoints. Though it crossed rock slabs that are steep and exposed where use of hands is required, it was not a rock climb in the technical sense, nor was it more difficult than some other officially maintained trails, such as the North Slide of Tripyramid or the Huntington Ravine Trail or the Holt Trail on Cardigan, although like those trails it was hazardous in wet or icy weather. (The only recorded hiking fatality on this mountain occurred on the slippery slabs below the former trail junction, along which the trail still passes.) The route can probably still be followed by those interested in undertaking a rewarding challenge at their own risk; particular caution should be exercised on wet spots, and the much steeper slabs to the south (right side) of the route should be avoided.

South Percy, which offers interesting views from a number of ledges near the summit, has no maintained trail, but an obscure footway with some flags leads to it from the col between the peaks. It is also a very steep but fairly short and relatively easy bushwhack that is within the capacity of many cautious though inexperienced bushwhackers; the route-finding is quite straightforward—as a matter of fact, the route seems to be nearly straight up—but one must be careful to stay away from some low cliffs and excessively steep ledges, particularly on the descent. For those interested in making this ascent, it might be best to climb North Percy first, then study South Percy carefully while descending back to the notch.

Leaving Nash Stream Rd., the trail ascends moderately for 0.3 mi., then bears right, crosses a small stream, and follows logging roads at easy to moderate grades, generally parallel to and north of Slide Brook. At 1.0 mi. the trail turns left at a large boulder, becomes steeper, and soon reaches the base of the lower slabs. The slabs in this area are mossy and extremely slippery when wet; stay to the right (south) of the slabs, ignoring any remaining blazes painted on the rocks to the left (such blazes were placed in an unusually dry year). At 1.2 mi. the trail reaches the former trail junction, where the old trail continued straight up the ledges; the current trail now turns right and follows the former Notch Trail.

The trail now traverses several ledges, staying north of the low point in the notch. Toward the east side of the notch a flagged route to South Percy leads right (south). Leaving the notch at 1.7 mi., the trail swings left (north) and ascends along a rocky outcrop with increasingly wide views. It comes out on open ledges with scattered scrub and follows blazes and cairns to the summit, from which there are good views in all directions.

Percy Peaks Trail (map 6:B7)

Distances from Nash Stream Rd. (1242')

> *to* former Notch Trail junction (2500'): 1.2 mi., 1250 ft., 1 hr. 15 min.

> *to* North Percy summit (3410'): 2.2 mi. (3.5 km.), 2150 ft., 2 hr. 10 min.

Sugarloaf Trail (WMNF)

This trail provides access to the bare rock summit of Sugarloaf Mtn., which commands sweeping views of the Nash Stream valley and surrounding areas. The trail ascends the east side of the mountain by a direct route, following a logging road that was the firewarden's trail to the former fire tower. From NH 110 2.6 mi. east of Groveton, take Emerson Rd. north until it swings right (east) at 2.2 mi., then follow the gravel Nash Stream Rd. left (north) for 8.3 mi. to a point 60 yd. beyond its crossing of Nash Stream. Park off the road in a grassy area. Refer to the USGS Percy Peaks quad.

The trail (sign) passes to the left of a camp, crosses a small brook, and continues through an open field. It then enters the woods and swings northwest, ascending at a steady grade to the firewarden's cabins (abandoned) at 1.6 mi. A short distance above the cabins, near a spring, the trail bears right at a fork (the left branch is an overgrown alternate route to the summit). It climbs to the ridge north of the summit, turns left (south), and reaches the summit ledges.

Sugarloaf Trail (USGS Percy Peaks quad)

Distances from Nash Stream Rd. (1530')

> *to* the warden's cabins (3220'): 1.6 mi., 1700 ft., 1 hr. 40 min.

> *to* Sugarloaf Mtn. summit (3710'): 2.1 mi. (3.4 km.), 2200 ft., 2 hr. 10 min.

Diamond Peaks Trail (DOC)

The Diamond Peaks are three small peaks (West Peak, 2010 ft., East Peak, 2050 ft., and South Peak, 1994 ft.) that cap a nearly semicircular ridge which rises between the Dead Diamond and Magalloway rivers. Their most attractive feature is a high cliff on the concave side of the ridge, facing south, with a number of viewpoints. Refer to the USGS Wilsons Mills quad.

The trail begins 1.5 mi. from the gatehouse, on the north side of the clearing across the road from the Dartmouth Management Center. It crosses a cutover area, then enters the woods and begins to ascend. At 0.3 mi. a side trail leads left 80 yd. to Alice Ledge, with a view of the Management Center area. The main trail turns gradually more to the south and climbs over the relatively flat west peak with several good outlooks, descends slightly, and climbs to the slightly higher and much sharper east summit, where there is another viewpoint.

Diamond Peaks Trail (USGS Wilsons Mills quad)

Distance from the Management Center (1350')

   to Diamond Peaks, East Peak (2050'): 1.1 mi. (1.8 km.), 700 ft., 55 min.

Table Rock Trail (NHDP)

This short, rough loop path begins and ends on NH 26 and gives access to Table Rock, which is perhaps the most spectacular viewpoint in the White Mtns., consisting of a narrow ledge rising several hundred feet over a cliff face. There may be better scenery in the White Mtns., but few trails reach airier spots from which to view it. The area is covered by the USGS Dixville Notch quad, but the trail is not shown on it. The east trailhead, which gives access to the much steeper section of the loop (called by the Balsams' map the Table Rock Climbing Trail, trail "D2," and now a part of the New Hampshire Heritage Trail), is in a parking lot 0.1 mi. east of the main entrance to the Balsams. The west trailhead (where the trail is called the Table Rock Hiking Trail, trail "D1," and is also designated as part of the Dixville Heritage Trail loop) is 0.4 mi. west of the main entrance to the Balsams near a "Pedestrian Crossing" sign. Due to the recent and ongoing expansion of the Balsams trail network, hikers may encounter more trail junctions and different trail designations than those described below, but the Table Rock Trail is now well signed and marked and can be easily followed.

Beginning at the west trailhead, the trail follows a cross-country ski trail (signed as "E", or #5) for 25 yd., then diverges left on the trail signed as "D1" and climbs moderately to the height-of-land. From there it descends gradually 50 yd., then turns left on the trail signed "D2" and follows this trail 25 yd., passing a junction on the right with the Three Brothers Trail (a part of the Dixville Heritage Trail loop), to the junction with the spur path that leads 50 yd. to the left out onto Table Rock. From the spur junction, continuing to the east trailhead, the trail turns right and virtually plunges down to NH 26. There are several intersecting paths in this area and caution should be used, particularly in descending, as the signs are placed for ascent only. In descending by the easier western route, enter the woods above Table Rock, avoid a path west, and take the next right (west) fork.

Table Rock Trail (USGS Dixville Notch quad)

Distances from parking area for east trailhead (1930')

> *to* Table Rock (2510'): 0.3 mi., 600 ft., 25 min.

> *to* west trailhead (1870'): 1.0 mi. (1.6 km.), 600 ft. (rev. 650 ft.), 50 min.

Sanguinary Ridge Trail (NHDP)

This trail provides access to the spectacular views from the open rocks of Sanguinary Ridge. Beginning and ending on NH 26, it is marked with directional signs and long pale yellow paint blazes, and is designated as part of the Dixville Heritage Trail loop. It is shown on the USGS Dixville Notch quad. The western trailhead is at the main entrance to the Balsams. The eastern trailhead is 1.0 mi. to the east at the Flume Brook picnic area of the Dixville Notch State Wayside, a rest area on the north side of NH 26 east of the notch, where there is also a short trail to the small flume on Clear Stream. The lower end of the eastern part may be signed as the Flume Brook Trail.

Leaving the picnic area, it climbs a scenic ridge, following an old 1920s trail in places as well as the blue-blazed state park boundary, through balsam and spruce forests with some hardwoods. Along the ridgecrest and overlooking the notch are outlook points with views of Table Rock and Old King cliffs, and also toward Errol and the Mahoosuc Range. At 1.0 mi. it crosses the height-of-land and switchbacks down to the most spectacular viewpoint, a rocky pinnacle overlooking Lake Gloriette and the Balsams Hotel. The trail continues to descend by graded switchbacks past Index Rock to the entrance road at the Balsams Hotel.

Sanguinary Ridge Trail (USGS Dixville Notch quad)

Distances from the Flume Brook picnic area (1600')

> *to* the height-of-land (2530'): 1.0 mi., 950 ft., 1 hr.

> *to* the Balsams Hotel entrance road (1860'): 1.5 mi. (2.4 km.), 950 ft. (rev. 700 ft.), 1 hr. 15 min.

Mount Magalloway Trail

To reach the trail to the fire tower on this peak, take the gravel road that turns southeast from US 3 4.7 mi. north of the First Connecticut dam. This is a main-haul logging road on which trucks have the right of way. At 1.2 mi. cross the Connecticut River on a bridge and continue straight. Bear left at 2.3 mi. and again at 2.9 mi. Turn right at 5.3 mi. and again at 6.3 mi. At 8.7 mi. from US 3 the good road ends at a turnaround, and the trail continues on the firewarden's jeep road to the summit. It may be possible to drive another 0.4 mi. up the road. The Bobcat Trail, an alternate route to the summit, is a footpath that may offer better footing than the old jeep trail, although it has been maintained only sporadically in the past. Refer to the USGS Magalloway Mtn. quad. This is a remote area, and in the past trail conditions have changed significantly over relatively short periods of time, but the principal trail (the old jeep road) has almost always been fairly easy to find and follow.

The trail continues on the rough, eroded jeep road, passing a cabin and a spring in 0.1 mi. Beyond the cabin, the trail ascends moderately on the old road with a few relatively steep grades to the summit, reaching the fire tower at 0.8 mi. There are excellent views southeast toward Aziscohos Lake and northeast to Rump Mtn. A short trail behind the warden's cabin (signed "Overlook") leads to the top of the ledges, from which there is also a good view.

Mount Magalloway Trail (USGS Magalloway Mtn. quad)
Distance from gravel road (2400')

> *to* Mt. Magalloway summit and fire tower (3384'): 0.8 mi. (1.2 km.), 1000 ft., 55 min.

Fourth Connecticut Lake Trail

This path begins at the US Customs station at the Canadian border on US 3. Hikers are asked to register at the customs office. Parking is available nearby. Refer to the USGS Second Connecticut Lake and Prospect Hill quads. From the boundary marker just north of the customs building, follow the international boundary uphill to the left (west). The boundary is a wide swath cut through the forest and marked at irregular intervals by brass discs set in concrete. At 0.6 mi. leave the boundary on the left (south) on a well-defined path (sign) and descend gradually 200 yd. to Fourth Lake.

Fourth Connecticut Lake Trail (USGS Second Connecticut Lake quad)
Distance from US Customs station (2360')

> *to* Fourth Connecticut Lake (2670'): 0.7 mi. (1.2 km.), 300 ft., 30 min.

Section 13

Middle Connecticut River Mountains

This section covers the chain of medium-sized mountains that rise east of and roughly parallel to the Connecticut River between Hanover and Glencliff. This range, which includes Moose Mtn., Holts Ledge, Smarts Mtn., Mt. Cube, Mt. Mist, and Webster Slide Mtn., is traversed by the Appalachian Trail and the network of side trails maintained by the Dartmouth Outing Club (DOC). A substantial portion of this network, both Appalachian Trail and side trails, has been relocated in the last decade, and a considerable amount of completely new trail has been constructed. The boundaries of this region are NH 10 on the west, US 4 on the south, NH 118 on the east, and NH 25 on the east and north. The northeastern part of this section, including all the trails described in this section that are located north of NH 25A, is shown on the AMC Moosilauke–Kinsman map (map #4). The region south of NH 25A is covered by USGS quads, but the most useful maps for this section are the Appalachian Trail Conference's map of the AT from Hanover to Glencliff and a map published by the DOC showing the DOC trail network, which consists of the Appalachian Trail and its side trails from Pomfret VT to Kinsman Notch in New Hampshire. This map—which may be obtained from Director of Trails and Shelters, Box 9, Robinson Hall, Dartmouth College, Hanover, NH 03755—includes all trails described in this section. Unless otherwise noted, all sections of the Appalachian Trail are described from south to north.

After reaching the New Hampshire boundary at the bridge over the Connecticut River, close to the western edge of both the town of Hanover and the campus of Dartmouth College, the Appalachian Trail passes through Hanover and proceeds eastward out of town to a region of low hills, then finally reaches Moose Mtn., the southernmost mountain of consequence in the chain. From here northward the AT is never far from the divide between the Connecticut and Pemigewasset drainages, but the mountains that it passes over do not really form a range, since they are mostly clearly separate peaks rising from a hilly upland with no significant connecting ridges between them. **Moose Mtn. (North Peak,** 2313 ft.; **South Peak,** 2293 ft.), is located in Hanover; the Moose Mountain Trail (new route of the AT) now crosses the South Peak and passes near the summit of the North Peak. Passing through the notch between the two peaks is the old Province Rd. (known in the Hanover area as Wolfeboro Rd.), laid out in 1772 to connect Governor Wentworth's residence in Wolfeboro with the Connecticut Valley towns, where the residents were becoming disaffected with the royal government in New Hampshire. **Holts Ledge** (2110 ft.) has good views to the east and southeast, though access to the outlook is often restricted during the season when peregrine falcons, who nest on the cliffs below the ledge in most years, are raising their young. **Smarts Mtn.** (3238 ft.), located in Lyme, affords interesting views of a less-known country from its abandoned fire tower. **Mt. Cube** (2909 ft.), located in Orford, has several fine viewpoints and is one of the more rewarding small mountains in this part of New Hampshire. **Webster Slide** Mtn. (2184 ft.) rises steeply above **Wachipauka Pond,** with excellent views from the top of the ledge that plunges toward the shore of the pond, while nearby **Mt. Mist** (2230 ft.) is wooded but has a fine outlook.

CAMPING

Most of this area is private land, where camping and fires are permitted only at official campsites. On the publicly owned lands of the Appalachian Trail corridor—all the way from Hanover to Glencliff—camping is permitted, but not within 200 feet of the Appalachian Trail itself except at the official campsites. The northern part of this section—north of NH 25A—is mostly in the WMNF, where camping is permitted in accordance with the usual restrictions.

Forest Protection Areas

The WMNF has established a number of Forest Protection Areas (FPAs)—formerly known as Restricted Use Areas—where camping and wood or charcoal fires are prohibited throughout the year. The specific areas are under continual review, and areas are added to or subtracted from the list in order to provide the greatest amount of protection to areas subject to damage by excessive camping, while imposing the lowest level of restrictions possible. A general list of FPAs in this section follows, but since there are often major changes from year to year, one should obtain current information on FPAs from the WMNF.

(1) No camping is permitted above treeline (where trees are less than 8 ft. tall), except in winter, and then only in places where there is at least

two feet of snow cover on the groundæbut not on any frozen body of water. The point where the restricted area begins is marked on most trails with small signs, but the absence of such signs should not be construed as proof of the legality of a site.

(2) No camping is permitted within a quarter-mile of any trailhead, picnic area, or any facility for overnight accommodation such as a hut, cabin, shelter, tentsite, or campground, except as designated at the facility itself.

Established Trailside Campsites

Velvet Rocks Shelter (DOC) is located 1.8 mi. north of the center of Hanover on a spur path 0.2 mi. from the Velvet Rocks Trail (AT).

Moose Mountain Shelter (DOC) is on the Clark Pond Loop on the east side of Moose Mtn., 0.3 mi. east of the Moose Mountain Trail (AT).

Trapper John Shelter (DOC) is near Holts Ledge, 1.0 mi. from Cummins Pond Rd. via the Holts Ledge Trail (AT) and a spur path.

Smarts Campsite (DOC), with tent platforms, is near the summit of Smarts Mtn. The former firewarden's cabin is also maintained as a shelter by the DOC.

Hexacuba Shelter (DOC) is an innovative hexagonal shelter for ten people on a spur path 0.2 mi. off the Kodak Trail (AT), 1.6 mi. south of the south peak of Mt. Cube. The former Mount Cube Shelter, 0.2 mi. from Quinttown Rd. via the South Cube Trail, still exists.

THE TRAILS

Velvet Rocks Trail (DOC)

This section of the Appalachian Trail passes through the town of Hanover and continues through the more rural outskirts of the town to the foot of Moose Mtn., passing Velvet Rocks Shelter. Strictly speaking, only a 3.7-mi. segment in the middle of this trail is officially known as the Velvet Rocks Trail, but for convenience the remaining sections of the AT between the Connecticut River and Three Mile Rd. at the base Moose Mtn. are included here. As this is generally a moderately populated area, a great deal of the trail is necessarily on roads of various kinds, and though there are interesting segments, the main purpose of this part of the AT is to cross the Connecticut Valley and connect the mountains of Vermont with the mountains of New Hampshire.

Beginning at the state line on the Connecticut River bridge between Hanover NH and Norwich VT, the AT follows West Wheelock St. to the square at the town common in Hanover. Turning right on North Main St., it soon turns left onto Lebanon St. and merges into NH 120 at 1.2 mi. In 100 yd. it turns left (sign) toward Chase Field and traverses the south end of the field on a gravel road, passes a gate, and enters the woods at 1.4 mi. At this point the segment officially known as the Velvet Rocks Trail begins. The trail swings left and ascends past a limited north outlook, and at 2.1 mi. a spur path leads left 0.2 mi. to Velvet Rocks Shelter, where the Old Velvet Rocks Trail continues another 0.5 mi. to East Wheelock St. just west of Balch Hill Rd. At 2.6 mi., a spur path leads left 0.1 mi. to the Old Velvet Rocks Trail 0.3 mi. above East Wheelock St., and another spur path descends left 0.2 mi. to a spring. At 3.1 mi. the Trescott Road Spur descends 0.4 mi. to Trescott Rd. (the continuation of East Wheelock St.). The main trail passes a campsite, crosses the height-of-land, and descends with some ups and downs to Trescott Rd. at 5.1 mi., where the official Velvet Rocks Trail ends.

The trail now ascends through a pine plantation, turns left on an old logging road at 5.8 mi. and follows it for 100 yd., then bears left off the road and ascends, turning sharp right at a stone wall, then sharp right again onto Paine Rd. (dirt). At 6.5 mi. it turns right onto Dogford Rd. (paved), and at 7.0 mi. it turns right onto the Etna–Hanover Center Rd. (paved). It passes a cemetery and turns left into the woods, then ascends gradually through a region of old fields with stone walls. At 9.2 mi. it turns right onto an old trail segment, then bears off it to the right at 9.6 mi. and soon reaches Three Mile Rd. at a spot that can also be reached by following dirt roads east, then south from Hanover Center.

Velvet Rocks Trail (DOC map)
Distances from Connecticut River bridge (390')

- *to* Velvet Rocks Trail, official west end (530'): 1.4 mi., 150 ft., 45 min.

- *to* Velvet Rocks Shelter spur (1000'): 2.1 mi., 600 ft., 1 hr. 20 min.

- *to* Velvet Rocks Trail, official east end (940'): 5.1 mi., 1200 ft. (rev. 650 ft.), 3 hr. 10 min.

- *to* Three Mile Rd. (1400'): 9.7 mi. (15.6 km.), 2050 ft. (rev. 400 ft.), 5 hr. 55 min.

Moose Mountain Trail (DOC)

This is the Appalachian Trail from Three Mile Rd. to Goose Pond Rd. Leaving Three Mile Rd., the trail descends across Mink Brook and then ascends to a junction at 0.4 mi. Here the Fred Harris Trail leaves left for Goose Pond Rd. The Moose Mountain Trail climbs moderately past a clearing with views to the southeast and reaches the summit of the South Peak of Moose Mtn. at 1.9 mi. It then descends to the notch between the two peaks of Moose Mtn., where it crosses the Clark Pond Loop at 2.4 mi. The Clark Pond Loop leads left (west) 0.6 mi. to the Fred Harris Trail and right (east) 0.3 mi. to Moose Mountain Shelter. This short path, the remnant of a much longer trail that is no longer maintained, now consists entirely of a segment of the historic old Province Rd. (known locally as Wolfeboro Rd.).

Ascending from the notch, the trail ascends at easy to moderate grades with a few minor descents to its high point on the North Peak of Moose Mtn. at 3.9 mi., where there is a view to the southwest. It then descends past a fine northeast outlook toward Smarts Mtn. (the best viewpoint on the mountain), crosses Hewes Brook at 5.2 mi., and continues to Goose Pond Rd., which it reaches at a point 3.5 mi. east of NH 10.

Moose Mountain Trail (DOC map)
Distances from Three Mile Rd. (1400')

- *to* Clark Pond Loop (2000'): 2.4 mi., 1000 ft. (rev. 400 ft.), 1 hr. 40 min.

- *to* Goose Pond Rd. (930'): 5.6 mi. (8.9 km.), 1450 ft. (rev. 1550 ft.), 3 hr. 30 min.

Fred Harris Trail (DOC)

This trail begins on Goose Pond Rd., 3.1 mi. east of NH 10 and 0.4 mi. west of the Appalachian Trail crossing, and runs west of Moose Mtn. to the Moose

Mountain Trail (AT) 0.4 mi. east of Three Mile Rd., making possible a loop hike over Moose Mtn. This is the former route of the AT and makes use of a variety of logging roads and country dirt roads. Although signs are still in place, the part of the trail north of the Clark Pond Loop has received no maintenance for several years. There is a great deal of blowdown, but most of the trail is not difficult to follow since the old roads it uses are fairly plain. However, it is poorly marked and the correct route is hard to find at several old road junctions (though a wrong turn in most cases simply leads to the road that parallels the trail to the west).

The trail follows a series of roads south from Goose Pond Rd., climbing moderately to a height-of-land, then descending at mostly easy grades to a road that is passable to autos. It then turns left off this road just past a house on the left and passes just to the right of the house, almost through the yard. At 3.1 mi. the Clark Pond Trail diverges left (east) to cross the AT between the two peaks of Moose Mtn. and continue to Moose Mountain Shelter. The Fred Harris Trail passes Harris Junction at 3.7 mi., where a side trail leads left to Harris Cabin (private). The Fred Harris Trail then passes a junction on the right with an old route of the AT, crosses Mink Brook and a DOC ski trail, and continues to the Moose Mountain Trail (AT) 0.4 mi. from Three Mile Rd.

Fred Harris Trail (DOC map)

Distances from Goose Pond Rd. (890')

> *to* Clark Pond Loop (1600'): 3.1 mi., 900 ft. (rev. 200 ft.), 2 hr.
>
> *to* Moose Mountain Trail (1400'): 4.0 mi. (6.4 km.), 900 ft. (rev. 200 ft.), 2 hr. 25 min.

Holts Ledge Trail (DOC)

This is the segment of the Appalachian Trail that crosses between Goose Pond Rd. and Cummins Pond Rd. (Lyme–Dorchester Rd.), passing over Holts Ledge. The endangered peregrine falcon has nested there in recent years, and portions of the ledge may be closed during the nesting season to prevent disturbance to the birds. The northern terminus is on Cummins Pond Rd., just west of the Dartmouth Skiway, and the south terminus is on Goose Pond Rd., 3.5 mi. east of NH 10. Because Holts Ledge is more frequently ascended from the north, this trail is described in the north to south direction.

Note: For AT through-hikers or others interested in a walking route between the north trailhead of the Holts Ledge Trail and the south trailhead of the Lambert Ridge Trail, there is a section of the AT 1.9 mi. long that runs roughly parallel to Cummins Pond Rd. At the fork in the Cummins Pond Rd. 3.2 mi. east of NH 10, near the base of the Dartmouth Skiway, the trail follows the left (northeast) fork for 0.2 mi. to the edge of an overgrown field, which it enters, marked by a blazed post, and crosses a snowmobile trail. It ascends gradually, crosses a brook, then descends gradually until it enters an old road at a granite AT mileage post. It follows this old road to Cummins Pond Rd., where it turns left and crosses a bridge to the trailhead for the Lambert Ridge Trail (AT) and Ranger Trail.

Leaving Cummins Pond Rd., the trail ascends, much of the time parallel to a ski trail (do not hike on ski trail). At 0.8 mi. it passes a side path to the right that leads in 0.3 mi. to Trapper John Shelter and continues to ascend, turning sharp right onto the Papoose Ski Trail and following it for 0.2 mi., then leaving it on the right. The trail turns sharp right where a fence 50 yd. to the left protects the falcon nesting area, and climbs past an excellent northeast outlook to the crest of Holts Ledge at 1.7 mi. The trail descends, turning sharp right at 1.9 mi., then follows a wood road, swinging east and then south past a beaver flowage before ascending gradually to Goose Pond Rd.

Holts Ledge Trail (DOC map)
Distances from Cummins Pond Rd. (870')

> *to* crest of Holts Ledge (2100'): 1.7 mi., 1250 ft., 1 hr. 30 min.

> *to* Goose Pond Rd. (930'): 3.7 mi. (5.9 km.), 1250 ft. (rev. 1200 ft.), 2 hr. 30 min.

Lambert Ridge Trail (DOC)

This is the segment of the Appalachian Trail between Cummins Pond Rd. (Lyme–Dorchester Rd.), 2.9 mi. east of Lyme Center, and the summit of Smarts Mtn. Ascending from the road moderately by switchbacks, it reaches a ledge with a view east at 0.8 mi. and continues along the ridge with occasional views. At 1.8 mi. there is a fine view of the summit ahead, and the trail descends into a sag with a small stream at 2.3 mi. It then swings right (east) and ascends again to join the Ranger Trail at 3.3 mi. At 3.7 mi. a spur leads right 50 yd. to a tent platform with a fine view, and at 3.9 mi. the J Trail diverges right and carries the Appalachian Trail northward. The Ranger Trail continues another 50 yd. to the fire tower, passing a spur 30 yd. right to the warden's cabin. Water is often available in a spring 0.2 mi. north of the summit on the blue-blazed Daniel Doan Trail, which descends to Quinttown Rd.

Lambert Ridge Trail (DOC map)

Distances from Cummins Pond Rd. (1110')

   to Ranger Trail (2600'): 3.3 mi., 1800 ft. (rev. 300 ft.), 2 hr. 35 min.

   to J Trail/Daniel Doan Trail (3230'): 3.9 mi. (6.2 km.), 2400 ft., 3 hr. 10 min.

Ranger Trail (DOC)

This trail, the old firewarden's trail to the fire tower on Smarts Mtn., ascends to the summit from Cummins Pond Rd. (Lyme–Dorchester Rd.) 2.9 mi. east of Lyme Center (the same place where the Lambert Ridge Trail begins). The upper 0.6 mi. coincides with the Lambert Ridge Trail and is part of the Appalachian Trail. The lower section, which may not be maintained, is not signed or blazed but is easy to follow.

   The trail starts up a woods road, with Grant Brook on the right (east). The road ends at a garage at 1.9 mi., and the trail turns right across the brook. The brook is recrossed at 2.3 mi. (last reliable water), and the grade steepens as the trail becomes rough, eroded, and slippery in places. At 3.0 mi. the Lambert Ridge Trail (AT) enters on the left, and the Ranger Trail coincides with it from here to the summit. At 3.5 mi. a spur leads right 50 yd. to a tent platform with a fine view, and at 3.6 mi. the J Trail diverges right and carries the Appalachian Trail northward. The Ranger Trail continues another 50 yd. to the fire tower, passing a spur 30 yd. right to the warden's cabin, where the Daniel Doan Trail descends to Quinttown Rd.

Ranger Trail (DOC map)

Distances from Cummins Pond Rd. (1110')

   to Lambert Ridge Trail (2600'): 3.0 mi., 1500 ft., 2 hr. 15 min.

   to Smarts Mtn. summit (3238'): 3.6 mi. (5.8 km.), 2100 ft., 2 hr. 50 min.

Daniel Doan Trail (DOC)

This recently restored trail along the route of the former Mousley Brook Trail ascends Smarts Mtn. from the northwest along the valley of Mousley Brook. It is named in honor of Daniel Doan, the author of the first of the popular *Fifty Hikes* series, who was a Dartmouth alumnus. It uses old logging roads for most of its length and is easy to follow on the descent, but has several poorly marked junctions where care must be used to follow the trail when ascending. From NH 25A 3.9 mi. east of its junction with NH 10 (where there are signs for "Quinttown Rd." and "Thomson Tree Farm"), follow Jacobs Brook Rd. 1.8 mi. east to a crossroads called Quinttown. Jacobs Brook Rd. continues east (straight ahead) from Quinttown past a locked gate to the J Trail (AT south) and Kodak Trail (AT north). For the Daniel Doan Trail, follow Quinttown Rd. south from Quinttown for 1.0 mi., past a large farm (right) and several small camps (left), to the trailhead. The road may not be passable in winter, and several bridges are in poor condition, so it may be necessary to walk at least part of the way from Quinttown.

The trail leaves the left (east) side of Quinttown Rd. and follows an old woods road, bearing right in 0.1 mi. at an unmarked fork. It passes an old grassy road (right) and almost immediately bears right again and passes the ruins of an old camp. Beyond this point the trail is easy to follow. At 1.3 mi. it bears left to bypass a wet, eroded section of the old trail, then rejoins the old route just before crossing Mousley Brook at 1.7 mi. It ascends along the south bank of the brook, then veers away to the right and becomes steeper, narrowing to a footpath as it ascends over scattered ledges. At 2.7 mi. the grade eases and the trail passes several springs (left) and the old warden's cabin (right) before reaching the summit and the renovated fire tower, which provides fine views. Here the J Trail turns left and the Lambert Ridge Trail (along with the coinciding Ranger Trail) continues straight.

Daniel Doan Trail (DOC map)
Distances from Quinttown Rd. (1350')

to Mousley Brook crossing (2200'): 1.7 mi., 850 ft., 1 hr. 15 min.

to Smarts Mtn. summit (3238'): 3.0 mi. (4.8 km.), 1900 ft., 2 hr. 25 min.

J Trail (DOC)

This is the segment of the Appalachian Trail from the summit of Smarts Mtn. to Jacobs Brook Rd. 2.9 mi. from NH 25A. Jacobs Brook Rd. leaves NH 25A 3.9 mi. east of its junction with NH 10 (where there are signs for "Quinttown Rd." and "Thomson Tree Farm"); at 1.8 mi., at the crossroads called Quinttown where Quinttown Rd. diverges right (south), Jacobs Brook Rd. continues straight through the crossroads and reaches a locked gate at 2.4 mi. The trailhead is 0.5 mi. past the gate; in winter or mud season, it may be necessary to walk the 1.1 mi. from Quinttown Rd. This trail is described from north to south.

The trail descends gradually and crosses a suspension bridge over the South Branch of Jacobs Brook and ascends through long-overgrown pastures. It reaches evergreen woods as the grade becomes easier on the J-shaped ridge at 2.3 mi. At 4.0 mi. the trail swings right (west) and descends slightly, passes a spring located on the left, then continues to the coinciding Lambert Ridge and Ranger trails at 4.3 mi. The Ranger Trail continues another 50 yd. to the fire tower, passing a spur that leads to the right 30 yd. to the warden's cabin. Water is often available in a spring 0.2 mi. north of the summit on the blue-blazed Daniel Doan Trail, which descends to Quinttown Rd. and offers a alternative return route to the J Trail trailhead.

J Trail (DOC map)

Distance from Jacobs Brook Rd. at locked gate (1300')

   to Lambert Ridge Trail (3230'): 4.3 mi. (6.9 km.), 1950 ft., 3 hr. 10 min.

Kodak Trail (DOC)

This is the segment of the Appalachian Trail from Jacobs Brook Rd. 2.4 mi. from NH 25A to the main (south) peak of Mt. Cube. Jacobs Brook Rd. leaves NH 25A 3.9 mi. east of its junction with NH 10 (where there are signs for "Quinttown Rd." and "Thomson Tree Farm"); at 1.8 mi., at the crossroads called Quinttown where Quinttown Rd. diverges right (south), Jacobs Brook Rd. continues straight through the crossroads and reaches a locked gate at 2.4 mi. The trailhead is 0.5 mi. past the gate; in winter or mud season, it may be necessary to walk the 1.1 mi. from Quinttown Rd.

   The trail ascends moderately from the road, swinging right as it climbs to the top of Eastman Ledges at 1.1 mi., where there is a fine view of Smarts Mtn. The trail descends and swings to the north, passing over a low ridge and descending to cross the North Branch of Jacobs Brook at 1.6 mi. At 2.0 mi. a spur path leads right uphill 0.2 mi. to hexagonal Hexacuba Shelter; the water source for the shelter is the brook at the spur path junction. The main trail soon ascends roughly by switchbacks to the southwest ridge of Mt. Cube and reaches ledges with southwest views. It descends into a sag at 3.1 mi. and then climbs on scattered ledges to the bare summit of Mt. Cube, where the South Cube Trail enters from the left and the Mount Cube Trail from the right.

Kodak Trail (DOC map)

Distance from Jacobs Brook Rd. at locked gate (1300')

   to Mt. Cube summit (2909'): 3.5 mi. (5.6 mi.), 1800 ft. (rev. 200 ft.), 2 hr. 40 min.

Mount Cube Trail (DOC)

This is the segment of the Appalachian Trail from the main (south) summit of Mt. Cube to NH 25A at a point 4.6 mi. west of its junction with NH 25 and 1.9 mi. east of its high point near Mt. Cube Farm. It is described here from north to south.

Leaving NH 25A, the trail ascends gradually on an old woods road past stone walls and a cellar hole, then crosses a gravel road at 0.5 mi. and swings right and narrows. At 1.5 mi. it turns left onto an old logging road, follows it for 50 yd., then turns right off it and soon crosses Brackett Brook. At 2.5 mi. there is a stone chair on the right. At 3.3 mi. the trail reaches the old route of the AT along the ridge between the two peaks of Mt. Cube. Here a spur path follows a segment of the old AT to the right 0.3 mi. from the junction, past the fine northeast outlook, to the north peak, where there is a view to the northeast toward Moosilauke. The Mount Cube Trail turns left at this junction and follows the old route to the summit of the bare south peak, where it meets the Kodak Trail and the South Cube Trail.

Mount Cube Trail (DOC map)

Distance from NH 25A (900')

    to Mt. Cube summit (2909'): 3.4 mi. (5.4 km.), 2000 ft., 2 hr. 40 min.

South Cube Trail (DOC)

This is the blue-blazed former route of the Appalachian Trail to the main (south) summit of Mt. Cube from Baker Rd. (often called Quinttown Rd.), which runs south from NH 25A 1.7 mi. west of the height-of-land near Mt. Cube Farm and reaches the trailhead in about 1 mi. The section of this road that runs south between this trailhead and the crossroads called Quinttown is not usually passable to ordinary vehicles. Though the South Cube Trail is severely eroded, it provides the shortest route to the summit of Mt. Cube. The trail leaves Baker Rd. on an old logging road and ascends past a short spur left to the old Cube Shelter at 0.2 mi. It continues to ascend steadily, reaching ledges 100 yd. below the bare summit. From the summit, the Kodak Trail runs south and the Mount Cube Trail north; the fine northeast outlook and the east outlook from the north peak can be reached by following the Mount Cube Trail and a spur path (part of the former AT) north for 0.4 mi.

South Cube Trail (DOC map)

Distance from Baker Rd. (1400')

    to Mt. Cube summit (2909'): 1.5 mi. (2.5 km.), 1500 ft., 1 hr. 30 min.

Atwell Hill Trail (DOC)

This is the segment of the Appalachian Trail from NH 25A to Atwell Hill Rd. opposite the Ore Hill Trail, 3.3 mi. south of NH 25C and 2.1 mi. north of NH 25A. The trailhead on NH 25A is 4.5 mi. west of NH 25 and 0.1 mi. east of the Mount Cube Trail. The trail ascends gradually from NH 25A and bears left onto an old woods road at 0.2 mi. At 1.2 mi. it bears right (east) off the woods road and continues to Atwell Hill Rd.

Atwell Hill Trail (map 4:K1)

Distance from NH 25A (900')

   to Atwell Hill Rd. (1500'): 1.7 mi. (2.7 km.), 600 ft., 1 hr. 10 min.

Ore Hill Trail (DOC)

This is the segment of the Appalachian Trail from Atwell Hill Rd. opposite the Atwell Hill Trail, 3.3 mi. south of NH 25C and 2.1 mi. north of NH 25A, to NH 25C at a point 3.5 mi. west of NH 25 and 0.1 mi. west of the Wachipauka Pond Trail. It ascends under power lines and through a part of Sentinel State Forest to the height-of-land on Sentinel Mtn. at 0.8 mi., then descends. At 2.0 mi. it crosses a small stream on a log bridge and swings right (east) on an old woods road for 0.1 mi., then leaves it left (north) and ascends to its high point on Ore Hill at 2.8 mi., where it bears right and descends to NH 25C.

Ore Hill Trail (map 4:K1–J1)

Distance from Atwell Hill Rd. (1500')

   to NH 25C (1500'): 3.4 mi. (5.4 km.), 700 ft. (rev. 700 ft.), 2 hr. 5 min.

Wachipauka Pond Trail (DOC)

This segment of the Appalachian Trail, which runs from NH 25C to NH 25, leaves NH 25C at a point 3.4 mi. west of NH 25 and 0.1 mi. east of the Ore Hill Trail. Its trailhead on NH 25 is 1.4 mi. west of the junction of NH 25 and NH 112 and 0.6 mi. west of the Glencliff Post Office, and 150 yd. south of the western terminus of the Town Line Trail. It is described here from north to south. Leaving NH 25, it begins as a woods road but soon becomes a foot trail and climbs moderately to its high point on Wyatt Hill at 1.2 mi., then descends west gradually to the north end of Wachipauka Pond. The trail contours around the base of Webster Slide Mtn. above the west shore of the pond, and at 2.3 mi. the Webster Slide Trail leaves right for the spectacular summit ledges of Webster

Slide Mtn. The main trail passes Hairy Root Spring, then climbs gradually, passing a short spur path left to an excellent east outlook. It crosses the wooded summit of Mt. Mist at 3.1 mi. and descends gradually, then rises slightly as it passes around a low hill and continues across Ore Hill Brook to NH 25C.

Wachipauka Pond Trail (map 4:J1-J2)

Distances from NH 25 (1050')

> *to* Webster Slide Trail (1500'): 2.3 mi., 650 ft. (rev. 200 ft.), 1 hr. 30 min.
>
> *to* NH 25C (1500'): 4.9 mi. (7.9 km.), 1400 ft. (rev. 750 ft.), 3 hr. 10 min.

Webster Slide Trail (DOC)

The spectacular outlook from this mountain's east ledges, which look straight down onto Wachipauka Pond, is reached by a spur trail that leaves the Wachipauka Pond Trail (AT) right (west) 2.3 mi. from NH 25. It follows an old woods road (a former route of Appalachian Trail) for 0.2 mi., then turns sharp right and climbs rather steeply to the summit at 0.6 mi. and continues down past the ruins of the former shelter to the ledgy viewpoint.

Webster Slide Trail (map 4:J1)

Distance from Wachipauka Pond Trail (1500')

> *to* Webster Slide Mtn. ledge outlook (2180'): 0.7 mi. (1.2 km.), 700 ft., 40 min.

Appendix A

Four Thousand Footers

The Four Thousand Footer Club was formed in 1957 to bring together hikers who had traveled to some of the less frequently visited sections of the White Mountains. At that time, such peaks as Hancock, Owl's Head, and West Bond had no trails and were almost never climbed, while other peaks on the list that had trails were seldom climbed, and the problem of over-use was unknown, except in the Presidentials and Franconias. Today the Four Thousand Footer Club is composed of active hikers whose travels in the mountains have made them familiar with many different sections of the White Mountain backcountry, and with the problems that threaten to degrade the mountain experience that we have all been privileged to enjoy. The Four Thousand Footer Committee hopes that this broadened experience of the varied beauties of our beloved peaks and forests will encourage our members to work for the preservation and wise use of wild country, so that it may be enjoyed and passed on to future generations undiminished.

The Four Thousand Footer Committee recognizes three lists of peaks: the White Mountain Four Thousand Footers, the New England Four Thousand Footers, and the New England Hundred Highest. Separate awards are given to those who climb all peaks on a list in winter; to qualify as a winter ascent, the hike must not begin before the hour and minute of the beginning of winter or end after the hour and minute of the end of winter. As of April 1997, these clubs had the following number of officially registered members: White Mountain Four Thousand Footers, 5857 (winter, 213); New England Four Thousand Footers, 1510 (winter, 72); New England Hundred Highest, 386 (winter, 39). To qualify for membership, a hiker must climb on foot to and from each summit on the list. The official lists of the Four Thousand Footers in New Hampshire, Maine, and Vermont are included at the end of this appendix. Applicants for the White Mountain Four Thousand Footer Club must climb all 48 peaks in New Hampshire, while applicants for the New England Four Thousand Footer Club must also climb the 14 peaks in Maine and the five in Vermont.

As of April 1998 the Four Thousand Footer Committee has issued newly revised lists for these clubs. For most climbers the most significant changes will be the substitution of Wildcat "D" for Wildcat "E" and the elevation of Spaulding Mtn. and Mt. Redington in Maine to Four Thousand Footer status. There will be a three-year grace period during which hikers will be allowed to use either the old or the new list; after April 1, 2001, all hikers applying for membership in any of the clubs must have climbed all the peaks on the new list for that club.

The New England Hundred Highest Club list differs substantially from the other two because it includes a considerable number of peaks without trails; several of these peaks require advanced wilderness navigation skills of the group leader, and two are on private land where written permission to enter may be required. Peaks on this list for which routes are described in this guide include: Sandwich Mtn. (3880 ft.), with several trails in Section 7; the Horn (3905 ft.), on a spur path from the Kilkenny Ridge Trail; the East Sleeper (3860 ft.), just off the Sleeper Trail; and the Northeast Cannon Ball (3769 ft.), on the Kinsman Ridge Trail. A copy of the full list and related information is available from the Committee.

If you are seriously interested in becoming a member of one or more of the clubs sponsored by the Four Thousand Footer Committee, please send a self-addressed stamped envelope to the Four Thousand Footer Committee, Appalachian Mountain Club, 5 Joy Street, Boston, MA 02108, and an information packet including application forms will be sent to you. If you are interested in the New England Four Thousand Footer Club and/or the New England Hundred Highest Club, please specify this, since these lists are not routinely included in the basic information packet. After climbing each peak, please record the date of the ascent, companions, if any, and other remarks.

Applicants for any of the clubs need not be AMC members, although the Committee strongly urges all hikers who make considerable use of the trails to contribute to their maintenance in some manner. Membership in the AMC is one of the most effective means of assisting these efforts.

Criteria for mountains on the official list are: (1) each peak must be 4000 ft. high, and (2) each peak must rise 200 ft. above the low point of its connecting ridge with a higher neighbor. The latter qualification eliminates such peaks as Clay, Franklin, North Carter, Guyot, Little Haystack, South Tripyramid, Lethe, Blue, and Jim. All 65 Four Thousand Footers are reached by well-defined trails, although the path to Owl's Head and some short spur trails to other summits are not officially maintained.

On the following lists, elevations have been obtained from the latest USGS maps, some of which are now metric, requiring conversion from meters to feet. Where no exact elevation is given on the map, the elevation has been estimated by adding half the contour interval to the highest contour shown on the map; elevations so obtained are marked on the list with an asterisk. The elevations given here for several peaks in the Presidential region differ from those given elsewhere in this book, because the Four Thousand Footer Committee uses the USGS maps as the authority for all elevations, while in the rest of the book the Bradford Washburn map of the Presidential Range supersedes the USGS maps in the area it covers.

Four Thousand Footers in New Hampshire

Mountain	Elevation		Date Climbed
	(feet)	(meters)	
1. Washington	6288	1916.6	_____
2. Adams	5774	1760	_____
3. Jefferson	5712	1741	_____
4. Monroe	5384*	1641*	_____
5. Madison	5367	1636	_____
6. Lafayette	5260*	1603*	_____
7. Lincoln	5089	1551	_____
8. South Twin	4902	1494	_____
9. Carter Dome	4832	1473	_____
10. Moosilauke	4802	1464	_____
11. Eisenhower	4780*	1457*	_____
12. North Twin	4761	1451	_____
13. Carrigain	4700*	1433*	_____
14. Bond	4698	1432	_____
15. Middle Carter	4610*	1405*	_____
16. West Bond	4540*	1384*	_____
17. Garfield	4500*	1372*	_____
18. Liberty	4459	1359	_____
19. South Carter	4430*	1350*	_____
20. Wildcat	4422	1348	_____
21. Hancock	4420*	1347*	_____
22. South Kinsman	4358	1328	_____

Mountain	Elevation		Date Climbed
	(feet)	(meters)	
23. Field	4340*	1323*	_____
24. Osceola	4340*	1323*	_____
25. Flume	4328	1319	_____
26. South Hancock	4319	1316	_____
27. Pierce (Clinton)	4310	1314	_____
28. North Kinsman	4293	1309	_____
29. Willey	4285	1306	_____
30. Bondcliff	4265	1300	_____
31. Zealand	4260*	1298*	_____
32. North Tripyramid	4180*	1274*	_____
33. Cabot	4170*	1271*	_____
34. East Osceola	4156	1267	_____
35. Middle Tripyramid	4140*	1262*	_____
36. Cannon	4100*	1250*	_____
37. Hale	4054	1236	_____
38. Jackson	4052	1235	_____
39. Tom	4051	1235	_____
40. Wildcat D	4050*	1234*	_____
41. Moriah	4049	1234	_____
42. Passaconaway	4043	1232	_____
43. Owl's Head	4025	1227	_____
44. Galehead	4024	1227	_____
45. Whiteface	4020*	1225*	_____
46. Waumbek	4006	1221	_____
47. Isolation	4004	1220	_____
48. Tecumseh	4003	1220	_____

Four Thousand Footers in Maine

Mountain	Elevation		Date Climbed
	(feet)	(meters)	
1. Katahdin, Baxter Peak	5268	1606	_____
2. Katahdin, Hamlin Peak	4756	1450	_____
3. Sugarloaf	4250*	1295*	_____
4. Old Speck	4170*	1271*	_____
5. Crocker	4228	1289	_____
6. Bigelow, West Peak	4145	1263	_____
7. North Brother	4151	1265	_____
8. Saddleback	4120	1256	_____
9. Bigelow, Avery Peak	4090*	1247*	_____
10. Abraham	4050*	1234*	_____
11. Saddleback, the Horn	4041	1232	_____
12. South Crocker	4050*	1234*	_____
13. Redington	4010*	1222*	_____
14. Spaulding	4010*	1222*	_____

Four Thousand Footers in Vermont

Mountain	Elevation		Date Climbed
	(feet)	(meters)	
1. Mansfield	4393	1339	_____
2. Killington	4235	1291	_____
3. Camel's Hump	4083	1244	_____
4. Ellen	4083	1244	_____
5. Abraham	4006	1221	_____

Appendix B

Accident Report

Your Name_____**Date** _____**TIme**_____

DESCRIPTION OF LOST OR INJURED PERSON:

Name_____**Age/Sex:** _____

Address: _____**Hair:** _____

_____**Fac. Hair** _____

Phone: _____

REPORTING PERSON:

Name _____**Phone:** _____

Address _____

WHAT HAPPENED:

_____

_____

_____

_____

_____

POINT LAST SEEN:

Car Description _____**Date** _____

Car Location _____

Itinerary _____

WEARING (color/style/size):

Jacket _____ Shirt _____

Shorts/Pants _____ Hat/Gloves _____

Glasses _____ Pack _____

Footgear _____ Crampons _____

CARRYING (color/style/size/quantity):

Map _____ Sleeping Bag _____

Tent/Bivy _____ Rand/Windgear _____

Flashlight/Batts _____ Extra Clothing _____

Food/Water _____ Ski Poles/Ice Axe _____

Experience _____

Physical/Mental Conditions _____

ESSENTIAL PATIENT EXAMINATION

PROBLEM AREAS/INJURIES

❏ Head   ❏ Neck   ❏ Shoulders   ❏ Chest
❏ Abdomen   ❏ Back   ❏ Pelvis

❏ Left Upper Leg   ❏ Left Lower Leg   ❏ Left Foot
❏ Right Upper Leg   ❏ Right Lower Leg   ❏ Right Foot

❏ Left Arm   ❏ Left Hand   ❏ Right Arm   ❏ Right Hand

Chief Complaint and Plan

_____

_____

_____

Problem 2 and Plan

_____

_____

_____

Problem 3 and Plan

_____

_____

_____

BACKGROUND INFORMATION

Allergies _____

Medication _____

Previous Injury/Illness _____

Last 24hr food/water intake _____

Medical Conditions/Other _____

_____

FOR BACK, CHEST, OR ABDOMINAL PAIN, DETERMINE:

History _____

Duration _____

Intensity _____Changing +/- _____

VITAL SIGNS

ESSENTIAL				HELPFUL		
TIME	LEVEL OF CONSCIOUSNESS	BREATING RATE	PULSE	BLOOD PRESSURE	SKIN	PUPILS

NOTES

DATE/TIME	WEATHER/LOCATION AND FINDINGS	ACTION TAKEN

Appendix C

Short to Moderate Hikes

This section is intended to supply readers with a certain number of suggestions for short and moderate hikes in the areas covered by this guide. No attempt has been made to create and apply strict criteria for these classifications, but the upper limit is roughly set at what an "average" hiker can expect to accomplish in seven or eight hours. Since we expect that in many cases readers will be looking for a trip within a reasonable driving distance of their present or planned base of operations, this section has been organized into regions by road access to trailheads rather than following the pattern of the body of this book, which is organized by mountain ranges. These regions have been created for convenience and have not been strictly defined. The numbers in brackets indicate distance, elevation gain, and time calculated by the normal formula; "ow," "rt," and "lp" mean "one way," "round trip," and "loop," respectively. It should be repeated that the time allowances are merely a very rough estimate–many parties will require more time, and many will require less–and they do not include time for extensive stops for scenery appreciation or rest.

Whoever compiles a list like this one faces certain problems that should be understood by the user. Many of the obvious candidates for inclusion on such a list naturally attract large numbers of people, and many hikers who visit one of them are likely to find a beautiful spot that is simply too crowded for them to enjoy. One of the most important criteria used in choosing these suggested hikes has been whether the places, and the trails that lead to them, can withstand any likely increase in use. All of us should be thoroughly aware of our role in protecting the beauty of the lands we pass through–the capacity of the land increases when we walk through it lightly and quietly.

508

GORHAM—PINKHAM NOTCH REGION

Short trips

In the vicinity of Pinkham Notch a number of good short hikes are available.

Lost Pond is a pleasant spot with excellent views across to the east face of Mt. Washington, reached by the Lost Pond Trail, which is part of the Appalachian Trail [rt: 1.0 mi., 100 ft., 0:35].

The Thompson Falls Trail, which begins at Wildcat Mtn. Ski Area, visits attractive cascades flowing over flat ledges [rt: 1.4 mi., 200 ft., 0:50].

Square Ledge, a rocky lookout on the east side of Pinkham Notch, is a fairly rugged but short trip [rt: 1.2 mi., 400 ft., 0:50].

Lowe's Bald Spot provides an interesting outlook up to Mt. Washington, and makes an attractive walk from Pinkham Notch Camp via the Old Jackson Road and Madison Gulf Trail [rt: 4.2 mi., 900 ft., 2:35].

The Crew-Cut Trail, George's Gorge Trail, and Liebeskind's Loop offer a number of opportunities for interesting short hikes. The basic loop [lp: 1.8 mi., 550 ft., 1:10] can be extended in a number of ways, and parts of these trails can be used as an alternative route to part of the Old Jackson Road for those going to or coming from Lowe's Bald Spot.

On the north side of the range the RMC trail system provides access to a number of falls and cascades. It should be emphasized that all these falls are essentially small cascades on rocks and ledges or in small gorges formed by the steep mountain brooks, and are not spectacular in any sense. However, they do provide pleasant walks along the banks of sparkling, splashing brooks. The dense trail network makes an almost infinite variety of walks possible–it is quite feasible to simply wander on the paths along brooks and through the woods until one's capacity for the day is reached.

Triple Falls on Evans Brook can be visited in a very short trip, though the trail to these cascades is fairly steep [rt: 0.4 mi., 200 ft., 0:20].

One of the best possibilities for an easy hike is the loop via the Fallsway and Brookbank, which passes Gordon, Salroc, and Tama falls [lp: 1.5 mi., 400 ft., 0:55].

Another possibility is the lower end of the Howker Ridge Trail, which passes Coosauk and Hitchcock falls, as well as some smaller falls and the interesting little gorge called the Devil's Kitchen [rt: 2.0 mi., 400 ft., 1:10].

A good trip involving many waterfalls can be made by taking the Amphibrach past Cold Brook Fall, and then making the side trips to the pleasant, broad Coldspur Ledges via the short eastern extension of the Monaway and to Spur Brook Falls via the Cliffway. One can return by the same route [rt: 4.8 mi., 1300 ft., 3:05] or lengthen the trip by continuing to the end of the Amphibrach at the junction called the Pentadoi, then following the Randolph Path down to the Valley Way and soon diverging on either the Fallsway or the Brookbank [lp: 5.3 mi., 1700 ft., 3:30].

Another good trip follows the Maple Walk and Sylvan Way to the Howker Ridge Trail near Coosauk Fall, then ascends the Kelton Trail and descends past the fine views of the Inlook Trail, then follows the Brookside, Valley Way, and either the Fallsway or the Brookbank out to the parking area [lp: 4.0 mi., 1500 ft., 2:45]. It is also possible to return past the excellent viewpoint called Dome Rock via the Inlook Trail and Valley Way (although the best of the brookside walking is missed) [lp: 3.7 mi., 1500 ft., 2:35]. The Kelton Trail and Inlook Trail both have fairly steep sections with rough footing.

Pine Mtn., at the northeast end of the Presidential Range, probably offers the best views in this region for the effort required. Its principal shortcoming is that the main trail is a good gravel road, closed to public vehicular use but open to hiking [rt: 4.0 mi., 800 ft., 2:25]. This may be an asset for people who may lack the agility to enjoy the rough footing on most mountain trails (such as the very young or the old), but many hikers will find this route boring in spite of the rewards to be gained at the summit; for such people a shorter and more sporty ascent on the branch trail over the south ledges is available [lp: 3.5 mi., 800 ft., 2:10].

Lookout Ledge, reached by the Ledge Trail [rt: 2.6 mi., 450 ft., 1:30] or several longer routes, provides excellent views into King Ravine.

Mossy Glen, located on Carlton Brook between Durand Rd. and Randolph Hill Rd., is easily reached from Durand Rd. by the Burnbrae and Glenside [rt: 0.8 mi., 200 ft., 30 min.]. There are many other short, easy paths in this area that may be explored in order to extend the walk.

The Devil's Hopyard, which lies well to the north of the Presidentials and is reached from NH 110 via the access road to South Pond [rt: 2.6 mi., 500 ft., 1:35], provides an easily-visited miniature version of the more spectacular but much more difficult similar gorges, the Ice Gulch and Mahoosuc Notch.

Moderate trips

King Ravine is usually regarded as a route to the summit of Mt. Adams, and in that role its three trails each make up a part of three of the most strenuous and beautiful routes to Mt. Adams. But this wild ravine, with its rugged scenery and its fascinating boulders and boulder caves, is a completely worthy objective in its own right. The shortest, easiest route to the ravine floor is via the Air Line, Short Line, and King Ravine Trail [rt: 6.2 mi., 2400 ft., 4:20]. It is also feasible to visit King Ravine as an extension of a trip mentioned in the Short section, following the Amphibrach to the Pentadoi and the King Ravine Trail from there to the floor of the ravine, then descending on the Short Line to the Randolph Path, Valley Way, and Fallsway or Brookbank [lp: 7.0 mi., 2400 ft., 4:40].

The Imp Face, a cliffy outlook on the northern part of the Carter Range, is a worthwhile objective reached by a loop path [lp: 6.3 mi., 2300 ft., 4:10] of which the northern half is both shorter and more interesting [rt: 4.4 mi., 1700 ft., 3:05].

Several peaks that are somewhat distant from Gorham but are readily reached by NH 110 also offer very rewarding moderate trips.

In the Nash Stream valley northeast of Groveton, Percy Peak [rt: 4.4 mi., 2200 ft., 3:20] and Sugarloaf [rt: 4.2 mi., 2200 ft., 3:10] offer fine views.

Rogers Ledge, a spectacular, remote, and seldom-visited viewpoint, can be reached from South Pond via the Kilkenny Ridge Trail [rt: 8.2 mi., 1900 ft., 5:05] or from York Pond via the Mill Brook and Kilkenny Ridge trails [rt: 8.8 mi., 1500 ft., 4:40].

An excellent hike to Unknown Pond and the Horn can be made from NH 110 via the Unknown Pond and Kilkenny Ridge trails [rt: 9.8 mi., 2400 ft., 6:05]; Mt. Cabot, the northernmost four-thousand-footer that virtually everyone climbs from East Lancaster, can be added to this trip [rt: 12.0 mi., 3400 ft., 7:40].

On the larger mountains in the area, there are a number of trips that seem particularly worthy of mention.

A very good loop can be made by following the Nineteen Mile Brook Trail to the Carter Lakes, then taking the Carter-Moriah Trail over Carter Dome and Mt. Hight (the best viewpoint on the Carter Range) and descending via the relatively easy Carter Dome Trail [lp: 10.2 mi., 3400 ft., 6:50].

The ascent of Mt. Moriah via the Stony Brook and Carter-Moriah trails is very scenic, affording excellent views from ledges along the way as well as at the summit [rt: 10.0 mi., 3100 ft., 6:35].

Shelburne Moriah via the Rattle River and Kenduskeag trails also offers exceptional views from ledges at the summit and on the upper part of the ridge [rt: 11.2 mi., 2900 ft., 7:05].

In the Mahoosuc Range area, a particularly rewarding loop trip can be made by the Goose Eye, Mahoosuc, and Carlo Col trails [lp: 7.6 mi., 2700 ft., 5:10].

Another fine trip is the ascent of Mt. Success from Success Pond Rd. [rt: 6.0 mi., 1950 ft., 4:00]. The beautiful, unusual Outlook reached by the side path on the way up the mountain must not be missed.

Mahoosuc Notch is also a very attractive feature, but while the normal loop route via the Notch, Mahoosuc, and Speck Pond trails is extremely scenic, it is also very strenuous and requires a car spot or road walk at the end [lp: 9.4 mi., 2500 ft., 5:55 (but probably much longer)]. The alternative is to come back through the notch from the far side, thus going through it twice, something that most hikers find daunting to contemplate [rt: 6.6 mi., 1200 ft., 3:55 (but could easily take as much as twice that long)].

While Mt. Washington and the three major Northern Peaks–Madison, Adams, and Jefferson–are very close to the upper margin of the moderate trips classification, if not over it, they are likely to prove extremely tempting to most hikers. One should never underestimate the potential severity of above-treeline weather or the strenuousness of the usual elevation gain of over four thousand feet. Possible routes of ascent are nearly limitless, considering all the side trails and the variations and linkings they permit. Some suggestions for interesting routes to these peaks follow.

Mt. Washington. From the east side, the Tuckerman Ravine Trail is the easiest and most popular route to the summit [ow: 4.2 mi., 4300 ft., 4:15; rt: 8.4 mi., 4300 ft., 6:20]. There are many other routes available, but though all of them are substantially less crowded they are also either longer or more strenuous. In good weather, the Boott Spur Trail offers better views, and though it is longer it is not substantially more difficult; one can ascend by this trail and then descend through Tuckerman Ravine with the crowds, or make the easier, faster ascent through Tuckerman Ravine and then make a leisurely descent via Boott Spur [lp: 9.6 mi., 4300 ft., 6:55]. The Lion Head Trail is about the same length as the Tuckerman Ravine Trail and also offers better views, but it has steeper sections and is generally rougher; for most people, it is probably a better route for the ascent than for descent [ow: 4.1 mi., 4300 ft., 4:10].

Jefferson. Although the Caps Ridge Trail has some fairly steep, rough sections, the relatively short distance and elevation gain make it the route of choice for most hikers [rt: 5.0 mi., 2700 ft., 3:50]. The Castle Trail is a beautiful but much longer and more strenuous route requiring equally difficult scrambling on its ledges [rt: 10.0 mi., 4200 ft., 7:05]. The loop involving the Caps Ridge and Castle trails and the Link is beautiful and very entertaining, but one must take into account the roughness of the Link–where one must beware of numerous ankle-twisting holes between rocks and roots, requiring an adequate supply of energy and daylight [lp: 6.7 mi., 2900 ft., 4:50].

Adams. There are numerous direct routes to Mt. Adams, such as Lowe's Path [ow: 4.8 mi., 4400 ft., 4:35] and the Air Line [ow: 4.3 mi., 4500 ft., 4:25], not to mention the routes via Madison Hut; the most popular route via the hut combines the Valley Way, Gulfside Trail, and Lowe's Path [ow: 5.0 mi., 4500 ft., 4:30]. The King Ravine Trail (including the variations afforded by the Great Gully Trail and the Chemin des Dames—Air Line combination) provides what are probably the most scenic routes to the summit, but these are all extremely strenuous routes. One attractive route that is no more strenuous than the direct trails follows the Valley Way, the Scar Trail and Loop, and the Air Line, thereby including the fine ledge outlook called the Scar and the long open knife-edged section of Durand Ridge [ow: 5.0 mi., 4300 ft., 4:40]. Another route, perhaps a bit steeper and rougher than the direct routes, follows the Amphibrach, Randolph Path, and Spur Trail to Thunderstorm Junction, passing the Knight's Castle, an unusual and spectacular viewpoint on the brink of King Ravine's cliffs [ow: 5.2 mi., 4300 ft., 4:45].

Madison. The easiest route to the summit is probably via Madison Hut, using the Valley Way [rt: 8.4 mi., 4100 ft., 6:15]. The Daniel Webster—Scout Trail [rt: 8.2 mi., 4100 ft., 6:10] and the Osgood Trail [rt: 10.2 mi., 4100 ft., 7:10] offer routes of somewhat greater difficulty, rougher and much more exposed to weather. The Howker Ridge Trail is a beautiful, wild route, but it is much rougher and requires some care to follow, particularly above treeline [rt: 9.0 mi., 4500 ft., 6:45].

CONWAY—CRAWFORD NOTCH REGION

Short trips

Arethusa Falls and Ripley Falls are the two highest waterfalls in NH. Arethusa Falls [rt: 2.6 mi., 1000 ft., 1:50] is somewhat more demanding than Ripley Falls [rt: 1.0 mi., 500 ft., 0:45]; on a visit to Arethusa Falls, the Bemis Brook Trail can be used either ascending or descending to obtain additional views of other falls in Bemis Brook. With a car spot, both of the big falls can be visited in one trip via the Arethusa-Ripley Falls Trail [lp: 4.3 mi., 1100 ft., 2:40]. It is also possible to use the Frankenstein Cliff Trail to make a loop that includes Arethusa Falls and Frankenstein Cliff [lp: 4.7 mi., 1400 ft., 3:05].

Sawyer Pond, reached by the Sawyer Pond Trail, is an attractive and popular mountain pond situated at the base of Mt. Tremont [rt: 3.0 mi., 500 ft., 1:45].

Church Pond is another attractive but far less popular pond reached by a loop path from the Kancamagus Highway [lp: 2.8 mi., 100 ft., 1:25]; it lies in a flat region of swamps and poorly-drained woodlands, very different from the terrain usually crossed by hiking trails–visitors should expect wet feet.

The Rob Brook Trail is a somewhat similar trail that follows an old railroad grade through an area of swamps and beaver ponds [rt: 4.6 mi., 100 ft., 2:20].

The Boulder Loop Trail is an interpretive nature trail that ascends a small mountain, a spur of the Moat group, that has good views from a ledge [lp: 3.1 mi., 900 ft., 2:00].

Big Rock Cave, an interesting boulder cave on a southern spur of Mt. Paugus reached by the Big Rock Cave Trail, is an interesting objective for young children [rt: 3.2 mi., 1100 ft., 2:10].

Iron Mtn., reached by the Iron Mountain Trail, has a broad ledge with an excellent view on its south end [rt: 3.2 mi., 1000 ft, 2:05].

Mt. Stanton and Mt. Pickering are two small mountains that offer beautiful red pine woods with scattered ledges, each with a different interesting view [rt: 4.2 mi., 1800 ft., 3:00]. They are on the Mount Stanton Trail, which continues over several small ledgy peaks called the Crippies; the trail is not recommended beyond the last Crippie [rt: 6.6 mi., 2400 ft., 4:30].

Mt. Crawford, reached by the Davis Path, is a beautiful rock peak with extensive views [rt: 5.0 mi., 2100 ft., 3:35]; it is also part of an excellent longer trip that includes Stairs [rt: 9.8 mi., 3000 ft., 6:25] or Resolution [rt: 9.2 mi., 2800 ft., 6:00] or both [rt: 11.0 mi., 3400 ft., 7:10].

Mt. Willard has long been celebrated for the view of Crawford Notch from the brink of its impressive cliffs [rt: 3.2 mi., 900 ft., 2:05].

The best view available from the Willey Range is found on the little crag called Mt. Avalon, reached by the Avalon Trail [rt: 3.6 mi., 1600 ft., 2:35]; visitors should make the short side trip on the loop to Beecher and Pearl cascades on the way.

Sugarloaf Mtn. near Twin Mtn. NH offers excellent views for modest effort from its two open summits [rt: 3.4 mi., 1100 ft., 2:15].

South Moat is a bare summit with excellent views in all directions [rt: 4.6 mi., 2200 ft., 3:25].

In the Green Hills Range, the new trail system offers many interesting hikes, including ascents of Black Cap [2.2 mi., 650 ft., 1:30], Peaked Mtn. [4.2 mi., 1200 ft., 2:40], and Middle Mtn. [4.2 mi., 1300 ft., 2:45].

Hedgehog Mtn., reached by the UNH Trail, which is a loop [lp: 4.8 mi., 1700 ft., 3:15], and Mt. Potash, reached by the Mount Potash Trail [rt: 4.4 mi., 1500 ft., 1:55], are two small peaks on the north side of the Sandwich Range that offer excellent views from their ledges.

Moderate trips

Mt. Chocorua is one of the most popular peaks in the White Mtns., and the easier trails usually have heavy traffic, but the crowds can often be avoided except at the summit. One of the better routes available is to ascend via the Piper, Nickerson Ledge, Carter Ledge, Middle Sister, and Piper trails, and descend by the Liberty, Hammond, Weetamoo, and Piper trails [lp: 10.7 mi., 3300 ft., 7:00].

The trip over North Moat via the Red Ridge and Moat Mtn. trails is one of the most beautiful trips in this region, traversing large amounts of open ledge [lp: 10.0 mi., 2800 ft., 6:10].

Kearsarge North, reached by the Mount Kearsarge North Trail, offers one of the finest views in the White Mtns. [rt: 6.2 mi., 2600 ft., 4:10].

Mt. Tremont offers excellent views but is far less frequently climbed; the Mount Tremont Trail must therefore be followed with care [rt: 5.6 mi., 2600 ft., 4:05].

Mt. Carrigain, which many people believe has the best view of all in the Whites, is reached by the Signal Ridge Trail [rt: 10.0 mi., 3200 ft., 6:35]. (As of 1997, the Sawyer River Rd. was closed, and until it is reopened the trip will be 4.1 mi. longer.)

The trip on the Nancy Pond Trail to Nancy Cascades [rt: 4.8 mi., 1200 ft., 3:00] is attractive in itself, but it is worth the effort to continue to the unusual ledge that dams Norcross Pond and affords a fine view into the Pemigewasset Wilderness [rt: 8.6 mi., 2100 ft., 5:20].

Mt. Whiteface, located at the southern edge of the high mountain region, offers an excellent view over the lake country to the south from the broad ledges south of the summit; it can be ascended by the moderately challenging Blueberry Ledge Trail [rt: 7.8 mi., 3000 ft., 5:25] or by a longer but more routine route via the Flat Mountain Pond and McCrillis Trails [rt: 9.8 mi., 3200 ft., 6:30].

Mt. Jackson is reached by the Jackson branch of the Webster-Jackson Trail [rt: 5.2 mi., 2200 ft., 3:35]; Mt. Webster by the Webster branch of the Webster-Jackson Trail [rt: 5.0 mi., 2000 ft, 3:30]; a loop can be made over both summits [lp: 6.5 mi., 2500 ft, 4:30]. If a car spot is available, one can ascend Mt. Webster by the Webster-Jackson Trail and then make a leisurely descent of the magnificent Webster Cliff Trail down to the notch [lp: 5.8 mi., 2000 ft., 3:55].

Mt. Hale can be climbed by the Hale Brook Trail [rt: 4.4 mi., 2300 ft., 3:20]; an interesting longer loop can be made by following the Lend-a-Hand Trail from the summit to Zealand Falls Hut, then following the Zealand Trail back out to Zealand Rd. [lp: 8.7 mi., 2400 ft., 5:35].

Zeacliff is a perch at the northern end of the Pemigewasset Wilderness that commands one of the finest outlooks in the Whites; it can be reached by the Zealand Trail and Twinway [rt: 7.8 mi., 2100 ft., 4:55].

The Evans Notch region is one of the less frequently visited corners of the White Mtns., but the Baldface Circle trip is one of the finest ridge traverses in the Whites. One can either do the trip on the Baldface Circle Trail all the way [lp: 9.8 mi., 3200 ft., 6:30], or avoid the steep ledges on South Baldface by using the Slippery Brook and Baldface Knob trails [lp: 10.6 mi., 3300 ft., 6:55].

East Royce Mtn. via the East Royce Trail [rt: 3.0 mi., 1700 ft., 2:20] offers a steep and rough but relatively short ascent to excellent views.

Mt. Washington. Few hikers will be able to resist the urge to climb the highest mountain in the northeast, despite the crowds on the popular trails and the hordes of tourists on the summit. The easiest way to climb it is probably the Jewell Trail-Gulfside Trail combination on the west side [rt: 10.2 mi., 3800 ft., 7:00], which begins at a parking lot on the road to the Cog Railway. Most hikers climbing from this side will be tempted to turn the hike into a loop by combining the Jewell and Gulfside trails with the Ammonoosuc Ravine Trail, which begins at the same parking lot [lp: 9.6 mi., 3800 ft., 6:40]. The Ammonoosuc Ravine Trail [rt: 9.0 mi., 3800 ft., 6:25] is a much more interesting and beautiful route to Mt. Washington than the Jewell Trail, but the steep section between Gem Pool and Lakes of the Clouds Hut can be extremely discouraging to a person in poor physical condition, to whom it may seem that little or no progress is being made. On the descent, this section passes mostly over ledges and rocks, some of which are wet and slippery, and it can be quite tedious and tiring for a person whose agility is limited. On the whole, it is probably better to ascend the Ammonoosuc Ravine Trail and descend the Jewell Trail, but if afternoon thunderstorms are threatening, the descent by the Jewell Trail is probably more hazardous, as it is far less sheltered; on the other hand, in rain without lightning the steep wet rocks on the Ammonoosuc Ravine Trail may be more of a problem, but if it is both cold and rainy the exposure on the Jewell Trail may be more hazardous.

LINCOLN—FRANCONIA NOTCH REGION

Short trips

Bald Mtn. is a scale model mountain; very impressive in appearance, it can be climbed very easily [rt: 0.6 mi., 300 ft., 0:25]. Unfortunately, the view from its once highly admired neighbor, Artists Bluff [lp: 1.3 mi., 400 ft., 0:50], has been severely marred by the extensive interchanges of the Franconia Notch Parkway at its foot.

The Basin-Cascades Trail follows Cascade Brook from the Basin area to the Cascade Brook Trail; there are many broad ledges and small cascades, and one can stop, enjoy, and turn back at any point or continue all the way to Rocky Glen Falls [rt: 2.0 mi., 600 ft., 1:20].

Eagle Pass, reached by the Greenleaf Trail, is a narrow rocky cleft between Mt. Lafayette and Eagle Cliff that merits exploration [rt: 3.0 mi., 1000 ft., 2:00].

Lonesome Lake, a very popular objective, offers fine views of the Franconia Range [rt: 3.2 mi., 1000 ft., 2:05].

The Kinsman Ridge Trail provides access to a fine broad ledge on the east peak of Cannon that commands a spectacular view across the notch [rt: 3.0 mi., 1800 ft., 2:25]; one can easily extend the trip to the tourist trap on the summit [rt: 4.4 mi., 2100 ft., 3:15].

Indian Head, offering an excellent outlook from a prow-like cliff, is reached from the Flume Visitor Center by the Mount Pemigewasset Trail [rt: 3.6 mi., 1200 ft., 2:25].

Bridal Veil Falls, one of the more attractive waterfalls in the White Mtns., is reached by the Coppermine Trail [rt: 5.0 mi., 1000 ft., 3:05].

Moderate trips

Cherry Mtn., located north of Twin Mtn. village, has some good views from the summit, where a fire tower used to stand; but the most interesting viewpoint by far is the ledge on Owls Head, the lower north summit. Since the Owls Head Trail, the direct route [rt: 3.8 mi., 2100 ft., 2:55], has parts with poor footing, it is probably easiest to follow the Cherry Mountain Trail from NH 115 to the main summit [rt: 3.8 mi., 2000 ft., 2:55], then follow Martha's Mile to Owls Head [rt: 5.4 mi., 2600 ft., 3:30], in spite of the extra elevation gain.

Mt. Garfield offers one of the best views in the Whites from summit ledges perched high above the Pemigewasset Wilderness; the Garfield Trail, though long, is easier (except for the last 0.2 mi.) than most mountain trails, with generally good footing and moderate grades [rt: 10.0 mi., 3000 ft., 6:30].

North Kinsman has a spectacular view out to the Franconia Range and almost straight down to picturesque Kinsman Pond at the foot of its cliffs; an interesting and varied trip can be made using the Mount Kinsman Trail from NH 116 and including the spur paths to Kinsman Flume and Bald Knob and a side trip to Kinsman Pond [rt: 9.4 mi., 3600 ft., 6:30]. South Kinsman, with its fine views particularly to the south, can be added to this trip [rt: 11.2 mi., 4200 ft., 7:35].

Though virtually everyone agrees that there is too much traffic on the Franconia Ridge, it is hard to imagine a serious hiker with enough resolve to forego one of the most spectacular walks in the East. The standard loop via the Old Bridle Path and Falling Waters Trail is probably unbeatable [lp: 7.9 mi., 3900 ft., 5:55]; it is a good trip in either direction, but most people will prefer the excuse to rest while ascending that is offered by the excellent outlook ledges on the Bridle Path, and appreciate the cold brooks for soaking heads and feet on the descent of the Falling Waters Trail.

Nearby Mt. Liberty offers equally good summit views but much less open ridge walking; the Liberty Spring Trail is the usual route [rt: 8.0 mi., 3200 ft., 5:35]. Many hikers will wish to visit Mt. Flume in the same trip and make a loop by using the Flume Slide Trail [lp: 9.9 mi., 3600 ft., 6:45], but descent by this trail is a tricky endeavor, and even its ascent will be less than pleasant for many people. Hikers wishing to do Liberty and Flume together should consider backtracking to the summit of Liberty [rt: 10.2 mi., 4200 ft., 7:10]; the separate ascent of Mt. Flume via the Osseo Trail [rt: 11.2 mi., 3200 ft., 7:10] is also strongly recommended for consideration.

MOOSILAUKE REGION

Short trips

An interesting loop through a region of ponds and swamps can be made via the Three Ponds Trail, Mount Kineo Trail, and Donkey Hill Cutoff [lp: 5.1 mi., 500 ft., 2:50]; the trip can be lengthened as much as desired by walking on the Three Ponds Trail or Mount Kineo Trail beyond the loop.

Black Mtn. in the Benton Range is a fine viewpoint reached by the attractive Chippewa Trail [rt: 3.6 mi., 1600 ft., 2:35].

Rattlesnake Mtn. is easily climbed, and the new loop trail offers interesting views of the Baker River valley [lp: 2.5 mi., 1000 ft., 1:45].

Mt. Cube is a very attractive small mountain in the Connecticut Valley; it can be ascended most easily via the South Cube Trail [rt: 3.0 mi., 1500 ft., 2:15], and it is worth while to include the trip on the spur trail to the viewpoints on the north peak [rt: 3.8 mi., 1600 ft., 2:40].

Moderate hikes

Moosilauke is the dominating peak of this region. Unless the brook at the start is high, the Benton Trail on the west side is probably the most attractive route [rt: 7.2 mi., 3200 ft., 5:10]. Another good choice is the Gorge Brook Trail on the east side, newly relocated to eliminate steep sections on the former route and include several excellent viewpoints [rt: 7.4 mi., 2600 ft., 5:00]. A good long loop with a wide variety of scenery can be made via the Glencliff, Tunnel Brook, and Benton trails [lp: 13.3 mi., 4000 ft., 8:40].

The trip on the Wachipauka Pond Trail (a part of the Appalachian Trail) to Wac hipauka Pond and the spectacular cliff-edge outlook on Webster Slide Mtn., in an area just to the west of Moosilauke, is particularly appealing [rt: 6.0 mi., 1800 ft., 3:55].

WATERVILLE VALLEY REGION

Short trips

Hikers interested in very short trips should obtain a map of the WVAIA trail system and make use of it. The possibilities for walks of any desired length and difficulty are practically endless.

One of the most popular objectives in this region is the Greeley Ponds, easily reached from the Kancamagus Highway by the Greeley Ponds Trail [rt: 4.4 mi., 600 ft., 2:30]. However, the trip from the Waterville Valley side [rt: 6.8 mi., 800 ft., 3:50] is more interesting and permits exploration of some of the side paths to local attractions such as the Scaur, Goodrich Rock, and the flume on Flume Brook.

Osceola can be ascended easily from the high point on Tripoli Rd. [rt: 6.4 mi., 2000 ft., 4:10]. Hikers should be aware that the trail to Osceola from Greeley Ponds is one of the steepest and roughest in the mountains.

The loop trip including both East Pond and Little East Pond [lp: 5.0 mi., 1300 ft., 3:10] is a pleasant walk, but finding the trailhead is often a problem due to lack of a sign–the trails themselves are easy to follow.

The loop over Welch Mtn. and Dickey Mtn. [lp: 4.4 mi., 1900 ft., 3:10] is a local favorite, offering a great deal of open ledge walking. It is one of the finest half-day walks in the White Mtns., a short trip over fairly rugged terrain with excellent views for an unusually large portion of the way.

Mt. Israel, located south of the main peaks of the Sandwich Range, offers an impressive view of its higher neighbors; its ascent via the Guinea Pond and Mead trails provides a pleasant, varied walk [rt: 6.6 mi., 1100 ft., 3:50].

West Rattlesnake, with its fine, easily attained view over Squam Lake, is one of NH's most popular peaks. Hikers using the most popular route, the Old Bridle Path [rt: 1.8 mi., 400 ft., 1:05], may find that they have to walk farther from their parking spot to the trailhead than from the trailhead to the summit; the Pasture Trail is a good alternative [rt: 1.2 mi., 600 ft, 0:55].

Directly across NH 113, the loop hike over Mt. Percival and Mt. Morgan via the Mount Percival, Crawford-Ridgepole, and Mount Morgan trails offers exceptional views for the effort required [lp: 5.1 mi., 1600 ft., 3:20].

Red Hill offers fine views north to the Sandwich Range; the Red Hill Trail, being an old jeep road, has much easier grades and footing than most mountain trails, making it suitable for hikers with limited agility [rt: 3.4 mi., 1300 ft., 2:20]; the Eagle Cliff Trail provides a more interesting route, but it is much steeper and rougher, particularly in the vicinity of the cliff [rt: 5.2 mi., 1800 ft., 3:30].

Moderate trips

Sandwich Mtn. at the south end of the Waterville Valley has a good view, but is upstaged by the little rock peak called Jennings Peak on its north ridge. One can follow the Sandwich Mountain Trail to Jennings Peak [rt: 6.0 mi., 2000 ft., 4:00], then decide whether to continue to the main summit [rt: 8.2 mi., 2600 ft., 5:25]. For a direct ascent of Sandwich, the Algonquin Trail is an extremely scenic route [rt: 9.0 mi., 3000 ft., 6:00].

Index

Note: **Boldface** type is used for trail names to distinguish trails from other indexed items. Trails marked by an asterisk do not have a separate description, but are discussed or mentioned in groups or within other trails' descriptions. Some trails are primarily (or were formerly) ski trails but are also maintained for and open to hiking in the snowless seasons; these trails are also boldfaced. Many ski trails are mentioned where they intersect hiking trails, but are not maintained for or open to hiking in the snowless seasons; some of these trails are indexed but they are not boldfaced.

About the
Appalachian Mountain Club

Begin a new adventure!

Join the Appalachian Mountain Club, the oldest and largest outdoor recreation club in the United States. Since 1876, the Appalachian Mountain Club has helped people experience the majesty and solitude of the Northeast outdoors. Our mission is to promote the protection, enjoyment, and wise use of the mountains, rivers, and trails of the Northeast.

Members enjoy discounts on all AMC programs, facilities, and books:

Outdoor Adventure Programs

We offer over 100 workshops on hiking, canoeing, cross-country skiing, biking, and rock climbing as well as guided trips for hikers, canoers, and skiers.

Facilities: Mountain Huts and Visitor Centers

The AMC maintains backcountry huts in the White Mountains of New Hampshire and visitor centers throughout the Northeast, from Maine to New Jersey.

Books & Maps

Guides and maps to the mountains, streams and forests of the Northeast — from Maine to North Carolina — and outdoor skill books from backcountry experts on topics from winter camping to fly fishing. Call 1-800-AMC-HILL to request a complete catalog.

The Appalachian Mountain Club
5 Joy Street
Boston, MA 02108
617-523-0636

Find us on the web at www.outdoors.org to order books, make reservations, learn about our workshops, or join the club.

542